COAST·TO·COAST

Dining
Guide

# *Mariani's*

## COAST-TO-COAST

# Dining Guide

### EDITED BY JOHN MARIANI

**Times** BOOKS

Library of Congress Cataloging-in-Publication Data

Mariani's coast-to-coast dining guide.

    1. Restaurants, lunch rooms, etc.—United States—
Directories. I. Mariani, John F.
TX907.M35   1986    647'.9573     85-41003
ISBN 0-8129-1309-4 (pbk.)

    Coordinating Editor: Rosalyn T. Badalamenti
    Cover and book design: Marjorie Anderson
    Calligraphy: Royce Becker
    Interior illustrations: John Hurst

Manufactured in the United States of America
98765432
First Edition

# CONTENTS

# INTRODUCTION

"Why is there no authoritative restaurant guide to the United States?"

It's a question the authors of this book and I have been asked week after week by travelers who come to our cities, by serious gourmets who want to sniff out the best America has to offer, and by a citizenry suddenly impassioned by good food and by the thrill of dining out.

Actually it's a pretty easy question to answer: The United States is just too darn big to be covered successfully in a guidebook along the lines of France's *Guide Michelin,* which, I'm told, has twelve inspectors to cover a geographic territory smaller than the state of Texas. Then again, how do you cover a country whose gastronomy ranges from spiced Maryland crabs to oysters Rockefeller, from *haute cuisine* to down-home cookery, from Dagwood sandwiches to "dirty rice"? In France, 99 percent of the restaurants are French, in China 99 percent are Chinese, and in India 99 percent are Indian. America's ethnic heritage makes the idea of classical standards an exercise in frustration. The country is just too darn diverse.

There have been guidebooks published that try to give an indication of the range of restaurants in America, but in almost every case, the authority of the venture is undermined by the reader's lack of certainty as to just who it is who is writing up these restaurants. The reader knows that no one food writer—despite his name emblazoned alone in the title of the book—could possibly cover all the restaurants in one state much less in fifty of them.

Unfortunately the reader has little way of knowing whether inclusion in some guides is dependent upon how many ads were bought in the magazine that year.

Just as serious is the objection that too many restaurant guides exalt expensive deluxe dining rooms while completely ignoring inexpensive, informal restaurants serving good regional or ethnic food—barbecue places, hamburger stands, pizzerias, diners, delicatessens—which may in fact constitute some of the most interesting eats in town.

How, then, would it be possible to cover America's best restaurants except by drawing on the acknowledged expertise of those who cover the territory on a daily basis? This is precisely what I sought to do: to go to America's best critics in scores of cities around the country and to ask them to write a chapter describing the best places to eat in and around their own hometowns. These are men and women who eat out professionally several days a week, bring to their job talent, experience, and enormous enthusiasm for their beat as well as a distinct local pride in telling out-of-towners about eating well in categories that range from the deluxe to the deli. Many of these authors have been food or restaurant critics in their towns for years, even decades, and no one knows what's new and interesting or old and dependable better than they. And, since none is under the constraints of the ad department or asked to do favors for a restaurant, these are critics you can trust.

They are a tough bunch, too. They don't pull punches and I've encouraged them to criticize when necessary and to cavil when it's deserved, on the assumption that no restaurant is perfect and some may have only the virtue of one or two good dishes that make them worth including here.

But our main design has been to point you, the reader, toward the best restaurants in this country, not to waste space writing about the worst. Which is why you'll find a good number of famous restaurants in various cities not listed at all. The reader should not assume, however, that omission means deliberate exclusion: Some cities have so many fine restaurants that there just isn't space to write them all up. All I asked of the authors was to write a chapter that gives a reasonable sense of their cities' gastronomic strengths and, in some cases, unique character. So, as the reader will immediately see, you can eat Thai food in Seattle, Sri Lankan food in Minneapolis, and Tibetan food in Los Angeles. You'll also be told where the natives go for breakfast or for a local specialty—like Louisville's Hot Brown sandwich—found almost nowhere else on the continent.

There has never been a time in America's history when going out to dine has been so exciting for so many people in so many cities. Not long ago you had to go to New York, New Orleans, or San Francisco to find first-rate dining rooms in this country, while American regional cuisine languished under a reputation of being too common for consideration. Sophisticated people wanted to eat in restaurants with red banquettes, silver carving carts, menus with tassels, and eponymous dishes such as veal Orloff, beef Welling-ton, and peach Melba. The alternatives were assumed to be little more than steak, lobster, or fast food—especially in cities where alcohol and wines were still banned for restaurant sale by blue laws left over from Prohibition.

Actually, things were never as bad as it seemed to snobbish gourmets. The great regional cooking of Americans was completely overlooked—North Carolina barbecue, New England chowders, Arizona chili, Florida Key lime pie, Pennsylvania Dutch pastries, Louisiana gumbos, and scores of other items never found at Chez André, The Escoffier Room, and similarly pompous-sounding restaurants in big cities.

It was not until the 1970s that American wines began to be taken seriously, whereas today we produce Chardonnays, cabernets, zinfandels, and other varietals that are a match for the best from France, Germany, and Italy.

Internationalism has made Americans far more familiar with the fine restau-rants of Rome, Madrid, Paris, and London than might have been imagined twenty years ago, and the result has been an explosion of good European restaurants—often with American-born, European-trained chefs—in every major city in the U.S.A., so much so that now it is to America that French and Italian chefs come to see what is going on in gastronomy. *Nouvelle cuisine* became fashionable and traveled well, so that its concepts and precepts turned up in kitchens from Portland, Oregon, to Boston, Massachusetts, within months of first being sighted in New York and Los Angeles.

Out of this infatuation with the new and the novel, urged on by the editors of well-produced, stylish food and wine magazines, came the so-called New American Cuisine, an idea so ill-defined as to count virtues like "freshness" and "seasonability" as bona fide hallmarks. Nevertheless, young American chefs—through trial and error—have developed certain styles of cooking that seem part of a trend: grilling over hard woods, pan-blackening of fish and meats; utilization of native ingredients such as corn, tomatoes, pecans, bourbon, and chile peppers; a serious interest in such regional items as smoked country hams, sturgeon caviar, farm-raised chickens, barbecue sauce, and fresh duck liver; and a headlong American exuberance for strong seasonings and flavors—from Vermont maple syrup to Louisiana Tabasco sauce. There *is* an emerging American cuisine, and it is reflected in the scores of restaurants now opening across the country that feature these kinds of foods and cooking methods.

The authors of this book hope that their efforts reflect this growing diversity and that our recommendations will go a long way to answering the question of where a person can find the best food in America these days. We sincerely hope, too, that we shall hear from you readers as to your own personal favorites across the country. In the meantime, eat wisely and well.

# A GUIDE TO THIS GUIDE

The authors of this book have tried to answer the kinds of questions serious and casual eaters want to know about the best restaurants in a city. Therefore, beyond the obvious information on address, phone number, and credit card information, we have tried to give you a sense of atmosphere, style, menu, special dishes, and, in many cases, the reasons that so many locals flock there. If a dish was created at a restaurant, we'll tell you. If the chef has achieved national eminence, you'll find that out too. If the place is far beyond what you wish to spend that night, you get an indication of the dinner price in figures, rather than a description of the menu as "moderate" or "expensive." We've indicated when a restaurant serves a specific purpose, such as for a late-night meal. We've also alerted you to the most interesting wine lists in the city. Be aware, however, that many restaurants change their menu frequently—some daily—and that in many cases we are only alluding to the kinds of dishes you may find on a menu of a given evening. Obviously in the summer you won't find much game served, and out of season shellfish is not likely to be the best thing on any menu. Most of all, we've tried to be as up-to-date as possible within the constraints of publishing deadlines. If you do hear of or experience a change of chef, days of opening, prices, or anything else you think reflects seriously on the restaurant described, please write to us at:

MARIANI'S COAST-TO-COAST
DINING GUIDE
Times Books
201 East 50 Street
New York, NY 10022

Here's a quick guide to the guide:

At the very beginning of each chapter there is a list that includes all the restaurants in various categories you may be looking for. We've provided as many categories as we think fit within a city's gastronomy, and sometimes a restaurant may appear under several headings—for instance, a French restaurant in a hotel with a particularly good view of the city may be listed under French, Hotel Dining Room, and Panorama.

A few of the headings may need a bit of explanation:

## AMERICAN

For the most part this category includes restaurants serving traditional American cookery, although it does not exclude certain restaurants that are doing quite modern dishes along traditional American lines. It also does not include the numerous categories of distinctive American foods like barbecue, steaks and chops, deli fare, seafood, hamburgers, and hot dogs, which all have their separate categories.

## CONTINENTAL

This indicates a restaurant that serves a menu of by now fairly standard European dishes (mainly French and Italian, with some steaks and chops thrown in).

## ECLECTIC

These are restaurants that serve a menu that may include dishes or preparations from all over the globe—*shiitake* mushrooms on Pacific salmon, *fettuccine* with American caviar, French turbot cooked with sesame oil, and so on. This style of cooking took its inspiration from French *nouvelle cuisine,* but in the United States it has often been called the "New American Cuisine" because young American chefs are making it, often utilizing native ingredients in novel ways. But the term is still vague (see my comments in the introduction of this book) and a cover-all for an eclectic style of cooking that at its best is innovative and refreshing but at its worst merely flashy and experimental. For the time being, then, let's term this style "eclectic" and see what develops in the years to come.

## UNIQUE PROPERTIES

This indicates a restaurant or food item that is unique to a particular city or that originated in a specific restaurant. The category also includes restaurants that have a unique quality that is part of the special character of that city—perhaps because of its position in the city's history or because it best expresses the vitality and spirit of its habitués. These are not always the best restaurants in a city, but we have included them because they are the kinds of places you wouldn't want to miss if you wish to know a city well.

# PRICES

The price indicated here is an average for the cost of a three-course dinner —appetizer, entrée, and dessert—unless otherwise noted (*e.g.,* a hamburger stand, a place that sells *dim sum* only, etc.) and does NOT include cocktails, wine, drinks, extra courses, tax, or tip. Also keep in mind that lunch prices may be considerably cheaper than dinner prices. We've also noted when there is a "fixed-price" menu—which is usually a good buy, and on rare occasions may include wines—or a *menu dégustation,* which is usually a tasting of five or more courses. If you add on beverage, wine, tax, and a tip of between 15 and 20 percent, you may easily up your bill far beyond what is indicated here, so that a dinner price of "About $25 per person" can easily run up to an $80 meal for two after wine, tax, and tip are added.

# OPEN

Restaurants are notorious for changing opening and closing times at the drop of a fork. Our listings reflect the current opening and closing times as of the time we go to press, so it is always a good idea to call ahead and find out if things have changed.

# CREDIT CARDS

"Accepts all major credit cards" indicates that a restaurant accepts a majority of nationally and internationally accepted credit cards such as American Express, Visa, MasterCard, Diners Club, and Carte Blanche. Otherwise, we have indicated which specific cards are accepted. In those cases where credit cards are not accepted at all, it's a good idea to telephone to see if they'll take personal or traveler's checks or accept cash only.

# *Mariani's*
## COAST-TO-COAST
# Dining
# Guide

# ATLANTA

## BY BILL CUTLER

**AMERICAN**
Lickskillet Farm
The Planters
Ye Olde Colonial

**BAR**
U.S. Bar y Grill

**BARBECUE**
Old South Bar-B-Que

**BREAKFAST**
The Café at the Ritz-Carlton
Hotel
Yen Ching

**CAJUN**
Lennox's

**CHINESE**
First China
Ho Ho
House of Chan
Yen Ching

**CONTINENTAL**
The Hedgerose Heights Inn
Ma Maison
103 West
Pano's & Paul's
Patrick's

**CUBAN**
Havana Sandwich Shop
Sarita

**ETHIOPIAN**
Blue Nile

**FAMILY RESTAURANT**
Mary Mac's

**GREEK**
Niko's

**HOTEL DINING ROOM**
The Dining Room at the
Ritz-Carlton Hotel

## INDIAN
Raja

## ITALIAN
Bambinelli's
La Grotta
Mama Mia's

## JAPANESE
Gojinka

## KOREAN
Korea House

## MEXICAN
Mexico City Gourmet

## MIDDLE EASTERN
Lawrence's Café
Nicola's

## NEW AMERICAN
Carsley's

## NIGHTCLUB/RESTAURANT
Dante's Down the Hatch

## PIZZA
Everybody's

## SEAFOOD
Savannah Fish Company

## SOUL FOOD
Annie Keith's

## STEAKS AND CHOPS
Bone's

## SUBURBAN
Lickskillet Farm (Roswell)
Old South Bar-B-Que (Smyrna
   and Roswell)
Ye Olde Colonial
   (Madison)

## VEGETARIAN
Rainbow Grocery

When I moved to Atlanta fifteen years ago, a decent meal in a restaurant was hard to find. Forget ethnic. Veal or lamb or any unwhiskered fish was an oddity on a local menu. This was still a beef, chicken, and turnip greens town, and trying to change the eating habits of Southerners was a perilous enterprise for any adventuresome restaurant operator. The mid-seventies, however, saw a hectic rush to transform Atlanta from a cow town into a major convention center. Hotels, staffed by chefs imported from Europe, the West Indies, and the Orient, sprang up all over the central business district. Several of these kitchen masters subsequently left hotel employ to open their own restaurants, which have continued to offer some of the best food in the city. During the same period, the attractions of the Sunbelt brought in from other parts of the country waves of sophisticates who appreciated and demanded a wide range of culinary experiences. As a result, Atlanta restaurants very rapidly passed through a period of gastronomic growing pains and now offer visitors excellent versions of many exotic cuisines, as well as some of the latest breakthroughs in American cooking. A negative side effect of the city's new cosmopolitanism is the disappearance of the old-fashioned Southern boardinghouse from urban neighborhoods. Now, visitors must travel an hour or so into the surrounding countryside to sample authentic regional cooking.

*Bill Cutler has been reviewing Georgia restaurants for local publications since 1972. He is currently restaurant critic for* Georgia Trend Magazine *and editor of a monthly newsletter,* Knife & Fork: The Insider's Guide to Atlanta Restaurants.

---

## ANNIE KEITH'S
649 Willoughby Way *(no sign outside the red-trimmed brick house, third on the right off Ralph McGill Boulevard, east of Glen Iris Drive)*
404-521-3651

Customers in all hues and types of garb crowd onto the front porch waiting for seats at one of the five tables in the small living room, while others walk around the side of the house to sit in a covered carport. A blackboard lists the day's lunch choices—four or five meats, often including sumptuous oxtails, plus special vegetables and fried pies not listed on the printed menu. The meats are generously cut, the macaroni and cheese is dependably good, and the pinto beans come with large chunks of yummy fatback. Other vegetables, such as English peas, are dumped straight from cans. Avoid the excessively dry cornbread muffins, but don't miss the mule ears (lardy fried pies, just oozing with cholesterol). Superior breakfast meats are served until 11:30 A.M. The giant pork chop, puffed up with peppery breading, is a glory. Best grits in town.

Service is prompt and cheerful. After your meal you pay at a counter separating the funkily decorated living room from the kitchen. No reservations are accepted.

*Price: Under $5 per person*
*Open Mon.–Fri. for breakfast and lunch only; closed Sat. and Sun.*
*No credit cards accepted*

---

# BAMBINELLI'S
## In Northlake II Shopping Center (*off Briarcliff and Henderson Mill roads behind Northlake Mall*)
### 404-493-1311

Until Sal and Bonnie Bambinelli moved South from the environs of New York and opened this unpretentious, low-budget place five years ago, Atlanta had a series of quaint mom-and-pop Italian eateries just oozing with charm and reeking of burnt garlic, canned tomato sauces, and soggy noodles. The Bambinellis introduced the city to the sort of honest, no-nonsense pasta and *calamari* dishes residents of other American towns expect to find routinely around the corner. They also serve fine heroes (both hot and cold) and pizzas, an excellent entrée of sausage and peppers, unpredictable *calzone,* and a nicely textured cheesecake. A few wines are offered, but no hard liquor. An accordionist makes a racket in one corner. Travel posters and a few trinkets on the walls. No reservations are accepted.

*Price: About $15 per person*
*Open Mon.–Sat. for lunch and dinner; closed Sun.*
*No credit cards accepted*

# BLUE NILE
## 810 North Highland Avenue at Greenwood Street
### 404-872-6483

Former residents of Ethiopia claim that the seasonings at Atlanta's only restaurant serving that country's food are toned down from the originals, while most local patrons unfamiliar with the fare say, "It's interesting, but too hot for me." Compared with the best-known counterparts in Washington, D.C., the spices here are more assertive, authoritative, and varied. Since all the meat and vegetable concoctions are eaten by being sopped up with a curious spongy fermented dough called *injera,* that richness of seasoning is essential to counter the sensation of bland clamminess imparted by the thick, white, pancake-like substance. Especially good choices on the very small menu are the chicken entrée *(doro wot),* the lentils *(yemisir wot),* the lamb entrée *(yabeg wot),* and an appetizer of vegetables wrapped in dough *(sambusa*—somewhat like Indian *samosas).* All side dishes accompanying main courses—kale, cabbage, split peas with turmeric, and lentil salad with lemon juice—are piquantly thrilling.

A statuesque beauty, wrapped in white cloths, moves with lethargic grace from dining room to kitchen. If you're in a hurry, her charms diminish. The decor includes travel posters, native musical instruments and religious symbols, plus two very handsome ostrich eggs. Full bar. Reservations are accepted only for parties of six or more.

*Price: About $10 per person*
*Open daily for lunch and dinner*
*Accepts all major credit cards*

# BONE'S
## 3130 Piedmont Road (*just south of Peachtree Road*)
### 404-237-2663

This version of a New York men's grill features the expected trappings: plain tables and chairs, relaxed waiters in mustard-colored jackets, thickly clustered photographs illustrating Atlanta's growth upstairs, along with autographed caricatures of Ted Turner and other local personalities downstairs. At the tables, John O'Hara types in corporate outfits are interspersed with Hemingwayesque parodies gnawing on great slabs of meat and downing stiff drinks. Trust the regulars. They know enough to limit themselves to the T-bone or the veal chop, plus the Seabreeze potato (dipped in kosher salt and baked) or the home fries with onion. Forget the sloppily prepared rest of the menu— all the seafood, appetizers, soups, salads, vegetables, and desserts. All the garnishes, even the sauces, cost extra—*lots* extra. The basic, no-frills meats have no peers in town. At prices up to $23.95 for a plain, ungarnished steak, one would hope so. Reservations are suggested.

*Price: About $35 per person*
*Open Mon.–Fri. for lunch and dinner; Sat. and Sun. for dinner only*
*Accepts all major credit cards*

---

# THE CAFÉ AT THE
# RITZ–CARLTON HOTEL
### 3434 Peachtree Road, Buckhead
#### 404-237-2700

The town's most alluring morning menu is to be found at this pleasantly airy room decorated with old-fashioned prints. Main courses include delectable *sennen rösti* (potato pancake, ham, Gruyère cheese, and fried egg), cheese blintzes with a delicate French character (not the heavy deli variety), and saltily robust, authoritative corned beef hash with poached eggs. Fruits, juices, and buckwheat hotcakes are other significant strengths here. Mistakes like oversalting occasionally occur, but the well-trained kitchen and dining room staffs take pains to rectify errors. So-so coffee. Don't look for the same food quality or menu selection at breakfast in the Ritz–Carlton's downtown café.

*Price: About $15 per person*
*Open daily for breakfast*
*Accepts all major credit cards*

---

# CARSLEY'S
### In Tower Place, 3340 Peachtree Road (*entrance off Piedmont Road*)
#### 404-261-6384

The arrival here in May 1985 of French chef Guy Leroy, a disciple and friend of New American pioneers Wolfgang Puck and Jonathan Waxman, has taken the town by storm. Such banal foods as pizza and Vidalia onions and mesquite-grilled chicken seem to have been invented or discovered by Leroy minutes before your plate arrives at table. Leroy's bowl of honey-yellow butternut squash soup bears at its center a small circle of *crème fraîche* in which four tarragon leaves form a symmetrical pattern. Not enough of the herb to flavor the dish, you might say, until the taste of just one of those leaves explodes in your mouth like a nova in the heavens, revealing a source of energy that had long existed but had not been perceptible to your senses. The miracles seem endless, in part because Leroy keeps changing his menu, making repeat visits an absolute necessity.

Carsley's has a breezy, modern, California feel quite unlike any other Buckhead restaurant's. Pastels wash across walls and zigzag along Art Deco seat-cover fabrics. The Hollywoodish serving staff wear colorful and expensive designer shirts. Too bad their duties are not better coordinated. Late in the evenings, jazz musicians make the brightly lit dining room throb.

*Price: About $35 per person*
*Open Sun.–Fri. for lunch and dinner; Sat. for dinner only*
*Accepts all major credit cards*

---

# DANTE'S DOWN THE HATCH
## 3380 Peachtree Road (*across from Lenox Square*)
### 404-266-1600

Crocodiles (some born on the premises) swim in a moat here surrounding the polished hull of an eighteenth-century sailing vessel (a real one, not a replica). On the ship, a stellar jazz trio holds forth every night except Monday, while folksingers croon in the area of the club known as the "wharf." Lots of fun things to look at, including stained glass windows originally from Lloyd's of London. Female patrons must not miss the witch waiting to greet them with a cackle in the ladies' room. The wine list is among the city's most extensive and interesting. Food is restricted to fondues and cheese platters—among the least of the attractions at this delightfully eccentric spot.

*Price: About $30 per person*
*Open daily for dinner*
*Accepts all major credit cards*

---

# THE DINING ROOM AT THE RITZ–CARLTON HOTEL
## 3434 Peachtree Road, Buckhead
### 404-237-2700

German-born Günther Seeger took over the kitchen here in late September 1985, instantly turning what had been a good but uneven operation into a breathtakingly brilliant one. Tact and artistic economy are Seeger's stock in trade. His dishes never loudly announce the presence of their ingredients, but whisper with the most refined subtlety of precious condiments and spices. Imagine a German preparing red cabbage softly, gently, without the usual aggressive vinegary seasoning. Imagine describing a soup as "cream of *cilantro*," not even mentioning that succulent chunks of lobster float in the heavenly broth. Seeger writes out his own menus daily and cooks both lunch and dinner. Hotel employment practices being what they are, rush to the Buckhead Ritz to revel in a genius's gifts before he's shipped off to some new location.

Stunning wines, including properly aged *grands crus* may be ordered by the glass from the gleaming Cruvinet in a corner of the polygonal dining room. The absence of columns or other room dividers gives all patrons unobstructed views of the entrance, the glass-walled sautéing kitchen with its imposing collection of copper pans, and an 18-seat bar tucked against one wall. Mahogany and marble add to the dark, sumptuously clubby environment defined by traditional hunting prints and other safely old paintings.

*Price: About $40 per person*
*Open Mon.–Fri. for lunch and dinner; Sat. for dinner only; closed Sun.*
*Accepts all major credit cards*

---

## EVERYBODY'S
### 1593 North Decatur Road, Emory Village
#### 404-377-7766

This hangout for students and young families is jammed on weekends and often raucous with beer drinkers. The eclectic and silly menu features a good deal of silly food, but the house special, "Everybody's Pizza," is truly distinctive. Not a classic zesty union of tomato sauce, cheese, and herbs, it's a curiously—deliciously—austere, dry juxtaposition of mushrooms, pepperoni, green peppers, and sliced tomatoes, each of which retains its individual fresh flavor on top of superbly crunchy dough. Even chronic crust-leavers are likely to gobble up every last bite. Have with the gigantic "Everybody's Salad," another heap of truly fresh, attractive ingredients, enhanced, in this case, by a splendidly sharp dressing of Italian descent. No reservations are accepted.

*Price: About $10 per person*
*Open Mon.–Fri. for lunch and dinner; Sat. and Sun. for dinner only*
*Accepts American Express, Visa, and MasterCard*

---

## FIRST CHINA
### 5295 Buford Highway, Doraville
#### 404-457-6788

The Mui family, recently of Hong Kong, demonstrate the subtlety and brilliance underlying Cantonese cooking, a cuisine often represented in this country as bland and boring. Mrs. Mui makes her own noodles from scratch, and her talented sons assemble exquisite arrangements of colors and textures in complicated dishes, such as bird's nest chicken (built upon a base of taro root noodles). Try also *gon gim foon* (hand-rolled rice noodles topped with shrimp, roast pork, black mushrooms, onions, and celery) and two of the steamed dishes: chicken with black mushroom and Chinese sausage, and pork with Chinese sausage. Kenny Mui, who presides with patient, smiling courtesy over the dining room, will lead you to the day's best treats—sometimes oysters so plump and bursting with juice you can barely fit them in your mouth. Even desserts are special here: unsweet and crumbly almond cookies and a tender white layer cake filled with fruit and frosted with whipped cream. The *dim sum* brunch, served Saturday through Monday, lacks the ceremony of rattling carts, but the quality of the limited steamed-dumpling selection is the highest in town. There is scrupulous regard here for patrons with dietary restrictions, such as no salt. Full bar. Reservations are accepted.

*Price: About $15 per person*
*Open Wed.–Mon. for lunch and dinner; closed Tues.*
*Accepts American Express, Visa, and MasterCard*

---

# GOJINKA
## In Pinetree Plaza, 5269-3 Buford Highway, Doraville
### 404-458-0558

Chef Yukio Watanabe, co-owner of this austerely bare place with adjoining *sushi* bar, enjoys a worldwide reputation, which brings customers and cooks from all over to marvel at and learn his skills. If he prepares a *sushi* or *sashimi* platter personally, its colors and shapes will ravish the eyes before exploding on the palate with startling freshness. His *sushi* chef is no slouch. Ask for your *sushi* assortment to exclude the boring boiled shrimp, but don't miss the sea urchin and flying fish roe. The *tempura* platter may be safely dispensed with in favor of the *sushi*-sized cylinders of beef wrapped around green onions, the fish dishes steamed with strips of vegetables, and the thin strips of raw beef served with garlic soy sauce *(gyuniku sashimi)*. A number of unusual appetizer items are not translated into English on the menu, and good luck getting your amiable waitress to explain them to you. They include such recommended individual pickled delicacies as squid with fish roe inside, ground radish served with various fish, Japanese mushrooms, seaweed, and dried bonito with spinach. No tourist fanfare such as teppan steak houses provide and there's little charm to the decor. Full bar. Reservations are accepted.

*Price: About $25 per person*
*Open Mon.–Sat. for dinner only; closed Sun.*
*Accepts all major credit cards*

# HAVANA SANDWICH SHOP
## 2905 Buford Highway (*near North Druid Hills Road*)
### 404-636-4094

No romance at this counter-service spot, pulsating with rock music, irradiated by fluorescent lighting, and decorated with beer emblems, a poster for *Gone with the Wind,* and another poster showing two pigs smooching. Order a Cuban sandwich (plentiful, tender slices of pork in a tangy sauce on fine crusty bread) or the steak sandwich made from thin slices of excellent beef or the *boliche* (pot roast) sandwich. Also recommended: the thick, smoky garbanzo bean soup and the pork platter, accompanied by yummily sautéed and browned thick slices of onion. Avoid all the desserts except the cinnamony, sweet rice pudding. No reservations are accepted.

*Price: About $10 per person*
*Open Mon.–Sat. for lunch and dinner; closed Sun.*
*No credit cards accepted*

# THE HEDGEROSE HEIGHTS INN
## 490 East Paces Ferry Road, Buckhead
### 404-233-7673

The restrained elegance of this small house and the impeccable refinement of chef-owner Heinz Schwab's opulent dishes have set the standard for excellence in Atlanta dining since April 1981. For more than four years before that, Swiss native Schwab's culinary gymnastics at Nikolai's Roof on top of the Atlanta Hilton made getting seats there (without waiting six months) the ultimate proof of prestige and power. (Nikolai's continuing reputation owes more to Schwab than to any of his successors.) Across-the-board brilliance is the hallmark here. No letdowns halfway through a meal, no faltering in the treatment of garnishes or small details. Bravado presentations of pheasant, buffalo, venison, and other powerful game dishes are Schwab's stock in trade, but his light touch is just as sure: classic perfection in a Dover *sole à la meunière,* delicate grace in the colorings of vegetable *terrines* and salads, levitating magic in sherbets. Don't look for much that is *nouvelle,* though. The grand gestures are the telling ones: intensely flavored *soufflés* and an exotic appetizer concoction of goose and chicken livers creamed and enriched into a *mousse* and rolled in truffles.

Patrons who demand to be fussed over and made constantly aware of their waiters' ministrations will not be happy with the unobtrusive service. Flowers are everywhere, in giant sprays spilling from celadon vases, reproduced in low mirrors behind a row of banquettes, and in the stunning service plate that unites the basic colors in the restaurant's design: greens, peach shading into terra-cotta, and off-whites. The wine selection, about equally divided between California and Europe, is on a par with the food and atmosphere. Reservations are a must.

*Price: About $35 per person*
*Open Tues.–Sat. for dinner only; closed Sun. and Mon.*
*Accepts all major credit cards*

---

## HO HO

### 3683 Clairmont Road (*between Buford Highway and Peachtree-DeKalb Airport*), Chamblee
#### 404-451-7240

Owner Chiu Ho Cheung comes from a coastal region of China opposite Hong Kong which is renowned for its preparation of seafood. It is not unusual to see owners of the town's other Chinese restaurants sampling here such rare dishes as seasoned jellyfish, fried oyster pancakes made with water chestnut flour, and pig nose marinated in *cilantro* and vinegar. Some of these delicacies may have textures unpleasing to Western palates, but ask Cheung's daughter Polly (the only reliable English-speaker around) for items off the "Special Menu" that are not quite so challenging. Braised mushrooms with bean curd, shrimp balls, fish cakes, whole fish in ginger or hot bean sauce, and beef stew pot with bean curd flavored with star anise are all delicious and approachable. Beware of the "Honey-Comb Stripe," a strong-tasting and misspelled version of tripe almost certain to displease. The standard Chinese dishes enumerated on the regular menu are no better than counterparts all over town. Beer and wine only; no hard liquor. No reservations are accepted.

*Price: About $15 per person*
*Open Mon.–Fri. for lunch and dinner; Sat. for dinner only; closed Sun.*
*Accepts all major credit cards*

---

## HOUSE OF CHAN

### 2469 Cobb Parkway U.S. 41 (*across from Loehmann's Plaza*), Smyrna
#### 404-955-9444

A tiny, glass-fronted space in an unassuming strip of shops is home to a wide range of specialties from various regions of China. Ask friendly Mr. Chan to guide you to dishes his wife has specially prepared that day, for example: fresh oysters stir-fried with green onions and ginger, or shrimp in bird's nest with crisp walnut meats and stir-fried snow pea pods, or shredded pork with sweet bean paste. The sweet-and-sour sauce is robust, not at all like the orange goo you may be used to. Ask if the savory steamed pork buns Mrs. Chan sometimes prepares for the staff are available. No danger of cornstarch or MSG overload here. Wine is available, but no mixed drinks. Reservations are accepted.

*Price: About $20 per person*
*Open Mon.–Fri. for lunch and dinner; Sat. for dinner only; closed Sun.*
*Accepts American Express, Visa, and MasterCard*

---

# KOREA HOUSE
## 831 Peachtree Street (*at Sixth Street*)
### 404-876-5310

A bewildering choice of dishes and flavorings assaults the newcomer to this large, dark establishment which is hung with all sorts of Oriental trappings. The staff's amiability toward and interest in strangers vary a good bit, and the menu contains a fair amount of fractured English. Push bravely on, nonetheless. Even timid palates will enjoy such charcoal-broiled meats as *bul koki* and *gal bee,* while braver souls will find mystery and enchantment in the wide range of pickled side dishes automatically brought to the table along with dinner orders. *Kim chee,* a strange fermented cabbage mixture, is Korea's national dish and sure to arouse strong sentiments, pro or con. Servers will warn Westerners against the cold buckwheat noodle dishes, very spicily flavored, but the adventuresome should not be dissuaded from an unusually exciting contrast of taste sensations. Some dinner choices come with an appetizer assortment. Try not to miss *bin due dduk* (starchy ground soybean pancakes studded with vegetables) and *goon mahn doo* (triangular wontons of meat in a fragile noodle wrapper). Recommended entrée selections include the mushrooms with beef and a startling concoction featuring a fried egg atop a scramble of meats and vegetables called *b bim bop.* Full bar. Reservations are accepted.

*Price: About $12 per person*
*Open Mon.–Sat. for lunch and dinner; closed Sun.*
*Accepts American Express, Visa, and MasterCard*

# LA GROTTA
## 2637 Peachtree Road
### 404-231-1368

The name refers to the location of this hummingly vibrant place in the basement of an apartment complex. You emerge from a sterile residential environment into a dining room crackling with electricity under the management of co-owner and maître d' Sergio Favalli. His partner in the kitchen, Antonio Pecondon, specializes in inventive veal and pasta dishes that include unusual ingredients such as pumpkin. His mastery ranges as far afield as a stunning dish of trout and *prosciutto* in Barolo sauce. A cold appetizer combination of *carpaccio, vitello tonnato,* and *bresaola* is consistently engaging, as are the soups. Keep your tab down by forgoing the banal desserts. The city's best selection of Italian wines is no surprise, but choices from California and France are also very strong. Dinner reservations are hard to come by on weekends and lunch is not served.

Don't expect the same food quality or atmospheric excitement in the newer branch of La Grotta in the suburban town of Roswell. The menu is nearly identical and the dining rooms, inside an antebellum raised cottage, are charming, but the chemistry needed to unite and focus disparate elements is sadly lacking.

*Price: About $30 per person*
*Open Tues.–Sat. for dinner only; closed Sun.*
*Accepts all major credit cards*

# LAWRENCE'S CAFÉ
## 2888 Buford Highway (*just south of North Druid Hills Road*)
### 404-320-7756

The Israeli proprietor and his Honduran wife have worked their way cautiously into offering Atlantans a full line of ethnic specialties. They discovered, happily, that a public existed for food more daring than tuna salad and *teriyaki* chicken, and they now offer the most interesting selection of Middle Eastern fare in the region. Of unusual appeal is the whole snapper, Haifa style—fried and covered with *tahini* and pine nuts or with garlic-lemon sauce. The grape leaves are dry and fibrous, but the vegetarian plate—a changing assortment of cold and room-temperature vegetables combined with garlic, olive oil, onions, lemon juice, and *tahini*—is stunning. Also recommended strongly: the *baba ganooj, hummus,* soups, *kafta, kibbi,* homemade yogurt, and wide range of desserts. Beer and wine only; no hard liquor. No reservations are accepted.

*Price: About $15 per person*
*Open Mon.–Sat. for lunch and dinner; closed Sun.*
*Accepts American Express, Visa, and MasterCard*

---

## LENNOX'S
### 2225 Peachtree Road (*south of Peachtree Battle*)
#### 404-351-0921

Blackened redfish has become *de rigueur* at local restaurants affecting to be "With It," but this place knows, unlike counterparts around town, how to sear the flesh so that the inside remains succulently moist and bland—an exquisite contrast to the resistant, powerfully seasoned exterior. Owner Lennox Gavin studied with Paul Prudhomme in New Orleans, and the lessons have evidently stuck. *Etouffés* and eggplant Bayou Teche are almost as good choices for main courses as the redfish. Cane River Pies (lardy Southern turnovers filled with shrimp, onions, and rich spices) can be enthusiastically recommended as appetizers for patrons reckless with calories. Entrées come with ignoble salads. Desserts, such as chocolate-pecan pie, have all been either lusciously wonderful or drearily bungled, depending on Gavin's luck in corralling makers of sweets.

Reservations accepted only for parties of five or more. Come as you are. Patrons wear everything from cutoffs to cutaways. The staff manner is appropriately casual—more Atlanta exuberant than French Quarter laid-back. Soft, soft pink is the dominant color of the suavely sophisticated dining room, down a level from the shiny Art Deco bar which is decorated with jazz posters. A few tiny tables on a quarter-moon-shaped balcony in the back provide outdoor seating overlooking Peachtree Creek, almost hidden by a jungle-like riot of vines.

*Price: About $25 per person*
*Open Sun.–Fri. for lunch and dinner; Sat. for dinner only*
*Accepts all major credit cards*

---

## LICKSKILLET FARM
### Old Roswell Road (*at Rockmill Road off Holcomb Bridge Road*), Roswell
#### 404-475-6484

From downtown, you'll have to drive for about three quarters of an hour to reach this charming old farmhouse nestled on the banks of a picturesque creek.

Giant oaks shade the gray frame structure and flowerbeds border the brick paths. Be sure to wander down the slope to the creek behind the restaurant, either before or after dinner. A rustic platform provides a good vantage point for admiring the golden fields stretching away from the farmhouse. Inside, low ceilings, wide-planked walls painted an intense blue-gray, and an accomplished pianist maintain the mood of cozy security.

The food isn't bad, but it adds little to an evening's entertainment. The nicest touch is the cornbread with cracklin's brought to the table in a skillet. Soups, meats, vegetables, and desserts are the sort your untalented mom or maid might have thrown together in the fifties. If you want wine with your meal, the host ushers you into a small room where bottles are stored at approximately kitchen temperature, and you pick out what looks best to you. Dinner only, every night except Monday, plus Sunday brunch (the latter not recommended). Reservations are suggested, especially on weekends.

*Price: About $25 per person*
*Open Sun. for brunch and dinner; Tues.–Sat. for dinner only; closed Mon.*
*Accepts all major credit cards*

---

# MA MAISON
## 2974 Grandview Avenue (*south of Pharr Road*), Buckhead
### 404-266-1799

Chef-owner Wolfgang Stoffer's instinct for food that is visually stimulating has always been sharp, but he has overcome an earlier tendency to let striking combinations of colors and shapes provide all the excitement while his seasonings provided almost none. The stylishly eclectic offerings here keep getting better, and Stoffer couldn't care less if traditional chefs question his experiments with classic preparations. He doesn't hesitate to mix vodka with cream in a fish *velouté* served on a julienne of beets or to combine such French staples as *beurre blanc,* leeks, and caviar with two Japanese standbys, *sake* and ginger, in his *"saumon japonais."* Sour cream and bacon show up in a wonderfully successful version of onion strudel in puff pastry. The desserts, for some reason, continue to be all show and absolutely no substance.

The building, once a residence in the middle of a quiet, shady block where other businesses have taken over private homes, has had its ceiling raised and a skylight put in. Walls and chairs are covered with dark-green patterned fabric. A tiny patio in front offers unusually pleasant lunchtime seating. Reservations are recommended.

*Price: About $30 per person*
*Open Tues.–Fri. for dinner only; Mon. for lunch only; Sat. for dinner only; closed Sun.*
*Accepts all major credit cards*

# MAMA MIA'S
## 5805 Buford Highway, Doraville
### 404-457-1113

The shrimp *fra diavolo* here is one of the higher seafood pleasures in town: enormous crustaceans cooked to that point of perfection you thought only home cooks could master. Another classically simple success is the appetizer plate of salami, cheese, and black and green olives. Also recommended: the veal and pasta dishes, the *minestrone,* an anise-scented green salad, the *caponata* (eggplant salad), and the entrée of sausage and peppers. Forest-green side walls, a mirrored back wall, eclectic art posters, and patterned oilcloths on tables create a cozy environment. There is a small wine selection, but no hard liquor. No reservations are accepted.

*Price: About $15 per person*
*Open Mon.–Fri. for lunch and dinner; Sat. and Sun. for dinner only*
*Accepts American Express, Visa, and MasterCard*

# MARY MAC'S
## 224 Ponce de Leon Avenue (*at Myrtle Street*)
### 404-875-4337

No visit to Atlanta is complete without taking time to crumble the area's best cornbread in pot likker—a saporous liquid extracted from turnip greens. The bread soaks up juices from this quintessential sweetly tart Dixie vegetable, which, at Mary Mac's, lacks the bitterness often underlying its taste. Much of the rest of the food, especially the desserts, more resembles bland Middle American fare than the saucy piquancy of the South. You write out your own order on a meal ticket, which one of the establishment's famously friendly waitresses will pick up and expeditiously attend to, perhaps addressing you as "Dear" and administering a pat or rub on your back. Pay close attention to your fellow patrons, who represent the widest possible cross section of Atlanta's elite and ordinary citizens. Politicians and other local celebrities are depicted in cartoon form on one of the restaurant's walls, while the wall farthest from the entrance sports a gigantic mural of the Atlanta skyline. Some of the establishment's four rooms are reserved for non-smokers. Mixed drinks available. No reservations are accepted.

*Price: About $8 per person*
*Open Mon.–Fri. for lunch and dinner; closed Sat. and Sun.*
*No credit cards accepted*

# MEXICO CITY GOURMET

2134 North Decatur Road (*at Clairmont Road*)   404-634-1128
In Shops of Dunwoody Plaza, 5500 Chambles-Dunwoody
Road   404-396-1111

Not Tex–Mex, New Mex–Mex, Cal-Mex, or Colo–Mex, Paco Rodriguez' dishes derive from various regions of Mexico, with occasional alien touches from fancy continental cooking. A clump of pâté and a mushroom-wine sauce tart up the "filet Mexicali," for example (with surprising success), and sirloin instead of the traditional skirt steak is used to make the excellent *fajitas* rolled in flour tortillas and served with a pungent *pico de gallo* sauce of onion, tomato, and *cilantro*. Order from among the daily specials rather than the menu, especially any of the soft *tacos* encasing various meats or the chicken *Michoacana* (lightly grilled *suprêmes* in a red tomato sauce with *chipotle* pepper, topped with cheese). The nearly omnipresent use of *cilantro* will seem overpowering to some palates. First-rate *seviche* and *guacamole* dip appetizers, grandly heavy *flan* in a rich, syrupy caramelized sauce. Owner Rodriguez divides his energies between the two locations, and his assistants are fully competent to replace him. Full liquor license in Dunwoody (order an "upside-down margarita" to show off your bar prowess); beer and wine only at North Decatur. A guitarist holds forth most evenings in the latter location.

*Price: About $20 per person*
*Open Mon.–Sat. for lunch and dinner; closed Sun.*
*Accepts American Express, Visa, and MasterCard*

# NICOLA'S

1602 LaVista Road (*near Briarcliff Road*)
404-325-2524

The menu at this cheerful, sparsely decorated spot looks misleadingly "continental," but owner-chef Nicola Ayoub gives a distinctive Lebanese flavor to, for example, his "Philadelphia Steak Sandwich" (unrecognizable in Philly). Proportions of ingredients in the *hummus* and *tabbouleh* vary widely from day to day, but always manage to stay within a more than acceptable range. Salting may seem excessive to people with low tolerance, but is appropriate to the spiciness of the food. Main courses are less appealing than salads, appetizers, and desserts. Reservations are accepted.

*Price: About $12 per person*
*Open Tues.–Fri. for lunch and dinner; Sat. and Sun. for dinner only; closed Mon.*
*Accepts all major credit cards*

# NIKO'S

## 1803 Cheshire Bridge Road (*near Piedmont Road*)
### 404-872-1254

The heat and noise levels in this low-ceilinged former fast-food establishment can startle, accentuated when a waiter sets on fire a *saganaki* appetizer of cheese and brandy, roaring *"Opa!"* as flames shoot all the way to the acoustic tiles. Almost everything is dependably good here, but among the appetizers, special praise belongs to the baby octopus in a lemon-wine sauce and the luscious spread of fish roe, potatoes, and olive oil called *taramasalata;* for main courses, try the eggplant stuffed with meat and seasoned with cinnamon, pan-fried codfish smeared with *skordalia* (a glorious heavy sauce of garlic, lemon, and potato), lightly floured pan-fried smelts, and the stuffed cabbage with egg-lemon sauce. The house special is *gyro* meat covered with a delightful cucumber-garlic sauce *(zazeeki)* and served with crispy, oregano-flecked fried potatoes. The desserts and house salad are not special (as a replacement for the latter, ask for the "Greek country" salad). A few Greek wines and a single Greek beer are available. No reservations are accepted.

*Price: About $20 per person*
*Open Mon.–Sat. for lunch and dinner; closed Sun.*
*Accepts Visa and MasterCard on checks over $10*

---

# OLD SOUTH BAR-B-QUE

## 601 Burbank Circle at Cherokee Road, Smyrna   404-435-4215
## 115 Norcross Street (*off U.S. 19, north of the town square*), Roswell   404-998-0816

A rare exception to the rule that you can't duplicate restaurant success. The ribs at both locations are tender, juicy, and generously meaty; the barbecued meats moist and perfectly trimmed. Most side dishes are excellent as well (especially the meaty, fresh-tasting Brunswick stew), and the chocolate-pecan pie is a decent version of this frequent abomination. The Smyrna decor is quintessential funky, Roswell's more self-consciously cutesy rural. Beer and soft drinks available; no hard liquor.

*Price: About $8 per person*
*Open Tues.–Sun. for lunch and dinner; closed Mon.*
*No credit cards accepted*

# 103 WEST

103 West Paces Ferry Road, Buckhead
**404-233-5993**

This is the third venture by the team of Albrecht and Karatassos, featuring by far the most sumptuous interior in town. Marbleized columns, Aubusson tapestries, an eighteenth-century Italian porcelain of Zeus in action, *trompe l'oeil* murals, and a glittering gold espresso machine are only a few of the diversions for the eye. The service is fittingly reverential and food presentation is intricate and mannered, sometimes to the point of fussiness. If chef Albrecht himself oversees the preparation of your meal, you can expect to savor dishes of extraordinary finesse and excitement, but the place is so vast, and some of his assistants newly recruited from the Culinary Institute of America so inexperienced, that dependable excellence is not to be counted on. Wines are high priced and classy. Reservations required, as are jackets for men.

*Price: About $40 per person*
*Open Mon.–Sat. for dinner only; closed Sun.*
*Accepts all major credit cards*

# PANO'S & PAUL'S

1232 West Paces Ferry Road (*at Northside Parkway and I-75*)
**404-261-3662**

The opening in 1979 of this elaborately decorated joint venture by chef Paul Albrecht and maître d' Pano Karatassos marked a milestone in Atlanta restaurant history. Richly textured fabrics, swirls of paisleys, and swaths of stripes dazzled patrons used to more restrained and coherent decors. The food was richly bewildering and heavy as well, while the atmosphere was full of bustle and excitement. Sensual overload as a form of entertainment made an immediate and lasting impact upon Atlanta.

Albrecht and Karatassos have since gone on to launch other ambitious and successful enterprises in town, and the rough edges have worn off their first operation. The serving staff are almost invisible, but customers in need of cosseting will appreciate the sedulous attention to their every need or whim. The menu is rich with choices, amplified by the kitchen's readiness to provide other sauces and even types of fish and flesh requested by patrons. Wines are expensive and splendid. Don't miss a visit to the bar, done over in tones of plum, cinnamon, and violet to evoke the self-indulgent exoticism of Paris in the 1920s. Reservations required, as are jackets for men.

*Price: About $35 per person*
*Open Mon.–Sat. for dinner only; closed Sun.*
*Accepts all major credit cards*

---

# PATRICK'S
## In Little Five Points, 484 Moreland Avenue
### 404-525-0103

If "continental" and "international" as restaurant terms suggest to you pretense and affectation, this loosey-goosey neighborhood spot will never fit the mold. The inspiration for chef-owner Patrick Burke's continually changing array of dishes comes from all over the world, borne by whatever winds of chance happen to blow his way. For a while, he was serving delicate corn flour *empanadas* because he had a Venezuelan helper in the kitchen. Much of his most creative work derives from combining distinctively American ingredients, such as wild rice and pistachios, with products of other cultures (feta cheese or Dijon mustard). Burke belongs to no school; he claims no masters. He's a genuinely free spirit whose inventions are almost always successful. In the mid-range price category, Patrick's has no peers for both consistency and daring. Dinner offers the best opportunities to sample Burke's talents, but breakfast and lunch are also recommended. Wines are few and moderately priced; no hard liquor.

The narrow rectangular space is crowded with small tables and functional wooden chairs. There are a few seats on an arbor-covered patio with views of a parking lot. The work of local artists decorates the walls inside. There's no telling whether your server will be with it or entirely out of it. Reservations are accepted.

*Price: About $20 per person*
*Open Mon.–Sat. for lunch and dinner; Sun. for lunch only*
*Accepts all major credit cards*

# THE PLANTERS

### 780 South Cobb Drive (*opposite Dobbins Air Force Base, Cobb County*)
#### 404-427-4646

Two glass-walled wings have been added to a Greek Revival mansion built in 1848, lovely places to dine while looking out over the grounds of a 13-acre estate. Roses from a garden behind the house embellish the halls and individual tables. Wallpapers are authentic reproductions of antebellum patterns. Antiques from the collection of owner Calvin Adams, including the handsome table settings, add to the appeal of the rooms that flank the main entrance. (Be sure to reserve tables in one of these front rooms. The smaller rear chambers have no view and very limited charm.) After dinner, stroll upstairs to see displays of Civil War artifacts found on the property and two bedrooms filled with European antiques.

The serving staff works hard to maintain the illusion of gracious elegance imparted by the environment. The departure as well as arrival of guests is handled with unaffected warmth. Wine service manages to be professional without snootiness. Wines are well chosen and fairly priced. The food is no disgrace to all of these fine trappings, though it too often resembles the bland pomposity of country club fare. Strongest elements are the breads (superb corn sticks, superior Parker House rolls) and salads. The baked goods, surprisingly uncloying, tend to be better bets than fruit choices for dessert. The price printed on the menu next to the entrées is the cost of an entire five-course meal. Reservations are requested.

*Price: About $25 per person*
*Open Mon.–Sat. for dinner only; closed Sun.*
*Accepts all major credit cards*

# RAINBOW GROCERY

### 2118 North Decatur Road (*at Clairmont Road*)
#### 404-633-3538

The dining room is a clean and cheerful cubbyhole in back of a meticulously scrubbed grocery. The basic menu of salads, sandwiches, and rice with vegetables is supplemented by daily specials, printed up on weekly menus. Monday might offer seven-bean soup and *polenta* with Italian vegetables, Wednesday potato soup and zucchini *risotto,* Thursday golden squash soup and Bulgarian cheese casserole, and so on. Inventive surprises, also, in the regular soups: mushrooms mixed in with the split peas, corn in the cauliflower, *miso* with the lima beans, and cashew milk with the cream of tomato. Only a health-food fanatic could love the cheesecake here. Plain wooden tables and chairs. Limited table service: You place your order at a counter. No reservations are accepted.

*Price: About $7 per person*
*Open Mon.–Sat. for lunch and dinner; Sun. for lunch only*
*No credit cards accepted*

---

# RAJA
## 2919 Peachtree Road (*north of Peachtree Battle*)
### 404-237-2661

Homey cooking—hearty, assertive, and copious—is the special province of this plain, rather dreary room. Elegant fare is not to be expected, but the thick curry sauces on house specialties are very much worth sampling. Cottage cheese makes its way into two of owner Raman Saha's fascinating inventions, embellished with nuts and raisins. Also try Lamb Ceylon in a fiery coconut-based sauce and chicken *rogan josh* in a spicy tomato-curry sauce. Avoid the *tandoori* chicken and the *biryanis*. Stick to plain *basmati* rice to accompany curries. Beer and wine only; no hard liquor. Reservations are accepted.

*Price: About $20 per person*
*Open Tues.–Sat. for lunch and dinner; Sun. and Mon. for dinner only*
*Accepts American Express, Visa, and MasterCard*

---

# SARITA
## In Howell Mill Village Shopping Center, 857 Collier Road
### 404-355-9552

Caribbean posters and blue-and-white tablecloths decorate a sparkling clean space with a counter in the back and a refrigerated case holding huge roasted hams and trays of Cuban pies. Disposable tableware detracts somewhat from the elegance of Sarita Gonzalez' lush black bean soup laced with cumin and her multilayered Cuban sandwiches. Don't miss her *picadillo,* a soupy ground beef stew with raisins, olives, garlic, and cumin. Even her *ropa vieja* (beef stewed until it falls apart into shreds) only *looks* stringy; it tastes juicy. From a Cuban bakery come delicious rectangular pies called *pasteladas* which are filled with cheese and a variety of meats and vegetables. Good *sangría,* Cuban coffee, and dark, dark *flan.* No reservations are accepted.

*Price: About $15 per person*
*Open Mon.–Sat. for lunch and dinner; Sun. for dinner only*
*No credit cards accepted*

# SAVANNAH FISH COMPANY

Below-sidewalk level of the Westin Peachtree Plaza Hotel,
Peachtree Street at International Boulevard
404-523-2500

Yes, this is a hotel dining room, but it's *nothing* like the common garden variety. No astronomical prices, ho-hum staff, expensive appointments, and predictably drab food. The menu is printed in the style of a tabloid newspaper, on cheap, thin stock. The outlines of fish appear next to menu items, stamped daily either "FRESH" or "DIDN'T BITE." The day's price for each of the former is inked inside the fish's outline. That price (identical at lunch and dinner) includes a large helping of a superbly pungent fish stew in which the flesh, miraculously, is still firm and flavorful, plus a salad of Boston lettuce. Avoid *à la carte* items, which are overpriced and undependable. If hunger still grips you, have a Hot Puff for dessert—delicious fried pastry served with vanilla or chocolate sauce or whipped cream. Wines are somewhat pricey, but many of them are available by the glass.

An enormous, tempting display of shrimp and various mollusks is heaped by the restaurant's entrance. A towering waterfall just outside the bank of windows is matched by oversized masonry columns between the tables, but these heavy trappings are softened by casual furniture and extensive greenery. Amiable, unstuffy servers. Reservations are accepted at 5:30 only.

*Price: About $25 per person*
*Open daily for lunch and dinner*
*Accepts all major credit cards*

# U.S. BAR Y GRILL

2002 Howell Mill Road (*at Collier Road*)
404-352-0033

The town's best margaritas distinguish this lively spot frequented by condominium dwellers in the neighborhood. On Wednesday and Sunday evenings, mariachi players stroll through the restaurant with guitars, violins, and well-tuned voices. The mushed-together food, served at plain wooden booths the color of wet Georgia clay under wide green lamps that hang exactly at eye height, is not among the establishment's attractions.

*Price: About $12–$15 per person*
*Open daily for lunch and dinner*
*Accepts American Express, Visa, and MasterCard*

# YEN CHING

1701 Church Street (*at Scott Boulevard in Scott Village Shopping Center*), Decatur
404-296-0101

Communication with servers is something of a problem at this anonymously decorated spot, which serves standard Chinese fare at all meals except breakfast. A few of the doughy wonders are offered on Saturdays and Sundays only: long crisp crullers inserted into flat, steaming hot sesame-seed cakes; wontons dipped in a chili oil sauce; flat, crisp, flaky green onion bread stuffed with fried egg; and pan-fried potstickers. Two people can share a large bowl of salty soybean milk soup laden with pieces of dried shrimp, hunks of fried cruller, coriander leaves, and hot chili oil added to taste at the table. No reservations.

*Price: About $10 per person*
*Open Sat. and Sun. for breakfast*
*Accepts American Express, Visa, and MasterCard*

# YE OLDE COLONIAL

On the Square in Madison
404-342-2211

The name is absurd and misleading, but the food served on a cafeteria line from steam tables almost always provides the peppery, lardy authority of authentic Southern cooking. Load up your tray with crisp yet tender fried chicken, a variety of vegetables, properly moist cornbread, iced tea, and a sweet fruit cobbler. You pay by the item, at the end of your meal. The dining room once housed a bank, with a pressed metal ceiling above ledges holding collections of arrowheads and old bottles. Ask the proprietor to show you the former bank vault, papered with Reconstruction-era railroad bonds. No reservations.

The town of Madison (an hour east of Atlanta off I-20) contains the most impressive array of antebellum homes in the state.

*Price: About $5 per person*
*Open Mon.–Sat. for lunch and dinner; closed Sun.*
*No credit cards accepted*

# ATLANTIC CITY

## *BY DEBORAH SCOBLIONKOV*

**CASINO DINING ROOM**
  The Meadows
  Prime Place

**CONTINENTAL**
  Johan's Zelande Restaurant

**CHINESE**
  Peking Duck House

**DELICATESSEN**
  Harvey's Deli

**ECLECTIC**
  Café One Flew Over
  Louisa's Café
  The Mad Batter

**ENVIRONS**
  Café One Flew Over (Ventnor)
  Louisa's Cafe (Cape May)
  The Mad Batter (Cape May)

**FAST FOOD**
  White House Sub Shop

**FRENCH**
  The Meadows

**ITALIAN**
  Angelo's Fairmount Tavern

**OPEN LATE**
  White House Sub Shop

**SEAFOOD**
  Abe's Oyster House
  Dock's Oyster House
  The Knife and Fork Inn

**STEAKS AND CHOPS**
  Prime Place

**UNIQUE PROPERTY**
  White House Sub Shop

In its heyday as the "playground of the world," people flocked to Atlantic City for the beach, the salt air, and the carnival ambience of the Boardwalk. Food was an afterthought. In between amusement rides and ocean dips, they devoured peanuts and hot dogs, cotton candy and fudge, macaroons, and Atlantic City's most famous contribution to gastronomy—saltwater taffy. And after the belly ache subsided, vacationers in search of a good dinner would find it in one of the city's many family-run seafood or Italian restaurants.

Then in the sixties, the town went into a steep decline, only to be dramatically rescued by the advent of legalized gambling in 1978.

Today, with over thirty million visitors a year drawn to the glitter and glamor of Atlantic City's eleven gambling parlors, feeding the masses has become an enormous industry dominated by the casinos. Their arrival introduced a new eating style to the area: theatrical food feasts designed to feed the players' fantasies, their hungry egos, and, only incidentally, their palates. Luckily, one's odds at the casinos' dining tables are improving, thanks to the importation of European-trained chefs and the Institute of Culinary Arts, a food-service program at the local community college that supplies the casinos' kitchens with a cadre of knowledgeable young professionals.

The casinos' impact on other local restaurants has been tremendous. Unable to compete with their gluttonous buffets, many of the city's eateries that would normally thrive on an increase in tourism instead starved to death. The truly outstanding restaurants (now run by second- and third-generation owners) have been able to survive by doing things the way their parents did: delivering refreshingly simple but excellent food at moderate prices.

A few adventurous newcomers have established themselves as well, offering exciting alternatives to straightforward old-world and glitzy new-world dining experiences. The most creative of these *nouvelle* eating houses are located about an hour south of Atlantic City, in the quaint Victorian village of Cape May. The restoration of this historic landmark resort has revived the art of inspired and imaginative dining as well.

*Deborah Scoblionkov is food editor for* Atlantic City Magazine *and writes a wine column for* Philadelphia Inside Magazine.

# ABE'S OYSTER HOUSE
## 2031 Atlantic Avenue
### 609-344-7701

Opened in 1935 as Atlantic City's first crab house. Don't let the name fool you. They've expanded their menu and put in a new lounge, but walk through the new wing into the old-fashioned, white-walled dining room with the mounted fish and neon beer signs. Sit down at the table festooned with fresh white linen tablecloths and order crabs, hard or soft shell, and an icy brew.

The fried jumbo soft-shells are coated with ground, crustless white bread known as "green crumb." It gives a nice fluffy texture without getting hard or crunchy; and, yes, a man comes in daily to slice the crusts off fresh Stroehman's bread.

Service is relaxed and gentle. Waitresses are motherly and, even, grand-motherly. It's a wholesome family place, one of the few restaurants where children's platters are served, though kids might have fun choosing their own lobsters from the tank.

*Price: About $15 per person (lobster more)*
*Open Tues.–Sun. for lunch and dinner; closed Mon.*
*Seasonal—mid-May to mid-September*
*Accepts all major credit cards*

# ANGELO'S FAIRMOUNT TAVERN
## 2300 Fairmount Avenue
### 609-344-2439

A former speakeasy in the Italian neighborhood known as Ducktown (for the ducks and geese that wandered in from the bay). It's known to the local politicians, godfathers, police, and press, who regularly lunch there, as "Sonny's" for the earthy, outspoken, cigar-chomping, Chivas-guzzling Angelo "The Meatball" Marcuso, Jr., who presides over the kitchen.

The music is Frank or Perry or Luciano, with maybe a little Barbra. The decor is simple wood walls and pictures of famous athletes, Miss America, and St. Francis of Sinatra.

Look on the blackboard for hand-scrawled specials, or better yet, ask Sonny what's good. You'll see a grumpy face light up as he delivers an ebullient account of the sausage he stuffed, the meatballs he rolled, or the *marinara* (made from hand-picked tomatoes—*his* hands!) simmered that morning. Go for the soups and homemade Sicilian specials.

The vino is terrific—it's Sonny's own pressing.

Desserts may be avoided. Finish up with *espresso* "from the pot." No one seems to have figured out how to work the new machine.

*Price: Under $15 per person*
*Open daily for lunch and dinner*
*No credit cards accepted*

---

# CAFÉ ONE FLEW OVER
## 5214 Atlantic Avenue, Ventnor
### 609-823-4411

Just a few blocks from "the strip," in the quiet suburb of Ventnor, a bird of a different feather has landed. The Café One Flew Over (right across from the Cuckoo's Nest boutique) serves creative California-inspired cuisine in a delightfully casual but elegant atmosphere. Original artwork (changed periodically) hangs next to the colorful handwritten menu that changes twice daily. Lunch is restricted to simple stir-frys, crab meat *croissants,* fresh fruit blintzes, seafood omelets, and the like. But they are prepared with respect and usually garnished with such treats as baby vegetables or oven-warmed muffins.

Dinner features more ambitious and imaginative dishes; grilled meats, exotic fishes, and vegetarian combinations are served with light tasty sauces. The Thai specials with their subtle Oriental flavors are the most exciting choices.

Desserts are marvelous, and *espresso* and *cappuccino* are available. But an annoying local ordinance prohibits serving liquor. If you forget to BYOB, don't fret; you can run across the street and pick up some wine at the corner drugstore.

*Price: About $20 per person*
*Open daily for lunch and dinner*
*Accepts all major credit cards*

---

# DOCK'S OYSTER HOUSE
## 2405 Atlantic Avenue
### 609-345-0092

You would never know it from the extensive blond-oak refurbishing the owners are so proud of, but Dock's is the oldest seafood house in Atlantic City (est. 1897), and run by a third generation of Doughertys. As you walk in, the mirror behind the bar is etched with Poseidon (or Neptune, depending on your persuasion), a design repeated on the menu and sign; and the pretty floral-and-seashell stained-glass motif is echoed everywhere. The decor may be a bit labored, but the food is simply terrific.

*Linguine* with clam sauce is made from homemade pasta; the clams are opened and chopped and then cooked in garlic and their own juice for each order. Fried dishes are covered with a light *tempura*-style batter, and the oyster stew deserves a pearl. Ask for Roquefort dressing, and you won't be "blue"; you'll get chunks of the real stuff. Room should be reserved for Joe's cheese pie.

Reservations are advised, but if you have to wait at the busy bar, there's a piano player on hand. He'll play your sentimental favorites. Dress is casual. You won't feel out of place in a leisure suit or a Hawaiian shirt.

*Price: About $20–$25 per person (more for lobster)*
*Tues.–Sun. for dinner only; closed Mon.*
*Seasonal—mid-March to mid-November*
*Accepts Visa and MasterCard*

---

# HARVEY'S DELI
In the Trump Plaza Hotel Casino, Mississippi Avenue and the Boardwalk
### 609-441-6000

Nearly every casino has a thinly-disguised coffee shop masquerading as a New York-style deli, but if you follow the *yentas* and Jewish mothers around until they get hungry, you'll probably end up at Harvey's to nosh on chopped liver, gefilte fish, stuffed cabbage, hot pastrami, and blintzes. The decor is nothing special, but the beef tongue is the "silkiest" in town.

*Price: About $12 per person*
*Open daily for lunch and dinner*
*Accepts all major credit cards*

---

# JOHAN'S ZELANDE RESTAURANT
3209 Fairmount Avenue
### 609-344-5733

Outside, it's a modest white home with a flower box under each shuttered window. Inside it looks like grandmother's house, a cozy combination of vintage Victoriana. In the kitchen is Johan Vroegop, an arrogant, flamboyant, temperamental master-chef, born in the Zelande region of the Netherlands and trained in Lausanne, who crossed the ocean in the galley of the S.S. *Rotterdam* and landed in Atlantic City.

Naturally, Johan expected that, as in Europe, the casinos would attract a sophisticated clientele who would appreciate his extravagant high-style cuisine. But it's not the gamblers who applaud his seven-course *prix-fixe* feasts, as much as the casino honchos and chefs who enjoy a little respite from their own brand of culinary theater. While he rarely rates a perfect seven, Johan tries, and when he's good, he's marvelous. Sauces can be heavy and service is pretentious—but never rude. Dinner at Johan's won't leave you feeling that the evening or the money was ill spent.

The wine list is adequate, and his house selection is a marvelous 1983 Hospices de Beaune Meursault.

*Price: Fixed price at $47.50 per person*
*Open daily for dinner only*
*Accepts all major credit cards*

---

# THE KNIFE AND FORK INN
## Albany and Pacific avenues
### 609-344-1133

This Dutch gabled inn with stucco walls studded with crossed knives and forks is undeniably the finest seafood house in Atlantic City.

The interior has a cluttered European *bistro* character, but the food is wonderfully prepared in no-nonsense, traditional American (or adapted American) styles like Newburg, Thermidor, *bouillabaisse,* as well as being simply broiled. Fish include flounder, swordfish, salmon, nightly specials, and a wide range of shellfish. Don't be afraid to order a fried dish; it'll be coated with delicious, waterground cornmeal. Chicken is "panned," not deep-fried; baby lamb chops are aged and butter-tender; vegetables are steamed to order; and corn fritters are made from fresh-cut corn. Feel free to order anything on the menu—except the tomato soup.

The wine list is superior, designed to match the quality of the seafood and steaks.

Reservations are strongly advised, and you might as well request the corner table on the enclosed porch. But be forewarned that it's the hottest table in town. Jackets are required for men—no exceptions—and they do specify "tailored," which means suit or sport—no denim.

*Price: About $25–$30 per person*
*Open daily for dinner*
*Accepts American Express*

# LOUISA'S CAFÉ
## 104 Jackson Street, Cape May
### 609-884-5882

What this tiny (18-seat) café is serving on a given day depends on what is fresh and ripe from Louisa's local sources, friendly farmers and fishermen, or her own garden. She thoughtfully prepares the fine ingredients with imagination and flair to produce such marvels as wild mustard soup, smoked fish *mousse,* fresh grilled tuna (marinated in *tamari,* sherry, and sesame oil), and desserts such as fresh peach, nectarine, and walnut pie.

The decor is simple and lovely. Outside, flower boxes overflow with impatiens, and arched gingerbread molding (carpenter's lace) frames the vitrine. Husband Doug's exuberant paintings color the walls inside.

Louisa does not advertise or care for publicity, but her café is one of the most popular, always crowded and rather noisy. Get there early or be prepared for a long wait. And bring your own wine.

*Price: About $15 per person*
*Open daily for dinner only*
*Seasonal—May to September*
*No credit cards accepted*

# THE MAD BATTER
## 19 Jackson Street, Cape May
### 609-884-5970

The town of Cape May is a Wonderland, and a meal at the Mad Batter will further convince you that you can eat well, too. Featuring a wildly imaginative mix of international cuisines, the menu is "a daily guessing game," as owner Harry Kulkowitz will tell you. Every few weeks, a new menu is conceived, and the daily additions can double the already numerous selections.

It's the kind of place where you hear, "Hi, my name is Mark and I'll be your waitperson for this evening," and then Mark leads you through a whirlwind tour of the exotic and adventurous specials inspired by far-flung cuisines, or dishes invented on the premises and given names like Crab Lalique, *Crêpes* Liliuokolani, or Da Fei's Duck. The staff is sent to various regions and countries (France and Thailand, for example) to study the local cuisines, so the creations can be surprisingly authentic and never boring.

But it takes time to prepare such extravaganzas, so prepare to relax. Service is attentive, if not overly so.

They have a wide selection of non-alcoholic wines, "mocktails," and juicy beverages, but no hard liquor. You may bring your own, of course, and champagne wouldn't be a bad choice.

There are three dining areas: an indoor garden terrace, a skylighted dining room, and a wide veranda. The latter is preferred when the weather is fine. It's the ideal spot to take a luscious dessert and one of the dozen or more variations on a cup of coffee, including Turkish coffee (brewed seven times), served with or without cardamom.

*Price: About $30 per person*
*Open daily for breakfast, lunch, and dinner*
*Seasonal—April through October*
*Accepts Visa and MasterCard*

---

# THE MEADOWS
## In Harrah's Marina Hotel Casino, Brigantine Boulevard and the Bay
### 609-441-5000

It's safe. This is one casino "gourmet" room where you won't be placed in a Hollywood movie set, served by costumed extras from some psychotic's fantasy, or serenaded by strolling violinists or harpists. Its elegance is rather understated. With a simple color scheme of burgundy and beige, the soothing ambience is enhanced by a glass wall that offers a stunning view of the bay harbor and peaceful salt marshes.

The menu is standard "high-roller" fare, featuring *terrine de foie de veau, escargots, soupe à l'oignon, bisque d'homard, tournedos Rossini, chateaubriand,* and *crêpes Suzette.* But the French chef has a genuine regard for quality and will accommodate requests for special preparations. The oysters are imported belons (when available), the Caesar salad is exquisite, and the rack of lamb is outstanding.

Food presentation is gorgeous and service is expert, not overly fussy or intrusive. Here, as in every casino restaurant, the majority of diners are gambling guests of the house. This is where gastronome gamblers place their bets, and the paying public should book reservations several days in advance (longer for weekend nights).

*Price: About $40 per person*
*Open daily for dinner only*
*Accepts all major credit cards*

# PEKING DUCK HOUSE
## 2801 Atlantic Avenue
### 609-344-9090

In 1981, Hong Kong-born Kenny Poo had the "naïve" idea to open a Chinese restaurant where Oriental food was presented with the style and respect once reserved for French cuisine. At the Peking Duck House, you won't find any dragons, lanterns, or gold-leaf moldings, and the color red appears only in the anthurium flowers. Walls are beige; lighting is soft and highlights the carved stone Oriental figures mounted along the walls. Amid the hushed elegance, you can actually hear the classical chamber music or Chinese folk instrumentals.

The namesake duck is legendary in this town. Fresh Long Island ducks are marinated for at least eight hours, blanched with honey and spices, roasted crisp, and carved at tableside. It's best to request this dish in advance (while making your reservation), so you won't be disappointed if they run out. Other delicacies include shark's fin soup, chicken dusted with lotus root flour, and beef with tiger lily flowers. Standards such as shrimp *lo mein* and pork fried rice are also available, but get them from your favorite take-out joint.

The wine list's not bad. The deep-fried ice cream for dessert is a dramatic experience.

*Price: About $25 per person*
*Open daily for lunch and dinner*
*Accepts all major credit cards*

# PRIME PLACE
## In Bally's Park Place Casino Hotel, Park Place and the Boardwalk
### 609-340-2000

This spacious, clean, well-lit room looks out onto the city on one side and into a red-tiled kitchen on another, where 20-ounce dry-aged New York strip steaks are being seared on an open charcoal hearth. The prime steaks are shipped daily from Chicago; they should be ordered blood-red to match the velvet walls.

And what's a steak without potatoes? The selection is staggering. They're prepared French fried or skinned, cottage style, mashed with chicken fat and onions, baked, Jewish *latke* style; there are even baked sweet potatoes. The salad bar is fresh and lively, and so is the wine list.

Jackets are required for men, but if you come in your shirtsleeves, you can borrow one from the house—even if you're a size 54. This room is heavily frequented by high-rollers whose appetite for blood knows no limits.

*Price: About $30 per person*
*Open Tues.–Sun. for dinner only; closed Mon.*
*Accepts all major credit cards*

---

# WHITE HOUSE SUB SHOP
## 2301 Arctic Avenue
### 609-345-1564

In Philadelphia, where they were invented, they're called "hoagies"; in New York, they're "heroes"; in Atlantic City, they're "submarines." And here the White House is their seashore base. Each is a meal wrapped in a 15-inch Italian roll. The doughy center is pulled out and filled with a tasty mix of salami, *capicolla, cotechino* (made from garlicky pigs' snouts), Provolone cheese, lettuce, tomato, onion, oregano, oil, and vinegar (other types like turkey and tuna are available—but *this* is the "REGULAR"). The Art Deco grill also serves up thinly sliced sirloin steak sandwiches, Philly-style.

There's usually a line of eaters who want to sit in a booth and gaze up at the wall plastered with photos of the stars and their favorite subs (many are faded relics from the forties and fifties), and you'll probably want to soak up the nostalgic ambience, too. But, if you can refrain from eating a whole sub, order half "to go," and savor it later when the flavors have had a chance to blend together into a greasy, garlicky delight. It peaks after about an hour and then gets soggy.

For dessert, try a Tastykake. And when you get up to leave, check out the photos on the wall behind the cashier—vintage 1964 Beatles holding a four-foot (yellowing) submarine.

*Price: About $5 for a whole sub*
*Open daily for lunch and dinner*
*No credit cards accepted*

# AUSTIN AND SAN ANTONIO

## By David Gaines

## AUSTIN

**AMERICAN**
Night Hawk
Scholz Garden
Threadgill's

**BARBECUE**
County Line on the Hill
Old Coupland Inn

**ECLECTIC**
Clarksville Café
Jeffrey's

**FRENCH**
Chez Nous

**MEXICAN**
El Azteca
Fonda San Miguel
Las Manitas

## SAN ANTONIO

**BAR**
Roosevelt Bar

**FRENCH**
Crumpets

**ITALIAN**
Paesano's

**MEXICAN**
La Fogata

Not so long ago Austinites used to check the phonebook for restaurants, narrow their hardly numerous choices to the standard three or four (always Tex–Mex or "down-home" places), relish the pseudo-decision-making process, and wait (at the most) ten to fifteen minutes for a table. The ribs and potato salad, the chicken-fried steak and mashed potatoes under white gravy, or the *enchiladas* with *salsa* they ate and the five-dollars-per-person (beer included) they spent were as predictable as the way they always ended up at the same few places. Out-of-towners occasionally commented upon a lack of variety and bustle about it all. Which, their hosts nodded, was precisely the point: Life in America's least expensive city was supposed to be laid-back. Whatever the state's capital lacked in culinary variety it made up for in casual places and inexpensive fare.

In the last few years, however, that has changed quite a bit, thanks to silicon chips and Sunbelt economics. Baby boomers have come of age and Northeasterners have moved to town. "Controlled growth" is Austin's all-purpose buzz phrase these days, but it rings pretty hollow in the face of twenty Yellow Pages on eateries. The bottom line, as these new folks call it, is that lots of money is being made and spent in once-lazy Austin. And, among other things, that means restaurants aplenty.

Although people now easily spend $20 per person (wine not included) and wait up to an hour—on a week night, at that—local cognoscenti still dance with the ones that brung them. Which means the "real things" in Austin are still Mexican food, barbecue, and almost anything battered and fried. A handful of new, romantic bistros can be found off the beaten path of downtown's Restaurant Row, Sixth Street, but let's face it: Blackened redfish and chilled Vouvray will never replace *chiles rellenos* and *cerveza* or liver and onions followed by banana pudding as the kinds of things Austinites prepare and eat best.

Progress has been great and fast, and Austin's newfound restaurant variety spices up gastronomic life here. But, as the following suggestions in the section covering Austin reflect, it's still the fundamental things that apply—the old reliables that put metaphorical meat on your bones and smiles on your faces.

San Antonio is the oldest and most charming city in Texas, the place Charles Kuralt (when he was reporting from "the road" for CBS) deemed his personal favorite. Kuralt—and San Antonio's less famous boosters—rightly celebrates the city's genial pace and old-world downtown. But they rarely mention the cuisine, because in this South Texas convention and tourist center a superb meal is often hard to find, particularly if you choose to dine where all sightseeing rightly begins and ends, along the River Walk. The best way to enjoy your food and expand your appreciation of San Antonio is to take a short cab ride to the local favorites mentioned in the section on that city.

*David Gaines writes about food and restaurants for* Third Coast: The Magazine of Austin. *He is Assistant Professor of English at Southwestern University in Georgetown, Texas, and is a freelance writer.*

# AUSTIN

## CHEZ NOUS
### 510 Neches
### 512-473-2413

If you are going to stick to Sixth Street and downtown, this pricey café will serve the most satisfactory and romantic meal you'll find among the trendy spots. There are many tables for two in this soothing atmosphere, where French music and waiters are the rule. The bread and marinated olives will keep you busy as you peruse the country French menu. The meal often lends itself to eating with your fingers as much as with knives and forks. Salmon done in a seafood stock, white wine, and cream and then topped with shrimp is only slightly less exciting than the tenderloin topped with butter and mustard. The generous portions of accompanying vegetables hardly leave room for dessert, and certainly not enough room for the custard that comes in a large bowl rather than a dainty ramekin. The list of French wines is impressive. Although you may have to wait for a table, you'll never feel rushed to leave once you're seated. That fact—and the food—makes the wait worthwhile.

*Price: About $25 per person*
*Open Tues.–Sat. for lunch and dinner; closed Sun. and Mon.*
*Accepts all major credit cards*

## CLARKSVILLE CAFÉ
### 1202 West Lynn
### 512-474-7279

The Clarksville Café's menu is as *nouvelle* as cuisine gets in Austin, and the restaurant is getting more popular by the month. This neighborhood café, where an ice cream parlor once stood, has become a city-wide phenomenon. Although this has meant increased crowds, the food and service have remained consistently satisfactory. The soups—two of which are available each day—range from a *sopa de tortilla* to a crab bisque and a black bean creation. The house *pâté* goes down nicely with locally baked French or whole wheat bread. A chicken salad with peanut butter and soy sauce over cold pasta is just right for someone who is a bit more adventurous than hungry. The Clarksville Broil is always perfectly cooked and served with new potatoes and carrots or green beans. Very good wine, French and Northern Californian, may be bought by the bottle or glass. As desserts go, the well-named "Chocolate Intemperance" has few rivals in town.

*Price: About $20 per person*
*Open Mon.–Sat. for dinner only*
*Accepts Visa and MasterCard*

---

# COUNTY LINE ON THE HILL
## 6500 West Bee Caves Road
### 512-327-1742

---

# COUNTY LINE ON THE LAKE
## 5204 Farm Market Road 2222
### 512-346-3664

The County Line on the Hill was so successful when it opened that its twin opened a few years later in an even more pleasant spot on Lake Austin, and these two have spawned a State Line restaurant in El Paso. The recipe for such success has been a clean, well-lighted dining room with burly wood tables. The upholstered booths are comfortable, and the upscale, family-style picnic tables in the centers of the rooms encourage bonhomie and hearty appetites. The available scenery—whether it be the hills of West Austin (which are a bit less breathtaking than they were before development set in) or the boat dock, where some diners sail in to dinner—makes the inevitable wait pleasant enough, particularly in the spring and fall. The food, especially the rib platter, is a carnivore's delight; the ribs, sausage, and brisket are accompanied by beans, potato salad, and coleslaw, or any combination thereof. Homemade ice cream and bread are also usually available until mid-evening.

*Price: About $15 per person*
*Open daily for dinner only*
*Accepts all major credit cards*

# EL AZTECA
## 2600 East 7 Street
### 512-477-4701

University students, young and aging professionals, legislators, and writers have been crossing the freeway since 1963 to eat simple Tex–Mex food beneath the velour paintings in this family-owned restaurant. The decor is busy and eclectic, the kind of comfortable tackiness that signals you are paying only for the food. The tortilla chips are always fresh and the *salsa* wonderfully piquant. The menu, which is printed on the paper placemat, runs the gamut from combination plates (always a solid bet) to more adventurous dishes made with *cabrito* (goat). The margaritas tend to be too sweet, but the Mexican beers are always just the right temperature. And the waiters are commendably efficient and unobtrusive.

*Price: Easily under $10 per person*
*Open Mon.–Sat. for lunch and dinner; closed Sun.*
*Accepts Visa and MasterCard*

# FONDA SAN MIGUEL
## 2330 West North Loop
### 512-459-4121

In the 1970s, Fonda San Miguel introduced the cuisine of Mexico's interior to an eating public accustomed to the Velveeta *con queso* and Ro-Tel *salsa* of Tex–Mex. San Miguel's white cheeses, black beans, and poached fish have made it one of Austin's most deservedly popular places for lunch, dinner, and Sunday brunch. The courtyard, with its numerous plants and cozy tables, is a pleasant place to spend the hour you can count on waiting most evenings between eight and ten o'clock, and the best margaritas in town and appetizers like seviche and *chile con queso* ease the wait considerably. In fact, they are so satisfying and generously portioned, that many people eat dinner out there. It's well worth the wait, though, to enter one of the two dimly lighted dining rooms with their soothing wall hangings and to sample the vegetarian *burritos* (a reliable combination of black beans and white cheese in flour tortillas) or the *pescado veracruzano* (broiled fish fillet with a tomato and caper sauce). The rice, studded with peas and corn, is always tasty, and the house coffee first rate.

*Price: About $15 per person*
*Open Sun.–Fri. for lunch and dinner; Sat. for dinner only*
*Accepts all major credit cards*

# JEFFREY'S
## 1204 West Lynn
### 512-477-5584

Many a person in Austin says that the best meal they have eaten in town has been next door to the Clarksville Café (see page 39). Which is just fine by all concerned, because the Café and Jeffrey's are owned, operated, and cooked for by the same people. The difference is that Jeffrey's is even more intimate and comfortable than its neighbor: Its menu contains more elaborate dishes with more variety every day (for example, the rib eye *aux cinque poivres* is a handsome steak rolled in five varieties of peppercorns, then broiled and topped with a brandy and champagne-vinegar cream sauce), and its waiters are the only ones in town who can compete with those next door for charm and knowledge of the business. Because reservations are not taken, the wait is long, but the stay at a table within the cream-colored walls is rarely less than two blissfully spent hours. Although you roll the dice each day on what will be on the menu, few people ever report losing. The Valentine's Day queue was nothing less than a street party, which is a difference in degree rather than one in kind from every other night at Austin's best, non-indigenous restaurant.

*Price: About $30 per person*
*Open Mon.–Sat. for dinner only; closed Sun.*
*Accepts Visa and MasterCard*

---

# LAS MANITAS
## 211 Congress
### 512-472-9357

This downtown brunch and lunch spot has begun serving dinner three times a week. Its atmosphere, accented by original Chicano art on the walls and liberal publications in the magazine rack up front, is relaxed, in spite of the growing crowds. You can sit at the counter and nurse a few cups of coffee with the morning paper. Or there is the courtyard through and behind the kitchen. Most brunchers and lunchers are willing to wait for a booth or part of a table to share with whoever happens to be there. The *huevos rancheros* are the authentic article, an Austin breakfast so ubiquitous as to rival fast food. And, at lunch, chicken and avocado *flautas* are a light alternative to the *enchiladas, carne guisada,* and daily specials.

*Price: Easily under $10 per person*
*Open daily for breakfast, lunch, and dinner*
*No credit cards accepted*

# NIGHT HAWK
## 336 South Congress
### 512-478-1661

This self-proclaimed "Austin Tradition Since 1932" was flooded in the late 1930s and burned down in 1985. Phoenix-like, it keeps rising from adversity to serve its biscuits at breakfast, burgers at lunch, and steaks-and-potatoes at dinner. Founded by the late Harry Aikin, a city council member and maverick liberal politician, "the Hawk" was redecorated for its fiftieth anniversary, when new brightly-patterned curtains and red leather booths were installed. The waitresses wear brown and beige uniforms, know at least half the people who come in, and let inquiring types know what kinds of pies are left. (The custard and chocolate icebox varieties are delicious.)

Lady Bird Johnson often eats here when she's in from the ranch, and many's the downtown worker who admits to eating two out of three meals a day here. Try the "Frisco"—the burger populi. The steaks are now even available as TV dinners at local grocery stores. For a blend of graciousness, basic food, and a dining crowd that averages about fifty years of age, this is the place.

*Price: About $5–$15 per person*
*Open daily for breakfast, lunch, and dinner*
*Accepts all major credit cards*

# OLD COUPLAND INN
## U.S. Highway 290E to Elgin, then North on Texas Highway to Coupland
### 512-856-2632

Like so many of the truly authentic barbecue places in Central Texas, this is a bit over half an hour's drive from downtown Austin. (The Salt Lick near Driftwood and Kreuz's Market in Lockhart are two other destinations of local pilgrims.) The drive is well worth it, for the scenery as well as the beef. Toward dusk, the hills, cedar trees, and creeks can stir feelings akin to the Great Gatsby's as he looked across at Daisy Buchanan's dock on Long Island, New York, sixty years ago. And the eating halls one finds upon arrival—an old saloon in Coupland, a rock house with screen porch at Driftwood, and a turn-of-the-century counter in Lockhart—make the journey all the more memorably picturesque.

Large groups tend to eat the ribs, sausage, and brisket family style, which means paying a slightly higher price per head and watching the platters come out for as long as anyone is still hungry. It's always wise to call ahead to make sure of hours: Coupland is only open on weekends and takes reservations. Reservations are advisable.

*Price: About $10 per person*
*Open Fri.–Sun. for dinner only; closed Mon.–Thurs.*
*No credit cards accepted*

---

## SCHOLZ GARDEN
### 1607 San Jacinto
### 512-477-4171

This 120-year-old restaurant and beer garden is quintessential Austin. A short walk from downtown, the Capitol, and the University, it is the longest-lived and most diverse watering hole in town. Although the food is mediocre at best, enjoying the pitchers of beer while sitting beneath the trees is de rigueur on spring afternoons. Legislators, academics, laborers, and softball players fill the outdoors from about 4 P.M. on. If you must eat, the *nachos* improve with each pitcher of beer and the fried chicken sometimes has its moment. Go for the Texas Populist nightcap.

*Price: Under $10 per person, depending upon the length of stay*
*Open Mon.–Sat. for lunch and dinner; closed Sun.*
*Accepts Visa and MasterCard*

---

## THREADGILL'S
### 6416 North Lamar
### 512-451-5440

This old roadhouse, where people used to go to hear music at a time when this locale was considered far north Austin, has been renovated and rejuvenated by Eddie Wilson, a local music and restaurant visionary. It's named after a guitar picker whom Janis Joplin used to visit here on Wednesday nights. The main show in the wood-floor, boisterous place is the food—lots of it at some of the best prices in town. Pork roast with jezebel sauce (pineapple, apple jelly, horseradish, and mustard), liver and onions, or chicken-fried steak are the leading entrée choices, each accompanied by two vegetables—mashed potatoes, black-eyed peas, stewed okra, and garlic-cheese grits being the best among them. Try to save room or at least go halves with someone on a pudding or piece of pie à la mode. Also try to get one of the bluejean-clad waitpeople to seat you in the new Art Deco addition that was the backdrop for recording artist Marcia Ball's latest album.

*Price: About $10 per person*
*Open daily for lunch and dinner*
*Accepts Visa and MasterCard*

# SAN ANTONIO

## CRUMPETS
### 5800 Broadway
**512-821-5454**

Although French food is not the regional *métier,* this congenial, unaffected restaurant in Alamo Heights consistently pleases the eclectic crowd it draws. The menu, with entrées such as green *fettuccine* with scallops or tenderloin of beef with green peppercorn sauce, changes regularly and is guaranteed to please a discriminating palate. An average wine list is more than made up for by a dessert cart many *cognoscenti* consider the best in town. Save room for a pastry and try anything made with peaches during the summer season.

*Price: About $15 per person*
*Open daily for lunch and dinner*
*Accepts American Express, Visa, and MasterCard*

## LA FOGATA
### 2427 Vance Jackson
**512-341-9930**

Doing best what San Antonio restaurants do best—that is, preparing and serving Tex–Mex (or, more accurately in La Fogata's case, Mex–Mex)—this small place is always very crowded and incredibly good. Anything with flour tortillas (particularly the *tacos al carbon*) will be the real thing. The temptation to order three or four dishes is easily justified by the reasonable prices and generous portions. Old standby dishes include the grilled green onions and the *charro* beans. The margaritas tend to be disappointing, but the Tecate beer with lime is chilled to perfection. The decor is appropriately simple and the staff wonderfully helpful and competent.

*Price: About $10 per person*
*Open Tues.–Sat. for breakfast, lunch, and dinner; Sun. for breakfast and lunch only*
*No credit cards accepted*

# PAESANO'S
## 1715 McCullough
### 512-226-9541

Little League coaches and bigtime politicians regularly help to fill one of the city's most popular restaurants. A big expansion a few years back (which brought in more red leather and black Formica tables while preserving the crowded bustle) helped cut the almost-guaranteed wait from thirty minutes to fifteen. The queue is for "shrimp Paesano," a dish with a cream-and-lemon sauce that was voted by local newspaper readers as the best in town. The veal dishes are consistently fine, too. After enjoying a workman-like dinner salad, the usual side of pasta, and a rich (visually and calorically) *spumoni* ice cream, you'll easily see why Paesano's has such a large and loyal following.

*Price: About $15 per person*
*Open Tues.–Fri. for lunch and dinner; Sat. and Sun. for dinner only; closed Mon.*
*Accepts Visa and MasterCard*

# ROOSEVELT BAR
## In the Menger Hotel, 204 Alamo Plaza
### 512-223-4361

A touch of the Old World turned to funk along the River Walk, this is a good place to come into out of the San Antonio heat. According to local lore, Teddy Roosevelt signed up many of his Rough Riders here in 1898. Many's the luminary who drank and slept in this 125-year-old hotel, which has slipped from being one of the most opulent establishments between New Orleans and San Francisco to something vaguely reminiscent of a hang-out in Raymond Chandler's world. Which makes it all a better place to recapitulate a Spurs' basketball game or plan the next outing. And if you have an adventurous sweet tooth, you might ask the kitchen to send over some of the hotel's homemade, ineffable mango ice cream. The bar is closed on Sundays.

*Accepts all major credit cards*

# BALTIMORE

## *BY ROB KASPER*

**BAR**
  Jean Claude's Café
  The 13th Floor Lounge

**BARBECUE**
  Café Tattoo

**BREAKFAST**
  The Women's Industrial
    Exchange

**BRUNCH**
  Hamilton's Landing

**CHINESE**
  Uncle Lee's Szechuan Restaurant

**CONTINENTAL**
  The Brass Elephant

**CRAB HOUSE**
  Bud Paolino's Restaurant
  C-J's Restaurant
  Gunning's Crab House
  Obrycki's Crab House

**DELICATESSEN**
  Attman's Delicatessen
  Bun Penny (see Harborplace)

**ECLECTIC**
  The Pimlico Restaurant

**ENGLISH**
  Bertha's Dining Room

**FAMILY RESTAURANT**
  Glenmore Gardens

**FAST FOOD**
  Harborplace
  The Lexington Market

**FRENCH**
  Chez Fernand
  The Conservatory
  Jacqueline

**HAMBURGERS**
  The Irish Pub

**HOTEL DINING ROOM**
  The Conservatory
  Jacqueline

**IRISH**
  Angelina's Restaurant
  McGinns's

**ITALIAN**
  Trattoria Petrucci

**MEXICAN**
  Pancho's (see Lexington Market)

**NIGHTCLUB/RESTAURANT**
  Ethel's Place

**OPEN LATE**
  Gampy's

**PANORAMA**
  Berry and Elliot's

**PIZZA**
  Bella Roma

**SEAFOOD**
  Faidley's (see Lexington Market)
  Marconi Restaurant Inc.

**SPANISH**
  Tio Pepe Restaurante

**STEAKS AND CHOPS**
  The Prime Rib

**SUBURBAN**
  Attman's Delicatessen
    (Pikesville)
  C-J's Restaurant (Owing Mills)
  The Pimlico Restaurant
    (Pikesville)

**THAI**
  Thai Restaurant

**UNIQUE PROPERTIES**
  Lexington Market
  The Women's Industrial
    Exchange

**WINE BAR**
  Jacqueline

When people come to Baltimore, they want to eat crabs and fish. I know this is a tremendous oversimplification. It's like saying the only reasons for living are to enjoy good food and good sex. You know these pleasures aren't the whole story, but you sure as shooting wouldn't want to miss out on them either.

The reason visitors to Baltimore want to eat seafood is a good one: geography. The Chesapeake Bay, source of crabs in the summer and oysters in winter and spawning ground for a boatload of Atlantic Ocean fish, is a short boat ride from downtown Baltimore.

Some of the locals don't even leave their neighborhood for crabs. In the summertime, folks in south Baltimore drop hand lines, pieces of string tied to chicken necks, from the narrow Hanover Street Bridge down into the waters of the Patapsco River. When these urban crabbers haul in big jimmies (male crabs), they become sources both of local color and local traffic congestion on the bridge. Baltimore is a crab town. Almost every Baltimore neighborhood has a restaurant that fills the air with the sweet perfume of steamed crabs. In some sections of the city—sections I regard as the better neighborhoods—there is a crab house on every block.

Three factors figure in the decision of which crab house to go to. The first is how hot is the seasoning? As they are steaming, hard-shell crabs are covered with a spicy mixture of salt, paprika, mustard, and pepper. While crab house operators get the basics of the seasoning from suppliers, they add their own touches. Some of these touches are more fiery than others. The second factor is the size of the crabs. Hard shells are priced by size and by the dozen. When the waitress says "the crabs are running 11, 16, 20, 24, and 28," it means the price escalates from $11 a dozen for small crabs up to $28 a dozen for jumbos. The advantage in buying the less expensive crabs, besides the price, is that their meat is often very sweet. The advantage in buying the large crabs is that they yield plenty of crab meat without having to hammer through lots of shell. Size and price vary from crab house to crab house. The third factor is finding out how a place cooks soft-shell crabs. A soft-shell crab is caught during the few days of the year when a crab has shed its old hard shell and is growing a papery new one. One of the great joys of life is eating a soft-crab sandwich. An entire crab is lightly fried or sautéed and then served as a sandwich with a thick slice of tomato. The tomato should be so juicy it squirts.

Because the city is a seaport, waves of immigrants have arrived in Baltimore, bringing with them their foods from the other side of the ocean. The city's Little Italy, Greektown, and fledgling Asian restaurant sections are evidence of the effect immigration has had on local eating.

But lately the biggest change in local eating patterns has been caused by renovation, not immigration. Beginning around 1980 with Harborplace, two harborfront pavilions consisting mainly of restaurants and food stands, downtown Baltimore has sprouted all sorts of new spots to eat. There has been growth not just in places where you sit down and eat, but in places where you stand up and eat something that needs little preparation, such as a raw oyster.

In the "Happy Eater" column I write for *The Baltimore Sun,* I don't restrict myself to sit-down places. I write about eating, drinking, and having a good time wherever I find it, with or without silverware. It is that spirit I bring to this chapter.

*Rob Kasper writes the "Happy Eater" column for* The Baltimore Sun.

---

## ANGELINA'S RESTAURANT
### 7135 Harford Road
### 301-444-5545

Angelina's (30 minutes northeast of downtown Baltimore) is the quintessential Baltimore–Irish restaurant. Downstairs there is singing; upstairs there is crab. One dish, tomato stuffed with crab, is named after one of the sons of the late owner. It is called Crab Brendan.

*Price: About $10 per person*
*Open Mon.–Sat. for lunch and dinner; Sun. for dinner only*
*Accepts all major credit cards*

---

## ATTMAN'S DELICATESSEN AT PAMONA
### 1700 Reisterstown Road, Pikesville
### 301-484-8477

---

## ATTMAN'S DELICATESSEN
### 1019 East Lombard Street (*east of downtown Baltimore*)
### 301-563-2666

Attman's started in Corned Beef Row, an east Baltimore neighborhood that once was the center of deli-style eating. Now the deli stronghold is Pikesville, a western Baltimore suburb. There still is an Attman's deli on Corned Beef

Row, but it is much smaller than the new one in Pikesville. The one in Pikesville offers more comfort, but the counter help on Corned Beef Row has better wisecracks. Both places serve cafeteria style. You get your tray and work your way down the line, deciding among the corned beef, which almost everybody else is ordering, the oversized hot dogs, or the hot pastrami. You get a big chocolate-chip cookie and maybe a beer. You eat, pat your middle, and smile.

*Price: About $5 per person*
*Pikesville open Mon.–Sat. for lunch and dinner; Sun. for dinner only; Lombard Street open daily for lunch; Mon.–Sat. for dinner*
*No credit cards accepted*

---

## BELLA ROMA
### 3600 Keswick Road
**301-235-2595**

In other parts of the country people may be putting whole zucchini on their pizza, but in Baltimore, pizza is still simple and tasty. This one has a thin crust, cheese, and tomato sauce. Takeout is a good idea, even though Bella Roma does deliver.

*Price: About $5 to $7, depending on toppings*
*Open Mon.–Sat. for lunch and dinner; Sun. for dinner only*
*No credit cards accepted*

---

## BERRY AND ELLIOT'S
### Atop the Hyatt Hotel, 300 Light Street
**301-528-1234**

First there is the panorama. The view is all Baltimore. Boats ease through the Inner Harbor. East Baltimore stretches out in neat lines. Federal Hill looks like a great vantage point for a cannon, which is exactly what it was used for during the Civil War when the Northern troops wanted to keep the rebels in Baltimore quiet.

Then there is the dancing: A deejay spins records and keeps the dance floor hopping. And last there is the food, a casual sampling of American eats: *nachos* with *guacamole* from the West and row oysters from the East; blackened red snapper from New Orleans and pizza topped with crab meat, from who knows where. The idea here is to dance and enjoy the view.

*Price: About $20 per person*
*Open daily for lunch and dinner*
*Accepts all major credit cards*

# BERTHA'S DINING ROOM
## In Fells Point, 734 South Broadway
### 301-327-5795

Fells Point is the section of town that the tugboats call home. Most of the time Bertha's is a waterfront seafood place known for its bumper sticker that reads: "Eat Bertha's Mussels." On the whole that is good advice. But in the afternoons, from 3 to 5 P.M., by reservation only, Bertha's serves tea—the whole spread, from scones to Scotch eggs to plates of assorted pastries. Reservations are required by noon for 3 P.M. tea.

*Price: About $5.50 per person for tea*
*Open Mon.–Sat. for lunch and dinner; closed Sun.*
*Accepts all major credit cards*

# THE BRASS ELEPHANT
## 924 North Charles Street
### 301-547-8480

Not only does The Brass Elephant do a good job with dishes from the European continent, it also provides the kind of elegant setting continental travelers are supposed to be seen in. The restaurant was once the stately nineteenth-century mansion of an old Baltimore family. Polished wood, gilded mirrors, and even a brass elephant decorate the dining rooms.

Sit anywhere other than at the very front tables and look right out onto Charles Street. The spot on the continent that the chef seems to like best is Italy. Even *lasagne,* which could be a mundane dish, comes out of the kitchen looking and tasting classy. You will see the dessert cart in the hallway as you walk in. You'll wonder if those cakes are as dark and rich and chocolate-tasting as they look. They aren't. After dinner go upstairs to the bar. Have an after-dinner drink or simply feel the bar's cool marble.

*Price: About $40 per person*
*Open Mon.–Fri. for lunch and dinner; Sat. and Sun. for dinner only*
*Accepts all major credit cards*

# BUD PAOLINO'S RESTAURANT
## 3919 East Lombard Street
### 301-732-4080

"Bud's," as the regulars refer to it, is the crab house softball players, bowlers, and major-league umpires feel comfortable in. The walls in the back dining room are devoted to sports memorabilia, autographed baseballs, autographed bats, and bowling trophies. The kitchen is devoted to crabs. At Bud's, the cook adds a little extra rock salt to the spice mix that covers the hard crabs. Bud's small crabs are some of the sweetest that ever swam.

*Price: About $20 per person*
*Open daily for lunch and dinner*
*Accepts all major credit cards*

## CAFÉ TATTOO
### 4807 Belair Road
**301-325-7427**

The ribs aren't cooked over wood, they're cooked in an electric smoker. But the sauces that go on top of them are pungent. The best, which has picked up a couple of prizes for the Café Tattoo owners in regional barbecue contests, is the Black Jack sauce. One of the ingredients is a shot of Jack Daniels whiskey. Strangely enough for a barbecue joint, the vegetables are good: The eggplant with feta cheese makes you forget you're eating eggplant. And the peanut butter pie is a perfect ending for a heavy rib feast. But, shucks, there is no beer here, though you can get a tattoo right next door. As of this writing, the café may be moving.

*Price: About $10 per person*
*Open Wed.–Sun. for dinner only; closed Mon. and Tues.*
*No credit cards accepted*

## CHEZ FERNAND
### 805 East Fayette Street (*next to the Baltimore Shot Tower*)
**301-752-8030**

Some time ago a fire forced Chez Fernand to leave the suburbs and relocate near a downtown Baltimore building once used to make shot for muskets. To some Baltimore eaters, Chez Fernand's move ranked right up there with Lafayette's arrival as one of history's most significant movements of friendly French forces. Sit in the dining room that overlooks a small park. Order *foie gras,* which will convert anyone into a liver lover. Taste the fish, such as ocean perch *meunière,* and note how it doesn't get lost in the butter sauce. The fowl is firm but not dry. Ask Fernand to pick the wine, and finish off with strawberries dipped in chocolate or the dark chocolate *mousse.* You'll leave humming "La Marseillaise."

*Price: About $35 per person*
*Open Mon.–Fri. for lunch and dinner; Sat. and Sun. for dinner only*
*Accepts all major credit cards*

# C–J'S RESTAURANT
## 10117 Reistertown Road, Owings Mills
### 301-363-6694

The building used to be a Burger Chef outlet, but nowadays crabs—big ones —come out of the kitchen of C–J's in Reistertown, a suburb about half an hour west of downtown Baltimore. C–J's is noted for having big crabs. In the summer, the big boys are homegrown, coming from the Chesapeake Bay, but in the winter C–J's has to get its jumbo crabs from Louisiana. Wherever they hail from, the crabs are treated the same. They are tossed in ice water to stun them, covered with a relatively mild seasoning, and then steamed.

*Price: About $20 per person for medium-sized crabs; $25 for large*
*Open daily for lunch and dinner*
*Accepts most major credit cards*

---

# THE CONSERVATORY
## Atop the Peabody Court Hotel, 612 Cathedral Street
### 301-727-7101

It's new, it's French, and it's fancy. Georges and Danielle Mosse converted a downtown apartment building into the luxury Peabody Court Hotel and topped it off with a posh 16-table restaurant.

Baltimore never looked better than from a table on top of the Peabody Court. The nineteenth-century mansions of the surrounding Mount Vernon neighborhood look stately and clean. The rooftops of the neat rows of east and west Baltimore stairstep to the horizons. Even the Maryland State Prison looks architecturally, if not residentially, pleasing.

The presentation of the food, from the champagne bubbling ever so temptingly out of the top of Italian crystal glasses to the waiters making sure that they simultaneously deliver the entrées, is a joy to behold.

The seafood entrées have two surprises: First no crab, not even in the summer; and second, the lobster in vanilla sauce, a bad idea. But the duckling, that comes complete with a decorative puff pastry duckette, and the chocolate *mousse* cake drowned in raspberry sauce, will leave you sighing with pleasure and thanking the creator for making duck and *mousse*.

The Conservatory has been billed as the city's most expensive restaurant. Entrées average $30. The wine list starts there, too, and quickly ascends. (There is another restaurant, The Brasserie, on the first floor of the hotel where the food, setting, presentation, and prices are less celestial.) The food at The Conservatory is superb. You'll have a hard time meeting a puff pastry item there you won't like. Especially tasty is the hors d'oeuvre of

California goat cheese in puff pastry served with Devonshire cream sauce. The sauce is decorated to look like a piece of china; it tastes like a piece of heaven.

*Price: About $75 per person*
*Open Tues.–Sun. for dinner only; closed Mon.*
*Accepts most major credit cards*

---

# ETHEL'S PLACE
## 1225 Cathedral Street *(across from Joseph Meyerhoff Symphony Hall)*
### 301-727-7077

This place defies the rules. Establishments that do more than two things at once, like sing and serve dinner, are not supposed to have good food. The food at Ethel's is among the best in the city. Their shrimp and mussels with garlic and cayenne and their veal dishes paired with crab meat or scallops are front-row fare. Even the vegetables, which often don't matter in restaurant meals, arrive at the table firm and fresh.

You may eat either in the nightclub, which features jazz singers (among them one of the owners, Ethel Ennis, for whom the club is named), or you may dine in the greenhouse—a handsome glass-topped dome. Either way you get meals that make you want to shout "Encore!" There is a nice selection of wines by the glass, as well as a very good wine list.

*Price: About $20 per person*
*Open Tues.–Sun. for dinner only; closed Mon.*
*Accepts all major credit cards*

---

# GAMPY'S
## 904 North Charles Street
### 301-837-9797

Gampy's keeps its kitchen open until 2 A.M. and is a popular after-work spot for waiters and waitresses whose duties ended a few hours earlier. If you are hungry get the chili and an order of potato skins.

If you want a nightcap, get the Irish coffee. If you want conversation, sit at the bar and ask "Who is this Gampy anyway?" The name is an acronym for Great American Melting Pot. If some wiseacre knows the answer, then ask him what an acronym is.

*Price: About $10 per person*
*Open daily for lunch and dinner*
*Accepts all major credit cards*

# GLENMORE GARDENS
## 4813 Belair Road
### 301-488-2366

An ideal spot to take the family to eat is an outdoor crab garden. The kids can wield hammers at the table without getting reprimanded. Neatness doesn't count. And mom and dad can eat fresh crab and drink cold beer and maybe even talk to each other. Glenmore Gardens is such a place. There are about 35 picnic tables in a courtyard outside the restaurant. That means there is no ceiling on which the sounds of kids hammering will reverberate.

The tables are covered with sheets of brown paper. At the end of a meal the table is cleared by rolling the brown paper up in a bundle and throwing it away. There are even outdoor sinks, for washing off hands, a few steps away from the tables. Eating there with kids is such a pleasant change from eating at home, that it may make you think about covering your own kitchen table with brown paper.

*Price: About $8 per person*
*Open daily for lunch and dinner*
*Accepts all major credit cards*

# GUNNING'S CRAB HOUSE
## 3901 South Hanover Street
### 301-354-0085

Gunning's is in South Baltimore, one of those neighborhoods that has a crab house on just about every corner. Nonetheless, Gunning's thrives, drawing eaters from all over the city. One reason is that Gunning's still cooks crabs the old-fashioned way—steaming them in the equivalent of a giant double boiler.

The hotly seasoned crabs sit in the top part of the boiler, drawing heat and flavor from the boiling water beneath them. Other crab houses cook the crabs using "live steam" piped into stainless steel pots from a central boiler. Order the $20-a-dozen crabs, several beers, and finish off with an order of deep-fried green pepper rings dusted with powdered sugar. In tomato season, order the soft-crab sandwich. The crab is deep-fried, instead of sautéed, but the tomato slice that comes with the crab is so juicy, all fried faults are forgiven.

*Price: About $20 per person*
*Open daily for lunch and dinner*
*Accepts all major credit cards*

# HAMILTON'S LANDING
In Fells Point, 1700 Thames Street
301-522-6766

Hamilton's Landing is right across the street from where the Baltimore harbor tugboats tie up for the night. And on Sundays the brunch spread that the kitchen puts out could satisfy even the legendary appetites of tugboat captains. There are Louisiana shrimp, pan-roasted oysters, spiced scrambled eggs, baked apples, and grits. It is served buffet style and called a "Southern brunch," but it's more like a Sunday dinner. There are two seatings, noon and 2 P.M. Reservations are suggested.

*Price: About $12 per person for brunch*
*Open Mon.–Sat. for dinner only; Sun. for brunch and dinner*
*Accepts all major credit cards*

# THE IRISH PUB
249 West Chase Street
301-752-4059

The Pub's three sandwiches—the basic burger, the blue burger (with blue cheese, bacon, and optional fried onions), and the Pubburger (with Swiss cheese and Russian dressing) are the ruling burgers. They are big, beefy, and almost a meal in themselves. Sit in the back room and order the onion rings. Don't worry about dressing up; the Pub is a neighborhood tavern.

*Price: Burgers are about $4 each*
*Open daily for lunch and dinner*
*No credit cards accepted*

# JEAN CLAUDE'S CAFÉ
Light Street Pavilion of Harborplace 301 South Light Street
301-332-0950

# THE 13th FLOOR LOUNGE
Atop the Belvedere Hotel, 1 East Chase Street
301-547-8220

There are two cocktail seasons in Baltimore: the indoor season and the outdoor season. The time for indoor cocktails is when the weather outside is forbidding. In Baltimore's climate that means all winter, when it's too cold to go outside, and most of August, when it is too humid to go outside. During this season the place to enjoy cocktails is the 13th Floor Lounge in the Belvedere Hotel. The Belvedere is a grand old building and the thirteenth floor offers comfortable chairs, good drinks, and a grand view of the city. Try to get a seat on the south side (to your right as you get off the elevator). That side shows you the steeples, gables, and cornices of the older section of downtown. The other side of the lounge isn't disappointing either. From it you can look down on the silver trains sliding in and out of Baltimore's Penn Station.

The outdoor cocktail season begins in spring and, forgetting about the month of August, runs until October. In 1980, this season got a real boost when Harborplace opened and quickly added about ten spots to sit outside and sip. The best of these is Jean Claude's. In the evening, sit out on the terrace and watch the promenade, as tourists and fun-seekers stroll along the promenade next to the water's edge. You won't actually think you're in Paris, but you might feel a burst of *joie de vivre*.

*Belvedere is open every evening for cocktails only;*
*Jean Claude's open daily for lunch and dinner*
*Prices: $3 per drink at the Belvedere;*
*$2 per drink at Jean Claude's*
*Both accept all major credit cards*

---

# THE LEXINGTON MARKET
## 400 West Lexington Street
### 301-685-6169

---

# HARBORPLACE
## 301 South Light Street
### 301-332-4191

Fast food means good food that you get in a hurry and in Baltimore that means the Lexington Market or the Light Street Pavilion of Harborplace. Both are indoor food markets.

Harborplace is neat and clean and has been on the cover of *Time* magazine. The best fast eats it has to offer are Thrasher's French fries, the rare roast beef on rye at the Bun Penny deli, the lemon stick (half a lemon with a peppermint stick in it, a Baltimore favorite) at the Oasis, and the carrot cake at Ms. Desserts.

The Lexington Market is older and not as clean as Harborplace, but the food is better. Get a fresh ham sandwich from the Mary Mervis deli stand and enjoy that fresh pig taste. Get a *gyro* from Mount Olympus; it'll make you rethink your position on lamb. For Korean food, try the beef-and-noodle platter at Bulkoki Corner. The East part of the market (across Paca Street) not only has a *burrito* you could write home about, at the combo at Pancho's, it also offers an excellent photo opportunity—you standing next to a lifesize mural of Babe Ruth, a Baltimore boy. The mural is on the north wall of the market, around the corner from Pancho's.

But the best fast food in Baltimore is raw oysters, and among the best places to eat them is at the oyster bar at Faidley's Seafood in the market. When the shucker nods at you, tell him you want three primes (large oysters). Put a little horseradish on them and count your blessings.

*Closed Sun.*

---

# JACQUELINE
## 101 West Fayette Street (*in the Omni Hotel*)
### (301) 685-8100

When Jacqueline opened in the fall of 1985, it was a breath of fresh air and a gulp of fresh wine for downtown Baltimore. The big, round bar in the middle of the airy restaurant serves 18 wines by the glass, making it the city's most serious wine bar. Most of the wines, priced from $2.50 to $4.00 a glass, are from California. The restaurant's exclusive wines, La Crema Vinera Chardonnay and Pinot Noir, have a rare vanilla flavor, and the Domaine Chandon Blanc de Noirs is a real sparkler.

The restaurant is a bistro, serving sandwiches, sausages, and entrées in a setting of brass, glass, and polished wood. The sausages, made by a transplanted German known as the "Sausage Doctor of Baltimore," are exceptional. *Choucroute Alsacienne* for two—*sauerkraut, bratwurst,* garlic sausage, smoked pork, and steamed potatoes—is served with a split of champagne, but also goes well with a glass of Johannisberg Riesling. For dessert, try either the *dégustation* of desserts (something rare in Baltimore), or the chocolate ice cream made on the premises.

*Price: About $15 per person*
*Open daily for breakfast, lunch, and dinner*
*Accepts all major credit cards*

# MARCONI RESTAURANT INC.
## 106 West Saratoga Street
### 301-752-9286

Baltimore has many seafood restaurants, but only one like Marconi's. It is old and quirky. It doesn't take reservations. It closes early, around 8 P.M. The menu is mimeographed. It simply serves good seafood.

The soft-shell crabs are sautéed. The fish, usually bay trout and red snapper, is neither overcooked nor oversauced. And when oysters are in season, that is in months with an "R" in them, they are treated like royalty. On Fridays in oyster season, the chef makes Oysters Pauline, oysters stuffed with lobster meat and Parmesan cheese and baked in the shells—reason enough to stay in town until Friday. Be sure to save room for the ice cream sundae—a mound of vanilla ice cream served with a bowl of homemade chocolate sauce. Most diners ladle the sauce on the ice cream and some fantasize about injecting it into their veins.

*Price: About $20 per person*
*Open Tues.–Sat. for lunch and dinner; closed Sun. and Mon.*
*Accepts most major credit cards*

# McGINNS'S
## 328 North Charles Street
### 301-539-7504

McGinns's is the kind of place you would take your Irish mother. The fare is corned beef and potatoes served on tables covered with white tablecloths. The bar is woody and conversational. On weekends the bands and singers come in and the lads get lively.

*Price: Under $10 per person*
*Open Mon.–Sat. for lunch and dinner; closed Sun.*
*Accepts all major credit cards*

# OBRYCKI'S CRAB HOUSE
## 1729 East Pratt Street
### 301-732-6399

Regarded as the grande dame of Baltimore crab houses, Obrycki's is the place crab eaters go when they are dressed up. The restaurant occupies an old Baltimore row house that has been restored to Colonial splendor. But it is

Obrycki's crabs, and not just its candlelight charm, that keep the customers coming. During the winter, when other restaurants are importing their crabs from Louisiana and Texas, Obrycki's closes down. Its reopening, every April, is a sure sign that the arrival of warm weather and Maryland crabs are just a few weeks away. Their soft-shell crab sandwich, which they pan-fry rather than deep-fry, is reason enough to wait in line for a table, which you might have to do on weekends. The hard-shell crabs, which tend to be medium size, are hot. Hard-shell crabs are served at dinner and sometimes for lunch. Call ahead to make sure they are on the menu.

*Price: About $20 per person*
*Open Mon.–Sat. for lunch and dinner; Sun. for dinner only*
*Seasonal—May through October; check days when crabs are served*
*Accepts all major credit cards*

---

# THE PIMLICO RESTAURANT
## 1777 Reisterstown Road, Pikesville
### 301-486-6776

The decor of this suburban restaurant is bright and airy, with lots of glass, flowers, and modern paintings. The food is a mixture of American—Maine lobster, Maryland crab, Midwestern beef—and Chinese, mostly Cantonese. The Pimlico egg roll, about the size of a yule log, is among the best in Baltimore.

The Pimlico is a reliable restaurant that handles every dish well. The dishes that have the least done to them—the simple lobster meat cocktail and the grilled swordfish—are the ones that come out the best. The servings are gigantic. The entrées come with enough vegetables to feed a family of four. That is part of the Pimlico style.

The wine list, mainly French with splashes of American and Italian wines, is well organized. The desserts are legendary, thanks in part to the habits of a local savings and loan mogul who ate pieces of the Pimlico's Mile High Pie —an ice cream pie covered with whipped cream—as his financial empire sank six feet under.

Reservations are a must. The Pimlico is a fixture in Baltimore's Jewish community, and many of the restaurant's patrons know each other. Don't be alarmed if somebody's mother is seated ahead of you. She not only knows the maître d'; she knows his mother.

*Price: About $25–$30 per person*
*Open daily for lunch and dinner*
*Accepts most major credit cards*

# THE PRIME RIB
## 1101 North Calvert Street (*enter on Chase Street*)
### 301-539-1804

The best piece of beef in the city is at The Prime Rib. The beef, a hunk of aged sirloin, is also so big it could probably feed a small city.

The Prime Rib has a dark and masculine decor. The waiters are coolly efficient, like presidential aides. They are there when you want them, they are gone when you don't.

The menu is long, but the emphasis is on beef—aged beef. If you are feeling like a he-man, order the big 16-ounce sirloin, black on the outside, pink in the middle, with a lot more taste than average beef. You won't finish it. But don't be shy about taking the remainder home. At the price you're paying for this beef, about $25, you should get more than one meal out of it. You must also have the potato skins; The Prime Rib invented them. The wine list has plenty of sturdy reds.

*Price: About $45 per person*
*Open daily for dinner only*
*Accepts all major credit cards*

# THAI RESTAURANT
## 3316 Greenmount Avenue
### 301-889-7303

"This food," the waiter tells newcomers, "is very hot and spicy." It is also delicious and inexpensive. Using ingredients such as coconut milk, cucumbers, and lime juice on pork, fish, and meat, the kitchen turns out dishes such as *yum koon chiang,* sweet sausages bathed in cucumbers and lime juice, and *pia rad prik,* a whole fried fish (often flounder) topped with chilies.

This is not a place for folks with timid tongues. But the delightful discovery of the sweet and hot tastes of the sausages, for example, makes up for the fish cakes, which still taste strong no matter how much cucumber you pile on them. There is wine on the menu, but stick to beer.

Located in a pocket of Asian food outlets near Memorial Stadium, the Thai Restaurant is an easy six-block walk to the baseball game. Parking can be a problem, especially on game days. In the rear of the restaurant there is a small parking lot, which can be reached by turning into the alley that runs behind the Waverly branch of the public library.

*Price: About $10 per person*
*Open Mon.–Sat. for lunch and dinner; Sun. for dinner only*
*Accepts all major credit cards*

# TIO PEPE RESTAURANTE
## 10 East Franklin Street
### 301-539-4675

It's ironic that Tio's, which is probably Baltimore's most famous restaurant, thrives in a city that has no significant Spanish population. It does so in part because its easily identifiable Spanish items—a good fruity *sangría,* a zesty *gazpacho,* and exceptional roast pork—are tasty yet don't scare off cautious eaters. Moreover, the chef at Tio's knows how to handle shellfish: The shrimp in garlic sauce, for instance, is so pleasing that you'll not only finish off all the shrimp, but all the sauce as well. Tio's does very well with fish, too, teaming up, for example, fresh cod and pimiento for a rewarding entrée. Garlic, of course, is everywhere.

The service at Tio's can be cool. And getting in on a Saturday night is a real accomplishment. But once you are in and drinking the *sangría,* munching on garlicky shrimp and deciding between the *flan* or the pine nut cake for dessert, it's hard not to feel festive.

*Price: About $40 per person for dinner*
*Open Mon.–Fri. for lunch and dinner; Sat. and Sun. for dinner only*
*Accepts all major credit cards*

# TRATTORIA PETRUCCI
## 300 South High Street
### 301-752-4515

Baltimore's Little Italy consists of about a dozen Italian restaurants crammed into about ten square blocks. Regulars float from one eating establishment to another. They know that the pasta at Chiapparelli's is made in the basement kitchen with ricotta cheese. They know that Capriccio's is kind to mussels, and that Sabatino's "bookmaker salad" is large enough to feed several horses.

Petrucci's covers the basics of Little Italy—good bread, good pasta, and a giant cheesy salad—and then goes on to distinguish itself with its grouper. The fish comes submerged in a sauce of tomato and green olives. Also, don't miss the mussels.

The fare at Petrucci's, like most of Little Italy, is Italian–American and is anything but light. Indeed, the key word in Little Italy is "lotsa." Lotsa pasta. Lotsa cheese. Lotsa sauce. On weekends Little Italy gets very busy. Reservations are a must. Folks who haven't made them hurry from restaurant to restaurant, comparing waiting times. On week nights the pace is more relaxed.

*Price: About $20 per person*
*Open daily for lunch and dinner*
*Accepts all major credit cards*

# UNCLE LEE'S SZECHUAN RESTAURANT
## 3317 Greenmount Avenue
### 301-366-3333

The 3300 block of Greenmount Avenue is probably the best-smelling block in the city. From one side of the street come the sweet aromas of coconut from the Thai Restaurant. And from the other side of the street come the stir-fried perfumes of Uncle Lee's kitchen.

Uncle Lee's is one of those clean, well-run Chinese restaurants that have sprouted in American cities faster than beans. Uncle Lee's empire includes an Asian food store next to the restaurant and a downtown restaurant that, strangely, occupies a former bank. The standard dishes, such as *moo shu* pork and spicy beef with orange rinds, are done well, although the beef dish is a might fiery. The exceptional dishes are the bird's nest soup and the lobster entrées. The hot food makes it easy to drink a lot of beer. And at $2 a beer, it's easy to run up the bill.

*Price: About $25 per person*
*Open daily for lunch and dinner*
*Accepts all major credit cards*

# THE WOMEN'S INDUSTRIAL EXCHANGE
## 333 North Charles Street
### 301-685-4388

This is a great find. Everyone who likes to eat in Baltimore has eaten lunch —crab cakes, chicken salad sandwiches, and homemade pie—at The Women's Industrial Exchange. Surprisingly few folks know that it's also open for breakfast.

The fare is straightforward: eggs, pancakes, homemade biscuits—you gotta have the biscuits—and dark coffee in thick white mugs. It's the kind of breakfast you used to get in restaurants before the restaurateurs read about egg substitutes and you read about cholesterol. This is within easy walking distance of many downtown hotels; breakfast is served from 7 to 11 A.M. The handicraft store in the front of the building sells handmade items, such as quilts and baby clothes. All the profits go to charity.

*Price: About $5 per person*
*Open Mon.–Fri. for breakfast and lunch*
*No credit cards accepted*

# BOSTON

## *By Steven Raichlen*

**AMERICAN**
Durgin-Park
East Coast Grill
Locke-Ober Café

**BAR**
Division 16
The Plow and Stars

**BREAKFAST**
The Café Plaza

**BRUNCH**
Imperial Teahouse Restaurant
Ritz-Carlton Dining Room

**BURMESE**
Mandalay

**CAFÉ**
Harvard Bookstore Café

**CAJUN**
Cajun Yankee

**CHINESE**
Chef Chang's House
Imperial Teahouse Restaurant
Pak Nin
Sally Ling

**CONTINENTAL**
Bay Tower Room
Café Calypso
Hampshire House
Locke-Ober Café

**DELICATESSEN**
Rubin's Delicatessen and
Restaurant

**ECLECTIC**
Another Season
Devon on the Common
East Coast Grill
Harvest
Panache
Restaurant Jasper

## FRENCH
Icarus
Julien
L'Espalier
Restaurant le Marquis de
  Lafayette

## HAMBURGERS
Division 16

## HEALTH FOOD
Five Seasons Restaurant

## HOTEL DINING ROOM
The Café Plaza
Julien
Restaurant le Marquis de
  Lafayette
Ritz-Carlton Dining Room
Seasons

## HUNGARIAN
Café Budapest

## ICE CREAM
Il Dolce Momento
Toscanini's

## ITALIAN
Allegro
Davio's
European
Il Capriccio
Upstairs at the Pudding
Vin and Eddie's Ristorante and
  Wine Bar

## JAPANESE
Nara

## KOREAN
Korea House

## KOSHER
Rubin's Delicatessen and
  Restaurant

## MEXICAN
Sol Azteca

## OPEN LATE
Moon Villa

## PANORAMA
Bay Tower Room

## PIZZA
Bertucci's Pizza and Bocce

## SEAFOOD
Dover Sea Grille
Legal Sea Foods

## SOUL FOOD
Bob the Chef

## STEAKS AND CHOPS
Boodle's
Grill 23 & Bar

## SUBURBAN
Allegro (Waltham)
Country Inn at Princeton
  (Princeton)
Il Capriccio (Waltham)
Vin and Eddie's Ristorante and
  Wine Bar (North Abington)

## TEX–MEX
Rudy's Café

## THAI
Thai Cuisine

## WINE BAR/RESTAURANT
Back Bay Bistrot

"The aboundance of Sea-Fish are almost beyond beleeving, and sure I would scarce have beleeved it except I had seen it with mine owne Eyes," wrote seafarer Francis Higginson on a visit to New England in 1630. Since Pilgrim times, Boston has been blessed with superlative seafood and a rich culinary heritage. The first American cookbooks were published in Boston (Paul Revere engraved the plates for one), and cooking authorities from Fanny Farmer to Julia Child have made this New England capital their home. The past meets the present at the Faneuil Hall Marketplace, a historic warehouse complex filled with hundreds of modern boutiques and food shops.

Boston is a fish-lover's paradise—try it fried at one of our popular fish houses, pan-blackened at a Cajun restaurant, or even raw at one of an ever-growing number of *sushi* bars. Local seafood delicacies include lobster (cheaper here than almost anywhere else in the U.S.), scrod (baby cod), fried clams (invented in the nearby town of Ipswich in 1916), chowder (always without tomatoes!), and succulent Wellfleet oysters. Avoid such tourist traps as Anthony's Pier Four and the No Name Restaurant, where you will wait for up to one and a half hours for the privilege of being rushed through your meal.

Boston may be called the "Athens of America," but our ethnic neighborhoods are thriving. The North End—our Italian quarter—boasts innumerable restaurants, cafés, and open-air markets. (Let the squeamish beware: Freshly slain rabbits hang in the shop windows.) Our Chinatown is the fourth largest in the U.S.; our Armenian community (centered in Watertown) is the third largest in the world. The South End boasts soul food and Middle East restaurants; East Cambridge has a large Portuguese population; Brighton has attracted Vietnamese immigrants; while Central Square has become a hotbed of Indian culinary delights. Don't expect much in the way of atmosphere in most of these places, as our best ethnic chefs put their energy into the cooking, not the decor.

Boston has its fair share of formal dining establishments, including L'Espalier, Panache, Jasper, the Seasons, and Devon on the Common. As befits a university town, we have hundreds of inexpensive eateries, ranging from Cantonese restaurants in Chinatown to sandwich shops in Harvard Square. Ice cream is a strong point of local pride: New Englanders boast the nation's highest per capita consumption. We are famous for our "mix-ins"—ice cream kneaded with nuts, chopped candy bars, and fruit. Other local specialties include baked beans, fiddlehead ferns (available in May), blueberries, Boston cream pie, and Indian pudding (made with cornmeal and molasses). You may wish to sample some New England wine: My favorites are the whites of Rhode Island's Sakonnet Vineyards and the fruit wines of the Nashoba Valley Winery. A locally brewed beer—Samuel Adams—recently took first prize in a national competition.

Some specific advice for out-of-town visitors: When possible, get around by subway or on foot; traffic here is a nightmare. Boston is surprisingly small and walking is the best way to savor our narrow streets and historic architecture. Many of the better-known Boston restaurants do not accept reservations (a practice I deplore), so make every effort to visit them at off-hours.

*Steven Raichlen is the restaurant critic for* Boston Magazine *and author of the* Taste of the Mountains Cooking School Cookbook *(Poseidon Press, 1986) as well as owner of the same school.*

---

# ALLEGRO
## 458 Moody St., Waltham
### 617-891-5486

Don't judge this boutique restaurant by its working-class neighborhood, for behind its unassuming facade is served Northern Italian food of considerable distinction. Allegro owner Jim Burke makes his pasta fresh daily, and builds his sauces on the starchless reductions of French *nouvelle cuisine.* His genius lies in the deceptive simplicity of his monthly-changing menu and his knack for bringing out the essence of every flavor. Recent creations include cold smoked lamb salad, bell pepper pasta with chicken and balsamic vinegar, and *ricotta gelato* (Italian ice cream) for dessert. The high-ceilinged dining room is decorated with exposed brick walls, high-tech lights, and Italian travel posters. Three serious complaints: The service is uneven, the pace of dining rushed, and there's no place to wait in the all-too-likely event that your table is not ready when you arrive. About a 30-minute drive from Boston.

*Price: About $40 per person*
*Open Tues.–Sun. for dinner only; closed Mon.*
*Accepts all major credit cards*

# ANOTHER SEASON
## 97 Mt. Vernon Street (*Beacon Hill*)
### 617-367-0880

Don't complain to Odette Bery about the infelicities of English cooking. For the past twenty years, the London-born chef has endeavored to improve the culinary reputation of her countrymen. Dinner might include a chilled cucumber-shrimp soup, halibut with mussels and saffron, or beef tenderloin sauced with Roquefort cheese and roasted red peppers. Desserts are uncommonly light, ranging from plum meringue tart to peaches stuffed with pistachio nut-blueberry ice cream. The charming dining room is decorated with murals portraying the Gay Nineties in Paris. You'd never guess the restaurant seats 72, divided as it is into four intimate dining areas, which are separated from each other with French doors. After dinner you can take the night air, strolling the gas-lit sidewalks of historic Charles Street.

*Price: About $30–$35 per person*
*Open Tues.–Fri. for lunch and dinner; Mon. and Sat. for dinner only; closed Sun.*
*Accepts American Express, Visa, and MasterCard*

---

# BACK BAY BISTROT
## 565 Boylston Street
### 617-536-4477

The Back Bay Bistrot's wine list features eighty vintages, thirty available nightly by the glass. But to come here for liquid sustenance alone would be to overlook a fine bill of fare that varies with what ingredients are in season. (On a recent visit we enjoyed the Cheddar cheese soup, sole stuffed with smoked scallops, and chocolate cake laced with Grand Marnier.) Recognizable by its pink neon sign, the Back Bay Bistrot seats 80 on bentwood chairs at tables draped with pink cloths. The private room above the main dining room (decorated in pink and gold) can accommodate 24.

*Price: About $15–$20 per person*
*Open daily for lunch and dinner*
*Accepts American Express, Visa, and MasterCard*

# BAY TOWER ROOM
## 60 State Street
### 617-723-1600

The food at the Bay Tower Room is really no better than that at any middling Continental restaurant. It just tastes better, seasoned by a spectacular, thirty-third floor view of the business district, the Boston harbor, and jets departing from Logan Airport. Stick to the simpler items on the menu: smoked salmon, grilled meats, and predictably rich desserts. The gold-rimmed china, heavy silver, and hovering waiters help explain why this glass-enclosed, tiered dining room is considered one of the most romantic spots in town. After dinner you can whirl beneath the stars on a postage-stamp-sized dance floor. This is where the Bay Tower Room *really* shines.

*Price: About $40–$50 per person*
*Open daily for dinner only*
*Accepts all major credit cards*

# BERTUCCI'S PIZZA AND BOCCE
## 799 Main Street (*near Central Square*), Cambridge
### 617-661-8356

The hottest new trend in pizza is as old as the hills: using wood-fired ovens for cooking. Our heartfelt thanks to Joey Krugnale (the man who forged Steve's Ice Cream into an empire) for bringing the wood-cooked pizza to Cambridge. The best seats in the house face a vast marble counter, where white-toqued chefs assemble such delights as pizza *sporkie* (topped with Italian sausage and *ricotta* cheese), *formaggio* (with four kinds of cheese but no tomato sauce), and *quattro stagioni* (a "four seasons" pizza with mushrooms, peppers, artichokes, and prosciutto). The pizzas, *calzone,* and pasta casseroles are baked in wood-fired ovens—Papa Gino's never tasted so good! After dinner, try your hand at bocce ball (Italian bowling) in the sand pit next to the window.

*Price: About $6 per person for pizza*
*Open daily for lunch and dinner*
*Accepts American Express*

# BOB THE CHEF
## 604 Columbus Avenue
### 617-536-6204

Bob the Chef may be the only soul food restaurant in America to have been honored by the visit of a U.S. president, Jimmy Carter, who dined here in 1979. For over a quarter of a century, Bob Morgan of Raleigh, North Carolina, has been packing 'em in for his smothered chicken, smoked ham hocks, black-eyed peas, and barbecued spareribs that are so tender the meat falls right off the bone. Don't expect much in the way of atmosphere—the decor is strictly Formica. And don't leave without sampling the delectable sweet potato pie.

*Price: About $10–$12*
*Open Tues.–Sat. for lunch and dinner; closed Sun.*
*No credit cards accepted*

# BOODLE'S
## In the Back Bay Hilton, 40 Dalton Street
### 617-266-3537

This unusual chop house raises the barbecue to a high art form. Guests have a choice not only of the cut of meat to be grilled, but of the wood (mesquite, hickory, cherry, and sassafras, to name a few) for the actual cooking. Nor are the fireworks restricted to beef: Fish, shrimp, clams, oysters, and even vegetables acquire a unique smoke flavor from grilling. There are over twenty different sauces and butters to choose from by way of accompaniments, and, to wash them down, seventeen different beers. Globe lights, brass rails, and etched glass create the atmosphere of a swank London men's club of the Twenties. The service is suitably efficient.

*Price: About $40 per person*
*Open daily for lunch and dinner*
*Accepts all major credit cards*

# CAFÉ BUDAPEST
## 90 Exeter Street
### 617-734-3388

The bar of the Café Budapest—with its live violin music and dimly lit alcoves —must surely be one of the most romantic watering holes in Boston. But to come here for love alone would be to overlook a tart cherry soup, chicken *paprikás crêpe*, and *sauerbraten à la St. Hubert* that have been known to reduce epicures to tears. My favorite dining room is the Weinstube, with its leaded glass windows and hand-painted rafters. Avoid the main dining room, where guests tend to be herded in and out like cattle. The Café Budapest is run by Edith Ban, a majestic woman in a flowing white dress, who rules her staff with dictatorial discipline. The service will be better if you avoid the 8 P.M. rush on the weekend.

*Price: About $45 per person*
*Open Mon.–Sat. for lunch and dinner; closed Sun.*
*Accepts all major credit cards*

---

## CAFÉ CALYPSO
### 578 Tremont Street
### 617-267-7228

The Calypso of old was an enchantress who kept Odysseus captive for seven years on her island. The Café Calypso, a café/restaurant in the South End, has captivated us with its refined country cooking, seductive pastries, and surprisingly reasonable prices. The cooking manages to be contemporary, yet firmly rooted in a European peasant tradition. The menu changes weekly: A typical meal might include a *torta valdostana* (onion and goat cheese pie), grilled lamb with balsamic vinegar sauce, and silken lemon-rum *mousse*. The rear dining room has peach-colored walls and lavender tabletops; the front dining room, a nice view of the kitchen. The art, which is changed monthly, features local artists. The staff is friendly and efficient.

*Price: About $15–$20 per person*
*Open Tues.–Sun. for lunch and dinner; closed Mon.*
*Accepts all major credit cards*

---

## THE CAFÉ PLAZA
### In the Copley Plaza Hotel, Copley Square
### 617-267-5300

The breakfast served in the formal dining room of the grande dame of Boston hostelries is not substantially better than that dished up by a very good greasy spoon. It just tastes that way, served by epauletted busboys amid the Waterford chandeliers, marble floors, and soaring ornate stucco ceiling of the magnificent Café Plaza. (Other matitudinal amenities include freshly squeezed orange juice and tiny jars of imported Tiptree jam.) There is no classier drink spot in town than the Plaza Bar, with its gilded cornices, deep leather chairs, and silver-plated complimentary hors d'oeuvres cart. (Try the "ice blue" martini, which is flavored with curaçao and served in an individual ice bucket.) For dinner you can repair to the Victoriana-filled Copley's for a first-rate steak.

*Price: About $15 per person for breakfast*
*Open daily for breakfast, lunch, and dinner*
*Accepts all major credit cards*

## CAJUN YANKEE

1193 Cambridge Street (*near Inman Square*), Cambridge
**617-576-1971**

Move over Paul Prudhomme. Make way for John Silverman. Five nights a week, the youthful owner of the Cajun Yankee draws capacity crowds for his pan-blackened redfish, fiery jambalaya, piquant shrimp *rémoulade,* Cajun "popcorn" (fried crawfish with cumin sauce), and garlicky crawfish *etouffé.* The baker (Mary Silverman) deserves sainthood for her bread pudding and sweet potato-pecan pie. The tiny dining room isn't much to look at, with its clunky tables and rec-room-style paneling. The extraordinary New Orleans cooking speaks loudly enough for itself. Reservations are a must—expect a two-week wait—the phone is manned only between 4:30 and 5 P.M.

*Price: About $25 per person*
*Open Tues.–Sat. for dinner only; closed Sun. and Mon.*
*No credit cards accepted*

## CHEF CHANG'S HOUSE

1004–1006 Beacon Street, Brookline
**617-277-4226**

To come to Chef Chang's without sampling the Peking duck would be like visiting Agra and missing the Taj Mahal. The duck is roasted to audible crispness, carved at the table by the venerable chef himself, and served with tangy *hoisin* sauce and Mandarin pancakes—and you don't have to order it the day ahead. A similar flair for theatrics is evident in the sizzling rice soup, General Gau's chicken (fried in chestnut batter), and the spectacular fried whole cod. Unlike most Chinese restaurants, Chef Chang's offers the niceties of bentwood chairs and tables draped with linens. A patterned screen sections off a private dining area—a fun place to bring a group for a Chinese banquet. Expect a 30-minute wait, as reservations are not accepted.

*Price: About $15 per person*
*Open Tues.–Sun. for lunch and dinner; closed Mon.*
*Accepts all major credit cards*

# COUNTRY INN AT PRINCETON
## 30 Mountain Road, Princeton
### 617-464-2030

High on a hill, overlooking the Boston skyline, stands a Queen Anne Victorian mansion that is now a country inn. But the six luxurious suites, each furnished with period antiques, are only part of what makes the Country Inn at Princeton such a romantic retreat. The chef tempers the innovative spirit of *nouvelle cuisine* with *haute* culinary classicism. The menu changes daily: A typical meal might feature crab meat and wild mushroom *ravioli,* three freshwater fishes with champagne-caviar sauce, and white chocolate *mousse* with fresh raspberries. There are three dining rooms—one done in navy and rose, one on a sun porch, and one a private library room that can be reserved for a party as small as two. Cocktails are served on a sunny veranda; after dinner you can relax by the fire in a parlor furnished with Victorian Chippendale, before trundling off to bed! About 1½ hours west of Boston.

*Price: About $40–$50 per person*
*Open Wed.–Sun. for dinner only; closed Mon. and Tues.*
*Accepts American Express, Visa, and MasterCard*

---

# DAVIO'S
## 269 Newbury Street
### 617-262-4810

This charming Newbury Street basement must be one of Back Bay's best kept restaurant secrets. The traditional Italian cooking here—from the *antipasto caldo* (hot antipasto) to the spicy shrimp *fra diavolo*—has a refinement simply not found in the restaurants of the North End. Antique prints, glimmering sconces, and velvet curtains set a mood of romance; the black-tie staff is professional, although not always prompt. When you order *zabaglione* for dessert, the waiters themselves whisk the sugar, eggs, and Marsala to an ethereal foam. The café upstairs serves first-rate "designer" pizzas.

*Price: About $30 per person*
*Open Mon.–Sat. for lunch and dinner; Sun. for dinner only*
*Accepts all major credit cards*

# DEVON ON THE COMMON
## 150 Boylston Street
### 617-482-0722

The owner is Dutch and the chef French-trained, but the cuisine is thoroughly American. The place is a sophisticated restaurant in the heart of the theater district: Devon on the Common. We have no beef with any establishment that grills well-aged sirloins and double-thick lamb chops over smoky mesquite. But to come here for the meat alone would be to miss such Cajun-inspired creations as "blackened" yellowfin tuna, quail with cornmeal stuffing, and an unusual sweetbread and truffle *boudin* (a kind of sausage). Wine buffs can order the $39 tasting menu: Each of the five courses is served with a glass of appropriate wine. The best seats in the house are those next to the picture window overlooking the Boston Commons. An understated elegance is achieved by sprays of fresh flowers, exposed brick walls, and Chinese Chippendale furniture. The service manages to be both professional and friendly. The Cajun Café downstairs serves informal New Orleans-style fare. Another plus is the valet parking.

*Price: About $35–$40 per person*
*Open daily for lunch and dinner*
*Accepts American Express, Visa, and MasterCard*

# DIVISION 16
## 955 Boylston Street
### 617-353-0870

The homemade French fry has gone the way of the dodo bird and the buffalo-head nickel. That's why we're willing to endure long waits and a pick-up scene as sticky as quicksand to get a table at this popular Back Bay singles bar. Ten-ounce burgers come as rare as you order them, available with bacon, Cheddar cheese, and other toppings. The upwardly mobile can nibble sherried cheese soup or *fettuccine all'Alfredo,* while down-to-earth folks will find plenty of Tex–Mex items, including chili and *quesadilla* (tortilla with cheese). Once a police station, this lively bar has the Art Deco trappings of neon lights, black lacquered tables, and a hostess in a slinky dress.

*Price: About $8–$15 per person*
*Open daily for lunch and dinner*
*Accepts all major credit cards*

# DOVER SEA GRILLE
## 1223 Beacon Street, Brookline
### 617-566-7000

As far as we're concerned, there is one sort of restaurant Boston will never have enough of: a good fish house. Serious seafood buffs have at least three reasons to rejoice about the recent opening of the Dover Sea Grille. The fish is fresh, the menu, imaginative, and, unlike so many Boston fish houses, it accepts reservations. The fried haddock and broiled scrod of traditional seafood restaurants have given way to pan-blackened tuna, mesquite-grilled swordfish, and *tortellini* with smoked salmon and cream sauce. As an alternative to chowder (a very respectable one, we might add), there's a lobster gumbo; we also like the unusual smoked bluefish pâté. The dining room, set in what was once a hotel lobby, boasts the Victorian appointments of gilded cornices, glimmering chandeliers, and Corinthian columns. The service is pleasant and efficient.

*Price: About $20 per person*
*Open Mon.–Fri. for lunch and dinner; Sat. and Sun. for dinner only*
*Accepts all major credit cards*

# DURGIN–PARK
## 340 North Market Street (*Faneuil Hall Marketplace*)
### 617-227-2038

Boston has changed a lot since John Durgin and Eldridge Park joined forces to start a restaurant in 1827. But at the renowned Durgin–Park, time has all but stood still. This is the only restaurant within a half mile radius of Quincy Market that does *not* have hanging plants, exposed-brick walls, and butcher-block tables. What it does have is long communal tables, planked floors worn by legions of brusque waitresses, and a noise level that would make the Park Street subway stop at rush hour seem quiet. It also serves some of the last real New England food anywhere: hearty chowders, roast duck with bread stuffing, and a prime rib that literally buries the plate. The cornbread is supposed to be complimentary, but you often have to ask for it. Be sure to save room for the Indian pudding and strawberry shortcake. As the locals know, you can avoid the long waiting line by ascending to the dining room directly from the bar.

*Price: About $12–$15 per person*
*Open daily for lunch and dinner*
*No credit cards accepted*

# EAST COAST GRILL

## 1271 Cambridge Street (*near Inman Square*), Cambridge
### 617-491-6568

"Grills just want to have fun" read the waitresses' t-shirts. Since its opening last summer, this lively bar and grill has drawn capacity crowds for a bill of fare that combines the innovations of California cuisine with the bounty of old-fashioned home cooking. When they say grill, they mean it: There's an open pit barbecue in the rear of the dining room, where ribs, duck, even vegetable kebabs are grilled over fruitwood fires. Barbecue buffs have three kinds to choose from: Texas-style (smoky beef brisket), North Carolina-style (shredded beef with vinegar), and Missouri-style (traditional ribs). Nightly specials are more unusual: tuna with tequila-lime butter and swordfish with *chipotle* vinaigrette. Be sure to save room for the bread pudding, grated apple pie, and blue frozen margaritas. Located in an old diner, the East Coast Grill is decorated with high tech lights and neon.

*Price: About $15 per person*
*Open Mon.–Fri. for lunch and dinner; Sat.–Sun. for dinner only*
*Accepts all major credit cards*

# EUROPEAN

## 218 Hanover Street
### 617-523-5694

Founded in 1917, the European is probably the oldest Italian restaurant in Boston. It's certainly the largest, seating 500 people in its five dining rooms. Pizza is a house specialty—more than 3,000 are served here each week. Other perennial favorites include *calamari* (squid) simmered in tomato sauce and a *lasagne* that will keep you sated for days. The European is as childproof as a restaurant can be: The paper mats absorb spills and no baby could out-scream the general noise level. After dinner you can stroll the narrow streets of the North End, Boston's Italian quarter.

*Price: About $6–$12 per person*
*Open daily for lunch and dinner*
*Accepts all major credit cards*

# FIVE SEASONS RESTAURANT
## 699A Centre Street, Jamaica Plain
### 617-524-9016

Who said that for food to be good for you, it has to taste like birdseed? The Pell brothers, owners of this popular Jamaica Plain restaurant, may well spurn butter, sugar, white flour, and other untouchables. But their colorful *nori tempura* roll (a sort of New Age egg roll), bluefish *teriyaki,* and *tofu* cheesecake rival the food at many high-priced establishments downtown. Serious ale drinkers will appreciate the availability of Anchor Steam beer. Unless you like maple syrup in your coffee (freshly ground and brewed), you'll have to bring your own sugar. The storefront dining room is decorated with clean pine walls, hanging plants, and red oak tables.

*Price: About $12–$15 per person*
*Open Tues.–Sun. for lunch and dinner; closed Mon.*
*Accepts all major credit cards*

# GRILL 23 & BAR
## 161 Berkeley Street
### 617-542-2255

The Grill 23 is Boston's version of a classic New York steak house. Located in the historic Salada Tea building, it offers the Roaring Twenties elegance of marble pillars and burnished lamps. Beef is aged for three weeks. But don't overlook the estimable steak tartare, seafood, unusual grilled fruits and vegetables, and an Indian pudding that rivals the one at Locke-Ober. The split-level dining room seats 150 at tables set with white linens, heavy silver, and marble salt and pepper shakers. The chief drawback is the noise level, which makes it almost impossible to hear your companions on a busy Friday or Saturday night.

*Price: About $40 per person*
*Open daily for lunch and dinner*
*Accepts all major credit cards*

# HAMPSHIRE HOUSE
## 84 Beacon Street
### 617-227-9600

It's hard to believe, as you ascend the vast marble staircase lined with medieval tapestries, that this was once a private domicile. For an evening, at least, you can experience what it must have been like to be wealthy Brahmin at the turn of the century, dining in a library complete with a blazing fireplace and window-side seats overlooking the Boston Commons. In keeping with the setting, the food in The Swan Dining Room is conservative and hearty: baked stuffed mushroom caps, Boston scrod, steak *au poivre,* prettily garnished *chateaubriand* for two. For more informal dining, you'll find omelets, salads, and sandwiches at the Oak Room Bar and Café on the first floor. The Bull and Finch Lounge in the basement (the model for the bar in the TV series *Cheers*) draws wall-to-wall crowds on the weekend.

*Price: About $20–$30 per person*
*Open daily for lunch and dinner*
*Accepts all major credit cards*

---

## HARVARD BOOKSTORE CAFÉ
### 190 Newbury Street
### 617-536-0095

There are few experiences more pleasant than dining *al fresco* at a sidewalk café. One of our favorites is the Harvard Bookstore Café, located on Newbury Street in Back Bay. There's plenty of food for thought in the tomes lining shelves of this actual bookstore. But I prefer sustenance of a different sort— *saganaki (kasseri* cheese flamed with *ouzo),* scrod *Orientale,* and confetti spaghetti—to name just a few of the house specialties. Long a popular breakfast spot, the Café is now also open for Sunday brunch. In the event that bad weather should force you inside, you'll find butcher-block tables and smartly framed lithographs.

*Price: About $15 per person*
*Open Mon.–Sat. for lunch and dinner; closed Sun.*
*Accepts all major credit cards*

---

## HARVEST
### 44 Brattle Street (*near Harvard Square*), Cambridge
### 617-492-1115

When it comes to an upscale social scene, we cast our vote for Ben's Corner Café at the Harvest. We hasten to add that the cooking here is as sophisticated as the young professional clientele. There are three dining areas: a shady terrace, a boisterous café, and a pricey formal dining room decorated with Marimekko wall hangings. The daily changing menu reflects an interest in regional American cooking: Recent innovations include chilled grilled peppered shrimp, *jalapeño fettuccine,* pear and goat cheese salad, pan-blackened fish, and unusual grilled lamb sausages. The pastry chef is beloved by chocoholics from all over town. Other Harvest attractions include annual wild game and Mardi Gras festivals, a popular Sunday brunch, and excellent homemade French bread.

*Price: About $15 per person in the café; $40–$50 per person in the formal dining room*
*Open daily for lunch and dinner*
*Accepts all major credit cards*

---

## ICARUS
### 540 Tremont Street
**617-426-1790**

Make your way through a stunning Art Nouveau portal to a dining room furnished with antique mantelpieces, turn-of-the-century lamps, and Mission oak tables, no two of which match any more than do the antique plates and silverware that adorn them. Welcome to one of the South End's best kept secrets, Icarus, which has evolved from a neighborhood haunt into a restaurant of citywide distinction. The menu changes daily: Typical dishes might include bay scallops with Roquefort sauce, soft-shell crabs with tarragon, and roast rack of lamb with rosemary. The pasta is properly *al dente;* so are vegetables. The flourless chocolate *gâteau* warrants a visit all by itself. Icarus serves a delightful brunch, with specialties ranging from the usual eggs Benedict to ham *pithiviers* (puff pastry cake) and French toast with strawberries. The service is leisurely but amiable.

*Price: About $40 per person*
*Open Tues.–Sat. for dinner only; Sun. for brunch only*
*Accepts all major credit cards*

---

## IL CAPRICCIO
### 53 Prospect Street, Waltham
**617-894-2234**

This boutique restaurant gives credence to the saw that good things come in small packages. Il Capriccio seats a mere 38 people in a dining room decorated with white walls and red geraniums. But the quality of the nightly-changing, fixed-price menu is inversely proportional to the diminutive size of the restaurant. Inspired by the cooking of Northern Italy, Capriccio chef Maurie Warren specializes in such simple but flavorful innovations as *polenta* with Gorgonzola cheese, monkfish with lobster, and beef tenderloin sauced with

Scotch whiskey. The wine list offers a balanced selection of Italian vintages. About a 30-minute drive from Boston.

*Price: About $35 per person*
*Open Tues.–Sun. for dinner only; closed Mon.*
*Accepts all major credit cards*

---

## IL DOLCE MOMENTO
### 30 Charles Street
**617-720-0477**

The hottest new trend in frozen desserts is *gelato*, Italian ice cream. The merest spoonful of such cooling concoctions as *nocciola* (hazelnut ice cream), *torrone* (Italian nougat), or "After 8" (chocolate mint) explains why the other Charles Street ice cream parlors have been abandoned for the appropriately named Dolce Momento (literally "sweet moment"). Ice cream and ices are but half the story, as you will also find here buttery pastries, frothy *cappuccino*, and unusual salads and sandwiches. Quarry tiles and red oak tables lend the place the air of an Italian café.

*Price: About $2–$4 per person*
*Open daily for lunch and dinner*
*No credit cards accepted*

---

## IMPERIAL TEAHOUSE RESTAURANT
### 70 Beech Street
**617-426-8439**

*"Dim sum,* lose some" is an apt saying for Chinatown. We found mostly winners at the Imperial Tea House, home of a *dim sum* spread that draws Chinese–Americans from all over Boston. *Dim sum* are Chinese tea pastries, served in staggering profusion between 10 A.M. and 3 P.M. There is no menu; the waiters wheel around carts loaded with shrimp dumplings, barbecued pork-filled buns, curried shrimp, tiny spareribs steamed with spicy black beans, and even duck feet braised with star anise. Point with your chopsticks to whatever you want—you can order dozens of dishes without breaking the bank. A *dim sum* brunch is great fun, especially with a large group. On the weekend, expect a half-hour wait to gain access to the vast dining room, decorated with coffered ceilings and glittering lanterns.

*Price: About $8 per person*
*Open daily for lunch and dinner*
*Accepts all major credit cards*

# JULIEN AT THE HOTEL MERIDIEN
In Post Office Square, 250 Franklin Street
617-451-1900

Named for the owner of Boston's first French restaurant (opened in 1791), and set in the Old Federal Reserve building on Post Office Square, the Julien reflects Boston's historic heritage. There's nothing old-fashioned about the menu, which specializes in *nouvelle cuisine* and *diététique gourmande* (lowfat gourmet). Guests start their meal with a complimentary hors d'oeuvre—perhaps salmon *mousse* or a pair of herb-steamed mussels—and end in the manner of grand restaurants in France—with complimentary *petits fours* and chocolate truffles. Meanwhile, you'll pay top dollar for such culinary flights of fancy as lobster *ravioli* in ginger broth and veal *médaillons* with caviar and champagne. Unfortunately, sometimes the food is brilliant, sometimes it is merely adequate.

Located in the former "Members Court" of the Federal Reserve Building, the Julien boasts the splendor of corniced ceilings, high, limestone walls faced with espaliers, and stately wingback Queen Anne chairs at tables draped with snowy linens and set with heavy silver. The largely European staff is as attentive as can be. On weekends a spectacular buffet brunch, highlighted by a cook station where *crêpes* are made to order, is served in the sunny Café Fleuri. The well-spaced tables and convenient location make this a popular restaurant with businessmen.

*Price: About $50 per person*
*Open Mon.–Sat. for lunch and dinner; closed Sun.*
*Accepts all major credit cards*

# KOREA HOUSE
20 Pearl Street (*Central Square*), Cambridge
617-492-9643

If you happen to hail from Seoul (as do most of the customers), the food here will taste as good as Mom's home cooking. But Westerners, too, will enjoy such traditional Korean dishes as *mandoo-kui* (pan-fried dumplings), *bool-go-ki* (Korean beef barbecue), and fiery *kim chee* (Korean "sauerkraut"). Guests can dine Western style—sitting on chairs at Formica tables; if you come with a large party, it's fun to sit cross-legged at a low table in the private dining room. Beverages range from nutty "twig" tea to soda pop; wine or beer buffs are welcome to bring their own.

*Price: About $10–$12 per person*
*Open Mon.–Sat. for lunch and dinner; Sun. for dinner only*
*No credit cards accepted*

# LEGAL SEA FOODS
## In the Boston Park Plaza Hotel, 35 Columbus Avenue
### 617-426-4444

Much as I hate waiting on lines and restaurants that don't accept reservations, I would hate even more to miss out on the peerlessly fresh fish served at this, the crown jewel of the Legal Sea Foods empire. Custom-smoked Irish salmon, succulent broiled bluefish, moist fried clams, and homemade sherbets are but a few of the specialties that have made this one of the most popular fish houses in New England. The wine list (a long computer printout) offers an impressive selection of California boutique wines. There are two annoying house policies: You pay for your meal when you order it and you receive your food when it is cooked, not necessarily when your guests receive theirs. The high noise level of the dining room, with its South Seas decor of wicker chairs and brass railings, makes this a dubious place for leisurely or romantic dining.

*Price: About $18–$25 per person*
*Open daily for lunch and dinner*
*Accepts American Express*

# L'ESPALIER
## 30 Gloucester Street
### 617-262-3023

Last year, L'Espalier chef-owner Moncef Meddeb spent over $4,000 importing fresh truffles from Europe. But a free hand with such costly ingredients as fresh *foie gras,* beluga caviar, Dublin Bay prawns, and specially raised squab is only part of what makes this the most estimable French restaurant in town. L'Espalier is located in an elegant Back Bay townhouse: Guests enter through a wrought-iron gate and sip *apéritifs* in a high-ceilinged *salon* complete with blazing fireplace. The downstairs dining room offers the elegance of French stucco and a marble mantelpiece, while the upstairs room has the polished paneling of an English Country manor. The fixed-price menu features the starchless sauces and aesthetic plate presentations of France's *nouvelle cuisine,* but with an international array of ingredients. Finicky eaters may find it limited; anyone but a Rockefeller will find it expensive. On past visits I have enjoyed the lamb *ravioli,* grilled duck breast with orange, coriander, and green peppercorns, and an unusual cake flavored with *marc de gewürztraminer* (pommace brandy). The wine list is particularly strong in Bordeaux and Burgundies; the homemade rolls and lavish cheese tray also deserve honorable mention. The service is hovering, mannered, and pretentious.

*Price: About $50 per person*
*Open Mon.–Sat. for dinner only; closed Sun.*
*Accepts all major credit cards*

---

# LOCKE-OBER CAFÉ
### 3–4 Winter Place (*near the Commons*)
### 617-542-1340

What does a restaurant founded in 1875, which barred women from its main dining room until 1970, offer the twentieth-century restaurant-goer? Quite literally, a taste of history. Where else can you dine amid the hand-carved mahogany, the gilded wallpaper, the rich leather seats and unhurried splendor of a nineteenth-century men's club? Where else do you still find waiters—dressed in black jackets and long white aprons, like dignified penguins—who consider their work a respected profession? The chef shows little interest in mesquite grilling, pan-blackening, or other current American food trends. His solidly Continental menu has remained virtually unchanged for fifty years. Some dishes are a trifle heavy for modern palates, but you can't go wrong with the clams à la Gino, lobster stew (a favorite of JFK), superlative steak tartare, chicken Richmond *sous cloche* (served under a bell jar), and Boston's best Indian pudding. Newcomers should request to be seated in the Men's Bar (co-ed since 1970), although the Ober Room, decorated with furnishings from a Newport mansion, is quieter and a shade more elegant. The private dining rooms on the third floor are popular with local businessmen.

*Price: About $40–$50 per person*
*Open Mon.–Sat. for lunch and dinner; closed Sun.*
*Accepts all major credit cards*

---

# MANDALAY
### 329 Huntington (*near Symphony Hall*)
### 617-247-2111

In the old days, this Burmese restaurant (Boston's only) occupied a seedy soda shop with a non-existent decor and bathrooms accessible only by walking through the kitchen. Today, it's a proper restaurant, complete with prettily set tables, textured wallpaper, and even a wine list. Surprisingly, the food has survived both the march of progress and repeated critical acclaim. Fans of fiery food will enjoy the tongue-blistering curries, unusual noodle dishes, and *thokes* (fried noodle and vegetable salads). Other Burmese specialties include *sar tay* (spicy, marinated broiled beef kebabs), *sar moo sar* (Asian kreplach—fried dough triangles filled with curried onions and beef), and *chit dee kebah* (curry-filled pancakes). Located near Symphony Hall, this cozy basement serves a special dinner for people who have to make an early curtain.

*Price: About $13 per person*
*Open daily for lunch and dinner*
*Accepts all major credit cards*

---

## MOON VILLA
### 23 Edinboro Street
**617-423-2061**

Where do you eat when it's 3 A.M., and your cupboard is as bare as Mother Hubbard's? The venerable Moon Villa in Chinatown is one of the few places where night owls are never too late for supper. Gone are the days when an order of "cold tea" brought you surreptitious alcohol, but Moon Villa continues to draw a loyal crowd with its forthright Cantonese cooking. House specialties include clams with black bean sauce, eight-flavor winter melon soup, and salt-baked chicken marinated with wine. Adventurers can try the fish maw soup, or greasy steamed pork with salted egg. The dining room has the usual Chinatown decor of garish orange booths, brown Formica tabletops, and seashell collages on the walls. The service ranges in friendliness from Dr. Jeckyll to Mr. Hyde.

*Price: About $10 per person*
*Open daily for lunch and dinner*
*No credit cards accepted*

---

## NARA
### 85 Wendell Street
**617-338-5935**

This tiny restaurant is run by Koreans, but it serves some of the best Japanese food in town. The *sushi* chef is a wizard when it comes to assembling cakes of vinegared rice and raw fish: Ask for the cucumber "boat" filled with oysters. The *tempura* is uncommonly delicate; nor should you miss the *kalbi,* broiled beef short ribs. Nara is a pretty restaurant with exposed brick walls, trellised partitions, and a *tatami* room in the back.

*Price: About $15–$20 per person*
*Open daily for lunch and dinner*
*Accepts all major credit cards*

---

# PAK NIN
## 84 Harrison Avenue
### 617-482-6168

Small on atmosphere, big on value, this Chinatown hole-in-the-wall draws a predominantly Asian crowd for its flavorful Hong Kong-style cooking. *Pak nin* means "long life" in Chinese, and a steady diet of such house specialties as roast squab, frogs' legs with black beans, and Cantonese lobster (stir-fried with ginger and scallions) will assure a happy life, if not an eternal one. Paper pennons festoon the walls, listing the excellent daily specials, which, mercifully, are translated into English on the first page of the menu. A word of caution: The cooking is strictly authentic here, so some dishes, such as the braised beef or green beans with pork, contain more fat than most Westerners feel comfortable eating. Bring your own beer and wine.

*Price: About $12 per person*
*Open daily for lunch and dinner*
*No credit cards accepted*

---

# PANACHE
## 798 Main Street (*near Central Square*), Cambridge
### 617-492-9500

Since 1979, Panache-owner Bruce Frankel has drawn a cult-like following to his chic boutique restaurant, located in a run-down neighborhood in Cambridge. His cooking defies classification, weaving Oriental, French, North American, and even macrobiotic influences into a style of refined understatement that remains uniquely his own. A typical meal at Panache (the menu changes daily) might feature marinated Massachusetts goat cheese with sun-dried tomatoes and grilled flat bread, Maine shrimp with fennel, or salmon *quenelles* with nasturtium buds. The measured portions may seem a trifle small to people with hefty appetites. A small but select wine list complements a small but equally select choice of cheeses. Nor should you miss the grand "dessert Panache"—a medley of cakes and pastries, highlighted by *marquise au chocolat* —chocolate *mousse* cake with coffee sauce that will reduce you to sighs. The dining room is stylishly appointed with pink and gray walls, lavish flower sprays, and an unusual pattern projector that casts seasonal images on the wall.

*Price: About $40 per person*
*Open Thurs. and Fri. for lunch and dinner; Sat. for dinner only; closed Sun.–Wed.*
*Accepts all major credit cards*

---

## THE PLOW AND STARS
### 923 Massachusetts Avenue, Cambridge
**617-492-9653**

By night this Irish bar attracts a hard-drinking crowd for its two-fisted drinks and live jazz and Irish folk music. By day the tables are draped with red-checkered tablecloths, ready to receive a more soft-spoken clientele, who flock here for the cooking of a self-taught chef who trained with an excellent teacher. A limited menu offers such peasant-style fare as chicken *bouillabaisse* or lamb curry with chutney. The Sunday brunch is popular with Cantabrigians, too.

*Price: About $6 per person*
*Open daily for lunch only*
*No credit cards accepted*

---

## RESTAURANT JASPER
### 240 Commercial Street
**617-523-1126**

If restaurants were ranked solely on the basis of hype, this one would surely cap all the ratings. But despite enough rave reviews to turn the head of any restaurateur, Jasper White continues to succeed with a menu that combines the innovations of the "new" American cooking with the plentiful portions of a bygone era. Breadsticks are freshly baked each evening; a salad sports peppered pecans and blood-rare duck breast; a bluefish fillet comes with garlic pasta and grilled clams. The spacious dining rooms are decorated with George Escher prints, recessed lights nestled amid exposed ceiling beams, and brick walls painted with soothing shades of lavender and gray. The service is friendly, formal, and a wee bit self-righteous. The prices would make even a Kennedy think twice: Dinner for two with wine and drinks is apt to exceed $120.

*Price: About $40–$50 per person*
*Open Mon.–Sat. for dinner only; closed Sun.*
*Accepts American Express, Visa, and MasterCard*

# RESTAURANT LE MARQUIS DE LAFAYETTE

In the Lafayette Hotel, 1 Avenue de Lafayette
**617-451-2600**

Bostonians are wont to deride the architecture of the shopping area called Lafayette Place, but there's one thing here they take seriously: the formal dining room of the Lafayette Hotel—Le Marquis. Supervised by chef Louis Outhier (of the famed Restaurant L'Oasis on the Côte d'Azur), this 60-seat restaurant serves some of the most sophisticated French fare in New England. The kitchen tempers the unusual flavor combinations of *nouvelle cuisine* with classical French culinary purity. What results are such masterful creations as *l'oeuf au caviar* (shirred egg with beluga), *ravioles de "clams"* (delicate clam ravioli), and *canard à l'armagnac* (a stunningly presented duck with a suave brandy sauce). The current pastry chef, Alain Teillet, deserves sainthood for a dessert cart that's remarkable for its breadth of choice and the delicacy of each *gâteau*. The gray color scheme is a trifle cool, but beveled mirrors, sculpted lions, and glimmering chandeliers lend the room an aura of elegance. The service is satisfactory, if, on occasion, supercilious. Note: This fall the chef and pastry chef are supposed to move to another hotel owned by the same company. Whether their successors can maintain the current high level of excellence remains to be seen, although Outhier will continue to supervise the menus and kitchen with visits every two to three months to keep things consistent.

*Price: Menu dégustation at $58; à la carte, about $45–$50 per person*
*Open Mon.–Fri. for lunch and dinner; Sat. for dinner only; closed Sun.*
*Accepts all major credit cards*

# RITZ–CARLTON DINING ROOM

In the Ritz–Carlton Hotel, 15 Arlington Street
**617-536-5700**

The Sunday brunch at this classic hotel lends new weight to the expression "putting on the Ritz." There are five circles in this gastronomic paradise, including a stunning cold buffet, hot buffet served from gleaming silver chafing dishes, carving board, cheese spread, and bountiful dessert table. On arriving, guests receive Laurent-Perrier champagne and caviar. After that, they are on their own to sample the smoked scallops, spicy steak tartare, finnan haddie, roast lamb with fresh mint sauce, apple strudel, and ultra-rich chocolate *mousse* cake—to name a few of the more than seventy dishes available. Naturally, some of the items suffer from steam-table anemia, but the discreet but hovering service makes up for it. So does the grandiose dining room, with its high ceilings, potted palms, tinkling piano, and crystal and cobalt blue chandeliers which match the cobalt blue water glasses on the handsome tables.

*Price: About $27.50 per person for brunch only*
*Open daily for lunch and dinner*
*Accepts all major credit cards*

---

## RUBIN'S DELICATESSEN AND RESTAURANT
### 500 Harvard Street, Brookline
#### 617-731-8787

Rubin's is one deli where you *won't* find bagels and cream cheese. One of Boston's few true kosher restaurants, it refuses to serve meat with dairy products, and, as a result, there is no cream (only Coffee-Lite), no butter (only margarine), and no cream cheese (not even with bagels and whitefish). Not that customers feel deprived, because it takes both hands to manage the corned beef sandwiches, home-cooked brisket, and hand-sliced Rumanian pastrami. The red and silver wallpaper, Formica tables, and red Naugahyde banquets don't conform to our vision of a delicatessen decor. Then again, the *kiska* (beef gut filled with bread stuffing), *tzimas* (carrot stew), and *kugel* (noodle pudding) are as authentic as a Jewish grandmother's own.

*Price: About $6–$10 per person*
*Open Sun.–Thurs. for lunch and dinner; Fri. for lunch only;*
*closed Fri. night and Sat.*
*No credit cards accepted*

---

## RUDY'S CAFÉ
### 250 Holland Street (*Teele Square*), Somerville
#### 617-623-9201

This boisterous café is not for the tender of tongue, timid of speech, or people seeking to flesh out their expense accounts. The rest of us enjoy the animated atmosphere and fiery Tex–Mex food at prices so low, you wonder how the owners manage to turn a profit. An icy margarita or one of the beers *du jour* will help relieve the sting of the Buffalo chicken wings, "hot lips" (chicken chunks fried in a peppery batter), or *chalupas* (tortillas topped with *guacamole* and refried beans), and devilish *salsa*. Whatever you order, save room for dessert: Laurie's "deep, rich brownies" are a chocoholic triumph. The hanging plants and framed gallery prints create the mood of a California fern bar.

*Price: About $8 per person*
*Open daily for lunch and dinner*
*No credit cards accepted*

# SALLY LING
## 256 Commercial Street
### 617-227-4545

It doesn't look like your typical Chinese restaurant, not with valet parking, tuxedoed captains, and tables graced with fresh-cut flowers and snowy linens. It certainly isn't priced like a Chinese restaurant, not with appetizers costing $4 to $8.50, entrées $8 to $18, and a multicourse tasting menu starting at $32. Welcome to Sally Ling, a restaurant on the Waterfront that reflects a national trend toward *haute* Chinese dining. Once you recover from the initial shock, you'll enjoy such creations as wontons in Szechuan sauce, peony blossom beef, and garlicky, skewered, steamed prawns. All the while, liveried waiters provide hovering French service, filling your goblets with vintage wines. Sally Ling's is a pretty restaurant, decorated with Chinese artwork and tiny spotlights. Colorful tropical fish dart in the aquarium behind the bar.

*Price: About $30 per person*
*Open Mon.–Fri. for lunch and dinner; Sat. and Sun. for dinner only*
*Accepts all major credit cards*

---

# SEASONS
## In the Bostonian Hotel, Faneuil Hall Marketplace
### 617-523-4119

Well-spaced tables, gleaming silver, and Louis XV chairs set a tone of refinement, and the spectacular view of the Faneuil Hall Marketplace is a delight for anyone lucky enough to be seated at a table by the window. The kitchen specializes—and mostly succeeds—in a cuisine that has come to be called "American bounty." Chef Lydia Shire's interest in regional cooking and New England provender may be seen in such creations as warm salad of monkfish, lobster, and lamb's lettuce with red caviar butter and a mixed grill of baby lamb, chicken, and Irish bacon. The wine list is all-American (although French champagnes are available on request). Vintage ports are available by the glass to complement the excellent desserts. Some of the waiters are snooty, and some of the culinary creations a bit outlandish. It helps to dine here on an expense account, as the prices are astronomical!

*Price: About $50 per person*
*Open daily for breakfast, lunch, and dinner*
*Accepts all major credit cards*

# SOL AZTECA
## 914A Beacon Street
### 617-262-0909

Some like it hot, goes the old saying, and this authentic Mexican restaurant cheerfully obliges with spicy *salsa, mole poblano* (chicken with chilied chocolate sauce), and a *puerco en adobo* (pork with orange juice and smoked chilies) that jolts you like a bite of a high-voltage cable. The more tender of tongue will appreciate the *camarones al cilantro* (shrimp with coriander leaf), caramel-like *cajeta*, and eminently refreshing *sangría*. The colorful tile tables, wrought iron, and Mexican handcrafts belie the basement location of this popular restaurant. Reservations are not accepted after 6 P.M.

*Price: About $15 per person*
*Open daily for dinner only*
*Accepts American Express, Visa, and MasterCard*

# THAI CUISINE
## 14A Westland Avenue (*near Symphony Hall*)
### 617-262-1485

Not all the food at this popular Thai restaurant will send you diving for your water glass. The best dishes will, however, like such incendiary delights as *satay* (kebabs with peanut sauce), *pla rad prik* (whole fried fish with mushrooms and chilies), and curries available with yellow, red, or green sauces. Lower down on the temperature scale are the *tod man pla* (fried bluefish patties) and *pad thai* (stir-fried noodles). And to extinguish the fires, you can order Singha, a hopsy Thai beer. Located behind Symphony Hall, this narrow storefront usually has a waiting line for a table.

*Price: About $15 per person*
*Open Mon.–Fri. for lunch and dinner; Sat. and Sun. for dinner only*
*Accepts most major credit cards*

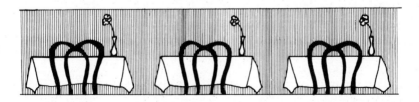

# TOSCANINI'S
899 Main Street (*near Central Square*), Cambridge
617-491-5877

If ice cream parlors were judged solely by chocolate, Herrel's in Harvard Square would take the prize for its chocolate pudding ice cream. But for overall performance, Toscanini's in Central Square gets our vote for an ever changing repertory highlighted by such exotic flavors as lemon-honey, kiwi-banana, and—my favorite—gingersnap-molasses. Many of the ice creams contain crumbled cookies; all are churned in the noisy salt- and ice-machines in the window. Circus chairs and wire tables line the windowed storefront for getting your licks on the premises.

*Price: About $2 per person*
*Open daily*
*No credit cards accepted*

---

# UPSTAIRS AT THE PUDDING
10 Holyoke Street, Cambridge
617-864-1933

The setting is the historic Hasty Pudding Club in the shadow of Harvard Square. But we've come for theatrics of an edible sort: the cooking of a chef named Michael Silver. Silver's Northern Italian menu reflects the latest trends in contemporary American cooking. What results are such innovative dishes as *tagliatelle* with Oregon slippery jacks and *boletus scaber* (two species of wild mushrooms), Topsfield rabbit with romaine and Gorgonzola cheese, and Jamaican Blue Mountain coffee ice cream. But unknown here is the *nouvelle cuisine* parsimony of six green beans or a single duck breast. Each generous entrée comes with half a dozen vegetables, ranging from fried sage leaves to exotic white eggplant. You pay dearly for such largesse: The fixed price menu costs $30 to $38. The dining room is handsomely appointed with pink table-cloths, brass service plates, and forest-green walls decorated with antique show posters. The service is Cantabrigian in its leisurely pace.

*Price: About $40–$45 per person*
*Open Tues.–Sat. for dinner only; closed Sun. and Mon.*
*Accepts American Express, Visa, and MasterCard*

# VIN AND EDDIE'S RISTORANTE AND WINE BAR

1400 Bedford Street (*Route 18*), North Abington
**617-871-1469**

The name of this place sounds like a sub shop, and North Abington is hardly a locale we associate with fine dining. But make no mistake, this thirty-year-old restaurant, now in its second generation, serves some of the best Italian fare in Greater Boston. You could start with veal *tonnato* (with chilled tuna sauce) or some astonishingly tender fried squid. Entrées range from sea bass *ravioli* with lobster sauce to a *fritto misto* ("mixed fry") that harbors tender nuggets of sweetbreads. Vin and Eddie's was one of the first area restaurants to install a Cruvinet—the nitrogen-pumped wine dispenser—and it is not wasted on ho-hum vintages. Wines available by the glass might include Château Margaux or Côte Rotie, not to mention an 1893 Armagnac. The four dining rooms are decorated with kitschy canvases; the waitresses are mercifully down to earth. I'll let you in on a further secret—the fried bananas are delicious. About a 30-minute drive from Boston.

*Price: About $30–$35 per person*
*Open Tues.–Sun. for lunch and dinner; closed Mon.*
*Accepts all major credit cards*

# CHARLOTTE

## By Dannye Romine

**AMERICAN**
Eli's on East

**BARBECUE**
Old Hickory House Restaurant

**CHINESE**
The Great Wall

**FRENCH**
Chez Daniel

**ITALIAN**
Zarrelli's Italian Restaurant

**MEXICAN**
La Paz

**SEAFOOD**
The Fishmarket

**STEAKS AND CHOPS**
The Epicurean

**UNIQUE PROPERTIES**
Bojangles Famous Chicken 'N
Biscuits

When George Washington visited Charlotte on his Southern tour in 1791, he described the town in his journal as "a trifling place." It might be that Washington was referring to his accommodations at Captain Cook's Inn on West Trade Street (he departed in such a hurry that he left behind his silver powder box). Or it might be that he was referring to the deeply rutted, red-clay roads or to the crude and corny speech of the natives. But more likely, if Washington dined in any of the local taverns or inns, he was referring to the food.

Until 1978, when Mecklenburg County voted in liquor by the drink, as far as dining out went, Charlotte was indeed a trifling place. Until then most people ate at Shoney's (salad bar and Friday night "all-you-can-eat" fish specials) or at the Pizza Hut or at the S&W Cafeteria or at Morrison's Cafeteria or at a fish camp or at a barbecue house. If you went for a night out at a steak house, you took your liquor bottle in a brown bag.

But Charlotte is growing up. Thanks to liquor by the drink, to a revitalization of the inner city, to a white-collar boom, dining out in Charlotte is flowering. It's still hard to find a can of black beans in the supermarket, but in restaurants you can find *gelato,* abalone, *calamari,* mesquite-cooked swordfish, sherry trifle, fried guinea squash, and quince *sorbet.*

Don't forget, though, that Charlotte was settled by Scotch–Irish Presbyterians, a feisty lot not about to let newfangled food get the better of them.

That's good news, because as Charlotte retains its traditions, it keeps some of its best food alive. Food like you find in such barbecue houses as the Old Hickory on North Tryon and the Old Original on Camp Greene Street.

As a matter of fact, if you want a real taste of the-way-Charlotte-was, drop into Wad's Soda Shop at 1608 East Boulevard. Hop up on one of those swirl-around barstools (circa 1955), rest your elbows on the Formica counter, and watch the waitress hand-pump lemons for fresh lemonade. Order a large lemonade and a BLT on whole wheat toast.

It may be trifling, but in Charlotte that often means it's terrific.

*Dannye Romine writes a "Dining Out" column for* The Charlotte Observer, *where she is also book reviewer.*

# BOJANGLES FAMOUS CHICKEN 'N BISCUITS

300 West Boulevard
3900 Brookshire Boulevard
140 Eastway Drive
231 East Woodlawn Road
5111 Central Avenue
1401 West Trade Street
110 West Sugar Creek Road
517 North Tryon Street
3301 Wilkinson Boulevard
8700 Matthews-Pineville Road
5525 East Independence Boulevard
**704-527-2675 (headquarters)**

Charlotte is the home of Bojangles fried chicken, the spicy, Cajun-style chicken that's very likely addictive. You'll find the spiciest Bojangles chicken at the West Trade Street location. The biscuits here are also a little lighter and a little fluffier. At this location, you can order your chicken to go or eat in the spanking-clean restaurant. (Some locations only offer takeout service.) Try the "quarter-fried white" dinner, which includes a breast and wing and a side order of "dirty rice," coleslaw, or fries. When you go back, try the chicken fillet biscuit and ask for three packets of hot sauce to dribble on the chicken. Eat it slowly. Wash it down with a huge paper cup of Bojangles sweetened iced tea. You're in business. You're in the South.

*Price: About $3–$5 per person*
*Open daily for breakfast, lunch, and dinner*
*No credit cards accepted*

---

# CHEZ DANIEL

1742 Lombardy Circle
**704-332-3224**

If you suddenly have a taste for quince *sorbet* or wild boar, you may be in luck. Chez Daniel, in a tiny house in a tiny shopping center, sometimes offers the *sorbet* between *premier* and *deuxième* courses. And frequently, it offers wild boar for the third course *(troisième)*. Chez Daniel, owned by Brittany natives

Patrick and Daniel Quillec, is a tucked-away jewel (you'll be wise to forget the Lombardy Circle address and enter the parking area of the Dilworth Cooperative off Garden Terrace, which is off East Boulevard). The place is decorated to the nines (Madame Bovary would've been in heaven) in hues of peach and blue, with fresh flowers and crystal candlesticks and flowered china, cloth-on-cloth table covers, and paintings by French masters. There's one seating in the evenings, so prepare to linger. The dishes are imaginative, delicately seasoned, and pristinely presented. First courses might include split pea, cream of leek, or fresh basil soup. Second courses: veal brains, *pâté,* snails with asparagus in white sauce. Entrées: veal with mushrooms, duck with orange sauce, roast pork with raspberry sauce, red snapper with tomato sauce. A typical fourth course is Brie with sliced apples. And for dessert, fresh raspberries or pears with praline sauce. Sometimes a little too-too, but generally delightful.

*Price: Fixed price at $30 per person*
*Open Mon.–Fri. for lunch and dinner; Sat. for dinner only; closed Sun.*
*Accepts all major credit cards*

---

# ELI'S ON EAST
## 311 East Boulevard
### 704-375-0756

In 1937, twenty-year-old Carson McCullers (author of *The Heart Is a Lonely Hunter*) and her new husband, Reeves, moved to Charlotte and briefly set up housekeeping at 311 East Boulevard—the present home of Eli's on East. McCullers was a first-rate character (sipping sherry from a Thermos in the Charlotte Public Library as she wrote), and perhaps her fleeting presence in the turn-of-the-century house inspired the charm and character that permeate the restaurant today. From the wide bevels on the panes of the double front doors to the glassed-in latticed sun porch to the bar that seems straight out of the film *Casablanca,* this place exudes a snappy and stylish grace. What's more, for lunch, for dinner, for Sunday brunch, the food is consistently imaginative and delicious. The fare is basically American—broiled calf's liver, cold boiled shrimp in a bucket, poached salmon, stuffed flounder, duck, veal Marsala, salads, burgers, *quiche.* But there's always a special touch, an unusual item or two—deep-fried dill pickles (surprisingly tantalizing), fried guinea squash sticks (eggplant), mulligatawny (an Indian soup of vegetables and apples), or deep-fried ice cream. A strolling Dixieland band plays at Sunday brunch. Do not leave Eli's without sampling its absurdly divine peanut butter pie with fudge sauce and whipped cream. Eli's is named for the great-grandfather of owner Robert Smoots. Wife Karen Smoots operates Eli's

Catering, which features the business-lunch-box express. She delivers with orders of eight or more (48 hours' notice). Prices: $6.50, $7.50, and $10.50; phone 704-529-1400.

*Price: About $15 per person*
*Open Tues.–Sat. for lunch and dinner; Sun. for brunch only*
*Accepts all major credit cards*

---

## THE EPICUREAN
### 1324 East Boulevard
#### 704-377-4529

In the not-too-long-ago days, when there was almost no place to eat in Charlotte, there was The Epicurean. The restaurant was twice (1983 and 1984) voted one of the nation's one hundred best restaurants for business dining in the U.S. and Canada by readers of *Sales & Marketing Management* magazine. There's nothing gimmicky or trendy here, nothing flashy. Since 1959, just good food—steaks, lamb chops, fish, mouth-watering biscuits—and consistently fine service. The Epicurean is fresh flowers and candlelight, low noise level, and intimate seating. The wine list—both domestic and foreign—is excellent. The Epicurean requires jackets for men, and the atmosphere is that of a private club. You'll find Greek touches in the flaky pastry pockets stuffed with meat paste one night and cheese the next and in the *dolmades* (beef and rice rolled inside grape leaves and cooked in lemon sauce).

Owners Jim and Dena Castanas were born in the Southern Greek village of Kayrai. When Jim was nineteen, in 1921, he came to New London, Connecticut, where he sold ice cream from a horse-drawn wagon. In 1926, he came to Charlotte and the next year he married Dena. Dena still makes the famous epicurean biscuits, and Jim selects and trims the meat each day, goes home for a nap, then returns to tend the grill each evening. Like Eaton stationery or a Hickey-Freeman suit, the Epicurean just doesn't go out of style.

*Price: About $15–$20 per person*
*Open Mon.–Sat. for dinner only; closed Sun.*
*Accepts all major credit cards*

---

## THE FISHMARKET
### 6631 Morrison Boulevard, Pavilion Mall (*across from South Park Shopping Center*)
#### 704-365-0883

Fine and fancy. That's the Fishmarket, a swanky seafood paradise that opened in 1983. On ribbon-cutting night, two high-powered searchlights drew the curious. Dinner guests that evening included the president of the Calvin Klein jeans company and the maître d' of New York's "21" Club. The decorations are plush with soft rose carpeting and misty pink linen, shimmery with crystal chandeliers and wall mirrors, dramatic with plants and a bigger-than-life aquarium. Sink into these sensations and relax, because the food is fabulous and the service is sometimes so-so. Never mind the veal, beef, and chicken selections. Head straight for the fish. Selections include abalone *amandine, calamari fritti* (fried squid), stuffed scrod, scallops in garlic butter with pasta, frogs' legs, broiled red snapper, poached salmon, stuffed turbot with shrimp, and fresh clams Casino. Imaginative salads include artichokes with black olives and feta cheese, white asparagus with *ravigote* sauce, hearts of palm vinaigrette, and the Fishmarket salad, a creamy combination of Bibb lettuce, crab, and small cold shrimp. For dessert, have a cup of *espresso,* and sample the rum cake, chocolate *mousse* cake, or cheesecake.

*Price: About $25 per person*
*Open daily for dinner only*
*Accepts all major credit cards*

---

# THE GREAT WALL
## 1600 Montford Drive (*near the Park Road Shopping Center*)
### 704-525-5803

There's an old-shoe ease at the Great Wall, likely born of the confident knowledge that this ten-year-old restaurant is a Charlotte institution. There are tables and booths (you can ask for a booth when you make your reservations), a red-and-black color scheme, a photomural of China's Great Wall, and scurry-scurry service. The fare, including Mandarin, Szechuan, Hunan, and Cantonese, is typically plentiful and impeccably prepared. One of the flashiest dishes is the *sa-cha* lamb—strips of tender lamb, red and green pepper, baby corn, and celery pieces, stir-fried in the tongue-tingling *sa-cha* sauce. If you're more than a party of one, be certain somebody orders the platter of mixed Chinese vegetables—sautéed (not steamed), crunchy snow peas, water chestnuts, broccoli, celery, carrots, and baby corn. For pre-dinner gnawing, try the barbecue spareribs. Eight meaty sticks—some actually plump—amply serve four. Owner Robert Lee, born near Peking, moved from Taiwan to Charlotte. His crew—natives of Taiwan, Hong Kong, Vietnam, and China—numbers about thirty-three. Lee and company close the restaurant one day a year—Thanksgiving—when they pile into a van and head out of town for a picnic of steaks, hot dogs, and potato salad. (Note: There's no longer any connection between this Great Wall and the ones on Carmel Road and Bradford Drive.)

*Price: About $10 per person*
*Open Sun.–Fri. for lunch and dinner; Sat. for dinner only*
*Accepts all major credit cards*

# LA PAZ
## 523 Fenton Place
### 704-372-4168

La Paz is in a converted two-story brick house on a quiet, tree-lined street on the seam of two of Charlotte's finer neighborhoods—Eastover and Myers Park. No question: This is the best Mexican restaurant in town. The appointments—serapes, pottery, and poppies—are cheerful but not raucous. A freestanding fireplace and a tiny side porch help to break up the floor space. Margaritas by the glass, pitcher, and half-pitcher are favorites here—generally served chilly and salt-rimmed. Trouble is, La Paz doesn't take reservations, and its popularity exceeds its seating capacity. So be prepared to wait in the upstairs bar for 20 to 45 minutes during peak hours (7 to 9 P.M.). While you wait, try the *nachos* with *jalapeño* peppers, melted Cheddar and Monterey Jack cheeses, refried beans, and a topping of sour cream and *guacamole*. But don't go overboard. You'll want to head downstairs with your appetite still functional. You can order from "specialties," "combinations," "*tacos* and *tostadas*," "*burritos*," "*enchiladas*," and "this side of the border." If you're out to satisfy a real Mexican-food craving, try the *chiles rellenos* (green chiles stuffed with Monterey Jack cheese). The "Steamboat chili" is fiery, and the dessert specialty—puffed pastry rolled in cinnamon sugar with ice cream and chocolate syrup—is gooey and good.

*Price: About $10 per person*
*Open daily for dinner only*
*Accepts Visa and MasterCard*

# OLD HICKORY HOUSE RESTAURANT
## 6538 North Tryon Street
### 704-596-8014

We're talking plain paneled walls, wobbly booths, no windows, miniature-covered-wagon wall lamps—and great barbecue. Old Hickory House serves Western (North Carolina)-style barbecue, which means the meat is cooked in a catsup-based sauce with lemon juice, butter, minced onion, brown sugar, Worcestershire, and hot pepper sauce. There's nothing like it. And don't let anyone trick you into thinking the vinegar-based Eastern (North Carolina) barbecue sauce is better. Hickory House claims to have introduced sliced barbecue (as opposed to minced) to North Carolina about 1956. The natives simply call the stuff " 'cue." But Georgia aunts visiting Charlotte typically ask to go get "bobba-coo." Pork or beef plates (sliced or minced) come with a choice of two: baked beans, Brunswick stew, sliced dill pickles, green salad, French fries, and coleslaw. Definitely order the Brunswick stew, an old-timey concoction of meat and vegetables that originally called for squirrel. If you order a sandwich, ask for sliced beef, outside meat—the crustiest, most savory part.

*Price: About $7–$10 per person*
*Open Mon.–Sat. for lunch and dinner; closed Sun.*
*No credit cards accepted*

---

# ZARRELLI'S ITALIAN RESTAURANT
## In the Park Place Shopping Center, 9101 Matthews-Pineville Road
### 704-541-3026

If you're interested in authentic (and subtle) Italian dishes, plus an evening's entertainment, Zarrelli's on the red-clay skirts of Charlotte is the place. Aniello (Neal) Zarrelli is a one-man show, extending a warm, oversized hand to guests, seating them, then crooning love songs in a tenor that in earlier days took him from the opera stage to the Copacabana. Some evenings a card magician also table-hops. It's pure Italian festival—and no place for intimate conversation. If there's a lull, a regular guest will stand and demand, "Sing, Zarrelli, sing!" The more interest you show in the fare, the more items will appear at your table. The chicken *scarpariello* (with banana peppers) is a tender combination of delicacy and zip. The *prosciutto* is thinner than fine paper, and the *zuppa di pesce* robust. Don't overlook the not-too-sweet *cannoli*. Those who like a one-big-happy-family atmosphere, with wine and beer but no mixed drinks, generally leave Zarrelli's glowing.

*Price: About $20 per person*
*Open Mon.–Fri. for lunch and dinner; Sat. and Sun. for dinner only*
*Accepts all major credit cards*

# CHICAGO

## BY JAMES WARD

**AMERICAN**
American Grill
Binyon's
Blue Mesa
Cricket's
Ed Debevic's
Gordon
Phil Smidt's
Printer's Row
Sinclair's
Wrigley Building Restaurant

**ARMENIAN**
Casbah

**BREAKFAST**
Lou Mitchell's

**CAFÉ**
Yvette

**CHINESE**
House of Hunan

**DELICATESSEN**
D.B. Kaplan's
Manny's
Mrs. Levy's

**DINER**
Ed Debevic's

**ECLECTIC**
American Grill
Arnie's
The Cottage
Gordon
Jimmy's Place
Jovan
Printer's Row
Sinclair's
Yoshi's Cafe

**FAMILY RESTAURANT**
Ann Sather's

**FAST FOOD**
The Great State Fare
Mr. Beef

**FRENCH**
Ambria
Bastille
Café Provençal
Carlos'
The Cottage
Jimmy's Place

Jovan
Le Français
Le Perroquet
Yoshi's Café

## GERMAN
Berghoff
Binyon's
The Golden Ox

## GREEK
Courtyards of Plaka
Greek Islands

## HAMBURGERS
Acorn on Oak

## HOTEL DINING ROOM
Cape Cod Room in the Drake
Hotel
Cricket's in the Tremont Hotel

## INDIAN
Bombay Palace

## ITALIAN
Avanzare
Chef Eduardo's
Club Lago
George's
La Strada
Riccardo's
Spiaggia

## JAPANESE
Hatsuhana

## MEXICAN
Boca del Rio
Dos Hermanos
Su Casa

## PIZZA
Pizzeria Due
Pizzeria Uno

## SEAFOOD
Cape Cod Room
Chestnut Street Grill
Maple St. Pier
Philander's
Shaw's Crab House
Tango

## STEAKS AND CHOPS
Lawry's—The Prime Rib
Morton's
Randall's for Ribs

## SUBURBAN
American Grill (Glenview)
Café Provençal (Evanston)
Carlos' (Highland Park)
The Cottage (Calumet City)
Le Français (Wheeling)
Philander's (Oak Park)
Phil Smidt's (Hammond,
Indiana)
Sinclair's (Lake Forest)

## SWEDISH
Ann Sather's

## THAI
Ananda
Siam Café

## UNIQUE PROPERTIES
Phil Smidt's
Riccardo's
Wrigley Building Restaurant

## WINE BAR
Bastille

Some reputations die hard. Consider Chicago's—cookery-wise or otherwise. It's no more the city of the Big Dumpling than it is of Big Al Capone. But Chicago's repute as a bastion of German and Middle European cooking hangs on, as does the legend of The Mob. Also the Windy City's moniker as a "meat and potatoes" town is decades past its prime. However, in the face of eat-light/drink-white dining trends, there has been something of an expensive steak house revival in recent years—rare beef at rare prices.

Chicago *does* live up to its reputation as America's convention capital, which means that the discriminating diner will have to dodge a lot of conventioneers and conventional dishes: beef Wellington and other things *en croûte,* pseudo-Caesar salads, and old-hat *nouvelle* stuff, and a few exploding desserts, too.

Finally, Chicago's reputation as a conservative restaurant town endures. Fortunately! Thus, the latest fad or *dernier cri* may come to Chicago belatedly (and, perhaps, lose something in translation), but if it plays in the Windy City, chances are it's good—taste-tested by sound sense and sensitive palate. The restaurants savored here are the best of what's good; and if the emphasis is on new American, French, Italian, and seafood establishments, so be it. Places such as Gordon, Maxim's, Spiaggia, and Philander's are *the* outstanding eateries.

But Chicago ain't entirely effete; there's still plenty of red meat. Although the city hasn't been "hog (or beef) butcher to the world" since the Union Stock Yards closed more than two decades ago, numerous links to yesteryear remain intact—look to Chicago's thriving neighborhood steak houses or to several popular Near North Side beef trusts, such as Eli's, the Chicago branch of NY's Palm, the rowdy (and rude) Gene & Georgetti's, and That Steak Joynt in Old Town. Yet there's one steak-out that tops them all—Morton's.

Excellent prime rib also still abounds in Chicago as at Don Roth's Blackhawk on Pearson, but with the closing of Roth's original landmark Blackhawk in the Loop two years ago, the imprimatur of "the best" now passes to another establishment, Lawry's.

Similarly, lip-smackin' barbecued ribs (pork baby backs and St. Louis spares or Texas beef ribs) can be found throughout the city from Leon's on the South Side to Bones in north suburban Lincolnwood as well as at Carson's (five locations) and the Santa Fe Café on the Near North Side. But again in this category, one place stands out, Randall's.

The one word that embraces the best of restaurants Chicago-style 1986 is "youth." And whether (as the expression goes) "Youth must be served" or not, the fact is that youth serves and cooks very well, indeed. Whatever its menu forte, "young" is the active adjective to describe the chefs, chef-proprietors, kitchen staffs, waiters and waitresses who tend Chicago's Good Table. They may be young but they know their business as seasoned professionals. They have fought the good fight against ennui and revitalized Chicago's dining-out tradition.

Although this chapter covers several excellent restaurants in the environs and in the far reaches of the city, most of Chicago's best dining is located on the Near North or Mid-North Side, where the vittle action is and always has been.

Also, you'll find that dining out in Chicago is distinguished by spacious settings and plenty of privacy for business or social chitchat. After all, Chicago is a horizontal city with a lot of room, including space for spectacular decor, which, for the most part, does not get in the way of the food—at least not in the restaurants recommended here.

The best in contemporary Chicago dining out is further marked by a certain indigenous pizzazz, and yes, by a singular brand of hospitality, that is unique to the Windy City. We're friendly folks. Come sample our style.

*James Ward is a food writer and editor, restaurant critic for Channel 7 (ABC, Chicago), author of* Restaurants Chicago-Style, *and was restaurant critic for the* Chicago Daily News *(1976–78) and the* Chicago Sun-Times *(1978–85).*

---

# ACORN ON OAK
## 116 East Oak Street
### 312-944-6835

There are many challengers, but most arguments end in agreement that the Acorn on Oak offers the best freshly ground burger in town. Worth having rare, on a great bun and with good garnish. It's also a very classy bar with generous drinks and lively entertainment from 11:15 P.M. to 4 A.M.

*Price: About $10–$12 per person*
*Open Mon.–Sat. for lunch; daily for dinner*
*Accepts American Express only*

# AMBRIA
In the Belden Stratford Hotel, 2300 North Lincoln Park West
312-472-5959

Although the restaurant is a favorite of the nouveau riche, to whom *nouvelle* cooking is still new, Chef Gabino Sotelino and his kitchen cohorts are capable of some dazzling presentations, even if marred hither and yon by telltale inconsistencies. Yet the place has youthful snap, pop, and crackle, despite Ambria's ambience: It looks like a restaurant in a French railway station somewhere in the provinces.

The menu changes frequently, but these dishes have become favorites: fresh *foie gras;* cheese and vegetable *mousse;* baby cabbage stuffed with crab meat; *salade* Ambria with shrimp, salmon, tomato, and *rémoulade* sauce; rare calf's liver with mustard seeds; grilled breast of chicken with *jalapeño* sauce; racks of lamb and veal; mallard and Muscovy ducks; and for dessert, pastries, mixed sherbets, white chocolate *mousse,* and delightful *soufflés.* There is an extensive, expensive wine list. The service is attentive and well-meaning but suffers from the juvenile exuberance of the apple-cheeked waiters.

*Price: About $40 per person*
*Open Mon.–Sat. for dinner only; closed Sun.*
*Accepts all major credit cards*

# AMERICAN GRILL
1913 Waukegan Road, Glenview
312-998-6070

In this two-year-old restaurant, trend-setting proprietor Roger Greenfield's forte is regional Americana, strongly influenced by *nouvelle* California. There are a lot of grillings and charrings, exotic thin pizzas, sublime, if curious, mixed vegetables, and higher-than-ever high-style pastas. Greenfield's handsomely redone restaurant (formerly a Sambo's chain link) has the free, spacious look of the West and Southwest, with a dash of California theater. The dramatic grill-kitchen, opened to the dining room, offers quite a show: A cast of four or five grill chefs and assorted kitchen folk work mesquite and other hardwood grills, flat tops, a high-fire brick pizza oven; a rotisserie turns chickens, ducks, and squab to a golden crisp.

On and beyond the printed menu, surprise is the order of the day. Yet despite the many variations there are these regional and seasonal themes. From Cajun country: marvelous Prudhomme-like blackened redfish, spicy gumbos, and pecan-breaded grouper. From the Midwest, there's Lake Superior whitefish with pine nuts and capers; a Wisconsin veal chop with port wine-fresh basil sauce; and grilled jumbo asparagus. From New England and the Mid-Atlantic, grilled sea scallops with saffron pasta; Maryland crab cakes and wild mushrooms; and tangy chowders. From Tex–Mex country, venison chili, BBQs of beef brisket and ribs, *fajitas* with *pico de gallo,* and a big T-bone with green chilies. And from California, seafood sausage with *pesto* sauce; smoked duck salad with *radicchio, arugula,* etc.; angel's hair pasta tossed with mussels, shrimp, and scallops. And on and on. The wine list is California, of course, and a good one. And the desserts are made on the premises, including these movable feasts: fresh fruit tarts and mango and raspberry *mousses.* About 30 minutes north of downtown Chicago.

*Price: About $18–$23 per person*
*Open daily for lunch and dinner*
*Accepts all major credit cards*

---

# ANANDA
## 941 North State Street
### 312-944-7440

Here's a Thai storefront with a difference—white clothed tables with good appointments, spotless contemporary interior, an extensive and descriptive menu in English, plus gracious service. Food is elegantly prepared and presented, and mild-to-very spicy, even if lacking the fire that takes the breath away. Recommended appetizers: grilled pork *satay;* fried fish cakes; deep-fried squid with spiced ground pork; mild-hot lemon grass soup with shrimp; and *yum-som,* a marvelous sweet-hot salad of shrimp, orange slices, peanuts, and peppers. As main courses: relatively torrid stir-fried chicken with basil and pepper sauce; the delicate special noodle Ananda; stir-fried pork with "young ginger"; whole deep-fried red snapper with a medley of sauces; marinated, then roasted, pork hock with greens; and curried chicken with a coconut-based sauce and its many-layered flavors. The set dinners for two to six persons offer an excellent introduction to Thai cooking for the novice. There is no liquor license, so bring beer or wine.

*Price: About $16 per person*
*Open Tues.–Sat. for lunch and dinner; Sun. for dinner only; closed Mon.*
*Accepts all major credit cards*

# ANN SATHER'S
## 929 West Belmont Avenue
### 312-348-2378

For breakfast, lunch, or dinner family-style, the local choice is Ann Sather's on the Mid-North Side. This old-timer is a fond reminder of Chicago's Swedish heritage. The setting is squeaky clean, the food simple and delicious (for example, chicken croquettes, Swedish meatballs, and thin pancakes with lingonberries). Children are very welcome.

*Price: Under $10 per person*
*Open daily for breakfast, lunch, and dinner*
*Accepts most major credit cards*

# ARNIE'S
## 1030 North State Street
### 312-266-4800

Arnie's is an "only-in-Chicago" showplace, the choice of locals as well as visitors who want a good time and a celebration, including dancing to live music. What the restaurant lacks in mere taste (the "Deco" decor is a bit much), it more than makes up for in panache and style. But Arnie's circuses get too much attention and the restaurant's excellent food too little. Pity! Because the eclectic chow is consistently *very* good.

The signature items are knock-out: *escargots* in pastry; fried Brie with tomato-basil sauce; Chicago's premier pasta *primavera;* Cajun blackened redfish; grilled swordfish with tequila-orange/basil-butter on *radicchio;* the succulent slab of BBQ baby backs; rack of lamb; a huge, lightly breaded "Sicilian" veal chop; prime steak; and any fresh fish of the day. Desserts are very rich and chocolatey. The wine list has a fine selection of fairly priced American reds and whites. If dinner at Arnie's is pop, lunch is power. There's also a lavish Sunday brunch at $11.95 per person.

*Price: About $25 per person*
*Open Sun.–Fri. for lunch and dinner; Sat. for dinner only*
*Accepts all major credit cards*

# AVANZARE
## 161 East Huron Street
### 312-337-8056

The place is undeniably urbane: a designer's dream of what Milan *should* look like—throw-away chic with a certain *dolce far niente*. Fine for business lunches, despite the hurly-burly and sometimes dawdlesome service.

The menu features "Northern Italian" fare as well as the more fanciful creations of Chef Dennis Terczak. As often as not, these daily flights-of-fancy should be grounded. Stick with the more familiar offerings on the printed card. Appetizers: *carpaccio* with tomato-vinaigrette, sun-dried beef with *arugula;* roasted peppers and anchovies. Pastas are imaginative: *fettuccine* with cured salmon and dill sauce; *ravioli* with duck, *porcini* mushrooms; spinach pasta filled with three cheeses. Entrées include several fresh fish of the day; calf's liver with sausage and lentils; a grilled veal chop; and steak roasted in *pesto* sauce, which is a joy to behold—and devour. There's a large and interesting wine list with some unusual Italian offerings. A pleasant sidewalk café is open during the summer months.

*Price: About $25 per person*
*Open Mon.–Fri. for lunch; daily for dinner*
*Accepts all major credit cards*

# BASTILLE
## 21 West Superior Street
### 312-787-2050

French brasserie fare, simple but superior food, much of it grilled, with sauce on the side, as one would find in Parisian bistros. Among the better offerings: any coarse *pâté,* robust onion soup, *boudin blanc,* and sausage *en croûte,* seafood *brochettes,* all fresh fish of the day, chicken and veal dishes. Most entrées are served with a basket of crisp *pommes frites.* Hearty *bouillabaisse, cassoulet,* and *couscous* are often featured. Bastille houses Chicago's first wine bar, which continues to serve outstanding vintages, many by the glass. Service is casual but efficient. Lunch is usually packed; dinner, more leisurely. Each July, Bastille celebrates its namesake holiday with a two- or three-*week* outdoor festival of food and entertainment. It's one of Chicago's best bashes.

*Price: About $18 per person*
*Open Mon.–Fri. for lunch and dinner; Sat. and Sun. for dinner only*
*Accepts all major credit cards*

# BERGHOFF
## 17 West Adams Street
### 312-427-3170

Established in 1898, Berghoff is the city's second oldest extant German restaurant and by far its most famous. As a Chicago institution it rivals the Chicago Symphony (founded only seven years earlier); as a great German restaurant —well, as noted, "the Berghoff" is venerable—and vulnerable. Although the food is only fair to good (and occasionally *very*), a visit to the establishment is a *must*. Chicagoans love it; and, without doubt, you will, too.

An unusually extensive menu offers everything from *sauerbraten,* boiled pork shank, and *Wiener Schnitzel* to *kassler ribchen,* smoked *thueringer* sausage, and roast goose (when available). Also note: Many locals enjoy Berghoff's fish and seafood—largely for good reason. Most entrées include potatoes and salad or vegetable. Of course there are great beers, light and dark, and a fair-to-good wine selection. The wood-paneled setting is incomparable (for Chicago); the service, down to earth; the ambience, hustle and rush.

*Price: About $10 per person*
*Open Mon.–Sat. for lunch and dinner; closed Sun.*
*No credit cards accepted*

---

# BINYON'S
## 327 South Plymouth Court (*between Jackson and Van Buren streets*)
### 312-341-1155

Binyon's is a long-time South Loop favorite: a solid American restaurant of strong German heritage. At lunch, the urbane upper and lively lower dining rooms are packed with politicos, lawyers, and judges from nearby offices and courtrooms. At dinner, Binyon's is cheek-to-jowl with before-the-event Blackhawk, Bulls, or Lyric Opera fans. The preferred vittles of several generations of Chicagoans should be your choice—turtle soup with sherry, grilled walleye pike, splendid sweetbreads and veal kidneys, short ribs with vegetables, and pork shank with sauerkraut. Desserts are unmemorable.

*Price: About $18 per person*
*Open Mon.–Sat. for lunch and dinner; closed Sun.*
*Accepts all major credit cards*

# BLUE MESA
## 1729 North Halsted Street
### 312-944-5990

"As American as the great Southwest" means delicious overlays of Indian, Mexican, and frontier cooking. Blue Mesa offers a very pleasant setting and food that is distinct yet not unfamiliar. White stucco, adobe-like walls, and native art supplement the kitchen's authenticity. The crowd is mostly young and smartly casual.

Recommended appetizers: the Frito pie; Blue Mesa fritter; fried *jalapeño* Jack cheese; and cactus salad served Cobb-style, with generous heapings of cactus, olives, tomatoes, beets, and avocado with a tart vinaigrette. Of main-course note: blue corn chicken *enchiladas, carne adovado* (roast pork marinated in red chile sauce and oven-roasted), honey-lime chicken, and veal sautéed with *piñon* nuts and wild mushrooms. À la carte light offerings include *chalupas* (with pinto beans, choice of pork or chicken, topped with cheese and *guacamole*), green chile cheeseburger, and a thick, hot New Mexico chili. Good list of imported beers.

*Price: About $15 per person*
*Open Mon.–Fri. for lunch; daily for dinner*
*Accepts all major credit cards*

# BOCA DEL RIO
## 917 West Belmont Avenue
### 312-281-6698

Alas, most of Chicago's Mexican restaurants are interchangeable: predictable and limited in offering and backdrop. This is the considered opinion of the writer, who is a passionate Mexicanophile. Yes, there are the little storefronts that are promising today, but unfortunately gone *mañana*. (The purpose of these recommendations—"the best"—is not to send the visitor to the further-most reaches of *madre y padre* land in search of the evanescent.)

One place, however, has proven itself by trial and success. Boca del Rio, on the handy Mid-North Side, does a fine job with fish and seafood specialties, and makes a commendable effort with the conventional Mexican dishes. The place, and the people who run it, are professional and pleasant. You'll enjoy all of the fresh seafood appetizers, plus nippy red sauce; *ceviche;* avocado filled with shrimp; red snapper or shrimp with a piquant sauce *Veracruzana*—onions, red and green peppers, plus tomatoes. Also try the crisp deep-fried fish or shrimp, first marinated in garlic sauce. Conventional Mexican dishes of note: chicken with heavy, flavorsome *mole* sauce; *enchiladas verdes;* various *tacos, sopes,* and *burritos,* plus *chiles rellenos*—big green peppers dipped in egg batter with beef or cheese. The margaritas are tart, salty, and adult. The Mexican beers are just the ticket.

*Price: About $15–$18 per person*
*Open Sat.–Sun. for late lunch; Tues.–Sun. for dinner*
*Accepts all major credit cards*

---

# BOMBAY PALACE
## 50 East Walton Street
### 312-664-9323

This beautiful restaurant—call it "Asian *Moderne"*—features spacious rooms with cinnamon-colored walls and alcoves that display brightly polished Indian treasures, trifles, and trinkets. Unlike all too many posh Eastern eateries, Bombay Palace doesn't sacrifice its offerings on the altar of (mid-) Western tastes. The menu highlights the subtly spiced food of India's northwest Punjab region—especially *tandoori* dishes. Appetizers of considerable note: vegetable *samosa* (crisp patties, stuffed with vegetables and spices); *pakoras* (chicken or vegetable fritters); and *shammi kebab.* As entrées, order *tandoori* specialties as well as curried whitefish; butter chicken; lamb cubes with ginger and onion; chicken or lamb *pasanda* (marinated in yogurt, then cooked in cream and spices). A dessert must: *kulfi,* a rosewater-flavored Indian ice cream with ground almonds. Daily luncheon buffet features an array of curries, *tandoori* and vegetable dishes with salads, rice, and other items.

*Price: About $18–$22 per person*
*Open daily for lunch and dinner*
*Accepts all major credit cards*

# CAFÉ PROVENÇAL
## 1625 Hinman Avenue, Evanston
### 312-475-2233

Over the past decade, especially with the spirited (if belated) victory of wet over dry, Chicago's northern suburbs, from the city line to Lake Forest, have blossomed with bistros, many of them French and some of them quite good. One of the best is Leslee Reis's Café Provençal in nearby Evanston. In addition to a tasty mélange of classic, *nouvelle,* and *bourgeois* food, chef-proprietor Reis offers an amazing list of wines at unbelievably low prices, with several by-the-glass offerings daily. It's almost as if La Reis were tweaking the noses of the WCTU—long headquartered in her suburb.

Opened in 1977, Café Provençal has a singular personality: part French provincial, part American colonial—and quite unlike that of Gallic restaurants in the city proper or improper. The small regular menu, changed quarterly, usually lists duckling in some delicious guise or other, veal chops or *médaillons,* a chicken dish—perhaps grilled breast stuffed with wild rice, mushrooms, and cabbage—and a lamb rack, often prepared with fresh herbs and sweet red pepper sauce. Because freshness and the chef's inventiveness are the order of the day at Café Provençal, there are many nightly specialties, all marked by gentle seasonings, light sauces, and dressings.

These dailies have included a *charcuterie* plate, a trio of fresh mushrooms, and various festive pasta dishes as first courses. As entrées, there might be fresh grilled tuna with saffron butter, roast halibut, or a veal chop with fresh sorrel. Desserts can be delightfully light or embarrassingly heavy.

*Price: About $30 plus per person*
*Open Mon.–Sat. for dinner only; closed Sun.*
*Accepts all major credit cards*

# CAPE COD ROOM
## In the Drake Hotel, 140 East Walton Street
### 312-787-2200

From sea to shining sea the Cape Cod Room is perhaps Chicago's best-known seafood restaurant—and perhaps the Windy City's best-known eatery, regardless of offering. Now it's rare that fame can be equated with "great," or even "good," but our beloved Cape Cod Room is tops. And it remains above and beyond seafood trends and fish fads. No mean catch! Since 1933, the Cape Cod has offered consistently fine dishes, such as seafood gumbo, Bookbinder's snapper soup, *bouillabaisse,* a variety of oyster treats, lake trout, pompano *en papillote,* crab meat Maryland, and rainbow trout. The almost immutable room is a classic with its checkered tablecloths and amusing marine clutter. It was —and is—a "must." Service is brisk but much friendlier than in days of yore.

*Price: About $25 per person*
*Open daily for lunch and dinner*
*Accepts all major credit cards*

---

# CARLOS'
## 429 Temple Avenue, Highland Park
### 432-0770

It's hard to find fault here, and frankly I've never tried. The quality of (great) pleasure is not strained. Carlos' is not perfect perhaps—it *merely* totters on the brink of greatness. Yes, indeed. Chef Roland Liccioni's menu strikes a consistently beautiful balance between French classic cuisine and *nouvelle* cooking. He always knows what he's about; his hallmark is controlled creativity— imaginative but informed—and his provisions are of the highest quality, of course. Favorites from the limited card, and list of extensive daily specialties, have included a light mushroom *pâté* with truffle sauce; fresh New York *foie gras,* beautifully garnished; a splendid seafood *cassolette;* various *feuilletée* "surprises"; and an *escargot brioche* with Roquefort and chives. The soups, including lobster bisque and duck consommé, are terrific; as are the super special salads. Entrées are robust or subtle, often both robust *and* subtle. Please consider salmon in perfect puff pastry; roasted lobster; any grilled or poached fish, often served over pretty pastas; duckling with sweet garlic sauce; or lovely pink liver with a sauce redolent of rosemary. The nightly changing dessert selection is wonderful, and has featured an elegant *profiterole* with ice cream and tangy chocolate sauce; gorgeous fruit tarts; and a Croesus-rich *sabayon* on sugar wafers with fresh raspberry sauce.

There is an adequate wine list, very fairly priced. The dining room is crisp, charming, private, and *quiet.* The service is intelligent, solicitous, and humane; these good people know *and* care. Considering everything, perhaps Carlos' has crossed the brink and *is* in the Elysian Fields of greatness! The restaurant is about a 45-minute drive north of downtown Chicago.

*Price: About $40 per person*
*Open Wed.–Mon. for dinner only; closed Tues.*
*Accepts all major credit cards*

# CASBAH
## 514 West Diversey Avenue
### 312-935-7570

Inexpensive, informal, and excellent! Chicagoans who hanker for the best in Armenian and Middle Eastern cooking have long made tracks to this hospitable Mid-North establishment with its Arabian Nights decor. The familiar menu arouses not startlement but satisfaction: Every dish offered is consistently and subtly prepared. Of particular note as appetizers: *baba ghanouj*, eggplant purée with *tahini* sauce; *kibbee nayyeh*, seasoned raw lamb and cracked wheat; spinach and cheese *beorak*; *yalanci sarma*, grape leaves liberally filled with walnuts, rice, and currants; and cold white beans with carrots in olive oil. Recommended entrées: *pastilla*, Cornish hen shredded and baked with a delightful egg-almond sauce in flaky pastry dough; *sarma-khashlama*, stuffed vine leaves, cooked with beautiful lamb; and *kibbeh* with ground lamb, onions, and walnuts; *tuss kabab*, stewed lamb presented over an eggplant-*béchamel* sauce. When offered as specials, order brook trout Leila, stuffed with puréed eggplant; and variations of *couscous*. Entrées are served with warm *pita* bread, smooth egg-lemon or cold cucumber soup, salad, and a rice pilaf, or vegetables. For dessert, the *baklava* is crisp, sweet, and elegant.

*Price: About $15 per person*
*Open daily for dinner*
*Accepts all major credit cards*

# CHEF EDUARDO'S
## 1640 North Wells Street
### 312-266-2021

In a high-ceilinged but still intimate Old Town setting chef-proprietor Eduardo Lougrini offers his pan-Italian menu of cooked-to-order specialties. Whether you choose the daily items or from the printed card, the selections are equally good. (And that's rare enough at a time when many restaurants push *du jour* and ignore the regular menu.) Eduardo's various pastas—especially the *tortellini alla panna*, the seafood *linguine* with *marinara* sauce, and savory *spaghetti alla carbonara* are toothsome, rich but light. Chicken breast with *pesto*, veal Marsala, *calamari*, sweetbreads, and knock-out frogs legs in garlic sauce are entrées of note.

*Price: About $18–$22 per person*
*Open Mon.–Sat. for dinner; closed Sun.*
*Accepts all major credit cards*

# CHESTNUT STREET GRILL

In Water Tower Place, Mezzanine Level, 845 North
Michigan Avenue

312-280-2720

Charcoal-grilled seafood has gone beyond the rage stage in Chicago, and the *cognoscenti* now talk of the relative merits of applewood, mesquite, hickory, and oak in hushed tones once reserved for California varietals. The Levy Organization's Chestnut Street Grill introduced the pleasures of gently grilled seafood to the city and they still do it best.

The restaurant—with its spiffy glass-walled cooking area, crisply set tables, and Louis Sullivan stencilwork—is a Chicago charmer. This tranquil backdrop whisks you far away from bustling Water Tower Place, where it is located. Just as the setting is honest, so the serving is intelligent and the seafood simply wonderful. Follow the trustworthy menu or ask about daily market specials that often include black sea bass, petrale and other soles, swordfish steak, New Zealand John Dory, shark, and salmon—all sparkling fresh. Begin with the city's best sourdough bread and sweet butter, and a bowl of steamed mussels and clams, or fried *calamari*—a cliché elsewhere, but heaven here. Also, the seafood salads are choice. And now there are a number of low-sodium, low-cholesterol "Spa" selections. Beyond fish, the calf's liver steak with bacon and onions is just swell. Desserts are rich and tasty: Try the *cappuccino* ice cream cake. Delightful Sunday brunch offers a changing menu of omelets, crab meat Benedict, fruit-filled chicken breast, among other pleasant surprises. A stunning wine list features over seventy California labels with at least four offered by the glass daily. No reservations are taken, but the Seafood & Raw Bar will hold you over until your table is ready at this very popular "first-come-first-served" eatery.

*Price: About $20–$25 per person*
*Open daily for lunch and dinner*
*Accepts all major credit cards*

# CLUB LAGO

Superior and Orleans streets

312-951-2849

A little west of the Gold Coast, in the increasingly arty but still blue-collar River North area stands this grand old Chicago saloon with a dining room in back serving spaghetti with *bolognese* sauce and other low-tab, high-quality pan-Italian dishes. For gala elbow-to-elbow lunches and early dinners (pre-Lyric Opera and pre-theater), Lago is a choice treat.

*Price: Under $10 per person*
*Open Mon.–Sat. for lunch; Mon.–Fri. for early dinner; closed Sun.*
*No credit cards accepted*

---

# THE COTTAGE
## 525 Torrence Avenue, Calumet City
### 312-891-3900

In the midst of the Sahara of the Culinary Arts that is the south suburbs of Chicago, The Cottage stands out as a refreshing oasis of fine food and good spirits. And *quel charme!* The restaurant is where it is and what it is because Calumet City is where the Busters, chef Carolyn and husband-host Gerry, live and fervently maintain an 11-year-old romance with their delightful, vaguely rustic bistro. The restaurant, like its owners, is both professional *and* amateur, but in the best "to love" sense of the word.

The Cottage menu has been called "Continental," perhaps because of the presence of several Austrian/Middle European dishes, but that's a misnomer: The subtlety, balance, and intelligence that informs the food is basically French. Yes, even with an *au courant* bow to California.

Menu items vary with the market and season, of course. And although the offerings are properly limited, the ten or so entrées plus appetizers, salads, and desserts provide much choice. Especially consider any fresh fish or seafood dish: Chef Carolyn's preparations range widely from Dover sole, scallops in cream sauce, and grilled garlic scampi to simple grilled salmon or complex salmon *en croûte,* for once airily encrusted and elegantly presented. Other favorite main courses: roast duckling (particularly good when served with raspberry sauce), spring lamb and fall game in season; veal Viennoise, garnished with twiced-fried onions; or steak Madagascar with a green peppercorn-cream sauce; and The Cottage pork *schnitzel.*

Appetizers and soups are lively or hearty or both; salads, distinctive; and vegetables beautifully cooked. It would be a shame not to have dessert—homemade ice creams; high-layered raspberry cake; bread pudding with Bourbon sauce; strawberries *cardinal;* rhubarb strudel; and an immensely delicious chocolate creation called "Chocolate Indulgence." When you ring for reservations, ask for driving directions. The Cottage is about a 30-minute drive south of the Loop.

*Price: About $25 per person*
*Open Tues.–Fri. for lunch and dinner; Sat. for dinner only; closed Sun. and Mon.*
*Accepts all major credit cards*

# COURTYARDS OF PLAKA
### 340 South Halsted Street
### 312-263-0767

A distinctive menu, friendly *and* efficient service, as well as a nifty contemporary look (no paintings of the Parthenon on velvet here) make this Chicago's most high-style Greek restaurant. Yes, there are all the usual Greek specialties (*taramasalata, pastitsio, moussaka,* and *dolmades* may be the choice items), but there are also a number of entrées unavailable elsewhere: for example, *tigania* (pork tenderloin slices in wine sauce) and *kreatopita* (lamb and beef in pastry). Appetizers include splendid *garidosalata,* a creamy shrimp salad; and *melizzanosalata,* spiced eggplant on sesame bread. If only the kitchen were steadier in its preparation of the familiar dishes! For dessert try the rich chocolate custard pastry called *sokolatina.* Lunch is crowded and less noisy than dinner. Indeed business people from the nearby Loop often enjoy a working lunch here.

*Price: About $14–$18 per person*
*Open daily for lunch and dinner*
*Accepts all major credit cards*

# CRICKET'S
### In the Tremont Hotel, 100 East Chestnut Street
### 312-280-2100

Is it French-American or American-French cookery that comes out of Cricket's excellent kitchen? The genre is usually a cliché but here it's presented with flair and style.

The clubby restaurant is as relaxed in a sophisticated way as it is low-key in appearance. The backdrop, the menu, the generally gracious French service, and the ministrations of suave maître d' Jean-Pierre Lutz make Cricket's one of Chicago's inner "in" spots for Old Money and quiet glitter—and a preferred place for upper power lunches *and* dinners.

The card is large (almost 75 items) and the food amazingly reliable for its consistency. Favorite dishes: hot onion or chilled senegalese soup, wilted spinach/bacon salad, crab *diablo* or baked oysters in Pernod for appetizers; terrific grilled salmon, sautéed Dover sole, halibut in pimiento butter—all the fish dishes are tops. And game is beautifully prepared. Also of note: *fettuccine* with *prosciutto* and shrimp, rack of lamb, a terrific mixed grill, kidneys *dijonnaise,* chicken hash, chops, wild game, and, yes, *the* hamburger, borrowed from New York's "21" Club, as is much of Cricket's decor. There is a good but expensive list of wines. For fine service, phone maître d' Lutz well in advance. Well worth a reward! The three-course New Orleans Brunch on Saturday and Sunday is $14.75 per person.

*Price: About $40 to $45 per person*
*Open daily for breakfast, lunch, and dinner*
*Accepts all major credit cards*

---

## D. B. KAPLAN'S
### In Water Tower Place, 845 North Michigan Avenue
**312-280-2700**

Chicagoans flock here for an almost endless variety of mountainous deli sandwiches and snacks in a light and bright surrounding.

*Price: About $6 per person*
*Open daily for lunch and dinner*
*No credit cards accepted*

---

## DOS HERMANOS RESTAURANTE & CANTINA
### In Sears Tower, 233 South Wacker Drive
**312-993-0527**

This large, festive, and attractive restaurant adds a much needed bright south-of-the-border accent to the South Loop area. If the food is Anglo–Mex and geared to pop taste, that's just fine because the *nachos grandes, chiles rellenos* with green sauce, beef *enchiladas,* and the *pollo fundido* are very good indeed. Also the beef and chicken *fajitas* are outstanding. And the all-you-can-eat *taco* bar is a real bargain. For dessert, skip the *flan*—it's topped with whipped cream. Have the silly-sounding but delicious fried ice cream.

*Price: About $6–$8 per person*
*Open Mon.–Fri. for lunch and dinner*
*Accepts all major credit cards*

---

## ED DEBEVIC'S
### 640 North Wells Street
**312-664-1707**

Ed's re-creates "American diner food" of the well-remembered 1950s to a madding crowd that ill remembers that era but has great nostalgia for it: A droll amalgam of Yuppies, young blue collars, and junior members of the coupon-clipping set. Of course, there's no Ed Debevic—it's a made-up name —but Ed's place is very real and tacky-chic, from its bubblegum-chewing waitresses to its aqua vinyl booths. The food includes burgers and fries, five-way chili, meat loaf, fried chicken, chicken-fried steak, cherry Cokes, and chocolate milk shakes. It's a vastly amusing, sadly accurate remembrance of things past—a big-buck re-creation by Chicago's Rich Melman of Lettuce Entertain You fame.

*Price: Under $10 per person*
*Open daily for lunch and dinner*
*No credit cards accepted*

---

# GEORGE'S
## 230 West Kinzie Street
### 312-644-2290

Finally completely and spiffily restored after 1984's big fire and water damage, George's is as striking in its cool Art Moderne appearance as ever. Yet despite all the severe green marble and glass brick, the place is cunningly curvaceous. It remains a "rage" restaurant—packed at lunch with buyers, designers, and rich clientele from the Merchandise Mart just across the way. At night, George's succeeds in the unlikely act of combining super North Italian cookery with American jazz. The performers are classic headliners; and the mellifluous sounds, the good spirits, and food work surprisingly well together. There is the matter of timing and pacing, however. Always call first (try to get "Casey") to match your schedule with George's. Note the wide selection of pastas—as appetizers or main courses—including a sensational *penne* with four cheeses. Of high note: *vitello tonnato,* salmon tartare, the veal chop *Valdostana,* sea bass with Gorgonzola cheese, or almost any seafood dish or fresh fish, especially those that are grilled. Outstanding Italian wine list.

*Price: About $30 per person*
*Open Mon.–Fri. for lunch; Mon.–Sat. for dinner; closed Sun.*
*Accepts all major credit cards*

---

# THE GOLDEN OX
## 1578 North Clybourn Avenue
### 312-664-0780

Teutonic tops! Whether The Golden Ox is the last gasp of Chicago's once dominant ethnic *küchen* or not, it remains the best—and not only by (sad) comparison. It is our most stylish German restaurant, combining traditional hospitality and fine food with contemporary vitality. The setting is rather preciously "Old World." If *gemütlichkeit* means anything in 1986 Chicago, this is the place to seek it out.

The menu is wide, high, and handsome, but (sigh) there are occasional problems of kitchen consistency. Recommended dishes: *hackepeter,* all the hearty soups, *sülze,* baked oysters—and then, *sauerbraten,* roast duck, *Wiener Schnitzel,* veal with lemon butter, *Kasseler rippchen,* and sweetbreads. Also try the liver dumplings, potato pancakes, and strudel. Usually the Bavarian pot roast and braised oxtails are worth writing home about, even if home is Munich. Splendid *hasenpfeffer* in season!

*Price: About $15–$18 per person*
*Open Mon.–Sat. for lunch and dinner; Sun. for dinner only*
*Accepts all major credit cards*

---

# GORDON
## 500 North Clark Street
### 312-467-9780

Here's gala glamor in a run-down neighborhood. Yet after decades of decay, the winos' "boulevard of broken dreams (and bottles)" is becoming the real estate developers' high-priced hope. With much daring and tongue-in-chic, restaurateur Gordon Sinclair opened this Haute Camp establishment ten years ago. It succeeded, fabulously. And just last year, he moved down the block into larger quarters. Happily, much is the same—stylishly, deliciously, and sweetly bizarre. Gordon is, as always, a very fashionable restaurant. Among the imaginative and yummy offerings: a paper-thin spinach *crêpe torte;* eggplant *duxelle;* artichoke fritters with *béarnaise;* roasted turbot with fresh thyme; *tournedos* with elephant garlic and mustard; roasted quail stuffed with veal *pesto mousse;* grilled lamb loin with chèvre and rosemary. For dessert, don't miss the superb flourless chocolate cake or coconut Bavarian cream. There is a good wine list.

*Price: About $25 per person*
*Open Sun.–Fri. for lunch and dinner; Sat. for dinner only*
*Accepts all major credit cards*

# THE GREAT STATE FARE

In the State of Illinois Building, 100 West Randolph Street
(*between Clark and LaSalle streets*)
312-280-3310

Although it's something of a misnomer to call the mostly fresh (not frozen), made-on-premise vittles featured at The Great State Fare "fast food," the delicious and attractively presented offerings *are* quickly served, popular, and moderate in cost (but not "cheap" in any sense of the word). GSF has three separate food centers. The Grill features barbecued ribs and chicken, South Carolina BBQ pork sandwiches, and a variety of gourmet-burger combos—and much more. The Kitchens offer baked stuffed potatoes, Chicago-style hot dogs and *würsts,* crispy fried chicken, fish treats such as Cajun popcorn, and individual pan pizzas, plus many other items: There is considerable choice.

Across the atrium, the walk-in Market features a deli, bakery (with fresh baked goods and a *quiche*-of-the-day), and fresh salads priced by the ounce. There are more than 600 comfortable chairs (at marble-topped tables) filled by a cross section of Downtown personalities: politicians, state and city employees, vested lawyers, construction workers, and tourists who come to gawk at the spectacular and controversial new State of Illinois Building.

*Price: Under $5 per person*
*Open Mon.–Fri. for breakfast, lunch, and takeout; Sat. for late breakfast and lunch; closed Sun.*
*No credit cards accepted*

# GREEK ISLANDS

200 South Halsted Street
312-782-9855

The best, hands down—or up. *Opa!* Slightly west of downtown's business and financial district is Chicago's most spectacular Greek restaurant—and one of the country's best. It draws everyone from professionals and ad-types at lunch to the family trade and visiting firemen at night. Opened in the early seventies, Greek Islands moved to its delightful, large new home (five dining rooms) in 1983. The gracious, and tasteful, new place offers the best of Greek hospitality and food at a very modest cost. There may be a few mishaps here and there, but mostly the proprietors and their kitchen staff well know what they're about. Practice makes (almost) perfect. Grilled fresh whole red snapper or sea bass with lemon juice, olive oil, and oregano; shrimp with feta cheese; a variety of loin or leg lamb dishes with wonderful (not overdone) vegetables; *pastitsio;*

*souvlaki; dolmades; moussaka*—gasp! All this is preceded by tart, flaming *saganaki, tadziki, gyro,* and *taramasalata*—as fine as you'll find anywhere! The place is noisy and friendly. A joy.

*Price: Under $10–$12 per person*
*Open daily for lunch and dinner*
*Accepts all major credit cards*

---

# HATSUHANA
## 160 East Ontario Street
### 312-280-8287

*Sushi:* Slick, quick, and made with such charm. Handsome Hatsuhana features Chicago's most impressive *sushi* bar, where a wide variety of beautiful raw seafood—tuna, salmon, yellowtail, shrimp included—is artfully crafted into *sushi, chirashi,* and *maki sushi,* with vinegared rice and/or seaweed and vegetables. Too often, this procedure is performed as a secret sacred right but not at Hatsuhana: The uninitiated are invited to behold—and enjoy.

Beyond these appetizers, there is a full menu of traditional dishes, ranging from the familiar to the obscure, and all of them good to excellent. Other recommended appetizers (hot) include spicy broiled steamer clams, fried salted chicken, fried bean curd and (cold) spinach in sesame and soy sauce and shredded radish with caviar. Also consider Hatsuhana's complete dinners, most notably the house "special" (*sushi* and *sashimi,* seafood *teriyaki,* shrimp *tempura,* broiled lobster, and many side dishes plus dessert). A smart buy, and a good way to graze across the menu. The setting is attractive and contemporary; the service, polite and welcoming.

*Price: About $20 per person*
*Open Mon.–Fri. for lunch; Mon.–Sat. for dinner; closed Sun.*
*Accepts all major credit cards*

---

# HOUSE OF HUNAN
## 535 North Michigan Avenue
### 312-329-9494

This large, comfortable, and cordial restaurant, done up in Hong Kong Victorian style, deserves kudos for its wide-ranging menu emphasizing spicy, hot Hunan and Szechuan cooking, as well as subtle Mandarin cuisine (plus many Shanghai and Cantonese dishes); and for the consistency of its preparation—always good to excellent—over the past nine years. It's no mean accomplishment for a kitchen to succeed in bravura boldness as well as in tasty understatement. The menu, arranged by food categories (seafood, pork, chicken, etc.), with regional dishes described in detail under each category, is immensely helpful to the informed as well as to the uninitiated. "Hot" items are marked as such, but if you like things really Chinese Hot (as opposed to Midwest Hot) you can specify "very" when you order. The kitchen and knowledgeable serving staff aims to please—and does.

Highly recommended appetizers: shrimp toast, pot stickers, hot tripe, the crunchy jellyfish, hacked chicken in a sesame and chile-pepper sauce, shrimp or chicken sizzling rice soup, or smooth but spicy hot and sour soup. Outstanding house specialties and other main courses: willow beef, steak sautéed in a medium-hot sauce; orange beef, with hot peppers, orange peel, and vegetables; the singular Hunan leg of lamb, first marinated then cooked with scallions in a really zippy sauce; spicy Szechuan frogs' legs or frogs' legs in a subtle Peking brown sauce; shrimp with garlic; surprisingly gentle Szechuan lobster or lovely lobster Cantonese, redolent of ginger and garlic; and deep-fried whole yellow fish, Hunan style. Also you will enjoy the restaurant's terrific version of that old Cantonese favorite, sweet and sour pork, or the sizzling Szechuan shredded pork; Szechuan chicken, diced with peppers and peanuts. Desserts are minimal, but apple or banana fritters glazed with syrup, then crystallized in ice water at table, are amusing. House of Hunan offers elegant family-style dining—the larger the group, the wider the sampling, but a twosome will be well satisfied.

*Price: About $20 per person*
*Open Mon.–Sat. for lunch and dinner; closed Sun.*
*Accepts all major credit cards*

---

# JIMMY'S PLACE
## 3420 Elston Avenue
### 312-539-2999

To those who are not familiar with Jimmy's Place and regard the address as far out, please be advised that this eight-year-old restaurant is smartly mainstream, and a speedy drive from the Loop. You are welcomed with the sound of opera in the background (a bit too Callas-strophic for some tastes) and greeted by friendly Jimmy Rohr and his gracious staff. The food is classically French educated, with a degree in *nouvelle* finesse, handsomely prepared and presented. Ironically, but only occasionally, certain light dishes become leaden.

The printed card varies monthly and there are daily specialties. Highly recommended signature dishes include: Belgian endive *à la flamande;* salads of mixed greens, goat cheese, and pine nuts, or of spinach, bacon, feta cheese, and mushrooms; halibut with poached oysters; grilled salmon or any other fresh fish of the day, neatly garnished and sauced. Other entrées of special note: sweetbreads with mustard-cream sauce; roast loin of lamb, marinated in garlic and olive oil, then embedded with cracked black pepper; and veal *en croûte* with port wine sauce. For dessert, have the *charlotte russe,* the lemon custard tart with apricot glaze, or the house favorite, caramel apples with rum, on coffee ice cream. Or *opera torte,* of course. There is a limited but fairly priced wine list. Ask for specific directions when you make your reservations at Jimmy's Place. Once there, you'll find plenty of free parking, unknown downtown.

*Price: About $30 per person*
*Open Mon.–Fri. for lunch and dinner; Sat. for dinner only; closed Sun.*
*Accepts most major credit cards*

---

# JOVAN
## 1660 North LaSalle Street
### 312-944-7766

Jovan is a phoenix gloriously risen from the ashes of the ho-hum original destroyed by fire several years ago. Owner Dieter Ahrens used the opportunity of starting anew to full advantage. He gave Jovan a lovely new home and an adventuresome new menu. Located at the point where the Gold Coast meets Old Town at Lincoln Park, Jovan is now one of Chicago's four or five most beautiful eating spots. A large space (150 seats) has been sculpted into intimate areas, and an aura of luxury created with rich fabrics and subtle lighting. If the setting of the new Jovan is more contemporary than the old, so is the food. It is neoclassic French, both lush and light, with the increasing imprint of California, regional Americana, and even a touch of the Orient. What could be an absurd mishmash is actually sane and subtle. The printed menu changes seasonally, and there are oodles of dailies. Among the delicious appetizers: *ravioli* filled with wild mushrooms and duck; sweetbreads and chèvre; salmon *tartare* with coriander; Brie soup; fresh lemon grass *consommé en croûte;* curried oysters with cucumber sauce; and a splendid hot seafood sausage with sorrel. Recommended entrées: rack of veal as well as lamb; duck with black peppercorns and apples; pheasant and sweetbreads; grilled sea bass; and honey-glazed fresh squab, grilled with ginger and garlic sauce. Desserts offer several luscious *soufflés,* premise-made ice creams and *sorbets,* and a fresh fruit *feuilletée* with caramel sauce. Order *à la carte* or the fixed-price dinner. There is an extensive wine list with some good red Bordeaux and distinguished California whites.

*Price: About $35 per person*
*Open Mon.–Sat. for dinner only; closed Sun.*
*Accepts all major credit cards*

# LA STRADA
## 155 North Michigan Avenue
### 312-565-2200

The service is quixotic, a windmill tilting from the solicitous to the officious; and the setting is more glitzy than grand, but the spacious room does offer privacy for business chats or trysting coos. Whatever your preoccupation, La Strada's Pan-Italian food can be glorious if you follow your tastes and not necessarily the waiter's recommendations. While dining here is sometimes a challenge, at least it's a lively one. The place has a certain style and it's fun.

About the food, this is the *strada* to glory: As appetizers, mussels *or* clams in a lovely light tomato, wine, and herb sauce; *bresaola,* mountain-dried beef, with oil and lemon; or fresh marinated shellfish. Pastas can be split or half portions ordered. In any case, these are outstanding: *vermicellini della Strada,* with *prosciutto* and mushrooms in a subtly spiced tomato sauce; or when available, *trenette al pesto—linguine* touched with garlic, fresh basil, and cheese. As entrées, most fish are good to splendid, including various shrimp preparations, red snapper, and striped bass with shellfish; but avoid the leaden *zuppa di pesce.* Order any veal dish with impunity and pleasure—whether thick or thin, scallops or chops. Also of considerable interest: calf's liver *alla veneziana.* Vegetables are imaginative, e.g., sautéed escarole; salads are indifferent; and dessert pastries weighty, but there are fresh fruits and a pleasant selection of cheeses. There is also a good regional Italian wine list.

*Price: About $30–$35 per person*
*Open Mon.–Fri. for lunch and dinner; Sat. for dinner only; closed Sun.*
*Accepts all major credit cards*

---

# LAWRY'S—THE PRIME RIB
## 100 East Ontario Street
### 312-787-5000

The setting is tatty *nouveau riche* implanted in an Old Money Chicago (McCormick) mansion. The menu is mid-America red meat with a vengeance; and rote-spiel characterizes the order-taking of the day. Yet it mesmerizes the poly-crowd from neighboring cornfields and environs as well as a classy crowd from wherever. Formula aside, these hungry hordes are amply rewarded. The single main course at dinner is prime rib of roast beef, served from monstrous, silver rolling carts. Three cuts are available, all amply Tudoresque. Dinner accompaniments: big, mostly green, but fresh salad in a bowl, real mashed potatoes, Yorkshire pudding, and whipped cream-horseradish sauce. Baked potato, choice of peas or creamed spinach (a must), plus several excessive desserts are also offered as extras. There is a fairly priced wine list of minor distinction. Lunch features a variety of dishes, including fresh fish! It's a welcome change of pace, and there's a fair amount of middle-level business entertaining.

*Price: About $20–$25 per person*
*Open Mon.–Fri. for lunch and dinner; Sat. and Sun. for dinner only*
*Accepts all major credit cards*

---

# LE FRANÇAIS
## 269 South Milwaukee Avenue, Wheeling
### 312-541-7470

*Haute*-hungry pilgrims, with well-padded pocketbooks, come from the world over to worship at the shrine of Le Français and to celebrate its high priest, chef Jean Banchet. If it's a culinary holy place within, from the outside the restaurant resembles a surburban roadhouse. Shrewdly located in the northwest suburb of Wheeling, Le Français is close to O'Hare International Airport and to Chicago's rich North Shore, and a relatively direct 45-minute drive from downtown.

Whatever the length of your journey, Le Français is worth it. It deserves the encomium "incomparable" for its subtlety of cooking as well as for its grossness of presentation. The menu is classic French but modern—a clever and sprightly updating of Escoffier. Banchet has a compulsion to dazzle with quantity *and* quality. Beyond the multitudinous menu items, there seem to be dozens of daily specialties, all of them displayed on a rolling cart or tray, course after course. Now, the mind may boggle at this embarrassment of *nouveaux riches,* but the palate and stomach will not—if you order with discretion.

Here are but a few vignettes from the brilliant Banchet kaleidoscope (dishes change seasonally, weekly, and daily): Appetizers include a king's ransom of *mousses,* from scallop, salmon, and lobster with three sauces, to pheasant *pâté* with *morels* and truffles, and sea scallops with their roe, mussels, and tiny noodles. Worth noting among the soups are the clam with saffron, cream of mussel, and the duck *consommé* with ginger.

A few of Banchet's glorious entrées are roast squab with cabbage; baked lobster; steamed turbot with cream, saffron, and basil, or with leeks and oysters; venison *Grand Veneur;* a stunningly simple rack of lamb marinated in thyme and garlic; heart of sweetbreads roasted with Belgian endives. Desserts touch on heaven's gate: raspberry, Grand Marnier, and other *soufflés,* fresh fruit *napoleons;* a palette of colorful smooth *sorbets;* fresh pears poached in red wine, and a peerless flourless chocolate cake.

Too much of a good thing? Can the superlative be superfluous? Curiously, the world-renowned Le Français is very much a "Chicago-style" restaurant, if not in its near perfection, then in its perfect overstatement.

*Price: $60–$75 per person*
*Open Tues.–Sun. for dinner only; closed Mon.*
*Accepts all major credit cards*

---

# LE PERROQUET
## 70 East Walton Street
### 312-944-7990

Long before the *nouvelle vague* inundated these shores, Le Perroquet had introduced an almost Proustian delicacy and symmetry of menu unknown in Chicago. And now that the wave has subsided, Perroquet's kitchen remains pacific: no fads, rages, or startlements, but on the other hand, few clichés—old or new. Over the years, the frequent changing of the guard in the kitchen, and, more recently, a change of owners have affected not a whit the delicious placidity of the place. (Anyway, the new owners, the brothers Nespoux, were with the restaurant from almost the beginning in 1971.)

The enchanting dining room, with its fine wall-hung kilims, is a study in graceful detail, from the *millefleurs* table lamps and the welcoming miniature *canapés* to the presentation of an after-dinner pear William (on shaved ice in a silver porringer) to the restaurant's adieu offering of chocolate truffles.

Beyond the staid printed menu, the *du jour* items are of most interest: Listen to the waiter's intelligent oral presentation of daily specialties. Excising certain indifferent dishes, here are a few perfect pleasures at Le Perroquet. For an appetizer, consider: A *mousse* of American mushrooms with Cape scallops; another subtle *mousse* of cauliflower with sea scallops in pimiento sauce, an Impressionist composition of white and pink; or a selection of four or five *pâtés,* dramatically played against each other in taste and texture. Exceptional entrées include scallops of sautéed swordfish in a gently reduced essence of fish stock, tomato, and carrots; roast lamb stuffed with *duxelles* and chopped lamb kidneys; braised duck breast, served with a sautéed duck leg in a honey-glaze and green peppercorn sauce; lobster with freshly made noodles with a tomato-Pernod sauce; or breast of goose Armagnac. Entrées are often served with a super pea purée and diced vegetables. For dessert, there's a precious offering of pastries, *sorbets,* and blueberry, raspberry, or other fresh fruit *soufflés.* The wine list is surprisingly only adequate.

Lunch is for some ladies who do just that every day (the meal's a steal);

but also for urbane business types who want attractive food, knowing service, and a quiet backdrop for conversation.

*Price: Fixed price at $44.50 per person*
*Open Mon.–Fri. for lunch and dinner; Sat. for dinner only; closed Sun.*
*Accepts all major credit cards*

---

## LOU MITCHELL'S
### 565 West Jackson Boulevard
### 312-939-3111

Lou Mitchell's is the fabled Chi-Town place for breakfast. Thick toast and fresh marmalade, earthy but airy omelets, always fresh coffee. It ain't fancy but it's *the* place where those-in-the-know go in the A.M. And Lou sends his customers off every morning with complementary Milk Duds to hold them through lunch. And if you're at Lou's for lunch, it's nifty, too.

*Price: About $5–$7 per person*
*Open Mon.–Sat. for breakfast and lunch; closed Sun.*
*No credit cards accepted*

---

## MANNY'S COFFEE SHOP
### 1141 South Jefferson Street
### 312-939-2855

Manny's, on the edge of the burgeoning South Loop area, is an old-time Jewish-American delicatessen *cum* cafeteria serving oxtail and other hearty soups, brisket of beef, stuffed peppers or cabbage, braised tongue, liver and onions—all of this heavy "comfort food" is consumed in the company of cabbies, cops, local merchants, and business people.

*Price: About $4–$5 per person*
*Open Mon.–Sat. for breakfast and lunch; closed Sun.*
*No credit cards accepted*

---

## MAPLE ST. PIER
### 1 West Maple Street
### 312-266-4810

This nine-month-old fish house has all of the spanking fresh appeal of a newly-shucked bluepoint or cherrystone. The setting is crisp, clean, and simple with porch wood walls and plank floors. Who cares whether it evokes California, Cape Cod, or the Keys? The feeling is good. Maple St. is the last and best word (for now) from restaurateur Arnie Morton. For good and delicious reasons, the menu offering recalls New York's great Grand Central Oyster Bar & Restaurant. The place can be spiffy or casual, so dress up or down. Sample a variety of oysters, clams, and crabs from Gulf Blue to Florida Stone or enjoy steamed mussels or clams, baked crab Imperial, conch chowder, tasty Maryland crab cakes (a new Chicago favorite), cold poached salmon with dill sauce, Cajun blackened redfish (yes, once again, but very good), or an oyster loaf sandwich inspired by New Orleans; and colossal, monster, giant, and jumbo shrimp served chilled, grilled, or stuffed and baked. Also there's a generous clambake with lobster (in two sizes), clams, mussels, grilled corn, potatoes, and coleslaw. Desserts are chewy, rich, and gross. Service is helpful and pleasant, and, sometimes, merely dopey. There is a good American wine list. No reservations are accepted.

Price: About $18 per person
Open Mon.–Sat. for dinner only; closed Sun.
Accepts all major credit cards

---

# MORTON'S
## 1050 North State Street
### 312-266-4820

The city's prime place for steaks (as well as for big broiled lobsters and thick veal chops) is, without doubt, Morton's. It's an attractive, clubby room of well-done understatement, rare for proprietor Morton, considering his propensity for decor excess (see Arnie's, page 108). Almost everything at Morton's is *à la carte* and expensive—prices are posted only on one small blackboard. And all items on the limited menu are superior, from the appetizers (usually fresh oysters, crab claws, or a shrimp cocktail) and the crisply-prepared vegetables and salads to hash browns or baked potatoes and the dessert *soufflés* (especially the Grand Marnier). Beyond the 2- to 5-pound lobster, veal chops, or fresh fish of the day, *the* big beef treat is the bountiful New York strip steak (about 20 ounces). All beef is USDA Prime, aged, house-trimmed—and all those good things you should expect at these prices. The wine list is exceptional, with many fair-to-medium-priced reds, including a plenitude of California boutique varietals. Morton's popularity and no-reservation policy can mean long waits, especially on weekends.

Price: $30–$35 per person
Open Mon.–Sat. for dinner only; closed Sun.
Accepts all major credit cards

# MR. BEEF
## 666 North Orleans Street
### 312-337-8500

At midday everyone who knows and wants the city's best Italian beef sandwich heads for Mr. Beef, a stone's throw from Club Lago (see page 116). Chow down while standing up on the premises or take out several sandwiches for sit-down wherever you go.

*Price: About $3 per person*
*Open Mon.–Fri. for lunch; closed Sat.–Sun.*
*No credit cards accepted*

# MRS. LEVY'S DELICATESSEN
## In Sears Tower, 233 South Wacker Drive
### 312-993-0530

Says Mrs. Levy on the menu, "I can't make all the deli food in the world, so I just make the *best* of it." A rather bold statement, but after tasting her sweet and sour cabbage soup, hot brisket of beef, *kasha varnishkes,* and meat blintzes, you'll probably agree that Mrs. Levy knows what she's talking about. And she knows what deli cooking is about: Many of the specialties have been created from Levy family recipes. Other notable selections from the very extensive menu are a fresh roast turkey sandwich (particularly good with mashed potatoes and *grivenes*), short ribs of beef, almost all of the deli sandwiches—especially the corned beef and pastrami. Also there are old-fashioned sodas, sundaes, and shakes; and Mrs. Levy's hot apple pie with cinnamon ice cream can only be called memorable. It's a great place for a nibble, a *nosh,* a complete meal, or a dessert treat. Located on the ground level of the "world's tallest building," the setting of Mrs. Levy's is in the grand tradition of delis—lively, friendly, and informal.

*Price: Under $6 per person*
*Open daily for breakfast, lunch, and dinner*
*No credit cards accepted*

# PHILANDER'S
## 1120 Pleasant Avenue, Oak Park
### 312-848-4250

There is only one outstanding restaurant of any eating idiom in Chicago's western suburbs, and this is it. Philander's is also, *at least,* the equal of any in-city fish house. It's well worth the quick trip—25 minutes, after the rush hour—via the Eisenhower Expressway (turn off at Harlem and go north) to Oak Park. The suburb is shady, green, hospitable, and, in the last few years, hospitably "wet," which makes a restaurant like Philander's profitably possible (generous drinks and fine wine and beer lists, by the way).

Chef Frank Chlumsky's menu is high, wide, and briny fresh. The printed card is as distinctive as the daily market specials. Order *anything* your taste or fancy dictates—and that's a rare directive. With a minimum of adjectives, here's a mini-list of Chlumsky's magic offerings: Port Chatham smoked salmon with onions, capers, cream cheese, and crackers; any fresh clam or oyster—often there's a fabled selection brought in from many bays; garlicky snails in the shell; and glorious New Orleans barbecued shrimp—rich as Croesus, in pepper butter. Soups and chowders are sublime, as are, yes, even the salads: How about shrimp or Maine lobster in avocado? Then there's Chlumsky's sensational *bouillabaisse* or spicy seafood gumbo as a main course, or seafood Maryland, Lake Superior whitefish, Dover sole (flown in, of course), scallops—ocean or bay; and steamed whole Dungeness crab. And for determined landlubbers, there are chops and steaks, including a New York strip stuffed with oysters.

*Price: About $25–$30 per person*
*Open Mon.–Sat. for dinner; closed Sun.*
*Accepts all major credit cards*

# PHIL SMIDT'S
## 1205 North Calumet Avenue, Hammond, Indiana
### 312-768-6686

This garish oldster done up in pink and black trim is justifiably famous for its frogs' legs, chicken, and boneless perch-in-butter dinners, served family style. It's a must for many generations of Chicagoans. A classic for locals and yokels. It's about a 45-minute drive from the Loop.

*Price: About $16 per person*
*Open Mon.–Sat. for lunch and dinner; closed Sun.*
*Accepts all major credit cards*

# PIZZERIA UNO

## 29 East Ohio Street
### 312-321-1000

# PIZZERIA DUE

## 619 North Wabash Avenue
### 312-943-2400

Windy City originals (Uno dates back to the early 1940s). This pair of casual and comfortable, if noisy, restaurants, a block apart, demonstrates with tasty élan what Chicago-style deep-dish pizza—invented here—is all about. The crust is thick and moist but light; the variety of ingredients, harmonious and generous. Good green salads with red onions, plus soups and sandwiches, too. Terrific straight-up martinis.

*Price: About $10–$15 per person*
*Pizzeria Uno open Tues.–Sun. for lunch and dinner; closed Mon.; Pizzeria Due open Mon.–Fri. for lunch; daily for dinner*
*Both accept all major credit cards*

# PRINTER'S ROW

## 550 South Dearborn Street
### 312-461-0780

Located in the city's intriguing new loft-apartment residential area south of the Loop, Printer's Row is a spacious, dark-wooded place devoted to "the new" American cooking, which features many highly original dishes and some highly experimental ones. Follow your good taste and sense of the appropriate. Among chef-owner Michael Foley's more successful creations are Brie cheese filled with vegetables; *crêpes* with corn and goat cheese on apple sauce; chicken liver *pâté* with Gorgonzola cream; smoked chicken with curry mayonnaise. Recommended entrées: beef tenderloin with vermouth and ginger; venison with walnuts; a ragout of venison shank; a mixed grill of various fish; and an outstanding *confit* of chicken with grilled breast. Desserts often include mocha cream pie, apple-crumb tart, and pear *charlotte* with custard sauce.

*Price: About $25 per person*
*Open Mon.–Thurs. for lunch and dinner; Fri. and Sat. for dinner only; closed Sun.*
*Accepts all major credit cards*

# RANDALL'S FOR RIBS

41 East Superior Street (*between Wabash Avenue and Rush Street*)

**312-280-2790**

In the great Chicago barbecue bonanza, only Randall's has elevated the baby back and Texas beef rib to the high plateau of fine dining. The baby backs are succulent but tactile; the huge beef bones, equally meaty, are not tough and seldom dry—an accomplishment. No St. Louis ribs or rib tips here, but there are Provimi veal ribs, quite lean but juicy. All are dressed with thick, smoky, snappy barbecue sauce. Simply put, Randall's is a very stylish rib restaurant that has not forgotten the honesty of country cookin'. Corn muffins, Cajun popcorn, barbecued shrimp in the shell, hot chicken wings, fried catfish fillets, and fiercely good beef chili are signature items. Also there are prime steaks, prime rib, and a grilled fish of the day. For dessert, have luscious pecan-peach cobbler on praline ice cream or some whiskey bread pudding. Takeout and delivery available.

*Price: About $18 per person*
*Open Mon.–Fri. for lunch; daily for dinner*
*Accepts all major credit cards*

# RICCARDO'S

437 North Rush Street

**312-944-8815**

Riccardo's, with its palette-shaped bar and seven lively arts murals, is a beloved Chicago eatery. The place dates back to the late great Ric Riccardo in the mid-1930s, and its still the dry-martini-and-green-noodles-*al-forno* paradise of the advertising and press crowd. You can't go wrong with the standbys: shrimp *Arno, ravioli,* chicken *tetrazzini* or *Vesuvio,* and any simple veal dish.

*Price: About $18 per person*
*Open Mon.–Fri. for lunch and dinner; closed Sat. and Sun.*
*Accepts most major credit cards*

# SHAW'S CRAB HOUSE

21 East Hubbard Street

**312-527-2722**

Shaw's Crab House (and adjacent Blue Crab Lounge) clearly recalls fish houses on the Eastern Shore of Maryland. And the huge 250-seat room does a nifty job of recreating another era as well, especially with the sounds of some superb forties recordings.

Shaw's menu lists more than forty seafood items—all are fresh and most good-to-very-good, although there is an inconsistency of preparation in some of the more "complicated" dishes, such as crab Imperial or crab cakes, or that original Chicago dish, shrimp *de Jonghe*. Especially notable: a wide variety of oysters, often including Chincoteague and Wellfleet; steamed mussels; seafood gumbo; scallop stew or pan roast; spicy barbecued shrimp; frogs' legs in garlic butter; and, when in season, soft-shell crab and authentic Maryland blue crabs (served only in the Lounge). Accompaniments: potatoes—swell hash browns with onions—to creamed spinach and coleslaw are outstanding. For dessert: delicious tart Persian lime pie masquerading as Key lime; Indian pudding; *crème brulée;* and pecan pie. Wines are white, mostly American, and inexpensive. No reservations are accepted.

*Price: About $20 per person*
*Open Mon.–Fri. for lunch and dinner in the Blue Crab Lounge; Mon.–Sat. for dinner only in Shaw's*
*Crab House main dining room; closed Sun.*
*Accepts all major credit cards*

# SIAM CAFÉ
## 4654 North Sheridan Road
### 312-989-0157

Very, er, casual; somewhat, er, communal. But quite hospitable, if rather hurried. And the Thai food is glorious—yummy-delicate, and/or wow-hot! *Everything* is definitely worthwhile. Enjoy the Siam barbecue (satays), charcoal chicken, lightly garlicked chicken, or egg salad with coriander touched off by red-hot sauce (on the table), as well as the gorgeous bean thread or shrimp soup, or fabulous nippy beef salad. Also delicious: Indian fried rice; pork with greens; fried mussels; fried greens with oyster sauce—and you must have a noodle dish. There is no liquor license, so bring beer *or* order the incredible Thai iced coffee. Simply, a great restaurant of the genre.

*Price: Under $10 per person*
*Open daily for lunch and dinner*
*No credit cards accepted*

# SINCLAIR'S
Westminster and Forest avenues, Lake Forest
312-295-8300

Immutable Lake Forest reeks of class and more than a soupçon of style. To contemporary eyes and palates, so does Sinclair's, the suburban outpost of dining impresario Gordon Sinclair (see Gordon restaurant, page 121). As proper and cordial as it is, Sinclair's lively ambience and "new American cookery" caused quite a few old-guard eyes to pop when it opened in the fall of 1982. After all, the restaurant is, as they say in Lake Forest, rather "different." Decidedly unstuffy.

"Change"—a word that evokes horror in the hearts of Lake Forest's *ancienne régime*—is Sinclair's order of the day, as dishes move daily and weekly following market availability; seasonally, to embrace the harvest of field, farm, stream, and lake; and, of course, there are always the "chef's whim" selections. Almost everything is very good to excellent: artichoke fritters with *béarnaise;* hot fried chicken salad with a stunning honey-mustard dressing; a salad of field lettuces and California chèvre; luscious Bahamian conch chowder, worthy of the Keys; fresh grilled fishes and other dishes (such as a veal chop with smoked garlic and a Creole mustard-cream sauce); genuine Cajun concoctions, not afraid to be bold and brave in the North. Then there's a marvelous pork loin, sometimes stuffed with cornbread and spicy *chorizo* sausage, served with black bean sauce; and pan-cooked lamb chops with fresh rosemary and *coli.* And for dessert, airborne flourless chocolate cake, fresh fruit tarts, pecan pie, and coffee *granita* with Sambuca cream. Sinclair's is worth the long trek to Lake Forest; as is Lake Forest itself. About a one-hour drive north of downtown Chicago.

*Price: About $25–$30 per person*
*Open Tues.–Sun. for dinner only; closed Mon.*
*Accepts all major credit cards*

# SPIAGGIA
In One Magnificent Mile Building, 980 North Michigan
Avenue (*at Oak Street*)
312-280-2750

Located on the high second level of One Mag Mile, Spiaggia offers a sweeping view of Lake Michigan and Lake Shore Drive—Chicago's Gold Coast. Chef Antonio Mantuano's menu emphasizes the light, lively, and always authentic dishes of Italy's northern regions. There are few, if any, clichés on this sophisticated menu (daily-changing at lunch; mostly *du jour* at dinner). Consider hearty lobster and *calamari* soup; beautiful *carpaccio;* genuinely Italian (not California) paper-thin brick-oven pizzas, with a variety of toppings from duck sausage and goat cheese to four cheeses. Delightful pastas include tomato *farfalle* with vegetables; scallion *fettuccine* with smoked salmon; and spinach *soufflé lasagne.* Among the entrées: grilled fish of the day with tomato-basil or lemon-olive oil sauce on escarole; duck breast with juniper berries; a veal chop with fresh sage; and calf's liver *alla Veneziana.* For dessert, do have the poached pear with bitter chocolate and pistachios or fresh fruit with *zabaglione.* An excellent, all-Italian wine list complements the menu. More informal dining is available at Café Spiaggia next door. It offers a neat *antipasto* bar and a menu for grazers, Italian style.

*Price: About $40 per person at Spiaggia; about $10 per person at Café Spiaggia*
*Spiaggia open Mon.–Sat. for lunch; daily for dinner; Café Spiaggia open daily*
*for lunch and dinner*
*Both accept all major credit cards*

---

# SU CASA
## 49 East Ontario Street
### 312-943-4041

Su Casa is *the* Mexican restaurant that most visitors and many folks in these parts think of as Mexico-in-Chicago. Without question, it's a very pretty place and a hospitable one. The *hacienda* touches may be a tad too "decorator," but after all, they are as real as San Miguel d'Allende. All the expected dishes are presented—from *guacamole, ceviche, chile con queso, tacos,* and *enchiladas* to *flan* and *crema de mango* for dessert—but they are prepared extremely well. Of special note: the *botanas* (assorted appetizers), sautéed trout with garlic and *cilantro,* shrimp *Veracruzana,* and chicken *poblano.* And a grand *carne asada* of high quality and virtue. As noted, service is welcoming, but occasionally it can be brisk or pokey. Interestingly, the proprietor of Su Casa is veteran Chicago restaurateur-entrepreneur Ike Sewell, who is also the *patron* of Chicago-style deep-dish pizza (see Pizzeria Uno and Due, page 133).

*Price: About $16–$18 per person*
*Open Mon.–Fri. for lunch and dinner; Sat. for dinner only; closed Sun.*
*Accepts most major credit cards*

# TANGO
## 3172 North Sheridan Road
### 312-935-0350

I find it hard to believe that I once called Tango's handsome design "audacious and avant-garde," but perhaps I've settled in—as has George Badonsky's restaurant. After 13 years, Tango's West African sculpture, Dali prints, and Warhol lithographs of Mao and Marilyn may seem almost nostalgic. Yet the restaurant's kitchen, which first introduced a vast variety of fresh seafood the likes of which Chicago had never seen, is, if anything, better than ever—more disciplined and precise, with fewer "pop" menu gimmicks.

The menu items and daily specials are staggering, and few of them are ever less than successful. Everything is fresh, and a new charcoal grill for fish adds a clear note of contemporary simplicity. Recommended dishes: salmon tartar; any smoked fish; handsomely garnished fresh oysters and clams; fried catfish and oysters New Orleans style; sea trout with ginger butter; broiled Lake Superior whitefish; charcoaled scampi; and shrimp *Grenobloise* (sautéed with capers in lemon butter sauce). Desserts are adequate, *comme ci, comme ça*. There is a splendid, comparatively inexpensive wine list.

*Price: About $25 per person*
*Open Tues.–Sat. for lunch and dinner; Sun. and Mon. for dinner only*
*Accepts all major credit cards*

# WRIGLEY BUILDING RESTAURANT
## 410 North Michigan Avenue
### 312-944-7600

Where Michigan Avenue crosses the Chicago River you'll find this well-established dining room, a Windy City classic that has long raised the ordinary to the "extra" classification. It's a brisk, busy place, where business people savor simple, honest fare at lunch: clams or oysters, crunchy salads, steak tartare, calf's liver and bacon, broiled whitefish—that sort of thing.

*Price: About $18 per person*
*Open Mon.–Fri. for lunch and dinner; closed Sat. and Sun.*
*Accepts all major credit cards*

# YOSHI'S CAFÉ
## 3257 North Halsted Street
### 312-248-6160

In Chicago chef-proprietor places are a late-blooming garden with a rich harvest, and this delightful 50-seat bistro is the preeminent example. Yoshi Katsumura, the young Jean Banchet-trained chef (see Le Français, page 127) who first made Jimmy's Place famous, heads the kitchen; and his charming wife, Nabuko, is in charge of the front of the house. Yoshi is one of the leaders in Chicago's neoclassical French revival. Still, his dishes are gracefully touched by his *haiku*-like Japanese elegance and simplicity. Printed menu items and favorite specialties of the day, reflecting the daily market and season, have included poached seafood sausage with prawns, *rillettes* of pork, frogs' legs *provençale,* exquisite hot venison *pâté,* sautéed fresh New York *foie gras* with oyster mushrooms in port wine sauce, an ethereal (and correct) two-bowl *bouillabaisse,* combination seafood entrées, rolled loin of lamb with artichokes and *béarnaise* sauce, and braised rabbit in mustard sauce. For dessert: feathersome pastries and an extraordinary green tea ice cream. There is a limited, fairly priced wine list.

*Price: $25–$30 per person*
*Open Tues.–Sun. for lunch and dinner; closed Mon.*
*Accepts all major credit cards*

# YVETTE
## 1206 North State Parkway
### 312-280-1700

Yvette may be a new Chicago classic-in-the-making. It's especially enjoyable in good weather when the stylish glass portals are open. Then it's sidewalk café time; come watch the Yuppie crowd preen and parade without, as well as within. There's good live music and mostly good, vaguely French, fare at moderate prices. But the *mis en scène* is everything.

*Price: $15–$18 per person*
*Open daily for lunch and dinner*
*Accepts all major credit cards*

# CINCINNATI

## By Ellen Brown

**AMERICAN**
The Golden Lamb

**BAR**
Palm Court of the Netherland
Plaza Hotel

**BARBECUE**
Walt's Hitching Post

**BRUNCH**
The Grand Finale

**CHINESE**
The China Gourmet

**ECLECTIC**
Coach and Four Restaurant
(Covington, Kentucky)
Delmonico's

**FRENCH**
Maisonette

**GERMAN**
Grammer's

**HOTEL DINING ROOM**
Delmonico's

**ITALIAN**
Edwards

**OPEN LATE**
The Diner on Sycamore
Grammer's

**PANORAMA**
Delmonico's

**STEAKS AND CHOPS**
La Normandie Taverne & Chop
House
The Precinct

**SUBURBAN/REGIONAL**
Coach and Four Restaurant
(Covington, Kentucky)
The Golden Lamb (Lebanon)
The Grand Finale (Glendale)
Walt's Hitching Post (Ft.
Wright, Kentucky)

**UNIQUE PROPERTY**
Skyline Chili

**WINE BAR/RESTAURANT**
Longworth's

The Chamber of Commerce dubs Cincinnati the "Blue Chip City," and the analogy to slow growth stocks extends to its dining spots. Cincinnati is a conservative city that respects quality and does not hop onto fads quickly.

This conservatism is part of the city's matrix. When other cities were gutting their urban cores, Cincinnati took a wait-and-see attitude about urban renewal, so when the historic-preservation movement hit during the 1970s, there were many fine structures as candidates for renovation, and many of them have found second lives as restaurants. Their interesting architectural details provide welcome lagniappe with meals.

The same attitude extends to the food served. When classic French cuisine was America's only option in fine dining well into the late 1970s, Cincinnati outshone much larger cities with places like the venerable Maisonette, which consistently deserves the constellation of stars it has won over the years. However, it was the late 1970s before a fine Italian or Chinese restaurant tossed its first pasta or *lo mein,* the early 1980s before the first *naan* was removed from a *tandoori* oven, and 1984 before a chef first seared over mesquite wood.

These options do exist today, and in general visitors will find that the cost of food is moderate and the portions large. You can definitely get some well-executed food in Cincinnati, even if contemporary culinary innovation is not one of the goals set by most restaurateurs.

Visitors are usually shocked to learn that the airport—and indeed a great percentage of the metropolitan area—is located in Kentucky. But with the exception of some great ribs, you won't find much Southern cooking. You will, however, find that the service in many restaurants has a noticeable twang. Northerners especially tend to be put off by the "Hi there, honey, what can I get for you?" But don't be. Cincinnati is a warm and friendly town.

*Ellen Brown is author of* Cooking with the New American Chefs *(Harper & Row, 1985) and* The Great Chefs of Chicago *(Avon Books, 1985). She is former restaurant critic and senior feature writer for* The Cincinnati Enquirer *and food editor for* USA Today. *She currently is a frequent contributor to the Home Entertaining column for the* Washington Post Sunday Magazine. *Cook's Magazine honored her in its Who's Who of Cooking in America awards for 1985.*

# THE CHINA GOURMET
## 3340 Erie Avenue (*Hyde Park*)
### 513-871-6612

About ten years ago, Bing Moy introduced authentic Chinese food to a city that never doubted the authenticity of chow mein, and the China Gourmet, located about 15 minutes from downtown, continues to be the city's best.

The menu offers such standard fare (all well-executed) as Szechuan *kung po* chicken, clams in black bean sauce, and Cantonese concoctions, such as a mélange of shrimp and crab meat served over sizzling rice cakes. But never look at a menu. Trust Bing or one of his captains to tell you what you should have that night. It can be perfectly fresh pike steamed with ginger and scallions, Chinese sausage stir-fried with *bok choy,* or a light salad of julienned chicken and cucumber in a fiery sauce laced with chile oil.

Although the restaurant is located in the basement of an office complex converted from a shopping mall, a skylit atrium provides sunlight during the day that nurtures a jungle of plants. The Ming-style dark wood chairs, soft beige booths, and silk paintings in the same muted tones create a gentle environment for a Chinese restaurant.

The tables are spread far enough apart to allow for private conversation, and, while the food is consistently good, the service can be a little lax when the restaurant is full. Reservations are suggested for weekend evenings.

*Price: About $15–$20 per person*
*Open Mon.–Fri. for lunch; nightly for dinner*
*Accepts all major credit cards*

# COACH AND FOUR RESTAURANT
## 214 Scott Street, Covington, Kentucky
### 606-431-6700

During the mid-nineteenth century, when the roads of Cincinnati were still mud paths, the ships' captains and barons of industry built grand mansions on the Kentucky side of the Ohio River. These were dilapidated slums in the mid-1970s when the historic-preservation movement caught on in the city, and suddenly Covington once again became chic. However, the dining options had not kept pace with the level of sophistication of the area's new residents until the Coach and Four opened in 1981.

The food served in this modest white, clapboard building, with an upbeat Bette Midler soundtrack and contemporary prints on the walls, has been attracting not only neighborhood folk but those who wouldn't have dreamed of crossing the river except to go to the airport a decade ago.

The food defies easy categorization, but all dishes are treated with a flair for seasonings and a light touch. The house specialty is a pecan chicken, which is served with a light Dijon-sour cream sauce. Also from the Southern tradition are a country ham with real redeye gravy and Maryland crab cakes topped with a New Orleans *rémoulade* sauce. But you will find dishes of Oriental inspiration, such as a sautéed monkfish with water chestnuts, and more than a nod to the Mediterranean in a wonderful version of Greek *spanakopita* and nightly pasta dishes.

As with most restaurants of this caliber, give heed to the nightly specials. Save room for the raisin-chess pie or cheesecake. The wine list is small, with a better selection from California than Europe, and the service can become bogged down on a crowded evening, which is almost every night. The restaurant is for a fun dinner, not an important one. You'll find the noise level is fairly high. Reservations are urged.

*Price: About $20 per person*
*Open Mon.–Fri. for lunch; nightly for dinner*
*Accepts all major credit cards*

---

# DELMONICO'S
## In the Westin Hotel, Fountain Square
### 513-241-3663

While dining options in Cincinnati include many spots that take advantage of the natural and man-made beauty of the city and its architecture, Delmonico's, on the second level of the new Westin Hotel, complements the changing human panorama with some of the best food the city offers.

The two-level dining room, with pale peach walls and crewelwork banquettes, overlooks Fountain Square, the city's hub. The fountain, titled the "Genius of Waters" and illuminated at night, was actually located on the site now occupied by the hotel and was moved across the street in the early 1970s when the Cincinnati skyline began jutting upward. The square is now surrounded by office towers, and the floor-to-ceiling windows at Delmonico's provide a wonderful bird's-eye view.

Delmonico's is part of the new breed of hotel dining rooms that is freeing the genre from its pejorative connotations. While the peach rose handed to female diners as they leave might be an overly gratuitous gesture, in general the basically *nouvelle* French food and attentive service are excellent.

The menu changes seasonally and always includes some variety of American game. It could be some perfectly roasted quails in a subtle morel sauce or a *pâté* of Texas smoked boar with a lively currant relish. Highlights as appetizers are the soups and *pâtés,* and while the roast meats have always been first rate, a few of the sauces tend to be overly thickened.

Desserts, presented on the familiar cart, are excellent, with a nightly selection of light pastries. The wine list is extensive and fairly priced.

For a small business dinner, there is a private room that can seat up to a dozen, and a staff very helpful in planning a menu.

If you don't want everyone in town to know you're having dinner at Delmonico's, request a table on the second tier. If you don't care, the front tables have the best view. It's one of the most romantic settings in town.

If you want to dance away some of the calories consumed at Delmonico's, Patterns disco is located right next door on the second level of the hotel, and features wines by the glass.

*Price: About $30 per person*
*Open daily for dinner*
*Accepts all major credit cards*

---

# THE DINER ON SYCAMORE
## 1203 Sycamore Street
### 513-721-1212

It could be any one of John Bader's paintings—a silver diner with black patent leather booths and maroon tables, playing off the pale pink-and-gray ceramic tile and polished stainless steel of the original interior. But The Diner is one of the few funky spots Cincinnati has to offer, and the strength of the menu is the "barfood" snacks and appetizers.

This is the perfect spot for a late-night graze, and, while the section of town in which the structure sits is not the greatest, it is a very convenient spot following events at Cincinnati's grand Music Hall or coming from musical events at the College–Conservatory of Music at the University of Cincinnati.

Avoid the entrées, and stick with the burgers, egg specialties (including a Kosher salami and scrambled eggs rarely seen away from the East Coast), and snacks, such as cubes of fried *mozzarella,* nicely spiced *nachos,* and crispy corn fritters, or just a platter of the homemade potato chips.

If you're into Yuppie exotic fruit drinks, there's everything from a frozen version of a screwdriver to a peach-almond shake, combining peaches, amaretto, and ice cream.

*Price: About $8 per person*
*Open daily for breakfast, lunch, and dinner*
*Accepts all major credit cards*

# EDWARDS
## 529 East Fifth Street
### 513-381-2030

The Edwards Manufacturing Company, a triangular red-brick building on the outskirts of the downtown area, was dilapidated and scheduled for the wrecking ball when chef Rob Fogel realized its potential for the Northern Italian restaurant he justly felt Cincinnati could support.

After entering the octagonal-tiled first-floor foyer, diners are ushered up a marble staircase into what was Mr. Edwards' board room. Antique hunting prints, extravagant urns of exotic flowers, and bentwood chairs enliven the rich wood paneling remaining from its previous incarnation.

Edwards' pastas are the best in town—always cooked perfectly *al dente*. During the winter months, there are some heartier Southern Italian specialties on the menu to complement the Northern, including a casserole of sausage. You can also count on the fact that Fogel's cross-cultural, non-Italian treatments, such as a *fettuccine* with a curried sauce topped with sour cream, will be excellent.

In addition to the pastas, you can always trust any veal dish: *Osso buco* served on saffron rice is a winter favorite.

The wine list is respectable and very moderately priced, strong in its selection of Italian wines. And no one dines at Edwards without saving room for dessert: The chocolate *mousse* was voted the best in town by the readers of *Cincinnati Magazine,* and the coconut pie in a lemon-rum crust and *cannoli* filled with mocha cream match it in flavor. The service is casual ("I'm Tom and I'm your waiter"), but remains professional.

*Price: About $20 per person*
*Open Mon.–Fri. for lunch; Mon.–Sat. for dinner; closed Sun.*
*Accepts all major credit cards*

# THE GOLDEN LAMB
## 27 South Broadway, Lebanon
### 513-932-5065

Few old inns remain in the Midwest, especially ones within an easy hour's drive of a major city, and the Golden Lamb is a regional treasure well worth the drive. In continuous operation since 1803, the inn features traditional American food prepared with the best-quality ingredients treated with a light hand.

The Golden Lamb, once a stagecoach stop between Cincinnati and Columbus, has played host to ten U.S. presidents, Mark Twain during his performances at the Lebanon Opera House, and Charles Dickens, who stayed here in 1842 during his first trip to America.

If you arrive early enough, or go for lunch, wander down to the Shaker Museum, or at least tour the upper guest rooms decorated in a variety of nineteenth-century styles, from Shaker plain to Victorian grand.

The dining rooms are filled with antiques, and the service from the costumed staff is professional and efficient. The inn is famous for its succulent duck preparations, and the loin of pork or rare leg of lamb should not be overlooked. A relish tray and vegetables are served family style. The pastry chef creates fine renditions of traditional Shaker desserts, including a Shaker sugar pie that should not be missed.

The best time to visit is around Christmas, when the inn is decorated to within an inch of its life, featuring a different theme each year. Reservations are advised but not required.

*Price: About $15 per person*
*Open daily for lunch and dinner*
*Accepts all major credit cards*

---

# GRAMMER'S
## 1440 Walnut Street
### 513-721-6570

Back in 1872 when Grammer's first opened its beveled-glass doors in a section of downtown called Over-the-Rhine (because of its concentration of German immigrants), it was the Upper East Side of the city. The neighborhood, which also includes the Gothic Revival Music Hall, hit the skids, but it is now experiencing the first signs of rejuvenation, and Grammer's has come up with the improvements.

The dark, shabby rooms were renovated in 1985 to reflect their nineteenth-century elegance, with a large rosewood bar dominating the tile-floored barroom, which is lit by converted gas globes. That's where it's the most fun to eat. In other rooms, the painted ceilings have been restored, and the stuccoed walls, inset with thick wood beams, give the spaces authority.

The food, which had slipped as the paint peeled, is now a mix of traditional German fare, such as light sauerkraut balls, pungent *sauerbraten,* and tender *Wiener Schnitzel,* and lighter choices, such as a cheese-and-herb *strudel* and a *fleisch teller* platter of smoked meat, liverwurst, beef tongue, and headcheese served on a bed of Bibb lettuce.

While the food is as solid as a town burgher, the service has not commensurately improved. On a few occasions it has verged on the nonexistent, while slow is the best that can be said. On a few occasions, there was also an accordion player who seemed to go on forever—and loudly at that.

The *strudels* are the best dessert choices, and change daily, and the Black Forest cake provides an ample chocolate fix.

Reservations are advised, especially for large groups. Another bonus is that an abbreviated dinner menu is served until 1 A.M., unusual in a city that goes to bed by 10 P.M.

*Price: About $15 per person*
*Open Mon.–Sat. for lunch, dinner, and Light Fare; closed Sun.*
*Accepts all major credit cards*

---

## THE GRAND FINALE
### 3 East Sharon Avenue, Glendale
**513-771-5925**

While *quiches* and *crêpes* may be forgotten foods in most parts of the country, they are still popular options at The Grand Finale, a restored Victorian mansion in one of Cincinnati's most exclusive suburbs. They are both featured on the daily menu and form the centerpiece for what is one of the loveliest brunches in the area, especially during the summer when it is served in a brick-walled garden of brilliant flowers with a blue-and-white striped awning which shields patrons from the sun.

The buffet features everything from the *crêpes* and *quiches* to eggs, buckwheat pancakes, Belgian waffles, cheese-and-garlic grits, and fried chicken livers. In addition, there is a sampler of the desserts for which the restaurant first became known—chocolate *mousse* pie in a pecan crust, trifle, hot fruit pies baked to order, and owner Cindy and Larry Youse's version of Key lime pie. Reservations are suggested, and brunch is served from 10:30 A.M. to 3 P.M.

*Price: About $7.95 per person*
*Open Tues.–Sun. for brunch, lunch, and dinner*
*Accepts all major credit cards*

---

## LA NORMANDIE TAVERNE & CHOP HOUSE
### 118 East Sixth Street
**513-721-2260**

La Normandie, located next door to the Maisonette (see page 148) and sharing some of its kitchen space, is hardly considered a stepchild, possessing a distinct identity of its own. La Normandie is a cozy English pub, with rough-hewn wood walls, pewter serving plates, plaid carpeting, and a roaring fireplace in the winter. It's one of the most popular bars in town; the bar also serves as a holding area as no reservations are accepted; in the evenings, you can count on more than enough time for a few drinks while you wait.

One of the benefits of sharing a kitchen with its venerable parent is the quality of the meat served—superb steaks and roast beef—as well as such touches as the delicate salad dressings and flaky pastries produced in the central kitchen.

Start with some peanuts at the bar—throwing the shells on the floor is the custom—and then dive into a steak, or note the blackboards for what fish has been flown in for the day. The wine list is very limited, but don't be shy about asking to see the entire Maisonette list. The waiter will be glad to oblige, and it's one of the best in the city.

*Price: About $17 per person*
*Open Mon.–Fri. for lunch; Mon.–Sat. for dinner;*
*closed Sun. and first two weeks of July*
*Accepts all major credit cards*

---

# LONGWORTH'S
## 1108 St. Gregory Street (*Mt. Adams*)
### 513-579-0900

Mt. Adams is the closest peak to downtown Cincinnati of the city's famous seven hills, and, by the number of bars alone, it justly deserves its reputation as the swinging singles zone.

Longworth's, housed in a building that has been a bar since the 1860s, features the town's best selection of wines by the glass, along with some fabulous burgers and other light fare. The garden, weather permitting, is the place to sit; if you visit late at night, Nick's Champagne Club on the second floor is a great place for dancing and drinking.

*Price: About $10 per person*
*Open daily from 11 A.M.–2:30 P.M.*
*Accepts all major credit cards*

---

# MAISONETTE
## 114 East Sixth Street
### 513-721-2260

Unlike many "institutions," the Maisonette, founded by the Comisar family more than thirty years ago, justly deserves its reputation as the best in Cincinnati. It is unmatched in terms of impeccable consistency in the quality of food and service.

A 1985 face-lifting changed the color scheme from one of the last bastions of "restaurant red" to a pale salmon tone that highlights to even a greater extent the fine nineteenth-century American art collection, specializing in paintings from the noted Cincinnati school and including works by Frank Duveneck. The dining room is broken into three sections, with the tables for four and banquettes for two in the center room as the places to be seen, although natives who are regulars have their favorite tables, and Alphonse Kaelbel, maître d' for the past decade, can recall a table preference even after a year's absence.

The menu has been lightened along with the decor. At last beef Wellington, which remained a popular entrée into the early 1980s, has been removed from the menu, although there's something wrapped in puff pastry almost every night. The cuisine can be considered conservative French, with some *nouvelle* touches in the sauces and presentations.

It is a perfect restaurant for a business dinner, as even the most fearful diners will have the best quality of beef or lamb as an option, and the more adventurous can take advantage of such specialties as veal with *shiitake* mushroom sauce, sweetbreads in a light paprika sauce, served with spinach pasta, or sautéed duck breast complemented by a braised leg in a well-reduced Beaujolais sauce.

All courses are served at tableside from rolling carts, augmented at lunch by rolltop silver servers from which sides of meat are offered and carved. The service is faultless and appears effortless.

Yet another cart arrives with the dessert selection, and, while chocolate *mousse* is probably still the most popular choice, the pastries can be stellar, if a bit tired by the end of a late seating.

The wine list is excellent for French wines, less so for California, although that section has been growing during the past few years.

Reservations for out-of-towners are highly recommended for both lunch and dinner, as natives get first choice on last-minute openings; reservations are a must for anyone on a weekend.

*Price: About $35 per person*
*Open Mon.–Fri. for lunch; Mon.–Sat. for dinner; closed Sun. and first two weeks of July*
*Accepts all major credit cards*

# PALM COURT OF THE NETHERLAND PLAZA HOTEL
## Fifth and Race streets
### 513-421-9100

You're sure Jean Harlow, dressed in slinky white satin, will be swooping down the staircase in front of the marble fountain, and it's the sort of environment that leaves you hankering for an apricot sour or a brandy Alexander.

The Netherland is a temple of Art Deco elegance; for decades the leaping metal antelopes around the frieze were allowed to tarnish and compete with some of the worst decor in the country, down to plastic flowers in the partitions. But after the face-lift the building so justly deserved, the Palm Court Bar, with a piano player for much of the day, is a glorious place to meet anyone for a drink—dramatic enough for a business client and romantic enough for a date.

There is a large bar in the center of the room, but try to snag one of the quilted floral banquets along the side walls. If you don't have time for a drink, at least make time to walk through the Netherland's lobby.

*Price: About $3.50 per drink*
*Open daily*
*Accepts all major credit cards*

# THE PRECINCT
## 311 Delta Avenue (*Hyde Park*)
### 513-321-5454

There are some veal dishes on the menu, and the "fresh catch of the day" is fresh. But the thing to order at The Precinct is steak. They do the best in town, and some learned carnivores consider the steaks to be the best in the Midwest.

The restaurant, about a 15-minute drive from downtown, is housed in a converted mid-nineteenth-century brick police station with a Romanesque revival turret. Upstairs is a jumping bar and disco, with a deejay spinning records late into the night. That's where you'll start your evening, regardless of the time of your reservations, which are a necessity on weekends if you are to get fed at all.

In addition to meat that is aged and broiled to perfection (ranging in size from a dainty 8-ounce filet mignon to a 22-ounce porterhouse that looks as if half a cow has been deposited before you), there are some interesting garnishes. The Steak Remington is topped with sautéed green peppers, onions, and mushrooms with an excellent *bordelaise* sauce; the pepper steak, dubbed au Roth here, is top-drawer.

Jeff Ruby, The Precinct's owner, is adamant that simple fare be done without shortcuts. You can taste the fresh garlic and herbs in his sauces, and the house salad is a Greek salad of romaine and endive with imported feta instead of the dreary wedges of iceberg lettuce offered by many steak houses.

While not known for its wine list, there are some excellent reds to accompany the steaks, from both French and California vineyards.

It's a noisy dining room, and the restaurant is the place to celebrate a business deal, not to make one.

*Price: About $20 per person*
*Open daily for dinner only*
*Accepts all major credit cards*

---

# SKYLINE CHILI
## 42 locations
### 513-761-4371 (*main office*)

There's no question that during a first visit to Cincinnati, someone will suggest trying the city's version of chili, the recipe for which, one writer suspected, was "marinate Alpo in kerosene, add a dash of cinnamon and *Voilà!,* you've got it."

Nicholas Lambrinides, a Greek immigrant, opened his first parlor in the Price Hill section of town in 1949. The chili would never be recognized as such by any Texan. It has a soupy consistency and is mildly spiced with a mixture of spices akin to the *moussaka* of its creator's youth.

Cincinnati chili, also served at other chains today, is eaten in two ways: as a "Coney Island" (named for an old amusement park on the Ohio River, not for the one in Brooklyn), in which the chili tops a rubbery hot dog and is smothered with grated yellow Cheddar and onion; the other way to eat it is as a topping for limp spaghetti. You must then decide among a "3-way" (with cheese), a "4-way" (with onions or beans and cheese), or a "5-way" (all the above).

I suggest the 5-way, since chances are you'll eat it only once in your life, and so you might as well get the full treatment.

*Price: About $3 per person, including soft drink*
*Open Mon.–Sat. for breakfast, lunch, and dinner; Sun. for lunch and dinner*
*only*
*No credit cards accepted*

# WALT'S HITCHING POST
## 3300 Madison Pike, Ft. Wright, Kentucky
### 606-331-0494

After leaving the expressway and traveling a winding country road, this white clapboard restaurant in surburban Cincinnati gives you the impression that you're far into the country, when in reality it's a mere 15 minutes from downtown.

You begin to enjoy the anticipatory aromas as your car is being parked, when you see a dozen slabs of ribs grilling over open fires. Walt's also serves excellent steaks and creditable barbecued chicken. But ribs are what you should order.

The interior of the crowded, noisy restaurant is filled with the prints and accouterments of horse racing, including photos of jockeys with winning horses, tacks, and saddles. It reminds visitors that the Blue Grass section of Kentucky is just a short drive away, and the diners at Walt's—from the Mercedes and pickup trucks in the parking lot—run the gamut from the movers and shakers who lunch at the Maisonette to the good ol' boys who are more interested in batting averages than stock quotations.

The casual atmosphere is great for rib eating. The slabs are served with a cup of sauce that bridges the gap between sweet and hot to perfection. Start with the hot slaw, a local specialty topped with bacon bits; then get into the main event. Rather than French fries, spring for the extra few cents for home fries with fried onions, a glass of cold beer (try the Christian Morlein, an excellent Cincinnati-based brewery), and your evening is set. Walt's doesn't take reservations, so expect a wait at the crowded bar.

*Price: About $13 per person*
*Open 10:30 A.M.–1:30 A.M. Mon.–Fri.; 5 P.M.–1:30 A.M. Sat.; 1 P.M.–1:30 A.M. Sun.*
*Accepts Visa and MasterCard*

# CLEVELAND

## BY IRIS BAILIN

**AMERICAN**
Ellawee's Restaurant
Miller's Dining Room

**BARBECUE**
Geppetto's Spaghetti & Steak
House
Rick's Café

**BREAKFAST**
Norton's

**BRUNCH**
Stouffer Inn on the Square

**CAFÉ**
Arabica
Tenth Street Café

**CHINESE**
Gourmet of China
Hunan in Coventryard
Szechwan Garden

**CONTINENTAL**
The Wine Merchant Restaurant

**DELICATESSEN**
Corky and Lenny's

**ECLECTIC**
Heck's Café
Noggin's
Sammy's
Watership Down
Z Contemporary Cuisine

**FAMILY RESTAURANT**
Miller's Dining Room

**FRENCH**
The French Connection
That Place on Bellflower

**GREEK**
The Mad Greek

**HAMBURGERS**
Heck's Café
Norton's
Our Gang

**HOTEL DINING ROOM**
The French Connection

**HUNGARIAN**
Balaton Restaurant
Csardas

**INDIAN**
The Mad Greek

**ITALIAN**
Giovanni's

**JAPANESE**
Otani
Shujiro

**KOREAN**
Korea House

**MEXICAN**
Lopez y Gonzalez
Marcelita's

**MIDDLE EASTERN**
Ali-Baba Restaurant
The Middle East Restaurant

**NIGHTCLUB/RESTAURANT**
Club Isabella

**OPEN LATE**
Club Isabella
Danny Boy's Old World Pizza
Diamond Grille
Heck's Café
The Mad Greek
Norton's

**PANORAMA**
Sammy's

**PIZZA**
Danny Boy's Old World Pizza
Mamma Santa's

**POLISH**
Renee's

**SEAFOOD**
Fins & Feathers

**SOUL FOOD**
Ellawee's Restaurant

**STEAKS AND CHOPS**
Diamond Grille

**SUBURBAN**
Diamond Grille (Akron)
Marcelita's (Hudson)
Rick's Cafe (Chagrin Falls)
Watership Down (Moreland
Hills)
The Wine Merchant Restaurant
(Akron)

**UNIQUE PROPERTIES**
Flat Iron Café
Jefferson Inn

**VIETNAMESE**
Minh-Anh

**WINE BAR/RESTAURANT**
Noggin's

Until the mid-seventies, dining out in Cleveland meant golden arches, corned beef on rye, a few ethnic holes-in-the-wall or, on dressier occasions, Continental cuisine at its gloomiest—frozen fish, overcooked meats in floury sauces, and too many flaming creations prepared tableside. Not even *quiche, nachos,* and *moo shu pork* were spoken here. But Cleveland has experienced a culinary renaissance that parallels the national obsession with food. As is true elsewhere in mid-America, it took a few years for trends to wend their way from the two coasts, but now foodies will find imaginative contemporary cooking styles using fresh American ingredients as well as a wide range of ethnic cuisines, including, of course, the foods that reflect Cleveland's strong Middle and Eastern European heritage.

Geography, demographics, and business economics profoundly affect Cleveland's culinary environment. The Cuyahoga River creates such a powerful mental, as well as physical, division of the city that east siders joke about how they need special visas to visit the west side and vice versa. The east side has long been considered the place for sophisticated, upscale dining, while the less affluent, more ethnic west side has tended to attract the inexpensive nationality restaurants. That still is true to a point, but the lines are fuzzier than they used to be. Because the downtown area is just beginning to undergo a rebirth, particularly in the Flats, along the lakefront, and in the environs of the Playhouse Square performing arts center, most of the city's best restaurants are in outlying neighborhoods about a ten- to thirty-minute drive from downtown. Cleveland's cultural arts center, University Circle, is about four miles east of Public Square. In addition, the development of a sprawling commercial park off Chagrin Boulevard (Route 422) in the eastern suburb of Beachwood has created a second "downtown" with a consequent several-mile-long "restaurant row."

Finally, because the Cleveland metropolitan area also includes Akron, the rubber industry center about thirty miles to the south, this chapter mentions two special restaurants in that city.

*Iris Bailin has been the restaurant critic and a contributing editor of* Northern Ohio LIVE *magazine since 1980, and was formerly a restaurant critic for* Cleveland Magazine. *She also is the chef for the executive dining room of Prescott, Ball & Turben, Inc., a Cleveland-based investment banking and brokerage firm, and freelances as a food consultant.*

# ALI-BABA RESTAURANT
## 12021 Lorain Avenue
### 216-251-2040

What is Gibran Slailati doing in this run-down near west side neighborhood operating an unassuming eight-table diner that has few apparent customers when he has a family and a well-known Lebanese restaurant in Montreal? You can dream up all manner of romantic/mysterious explanations as you dine on his exceptionally well-seasoned Lebanese cuisine. Start with one shared combination plate—six items which may include commendable *hummus,* outstanding *baba ghanouj,* thick/tangy *labnee,* and unusual fried *falafel.* The *tabbouleh* is so fresh you can hear Gibran's knife chop-chopping the parsley after his female partner takes your order. How unfortunate, then, that they toss microwaved *pita* bread on the table, still in its bakery bag. The kitchen also does a traditional *mazza* for seven dollars per person. If a complete dinner seems too much after all that, you can order most of the entrées as "sandwiches" for less than half the price. Finish with excellent Turkish coffee, served in a *jezve,* and *atayef* (Lebanese *crêpes*). You can't get silly here on booze—Gibran plans to acquire a license in the future—but you still can have a few laughs trying to guzzle water from the spout in the side of the *brik* without drizzling it down your chin.

*Price: About $10 or less per person*
*Open Tues.–Sun. for lunch and dinner; closed Mon.*
*No credit cards accepted*

# ARABICA
## 2785 Euclid Heights Boulevard (*at Coventry Road*), Cleveland Heights   216-371-4414
## 13216-18 Shaker Square (*southeast quadrant*)   216-283-8015
## 401 Euclid Avenue (*in The Arcade*)   216-621-1048

If you could eavesdrop on conversations at Arabica on any given day, you might hear arts activists and foundation bigwigs discussing grant money, high-level attorneys plotting trial strategy, joggers describing that fabulous new microscopic knee surgery, and best friends commiserating over a recently shattered love affair. Arabica is *the* place for east siders to meet over superb coffee in all its guises. (There also is a small downtown branch in the worth-a-special-trip Arcade.) People have been known to start the day at Arabica over *croissants* and addictive bran muffins, gab their way into a sandwich, stuffed *brioche,* or salad lunch, and about 4 P.M., having chatted with at least half a dozen different acquaintances, find that they're ready for a cup of herb tea and a pastry. Each Arabica has a different flavor: The original in the funky Coventry Road neighborhood attracts students and aging hippies, while the Shaker Square branch, with its outdoor tables, wine license, and more extensive menu, is a Yuppie outpost.

*Price: Under $5 per person*
*Open daily for breakfast, lunch, and dinner at Coventry and Shaker Square;*
*Mon.–Sat. at The Arcade*
*Accepts Visa and MasterCard*

## BALATON RESTAURANT
### 12523 Buckeye Road
### 216-921-9691

Cleveland's Buckeye Road Hungarian neighborhood has succumbed somewhat to urban decay, but, fortunately, nothing has changed, except the prices, at the famous Balaton. The storefront dining room is spare but sparkling clean, and the Hungarian home cooking is unassuming and well seasoned, if a bit greasy. The menu says small orders are available for persons with small appetites, but disregard both "smalls." The regular portions will defeat all but the voracious. The Hungarian platter includes delicious chicken *paprikás* (two Dolly Parton-size portions), a mountain of savory *gulyás,* an enormous stuffed cabbage roll (just okay), and two (two!) scoops of real mashed potatoes. The Balaton's fall-off-the-plate *Wiener Schnitzel* is legendary, and other good bets are the hearty *gulyás* soup, veal *paprikás* with wonderful *spätzle*-style dumplings, and, for dessert, *palacsinta* with four different fillings. Beer and several Hungarian wines are available. Service can be offhand and rushed, and, when business is slow, you might find idle waitresses chatting over coffee and staring at you as you eat.

*Price: Under $10 per person*
*Open Tues.–Sat. for lunch and dinner; closed Sun. and Mon.*
*No credit cards accepted*

## CLUB ISABELLA
### 2025 Abington Road (*south of Euclid Avenue*)
### 216-229-1177

Exposed brick walls, a wonderful old Art Deco bar, glass brick windows, and eye-catching modern art have made this chic renovated coachhouse in Cleveland's University Circle a favorite haunt for the pre-theater and -concert crowd and a mecca for jazz lovers in the later hours. The eclectic light menu offers lots of appetizers for grazers (try the *calamari fritti,* mussels *con basilico,* crisped Provolone, and homemade potato chips), pasta dishes, a superb deep-dish pizza, and entrées running the gamut from the popular beef Wellington burger to char-broiled ribs, steak, and fish to sautéed veal and chicken to roast duck and to fish and chips. Desserts are enticingly ooey-gooey, and most selections on the small, moderately priced wine list are available by the glass. There is live jazz nightly, with a cover charge only on Tuesdays, when the group Forecast holds forth. Except on Sunday and Monday, when it closes at 11 P.M., the kitchen is open till 1 A.M. There is *al fresco* dining in good weather.

*Price: About $18 per person, less for burgers, pasta, pizza, or shared appetizers*
*Open Mon.–Fri. for lunch and dinner; Sat. and Sun. for dinner only*
*Accepts all major credit cards*

---

## CORKY AND LENNY'S
### 13937 Cedar Road (*at Cedar-Center*), South Euclid
#### 216-321-3310
### In the Village Square Shopping Center, 27091 Chagrin Boulevard (*Route 422*), Woodmere   216-464-3838

There are other places in town to get a good corned beef sandwich, but a Jewish deli, after all, is theater, and Corky's produces the whole show. The Village Square branch in the tonier eastern suburbs attempts more "decor" than the original in the old Jewish neighborhood, but both are big, boisterous, and eminently tacky in their own fashion. And both are where you go for your jaw-breaking combo sandwiches, matzo ball soup, and Sunday morning lox and bagel.

*Price: Under $10 per person*
*Open daily for breakfast, lunch, and dinner at Cedar-Center; closed Mon. at Woodmere*
*No credit cards accepted*

---

## CSARDAS
### 11321 Broadway Road, Garfield Heights (*take I–480 to the Broadway exit; go right on Broadway*)
#### 216-883-6866

This roadhouse diner used to be the Mill Creek Inn, and, if you still can't envision the setting, let's just say you go for the dumplings, not the decor. At least the tables wear real linens, and besides, who needs atmosphere when a couple of rumbling tummies encounter a nice friendly waitress and heaps of honest Hungarian home cooking? Soups are satisfying, as are the juicy chicken *paprikás*, robust *székely gulyás*, crisp *Wiener Schnitzel*, and light, egg-battered veal called *Parizsi czelet*.

Entrées, both small and large portions, come with real mashed potatoes or ethereal *spätzle*-like dumplings. On Fridays, don't miss the homemade noodles mingled with cabbage and onions, a dish that will destroy one's gustatory sophistication for weeks afterward. Desserts are pretty decent. Ask the waitress to recite the Hungarian wine selections.

*Price: About $7 per person*
*Open Mon.–Fri. for lunch and dinner;*
*Sat. for dinner only; closed Sun.*
*No credit cards accepted*

## DANNY BOY'S OLD WORLD PIZZA
### 13411 Detroit Avenue, Lakewood
#### 216-228-4940

If this isn't the best pizza in Cleveland, contenders should come forth to challenge the puffy/chewy/crispy crust, outstanding spicy sauce, abundant gooey cheese, and strictly fresh toppings (mushrooms and hot peppers included). "This is almost the perfect pizza," said a 14-year-old aficionado, and who, after all, is a better judge? Danny Boy loyalists also love his *calzones* with stuffings traditional and bizarre (*gyro* pizza?) and the yummy "woogie-bear" pizza roll: three cheeses and *pepperoni* wrapped up in dough and baked until crisp. This west side storefront is nothing to look at, but you can view the steady stream of locals picking up their takeout orders. There's no license here, so no beer with your 'za. Danny Boy's is open till 1 A.M. Friday and Saturday.

*Price: A large (13-inch) pizza is $4.55 plain; $6.35 with three items*
*Open daily for breakfast, lunch, and dinner*
*No credit cards accepted*

## DIAMOND GRILLE
### 77 West Market Street, Akron
#### 216-376-1216

Northern Ohio's most famous steak house, the Diamond has hosted every major golf pro on the tour except Lee Trevino and has a solid membership in that rarified collection of establishments called "institutions." If you prefer a quiet white-tablecloth setting, ask to sit in the rather tacky dining room with its starburst chandeliers and *trompe l'oeil* windows overlooking a French park scene. But if it's action you want, sit in a wooden booth in the long barroom with the rubber industry execs, advertising honchos, visiting celebrities, and local movers and shakers. You won't love the salad, appetizers are no big deal, and there's no dessert but ice cream. But you're here for the he-man steaks, the humongous lamb chops, maybe a broiled lobster, and first-rate home fries (order 'em well done). And, while you're at it, if your gullet can take it, have an *à la carte* order of the hot pepper-laced Willie fries. There's not much available by the glass, but the wine list includes a fair smattering of Cabernets. Diamond Grille serves until about midnight on weekdays and 1 A.M. on Friday and Saturday. It's about an hour's drive from Cleveland.

*Price: $14–$18 for most entrées; more for large lobsters*
*Open Mon.–Fri. for lunch and dinner; Sat. for dinner only; closed Sun.*
*No credit cards accepted*

## ELLAWEE'S RESTAURANT
### 7701 Carnegie Avenue
#### 216-361-8456

Most girls learn cooking from their mamas, but Eloise Scott also had her Aunt Ellawee, who just happened to run a restaurant in Cleveland's black community. In 1982, Scott and her husband, Walter Monroe, took over the thirty-year-old operation and in 1985 moved it to a pleasant little brick and wood-paneled room on a busy commuter thoroughfare near the Cleveland Clinic and the Cleveland Playhouse. Walter, a most amiable guy, may wait on you, while Eloise turns out very fresh Southern cooking featuring ham hocks, neck bones, meat loaf, spicy fried pork chops, and tender savory short ribs. On Fridays, there is fried fish, the whiskered variety included. Of the ten possible sides, the best are the fried corn and just-right greens. The fried chicken, done in a skillet Mississippi style, is a bit dry, and the peach cobbler is okay if you love nutmeg and don't mind canned fruit.

*Price: About $7 per person*
*Open Tues.–Sun. for breakfast, lunch, and dinner; closed Mon.*
*No credit cards accepted*

## FINS & FEATHERS
### In the Van Aken Shopping Center, 20303 Van Aken Boulevard, Shaker Heights
#### 216-991-5454

Even before New Orleans' Paul Prudhomme was the hottest thing since Tabasco sauce, the partners of this seafood and poultry shop were serving up

Creole-style goodies in an adjacent ten-table café with tile floor and painted stucco walls adorned with charcoal drawings of jazz festivals. There are concessions to trends now—items such as *quiche,* fried zucchini, and pasta salad —and prices have climbed from cheap to moderate, but it still is a nifty place to get an earthy bowl of gumbo, sparkling shrimp salad, Prytania Street hot-peppered shrimp, irresistible fried potatoes, and about a dozen different deep-fried fish or crustaceans (grilled or sautéed, fifty cents extra). There are a couple of chicken dishes for the "nothing that swims" contingent, and good rum cake for the sweet freak. Domestic and imported beer and five house wines are available. Fins & Feathers is open only until 8:30 P.M. on weeknights and 10 P.M. Friday and Saturday.

*Price: About $10 per person*
*Open Mon.–Sat. for lunch and dinner; closed Sun.*
*Accepts American Express, Visa, and MasterCard*

---

## FLAT IRON CAFÉ
### In the Flats, 1114 Center Street
### 216-696-6968

Rub elbows with truck drivers, lawyers, politicians, and longshoremen at one of the Flats' best-known working-class bars as you crunch into a heap of just-fried Lake Erie perch, served every Friday from 11 A.M. to 8:30 P.M. You'll pick up your draft at the bar, wind through the cafeteria line, and then find an empty seat at one of the oilcloth-draped communal tables for eight. *Erin-go-braugh* streamers stretched behind the bar look like they're left over from St. Patty's Day, and the green shamrock on the sign outside confirms that this place ain't Italian. Don't be tempted to order the shrimp or scallop dinners; the perch is the reason to come here.

*Price: $7.25 for the fish dinner, $3.50 for the fish sandwich*
*Open Sat.–Thurs. for breakfast and lunch; Fri. for breakfast, lunch, and dinner*
*No credit cards accepted*

---

## THE FRENCH CONNECTION
### In Stouffer's Inn on The Square, 24 Public Square
### 216-696-5600

Named one of the ten most romantic restaurants in America in *USA Today,* this posh room in Cleveland's most elegant hotel is a popular spot for special occasion dining and, given its central downtown location, business entertaining. Some may find the formal service pompous at times, and the *nouvelle cuisine* can be a bit self-conscious, but for unabashed elegance, there is nothing like it in Cleveland. The 76-seat room has cranberry-rose walls, pink napery, pin-dot carpeting, velvet banquettes, French art and appointments (there is an original Dufy), and windows overlooking Public Square.

The menu, which changes yearly, offers such items as smoked tuna, sweetbreads *ravioli* with saffron sauce, lobster *crêpes* with chives and ginger, duck breast with oyster mushrooms and soy, poached salmon with vermouth butter and *enoki* mushrooms, veal with peppercorns and grapefruit, and, for the traditionalists, *chateaubriand* and rack of lamb. The kitchen is a bit conservative about cooking times, so if you want your duck or fish medium-rare, say so. Lovely, light desserts include *mousses,* Bavarian creams, and macerated fruits. The excellent, but rather expensive, wine list has a nice selection of California bottles, but is particularly strong on red Bordeaux and Burgundies. A few half bottles are available.

*Price: About $35 per person*
*Open Mon.–Fri. for lunch and dinner; Sat. and Sun. for dinner only*
*Accepts all major credit cards*

---

# GEPPETTO'S SPAGHETTI & STEAK HOUSE
## 3314 Warren Road
### 216-941-1120

If they awarded a prize for the Most Incongruous Restaurant Operation, it would have to go to a guy named O'Malley who serves barbecued ribs in a spaghetti and pizza joint. It's because of the ribs that this otherwise ordinary little neighborhood eatery appears in these pages. After winning Cleveland's local burnoff for two years running, the lean, sweet-spicy spareribs went on to place third in the nation in the 1985 National Rib Cookoff.

*Price: $8.95 for a half-slab rib dinner, $12.95 for a full-slab rib dinner*
*Open Mon.–Sat. for lunch and dinner; Sun. for dinner only*
*Accepts American Express, Visa, and MasterCard*

# GIOVANNI'S

25550 Chagrin Boulevard (*Route 422*), Beachwood
(*just west of I-271*)
216-831-8625

In this age of minimalist restaurant design, Giovanni's is something of a throwback. Plush and elegant in an Old World sense, the formal Italian provincial setting features lamp-shaded chandeliers, potted trees, emerald velvet banquettes, heavy linens, fine china, and a dramatic copper *espresso* machine. Some call the attentive service overbearing, but what's so bad about handsome Italian waiters who make a woman feel like the most beautiful in the world, and who present a pair of reading glasses on a silver tray to a guest who can't quite make out the menu?

Because of its proximity to the Beachwood commercial park, lots of important business deals are wrapped up over Giovanni's lunches. At night, there is more of the same, plus affluent east siders celebrating someone's birthday. Some people think you eat better at Giovanni's if you're known, but there is no doubt the kitchen is capable of excellence. Though the menu speaks Italian, the food has strong French overtones with *nouvelle* leanings. *Antipasti* range from the classic *(caponata, frutti di mare,* fresh *mozzarella, carpaccio)* to the unorthodox (smoked goose breast, scallops in raspberry and lime sauces). Pastas are excellent: *gnocchi verde alla Piemontese;* angel's hair with tomato and capers; and *linguine* with clam sauce the way it should be done. The kitchen specializes in fresh fish—lavish preparations with wine sauces and shellfish garnishes—and is famous for its enormous veal chop. The pastry cart brings rich confections which vary depending on who did them that day. Do try the *zabaglione* prepared tableside. The wine list, with extensive Italian, French, and California labels, should excite any oenophile, and there are Cognacs that cost more, per shot, than the whole dinner.

*Price: About $35 per person*
*Open Mon.–Fri. for lunch and dinner; Sat. for dinner only; closed Sun.*
*Accepts all major credit cards*

---

# GOURMET OF CHINA

28699 Chagrin Boulevard (*Route 422*),
at Eton Square Mall (*east of I-271*)
216-831-3955

Though half the fun of eating *dim sum* is anticipating the goodies on the next go-round of the cart, one still can have a grand time working through the list of nearly thirty items at this, Cleveland's only extensive tea lunch, available weekends only. Try the *shao mai*, shrimp dumplings, curried beef pie, sesame cakes, savory meat sauce noodles, and the well-executed *lo mein*. But be aware that the "buns" here are really dumplings. The regular menu at Gourmet of China is only partially successful, but the unusually fine Peking duck in three separate courses (special order) is worth the 30-minute drive. No alcoholic beverages are served.

*Price: About $7 per person*
*Open daily for lunch and dinner*
*Accepts all major credit cards*

---

# HECK'S CAFÉ
## 2927 Bridge Avenue (*in Ohio City*)   216-861-5464
## 19300 Detroit Road (*in Beachcliff Market Square*), Rocky River   216-356-2559

Like a woman with beauty *and* ability, Heck's could succeed nicely with either, but is dynamite with both. Can this be the same establishment that was just a little burger joint in Ohio City in the mid-seventies? That Heck's still is there, a landmark building in the gentrified old neighborhood (once a separate "city") near Cleveland's famous West Side Market. The cozy eatery has a friendly bar, an intimate room with copper-topped tables, and a skylit garden area. It offers a scaled-down version of the menu at Heck's at Beachcliff Market Square, a renovated suburban movie palace about 20 minutes west of downtown. People began to take Heck's seriously when this stunner debuted in 1981. The neoclassic entry features a white baby grand piano, an extravagant floral arrangement, changed three times weekly, and shell-shaped plaster of Paris remnants from the old theater lobby, refinished in *faux* jade and mounted on mirrored walls. The tropical courtyard area has Rousseau-like murals, stretches of white lattice, ficus trees, and planters filled with lush greenery.

Heck's cuisine defies categorization, ranging as it does from gravlax to *coulibiac* to blackened redfish. The latter, which works beautifully, hints at the kitchen's current passion for Louisiana cooking (would you believe a sauté of bayou alligator?). But what distinguishes the food most is its celebration of seasonal offerings: *cassoulet* in winter; sorrel, wild mushrooms, and fiddlehead ferns in spring, and, on a day in early summer, soft-shell crabs with squash blossoms. Soups, composed salads, and pastas are especially inventive. Heck's still does hamburgers—fourteen versions—and is also known for its lavish desserts. Either Heck's is a lovely place for Sunday brunch, which in summer is served only in Ohio City. Heck's at Beachcliff also has *al fresco* dining.

*Price: About $20–$24 per person*
*Open Mon.–Sat. for lunch and dinner; Sun. for dinner only at Rocky River;*
*Sun. for brunch and dinner at Ohio City*
*Accepts all major credit cards*

# HUNAN IN COVENTRYARD

2797 Euclid Heights Boulevard (*behind the Coventryard Mall*),
Cleveland Heights
216-371-0777

Great Chinese cuisine has yet to arrive in Cleveland, but if you are looking for decent, fairly priced regional Chinese cooking on the city's east side, this is the place to go. The kitchen is a bit timid with chile peppers, but the food is generous and attractively presented. Soups are excellent, as are the tung-ting shrimp, twice-cooked pork, stir-fried noodles, and Hunan fish. The subdued burgundy-and-white setting is several notches above standard issue red dragon decor, and the service must be the most congenial in the city. The place is tiny and accepts no reservations, so expect a wait during peak hours. There is full bar service.

*Price: About $12 per person*
*Open Tues.–Sat. for lunch and dinner; Sun. for dinner only; closed Mon.*
*Accepts American Express, Visa, and MasterCard*

---

# JEFFERSON INN

820 Jefferson Avenue
216-241-6635

Perhaps no food represents Cleveland's strong Middle European heritage better than *pierogi*. Alas, the best examples of the art are usually found in private homes and at church suppers. But on Fridays, you can kiss off misgivings about cholesterol and onion breath and sample the real thing. To experience the ultimate, you must venture into Cleveland's old Tremont neighborhood to a tavern setting not merely tacky but downright sleazy. There isn't even a sign outside one can discern. You will pass through a barroom, where the tattooed locals play pinball, into a cavernous dining room/pool hall/storage room where you will sit on a red vinyl chair at a stained Formica table and try to get the barmaid to pay you some attention. And finally, you will get a dozen little beauties—potato, sauerkraut, or cheese—swimming in fried onions and fat. Add a beer, and you'll roll out of there for three bucks and change. This could be the cheapest fill-up since thirty-cent-a-gallon gasoline. Jefferson Inn serves *pierogi* on Fridays from 9:30 A.M. to 6 P.M. They usually run out by mid-afternoon; if you plan to go later, call ahead and ask them to save some for you.

*Price: About $3 per person*
*Open Fri. from 9:30 A.M.–6 P.M. for* pierogi
*No credit cards accepted*

# KOREA HOUSE
## 3420 Payne Avenue
### 216-431-0462

Several young Korean businessmen who recently visited Cleveland on a Rotary Club exchange program stopped in at Korea House and pronounced its extensive menu authentic and good. If you are really adventurous, try something like buckwheat noodles in spicy sauce topped with wing fish salad. The delicious fried dumplings *(man du)* and char-broiled or marinated beef dishes will appeal to more timid palates, but either way, don't leave without at least tasting the pungent *kim chee.*

The atmosphere here is so awful it is almost camp. You enter through a bar with jukebox and cigarette machine by the door—this is a hangout for residents of the ethnic neighborhood—and pass through a beaded curtain into a more "formal" dining room with faded floral curtains, Chinese lanterns, wood paneling, and red vinyl table covers. Someone obviously tried to set the scene with whatever Oriental doodads they could get their hands on—Japanese calendars, travel posters, wooden dolls, china bric-a-brac, and the *pièce de résistance,* a commemorative plate inscribed "Han Yang soccer team, August 1982."

*Price: About $10 per person*
*Open Mon.–Fri. for lunch and dinner; Sat. for dinner only; closed Sun.*
*Accepts American Express, Visa, and MasterCard*

# LOPEZ Y GONZALEZ
## 2066 Lee Road (*north of Cedar Road*), Cleveland Heights
### 216-371-7611

Seekers of stuffed tortillas, go elsewhere. This is serious regional Mexican cuisine, and one of the best restaurants in Cleveland. Originally designed by Rick Bayless, star of a public-television cooking series, the menu features outstanding soups (perhaps a shrimp-corn chowder), irresistible appetizers *(guacamole,* ceviche, *queso fundido, quesadillas),* and such specialties as Pueblan-style chicken *mole, tacos al carbon,* and deep-fried *flautas.* But the kitchen is best known for its daily chicken and seafood dishes in complex sauces, which are careful blends of various spices, nuts, seeds, and chilies. The fresh fish is always perfectly grilled; frequently-featured tuna comes out rare. Not a place to stagnate, Lopez has been toying with novel inventions without sacrificing the integrity of the cuisine. Result: *cilantro "pesto,"* mesquite-smoked baby chicken with mustard-*jalapeño* sauce, grilled duck breast with red pepper cream sauce, and veal *pâté* with avocado sauce. Desserts, including homemade ice creams, are scrumptious, but the fried ice cream is just a novelty. There is a minimal wine list here; stick to margaritas or the four Mexican beers.

The understated south-of-the-border decor at Lopez features polished wood tables with terry cloth "napkins," stucco walls, terrazzo floors, flame-stitch banquettes, Mexican artifacts and pottery, and greenery suspended from a beamed ceiling in front of high rectangular windows. There are a few private booths, but don't plan on intimate conversation; the place is always jumping and so is the noise level. Service is friendly and competent. No reservations are accepted for parties under six; expect a wait on weekends.

*Price: About $18 per person with daily specials; $13 with regular items*
*Open Mon.–Fri. for lunch and dinner; Sat. for dinner only; closed Sun.*
*Accepts American Express, Visa, and MasterCard*

---

# THE MAD GREEK
## 2466 Fairmount Boulevard (*at Cedar Road*), Cleveland Heights
### 216-421-3333

In a city that has no East Indian eatery, The Mad Greek is a welcome hybrid —a nice little Greek restaurant with a dandy Indian menu reflecting the heritage of owner Loki Chopra (his wife is Greek). Try the *samosas,* the chicken *tikka,* or the delicious curries with a side of incendiary mint chutney. Ask for the food hot, and it'll tear your guts out. The Greek menu offers the usual dishes, including a good *gyro* sandwich, and some creative daily specials, but the most interesting choice is the *mezedakia* appetizer platter. Have it for dinner or share it as a late snack. The *hummus* and *baba ghanouj* are good, but always seem to leave an aftertaste of processed garlic. If you picture this as just another Formica hole-in-the-wall, you'll be delighted with the Greek's airy, multilevel courtyard setting with terrazzo floor, whitewashed brick, wrought-iron and ceramic tile accents, bentwood chairs, sophisticated black tablecloths, and plenty of greenery. The wine list also is better than you would expect at this sort of place. The restaurant's snazzy gray-and-salmon post-modern lounge offers live music Friday and Saturday, when the kitchen stays open until at least 1 A.M. Other nights, this is one of the nicest places around to meet a friend for a drink.

*Price: About $13 per person*
*Open Mon.–Sat. for lunch and dinner; Sun. for dinner only*
*Accepts American Express, Visa, and MasterCard*

# MAMMA SANTA'S
## 12301-05 Mayfield Road (*Route 322*)
### 216-231-9567 or 216-421-2159

Many are the university students and hospital residents for whom a Mamma Santa pizza was an essential element in the educational process. This Little Italy institution turns out a very good, not great, pie with a crisp crust, savory sauce, good toppings, and painless price tag. Skip the Sicilian food on the menu, but the *antipasto* salad is a worthwhile accompaniment. Unfortunately, Mamma Santa's expanded into three rather dingy dining rooms without a parallel addition of pizza ovens, so during peak hours there can be a long wait for food.

*Price: A 13-inch pizza is $2.90 plain; $4.85 with three items*
*Open Mon.–Sat. for lunch and dinner; closed Sun.*
*Accepts Visa and MasterCard*

---

# MARCELITA'S
## 7774 Darrow Road (*Route 91*), Hudson (*2 miles off I-480 near the Ohio Turnpike*)
### 216-656-2129 or 216-650-1121

Marcela McNeill left her family in Mexico City and, in 1978, with her gringo husband, Jack, and sister-in-law Jeanne, put together a wildly popular Mexican eatery in a roadhouse on the outskirts of Hudson, a charming New England-style bedroom community about thirty minutes from Cleveland. Despite an expansion to 150 seats, there can still be an hour's wait on the weekends, a period made more tolerable if you are sipping margaritas and dipping chips in Marcelita's three superb salsas. The extra-hot red sauce is for asbestos tongues only. The menu is a little silly ("Quesadilla [kay-sah-dee-ya]"; "Cheese Crisp [cheez krisp]"), but this is very serious Mexican and Tex–Mex food at unbelievably fair prices. Marcelita doesn't give you infinite variations on a theme with one all-purpose sauce; ten distinct sauces derive their character from many different chile peppers, including one specially shipped up from Mexico. Don't miss the *enchiladas suizas* and *rojas,* and try the *chimichanga, chiles rellenos,* and the popular wet *burritos.* Marcelita's doesn't look like much from the exterior, but inside are a cozy, dark lounge and three cheery dining rooms with stucco walls and just enough Mexican artifacts to set the scene.

*Price: About $8 per person*
*Open Tues.–Sat. for lunch and dinner; closed Sun. and Mon.*
*Accepts American Express, Visa, and MasterCard*

# THE MIDDLE EAST RESTAURANT
In the Carter Manor, 1012 Prospect Avenue
### 216-771-2647

When Arab royalty journey to the Cleveland Clinic for everything from bypass surgery to skin rashes, they make The Middle East their local palace kitchen. Located in a downtown residential hotel, the room is packed at lunchtime with Playhouse Square office workers, but often it is nearly deserted at dinnertime. It's not big on ambiance (Whoever chose powder-blue wall murals to go with the red and gold carpeting, chairs, and tablecloths?), but the $10.95 family dinner (for four or more) is one of the best values in town. In addition to tender lamb shish kebab and the usual Lebanese specialties, the kitchen also does lima beans simmered in a sauce of tomatoes, lamb, and cinnamon and, on the weekends, a roasted chicken stuffed with meat, rice, and pine nuts. The Middle East has full liquor service.

*Price: About $11 per person*
*Open Mon.–Sat. for lunch and dinner; closed Sun.*
*Accepts Diners Club, Visa, and MasterCard*

# MILLER'S DINING ROOM
16707 Detroit Avenue, Lakewood
### 216-221-5811

If they had searched for a Cleveland restaurant location for that film about the kid who travels back thirty years and meets his parents as teenagers, surely they would have chosen Miller's. In an age when American cuisine can mean suckling pig in black bean sauce with *foie gras* pot stickers, Miller's still serves a wholesome, all-American complete dinner for about what you would spend at a chichi hamburger emporium. You are barely settled in at your table in the vaguely Colonial, blue-and-cream dining room when the sticky bun lady whips by with the first of about five offerings of the gooey little gems. Then comes the salad lady with her tray of glittering confections: Waldorf salad, cabbage and carrot slaws, pears with marshmallows, and, of course, shimmering gelatin molds. The appetizer is a hearty soup, fruit cup, or juice. Then your roast pork or brisket of beef or veal cutlet in Creole sauce or not-to-be-missed chicken à la King in a freshly fried potato basket comes with two vegetables. But you're not finished yet. There still is dessert and coffee. None of the dinners mentioned costs more than—are you ready for this—seven dollars. Efficient

waitresses in burgundy dresses look like they've been at Miller's forever; so
does much of the clientele.

*Price: Under $10 per person*
*Open daily for lunch and dinner*
*No credit cards accepted*

---

## MINH-ANH
### 5428 Detroit Avenue
**216-961-9671**

You will have to work at spending more than six dollars per person on the
home-style Vietnamese cuisine in this spotless little west side storefront. The
food is mild, to be doctored to taste with *nuoc mam* (Vietnamese fish sauce),
*nuoc cham* (a gussied fish sauce blend), hot chile paste, and chunks of fresh
lemon and hot green chilies. The best soups are the *pho Saigon* (cinnamon beef
with rice noodles) and *hu tieu dai* (shrimp and pork with clear noodles); a large
bowl is a whole meal. Recommended entrées include an exceptional Vietnamese *crêpe,* stir-fried beef with lemon grass, chicken curry topped with fried
onions and crisp spring rolls (available alone as an appetizer) served in concert
with *vermicelli,* peanuts, vegetables, and mint. Other dishes are variations on
bits of meat atop various noodles and vegetables. Desserts are interesting but
perhaps an acquired taste, and unusual beverages include coconut soda pop and
sugar cane, guava, mango, and soybean juices. There is no liquor license.
Minh-Anh has been discovered following favorable reviews, so call for reservations.

*Price: About $6 per person*
*Open Tues.–Sun. for lunch and dinner; closed Mon.*
*No credit cards accepted*

---

## NOGGIN'S
### In the Shaker Shopping Center, 20110 Van Aken Boulevard,
### Shaker Heights (*near Routes 8 and 422*)
**216-752-9280**

If someone wanted to formulate the elusive mix that makes a restaurant a
phenomenal success, they might start by studying Noggin's. This is the quintessential Yuppie hangout—an informal butcher block/bentwood/basket-of-
plants space that happens to have a superb raw bar, a lively pub, an outstanding
California wine list, and unpretentious, creative food that is consistently good,
if not sensational.

The menu offers a mixed bag of nibbles, omelets, sandwiches, vegetarian items, salads, steaks, and chicken breast sautés. But the regulars come in for the splendid soups and the seafood and pasta specials. There might be grilled monkfish with fennel butter, halibut with dilled *mousseline,* soft-shell crabs, sea bass with sherry butter and trumpet mushrooms, gently deep-fried Pacific oysters, or grilled sea scallops on Bibb lettuce with herbed walnut vinaigrette. The kitchen uses high-quality imported macaronis, but on Tuesdays they turn out homemade fantasy pastas, such as lemon-parsley noodles with veal sausage; tarragon *fettuccine* with broccoli, feta, olive oil, butter, garlic, vermouth, and egg; and herbed *linguine* with crab meat, shrimp, and sun-dried tomatoes. Desserts are homey and good, and there are always at least ten wines by the glass, with three featured labels each week, and an exceptional list of vintage ports. Service is friendly and low-key.

*Price: About $20 per person, half that for a meal of soup, salad, pasta, and dessert*
*Open Mon.–Sat. for lunch and dinner; Sun. for dinner only*
*Accepts American Express, Visa, and MasterCard*

---

# NORTON'S
## 12447 Cedar Road, Cleveland Heights (*the parking lot is in the back off Surrey Road*)
### 216-932-2727

Walk into Norton's on a weekday morning and chances are you won't find one table without a briefcase resting next to it. Weekends, a heterogeneous Cleveland Heights clientele crowds in for the diet-destroying Miami French toast, fresh-squeezed orange juice, "Norton's scramble" (eggs with potato, onion, green pepper, and Cheddar), and the homemade fried cakes. This is one of those airy, woodsy, Scandinavian-feeling places that became so popular in the seventies. If you're not coming in for the famous breakfast, the soup/burger/omelet fare is nice the rest of the day, particularly if you get the post-concert hungries on the weekend. The kitchen is open till 1 A.M. on Fridays and Saturdays.

*Price: Under $5 per person for breakfast; under $10 per person for the regular menu*
*Open daily for breakfast, lunch, and dinner*
*Accepts Visa and MasterCard*

# OTANI

1625 Golden Gate Shopping Center (*on Mayfield Road—Route 322*) at the Mayfield Heights exit of I-271
**216-442-7098**

Considering that Otani is trying to be all things to all people, at least when it comes to Japanese cooking, it does a surprisingly good job. The dining room, decorated with the usual Japanese design elements and a few low tables with leg "pits," features the standard specialties; *tonkatsu, yakiniku, teriyaki,* and *gyoza* are all good. In the adjacent *teppanyaki* steak house, Japanese chefs perform dagger-knife dazzle at lower prices than the franchise competition (ginger pork is an especially good value). But the best thing about Otani is its Tokyo-style *sushi* bar. On a busy night, two chefs turn out standard items plus intriguing daily specials. The board might list red shrimp, cockles, soft-shell crab, or the popular new Otani roll, a *maki sushi* extravaganza with, among other things, grilled eel, *negihamachi,* cucumber, and Japanese pickle.

*Price: About $14 per person in the restaurant,*
*$11 in the teppanyaki room;* sushi *items average $2.50*
*Open Mon.–Sat. for lunch and dinner; Sun. for dinner only*
*Accepts all major credit cards*

---

# OUR GANG

20680 North Park Boulevard (*at Fairmount Circle*), University Heights   **216-371-4700**
19729 Center Ridge Road, Fairview Park (*off the Hilliard Road exit of I-90 at Rockport Plaza*)   **216-333-6211**

Upscale junk food surrounded by cutesy collectables isn't news anymore—every city big enough to have a McDonald's probably also has a gourmet burger—but Our Gang could write a textbook on the subject. It was the first of the genre in Cleveland (there are two branches now) and it's the best. All the now-classics are here: potato skins, *nachos, pita* sandwiches, "create-your-own-omelet," the tuna melt, the *taco* salad. Our Gang sundaes run out of ice cream before the hot fudge is gone. The burgers are fat and juicy and grilled the way you want 'em, the chili won the local Kidney Foundation cook-off, and the gargantuan onion rings are unbelievable. But what puts Our Gang on the map is their relatively recent foray into exotic beers. The owner conducts monthly tastings, and the menu now lists more than 100 brews, including Guinness and Bass on draft, and four Northern Ohio exclusives. This is where you can quaff an EKU Kulminator "28," temperature-controlled, of course. The east side Gang serves Sunday brunch.

*Price: Under $10 per person, a little more with regular entrées*
*Open Mon.–Sat. for lunch and dinner; Sun. for dinner only*
*Accepts American Express, Visa, and MasterCard*

---

## RENEE'S
### 5605 Fleet Avenue (*off I-77*)
#### 216-883-4747

In the heart of the renovated Slavic Village, a 1.6-square-mile enclave of ethnic butchers, bakers, and grocers on Cleveland's southeast side, Renee Kulacz produces authentic Polish cooking influenced by her origins in the coastal town of Gdansk. The cover of the menu presents a fascinating description of the cuisine, and inside it says, *"Witamy Was"*—"We Welcome You." Renee cooks classic Polish soups (white *barszcz, czarnina,* and tripe) and such specialties as rich, intense *bigos* (hunter's stew) and *zrazy zawijane,* bacon-and-cucumber-stuffed beef *roulades* with buckwheat groats and earthy beets. Try also the savory *gulasz,* the roast pork loin, and the two obvious choices— *golabki* (stuffed cabbage) and excellent *pierogi.* Noteworthy nightly features include *kielbasa* on Mondays, *nalésniki* (cheese *crêpes*) on Wednesdays, potato pancakes on Fridays, and roast duck Thursday through Saturday. The 18-table storefront has a large lounge and an unassuming brown-and-green color scheme, accented with Tiffany-style lamps, simulated marble-top tables, and a picture postcard mural on the back wall. A deejay plays contemporary hits and oldies for dancing after 10 P.M. Friday, Saturday, and Sunday.

*Price: Under $10 per person*
*Open Mon.–Sat. for breakfast, lunch, and dinner*
*No credit cards accepted*

---

## RICK'S CAFÉ
### 86 North Main Street, Chagrin Falls
#### 216-247-7666

Clevelanders take their barbecued ribs so seriously (this is the home of the National Rib Cookoff) that it is almost foolhardy to single out one rib joint. Ribs, after all, are as personal as the perfume one wears. Rick's may or may not be the best in town, but it has three things going for it. For one, they do serve up some mighty fine baby back and spare ribs in a fairly spicy, not-too-sweet sauce, along with great coleslaw and homemade fries. Rick's also has a neat Art Deco interior—outrageous walls of lavender and forest green, ceiling fans, low light from fabulous Deco fixtures, murals of dancing couples in thirties garb, and, the room's focal point, a mellowed Art Deco bar. The theme seems startling in a staid little town that looks as if it really belongs somewhere in Vermont. And that's the third reason for mentioning Rick's. Chagrin Falls itself entices visitors with its Victorian architecture, smart antique and clothing shops, and the rushing waterfall at the center of town. If you're energetic, climb down to the foot, then pick up a soft ice cream cone across Main Street and watch the world go by from a bench in the town square. Rick's has live jazz some nights and on Tuesdays features an all-you-can-eat rib feast for $10.95. It's about a 40-minute-drive from downtown Cleveland.

*Price: $9.95 for a half-slab rib dinner; $14.95 for a full-slab rib dinner*
*Open Mon.–Sat. for lunch and dinner; closed Sun.*
*Accepts Visa and MasterCard*

---

# SAMMY'S
## In the Flats, 1400 West 10 Street (*just off Superior Avenue*)
### 216-523-5560

Far below muslin-draped floor-to-ceiling windows, light shimmers hypnotically on the Cuyahoga, illuminating the looming contours of the river's many bridges. This is the stretch of railroad tracks and heavy industry known as the Flats, and two stories up in an old brick warehouse is what is one of the best restaurants in Cleveland. Sammy's has all the elements: slick warehouse chic with exposed ductwork, brick walls, and elegantly dressed tables; dazzling raw bar; cool jazz; knowing wine list; flamboyant waiters and a creative kitchen that is nearly obsessed with obtaining gorgeous raw materials.

Sammy's attracts a dichotomous mix: junior execs and suburban singles inhale Scotch and shrimp on the bar side, while over in the 80-seat, three-tiered dining area, well-heeled east siders and expense-account high rollers groan over exquisitely presented *nouvelle cuisine.* It might be a sauté of veal with sweetbreads, toasted pecans, and julienned carrots in Madeira sauce; *médaillons* of pork with shrimp on a Zinfandel/balsamic vinegar sauce with Napa and purple cabbage and an Oriental dumpling; or perhaps grilled tuna with cucumbers, peppers, and rosemary butter. Sammy's is one of few local restaurants serving fresh New York State *foie gras;* other appetizers include remarkable soups, *terrines,* pastas, and seafood. Portions, alas, are sometimes skimpy for their cost. Save room for the desserts, especially the signature *boule de neige* and the extraordinary ice creams, then mellow out with *espresso* and a glass of the house's selected barrel-aged port. A caveat, though: Request a table away from the music, or you will have to shout through dinner.

*Price: About $36 per person*
*Open Mon.–Sat. for lunch and dinner; Sun. for dinner only*
*Accepts all major credit cards*

---

# SHUJIRO
## 2206 Lee Road (*south of Cedar Road*), Cleveland Heights
### 216-321-0210

Since its debut in 1982, Shujiro has evolved into a first-rate Japanese dining room and one of Cleveland's outstanding restaurants. The tranquil setting, with its pale woods, attractive wall hangings, lilting background music, and subtle purple color scheme, is calming after the most frenzied day. Kimono-clad waitresses serve guests at Western-style tables set with stark black Formica mats and chopsticks (forks available upon request) or at *tatami* seating along one wall of the room. All of the appetizers here are wonderful, the *sashimi* is impeccably fresh, and the mammoth *shiitake* mushrooms, when available, are not to be missed. The standard Japanese dishes are all good—the *tempura* is exceptional—but what makes Shujiro special are items such as grilled eel with *kabayaki* sauce and fried soft-shell crabs with rice vinegar dressing. The kitchen also does some nice fish specials, but tends to cook the fish beyond medium-rare, so specify how you want it. Classically trained chef-owner Hiroshi Tsuji also has been dabbling in Sino–French creations. Result: sautéed veal sauced with sake and soy and roast duck with Japanese-accented sauces. Shujiro's *sushi* bar (closed Mondays) is small and shares space with the liquor, but the product is outstanding.

*Price: About $16 per person; sushi items average $3*
*Open Mon.–Fri. for lunch and dinner; Sat. and Sun. for dinner only; sushi bar closed Mon.*
*Accepts Visa and MasterCard*

# STOUFFER INN ON THE SQUARE
## 24 Public Square
### 216-696-5600

For pure grandeur there's nothing like the Sunday extravaganzas in the plush rose-toned lobby of this elegant hotel at the center of downtown Cleveland. The French-inspired decor features dramatic chandeliers, polished wood floors adorned with Oriental rugs, gilt-framed mirrors, marble columns, a bubbling fountain, and potted palms. Some tables have cozy upholstered armchairs facing on Public Square. The spectacular brunch requires several trips to the six buffet tables as well as a ravenous appetite. Chefs prepare omelets and waffles to order; another reheats gently poached eggs in simmering water before assembling your eggs Benedict. There is an enticing array of fresh fruits and pastries, a lox and bagel station, and chafing dishes filled with all the usual breakfast items plus some substantial meat dishes. Brunch is served from 9:30 A.M. to 2 P.M. No reservations are accepted, so expect a wait during peak hours.

*Price: Adults, $13.95; children 12 and under, $7.95; under 3, free*
*Open Sun. for brunch*
*Accepts all major credit cards*

# SZECHWAN GARDEN
## 13800 Detroit Avenue, Lakewood
### 216-226-1987

This spiffy little neighborhood restaurant has generated so much enthusiasm that many east siders regularly make the trek across the Cuyahoga to partake of its Szechuan and Hunan specialties. Hostess/waitress Anne Huang and her chef-husband Jang turn out food that is fresh, as spicy as you want it, and sauced with clear, distinct flavors. Good choices are empress chicken or shrimp, Hunan beef, pork with garlic sauce, *kung pao* chicken, broccoli with garlic sauce, fried noodles, and, to soothe the stinging palate, the delicate Lake Tung Ting shrimp. Skip the orange beef. The kitchen is less successful with appetizers—only the *satay* beef is memorable. The room, with its wallpaper, paneling, fitted vinyl table covers, and a few Oriental geegaws, is a cut above Early Ethnic. Beer and wine are available.

*Price: About $11 per person*
*Open Tues.–Sat. for lunch and dinner; Sun. for dinner only; closed Mon.*
*No credit cards accepted*

# TENTH STREET CAFÉ

In the Flats, 1400 West Tenth Street (*just off Superior Avenue*)

216-523-1094

If you want to sample the glories of Sammy's without facing a three-digit tab, visit this sleek black-and-white café for lunch, late-afternoon *cappuccino,* or a chic little pre-theater dinner. It offers the best of the upstairs restaurant—style, culinary sparkle, and "riv vu," and, if you're there at the right hour, you can watch the sun slip down behind the bridgescape of the railroad flats as you swoon over sublime soups, inventive pizzas, luscious pastas, and interesting salads. The chef might come up with a Mexican-accented chicken in *filo* on a creamy corn sauce with *cilantro,* and for dessert there are jewel-like pastries or a selection of Corné Toison d'Or chocolates from the adjacent food emporium. Sip sparkling water, *espresso,* or wine by the glass, and be sure to allow time afterwards for browsing through the Flats' fascinating shops.

*Price: About $15 per person*
*Open daily for lunch; dinner hours erratic*
*Accepts American Express, Visa, and MasterCard*

# THAT PLACE ON BELLFLOWER

11401 Bellflower Road

216-231-4469

As a game of musical toques goes on at That Place, its French cuisine swings from wildly creative, but inconsistent, to traditional, but sometimes dowdy. Still, That Place flourishes, probably because of its location in the heart of University Circle, the city's cultural and medical center, and probably because it's one of the best-looking restaurants in the city. The century-old converted carriage house has an open kitchen, white-washed brick walls, hanging Oriental rugs, and black-and-white paintings which are echoed in artsy table covers. Alas, crowded tables tend to negate the romantic atmosphere; if you are planning an *intime* dinner, request a more secluded table. On blustery days, try to sit by the wood-burning fireplace, and when balmy weather finally comes to Cleveland, the best place to be is on the tree-shaded deck.

At this writing, typical menu offerings are veal Oscar, breast of chicken in champagne sauce, filet mignon with Cognac and horseradish, and the popular salmon with spinach and Pernod *mousse* wrapped in puff pastry with lobster sauce. Appetizers include octopus salad, scallops in caper *rémoulade,* and an artichoke with black currant vinaigrette. If you like to share several appetizers for dinner, you won't get haughty glances from the stylish and usually efficient waiters. The wine list has a good selection of French and California bottlings and some interesting cordials for after dinner.

*Price: About $22 per person*
*Open Mon.–Sat. for lunch and dinner; Sun. for dinner only*
*Accepts all major credit cards*

---

# WATERSHIP DOWN
## 34105 Chagrin Boulevard (*Route 422 at Route 91*), Moreland Hills
### 216-831-5800

A captivating, hand-carved rocking rabbit greets visitors to this charming little white-frame country house in the affluent eastern suburbs about a 40-minute drive from downtown. The rabbit motif continues tastefully in several intimate downstairs dining rooms decorated with Provençal prints. There are flickering candles, real wood-burning fireplaces, and stunning Villeroy and Boch china, whose morning glory design is repeated on the handsome cream, green, and pink menus.

The food is best described as "international *nouvelle*." Not everything works all the time, but it's always inventive and usually delicious. Extensive daily specials emphasizing seafood and veal augment the eight starters and entrées on the seasonally changing menu. And yes, in case you were wondering, the rabbit theme turns up as a *terrine* or a *consommé* with vegetables. Typical appetizers are smoked scallops with *fettuccine* and *shiitake* mushrooms in *crème fraîche;* smoked salmon baked on homemade whole wheat with parsley, capers, and olive oil and served with *beurre blanc;* oysters with chili-coriander *pesto;* and chilled apple soup with toasted walnuts. Popular entrées include blackened redfish; lamb Wyoming, the loin and tenderloin wrapped with a forcemeat and napped with a brown truffle sauce; lobster sautéed with hazelnut oil, lemon, and wine and tossed with angel hair pasta and *pignoli* (pine nuts); veal chop on breaded eggplant with artichokes, mushrooms, and *béarnaise* sauce. The wine list is excellent, and there is a "captain's list," by request, with collector's items and special Cognacs, ports, and sherries. Desserts are uneven but generally good. Try the *sorbets* and don't miss the chef's chocolate truffles. The kitchen can be a bit slow, but service is professional and attentive.

*Price: About $28 per person*
*Open Mon.–Fri. for lunch and dinner; Sat. for dinner only; closed Sun.*
*Accepts all major credit cards*

# THE WINE MERCHANT RESTAURANT
## 1680 Merriman Road, Akron
### 216-864-6222

By seven o'clock every morning John Piscazzi is out making the rounds of his purveyors, hand-picking the ingredients for what is considered to be the best kitchen in Akron. Lusty, bold, and unpretentious, the Falstaffian Piscazzi enjoys sharing his indulgences with other *bon vivants,* frequently pulling up a chair, and, if they are more comfortable wearing blue jeans or tennis clothes, that's just fine with him.

Don't be misled by the rather conventional French and Italian veal and beef dishes on The Wine Merchant menu. The house specializes in fresh fish, usually eight and as many as twelve different species each night. Piscazzi prefers fish baked in a little olive oil and butter or poached in court bouillon, but diners may choose from four other preparations: broiled, fried, *amandine,* or *oreganato.* The first two styles, finished off with *buerre noir* or a sublime cucumber-champagne sauce, are best. With twenty-four hours' notice, Piscazzi will do *bouillabaisse, paella,* stuffed boneless duck, or a boneless double rack of lamb for one. He also welcomes special requests.

The restaurant's two plain, vaguely Spanish dining rooms won't win any design awards, but it really doesn't matter. Most of the atmosphere comes from a wall lined with wine bins. After all, as its name implies, this is a mecca for oenophiles. The primarily French and California list contains more than 500 wines, including some rare bottles. If you want a magnum of 1945 Talbot or a 1959 Lafite, they're here. Two full-time wine stewards also will inform you of the many newer acquisitions not on the list or simply bring you a liter ($7) of one of the four house wines without the slightest hint of intimidation. Ask for directions when you call for reservations. About an hour's drive from Cleveland.

*Price: About $23 per person*
*Open daily for dinner only*
*Accepts American Express, Visa, and MasterCard*

# Z CONTEMPORARY CUISINE
## 20600 Chagrin Boulevard (*Route 422*), Shaker Heights
### 216-991-1580

Zachary Bruell proved you can go home again with one of the most interesting and critically acclaimed restaurants to arrive in Cleveland in recent years. Native son Bruell learned his craft on the West Coast, then brought his personal cuisine to a spare, sophisticated, off-white space on the first floor of an office building designed by Bauhaus School founder Walter Gropius. The 75-seat main room and two 10-seat side rooms are textbook examples of the less-is-more concept. Not a candle or a single bloom clutters the white-clothed tables, and the only punches of color come from abstract art. Bruell is not a trendsetter; he won't startle you with daring innovations, but neither will he jar you with bizarre inedibles. You can count on the best available materials, impeccably cooked and sublimely sauced. The half-dozen or so starters will include a soup, a *terrine,* a pasta, a seafood, and whatever else suits Bruell's whimsy and the offerings of the marketplace. The entrées, all grilled, feature fish, veal, pork, beef, and chicken, each paired with a complementary reduction sauce and garnished with the chef's signature bouquet of vegetables. Desserts are notable for quality and variety, and the wine list is remarkable for selection and price.

*Price: About $26 per person*
*Open Tues.–Fri. for lunch; Mon.–Sat. for dinner*
*Accepts American Express, Visa, and MasterCard*

# COLUMBUS, OHIO

## BY DORAL CHENOWETH

**AMERICAN**
Circus Chef, a.k.a. EAT
The Refectory

**BARBECUE**
JP's Barbecue Ribs

**CAJUN**
Fifty-Five on the Boulevard

**CHINESE**
Hunan House
Sun Tong Luck Tea House &
Restaurant

**CONTINENTAL**
The Plaza
The Worthington Inn
Ziggy's Continental

**DELICATESSEN**
Katzinger's Delicatessen

**EASTERN EUROPEAN**
a la carte

**ECLECTIC**
Chutney's, a café

**FRENCH**
Buxton Inn
L'Armagnac

**GERMAN**
Schmidt's Sausage Haus

**HAMBURGERS**
Max & Erma's
Wendy's Old Fashioned
Hamburgers
White Castle

**HOTEL DINING ROOM**
A Taste of Wine
The Plaza

**ITALIAN**
Monaco's Palace
Moretti's Italian Foods

**JAPANESE**
Otani

**SEAFOOD**
   Fifty-Five on the Boulevard

**SLAVIC**
   Delikatesa Slavic Restaurant

**STEAKS AND CHOPS**
   The Clarmont
   A Taste of Wine
   The Top Steak House

**SUBURBAN**
   Buxton Inn (Granville)
   The Worthington Inn
   (Worthington)

**WINE BAR/RESTAURANT**
   Lindey's

W hen the City of Columbus was considering symbolic sculpture to impress visitors arriving through its international airport, one columnist suggested a bronzed hamburger. It didn't fly.

The Columbus metro trade market has almost 600 restaurants, but 450 of them are fast-food establishments. There is a good reason: Columbus is a hamburger test market with a tasty history.

*The Wall Street Journal* once said "credit for much of our fast food (seems) to belong to Columbus, Ohio." *The New York Times* profiled a single Columbus street as "fast-food wonderland," noting that the city's market supported those 450 fast-food eateries and was home plate for eight fast-food chains, not all of them hamburger oriented. Not all fast-food concepts are success stories, such as Wendy's and White Castle or Bob Evans Restaurants. In 1969, one called Turkey Trot opened to great fanfare only to close following the grand opening press party. Food poisoning from bacteria hospitalized several early patrons, including a restaurant reviewer. Verbalizing his review at the time, he opined: "This turkey will never get off the ground."

Hollywood's beach blanket movies gave California credit for drive-ins using roller skates for fast curb service. But, it all tested out in Columbus, Ohio. In 1939, a Coney dog and malt shop reasoned that individual car speakers on the parking lot would be good for takeout service. McDonald's' Ray Kroc once used the word "speedee" in his corporate signing and credited the origin to a mid-1940s Columbus malt shop advertising "speedy curb service." Kroc had sold equipment to the shop.

A "Coney stand" sold waxed paper-wrapped dogs from a "drive under," similiar to today's beer docks. It may not have been the first, even in the mid-1930s, but it was a concept eventually refined by such locals as Wendy's International and Sister's Chicken and Biscuits.

Columbus gave first exposure to the finest restaurant critic in our times, Clara Peller for Wendy's, when she searched for the beef. But she missed Wendy's hometown, where the popular gourmet hamburger was pioneered by a regional chain, Max & Erma's. In 1972, Max got Erma to create a 10-ounce, handmade beef patty with grilled adornments. Today, copycats include Flakey Jake's, Fuddruckers, Spoons, and others.

And Columbus is home frying pan for the cult-supported "slider," greased by White Castle Systems. You'll find sliders herein as one of the recommended culinary achievements in Columbus. So, too, you'll find a favored listing for fine downtown, ethnic, and suburban establishments. White tablecloths, candlelight, and the best of wines finally arrived in the midst of Hamburger High Tech.

*Doral Chenoweth has been restaurant critic and "The Grumpy Gourmet" for* The Columbus Dispatch *for twenty-six years.*

---

## A LA CARTE
### 2333 North High Street (*north of OSU campus*)
### 614-294-6783

This is Columbus' answer to Berkeley's Chez Panisse. Chef Coralene Dimovich, San Francisco-born and -trained, specializes in the food styles of Eastern Europe. Her menu offers only four nightly entrées, heavy with lamb and veal and some seafood. She changes the entrées every week.

The setting is a busy, converted funeral home with 70 chairs inside and, in decent weather, 20 more on the front porch. It caters to the Ohio State University faculty and campus community.

Besides the modest prices, a la carte is noted locally for the excellent wine selections and service of same. There is no wine list. Patrons select their bottle from shops on any of the three floors, pay a dollar for corkage, and enjoy. Paper napkin service with no reservations.

*Price: About $5.50–$6.95 per person*
*Open Mon.–Sat. for lunch and dinner; closed Sun.*
*Accepts American Express, Visa, and MasterCard*

# BUXTON INN
## 313 East Broadway, Granville
### 614-587-0001

To the inch, Buxton Inn is 31 miles due east of downtown Columbus: out Broad St., which turns into State Route 16, and you'll find an old stagecoach stop that first opened in 1812.

While this is Ohio's oldest, continuously operated restaurant, history has little to do with the cuisine and supporting wine cellar. As for the wine, the list and cellar are second in Ohio only to Cincinnati's famed Maisonette. Cuisine is considered French/American with emphasis on seafoods.

Granville is home for Denison University, which gives the town an Ivy League flavor and appearance. The town also supports two other noted restaurants: Bryn Mawr Restaurant and the Granville Inn. If you make just two trips to Granville, skip the latter establishment and leave it to the tourists.

An added attraction for Buxton Inn is the unsupported rumor that ghosts occupy the three sleeping rooms. If you register alone, you still pay single rates.

*Price: About $20 per person*
*Open daily for lunch and dinner*
*Accepts American Express, Visa, and MasterCard*

# CHUTNEY'S, A CAFÉ
## In the Great Southern Hotel, 310 South High Street
### 614-228-3800

We must discuss the chef when writing about Chutney's, a café. This is a small, intimate café in an old hotel saved from the wrecking ball by local support, federal monies, and an approving city government interested in historical landmarks.

Luck of the draw landed a native of Cyprus here, Chef Remy Berdy, who arrived in this country with dual citizenship: Israel and Great Britain. His culinary culture was honed in Vienna, home of his mother, and by an apprenticeship at the Savoy Hotel in London. His signature dish in Columbus is tri-cultural; called simply Wellington's. It is British beef Wellington, but made with lean ground beef and not a filet, American style, that is seasoned with French and Cajun sauces; thus, the three-cuisine description.

Most dinner entrées are under $10: pastas, chicken, turkey, bay scallops presented with an array of baby vegetables from nearby Michigan hot house farms (poached cucumbers, fiddlehead ferns, baby okra, non-acidic yellow tomatoes, baby eggplants, and pattypan squash). The most expensive entrée may be a quail with a truffle stuffing, usually in the $12 range when available.

A menu standard is called *"fettuccine* and goats" which is spinach *fettuccine* combined with goat's cheese from nearby Amish farms, fresh broccoli and cauliflower, thyme, various herbs, and a chicken stock.

The chef is noted by name because he is a student of Lyon's Paul Bocuse and Illinois' Paul Banchet. If there is a restaurant in Columbus striving for world class, it is Chutney's, a café.

Local gourmands speak quietly about Chutney's, a café, because they think the chef has everything down except the prices. They *are* down: They just don't want him to raise them to Bocuse or Banchet levels. Chutney's, a café, is for serious gourmets in this market.

*Price: About $15–$18 per person*
*Open daily for lunch and dinner*
*Accepts all major credit cards*

---

## CIRCUS CHEF, A.K.A. EAT
### 3260 South High Street
**614-491-7393**

When the Toddle House chain went out of business in Columbus, some units became real restaurants. Some thirty years ago, this one became listed in the Yellow Pages as Circus Chef. However, the only hint that you are approaching a place serving food is a wooden panel of fading boards with two-foot-high letters reading "EAT."

EAT is a command, not an invitation. There are nine stools topped with ripped plastic, a Formica counter, and nine ashtrays, all being used at the same time. If one can avoid breathing both grease and cigarette smoke for half an hour, one can walk away filled to the limit with good meat loaf, ground steak, country-fried steak, or fresh pork. Friday is for fried fish, usually perch. Everything comes with potatoes and gravy and ordinary sliced bread.

Approach the lot with caution. Usually, there are six to a dozen 18-wheelers in the lot. (EAT has stand-up accommodations for those unable to elbow their way to a stool.)

Chief cook and rule-enforcer (she openly displays a baseball bat over the boxes of cornflakes) Margie Wright sets culinary and service standards: "Honey, if you don't like my food, don't you come back in here, hear?" Burping and scratching are acceptable. Toothpicks come in handy.

*Price: Under $10 per person*
*Open Mon.–Sat. for breakfast, lunch, and dinner; closed Sun.*
*No credit cards accepted*

# THE CLARMONT
In German Village, 684 South High Street
614-443-1125

The Clarmont opened in 1936 and is the result of a well-known divorce settlement involving the late owner, Frank Kondos. At the time, he was the winner. Today, one would think Kondos got the short end of the award. The Clarmont, still highly proper with an older clientele, has to be the second ugliest restaurant in Columbus. Aging and fading plastic signs proclaim it to be a steak house. That, it is.

The steak-and-baker crowd still frequents The Clarmont. They still order their Manhattans and Old Fashioneds. Gin fizzes still have callers. The Perrier crowd missed The Clarmont.

Kondos and present owners always kept a fried perch on the menu for Fridays. However, since early in 1984, venerable Clarmont devotees have seen change swim into their midst. Some forty percent of volume is now coming from fresh seafood arriving daily on the premises. There's even a lobby board pointing to "catch of the day," which may be grouper or orange roughy. A year ago when New Orleans' famed chef Paul Prudhomme popularized a scorched piece of redfish with hot seasonings, this Cajun dish surfaced on The Clarmont's bill of fare. Credit the present owner, Barry Zacks, who has never boiled a pot of water, but has lived most of his adult life on an expense account in our finer cities.

Five or six years ago, he asked the customary expense-account question in New Orleans: "Where is the best restaurant in town?" He was pointed to and became infatuated with K-Paul's Louisiana Kitchen.

That's how conventional restaurants change for the better. When Kondos was alive, The Clarmont had a jug of muscatel. For some years under Zacks, wine bottles at The Clarmont were opened in the parking lot, or some such place out-of-sight. With the coming of the Perrier set and lighter eaters, The Clarmont even has an acceptable wine list.

As for the steak crowd, be advised The Clarmont still prepares some of the finest beef in the Midwest. It is the only Columbus restaurant consistently to offer the true certified Angus filet and strip. And The Clarmont has cooks, not chefs.

Avoid: House salads unless you like iceberg lettuce; tartar sauce; looking at the dusty, tasteless artwork offered for sale on all walls; exterior signing; and the whole place on any Saturday when Ohio State University plays football in Columbus. The restaurant has the city's most expansive cigar counter.

*Price: About $15–$20 per person*
*Open daily for lunch and dinner*
*Accepts American Express, Visa, and MasterCard*

---

## DELIKATESA SLAVIC RESTAURANT
In Lane Shopping Center, 1615 West Lane Avenue
**614-488-2372**

This intimate, tiny, frilly-curtained offshoot of something from the country provinces prepares Eastern European dishes and pastries for a select following in Columbus. You must call in advance for directions. Even though it's in a shopping center, you'll need a guide dog to get you there once you reach the parking lot. Try the *borsch*. Avoid the limited wine choices, unless you find a single bottle to fit your tastes, and ask the server to open the bottle at tableside. In spite of all the old-world customs in evidence, they still seem to open bottles in the parking lot . . . or someplace remote.

*Price: About $9.50 per person*
*Open Mon.–Sat. for lunch and dinner; closed Sun.*
*Accepts American Express, Visa, and MasterCard*

---

## FIFTY-FIVE ON THE BOULEVARD
55 Nationwide Boulevard
**614-228-5555**

This is a full-service steak, veal, and chops restaurant, but the emphasis should be placed on the Cajun-style seafood. I admit, many of the recipes come from Paul Prudhomme's Louisiana Kitchen (book and restaurant), but authenticity and reverence for the original exists.

Shrimp and crab *au gratin* in eggplant is pure Prudhomme. Two jambalaya variations using duck, chicken, and seafood draw customers. Of course, blackened redfish is the headliner, beautifully and correctly prepared.

In mid-1985, this restaurant started experimenting with *tasso* (Cajun smoked ham) using various pasta combinations. Today, *tasso,* shrimp, oysters, and pasta are sufficient reason to experience the place in another of those downtown Columbus landmark renovations.

Avoid the shrimp *tempura.* And complain if your veal dishes do not fit the menu description. This place should stick to what it does best—anything from Prudhomme's bayou.

*Price: About $20 per person*
*Open Mon.–Fri. for lunch and dinner; Sat. and Sun. for dinner only*
*Accepts all major credit cards*

---

## HUNAN HOUSE
### 2350 East Dunblin–Granville Road
### 614-895-3330

Hunan House is a gem in a city with 34 Chinese restaurants. It is not a chain operation and is chef-operated (Peter Lee and Jason Chang). The menu has 82 entrées, all Hunan and Szechuan with specialties leaning toward chicken. One of the *best* listed dishes is the chicken and cashews.

The major flaw is failure to accept reservations for parties of less than five. However, it has been noted that a patron making a second or third visit is recognized as "family" and usually pushed ahead of the crowd.

*Price: About $15–$20 per person*
*Open daily for lunch and dinner*
*Accepts all major credit cards*

---

## JP'S BARBECUE RIBS
### 1072 East Main Street
### 614-258-3756

If you want barbecued pork ribs, call ahead. JP's is a takeout place in a tough section of town. But, they fill orders that go into the posher sections of town and are noted for filling orders of 800 to a thousand slabs. Many Columbusites send a cab for their orders. (Owner J. P. Makar caters annual football coaches' conclaves at Ohio State University. And football coaching in Ohio is big business.)

There is nothing "secret" about Makar's sauce recipe. He once told a reporter that he used a commercial sauce (Open Pit) and spiked it with cheap burgundy and any pepper that happened to be on the shelf. His ribs are oven-baked.

*Price: For a slab of 12–14 bones, $8.95*
*Open Mon.–Sat. for lunch and dinner; closed Sun.*
*No credit cards accepted*

# KATZINGER'S DELICATESSEN
## 475 South Third Street
### 614-228-DELI

Dr. Brown's Cel-Ray Tonic, *boudin* sourdough, Gundelsheim sauerkraut, Usinger's sausages, balsamic vinegar, Marshall's (from New York City) smoked whitefish, salmon, chubs, sturgeon, and all those Yuppie beverages, such as LaCroix Natural Lime, Vine Grape Soda, and Natural 90 Raspberry Soda, make this deli a true New York first cousin. But this Ohio native is a master when it comes to making its own knishes, matzo balls, and kreplach. Breads: Rye, pumpernickel, and challah work on a paint-board listing of 26 combination sandwiches and 26 singles.

The place seats only 40 in tight quarters, but the staff doesn't mingle other than to clear tables. The only thing missing from this delightful deli is the required New York surliness. Blintzes and Danish available for breakfasts starting at 8:30 A.M. No eggs, please.

Suggested afternoon delight: the "Just for Benson" combo brisket of beef, Bermuda onion, schmaltz, and chopped liver on rye—$3.65.

Avoid the chef's salad ($3.95). It looks tired.

*Price: Under $10 per person*
*Open daily for breakfast, lunch, and dinner*
*No credit cards accepted*

# L'ARMAGNAC
## 121 South Sixth Street (*opposite Grant Hospital*)
### 614-221-4046

At first bite, L'Armagnac is not for the masses, even though it is *cuisine bourgeois*—homestyle cooking. *Coq au vin, boeuf à la bourguignonne* for lunch in downtown Columbus? Even though it's been there for years, it's a well-kept secret. Owners of the place once ran a small advertisement, but they didn't know what to do with the business which suddenly appeared off the street. Their patrons are regulars and, usually, known by social status, income level, blood type, and professional affiliation.

Last year, the *American Bar Association Journal* listed L'Armagnac as one of their favored establishments. L'Armagnac looks like a real-estate holdout in mid-Manhattan. It's a true copy of an old French farmhouse and offers a cuisine befitting the surroundings. Owner-chef Tom Johnson offers six or seven *à la carte* entrées nightly, light desserts, and a classic, though limited, wine list. Parking is a problem here.

*Price: About $25 per person*
*Open Tues.–Sat. for lunch and dinner; Mon. for lunch only; closed Sun.*
*Accepts all major credit cards*

---

# LINDEY'S
## In German Village, 169 East Beck Street
### 614-228-4343

This is a loud, busy European-style bistro with a good fixed menu plus daily specials based on the market. Everything served in the evening is *à la carte* and expensive, but lunches for the near-downtown mob are reasonably priced.

There is a coffee house atmosphere, even though a long bar and crowded seating tend to dominate. Serious diners and confirmed boozers mix readily. Veal and experimental seafood dishes are appealing because the top hand in the place, Sue Doody, is something of a perfectionist. She ramrods while training talented chefs who move on to open their own restaurants.

Lindey's is not meant for tourists or those attending conventions. Lindey's is for lovers (of fine and changing cuisines) who attend Doody services regularly to compare last week's dinner with tonight's. Don't even think about getting into Lindey's on Thursday nights. This is jazz night and becomes something resembling New Orleans' Preservation Hall—only cleaner and with windows for those left in the street.

Service is excellent in Lindey's, but you'll always get the suggestion that the most expensive off-the-menu entrée is best that evening. As the waiters tend to neglect price, ask.

Lastly, while Lindey's is considered to be a classy "wine bar" in the intended context, it ain't. It is classy, but wine choices are limited to less than the best available in the market. Servers know nothing about the wines, so trust your own opinions and the labels. You're dining next to a vodka martini drinker and being served by a St. Pauli Girl.

Avoid the house bread which is something akin to an Iranian terrorist—hard enough to break your face and flaky.

Enjoy any dessert with a chocolate base.

Lindey's is for natives of German Village who can walk there each evening. There is zero parking in the neighborhood, so call a cab. If you are an experienced car parker in Times Square or downtown Beirut, then you may survive a trip to Lindey's.

*Price: About $15–$20 per person*
*Open daily for dinner; Mon.–Fri. for lunch*
*Accepts all major credit cards*

# MAX & ERMA'S
## In German Village, 739 South Third Street
### 614-444-0917

In Columbus, graduates from sliders and Wendy's move to higher burger levels when they first enter Max & Erma's. Hamburger history will someday bestow a bronze plate in front of this place as birthplace of this generation's gourmet hamburger concept.

In 1972, this once-dingy neighborhood saloon dumped beef jerky and soggy potato chips in favor of a hamburger put together by hand. That first one was ten ounces of lean beef, grilled with all the intended juices and air intact. Lights were turned down and prices hiked to fit the product. Columbus is a major college town (Ohio State University has 55,000 students on one campus within the city limits); the more affluent graduate students made the place headquarters for the Yuppie-preppie-trendy set seeking good food and beer.

There are now five Max & Erma's in Columbus. Expansion was necessary because all the copycats bidding for the gourmet market—Fuddruckers, Spoon's, and Flakey Jake's—moved into town for a test market shoot-out. Max still has the best weapon—and it's *still* a just-six-ounces-short-of-a-pound hamburger.

*Price: Most expensive burger is $6.25; full meal about $12–$15 per person*
*Open daily for lunch and dinner*
*Accepts all major credit cards*

# MONACO'S PALACE
## 4555 Cleveland Avenue
### 614-475-4817

This is a Northern Italian restaurant with a cast of thousands . . . mostly the entire Monaco family under management direction of the mama in the family, Anna Monaco, who works the kitchen seven days a week.

All the Monaco kids have specific assignments: front of house, bar, entertainment, banquets, dining room. The place handles massive parties and banquets, but the finer culinary touches are left for the single dining room. Monaco's is not a meatball place. It specializes in several veal entrées and its own pastries and all breads are baked on premises.

Italian restaurants in Columbus are noted for having some of the worst wine selections in the country. For some reason, Ohio's Italian community takes pride in offering only the poorest products exported from the boot. Monaco's, however, received help and advice from Jon Christensen, wine writer for the city's classy monthly, *Columbus Monthly*. The list remains modest, but is well represented by labels beyond a gandy dancer's chow car cooking wine.

*Price: About $20–$25 per person; gourmet dinner from $22.95–$38.95*
*Open daily for dinner only*
*Accepts American Express, Visa, and MasterCard*

---

## MORETTI'S ITALIAN FOODS
### 1447 Grandview Avenue
### 614-488-2104

At first glance one might think this is just another olive oil-and-pasta *porta fuori* ("carry-out"), but it is the on-premises bakery that's the real neighborhood attraction. Moretti's seats only 24 at small tables, which means elbows get tightly tucked. The place doesn't take reservations, so search out street parking space and then stand in line. There is no wine list, and the place is dry. The attractions are the fine pastas, baked goods, sugary desserts, and spinach *lasagne.* Think about ordering the *cannelloni* (egg noodles filled with a meat-tomato sauce) to go.

*Price: Lunch specials $3.95–$4.95; dinner specials $4.95–$9.95*
*Open Mon.–Sat. for lunch and dinner; closed Sun.*
*Accepts Visa and MasterCard*

---

## OTANI
### 5900 Roche Drive (*vicinity of I-71 and Route 161*)
### 614-431-3333

Other than the West Coast, Columbus, Ohio, has one of the largest Japanese communities in the nation. (Honda makes automobiles nearby.) Otani is the true *sushi* bar for craftsmen who speak the language.

Otani offers only 14 stools for *sushi* and *sashimi,* but has a large dining room for table service of *sukiyaki* and *tempura* dishes. Tokyo-trained *sushi* chefs prepare all foods.

For natives, *omakase* style is suggested to learn the ways of Japanese cuisine. *Maguro* (beginner's *sushi*) is a two-bite delicacy of bright red tuna. The *sushi* menu is extensive for this inland locale. And both lunch and dinner are served seven days a week, something uncommon in Ohio. But, like Yankees, our Japanese eat daily. Reservations are not accepted for the *sushi* bar.

*Price: About $15–$25 per person*
*Open daily for lunch and dinner*
*Accepts all major credit cards*

# THE PLAZA
## In the Hyatt on Capitol Square, 75 East State Street
### 614-228-1234

A full-service dining room serves three meals overlooking the city's finest view, a second-level vantage point to see Ohio's crumbling, but beautiful State House.

The culinary attraction here is not real estate, however. It is a noted hotel chef, Hermann Hiemeyer, Hyatt's "1985 Chef of the Year" for the 70-unit international chain. German-born and -educated, the man prepped for his Columbus finals in Maui, Singapore, and Seoul Hyatts, thus the international flavor imparted in an establishment too many locals put down as "hotel food."

The Plaza's menu changes every six months to reflect local market availabilities. If wild pheasant or duck is offered on a given evening, Chef Hermann personally attends to the chore. If burgers and chicken are barbecued in the summery Fountain Court outside, the executive chef stokes the coals. The city's most expansive Sunday brunch has become a personal signature for the chef.

Hiemeyer's grim dining room demeanor once brought the comment that he "appears to have the humor of a cabbage." A patron countered: "Yes, but it'll be fresh and colorful."

(The Plaza first brought designer plates [of food] to Columbus.)

Service on all levels is exceptional, except for the wines. The wine list is a list, not a display, and is almost undersold in this otherwise perfect dining setting. One may have to pry away a wine list or be pleased with the J. Lohr special bottling done for all Hyatts.

For two years running, this restaurant has been spotlighted in the city's largest daily newspaper as "Columbus' Finest Restaurant."

One item to avoid: A luncheon crab meat *fettuccine*—all pasta and zero crab meat.

*Price: About $13.50–$22.50 per person*
*Open daily for breakfast, lunch, and dinner*
*Accepts all major credit cards*

# THE REFECTORY
## 1092 Bethel Road (*Northwest Columbus*)
### 614-451-9774

The Refectory is Columbus' most outstanding wine restaurant with a cellar containing more than 10,000 bottles representing more than 400 labels.

While a full American bill of fare is there, The Refectory is known locally for various veal entrées, select desserts displayed on a cart, and atmosphere. On the latter, dining areas are in a rebuilt church, while the bar crowd is kept in school—an old one-room schoolhouse adjacent to the sanctuary. Reservations are necessary.

*Price: About $20–$25 per person*
*Open Mon.–Sat. for lunch and dinner; closed Sun.*
*Accepts all major credit cards*

# SCHMIDT'S SAUSAGE HAUS
## In German Village, 240 East Kossuth Street
### 614-444-6808

German Village is a privately restored area befitting its name. It covers some forty square blocks of the near-downtown area of Columbus. Residents of the Village sometimes contend they reside in this pleasant tourist attraction for the sole purpose of giving directions to Schmidt's, also a legitimate landmark.

It's a true German restaurant with homemade sausages, fattening pastries, all the required national dishes, plenty of beer, and loud singing supported by an oom-pah band. Stuffed cabbage is a house specialty. The same menu serves both lunch and dinner.

There are two copies of this restaurant in other sections of Columbus, but stick with this address, where the best stuff is made. Off-street parking is available.

*Price: About $10 per person*
*Open daily for lunch and dinner*
*Accepts American Express, Visa, and MasterCard*

# SUN TONG LUCK TEA HOUSE & RESTAURANT
## In Blacklick Plaza, 6517 East Livingston Avenue
### 614-863-2828

Sun Tong Luck is Columbus' *dim sum* restaurant. It seats only 44 and offers a limited Chinese menu. The restaurant does not have a liquor license, but brown bagging is permitted, if one is quiet about it.

*Price: Under $10 per person*
*Open Tues.–Sun. for lunch and dinner; closed Mon.*
*Accepts Visa and MasterCard*

# A TASTE OF WINE
## 1213 East Dublin–Granville Road
### 614-885-4084

This is one of Columbus' least known finer restaurants, possibly because it is located in the nondescript Ramada Inn (North), known locally for the introduction of Cruvinet service of wines plus a select list of better California labels.

On the meaty side of things, the house specialty is the crusty preparation of a rack of lamb (for two, about $29). Otherwise, A Taste of Wine is just another steak-and-chop house, but a good one to discount the term of "hotel food."

*Price: $10–$15 per person*
*Open Mon.–Sat. for lunch and dinner; closed Sun.*
*Accepts all major credit cards*

# THE TOP STEAK HOUSE
## 2891 East Main Street
### 614-231-8238

Long noted as a fine beef house known for its excellent charcoaling of strips and filets, now The Top has become a very good rib house.

The Top's bar is a popular fixture in the city as it is a holding pattern for serious beef eaters who are willing to soak up suds and other spirits while the long wait for seating takes place.

Lunches are busy with the rib and sandwich crowd. Atmosphere is dark and smoky. No reservations are accepted. Free parking.

*Price: About $20 per person*
*Open daily for lunch and dinner*
*Accepts all major credit cards*

---

## WENDY'S OLD FASHIONED HAMBURGERS
### 257 East Broad Street (*and 55 other locations*)
### 614-224-2635

In 1969, R. David Thomas, who came to Ohio as Colonel Sanders' advance man for fried chicken, decided he wanted what he believed to be a "real, honest, all-beef hamburger made fresh." Mostly, he wanted it in downtown Columbus. In a building that had been a graveyard for a dozen other businesses (nightclub, used cars, etc.), Thomas personally prepared and cooked that first fresh beef burger and topped it with fresh tomato, lettuce, and onion. Patties were cooked in front of the waiting customer. They were (and still are) so juicy you'll need more than a few napkins. For a long while, many people thought Wendy's was selling napkins because of their advertising thrust. Clara Peller's nationwide cry of "Where's the Beef?" changed all that.

Thomas, who named the first Columbus store after his red-haired daughter, Wendy, went on to honor her with 2,999 more in several countries and with several stock splits.

Wendy's No. 1 is still in the same location, now serving breakfast, baked potatoes, and offering a salad bar.

*Price: About $3–$5 per person*
*Open daily for breakfast, lunch, and dinner*
*No credit cards accepted*

---

## WHITE CASTLE
### Downtown at 30 North High Street (*and 13 other locations*)
### 614-464-1755

*The Columbus Dispatch* rates restaurants and includes a list of "best" dishes in various culinary arts, even fast foods. The paper's *best* 3 P.M. hamburger is Wendy's; the *best* 3 A.M. hamburger helper is a sack of White Castle "sliders" —a colloquialism for grease ball. Sliders are sold around the clock, 365 nights a year.

White Castle, privately owned by employees, operates only 200 stores in the eastern half the nation, while their crosstown group, Wendy's International, runs 3,000. Among all hamburger chains, White Castle is tops nationally for per unit sales—an average of $1.3 million each.

Part of the reason is the 28-cent cost per slider. Then, again, a lot of people like burgers made from frozen beef, that are fried and steamed with chopped onion, and placed on a soft bun marinated in grease.

White Castle Systems stop in Kansas City, but their fame is bicoastal or within limits covered by Federal Express. Aficionados get their "hamburgers to fly" orders on time for microwaving in bulk. An Arizona city group dials a toll-free (1-800-W-CASTLE) number to fill annual orders. Six years ago the sunny citizens called for 9,999 hamburgers and one cheeseburger "to go." White Castle put all Columbus outlets (14 now, then 9) to work. Fried, then freeze-wrapped and ice packed, they were flown to the party.

Early in 1985, it took three Bekins' 18-wheelers to transport 585,000 sliders to various western states.

It is an unwritten belief among boozers that a sack of sliders will sober up anyone. Also, every Columbus publication rating food and restaurants always credits White Castle with having the *best* coffee. Slider coffee works as well for the late martini consumer as it does for the guy sitting next to you with a crumpled brown bag of Sweet Lucy. For those objecting to the Sweet Lucy set, the single drive-thru is provided at Second Avenue and North High Street, a tough neighborhood.

Columbus has few all-night restaurants, but you'll be contented with the gravy and biscuits, fries and sliders here. All go well with a cold beer in a hotel room.

*Price: 28 cents for a hamburger*
*Open daily for lunch and dinner*
*No credit cards accepted*

---

# THE WORTHINGTON INN
## 649 High Street, Worthington
### 614-885-7700

Here's another historical site (154 years old) expensively rebuilt to include 23 sleeping rooms and a restaurant headed by Belgian chef Raymond Ameye, who combines both Flemish and French touches in his recipes.

A hundred years ago, this inn was fried chicken and Sunday suppers. Today, it is fresh coho salmon poached and served with a white wine and basil sauce; fish and scallops casserole; or a rare breast of Long Island duckling, sliced thin on a raspberry-duckstock sauce.

Today, it has one of the major wine cellars in Ohio. Still, there exists an age set in Central Ohio that thinks The Worthington Inn should be serving fried chicken and hot biscuits. There is a fixed-price menu which stuns many locals, not by the price, but by the excellent entrées.

*Price: About $25 per person*
*Open daily for lunch and dinner*
*Accepts American Express, Visa, and MasterCard*

---

# ZIGGY'S CONTINENTAL
## 3140 Riverside Drive
### 614-488-0605

Columbus' premier French restaurant with a chef-owner (Ziggy Allespach) is known for country cuisine approaches and service. But, as the truth now surfaces, about five percent of volume comes from the closer attention being given to the fresh pasta and Northern Italian recipes seeping into the kitchen.

Top item is *osso buco alla milanese,* a slice of veal shank braised in a veal sauce with white wine and flavored with lemon peel and anchovies.

One of the most expensive entrées is lobster *ralioli*—a whole lobster filled with a fish *mousse* and lobster chunks.

Lunches are moderate in price and walk-ins will be served readily. In the evenings, however, it is best to call well in advance for reservations. Ziggy's is where the rich, high-rollers dine in culinary splendor. Seldom is the place shared with tourists. The place is very small, *à la carte,* and supported by a 160-label list heavy with French and California wines. There are a few select German labels, but one has to ask for them, as the chef keeps them to himself.

*Price: About $30–$35 per person*
*Open Mon.–Sat. for lunch and dinner*
*Accepts all major credit cards*

# DALLAS

## *By Liz Logan*

**AMERICAN**
Gennie's Bishop Grill
Good Eats Café
Rosemarie's

**BAKERY**
La Madeleine

**BAR**
Andrew's
The Bronx

**BARBECUE**
Sonny Bryan's Smokehouse

**BRUNCH**
St. Martin's

**CHINESE**
Forbidden City

**CZECH**
Bohemia

**ECLECTIC**
The Mansion on Turtle Creek
Routh Street Café

**FRENCH**
Enjolie
The French Room
West End Oasis

**INDIAN**
Kebab-n-Kurry

**ITALIAN**
La Tosca

**MEXICAN**
Café Cancun
Genaro's Tropical
Gonzalez

**MIDDLE EASTERN**
Mr. Shishkabob

**SANDWICHES**
Schlotzky's

**SEAFOOD**
Aw Shucks
Café Pacific
Turtle Cove

## STEAKS AND CHOPS
Hoffbrau Steaks

## THAI
Siam Orchid

## UNIQUE PROPERTIES
Highland Park Cafeteria
Tolbert's Texas Chili Parlor

## VEGETARIAN
Bluebonnet Natural Foods
Grocery

## VIETNAMESE
Mai's

## WINE BAR/RESTAURANT
The Grape

Depending on your perspective, "Dallas is money" (the erstwhile ad campaign of a local bank), "the city that still works" *(Time)*, or "Oz on the prairie" (French restaurant critics Henri Gault and Christian Millau). Whatever Dallas is, it isn't the Wild West, or even the *Dallas* of prime-time TV fame—J.R.'s ranch is in Plano, a suburb north of the city. In reality, according to Jim Schutze, a columnist for the *Dallas Times-Herald,* the true Dallas epic would be called *Salad,* and would feature an actuarial executive who dines on mineral water and salad and rises at 2:30 A.M. to get in a 15-mile run before work.

However, neither the old Protestant work ethic nor the new asceticism stands a chance of trouncing the timeless ethic of conspicuous consumption that characterizes dining out in Dallas at its priciest. But, happily, these days the quality of restaurant food frequently matches the price tag at the city's temples of cuisine. (*D Magazine,* Dallas' city magazine, explored the phenomenon of "restaurant religion" in a recent cover story.)

It was not always so. Ten years ago, or even five, "fine dining" in Dallas was, for the most part, a pretty grim matter of choosing among restaurants that suffered from what *The New Yorker* writer Calvin Trillin has dubbed the "Maison de la Casa House, Continental Cuisine" syndrome. It is a measure of how far big-deal dining in Dallas has progressed that the restaurant considered a decade ago to be the city's gastronomic *ne plus ultra*— the Old Warsaw—is now regarded by most restaurant-goers to be a dusty relic of times past. These days, Dallas' most ambitious restaurants are serving up the New American Cuisine with a Southwestern accent, and the results rival New York and L.A.'s best.

*Liz Logan is the restaurant critic for* D Magazine. *She was formerly the Dallas-based food editor of* Texas Homes *magazine and restaurant critic of the* Dallas Morning News *and the* Orlando Sentinel.

# ANDREW'S

3301 McKinney Avenue (*at Hall Street*)   214-521-6535
14930 Midway (at Belt Line)   214-385-1613

More bar than restaurant, Andrew's is a notable exception to the don't-eat-where-you-drink rule. Ignore the setting (imitation New Orleans French Quarter) and the entertainment (fairly pitiful folk-style stuff), and concentrate on the food and drink. The salad is made of Boston lettuce, the boiled shrimp is fresh, and the black bean soup is *muy bueno*. That's all you need to know, except this: The "banana Miranda," in spite of its silly name, makes for a great rummy dessert drink.

*Price: About $10 per person*
*Open daily for lunch and dinner*
*Accepts all major credit cards*

# AW SHUCKS

3601 Greenville Avenue (*at Longview Street*)   214-821-9449
4535 Maple Street   214-522-4498

If you think of landlocked Dallas as a terrible place for seafood, you're wrong. Aw Shucks trucks its own oysters and shrimp up from the Gulf coast of Texas to two Dallas locations, and serves them up fresh and simple (usually, battered in cornmeal and lightly fried). The decor, which features counter setting, is minimal.

*Price: Under $10 per person*
*Open daily for lunch and dinner*
*No credit cards accepted*

# BLUEBONNET NATURAL FOODS GROCERY

## Greenville Avenue at Belmont Avenue
### 214-824-1740

This Austin-style (which is to say laid-back) health-food establishment and café serves unusually flavorful fare. If you're a health-food non-believer, try a fresh "papaya smoothie" and black bean *nachos*.

*Price: About $5 per person*
*Open daily for breakfast, lunch, and dinner*
*Accepts all major credit cards*

# BOHEMIA

## 2810 North Henderson Avenue (*just east of North Central Expressway*)
### 214-826-6209

Have you heard the one about Czech food? A week later and you're hungry again. At Bohemia, the attraction is sturdy Eastern European food served in delicately charming surroundings (lace tablecloths, Viennese waltzes). The *Wiener Schnitzel* is peerless. However, unless you're heavily committed to authenticity, forget the weighty dumplings in favor of simple boiled potatoes. Don't miss the homemade apple strudel.

*Price: About $20 per person*
*Open Tues.–Sun. for dinner only; closed Mon.*
*Accepts all major credit cards*

# THE BRONX

## 3835 Cedar Springs Road (*north of Oak Lawn Avenue*)
### 214-521-5821

The Bronx, a sophisticated, comfortable neighborhood bar with substantially gay patronage, is a local blessing for late-night sustenance, especially as a source of good coffee and dessert. Daily specials are better bets than standard menu items.

*Price: Under $10 per person*
*Open Mon.–Sat. for lunch and dinner; Sun. for brunch only*
*Accepts American Express, Visa, and MasterCard*

# CAFÉ CANCUN

4131 Lomo Alto (near Lemmon Avenue), Highland Park
### 214-559-4011
Caruth Plaza, Park Lane at Central Expressway    214-369-3712

Two locations of Café Cancun offer the same heart-of-Mexico (as opposed to Tex–Mex) fare in relaxed, tropical settings. *Enchiladas verdes* (the *verdes* refers to a tangy green sauce made of *tomatillos*) accompanied by black beans and Mexican rice and followed by coconut ice cream are a wonderful starting point for *gringos*. One of the killer margaritas would not be out of place, either.

*Price: About $15 per person*
*Open daily for lunch and dinner*
*Accepts all major credit cards*

# CAFÉ PACIFIC

24 Highland Park Village
### 214-526-1170

Because Café Pacific is a local favorite, the wait for a table can be an ordeal. However, the experience tends to confirm that the restaurant's habitués are onto something. Service is generally smooth and helpful, and the setting is delightful: a gleaming assemblage of brass, glass, and tile. And the overall attention to detail is impressive: A pepper grinder with white peppercorns is on each table, and water arrives with a thin slice of orange. The food usually equals the surroundings, with the simpler fish dishes a better bet than the more elaborate pasta options.

*Price: About $30 per person*
*Open daily for lunch and dinner*
*Accepts all major credit cards*

# ENJOLIE

In the Mandalay Four Seasons Hotel, 221 South Las Colinas
Boulevard, Irving
### 214-556-0800

Located in Las Colinas, a development near Dallas/Fort Worth Airport, Enjolie is the top-of-the-line restaurant of the Mandalay Four Seasons Hotel.

The restaurant offers discreetly classy surroundings (banquettes, blond wood, chiaroscuro lighting, marble floors, and plush carpeting) and good-to-great *nouvelle* French food. Don't miss the lobster in champagne sauce, pheasant *mousse* with blueberry sauce, and the peerless desserts. The complimentary cheese tray and selection of *petit fours* add to the experience without adding to the tab.

*Price: About $45 per person*
*Open Mon.–Fri. for lunch and dinner; Sat. for dinner only; closed Sun.*
*Accepts all major credit cards*

---

# FORBIDDEN CITY
## 5290 Belt Line Road
### 214-960-2999

Although Dallas has plenty of Chinese restaurants, excellent Chinese restaurants are in mysteriously short supply. Forbidden City is a notable exception to that rule. Here, unusually classy decor is the backdrop for carefully prepared dishes. Spinach with bean curd soup is just what the doctor ordered for the won ton weary. Two standout entrées are chef's shrimp, with snow peas, mushrooms, water chestnuts, and broccoli, and Szechuan chicken, a pleasing paradox that is at once subtle and spicy.

*Price: About $15 per person*
*Open daily for lunch and dinner*
*Accepts all major credit cards*

---

# THE FRENCH ROOM
## In the Adolphus Hotel, 1321 Commerce Street
### 214-742-8200

The most luxurious-looking restaurant in town is situated downtown. With its roseate baroque decor, the French Room has easily maintained its status as a visual knockout since its opening in 1981. Cherubs fly on the ceiling, peasants flirt in the murals, and the captains flutter in the dining room, serving a wide-ranging, sumptuous feast. The food, however, has had its ups and downs. Happily, these days the French Room's *nouvelle cuisine* is usually as good as it is expensive. (*Langoustine bisque* for an appetizer and *feuilletée* of seasonal fruit for dessert are musts.)

*Price: About $50 per person*
*Open Mon.–Sat. for dinner only; closed Sun.*
*Accepts all major credit cards*

# GENARO'S TROPICAL
## 5815 Live Oak Street (*at Skillman Street*)
### 214-827-9590

The "tropical" menu at Genaro's translates to Mexican fare with an emphasis on seafood and lighter dishes. This, together with a slick, Art Deco-inspired setting, has endeared the place to Dallas' Yuppies. All in all, Genaro's is a fine Mexican-with-a-twist option. The first-class margaritas do much to contribute to the pleasures of a languorous lunch or dilatory dinner.

*Price: About $15 per person*
*Open daily for lunch and dinner*
*Accepts all major credit cards*

# GENNIE'S BISHOP GRILL
## 308 North Bishop Avenue
### 214-946-1752

Gennie's is a Calvin Trillin fan's dream: tiny, cheap, out-of-the-way (in distinctly un-chic Oak Cliff)—and terrific. The blackboard menu changes daily, but always includes yeast rolls and chicken-fried steak. For dessert, there is banana pudding or peanut butter pie, both definitive Southern versions. Don't go if you're standoffish; you can count on sharing any empty seats at your table with others.

*Price: About $5 per person*
*Open Mon.–Fri. for lunch only; closed Sat. and Sun.*
*No credit cards accepted*

# GONZALEZ
## 4333 Maple Avenue (*at Wycliff Avenue*)
### 214-528-2960

Gonzalez serves no-frills Tex–Mex. The beauty of the place is its successful combination of home-style cooking and fast-food-style service and prices. You can even drive through and order easily portable food, such as *chalupas* (crisp-fried corn *tortillas* topped with a choice of *guacamole,* chicken, or beef) or *gorditas* (a Mexican sandwich made with thick rounds of cornmeal, instead of bread), to go, if you're so inclined. Not that there's anything wrong with the restaurant's plain but soulful interior: It's clean and pleasant. Incidentally, Gonzalez has my nomination for best cheap breakfast in the state. The *burritos* (homemade flour *tortillas* stuffed with potatoes and eggs, among other choices) go for $1.50 each.

*Price: About $5 per person*
*Open daily for breakfast, lunch, and dinner*
*Accepts all major credit cards*

---

# GOOD EATS CAFÉ
## 3531 Oak Lawn Avenue
### 214-521-1398

Hippified, Yuppified Southern food by way of Austin, where the original Good Eats Café is located. Hence, one may have black-eyed peas and mashed potatoes to accompany one's mesquite-grilled fish. Good Eats does the basics —omelets and burgers—especially well.

*Price: About $10 per person*
*Open daily for breakfast, lunch, and dinner*
*Accepts all major credit cards*

---

# THE GRAPE
## 2808 Greenville Avenue (*at Goodwin Avenue*)
### 214-823-0133

One of Dallas' oldest bistro/wine bars is still its best. The mushroom soup and *pâtés* are first rate, and the selection of wines by the glass is thoughtful, if limited.

*Price: About $15 per person*
*Open daily for lunch and dinner*
*Accepts all major credit cards*

---

# HIGHLAND PARK CAFETERIA
## 4611 Cole Avenue (*at Knox Street*), Highland Park
### 214-526-3801
## 5100 Belt Line Road, Sakowitz Village   214-934-8025

If the Mansion and Routh Street Café represent the new Southwestern cuisine, then Highland Park Cafeteria stands for the plain old home cooking of the Southwest. This local legend isn't called the Cadillac of cafeterias for nothing. The setting sparkles, and the array of always-fresh offerings emphasizes traditional Texas favorites, such as fried chicken, chicken-fried steak with cream gravy, *jalapeño* cornbread, resolutely non-*al dente* vegetables, peach cobbler, and zucchini-walnut muffins.

One warning: HPC's upstart second location in Sakowitz Village (in the glitzy wilds of North Dallas) is not as consistent as the original HPC, situated in discreetly rich Highland Park. Be prepared for a daunting-looking line, which moves swiftly.

*Price: About $5 per person*
*Open Mon.–Sat. for lunch and dinner; closed Sun.*
*No credit cards accepted*

---

## HOFFBRAU STEAKS
### 3205 Knox Street
**214-559-2680**

Nine beef choices and a lone breast of chicken: That's a pretty plain-spoken indication of the priorities at the Hoffbrau. The steaks, pan-sautéed with lemon butter, are among the best and most reasonably priced in the city. The decor is Texan-to-the-tenth-power, the jukebox features Waylon and Willie and the boys, and the line is nearly always long, so go early if you don't want to join it. Possibly the best one-stop introduction to what Texans hold dear.

*Price: About $15 per person*
*Open daily for lunch and dinner*
*Accepts all major credit cards*

---

## KEBAB-N-KURRY
### 401 North Central Expressway (*between Belt Line and Arapaho roads*), Richardson
**214-231-5556**

An anonymous-looking strip shopping center in Richardson (a suburb north of Dallas) is an unlikely place to find extraordinary Indian food. But Kebab-N-Kurry, despite its unlikely sounding name, serves up the best local versions of curry and kebabs, not to mention *tandoori* chicken, lamb in spinach sauce, and *ras malai* (the Indian version of cheesecake patties similar to dry cottage cheese, served with a sweet cream sauce, flavored with crushed pistachios and cardamom). There's another Kebab-n-Kurry at 2620 Walnut Hill Lane.

*Price: About $12 per person*
*Open daily for lunch and dinner*
*Accepts all major credit cards*

# LA MADELEINE
## 3072 Mockingbird Lane   214-696-6960
## 3906 Lemmon Avenue   214-521-0182

Even if you hated reading Proust (from whose *Remembrance of Things Past* madeleines derive their literary significance), La Madeleine may make you want to stand up and sing *La Marseillaise*. Patrick Esquerre's bakeries are the *vraie chose,* as a result of the imported-from-France baking crew and wood-burning ovens. And to judge from the throngs of customers lined up at most times of the day, Dallasites appreciate Gallic authenticity. La Madeleine's hours —until 9 P.M. daily—make it *très* convenient to take a break and chase away any traces of an oncoming *cafard.*

*Price: About $5 per person*
*Open daily till 9 P.M*
*No credit cards accepted*

# LA TOSCA
## 7713 Inwood Road (*just south of Lovers Lane*)
### 214-352-8373

Minimalist-chic, black-and-white decor lends a New Wave accent to the homemade pastas and off-the-beaten-path specialties, such as octopus salad and *tortellini alla nonna.* La Tosca is inconsistent, but at its best, it is far and away the most impressive Italian restaurant in town.

*Price: About $30 per person*
*Open Tues.–Sun. for dinner only; closed Mon.*
*Accepts all major credit cards*

# MAI'S
## 4812 Bryan Street (*southeast of Fitzhugh Avenue*)
### 214-826-9887

Mai's offers cheap, filling food at its local best. Good bets are the *cha gio,* a crisp, oily version of egg rolls with thin pastry enclosing ground meat, shredded carrots, and bean threads; *pho,* a beef broth-based soup with beef slices, rice noodles, green onions, and coriander; and duck and rice, which is just that. The beverages are a bonus: fresh lemonade and wonderful, killer iced coffee.

*Price: About $6 per person*
*Open Wed.–Sun. for lunch and dinner; closed Mon. and Tues.*
*No credit cards accepted*

---

# THE MANSION ON TURTLE CREEK
## 2821 Turtle Creek Boulevard
### 214-526-2121

Housed in the restored home of cotton trader Sheppard King, The Mansion on Turtle Creek was built by Dallas oil heiress Caroline Hunt Schoellkopf (who also built The Remington in Houston and The Bel-Air in Los Angeles), and in Texas, nobody does it better. Wolfgang Puck of L.A.'s famed Spago has consulted here for some time, and recently, Dean Fearing, a supernova among young Dallas chefs, was hired away from the Verandah Club at the Loew's Anatole to head up The Mansion's kitchen.

Fearing's sophisticated interpretations of Southwestern cuisine—such as smoked pheasant salad, roast yellow bell pepper soup with *serrano* chile cream, and grilled Gulf red snapper with *tomatillo-cilantro* sauce and *jícama* relish— are always imaginative, but never outlandish. What's more, the people-watching is peerless, if you're at all interested in anthropological observation of Dallas' upper crust at table. At The Mansion, the tab for dinner can match New York's highest prices if you work at it, but the value received is never in question.

The mansion itself is an example of gracious Texas style and elegant opulence—romantic and dignified at the same time.

*Price: About $50 per person*
*Open daily for breakfast, lunch, and dinner*
*Accepts all major credit cards*

---

# MR. SHISHKABOB
## 9454 Marsh Lane (*just north of Northwest Highway*)
### 214-350-9314

For unknown reasons, Middle Eastern restaurants have traditionally had a hard time making a go of it in Dallas. But if any establishment can break this jinx, Mr. Shishkabob can. The basics—*hummus, falafel,* and *kibbee*—are all commendable, and the blue-hued setting is pleasant.

*Price: About $10 per person*
*Open daily for lunch and dinner*
*Accepts Visa and MasterCard*

# ROSEMARIE'S
## 1411 North Zang Boulevard
### 214-946-4142

Rosemarie's is run by the same family that owns Gennie's Bishop Grill, and the food is equally fine. Although the truck stop/diner decor may not be as satisfyingly soulful as Gennie's (see page 205), Rosemarie's is larger, which makes it easier to go through the serving line and secure a table.

*Price: About $5 per person*
*Open Mon.–Fri. for lunch only; closed Sat. and Sun.*
*No credit cards accepted*

---

# ROUTH STREET CAFÉ
## 3005 Routh Street (*at Cedar Springs Road*)
### 214-871-7161

Routh Street Café is the product of the vision of chef Stephan Pyles and partner John Dayton, young proponents of the new Southwestern cuisine (a delicious solution to the dilemma of Texans torn between their desire to eat indigenously and to consume conspicuously). In a coral-and-gray-hued minimalist setting (the effect is one of austere luxury) designed by Tonny Foy of Fort Worth, Pyles serves up such fare as catfish *mousse,* grilled redfish with smoked-tomato *salsa,* Texas wild boar with sweet potato pancake and *tamarindo-ancho chile* sauce, and chocolate-pecan cake with *cherimoya*-custard sauce. The wide selection of wines by the glass from the all-American wine list is a bonus. Reservations are essential: Since it opened in late 1983, Routh Street Café has been the hottest ticket in town.

*Price: About $40–$45 per person*
*Open Mon.–Sat. for dinner only; closed Sun.*
*Accepts all major credit cards*

---

# SCHLOTZKY'S
## Multiple locations; see White Pages

The Schlotzky's sandwich—a mélange of ham, salami, lunch meat, Cheddar cheese, marinated black olives, lettuce, and tomato served on fresh-baked sourdough bread—originated in Austin. Now there are Schlotzky outlets all over the state, but the sandwich itself still tastes far from franchised.

*Price: About $5 per person*
*Open daily for lunch and dinner*
*No credit cards accepted*

# SONNY BRYAN'S SMOKEHOUSE
## 2202 Inwood Road
### 214-357-7120

Legendary isn't a term to throw around lightly when it comes to Texas barbecue. I'll say it anyway: Sonny Bryan's is a legendary local institution. In fact, the sociology of the place may be more interesting than the ribs and sliced beef, which are tasty, but would be unremarkable without the tangy sauce. *Toute* Dallas, from the respectably rich to the recklessly redneck, can be found at Sonny's, or at least it seems so if you're there at lunchtime. The soot-covered shack that houses Sonny's must be seen to be believed, and the seating consists of school desks. Get there early; when Bryan's is out of barbecue, they close the doors.

*Price: About $5 per person*
*Open daily for breakfast and lunch (until late afternoon)*
*No credit cards accepted*

# ST. MARTIN'S
## 3020 Greenville Avenue
### 214-826-0940

There's nothing like baroque music and soothing blue decor to inspire a feeling of well-being on a Sunday morning. If St. Martin's didn't serve food at all, one could still enjoy its calming aura. But, happily, the brunch offerings are calculated to fuel euphoria. They're not cheap, but the enjoyment-to-the-dollar ratio is high. To start, your $10.95 brings orange juice and complimentary champagne that is reasonably dry and drinkable. This is followed by a fresh fruit *macédoine.* Then comes a *croissant* and a large French coffee cup full of good, strong coffee. All of this is prologue to the entrée from the blackboard menu, which always includes commendable eggs Benedict.

*Price: Under $15 per person*
*Open daily for lunch and dinner*
*Accepts all major credit cards*

## SIAM ORCHID
### 1730 West Mockingbird Lane
#### 214-631-6505

Siam Orchid, with its "interesting" location (near the Denmark Adult Bookstore), tests the mettle of the ethnic-food adventurer. However, once you get inside, all is perfectly civilized, and the *moo satay*––grilled pork on a skewer, served with peanut sauce—may change your life. Other standouts are *pad thai* (rice noodles, shrimp, shredded pork, and bean sprouts, garnished with chili peppers and peanuts) and *gang ped* (chicken curry with a rosy, coconut-based, fresh mint-garnished sauce).

*Price: About $10 per person*
*Open daily for lunch and dinner*
*Accepts all major credit cards*

## TOLBERT'S TEXAS CHILI PARLOR
### 4544 McKinney Avenue (*near Knox Street*)
#### 214-522-4340

Stick to "Texas red" (chili, in other words), burgers, or "donkey tails" (deep-fried, flour *tortilla*-wrapped hot dogs served with hot mustard), with a gargantuan side order of homemade French fries at this monument to Texana. The beverages of choice: Dr Pepper and Lone Star beer, both practically part of the Texas state charter. Frank X. Tolbert was one of the originators of the now legendary Annual World Championship Chili Cookoff in Terlingua, and his own recipe is one of the best in town.

*Price: About $7 per person*
*Open daily for lunch and dinner*
*Accepts all major credit cards*

## TURTLE COVE
### 2731 West Northwest Highway
#### 214-350-9034

If you think of landlocked Dallas as a terrible place for seafood, you're wrong. Turtle Cove was one of the first restaurants in the nation to catch on to the affinity of fresh seafood and the now-ubiquitous mesquite wood, and chef Jeff Troiola keeps the menu on the move with constant innovations, such as oysters in *chile pesto* and salmon in orange-butter sauce. Steak is also available, but coming here for steak is like going to a singles bar for a philosophical discussion. The setting is casually attractive (even if this isn't the best part of town), and the good American wine list is a plus.

*Price: About $25 per person*
*Open daily for lunch and dinner*
*Accepts all major credit cards*

---

# WEST END OASIS
## Pacific Avenue at Market Street
### 214-698-9775

The food (*nouvelle* French with occasional nods to the Southwest) doesn't always live up to the setting (in the turn-of-the-century Texas Moline Building, with abundant natural light, serious art, handsome woodiness, and enclosed patio garden with water wall). However, when it does, the result is a breathtaking experience. Proprietor-character Richard Chase is often on the premises, which bodes well for the future of the Oasis.

*Price: About $40 per person*
*Open Tues.–Fri. for lunch; Tues.–Sun. for dinner; closed Mon.*
*Accepts all major credit cards*

# DAYTON

## By Doral Chenoweth

**CONTINENTAL**
King Cole
Peasant Stock

**ECLECTIC**
The Courtyard

**FRENCH**
L'Auberge

**SEAFOOD**
Jay's Restaurant

**STEAKS AND CHOPS**
The Pine Club

D ayton is a big factory town—skilled high-tech and military personnel with tastes to match their pocketbooks.

If you're driving an American vehicle, chances are some of the instruments or batteries came from Dayton. When you go into a restaurant in any part of the world today, chances are the check you receive will be one of those newfangled computerized printout things that tell you price, time, tax, and what you had for dessert. National Cash Register is the major employer in Dayton. So, whether you dine in Dayton or Dallas, you are part of the local economy.

The day is with us when your server takes an order tableside, turns and codes in your instructions to the kitchen via a serving-station computer which transmits to the chef. If there is tax in your state on some items, not on others, Big Brother will be telling you in one of those current restaurant checks that print out like an old Chinese laundry list. Credit Dayton's National Cash Register.

Dayton is home base for Wright-Patterson Air Base which includes both the Air Force Museum and this nation's major strategic strike force of heavy bombers. As such, in-out restaurant traffic takes on a world-class flavor. There has to be something for every taste—and pocketbook.

Dayton is home for the Ponderosa System, a no-tipping, frontier-like steak place generally credited with offering an early version of the all-you-can-eat salad bar . . . "the world's biggest, best salad bar" as Ponderosa CEO Jerry Office says while playing his own television pitchman. Assembly-line steak is big in Dayton.

Dayton has a handful of good restaurants, two of them—Peasant Stock and L'Auberge—are outstanding.

Hotel dining rooms in Dayton have long been noted for giving a bum rap to hotel food. Both Stouffer's and the Marriott make up the downtown pickings. Both attempt to make the scene with tony-sounding menu items, but both are best left for the tourist who is room-bound in a snowstorm.

Fortunately, Dayton downtown has two very good restaurants within walking distance of most hotels—King Cole and The Courtyard.

It was in Dayton that Domino's Pizza discovered a market for hotel guest delivery. That tells part of the culinary story. But, there is a bright side. Dayton (not Cincinnati) could lay claim to having Ohio's finest French restaurant. The Maisonette in Cincinnati is the long-acclaimed Frenchy for

Ohio. Now, however, a former Maisonette chef, Dieter Krug, serves Dayton from his six-year-old L'Auberge.

*Doral Chenoweth has covered Ohio restaurants for* The Columbus Dispatch *for twenty-six years.*

---

# THE COURTYARD
## In Mead Tower, Second and Main streets
### 513-461-3211

The Courtyard is an innovative establishment. If blackened redfish is the rage, The Courtyard will perfect the dish for Dayton tastes.

The Courtyard is a high-traffic luncheon spot for the paper empire employees of the Mead Corp. and for the nearby financial district. It is below street level, loaded with fresh flowers in a trendy green-pink-gray setting.

The pace is slower in the evenings, though the hotels send over big numbers of people who know how to escape coffee shop steak-and-fries.

The Courtyard does good things to duck breast when available. One evening it was grilled with plums and cassis. Usually the finer entrées, such as a sautéed veal with morels, may be off the menu, depending on availability in the market. Cuisine is best described as American Light.

A good wine list, something new for Dayton, leans heavily toward California chardonnays and cabernets and a limited number of French and German labels.

House salads are fresh, not overwhelmed with iceberg lettuce, and best with a Dijon mustard-cream sauce. If there is anything to avoid, it's the bay scallops appetizer. For a nickel under a five spot, you get 24 by count. Preparation is good, but pricing is out of sight.

Service is brisk and bistro-like. If you go at night, take a taxi, and call one before departing.

*Price: About $25–$30 per person*
*Open Mon.–Sat. for lunch and dinner; closed Sun.*
*Accepts all major credit cards*

# JAY'S RESTAURANT
In the Historical Oregon District, 225 East Sixth Street
### 513-222-2892

It should be called Jay's Seafood because this is the way natives relate to Jay's Restaurant. There are a couple of New York strips and a filet mignon listed, but locals go to The Pine Club (see page 219) for four-footed stuff.

Jay's is loud and crowded. If there is a bistro atmosphere in Dayton, Jay has it. Best advice is to have a firm reservation, or don't attempt to get a table. Reservations are taken for any evening except Saturday.

Jay's is most noted for pioneering the raw bar concept for Dayton. Fish that was swimming several hours before is flown via Piedmont Airlines from Boston on a daily run. Oysters in every manner is a house specialty.

Jay's is just two blocks from Dayton's convention center, so you may be competing with Shriners, war veterans, or tool-and-die makers.

*Price: About $18–$20 per person*
*Open Mon.–Sat. for lunch and dinner; Sun. for dinner only*
*Accepts all major credit cards*

# KING COLE
In the Kettering Tower Lobby, Second and Main streets
### 513-222-6771

Every city has at least one restaurant that must be considered "an institution." Every major city has one outstanding restaurant that makes all the legitimate dining guides. The King Cole is as much a major part of downtown Dayton as traffic lights.

The King Cole is where all civic, social, and most of the political problems of the city are discussed. Since the restaurant is close to the heart of some of America's Fortune 500 biggies, a lot of power business gets chomped over during lunch and dinner.

Cuisine is best described as an American original. However, a good supply of top chefs over the last three decades has injected fine Continental flavors into the classy bill of fare. King Cole is very much *à la carte*. In surroundings looking more like a fine art gallery, one receives perfect service. It's a coat and tie place, as well as a steak and lobster place.

*Price: About $25–$30 per person*
*Open Mon.–Sat. for lunch and dinner; closed Sun.*
*Accepts all major credit cards*

# L'AUBERGE
## 4120 Far Hills Avenue
### 513-299-5536

Cincinnati was once noted for having *all* the best French restaurants in Ohio. However, one newspaper reviewer in that Ohio River town wrote that "the best French restaurant in Cincinnati may be in Dayton, Ohio." It was at a time when Dieter Krug had departed Cincinnati's noted Maisonette for Dayton to open his own place. He took with him Josef Reif from Cincinnati's other noted restaurant, The Gourmet Room. Krug cooks. Reif greets.

What they have done is to create for Dayton a true replica of a French countryside home both inside and out.

Maître d' Reif brought from France the lace tablecloths, the silver service (including the carts), hand-painted French china, and antique coppers.

Both worked to eliminate any taint of haughtiness associated with formality. Both make periodic rounds of the tables to speak with each patron, both regular and casual visitor. L'Auberge draws the corporate traveler coming to Dayton from around the world. On any given night, half a dozen languages are spoken by servers handling business persons from Japan, Europe, even some of the Iron Curtain countries that send buyers to Dayton's high-tech warehouses.

What will they be getting on the table?

Depending on the season, they may be taking a culinary tour of the French provinces. Chef Krug, for his salute to Alsace-Lorraine, brought in regional sausages and ham from Strasbourg and Colmar, a crawfish appetizer with a recipe from Strasbourg, and a Rhine River salmon or trout for poaching. Krug repeats to patrons the fact that Alsace is known as "the pantry and larder of Europe."

Krug introduced seafood *pâté* to Dayton. His lobster bisque is in a light golden *roux* with parsley and a lobster claw. On any given evening, Krug may offer venison from Lorraine or Canada, a *médaillon* of lamb loin marinated with fresh garlic and pink peppercorns. Krug loves pink peppercorns.

L'Auberge is increasingly popular with Ohio's mobile population. This inn of many serving rooms and levels has become one of those "worth driving to" places that Midwesterners need.

*Price: About $30 per person*
*Open Mon.–Sat. for lunch and dinner; closed Sun.*
*Accepts all major credit cards*

# PEASANT STOCK

In the Town & Country Shopping Center, Stroop and Far
Hills avenues, Kettering
513-293-3900

Peasant Stock is a cross between a European country home and the old
department store tearoom—depending on the hour of the day.

Luncheons of asparagus *Mornay, quiches,* vegetarian-stuffed zucchini and
*croissant* sandwiches draw affluent shoppers from nearby posh neighborhoods.
Later afternoons are given over to tea time amid a decor befitting the finest
greenhouses of California. Peasant Stock was one of the early feeding atriums
in this country. It gets heavy traffic, despite its hard-to-find location in the
back of a shopping center mini-mall. You may have to ask directions twice.
And cabbies may have a hard time locating the place because it is a secret
closely kept by locals.

You will experience excellent entrées, such as a seafood casserole, excellent
chicken dishes, vegetarian-stuffed pasta shells, and a unique veal *Cordon Bleu,*
which makes the trip worthwhile.

Chefs at Peasant Stock may vary the daily fare, with visits from Mexican,
Oriental, or California cooks.

Evenings also offer lighter sides, such as *fettuccine al dente,* several *quiches*
with salads, or a roast turkey breast.

Wines are limited in number, but there are good choices.

Nearby, this same restaurant operates a takeout called Peasant Kitchen,
where gourmet pastas, breads, and salads are popular. There is, however, a
daily variety of prepared duck, venison, and liver *pâtés.* If you're returning
to a downtown hotel room, take a box lunch or dinner with you. Think about
a late-night snack of honey-curried chicken.

*Price: About $15 per person*
*Open Mon.–Sat. for lunch and dinner; closed Sun.*
*Accepts all major credit cards*

# THE PINE CLUB
1926 Brown Street
513-226-9064

If there is a K-Paul's Louisiana Kitchen for steak eaters, it is The Pine Club.
Neither takes reservations. Neither bothers with a tablecloth. Neither gives
even scant attention to a wine list. Both are rather smoky and dingy, but clean.

Both herd in willing customers by number, on a first-come, first-serve basis. And you could be sitting with total strangers.

Dayton's Pine Club doesn't have a celebrated chef like Paul Prudhomme. But it does have a sixty-year-old reputation for putting out excellent cuts of steak and little else. Oh, yes, it does have heavy cuts of lamb loin chops for the few in Dayton who are not addicted to good beef.

The Pine Club always does things right. The same people keep coming back and standing in line. The owner's wife, Mrs. David Hulme, once became so upset with having to stand in line for a table in her husband's crowded place that she huffed out and went elsewhere. When the governor of Ohio (Richard Celeste) is in town and wants to eat there, he sends one of his bodyguards around to hold a place in line.

Every entrée arrives with your historical choice of baked, fries, or hash browns, plus onion rings once described by *Fortune* magazine as "gossamer curlicues."

And every plate comes with a serving of very sweet stewed tomatoes, really a purée that some regulars want for dessert.

The Pine Club doesn't bother with dessert. The original owner's reasoning, in form of a rhetorical question: "Have you ever heard of someone eating three pieces of coconut pie after a meal? No, but someone might easily drink three grasshoppers."

The Pine Club is one of those old-fashioned steak places emphasizing a well-stocked bar as a centerpiece. Pine Clubbers sit, stand, or lean around a 35-stool bar housing more than 360 bottles of hard stuff. Wine, on the other hand, is so limited that a patron ordering a bottle is immediately tagged as a tourist. There are 98 seats, and you're expected to finish your meal within 55 minutes. The Pine Club has steak and service down to a minute science. Don't dally. Pay your check with cash. Someone's waiting for your table.

*Price: About $20–$25 per person*
*Open Mon.–Sat. for dinner only; closed Sun.*
*No credit cards accepted*

# DENVER

## By Michael Carlton

**AFGHAN**
Khyber Pass

**AMERICAN**
Brendles

**BRUNCH**
Kilgore Trouts

**CHINESE**
Yen King

**CONTINENTAL**
Café Giovanni
Duesenberg
Marquis Room

**FRENCH**
Dudley's
John's
Sebanton

**HAMBURGERS**
Fuddruckers

**HOTEL DINING ROOM**
Marquis Room

**INDIAN**
Tandoor

**ITALIAN**
Gabriel's
Ristorante Boccalino

**PIZZA**
Bonnie Brae Tavern

**STEAKS AND CHOPS**
Emil-Lene's Sirloin House

**SUBURBAN**
Alexandre's (Englewood)
Gabriel's (Georgetown)
John's (Boulder)
Mirabelle (Beaver Creek)
Sebanton (Longmont)
Unicorn (Littleton)

**UNIQUE PROPERTIES**
Buckhorn Exchange

**VIETNAMESE**
Chez Thoa
Unicorn

When Horace Greeley told his readers to "Go west young man," it was obvious he had never eaten a meal in Denver. Denver—the "heart of the Rocky Mountain Empire," as boosters call it—is not a great restaurant town. It isn't even a good restaurant town. But it is improving, if only at an *escargot*'s pace.

In the past five years there has been a steady, if maddeningly slow, improvement in the quality and variety of dining in Denver. Five years ago there weren't more than half a dozen restaurants worth the time and expense for an evening out. Today, there are probably a score of establishments providing excellent value for your money, and perhaps two or three that rank with the best in any city.

There are developments on the restaurant scene that indicate Denver is finally growing up after a century of serving second-rate food at first-rate prices. The growth of interesting restaurants in the vicinity of 17 Street just east of downtown has given that once-blighted area a welcome boost; and the burgeoning development of downtown has fostered some exciting new restaurants.

The proliferation of ethnic restaurants—Vietnamese, Indian, and Japanese—is exciting, even if the restaurants sometimes miss their mark, and the diversity only helps to make the palates of Denverites more sophisticated.

But not all the signs are positive. The Mexican restaurant situation is particularly lamentable, given the healthy Hispanic community in the city. There simply is not a great Mexican restaurant. And, it's not easy to find a good piece of fish, nor is there a memorable barbecue place.

Still, there has never been a more optimistic time in Denver dining; never a greater chance for this city to be there when the roll call of the great restaurant cities is taken. For much too long Denver's culinary horizons ended at quasi-French gourmet cooking that was neither French nor gourmet. Today those horizons seem limitless, bright and very exciting to anyone who has suffered through the city's culinary doldrums. Greeley's advice can now be taken with the confidence that there will be a decent meal at the end of the trail.

*Michael Carlton is restaurant critic for* The Denver Post.

# ALEXANDRE'S

## 8081 East Orchard Road, Englewood
### 303-741-4444

Visitors to South Denver's Tech Center, where a second city of sorts is rapidly growing, have had to contend with pretty ordinary fare in that area's many restaurants. There is a mediocre Chinese place, an ordinary steak restaurant, and a lot of other bistros that have made money because of the number of people who live and work and eat here, not because of their food.

Thankfully, Alexandre's changed all that. It is located in the trendy Beau Monde shopping center, a place of boutiques, splendid architecture, and a lot of money.

Alexandre's is small, probably able to serve no more than sixty patrons at one time. Its colors of rose and burgundy, gold and sand, work well together, and tables are spaced far enough apart for privacy.

The food here is the best in the southeast suburbs, and as good as most in the city. The baby grilled lobster served with marinated sirloin *tartare* is an especially good appetizer, and the butterflied shrimp sautéed in hickory smoked butter, cracked pepper, and thyme gets my vote for the best entrée. Also special are the scallops, which are beautifully presented on a bed of saffron rice rimmed with chive flowers.

The wine list has very few American selections, but a limited number of French wines should do the trick. The bar is very comfortable and well stocked (the house chardonnay is Lambert Bridge) and the entire feel about Alexandre's is right.

*Price: About $30 per person*
*Open Mon.–Fri. for lunch and dinner; Sat. for dinner only; closed Sun.*
*All major credit cards accepted*

# BONNIE BRAE TAVERN

## 740 South University Boulevard
### 303-777-2262

Bonnie Brae is located near the University of Denver, and if there is one thing those kids know, it's pizza. For years, students from the university have been coming to Bonnie Brae, sitting down at one of its crummy old booths or unstable tables and eating Denver's best pizza. The sauce on the pizzas here is thick and rich, the ingredients are piled generously on top, and the crust is just thick enough and wonderfully crisp.

If you don't want to stick around and look at all the college kids, Bonnie Brae has takeout.

*Price: House special (with everything but the kitchen sink), $13.75*
*Open Tues.–Sun. for lunch and dinner; closed Mon.*
*No credit cards accepted*

---

# BRENDLES
## 1624 Market Street
### 303-893-3588

Brendles has long touted its "new American cuisine" and has successfully continued to serve food that is both innovative and perfectly cooked. Although it has gone through a change in ownership, the temporary loss of its liquor license, and an increasing amount of competition in the Market Street area, Brendles continues to prosper.

Located in the basement of an old warehouse, Brendles has warm brick walls and booths of rich wood and brass. This is a comfortable place for a rendezvous, a nice place to steal a kiss in a very private booth, and a perfect place for a confidential conversation.

The kitchen uses the freshest available produce, fish, and meats. In line with its American theme, you can usually get venison and elk, and trout fresh from Rocky Mountain lakes. Pine nuts are popular here, and there are a number of dishes for vegetarians. The wine list is long and the service is Colorado casual but efficient.

*Price: About $30 per person*
*Open Mon.–Fri. for lunch and dinner; Sat. for dinner only; closed Sun.*
*Accepts all major credit cards*

---

# BUCKHORN EXCHANGE
## 1000 Osage Street
### 303-534-9505

Everyone—and I mean everyone—who visits Denver should have lunch or dinner at the Buckhorn Exchange. An hour spent at the Buckhorn is an hour well spent, not so much for the food as for the atmosphere, the feeling of the Old West.

Buffalo Bill Cody used to drink here, a lot of cowboys got blind drunk at the Buckhorn in days past, and a lot of stockbrokers still do. The place creaks with history. Old wooden floors carry the scuff marks of a thousand boots, and the walls are hung with a wild menagerie of creatures. While you eat you will be stared at by hundreds of glassy eyes sitting in the stuffed heads of elk and antelope, buffalo and mule deer.

The food isn't bad, either. You can get a passable hamburger here; the buffalo steak is excellent and the Rocky Mountain oysters are the best you are likely to find in Colorado. The wine list is terrible, but there is plenty of beer and a shot of redeye or two to put you in the mood. Sometimes you expect Buffalo Bill himself to walk through the front door.

*Price: About $15 per person*
*Open Mon.–Fri. for lunch and dinner; Sat. and Sun. for dinner only*
*Accepts all major credit cards*

---

# CAFÉ GIOVANNI
## 1515 Market Street
### 303-825-6555

This restaurant has consistently been the best in Denver. Owners Jan and Jack Leone are always on hand to oversee service (Jan) and cooking (Jack), and the result is a very pleasant combination of both. The two restaurateurs were among the first to move into the old warehouse district of Denver and take advantage of the century-old architecture in the area. The restaurant is on three levels: The basement is used for special parties; the ground floor holds a handsome bar and a comfortable lounge area; and the second floor is the main dining room. Ask for a booth if you want real privacy, and insist on the front room, which overlooks Market Street. The back can be too crowded and noisy.

The menu changes with the seasons, but there is always a superb treatment of roast duckling, and always a light fish cooked in parchment paper. The desserts are the best in Denver; the wine list isn't. Make reservations well in advance, especially for weekends.

*Price: About $25 per person*
*Open Mon.–Fri. for lunch and dinner; Sat. for dinner only; closed Sun.*
*Accepts all major credit cards*

---

# CHEZ THOA
## 158 Fillmore Street
### 303-355-2323

Thoa Fink, a Vietnamese who married an American doctor during the Vietnamese war and moved to Denver, has made Vietnam's loss Denver's very great gain. Under her direction, Chez Thoa has become one of the most desirable places to eat lunch and dinner in the city.

Although offering both French and Vietnamese food, it is the Vietnamese side of the menu that is the most appealing. From light spring rolls to lemon grass chicken, the Vietnamese dishes are all first rate, a statement that can't be made for some of the French selections.

The restaurant is located in the basement of an office building, and parking in the popular Cherry Creek area is sometimes hard to come by, but your patience will be well rewarded. This is a very dressy restaurant, with hordes of society matrons crowding the place during lunch, and successful business-people making it a top dining spot in the evenings. A very worthwhile choice for a special night out, if only for the chance to talk with Madam Thoa.

*Price: About $25 per person*
*Open Tues.–Sat. for lunch and dinner; closed Sun. and Mon.*
*Accepts all major credit cards*

---

# DUDLEY'S
## 1120 East Sixth Avenue
### 303-777-2790

Innovation is the trademark of Dudley's, the favorite restaurant of the Yuppie crowd in Denver. It was the first to serve *nouvelle cuisine,* the first fine restaurant to move into the Sixth Avenue neighborhood, and the first to hire young, exciting chefs and allow them to experiment.

Some of the best food in Denver is served here, and certainly the most visually pleasing. The presentation is flawless in Dudley's dishes, tapestries of color and texture. Dudley's is justly famous for its sweetbreads, but nearly everything on the constantly changing menu is worth trying.

Decor is decidedly of secondary interest, with too-bright lights, dull decorations, and noise combining to numb the senses a bit. Service is very good, if a bit informal. The wine list is quite limited but intelligently selected and fairly priced.

*Price: About $25 per person*
*Open Mon.–Sat. for lunch and dinner; closed Sun.*
*Accepts all major credit cards*

# DUESENBERG
## 1745 South Acoma Street
### 303-698-1888

Duesenberg used to be better known for its collection of cars than for its food, but with a new management and a new direction, this restaurant is now serving some of the finest meals in Denver. The cars are still there—a splendid collection of vintage automobiles rivaling Harrah's Nevada collections—but they are no longer the focus for serious diners.

Today the restaurant pleases its customers with a salad of warm duck strips, pecans, *radicchio,* and endive; *médaillons* of lobster served in a light chive cream sauce is also popular. The wine list is enormous and well priced, but the service can be a bit amateurish for such an elegant place.

After a particularly satisfying meal, patrons often walk to the adjoining warehouse to look at the cars, but it is usually the food, not the automobiles, that impresses most.

*Price: About $25 per person*
*Open Tues.–Sat. for dinner only; closed Sun.*
*Accepts all major credit cards*

# EMIL-LENE'S SIRLOIN HOUSE
## 16000 Smith Road, Aurora
### 303-366-6674

This is a dumpy-looking place, and looks are not deceiving. It resembles an old roadhouse and there is a tree growing in the middle of the restaurant. The tables are rough and have no tablecloths and the napkins are paper. Sometimes when it rains you might get a little wet, and the parking lot will become mud. There are a lot of truckers eating here, some good ole boys who look like they came directly off the set of an old John Wayne movie, and the waitresses will probably outweigh you by at least fifty pounds.

Still, if you want a steak—a guaranteed thick, juicy Colorado piece of beef cooked to perfection—there's no other place that comes even remotely close to Emil-lene's.

With your steak you'll get a relish tray, a house salad, a big pile of spaghetti, and either French fries or a baked potato. Don't bother with the wine, just order a beer and enjoy one of the best pieces of beef in the West.

*Price: About $15 per person*
*Open Mon.–Sat. for lunch and dinner; Sun. for dinner only*
*Accepts Visa and MasterCard*

# FUDDRUCKERS
## 3055 South Parker Road
### 303-671-6020

How fresh is the beef at Fuddruckers? All you have to do is look into the adjoining butcher shop to see fresh slabs of beef being ground into hamburger to know how fresh it is. The hamburgers at Fuddruckers are plump, juicy, and grilled with a wonderful mesquite flavor that reminds you of the Texas hill country. There are cartons of ruby-red tomatoes, mountains of onions, and huge containers of cheese and other goodies you can put on your burgers. Each patron can be as creative as he wishes with his burger, and some of the resulting combinations are interesting, if a bit bizarre.

There's plenty of beer to be had, some indifferent wine, and tables that are more utilitarian than comfortable. You wait in line here to give your order and receive your burger, but a waiter will bring you a bucket of beer if you need help washing down the burgers.

After dinner have a brownie or a chocolate chip cookie while you watch the huge stream of people who, like you, have discovered a nearly perfect hamburger.

*Price: About $8 per person*
*Open daily for lunch and dinner*
*Accepts all major credit cards*

# GABRIEL'S
## 1025 Rose Street, Georgetown
### 303-569-2700

Georgetown is a small town of large charm, one of the leading weekend destinations for Denverites who want to escape the city smog and breathe the clean air at 9,000 feet. The town is liberally blessed with Victorian homes, Clear Creek runs clear and fast through the center of the town, and the antique stores beckon to avid shoppers.

But, perhaps, the best feature of Georgetown is Gabriel's, Colorado's finest Italian restaurant. The owner, Gabriel, used to cook at the nearby Berthoud Falls Inn, and his skill in the kitchen made it one of the most popular restaurants with visitors to the mountains. Now that he has opened his own place, Gabriel is helping keep Georgetown on the map.

His restaurant is in a very modest building and would win no awards from *Architectural Digest* for decor. Ah, but the food. Gabriel makes splendid pastas and his veal dishes are the thing of dreams. His prices are low, his wines are inexpensive, and his service is well intentioned, if a bit slow. His restaurant is the best reason to visit this historic little village. It is well worth the 1-hour drive from Denver.

*Price: About $20 per person*
*Open Mon.–Sat. for dinner only; closed Sun.*
*Accepts all major credit cards*

---

# JOHN'S
## 2338 Pearl Street, Boulder
### 303-444-5232

Denver's sister city, Boulder, is about a 45-minute drive away—a drive that can seem very long indeed, on a dark and stormy night when the snow shrieks out of the mountains. But, once you reach the warmth of John's, the weather is forgotten. A fireplace will warm you, the small dining rooms will welcome you, and the casual good taste of everything will relax you. And, best of all, the food will please you and make the drive to Boulder seem of no importance. The scallops sautéed with capers and lemon will start the meal nicely, and the boneless chicken in a creamy mustard sauce or the veal chop served with green peppercorns will provide a moment of intense pleasure.

John's is located in a house reminiscent of one you would find in the old South, and the atmosphere is properly relaxed—a nice change from the rushing to and fro in so many French restaurants. This place is more Provence than Paris and the food reflects that fact. The service is very friendly and efficient. The wine list is not extensive.

*Price: About $25 per person*
*Open daily for dinner only*
*Accepts all major credit cards*

---

# KHYBER PASS
## In the Galleria, at Colorado Boulevard
### 303-692-8500

In a city not known for its ethnic restaurants, Khyber Pass is a pleasant surprise. Although there aren't many Afghans in Colorado, the restaurant has found a loyal following of people who delight in unusual cuisine.

Located in a high-rise office building, Khyber Pass isn't easy to find, but the effort is well spent, for the restaurant is one of the small gems of Denver dining. Particularly pleasing are the various *kabobs*—lamb, beef, and chicken —and the curries, some of which are hot enough to send you screaming to the nearest water (perhaps that's why there is a splashing fountain in the middle of the dining room). For adventuresome diners, a good appetizer is lamb brains; for the less adventurous, fried eggplant served with a garlic-yogurt sauce is a good choice.

The dining room looks out over Denver and the mountains, and there are two small rooms for those who wish to sit on carpets and dine in the traditional Afghan way. Each night there is a demonstration of belly dancing by some of the most skilled practitioners.

*Price: About $15 per person*
*Open Mon.–Sat. for lunch and dinner; closed Sun.*
*Accepts all major credit cards*

# KILGORE TROUTS
## 30963 Hilltop Drive, Evergreen
### 303-674-0222

I'm tired of brunch buffets. I'm tired of standing in line while the little old lady in front of me spends 10 minutes deciding between the pickled eggs and the smoked eel. I like a brunch where I can sit down, sip a glass of champagne, and have someone wait on me.

And that's one reason I like the weekend brunch at Kilgore Trouts. The other reason I like it is that the food is good. There is even entertainment some Sundays, usually a couple of local musicians playing a piano and a flute.

From the outside, Kilgore Trouts isn't much, a small adobe building hunkering down on a hilltop. But inside, it is very warm in a rustic sort of way. There are wooden floors and lots of beams, wooden tables covered with lace tablecloths, and lots of baskets hang from the ceilings. The dining rooms are small and a certain intimacy is maintained to help relax you.

Brunch varies, but you can usually get some waffles, a good piece of salmon, and generous orders of eggs accompanied by spicy homemade sausage. There is a small but comfortable bar for waiting and a fairly priced but limited wine selection.

*Price: About $12 per person*
*Open Sun.–Fri. for lunch and dinner; Sat. for dinner only*
*Accepts all major credit cards*

# MARQUIS ROOM
## In the Fairmont Hotel, 1750 Welton Street
### 303-295-5825

The Marquis Room is easily the most elegant dining room in Denver. High-backed, plush chairs surround linen-covered tables in the middle of the room, while large, private banquettes range around the perimeter. Gold-plated place plates glitter, fine crystal and silver shimmer in the candlelight, and all is good with the world when you are dining at the Marquis Room. The service is flawless. Never is an ashtray allowed to receive more than one cigarette before it is removed, never is your wineglass allowed to empty, never is a knife used for more than one course.

The food, happily, is as good as the service and setting. The Marquis chefs are trained in the Fairmont tradition and offer excellent, if not particularly innovative, fare. The sole here is as good a piece of fish as you will get in Denver, and the steaks are consistently tender and flavorful.

Sometimes the room tends to go a bit overboard, such as serving *sorbet* in the middle of a lighted ice swan, but the experience is very special and allows Westerners to dress up for a change. The wine list is one of the best in town and although it tends to be pricey, it is extensive enough to please anyone.

*Price: About $30 per person*
*Open Mon.–Fri. for lunch and dinner; Sat. and Sun. for dinner only*
*Accepts all major credit cards*

# MIRABELLE
## Beaver Creek
### 303-949-7728

Beaver Creek is the most luxurious ski resort in Colorado. Gerald Ford lives there; so does the former oil minister of Mexico, comfortably encased in a 28,000-square-foot house that cost about $7 million. This—more than Vail, more than Aspen—is where the rich and famous come to play. It follows naturally enough that these folks want a first-rate restaurant when they come to the high Rockies.

And that is what Pierre and Catherine Luc have provided them. Mirabelle's is located in a ranch home dating to 1898 that positively oozes with charm. Polished cotton curtains crown the windows, fine linens cover the tables, surrounded by comfortable chairs, and placed far enough apart to ensure privacy while making that big deal.

The food is the stuff of culinary dreams. Particularly good starters are the veal and pork country *pâté* and the fish *mousseline* served with a lobster and *beurre blanc* sauce, while entrées run the gamut from a delicate poached salmon, garnished with mussels, mushrooms, and bay scallops, to grilled lamb chops served with a hollandaise sauce, lightly flavored with fresh mint. The desserts are the best in Colorado. If you are anywhere in the mountains, you owe it to yourself to try Mirabelle. Plan on about an hour and a half driving time from Denver.

Price: About $25 per person
Open Tues.–Sun. for dinner only
No credit cards accepted

## RISTORANTE BOCCALINO
### 158 Fillmore Street
#### 303-393-6544

This is perhaps the most consistently popular restaurant in Denver—and with good reason. This was one of the first restaurants in town to offer "gourmet pizza" and unusual pasta dishes. The angel's hair pasta with black mushrooms and *prosciutto* and the *bucatini* served with *porcini* mushrooms and a tarragon cream sauce are solid bestsellers. The small entrée menu features such items as chicken breasts rolled with *prosciutto* and *mozzarella* and baked with a tomato sauce, and grilled pork tenderloin in a Chianti sauce.

The decor includes lots of wood and brass and simple place settings on wooden tables; it is designed as a place to see and be seen. If you want a table, particularly one on the terrace in warm weather, show up early or be prepared to wait for a long time.

All the wines, with the exception of champagne, are Italian, to encourage diners to learn more about the little-known wines of the country. Dress is informal and patrons tend to be young and successful.

Price: $15 per person
Open Mon.–Sat. for lunch and dinner; closed Sun.
Accepts all major credit cards

## SEBANTON
### 424 Main Street, Longmont
#### 303-776-3686

Longmont isn't much of a town, a one-horse sort of place, a middle-class town where a big night out usually consists of grabbing a beer at the neighborhood bar and then going home to watch *Dynasty* or *Dallas*.

Why, then, did Sebanton, arguably the best French restaurant in Colorado, locate there? For one thing, it didn't cost much to put a restaurant in the simple storefront in which it sits, and the owner reasoned his food was so good people would drive the 45 minutes from Denver to try it. He was right.

Sebanton has a constantly changing menu, with that day's offerings posted on a small blackboard. There is usually some duckling, a steak or two, and

232 D E N V E R

some of the best veal around. The *Lyonnaise* sausage, when available, is splendid, and the French onion soup is as good as you're likely to find anywhere. The atmosphere is pure French bistro, with checkered tablecloths, uncomfortable chairs, lots of noise, and too many bright lights—in short, terrific!

*Price: About $20 per person*
*Open Tues.–Fri. for lunch and dinner; Sat. for dinner only; closed Sun.*
*Accepts all major credit cards*

## TANDOOR

### 1514 Blake Street
**303-572-9071**

If you will forgive the page of the menu that lists "Gunga Din's Special Drinks," featuring such horrid names as "Holy Cow," "Bombay Bomb," "Rogue Elephant," and "Bleeding Madras," you might like this place.

The curries are hot but not killing, and the *tandoori* specialties roasted in a traditional clay oven are outstanding. Particularly good is the shrimp *tandoori*. The restaurant also offers a number of vegetarian entrées and a wide selection of Indian breads freshly baked on the premises. Appetizers, such as *samosas* (fresh vegetables, potatoes, and meat in a crisp pastry shell) and *jhingha pakoras* (batter-fried shrimp) are served with a fine mint chutney.

Elephants are everywhere in sight. You open Tandoor's front door by pulling on a small, gold elephant trunk, and there are elephant murals and paintings on most of the walls. There is some fine woodwork decorating this restored warehouse, and much of the original brickwork is still visible. Wines are limited (Robert Mondavi is the house white), but there is a good selection of beers, which go better with curries.

*Price: About $10 per person*
*Open daily for lunch and dinner*
*Accepts all major credit cards*

## UNICORN

### 699 West Littleton Boulevard, Littleton
**303-794-6118**

Like Chez Thoa, Unicorn bills itself as a French/Vietnamese restaurant and, like Chez Thoa, you are better off staying with the Vietnamese.

Unicorn is run by an entire Vietnamese family—grandfathers, fathers, grandmothers, mothers, sons, and daughters. All are refugees from that sad country.

The restaurant is in a tiny house and tables are jammed together seemingly haphazardly. There is no atmosphere to speak of, and little romance to be had. But the food makes up for the lack of ambience. Shrimps on a skewer and imperial rolls to start, a white asparagus and crab soup next, followed by a chicken breast sautéed in soy sauce and served with three different kinds of Oriental mushrooms over steamed rice make a splendid meal. If you give 24-hours' notice you can have the house roast duckling prepared according to an old family recipe.

*Price: About $15 per person*
*Open Mon.–Fri. for lunch and dinner; Sat. for dinner only; closed Sun.*
*Accepts all major credit cards*

---

# YEN KING
### 3425 South Oleander Court
#### 303-692-0468

In a city that had, at last count, more than 150 Chinese restaurants, and in a city that has a significant Oriental population, there is a surprising lack of good Chinese food. The best of the lot is Yen King, a modest restaurant owned by a Hong Kong Chinese who previously worked in San Francisco and has brought his considerable skills over the Rockies. Although serving both Szechuan and Mandarin cuisine, Szechuan is your best bet. The chilies make the food wonderfully fragrant and spicy. Sizzling shrimp and rice is especially good and—given a day's notice—the restaurant's skilled chefs can turn out a very respectable Peking duck.

Like most Chinese restaurants, the decor isn't much, and the service can be quite slow on a busy evening, but the food is worth the inconvenience.

*Price: About $10 per person*
*Open Mon.–Fri. for lunch and dinner; Sat. and Sun. for dinner only*
*Accepts all major credit cards*

# DETROIT

## *BY MOLLY ABRAHAM*

**AMERICAN**
London Chop House
333 East

**BAR**
Flood's Bar & Grille

**BREAKFAST**
The Original Pancake House

**BRUNCH**
Harlequin Café

**CHINESE**
Wong's Eatery

**CONTINENTAL**
Golden Mushroom
The Lark
Mason-Girardot Manor
The Money Tree
Restaurant St. Regis
Sparky Herbert's

**FRENCH**
Elizabeth's
Pontchartrain Wine Cellars
Van Dyke Place

**GERMAN**
Jacoby's Since 1904

**GREEK**
Greektown

**HOTEL DINING ROOM**
Restaurant St. Regis
333 East

**INDIAN**
Royal Bengal

**ITALIAN**
Salvatore Scallopini

**JAPANESE**
Nippon Kai

**JEWISH**
Stage & Company

**KOREAN**
Koreana

## MIDDLE EASTERN
Phoenicia
The Sheik

## OPEN LATE
Greektown
Niki's

## PANORAMA
Park Terrace

## PIZZA
Maria's
Niki's

## POLISH
Polonia
Royal Eagle

## SEAFOOD
Benjie's Fish & Seafood
Joe Muer's

## STEAKS AND CHOPS
Carl's Chop House
London Chop House

## SUBURBAN
Benjie's Fish & Seafood (Sylvan Lake)
The Earle (Ann Arbor)
Nippon Kai (Clawson)
Park Terrace (Windsor, Ont.)
Wong's Eatery (Windsor, Ont.)

## VEGETARIAN
D.C. Watt
Garden Café

## WINE BAR/RESTAURANT
Traffic Jam

Despite our massive convention center and collective civic eagerness to attract visitors, even the most chauvinistic Detroiter would have to admit that this is not yet a tourist city. With our neglected waterfront beginning to blossom, our first festival marketplace, Trappers Alley, in full swing, the Renaissance Center standing as a silver symbol of urban survival, things seem to be in the process of changing dramatically.

The very fact that we have not been a prime destination for tourists has been a positive factor where restaurants are concerned. We simply do not have the gaudy, overpriced, tourist-trap sort of places that spring up where travelers are more prevalent. Restaurants depend primarily on locals, who value consistency above glitz.

Our restaurants tend to be, if anything, almost self-effacing. Aside from the venerable London Chop House, established by the late Lester Gruber in the 1930s and now run reverently in his footsteps by a devotee, Max Pincus, and

Joe Muer's seafood house, still going strong after fifty-seven years under one family, Detroit dining places are not well known nationally.

Yet there are some that will come as a revelation to those who think of Detroit solely as a blue-collar city. Because there is no real restaurant enclave here, the restaurants cannot easily be pinpointed on a map, but tend to be scattered throughout the tri-county area (Wayne, Oakland, and Macomb) which makes up Metropolitan Detroit, a sprawling area in southeastern Michigan.

Aside from downtown Detroit's Monroe Street, where the single block of vintage buildings houses a number of Greek restaurants (take your pick) as well as the five-level, skylit Trappers Alley festival market, a handsomely adapted red-brick edifice that once was a center for fur traders (thus its name), all within easy strolling distance, restaurants require something of a search by those not familiar with the area.

And since public transportation is virtually non-existent, a car and a map of Michigan are absolute necessities—something I suppose can be pardoned of the place that put America on wheels.

Many fine restaurants require a drive of 30 to 45 minutes from the center of the city. There are also interesting ones tucked along obscure streets in city neighborhoods where ethnic groups once settled. Some of the restaurants remain as the only vestige of those groups whose younger members long since moved to the suburbs.

Though restaurant trends are a year or two slower to arrive here than on the trendy coasts, they do arrive eventually. And so we have the inescapable pastas, the Cajun dishes, *sushi* bars, and emporia of things Szechuan. And, of course, fish and seafood even in neighborhood saloons. Some wonderful young chefs are turning out the new American cuisine in several restaurants.

But our city is really stronger in the classics. People here are less fickle than those in more trend-afflicted areas where restaurants come and go like the seasons. Detroiters are more likely to stick with a tried-and-true, and the newcomer has to be very good to woo them away from an old favorite.

In the long run, that's a plus. And another is the proximity of Windsor, Ontario, Canada, a town of 200,000 easily approachable by the Detroit–Windsor tunnel under the river or by the glowing Ambassador Bridge, decked by night with a graceful necklace of white lights.

Windsor adds its array of restaurants to the variety found in Detroit. In fact, Windsor restaurants depend upon the U.S. traffic, some estimating that as much as 70 percent of their business comes rolling across the river. This is really a tale of two cities, Detroit and Windsor.

*Molly Abraham is restaurant critic for the* Detroit Free Press *and was formerly restaurant critic for the* Detroit News. *She is author of* Restaurants of Detroit *(1985), published by the Detroit Free Press.*

# BENJIE'S FISH & SEAFOOD
## 2650 Orchard Lake Road, Sylvan Lake
### 313-682-7730

Seasonal, fresh fish and seafood and a well-stocked wine bar make an ideal combination, and that is exactly what's offered here in a simple room done in polished oak softened with dark-blue print tablecloths and candlelight. It is very unpretentious, in keeping with both its far suburban location and the personality of its owner, the rotund Benjie Pearlman, a former teacher, who makes frequent forays through the dining room in his chef's whites.

Methods of preparation include plain broiling, mesquite or char-broiling, frying, sautéing, or baking, allowing lots of room for personal preference. Accompaniments are redskin potatoes, stewed tomatoes, house-baked honey-wheat-caraway bread, and green salads. Dinner only, with a lavish seafood buffet on Sundays from late afternoon through early evening.

*Price: About $20 per person*
*Open daily for dinner*
*Accepts all major credit cards*

# CARL'S CHOP HOUSE
## 3020 Grand River Avenue
### 313-833-0700

Detroiters have been eating steak here for more than fifty years, and if there is a more classic American beef house around, I can't imagine it. The rooms are huge—seemingly big enough to house the blue-ribbon cattle that find their way to the plates—the atmosphere anything but soothing, the service no-nonsense rather than pampering, the artworks on the wall strictly flea market, and the foliage plastic. It seems as if everyone is on his or her way to the ballgame or the hockey arena—and that's often true.

Yet for standing prime rib roast of beef, porterhouse steak, or any number of other solid American dishes of the ilk, Carl's is dependable. The full-course meal survives here, from relish tray, cottage cheese, marinated herring, and soup through salad and choice of potato. The restaurant, which is the antithesis of trendy, is open every day of the year with one exception, Christmas Day.

*Price: About $20 per person*
*Open Mon.–Sat. for lunch and dinner; Sun. for dinner only*
*Accepts all major credit cards*

# D. C. WATT

## 10223 Whittier Avenue

### 313-372-7884

Diane Christine Watt is the person behind the name, and her small, rosy restaurant is her personal statement. The calm, soothing air about the place very much reflects Diane, a talented cook who prepares red meatless—but not fishless or chickenless—dishes from chili to pizza on either a *filo* or whole wheat dough base. Whole wheat *linguine* noodles are brightened with shrimp, mussels, clams, and lobster, clam chowder is outstanding, and there is none of that holier-than-thou attitude found in some vegetarian spots. No smoking here and no bar.

*Price: About $16 per person*
*Open Tues.–Fri. for lunch and dinner; Sat. for dinner only; closed Sun. and Mon.*
*No credit cards accepted*

---

# THE EARLE

## 121 West Washington at Ashley, Ann Arbor

### (313) 994-0211

The cellar-level, dinner-only restaurant in a hundred-year-old building in the heart of downtown Ann Arbor is dusky and romantically lit by flickering candles on bare-topped tables. The overall effect of the understated beiges and browns, the brick, rough-hewn stone, and dark wood is just right for the hearty menu which features country-French and country-Italian dishes.

Just ten choices of hors d'oeuvres, two soups, five salads, and the same number of pastas, and ten main courses are offered at The Earle. Occasionally, a dish runs out before the evening is over—a sign that the kitchen does indeed specialize in the fresh. The choice of vegetables is particularly imaginative— rutabaga purée, braised fennel, roasted peppers.

Chef Shelley Caughey Adams—a Culinary Institute graduate, who gets a credit line on the menu, as well she should—keeps the kitchen creative by changing the menu at least every three months.

The tone and theme remain the same, however: Where one menu offered bluefish sautéed with smoked salmon butter, another has bluefish with a creamy mustard sauce. Where the veal scallopine was served with garlic, lemon, and fresh rosemary, another version offers the veal scallops with a fresh sage butter. The fish stew differs slightly in embellishments from a previous one.

Both bread and ice cream are housemade and both are superlative, as is the wine list.

*Price: About $20 per person*
*Open daily for dinner only, except from late May to early September*
*Accepts all major credit cards*

---

## ELIZABETH'S
### 227 Hutton Street, Northville
### 313-348-0575

Fixed-price dinners and à la carte lunches are exquisitely served at this Victorian cottage, which is the domain of a talented husband-and-wife team, Doug and Elizabeth (Beth) Campbell, who visit France every year in search of inspiration and who even import their tubs of butter from Normandy. At $31 per person for a complete dinner from, say, *cassoulet* of *escargots* served in a silver pot with a lid topped with a silver snail (the Campbells collect snail pieces) right down to a poached pear drizzled with chocolate and napped with lemon sauce, the quality is exceptional. The cottage is immaculate and nicely decorated with appropriate artworks, including provincial handcrafts and photos of hot-air balloons, another of the Campbells' passions. Reservations are almost always necessary at dinner. No bar.

*Price: Fixed price at $31 per person*
*Open Mon.–Fri. for lunch; Mon.–Sat. for dinner only; closed Sun.*
*Accepts all major credit cards*

---

## FLOOD'S BAR & GRILLE
### 731 St. Antoine Street
### 313-963-1090

The beautifully preserved Detroit Cornice & Slate Building is a historic treasure on its own, and inside its first-floor space is a gathering spot which mixes antiques, Art Deco, and contemporary art wittily put together by the clever Ron Rea, who has begun to make his mark in Detroit restaurant design. A spectacular bar, topped with a reproduction of an ornate cornice, dominates the room, but there are also tables around the perimeter under antique French posters against brick walls for those who prefer to escape the bar action. A menu of pastas and chicken and shrimp dishes, as well as burgers and sandwiches, gives the interesting urban crowd something to choose from.

*Price: About $12 per person*
*Open Mon.–Fri. for lunch and dinner; Sat. for dinner only; closed Sun.*
*Accepts all major credit cards*

# GARDEN CAFÉ
301 Fisher Building, West Grand Boulevard at Second
Avenue
313-873-7888

An Art Deco treasure, the Fisher Building is simply gorgeous, a tribute to the Fisher Brothers of Fisher Body fame who built it in 1928, lavishing marble, terrazzo, mosaics, and brass everywhere. Tucked on the third floor within its marble hallways is a delightful café, part of a gallery of contemporary crafts, where pure vegetarian soups, salads, sandwiches, and house-made desserts are served at lunch only.

The building itself is worth a visit, and the café provides a respite after admiring the handiwork that has so handsomely survived the years.

*Price: About $10 per person*
*Open Mon.–Sat. for lunch only*
*No credit cards accepted*

# GOLDEN MUSHROOM
10 Mile Road (*just west of Southfield Road*), Southfield
313-559-4230

A most unlikely location for ambitious cuisine, set as it is at a busy intersection next door to a service station. But it is serene within and very much a reflection of the personality of its Czechoslovakian chef, Milos Cihelka, who regularly features game birds, venison, mallard ducks, and pheasant along with veal and seafood and is meticulous about the quality of his raw materials, from Michigan morels to seasonal green vegetables.

The French-dominated wine list is in keeping with a menu featuring caviar, house-smoked salmon, and fresh Dover sole.

Cihelka's staff of young chefs has become a poaching ground for other restaurants looking for help, a tribute to his teaching abilities.

*Price: About $35 per person*
*Open Mon.–Fri. for lunch; Sat. for dinner only; closed Sun.*
*Accepts all major credit cards*

# GREEKTOWN

The 501 block of Monroe Street (*between St. Antoine and Beaubien streets*)

Late is a relative term. And in Detroit, late means, with very few exceptions, a kitchen open until midnight. The best bet after 1 A.M. is to head for the Greek restaurants on this block, where a dozen or so are tucked into the squatty, painted brick buildings under vintage streetlights. The biggest and most glamorous is the Pegasus Taverna, on the first floor of the Trappers Alley festival market, and the one with the greatest local popularity is the New Hellas Café, perched on the corner of Monroe and St. Antoine. Most serve until 2 A.M., a few until 3. Menus range from lamb in dozens of variations to *moussaka, pastitsio,* spinach pie, flaming cheese, stuffed grape leaves, Greek salads, and the wonderful pale brown bread chopped into hunks and pulled apart with the hands.

*Price: About $10 per person*
*Accepts all major credit cards*

# HARLEQUIN CAFÉ

8047 Agnes Street
313-331-0922

The premises once housed an old-fashioned soda fountain/drugstore complete with wood and glass apothecary cabinets. The setting was made to order for a restaurant. The marble counter with its backless swivel stools has become the bar, and the lighted cabinets house small pieces of sculpture and other artworks by a local artist.

The continental cuisine, ranging from calf's liver Madagascar to sweetbreads, is served at tables covered in apricot and black. Sunday brunch is particularly appealing, offering freshly squeezed orange juice, champagne, fresh fruit, eggs Benedict, and a choice of seafood, veal, or turkey main dishes, salad, pastries, and coffee, at about $11 per person. Soft jazz accompanies the dining, from 11 A.M. to 4 P.M.

*Price: About $20 per person at dinner*
*Open Tues.–Sun. for lunch and dinner; closed Mon.*
*Accepts all major credit cards*

# JACOBY'S SINCE 1904
## 624 Brush Street
### 313-962-7067

While German food has fallen from favor here, and a couple of other German restaurants have shuttered, this vintage saloon continues to be a favorite, probably because of its rich vintage atmosphere and comfortable informality. This is the real thing, a tin-ceilinged saloon run by the descendants of Albert P. and Minnie Jacoby, who indeed started the whole thing in 1904. Dark beer is on tap at the mirrored mahogany backbar, tables are clustered together clubbily with a view of an open kitchen from which emanate excellent sandwiches on dark pumpernickel bread and more solid German dishes, including *sauerbraten* and potato pancakes, *knackwurst, bratwurst,* or *weisswurst* served with sauerkraut or red cabbage and German potato salad.

*Price: About $15 per person*
*Open Mon.–Sat. for lunch and dinner; Sun. for brunch only*
*Accepts all major credit cards*

# JOE MUER'S
## 2000 Gratiot Avenue
### 313-567-1088

The seven-table oyster bar established by the original Joe Muer in 1929 has now grown to a restaurant that seats 420. But that massive size is nicely disguised by the flowing series of dining rooms in which people are spread out through the brick-walled, softly lit building and the third and fourth generations of Muers are still in charge.

Fresh fish and seafood—on a daily dated menu—are very simply prepared here. This is not a house of sauces, but one which depends on the freshness of the raw materials rather than embellishments. Most of the fish is broiled in a special gas oven devised by a chef who was with Muer's for forty years. The service is highly professional, the tables covered with those heavy white linen cloths that aren't seen much anymore, the housekeeping exemplary.

If it swims and it's in season, it's on the menu here. An excellent, California-dominated wine list accompanies the menu, along with the sort of simple vegetables, salads, and ice cream desserts that befit the classic American seafood house theme.

*Price: About $35 per person*
*Open Mon.–Fri. for lunch and dinner; Sat. for dinner only; closed Sun.*
*Accepts all major credit cards*

# KOREANA
## 14537 Gratiot Avenue
### 313-372-6601

The room is redolent of the "three flavors of Korea," garlic, chile peppers, and sesame seeds, and the fare, influenced by China and Japan yet with a distinct character of its own, is assertive and spicy.

Lunches and dinners both include the house soup, meat-stuffed noodles in chicken broth dusted with bright bits of scallion, rice in little individual covered bowls, the national condiment, *kim chee* (pickled cabbage), as well as a bit of fresh spinach, bean sprouts, and salty strips of dried fish.

Main courses are varied, from Korean egg rolls served in multiples of eight to rice noodles with beef and vegetables and shrimp or vegetable *tempura*. Scallion-nut chicken is particularly tasty as is *bi bim bap,* a blend of beef, fresh spinach, rice, egg, and fiery sauce. Dishes can be adapted for vegetarians.

The setting for all this is a former steak house, now nicely disguised with Oriental trappings. Service is kindly and helpful, always a plus in an ethnic café.

*Price: About $10 per person*
*Open daily for lunch and dinner*
*Accepts all major credit cards*

# THE LARK
## Farmington Road (*just north of Maple Road*), West Bloomfield
### 313-661-4466

A country inn done up with Portuguese tile, terra-cotta pottery, and fresh flowers is the setting for fixed-price dinners beginning with a selection from the hors d'oeuvres cart, followed by soup, fresh pasta, or a hot appetizer. Salad is served following the chosen main course from a list that changes bimonthly but usually includes the house favorite fish, pickerel in varying treatments, as well as duck, rack of lamb, Chinese oven-roasted duckling, veal, and, often, abalone flown in from California.

The price of the main course determines the price of dinner ($28 to $42), with desserts extra. An especially nice feature is the selection of wines to fit each course, at $14 per person. The brick-walled garden produces herbs all summer, and in warm weather it's the setting for outdoor grilling over

mesquite. There are just a few seats for dessert and coffee *al fresco*.
The restaurant seats only fifty and reservations are almost always necessary.

*Price: About $50 per person*
*Open Tues.–Sat. for dinner only; closed Sun. and Mon.*
*Accepts all major credit cards*

---

## LONDON CHOP HOUSE
### 155 West Congress Street
#### 313-962-0277

The Chop House, as it's called by habitués, is noisy and cluttered, a jumble of colors and contrasting styles in a cellar room in which the bar parallels the somewhat serpentine dining area, where tables and some highly desirable banquettes are closely packed under caricatures of the celebrities who have passed through the doors over the past two generations.

At first glance it looks like anything but an ambitious restaurant. But, as is so often the case, looks are deceiving. It's possible to get pretty much what you want here, as long as it's in season someplace in the world.

Chef Jimmy Schmidt, the acclaimed protégé of late owner Lester Gruber, recently departed but has been replaced with Tom Varee, who respects his raw materials and who is perfectly comfortable presiding over a kitchen that turns out chopped beefsteak ($16.95) and, as the menu calls them, "a mess of perch" and a "heap of frogs' legs" as well as his airy seafood and veal dishes.

Desserts are equally impressive, especially the French vanilla ice cream with caramel-pecan sauce and the frozen hazelnut *soufflé*. The wine list and liqueurs list are outstanding.

*Price: About $50 per person*
*Open Mon.–Sat. for lunch and dinner; closed Sun.*
*Accepts all major credit cards*

---

## MARIA'S
### 19220 Grand River Avenue
#### 313-533-2910

Yes, it still exists, the classic little neighborhood Italian restaurant with red-and-white checked cloths, candlewax dripping over the sides of Chianti bottles, closely packed tables, cheery young help. It all works, and the hearty toppings on the chewy house crust rate with the town's best—and this is a town that loves its pizza.

Tossed salads with Caesar-style dressing come along with pizza at no extra charge and there are basic Italian pastas and veals in addition. There is an adequate Italian wine list. This is a very unpretentious and comfortable place.

*Price: Under $10 per person*
*Open Mon.–Fri. for lunch and dinner; Sat. and Sun. for dinner only*
*No credit cards accepted*

---

## MASON-GIRARDOT MANOR
### 3202 Peter Street, Windsor, Ontario, Canada
#### 519-253-9212

The three main-floor rooms of an appealing Victorian structure are decorated in keeping with the age of the circa-1877 house, and the setting, the courtesy, and the gentility of the founding family make this an especially interesting spot.

The small menu of classic dishes, such as fillet of sole *à la meunière,* steak Diane, and veal tenderloin, is as nicely served as it is carefully prepared. The Turkish touch evident in the chilled yogurt and cucumber soup and the *boerek* on the appetizer list only hints at the nationality of the owners, but upstairs, a full-fledged Turkish room spotlights the cuisine of their former home. Reservations are usually advisable.

*Price: About $18 per person*
*Open Tues.–Fri. for lunch and dinner; Sat. and Sun. for dinner only; closed Mon.*
*Accepts all major credit cards*

---

## THE MONEY TREE
### 333 Fort Street
#### 313-961-2445

A talented chef, Ed Janos, barely thirty, has made his mark in a downtown restaurant which has steadily improved since opening in 1971. Like so many chefs of his generation, Janos is a stickler for fresh, seasonal ingredients, and his menu is a constantly changing one, with fresh pastas, game, duckling, veal, and fresh salmon among his favorites.

The pastry tray is a focal point in a room that is basically quite casual, despite the sophistication of the fare. The copper-sheathed tables can be a little too close together for comfort sometimes, but the atmosphere, with its soothing light level and background music by a jazz flute–guitar duo, and window wall looking out on the passing city scene, are suitably soft. Service by a predominately young, shirt-sleeved staff is kindly and competent.

*Price: About $35 per person*
*Open Mon. for breakfast and lunch; Tues.–Fri. for breakfast, lunch, and dinner;*
*Sat. for dinner only; closed Sun.*
*Accepts all major credit cards*

---

# NIKI'S
### 735 Beaubien Street
### 313-961-4303

The pizza here is Greek: That simply means the cheese is *kasseri* instead of *mozzarella* and the sausage is the Greek version of *pepperoni*. It's the thick, square, chewy variety. The high-ceilinged, bare-tabled room is as basic as can be and the place stays open very late. Other good choices on the menu are *gyro* sandwiches and *pita* burgers.

*Price: About $7 per person*
*Open daily for lunch and dinner*
*Accepts all major credit cards*

---

# NIPPON KAI
### 511 West 14 Mile Road, Clawson
### 313-288-3210

A surprise awaits you inside what appears to be a nondescript building in this quiet suburb. The setting is Japanese to the smallest detail, even to the decorative covers on the coat hangers. The room is done in ivory and golden wood. A *sushi* bar stretches across one wall and there is table seating as well as *tatami* rooms on the other. Translucent rice paper masks windows, allowing the imagination to supply the Japanese garden outside. Waitresses wear brilliantly-hued kimonos and the proprietor's grandmother's red, metallic gold, and blue wedding kimono is hung as a work of art on one wall.

There are dining options ranging from the offerings at the *sushi* bar to *à la carte* dishes to a trio of complete dinners ranging from what the house calls "tidbit combination," through soup, salad of thin cucumbers, seaweed, and bits of seafood in a vinaigrette, *tempura*, *sukiyaki,* and lobster. Pickled vegetables, green tea, and dessert round out the assortment.

The covered lacquer bowls and footed cedar planks for *sashimi* and *sushi* and platters in a variety of patterns and textures are in keeping with the sense of harmony throughout.

*Price: About $25 per person*
*Open Mon.–Fri. for lunch and dinner; Sat. and Sun. for dinner only*
*Accepts all major credit cards*

---

## THE ORIGINAL PANCAKE HOUSE

### 20273 Mack Avenue, Grosse Pointe Woods   313-884-4144
### 19355 West 10 Mile Road, Southfield   313-357-3399

Whether you want breakfast at the traditional time of day or late afternoon or even in the evening (until 9 P.M.), these Early American dining rooms are always ready to serve it, from flapjacks, *crêpes,* baked fruit-laden pancakes that fluff up like *soufflés* to waffles and omelets, accompanied by that endangered species, freshly squeezed orange juice, and coffee with heavy cream. The pancakes are made from batters of unbleached, hard wheat flour. People wait in line, newspapers in hand, on weekends. The fare is worth the wait.

*Price: About $7 per person*
*Open daily for breakfast until 9 P.M*
*No credit cards accepted*

---

## PARK TERRACE

### In the Hilton International Hotel, 277 Riverside Drive, Windsor, Ontario, Canada
### 313-962-3834 (*in Detroit*)

A rare hotel dining room: first, for its view, a sweeping one of the Detroit River and the city from virtually every table in the bi-level room, second for its interesting regional menu, spotlighting Ontario and Great Lakes foods from fresh fish and local veal to quail and rabbit. The menu changes with each season, and features a complete, fixed-price "Heritage dinner," which is a notable bargain at from $20.75 to $23.75 (Canadian). With the exchange rate favoring the dollar, Windsor dining has become more appealing than ever.

*Price: Fixed price at $20–$23.75 (Canadian) per person*
*Open daily for breakfast, lunch, and dinner*
*Accepts all major credit cards*

# PHOENICIA
## 588 North Woodward Avenue, Birmingham
### 313-644-3122

The fare is Lebanese and absolutely authentic, from appetizers of fava bean salad, marinated olives, pickled turnips, eggplant stuffed with walnuts and garlic to numerous marinated, well-spiced lamb and chicken entrées and stickily sweet honey-bathed pastries.

Phoenicia is somewhat exotic for this chic town with its coterie of exclusive boutiques and expensive housing. Proprietor Sameer Eid, who virtually worked his way out here by putting in some hard years in a lesser location, is an experienced restaurateur who knows how to please a demanding clientele with well-prepared, nicely served food in a subdued setting of beige and forest green.

*Price: About $18 per person*
*Open Mon.–Sat. for lunch and dinner; closed Sun.*
*Accepts all major credit cards*

# POLONIA
## 2934 Yemans Street, Hamtramck
### 313-873-8432

The spirit of the Workmen's Cooperative, which originated in this tin-ceilinged room in 1927 in order to speak Polish and eat *pierogi* and stuffed cabbage, still imbues the place, and the menu is virtually the same. Peer into the kitchen, where old-fashioned Polish fare is being prepared: jellied pigs' feet, dough for *pierogi,* sausage, and sauerkraut are all there.

There are few amenities here—the atmosphere reminds you of a school lunchroom—but the food is the real thing and the price structure seems to have remained in place for years. Solid fare every day, except Tuesdays, through early evening. No bar.

Hamtramck is a town-within-a-city, a Polish-founded enclave surrounded on all sides by Detroit.

*Price: About $7 per person*
*Open daily for lunch and dinner*
*No credit cards accepted*

# PONTCHARTRAIN WINE CELLARS
## 234 West Larned Street
### 313-963-1785

In talking of Detroit perennials, the Wine Cellars, as Detroiters invariably call it, might well head the list. Though it does not have a pure French menu but one that is more correctly termed French-accented, it certainly does have the kind of dusky, *château*-country setting that simply exudes French ambiance.

It also has an owner on hand most of the time, a staff with years of service adding up to the age of the building (circa 1882), and a reliable kitchen that turns out such dishes as frogs' legs *Provençale,* grilled silver salmon, *noisettes* of lamb, and *tournedos* of beef tenderloin, accompanied by wines from a well-stocked cellar headed by Bordeaux and Burgundy bottlings. Wine and beer are the only beverages aside from coffee.

The dessert list includes the classic *pot de crème au chocolat,* peach Melba, and pears *Hélène,* as it has for more than fifty years.

*Price: About $25 per person*
*Open Mon.–Fri. for lunch and dinner; Sat. for dinner only; closed Sun.*
*Accepts all major credit cards*

---

# RESTAURANT ST. REGIS
## In the St. Regis Hotel, 3071 West Grand Boulevard
### 313-873-3000

The small, European-style hotel which looks as if it has the patina of great age (but actually hasn't) offers a more serene setting than large commercial hotels can manage. English-garden prints, overstuffed furniture, a pianist pouring out Gershwin, and deferential service add to the illusion in the dining room, which flows into the veddy British sitting room where afternoon tea is served.

The dinner menu ranges from steak and kidney pie (with a bow to the Rank Hotels which run the hostelry) to chicken breast Parmesan, broiled silver salmon, and veal shank in sherried cream sauce.

The restaurant serves all day, every day, and has such amenities as afternoon tea and a popular Sunday brunch for which reservations are usually necessary.

*Price: About $25 per person*
*Open daily for breakfast, lunch, and dinner*
*Accepts all major credit cards*

## ROYAL BENGAL

### 155 Wyandotte Street East, Windsor, Ontario, Canada
#### 519-253-2151

A storefront spot where the trappings are minimal but the fare is authentic, Royal Bengal offers what the proprietor calls "a general Indian menu." Outstanding dishes include onion *bhaji,* chicken *biryani, sag* lamb, and *sag aloo bhaji.* The restaurant offers three combination dinners, the easy way to go if the fare is unfamiliar.

*Price: About $12 per person (Canadian)*
*Open Mon.–Sat. for lunch and dinner; Sun. for dinner only*
*Accepts all major credit cards*

## ROYAL EAGLE

### 1415 Parker Street
#### 313-331-8088

Refined Polish dishes rather than the sturdy kind are the specialty in this former apartment hotel dining room, which has just the right touch of slightly shopworn elegance.

The costumed help, the big bouquets of flowers, and cut-glass pieces displayed around the lace-curtained room add to the vintage feeling. Dinner only, from a small menu of dishes, such as duckling with dumplings and raspberries, and veal cutlets stuffed with asparagus and cheese, with a lovely walnut torte for dessert. Iced vodka is the house drink, but there is a small wine selection as well.

*Price: About $17 per person*
*Open Wed.–Sun. for dinner only; closed Mon. and Tues.*
*Accepts Visa and MasterCard*

## SALVATORE SCALLOPINI

### 1650 East 12 Mile Road, Madison Heights
#### 313-542-3281

This fetching little Italian *delicatezza* with pastas made on the premises and the kind of gutsy, redolent-of-garlic fare typified by southern Italy has a personality bursting with vitality and cheeriness. It is an Italian kitchen/old-fashioned grocery store translated into contemporary terms, with a few oil-cloth-covered and some bare-topped tables clustered around the glassed-in counter where *mortadella* and artichoke salads are dispensed to the takeout trade. No reservations, but an admirably democratic first-come, first-serve attitude, and good service by the staff, wrapped in oversized white aprons.

*Price: About $12 per person*
*Open daily for lunch and dinner*
*Accepts Visa and MasterCard*

---

## THE SHEIK
### 316 East Lafayette Boulevard
#### 313-964-8441

Despite a remodeling that shocked some of the long-time patrons of this former frame house, now sheathed in sparkling sandstone, this restaurant retains its friendly, almost family-style quality. It is run by the daughters of the man who founded it in 1940, and they welcome diners as if to their own home.

Almost every dish revolves around lamb, and the bill of fare is absolutely authentic, and small enough that every dish qualifies as a specialty of the house, from shish kebab to *kibbee nya* (raw spiced lamb) to the salads topped with pickled turnips. The best way to order is to ask for a sampling of the appetizers, including *hummus, baba ghanouge,* and *tabouli,* to share prior to the lamb entrées. Rice pudding is a dessert must.

*Price: About $16 per person*
*Open Tues.–Fri. for lunch and dinner; Sat. and Sun. for dinner only; closed Mon.*
*Accepts Visa and MasterCard*

---

## SPARKY HERBERT'S
### 15117 Kercheval Avenue, Grosse Pointe Park
#### 313-822-0266

The pub-like bar in front is usually packed and convivial, the high-ceilinged, skylit dining room in the back is a bit more serene. The menu ranges from a notable burger (usually munched by the bar crowd) to such dishes as blackened red snapper, rack of lamb, grilled lake trout with *pesto* glaze, and sautéed calf's sweetbreads with wild mushrooms (the choice of the back-room diners).

Sparky's is typical of the hard-to-pigeonhole restaurant now beginning to crop up that uses fresh ingredients in imaginative ways and owes no particular allegiance to a cooking style. Like others of its kind, it has greatly expanded its wine list and offers a good selection by the glass. A notable Sunday brunch is served here.

*Price: About $18 per person*
*Open daily for lunch and dinner*
*Accepts all major credit cards*

---

## STAGE & COMPANY
### 6873 Orchard Lake Road, West Bloomfield
#### 313-855-6622

In an upscale setting of putty, deep purple, and gray, with theatrical lighting that allows a good view of fellow diners (seeing and being seen is important here), this glamorous deli with a full bar offers great variety, from towering combination sandwiches named for Broadway shows, salads named for local celebrities, and solid dishes, such as chicken in the pot, boiled beef flanken, and baked short ribs, served with baskets of irresistible rye bread.

*Price: About $12 per person*
*Open Sat. and Sun. for breakfast, lunch, and dinner; Tues.–Fri. for lunch and dinner only; closed Mon.*
*Accepts all major credit cards .*

---

## 333 EAST
### In the Omni International Hotel, 333 East Jefferson Avenue
#### 313-222-7404

An elegant new hotel was added to the downtown Detroit landscape in 1985, and its first-floor dining room, named for the hotel's address, is hung with surprisingly sophisticated contemporary silkscreens, Japanese paper pieces, etchings, and pastels. The flowing series of dining areas is furnished with varying colors and styles, and it looks no more like a traditional hotel dining room than does the menu suggest old-fashioned Continental clichés.

Egg-shell linens swath tables set with profusions of fresh flowers, crystal wineglasses, and creamy English china; the staff is nothing if not enthusiastic, and the fare is an imaginative American borrowing inspiration from the French.

Dishes on the *à la carte* menu include seafood appetizers served both hot and cold, and main courses of grilled Pacific salmon, sautéed veal, breast of duck or chicken with fresh herb and wine sauces, with lighter selections, of course, at lunchtime, when omelets, California-style pizza, and an assortment of *pâtés* and *terrines* are offered. A Cruvinet system houses twenty-eight different wines available by the glass.

*Price: About $40 per person*
*Open daily for breakfast, lunch, and dinner*
*Accepts all major credit cards*

---

## TRAFFIC JAM
### Canfield Street at Second Avenue
### 313-831-9470

Something new always seems to be happening at this former college hangout, which has developed into an interesting restaurant, with an in-house bakery turning out some of the best bread in town, and lately, house-made sausages and cheeses as well. Its California-dominated wine selection operates like a retail store: Bottles have wine-store price tags, and may be carried out or consumed at the tables for a slight additional corkage fee.

The menu focuses as much as possible on seasonal fruits and vegetables, many of them emanating from the West Coast, and there are good fish, pastas, herb-crusted pizzas made with fresh tomatoes, cheese, and the house sausage. Desserts are perhaps typified by one called Carlotta Chocolatta ice cream cheesecake—double chocolate cheesecake wrapped in coffee ice cream coated with bittersweet hot fudge and sprinkled with ground *espresso*.

*Price: About $12 per person*
*Open Tues.–Fri. for lunch and dinner; Mon. for lunch only; Sat. for dinner only; closed Sun.*
*Accepts Visa and MasterCard*

---

## VAN DYKE PLACE
### 649 Van Dyke Avenue
### 313-821-2620

A beautifully preserved 18-room townhouse built in the early part of this century became a fine restaurant in 1981, under owners who had never before been restaurateurs but who have taken to it with great flair. Physically, it's spectacular, with its intricate, hand-gilded plasterwork, silk-shaded carved wall sconces, dove-gray walls, Italian silk brocade draperies, and antiques from the owners' private collections.

The monthly changing menu, under the heading "An American Perspective on French Cuisine," offers hors d'oeuvres typified by house-smoked duck breast, three American caviars, or fresh artichokes with Gulf shrimp and bay scallops in cayenne mayonnaise, and such entrées as *médaillons* of abalone, veal scallops with wild mushrooms and heavy cream, rack of spring lamb, and fresh duckling in a daily changing variety.

House-made pastries and coffee are served in a series of upstairs sitting rooms, allowing those who have dined at the dozen tables in the three antique-bedecked rooms on the main floor to have a glimpse of the rest of the house, which is very much a part of the restaurant's appeal.

Table appointments, including Bavarian china dinnerware, service, and a good wine list, are of the grand luxe quality that befits the opulent house. Reservations are highly advisable, with Saturday evenings almost impossible to book unless you do so well in advance.

*Price: About $50 per person*
*Open Tues.–Sat. for lunch and dinner; Mon. for lunch only; closed Sun.*
*Accepts all major credit cards*

---

# WONG'S EATERY
## 1457 University West, Windsor, Ontario, Canada
### 313-961-0212 (*in Detroit*)

Probably the most popular Chinese restaurant on either side of the Detroit River, Wong's has become something of a standard by which others are judged.

The menu ranges through several regional Chinese cuisines, from Cantonese and Hong Kong style to Szechuan, with much emphasis on fish and seafood. *Dim sum* are served every day, by menu order during the week, and via rolling carts on weekends and holidays.

The clientele is an interesting blend of Oriental and non-Oriental diners, and proprietor Raymond Wong is very much in evidence, walking about the dining rooms and suggesting dishes to the numerous parties who are content to leave the ordering up to him.

The rooms are handsomely decorated with peacock chairs, artwork, and huge round tables.

*Price: About $15 (Canadian) per person*
*Open daily for lunch and dinner*
*Accepts all major credit cards*

# FLORIDA

*Miami and Dade County*
*Palm Beach County*
*Fort Lauderdale and Environs*
*Tampa Bay*

## By Robert W. Tolf

# MIAMI AND DADE COUNTY

**AMERICAN**
  Cye's Rivergate (Miami)
  Miracles on 41st Street (Miami)

**BELGIAN**
  Le Festival (Coral Gables)

**CHINESE**
  Christine Lee's Gaslight (Miami
    Beach)
  Fung Wong of Chicago
    (Miami)

**CONTINENTAL**
  Dining Galleries (Miami Beach)
  The Forge (Miami Beach)
  Grand Café (Miami)

**CUBAN**
  La Esquina de Tejas (Miami)
  Versailles (Miami)

**DELICATESSEN**
  Wolfie Cohen's Rascal House
    (Miami)

**ECLECTIC**
The Painted Bird (Coral Gables)

**FRENCH**
Café Chauveron (Bay Harbor Island)
Chez Maurice (Coral Gables)
Dominique's (Miami Beach)
Le Festival (Coral Gables)
Pavillon Grill (Miami)
St. Michel (Coral Gables)

**GERMAN**
Zum Alten Fritz (Miami)

**GREEK**
Nick and Maria's (Miami)

**HOTEL DINING ROOM**
Danieli (Miami)
Dining Galleries (Miami Beach)
Dominique's (Miami Beach)
Fish Market (Miami)
Grand Café (Miami)
Pavillon Grill (Miami)
700 Club (Coral Gables)

**HUNGARIAN**
Charda (Miami)

**ITALIAN**
Danieli (Miami)
Il Tulipano (Miami)
Tiberio (Miami Beach)

**JAPANESE**
Toshi (Miami)

**MEXICAN**
Señor Frog's (Miami)

**PIZZA**
My Pie (Miami Beach)

**SCANDINAVIAN**
Fleming (Miami)

**SEAFOOD**
East Coast Fisheries (Miami)
Fish Market (Miami)
Joe's Stone Crab (Miami Beach)
Monty Trainer's Bayshore (Miami)

**SPANISH**
Casa Juancho (Miami)
Centro Vasco (Miami)
Cervantes (Coral Gables)
El Bodegon Castilla (Miami)
El Minerva (Miami)

**STEAKS AND CHOPS**
Christy's (Coral Gables)
New York Steak House (Miami Beach)
Palm (Miami Beach)

**SWISS**
St. Michel (Coral Gables)
Vinton's (Coral Gables)

**THAI**
Bangkok, Bangkok (Coral Gables)

**UNIQUE PROPERTIES**
Joe's Stone Crab (Miami Beach)

# PALM BEACH COUNTY

**AMERICAN**
Banana Boat (Boynton Beach)

**BARBECUE**
Tom's Place (Boca Raton)

**BREAKFAST**
The Original Pancake House
(Delray Beach)

**CHINESE**
Feng Lin (Delray Beach)

**CONTINENTAL**
Café L'Europe (Palm Beach)
Gazebo Café (Boca Raton)
Petite Marmite (Palm Beach)

**DELICATESSEN**
Off Broadway (Boca Raton)

**ECLECTIC**
The Epicurean (Palm Beach)

**FRENCH**
Auberge Le Grillon (Boca
Raton)

La Vieille Maison (Boca Raton)
Le Monegasque (Palm Beach)

**HAMBURGER**
Hamburger Heaven (Palm
Beach)

**HOTEL DINING ROOM**
Café Palmiers (West Palm
Beach)

**ITALIAN**
Arturo's Ristorante (Boca
Raton)
Il Girasole (Delray Beach)
Raffaello's (Boca Raton)

**JAPANESE**
Fugi (Boca Raton)

**SEAFOOD**
Anchor Inn (Lantana)
Busch's (Ocean Ridge)
Joe Muer Sea Food (Boca
Raton)
Oar House (Lake Worth)

**THAI**
Siam Garden (Boca Raton)

# FORT LAUDERDALE
# AND ENVIRONS

**AMERICAN**
Café Max (Pompano Beach)
Gibby's (Oakland Park)
Pal's Captain's Table (Deerfield Beach)
Yesterday's

**BARBECUE**
Ernie's Bar-B-Que

**CAJUN/CREOLE**
Lagniappe Cajun House

**CHINESE**
Christine Lee's Northgate

**CONTINENTAL**
Café September
Celebrity Room (Hollywood)
French Quarter

**FRENCH**
Brooks (Deerfield Beach)
La Bonne Crêpe
La Ferme
Le Café de Paris
The Left Bank
Windows on the Green

**GERMAN**
Brauhaus
Gerd Mueller's Ambry
Wine Cellar

**GREEK**
Ambrosia (Pompano Beach)

**HOTEL DINING ROOM**
Celebrity Room (Hollywood)
Windows on the Green

**HUNGARIAN**
Nada's Dubrovnik (Davie)

**ITALIAN**
Casa Vecchia
Paesano

**JAPANESE**
Nobi

**PIZZA**
Pizzeria Uno

**POLYNESIAN**
Mai-Kai

**SEAFOOD**
Cap's Place (Lighthouse Point)
Crab Pot Café (Lighthouse Point)
15th Street Fisheries and Boat House
Old Florida Seafood House

**STEAKS AND CHOPS**
Ruth's Chris Steak House

**SWISS**
Café de Geneve

**THAI**
Yum Yum of Siam

**UNIQUE PROPERTIES**
Cap's Place (Lighthouse Point)

# TAMPA BAY

**AMERICAN**
  Cypress Room (Tampa)
  Heilman's Beachcomber
    (Clearwater Beach)
  rg's north (Tampa)
  Siple's Garden Seat (Clearwater)
  The Verandah (Tampa)

**CONTINENTAL**
  J. Fitzgerald's (Tampa)
  Sabals (Dunedin)

**FRENCH**
  Pasquet (St. Petersburg)

**GERMAN**
  The Wine Cellar (North
    Redington Beach)

**GREEK**
  Louis Pappas (Tarpon Springs)

**HOTEL DINING ROOM**
  Cypress Room (Tampa)
  J. Fitzgerald's (Tampa)

**ITALIAN**
  Donatello (Tampa)
  Lauro Ristorante (Tampa)
  Selena's (Tampa)

**SEAFOOD**
  Lobster Pot (Redington Shores)
  Miller's Seafood Center
    (Tampa)

**SPANISH**
  Columbia (Tampa)
  Don Quijote (Tampa)
  El Madrid (Clearwater)
  Pepin's (St. Petersburg)
  Tio Pepe (Clearwater)

**STEAKS AND CHOPS**
  Bern's Steak House (Tampa)

**THAI**
  Sukhothai (Tampa)

The premier eating experiences in the Sunshine State—super-luxe as well as ethnic exotica—are found along the Gold Coast, that strip of sand caressed by the Gulf Stream and glittering from Palm Beach in the north to Miami in the south. Fort Lauderdale, Pompano Beach, Boca Raton, and Delray Beach gleam along that strip and reflect in the diversity of their restaurants nationwide trends, from Cajun to California *nouvelle,* Thai to Tex–Mex. Only a few years ago there were no Thai eateries to be found on the Gold Coast; today there are close to forty. *Sushi* and *sashimi* bars have popped out of the sand almost as fast as the purveyors of Hunan and Szechuan specialties. And for every dozen fast-food feeders that open their doors, some newly arrived chef, manager, or enterprising couple find a place in the sun, doing their French, Italian, Greek, Scandinavian, even Indonesian and Vietnamese thing, joining Cuban cousins and Basque emigrés who have made Miami the Spanish eating capital of the country.

Second place in the Spanish sweepstakes belongs to Tampa, but their *arroz con pollo* servers go back a good many years before Fidel Castro. And, in recent years, other ethnic eateries have added their spices to the Tampa Bay restaurant whirl.

*Robert W. Tolf is restaurant critic for the* Fort Lauderdale News/Sun-Sentinel *and* Florida Trend *magazine and is the author of* Florida Restaurant Guide, Tampa Bay *and* Gold Coast *editions.*

# M I A M I   A N D   D A D E
# C O U N T Y

## BANGKOK, BANGKOK
### 157 Giralda Drive, Coral Gables
**305-444-2397**

One of the best-dressed of the three dozen Thai restaurants currently dotting the Gold Coast landscape; and the best served. While music from the Land of Smiles plays softly in the background, the jodhpur-clad waiters bring forth curries and spicy, peppery blends, prepared as hot or mild as the diner desires. There's a second Bangkok, Bangkok, at 12584 North Kendall Drive (telephone: 305-595-5839), but this one in the Gables is more convenient.

*Price: About $15 per person*
*Open daily for lunch and dinner*
*Accepts all major credit cards*

# CAFÉ CHAUVERON

9561 East Bay Harbor Drive, Bay Harbor Island (*near North Miami Beach*)

305-866-8779

When founder-perfectionist Roger Chauveron died in April 1983, there was considerable concern about the future of the Gold Coast's temple of *haute cuisine*. Partner Curtis Blank and super chef Marcel Challamel pulled out and opened another restaurant across the state in Naples; son André was left to carry on alone. But after some initial problems he demonstrated, with great aplomb, that he was made of the same Gallic championship "right stuff" as his Périgord papa. His café is back on the right track, and those who knew Chauveron and Chambord in Manhattan—before André moved to Miami in 1972—are convinced André's current incarnation is as good as the originals. That means pike *quenelles* almost too light to be held in place by the Nantua sauce, and salmon *mousse,* a *terrine* of duck, and a *bouillabaisse* that sparks memories of Marseilles. Truffles and *foie gras,* key ingredients in the Chauveron cookbook, are used with abandon. The wine list is excellent, the level of service superb, and the setting is straightforward elegant. The menu is extensive, containing most of the pre-*nouvelle* classics, and the *soufflé* Chauveron, made with Grand Marnier and chestnuts, is the perfect climax to an evening of highly civilized dining. Reservations are required. The restaurant is open only from mid-October to the end of May.

*Price: About $45 per person*
*Open daily for dinner only during the season*
*Accepts all major credit cards*

# CASA JUANCHO

2436 S.W. Eighth Street, Miami

305-642-2452

A bustling place that comes very close to capturing the *tapas* spirit and substance of Spain. Casa Juancho is almost always filled, and the up-front bar and lounge can get a mite overcrowded, but the ramble of dining rooms provides happy retreats. The red-vested staff moves with quick confidence. Order something from the grill, on view at the entrance, or some dried ham or *chorizo* sausages—in the best *tapas* manner—and then some of the roast lamb, the rabbit with seafood and rice, the traditional *paella,* or the suckling pig. And for finishers what could be more soothing to the stomach than a bowl of *crema Catalana?*

*Price: About $20 per person*
*Open daily for dinner only*
*Accepts all major credit cards*

# CENTRO VASCO
## 2235 S.W. Eighth Street, Miami
### 305-643-9606

The origins of this extremely popular noon and night feeder go back to Spain's Basque country and founder Juanito Saizarbitoria's opposition to Franco, and then, in a new country as refugee with a successful restaurant, to Castro. Since 1965 the Saizarbitoria clan has been safely ensconced in this ramble of Spanish *refugio*—all wood, stucco, and stone, usually filled with Miami's Spanish-speaking community, eating their fill of *paella,* sautéed snapper fingers in wine sauce, *tournedos* stuffed with ham and cheese, spiced potato soup, fried garbanzo beans. The wine list is reasonably priced and the *sangría* is excellent.

*Price: About $15 per person*
*Open daily for lunch and dinner*
*Accepts all major credit cards*

# CERVANTES
## 2121 Ponce de Leon, Coral Gables
### 305-446-8636

The Man of La Mancha is everywhere in evidence in this Spanish-owned and -operated treasure house of most things Spanish: in busts and books, in paintings and tiles, many of them from Talavera de la Reina, in decorated plates, and in quotations strung along the ceiling beams. The wines, brandies, weekend entertainment (complete with flamenco dancers on the small stage by the cave of a lounge), and, of course, the food are equally reflective of the best of the Old Country. Start with *tapas* taken in the Cave ("La Cava"), stimulating appetizers of fried squid, sausage broiled in olive oil and sherry, or those special *anguilas de aguinaga a la bilbaina,* tiny eels in garlic-spiked oil hotter than hot (and of necessity eaten with a wooden fork). With a bold Rioja wine at your plate, proceed to a platter of *paella*—no one in Little Havana does it better—or chicken and seafood with rice, or tripe in a tomato-based sauce, quail sautéed in a heady blend of buttered shallots doused with brandy, finished with heavy cream and freckled with grapes, or a whole fish baked in its own bed of salt to seal in the flavor. Reservations are mandatory on the weekends and plan to dine Spanish style—late—in order to catch the show.

*Price: About $20 per person*
*Open daily for lunch and dinner*
*Accepts all major credit cards*

---

## CHARDA
### 13885 Biscayne Boulevard, Miami
#### 305-940-1095

Owner George Fuzek is the heir of Hungarian restauranting traditions that go back seven generations. The experience shows on the walls with an attractive array of decorated plates and other mementos from home. There's live entertainment, usually with a violin tugging at the heartstrings with Gypsy melodies. The kitchen makes *gulyás,* cabbage rolls, dumplings, and those special pancakes known as *palacsinta* to perfection. Meals start with a spread of sheep's milk *körözött* cheese dotted with caraway seeds and scallions, best accompanied by a bold Hungarian wine, a Badacsonyi Kéknyelü or Egri Bikavér—"Bull's Blood."

*Price: About $20 per person*
*Open daily for dinner only; closed Mon. and Tues. in the summer*
*Accepts all major credit cards*

---

## CHEZ MAURICE
### 382 Miracle Mile, Coral Gables
#### 305-448-8984

The recent arrival of still more Frenchmen seeking a place in the Gables restaurant whirl has not bothered Maurice Cambin, an ample man of good spirit. Nor has *nouvelle* nonsense or other trends. Maurice merely continues in his country-French ways, providing a non-stuffy setting served by a smiling, accommodating staff, preparing the food of a rustic *auberge* rather than the three-star *haute cuisine.* That means smoked salmon and light soups or coarse-grained *pâtés* for starters; or better, the *ratatouille,* which has practically disappeared from restaurants these days. Entrées can be built around sautéed beef bits, chicken or shrimp in pastry, fresh fish surrounded by shallots and sweet peppers bathed in white wine, a *boudin* (a sausage served with crisp vegetables and rounds of potato). Desserts are freshly assembled. Maurice's favorite—and mine—is the *vacherin maison,* a high-cal collection of meringue, ice cream, and rich chocolate sauce.

*Price: About $20 per person*
*Open Mon.–Sat. for lunch and dinner; closed Sun.*
*Accepts all major credit cards*

---

## CHRISTINE LEE'S GASLIGHT
### 18401 Collins Avenue, Miami Beach
#### 305-932-1145

There's none of that red carpet-golden dragon-tassel lantern decor in this etched-glass, mirrored marvel with intelligently spaced tables and banquettes. But then there's none of the tired old chop suey, blue-plate-special approach either. Not in a superbly supervised kitchen that produces the best *moo shoo* pork in town; and the best Hunan whole fish, *dim sum,* chicken wings in oyster sauce, a remarkable dish created out of eggplant, shredded meat, peppers, and finely chopped scallions swimming in a zinger of a sauce with just the right touch of garlic. Then there's Christine's Special, a mishmash of just about everything delivered in dramatic style on a sizzling platter. It's her memory of the kind of fare assembled from whatever was available in her native Shanghai during the Second World War. Christine, an omnipresent lady with considerable charm and dedication, also knows how to order, age, and cut prime steaks. No other Chinese restaurant in the state can make that claim. Except Christine Lee's in Northgate, west of Fort Lauderdale, and the East Ocean in Boca Raton, a spinoff of her former manager and other staffers.

*Price: About $25 per person*
*Open daily for dinner only*
*Accepts all major credit cards*

---

## CHRISTY'S
### 3101 Ponce de Leon Boulevard, Coral Gables
#### 305-446-1400

This is a classic All-American steak house with more high-ceiling European influence in the decor than in Kansas City: The drapes are velvet, the cushy chairs leather, the napery crisply white. But the prime rib and the steaks are strictly Midwestern. The baked potato has no peer, the Caesar salad is super, and the desserts are as All-American as apple pie. The trio of double rib lamb chops are the best in the state. Reservations are a must, even at lunchtime, when the power brokers of the Gables congregate.

*Price: About $25 per person*
*Open Mon.–Fri. for lunch and dinner; Sat. and Sun. for dinner only*
*Accepts all major credit cards*

---

## CYE'S RIVERGATE
### 444 Brickell Avenue, Miami
### 305-358-9100

Cye's sits on the Miami River in the Rivergate Plaza Building, the heart of the financial institutions that have popped out of the sand in recent years. It's the best luncheon spot in the strip, one with a swinging bar at late afternoon during "attitude readjustment time" and then again in the wee hours, when they serve a late supper menu. There are some Mexican concoctions at lunch along with fat sandwiches and fresh salads, and, at night, prime meats, duckling, and rich chocolate cake. Noon or night there are reasonably priced wines.

*Price: About $20 per person*
*Open Mon.–Sat. for lunch and dinner; closed Sun.*
*Accepts all major credit cards*

---

## DANIELI
### In the Palm Bay Hotel, 2 Palm Bay Lane, Miami
### 305-757-3500

Although it's a newcomer, which opened in the spring of 1985, this marble-mirror super-luxe server with such sensational views of the bay is already sitting on the Miami Italian summit with Tiberio and Il Tulipano. The *terrines* are as seductive to look at as they are to eat; the goose liver *pâté* is more of a *mousse* freckled with white truffles; the veal possibilities are as delectable as they should be in a Northern Italian establishment with credentials, and the chocolate conclusions, especially the *fonduta,* are guaranteed to give you the waistline of a Pavarotti. We presume the wine list will improve as this class act settles into its second year.

*Price: About $35 per person*
*Open daily for breakfast, lunch, and dinner*
*Accepts all major credit cards*

# DINING GALLERIES
In the Fontainebleau Hotel, 4441 Collins Avenue, Miami
Beach
305-538-2000

The multi-level museum hovers on the precipice of Miami Beach Baroque
with Carrara marble statuary, a Steinway grand piano of exquisite inlay
design, schmaltzy violin music, and the kind of buffets that are the very
definition of eye-popping. But it is romantic, extremely well staffed and
served, the level of cooking superb, and the Sunday brunches (and noontime
during the season on the other days of the week) are the best in the state. Start
an evening meal with a platter of just about everything, from *scampi* to
*escargots,* stone crab to smoked salmon, *pâté de foie gras* to *fettuccine.* And then
work through entrées of pompano—Florida's answer to Dover sole—lamb
kissed with a zestful orange chutney, some of the veal dishes, or the full-blown
filet mignon. But remember to order that *soufflé* in advance. And don't worry
about the number of toasts you're making to salute such surroundings: The
wine tariffs are not out of line.

*Price: About $35 per person*
*Open Mon.–Fri. for lunch and dinner; Sat. and Sun. for dinner only*
*Accepts all major credit cards*

# DOMINIQUE'S
In The Alexander, 5225 Collins Avenue, Miami Beach
305-861-5252

Lyons native Dominique D'Ermo, with a singularly successful restaurant in
Washington, D.C., returned to the beach where for a half dozen years he
worked as pastry chef—at the Americana Hotel during the 1960s. As in the
nation's capital, he has filled his restaurant with a strikingly attractive collection of antiques, Oriental carpets, stained and etched glass, and recruited a
pleasant, accommodating staff. His menu is a shocker, with ostrich and rattlesnake salads, smoked buffalo, 'gator scallopine, and sausages made from kanga-
roo. But Dominique is a showman. He's also a farmer, growing his own
vegetables and raising pheasant and Peking ducks, mallards, quail, and lamb,
guaranteeing freshness and quality. He sells rack of lamb by the ton, offers a
seven-course gourmet dinner, along with superior calf's liver sautéed with
raspberry vinegar and garnished with crisp onions and apple slices, and *escargot-*
stuffed prime steak. Presentation is as elegantly pleasing as the setting, and in
the right kind of weather—just as in Washington—there's an outdoor terrace

for *al fresco* dining. Another plus for Dominique's new Dominique's—it's open for breakfast and lunch as well as dinner.

*Price: About $30 per person*
*Open daily for breakfast, lunch, and dinner*
*Accepts all major credit cards*

---

## EAST COAST FISHERIES
### 360 West Flagler Street, Miami
#### 305-373-5516

Only the Florida lobster and the bivalves on the half shell escape the deep-fryer in this wonderfully informal fish house, one that sports its own fishing fleet and retail store. But the fish is fresh, the service speedy, the vibes authentic, and it does sit smack on the Miami River.

*Price: About $10 per person*
*Open daily for lunch and dinner*
*No credit cards accepted*

---

## EL BODEGON CASTILLA
### 2499 S.W. Eighth Street, Miami
#### 305-649-0863

Since opening its doors in 1979, this *parador* of a place, owned and operated by a quintet of Spaniards, has been at the forefront of the parade of Spanish-Basque-Cuban restaurants dotting the avenue of "Calle Ocho," the main artery which runs through the heart of Miami's Little Havana. The wood and stucco structure and the Spanish murals on the walls—with a minimum of the bullfight and Don Quijote theme-ploitation—create a comfortable backdrop for meals that should commence with *caldo Gallego,* that marvelous melange of white beans, hearty sausage, ham, bacon, and turnip or collard greens, and end with a bit of *leche frita,* fried milk, otherwise described as a thick, milky custard showered with cinnamon. In between there's *arroz con pollo* or *arroz con mariscos* (rice with chicken or shellfish), fresh snapper in green sauce, ham and cabbage, and those sizzling hot silvery little baby eels called *anguilas.* The wine list is excellent, with a better selection of Spanish bottlings than usually encountered. The staff is only too happy to introduce their guests to the joys and special pleasures of Spanish cuisine.

*Price: About $15 per person*
*Open daily for lunch and dinner*
*Accepts all major credit cards*

# EL MINERVA
## 265 N.E. Second Street, Miami
### 305-374-9420

Two decades before Castro came to power and the Cubans started streaming to Miami, this simple downtown establishment was spooning out *arroz con pollo* and frying plantains. It's the oldest Spanish feedery on the Gold Coast and still a popular spot for lunch and dinner, serving a reliable menu in uncomplicated surroundings.

*Price: About $15 per person*
*Open Mon.–Sat. for lunch and dinner; closed Sun.*
*Accepts all major credit cards*

# FISH MARKET
## In the Omni Hotel, 1601 Biscayne Boulevard, Miami
### 305-374-0000

The name is far too simple a term for this elegantly attired establishment with an abundance of marble and mirrors, with white-jacketed waiters bringing the bounty of the deep: crab from the Chesapeake, swordfish from the Atlantic, squid from Monterey. The fresh slabs are grilled over lava rocks—like some leftover from Viking times in Iceland—or they're mingled with just about everything else from the sea in a *cioppino*, that fish stew devised by Italian fishermen in San Francisco searching for some riposte to the French *bouillabaisse*. The wine list is reasonable and replete with the kind of quality California whites needed for all that good seafood.

*Price: About $25 per person*
*Open Mon.–Sat. for dinner only; closed Sun.*
*Accepts all major credit cards*

# FLEMING
## 9050 South Dixie Highway, Miami
### 305-666-5181

Diners searching for a Danish approach to budget-stretching should head for this little highway hugger not far from Dadeland in South Miami. Jodi Johansen out front and husband Fleming behind the burners are the happy team that offers quality food at reasonable prices in a felicitous setting. From special marinated salmon served with a sharp dill-mustard sauce—*gravlaks*—to snapper in a sack, and duck treated to apples and prunes and served with a sensational red cabbage garnish. The Caesar salad that comes with all entrées is excellent, as is the Johansen soup of the night, brewed that day out back. But remember to save room for the desserts: They are equally fresh, and run the full gamut of Danish high-cal delights.

*Price: About $15 per person*
*Open Tues.–Sun. for dinner only; closed Mon.*
*Accepts all major credit cards*

---

## THE FORGE
### 432 Arthur Godfrey Road, Miami Beach
#### 305-538-8533

There's more stained glass here than most museums can boast, enough art on the walls to stock a good-size gallery, and the wine cellar is one of the finest in the land. The kitchen crew, now and then reflecting a bit of Gallic ingenuity, prepares glorious duck, splendid snapper, and memorable veal. But its loftiest laurels are earned by their T-bone and pepper steaks. There's a lot of action in the lounge, which sometimes raises the decibel level in the dining rooms to an unacceptable level, but that's all part of the beach bustle, and the professionals doing the serving do their best to maintain a tranquil mood.

*Price: About $35 per person*
*Open daily for dinner*
*Accepts all major credit cards*

---

## FUNG WONG OF CHICAGO
### 9796 S.W. Eighth Street, Miami
#### 305-226-8032

*Dim sum*—that endless parade of appetizers similar in spirit but not substance to the Spanish *tapas*—are the main attraction in this classic storefront operation, one of only three Chinese restaurants specializing in such items. (The other two, August Moon and Dim Sum, are in Broward County.)

*Price: Under $10 per person*
*Open daily for lunch and dinner*
*Accepts all major credit cards*

# GRAND CAFÉ

In the Grand Bay Hotel, 2669 South Bayshore Drive,
Coconut Grove, Miami
305-858-9600

There's been a game of musical chairs going on in the kitchen of this ultra-sophisticated hotel, the only such operation in the U.S. of the prestigious Italian C.I.G.A. hotel group, but somehow they have survived—and prospered. Serving inside and out, sponsoring special dinners in their handsome wine room, featuring luncheons built around cold pasta preparations, duck breast salads dressed with raspberry vinegar, veal *tonnato,* lobster with shrimp and squid; and dinners starting with marinated salmon and she-crab soup, and proceeding to a veal chop stuffed with *prosciutto,* spinach, and Romano cheese. The lamb chops are special, the grilled slabs of fish heavenly. And the wines are select.

*Price: About $30 per person*
*Open daily for breakfast, lunch, and dinner*
*Accepts all major credit cards*

---

# IL TULIPANO

11052 Biscayne Boulevard, Miami
305-893-4811

From A to Z, *antipasto* to *zabaglione,* this is a wondrous restaurant, professionally run, superbly cheffed, and happily served. Tiptoe past all those tulips on the islands of crisp-white napery and work through meals that start with snails tucked into pastry and coated with a fine tomato sauce, or a salad bristling with seafood, tomatoes, parsley, and peppers, or a marvelous presentation of pasta, spinach-*ricotta ravioli* in a rich creamy sauce. Then settle into a slab of snapper showered with chopped tomatoes, Maine lobster bedded down with angel's hair, or a giant veal chop with a slight suggestion of Fontina. Save space for a salad of *arugula,* fennel, and *radicchio,* select something special from the excellent cellar of Italian wines, and end it all with some of that *zabaglione* or maybe something sweeter in the shape of a tulip.

*Price: About $30 per person*
*Open Wed.–Mon. for dinner only; closed Tues.*
*Accepts all major credit cards*

# JOE'S STONE CRAB

## 227 Biscayne Street (at Washington Avenue), Miami Beach
### 305-673-0365

Long before realtors discovered the mangrove-filled strip of sand east of the mainland, the Gold Coast's oldest restaurant was dispensing food to the fishermen and a few tourists. That was 1913, and in a few years the locals convinced the owner to serve stone crab claws. The rest is history: the fishing fleet, the expanded menu, the long lines out front, the worldwide fame. Today, Joe's is still worth the trip: for the cold crab with that special mustard sauce for dipping, for the budget-priced fried oysters, the creamed spinach, fried potatoes, and atmosphere. To avoid the sardining during peak hours, arrive early for dinner or try lunch. There are no reservations, and the maître d' here has to be one of the wealthiest, for those who tip handsomely never wait in line. Open only during stone crab season—mid-October to mid-May.

*Price: About $25 per person*
*Open Tues.–Sun. for lunch and dinner; Mon. for dinner only; closed from May 15–October 15*
*Accepts all major credit cards*

---

# LA ESQUINA DE TEJAS

## 101 S.W. Twelfth Avenue, Miami
### 305-545-5341

A classic Cuban storefront, typical of the breed which has proliferated across the Miami landscape in the past three decades. They never seem to close (open daily from seven in the morning until midnight); they have food at bargain prices; the setting is simple; and the service is friendly. But this establishment jumped out of the pack when President Reagan stopped by for a meal, one which was built around chicken with rice, black beans, and fried plantains, followed by *flan* and some of that powerful Cuban coffee.

*Price: Under $10 per person*
*Open daily for breakfast, lunch, and dinner*
*No credit cards accepted*

## LE FESTIVAL
2120 Salzedo Street, Coral Gables
305-442-8545

The menu is predictable and includes most of the standard items one has learned to expect in a French restaurant this side of Marseilles—or Manhattan: *quiche,* onion soup, veal *Française,* pepper steak, and duckling *à l'orange.* But they also dazzle a bit with nightly specials, including a rather good version of *bouillabaisse,* fresh red snapper saluted with a shallot-showered wine-cream sauce or given that special *dugléré* treatment of cream and tomatoes. Pastries are worth the calories. The staff is unusually accommodating.

*Price: About $25 per person*
*Open Mon.–Fri. for lunch and dinner; Sat. for dinner only; closed Sun.*
*Accepts all major credit cards*

## MIRACLES ON 41ST STREET
4100 N.E. Second Avenue, Miami
305-573-3350

Designer David Harrison—a seminal force in the world of floral design—has created a garden of great delights, from the marble-and-mirror enchanted setting to the endless parade of dishes displaying their own kind of design genius. Thus, the conch fritters, usually delivered to the diner as a colorless collection of lonely blobs, are presented here with a nosegay of bean sprouts on a conch shell. Soups are ladled into ruggedly handsome bowls and garnished with fresh herbs; the snails are not delivered plain in shell or ceramic server or in mushroom caps or pastry puff, but on circles of zucchini spooned with garlic butter and garnished with walnuts. After such an eye-popping array, I'm always content to settle into something more routine for dessert, something such as their superb bread pudding.

*Price: About $30 per person*
*Open Mon.–Fri. for lunch and dinner; Sat. for dinner only; closed Sun.*
*Accepts all major credit cards*

## MONTY TRAINER'S BAYSHORE
### 2560 South Bayshore Drive, Coconut Grove, Miami
#### 305-858-1431

Extremely popular indoor-outdoor oasis for the Grove's younger set, but the outdoor raw bar under the palm fronds of a Seminole *chickee* appeals to all ages. Trainer has become a major force in the Florida restaurant whirl, with several other places in his portfolio; but this was the first and it's definitely the most fun. It also features just about everything and anything that calls the water home.

*Price: About $15 per person*
*Open Mon.–Fri. for lunch and dinner; Sat. for dinner only; closed Sun.*
*Accepts all major credit cards*

## MY PIE
### 239 Sunny Isle Boulevard, North Miami Beach
#### 305-945-1387

Best pizza—deep-dish Chicago style—in Miami, from a Chicago company that has established a mini-chain; other My Pies are found at 13856 S.W. 88th Street and 9545 South Dixie Highway.

*Price: Under $10 per person*
*Open daily for lunch and dinner*
*No credit cards accepted*

## NEW YORK STEAK HOUSE
### 17985 Biscayne Boulevard, North Miami Beach
#### 305-932-7676

A junior version of Miami's Palm, with Midwestern prime and humongous Maine lobsters the attraction, along with a straightforward setting with caricatures on the walls and friendly waiters. And, like Palm and other top-quality beef purveyors who fly in those super-size lobsters, the tariffs are not exactly budget-minded.

*Price: About $35 per person*
*Open daily for dinner only*
*Accepts all major credit cards*

## NICK AND MARIA'S
### 11701 N.E. Second Avenue, Miami
#### 305-891-9232

A simple, straightforward eatery that prepares, in highly competent fashion, all the classics we've come to expect in Greek restaurants with little or no pretense: *moussaka, pastitsio,* feta-freckled salads, garlic-kissed lamb, and *baklava.*

*Price: Under $10 per person*
*Open Mon.–Fri. for lunch and dinner; closed Sat. and Sun.*
*No credit cards accepted*

## THE PAINTED BIRD
### 65 Merrick Way, Coral Gables
#### 305-445-1200

The three Rangel brothers are responsible for this softly decorated, peach-plum retreat opened in 1980, which has flown to the high ground of culinary imagination and innovation. With a superbly selected wine list (with many wines available by the glass), they offer such delights as feta-spinach fritters freckled with walnuts and surrounded by tissue-thin *filo,* duckling swimming with apples and cashews, rack of lamb in a guava-garlic sauce, filet mignon crowned with Brie and figs or a butter bristling with chervil, and *médaillons* of veal layered with kiwi and *prosciutto.* The accompanying salads are blessed with a fine dill vinaigrette, and the vegetables are ever so gently cooked.

*Price: About $25 per person*
*Open Mon.–Fri. for lunch and dinner; Sat. and Sun. for dinner only*
*Accepts all major credit cards*

## PALM
### In Seacoast Towers East, 5151 Collins Avenue, Miami Beach
#### 305-868-7256

New Yorkers never use the article when describing the Second Avenue institution, parent of Miami's Palm, and they no doubt dismiss this mission to the tropics as a second-rate imitation. But they cannot deny the fact that the lobsters are as huge in Miami as in Manhattan, and that the steaks are Prime.

There's no sawdust on the floor, there's no corner vest-pocket bar as in New York, but there are caricatures on the walls and a corps of waiters slightly more accommodating than those in New York. The creamed spinach is still distinguished by a touch of nutmeg and a dash of garlic. Start with the special salad —lettuce, pimiento, and onion—and remember to order the fried onions with the steak. The steak Stone is a personal favorite, delivered sliced (and of course grilled precisely as ordered) with lots of onion and pimiento. There are also ten veal and seafood selections, but when at Palm or The Palm, I almost never get past the lobster and beef.

*Price: About $35 per person*
*Open daily for dinner only*
*Accepts all major credit cards*

---

# PAVILLON GRILL
## In the Pavillon Hotel, Chopin Plaza, Miami
### 305-374-4494

What better introduction to a world-class French restaurant than a giant sculpture in the lobby by Henry Moore? And what better prelude to a lunch or dinner than an apéritif in a British club of a lounge, all dark mahogany and leather? There's more damn-the-expense surroundings in the dining room: columns of green Italian marble, rosewood chairs, and ultra-elegant table appointments with heavy Italian silver and glistening crystal. The culinary accents here are definitely *nouvelle,* but without nonsensical exaggeration. Freshness and prime quality of ingredients are emphasized, and there are nightly specials, reflecting the market availability and inspiration of the chef. Crayfish is brought in from Louisiana, pigeons fly in from somewhere and are braised in a bracing sauce that is as uniquely appealing as the port wine and *foie gras* enhancement of the roast mallard. Turbot and venison are not found on many other menus in Florida, but they are here. Pompano, yellowtail, and sweetbreads are served in many other establishments, but rarely are they treated with as much respect and imagination as at this stunner of a place many Miamians argue is the finest restaurant in the South.

*Price: About $45 per person*
*Open Mon.–Fri. for lunch and dinner; Sat. for dinner only; closed Sun.*
*Accepts all major credit cards*

---

# ST. MICHEL
## 162 Alcazar Avenue, Coral Gables
### 305-444-1666

The Art Deco setting is sensational, the Sunday brunches with bass and piano are alone worth the trip, the duckling bathed in black currants and pears is close to Platonic, and the service, enthusiastically supervised by the tireless Stuart Bornstein, is admirable. Another plus is the fact that owner Bornstein is also an innkeeper: Upstairs in the 1920s structure are a dozen rooms he has carefully restored and filled with an interesting array of antiques and collectibles.

*Price: About $20 per person*
*Open daily for breakfast, lunch, and dinner*
*Accepts all major credit cards*

## SEÑOR FROG'S
### 3008 Grand Avenue, Coconut Grove, Miami
**305-448-0999**

There's been an explosion of outlets large and small for South of the Border fare lining the fast-food freeways of the Gold Coast, but here's one that is definitely not a chain reaction. It's the product of a quartet of Mexicans from Guadalajara who oversee a menu that offers the best *burritos, tostadas, tacos rancheros,* and *enchiladas* in a green sauce, all served with super-size margaritas and a good selection of Mexican beer. Also, there's an outdoor patio for fresh-air dining. The bar usually fills with the swingles set before the sun sets over the serapes.

*Price: About $10 per person*
*Open daily for lunch and dinner*
*Accepts all major credit cards*

## 700 CLUB
### In the David William Hotel, 700 Biltmore Way, Coral Gables
**305-445-7821**

High atop a hotel with a ground-floor imitation of the Paris Maxim's known as Chez Vendome, the handsomely wood-paneled 700 Club, with its splendid gallery of matador portraits, provides the perfect staging area for an evening in the city beautiful. Enjoy the panorama or huddle into that minuscule bar or spend some time at the comfortable tables, working through the uncomplicated menu. Beef and duckling are the specialties, served in generous portions, along with Frenchified desserts.

*Price: About $35 per person*
*Open Mon.–Sat. for breakfast, lunch, and dinner; closed Sun.*
*Accepts all major credit cards*

# TIBERIO
## 9700 Collins Avenue, Bal Harbour (North Miami Beach)
### 305-861-6161

The perfect restaurant for the sophisticated, pricey, ultra-chic Shoppes of Bal Harbour: The up-front bar has the feel of something intimate in Cannes; the explosion of yellow roses assuage the senses of sight and smell, and the menu bristles with marvelous pastas, impeccably prepared veal and liver dishes, delivered faultlessly by a highly professional staff of waiters and captains. The wine list is excellent and the desserts sheer delight.

*Price: About $30 per person*
*Open Mon.–Sat. for lunch and dinner; Sun. for dinner only*
*Accepts all major credit cards*

# TOSHI
## 5759 S.W. Fortieth Street (Bird Road), Miami
### 305-661-0511

The kimono-clad Samurai showman of a chef flashing those blades across all those fillets of fresh fish is owner Toshi Takamine, and he has created a Japanese oasis of great class, one complete with background music, floor cushions for testing your dexterity while dining, and a full range of the classics: *sushi* and *sashimi, sukiyaki* and *teriyaki* and, of course, *tempura.* But he goes further inside his bamboo walls: The menu advises that Tokyo officials have qualified him to be a *fugu* chef. *Fugu* is a blowfish, a toxin-loaded killer that has to be handled with great care to remove the poisons—some thirty steps in all, as required by law. But Toshi hardly ever takes the time and trouble: He doesn't like the blowfish available off the coasts of Florida.

*Price: About $12 per person*
*Open daily for dinner only*
*Accepts all major credit cards*

# VERSAILLES
## 3555 S.W. Eighth Street, Miami
### 305-445-7614

There are mirrors, but that's the only similarity with its French namesake outside of Paris. Here all is Cuban. And bustle up front, by the small takeout window, at the winding counter, in the large dining room with capacity of a couple hundred. It's a Little Havana landmark and a great place to be introduced to Miami's Hispanic community.

*Price: About $12 per person*
*Open daily for breakfast, lunch, and dinner*
*Accepts all major credit cards*

---

## VINTON'S
### 116 Alhambra Circle, Coral Gables
**305-445-2511**

The Eichman brothers from Switzerland are responsible for this romantic little gem with its staff of well-schooled waiters. René—with a distinctive "Le Chef" on his Coupe de Ville license plate—runs the kitchen while Hans is out front. Together they constitute a terrific duo, stocking one of the best wine cellars in the area, sponsoring Monday evening let-it-all-hang-out gourmet extravaganzas, insisting on fresh produce and seafood, and then handling it with great conscience and imagination. The *sorbets* are super and the changed-daily *quiche,* included as appetizer, is always tempting. Few other establishments are serving better fish dishes, saluted with such sensational sauces. The tariffs are among the highest in the state, and some guests have complained about the small portions. But this is not a place for *fressers* or food freaks who merely want to stuff. Vinton's is for those who want to dine in comfort and quiet, sipping select wines, embraced by the romance of the setting.

*Price: About $45 per person*
*Open Tues.–Fri. for lunch and dinner; Sat.–Mon. for dinner only*
*Accepts all major credit cards*

---

## WOLFIE COHEN'S RASCAL HOUSE
### 17190 Collins Avenue, Miami
**305-947-4581**

The best of the Florida delis, spotless and efficiently run, established by the same genius of a Wolfgang Cohen who also started the original Wolfie's and Pumpernick's. The line stretches for hours in the peak of the season.

*Price: Under $10 per person*
*Open daily for breakfast, lunch, and dinner*
*No credit cards accepted*

## ZUM ALTEN FRITZ
### 1840 N.E. Fourth Avenue, Miami
#### 305-374-7610

In the heat of the subtropics, German food is sometimes considered too heavy, but for those who worship *würst* and seek *Schnitzels* in any clime, this is the place. It's filled with memories of Berlin and, tucked into an old home with its own memories, is reminiscent of some *gasthaus* in the Old Country. The *sauerbraten* is authentic and the *strudel* superior.

*Price: About $15 per person*
*Open Tues.–Sun. for lunch and dinner; closed Mon.*
*Accepts all major credit cards*

# PALM BEACH COUNTY

## ANCHOR INN
### 2810 Hypoluxo Road, Lantana
#### 305-965-4794

In addition to the absolutely fresh seafood served at this water-hugging hideaway, the chowder is of championship caliber, the baked beans and whole grain breads that come with the meals excellent, and there's a good selection of California white wines. The back room knows how to handle the harvest of the deep and blends a good dill sauce, along with a Creole treatment of fish baked with tomatoes and onions and some Louisiana seasoning. The pies are also special.

*Price: About $20 per person*
*Open daily for dinner only*
*Accepts all major credit cards*

# ARTURO'S RISTORANTE
## 6750 North Federal Highway, Boca Raton
### 305-997-7373

In 1983 Arturo's of Long Island, New York, established a mission to the southern provinces in a villa of a structure, staffed it with veterans from the north, found a local crew of waiters and captains, and proceeded to take off. With a starter course of *torta primavera* (more than a dozen layers of pasta, salami, veggies, and *mortadella* beautifully assembled), the back room—partially on view through a window by the entrance—aims to please. The fried *calamari* is crunchy, and, when mixed with a little shrimp and olive oil, heavenly as an appetizer. My favorite entrée here is the veal chop, but I usually make sure someone at my table orders the fresh red snapper, dolloped with a tomato sauce that is equally fresh. Service is formal and, even in the crush of the season, friendly and eager to please. The made-fresh Hovis loaf is as welcome as the chariot of desserts and the presence of quality Italian wines in the cellar.

*Price: About $30 per person*
*Open Tues.–Sun. for dinner only; closed Mon.*
*Accepts all major credit cards*

# AUBERGE LE GRILLON
## 6900 North Federal Highway, Boca Raton
### 305-997-6888

A tiny gem of a place loyal to its cricket name, but a giant when it comes to taking the extra steps to create memorable dining experiences. Owners Harm Meyer from Holland and Malcolm Miller from England make this forty-seater soar, overseeing front and back rooms with generous portions of tender, lovin' care, cellaring good wines, regularly changing menus to reflect seasonal shifts and kindle the interest of their happy patrons. Among the highlights of this inn of the cricket are the Dover sole set with lobster and scallops with Pernod and glazed with *mousseline;* the fresh trout swimming in coconut butter with rafts of oranges; chicken breast filled with a *mousse* of veal with a sauce redolent of rosemary; appetizer pears with a walnut-sprinkled Roquefort sauce. The accompanying vegetable platter with its made-fresh pasta is clearly the best in the state and the white chocolate *mousse* carefully spooned onto a swirl of raspberry sauce is a joy to behold.

*Price: About $30 per person*
*Open Tues.–Sun. for lunch and dinner; closed Mon.; closed June–Sept.*
*Accepts Diners Club, Visa, and MasterCard*

# BANANA BOAT

## 739 East Ocean Avenue, Boynton Beach
### 305-732-9400

An island escape for lunch and dinner seven days a week, served by a cheerful crew of bouncing, leggy girls who smile their way from table to table, bringing from the back room fish fillets that are fresh and carefully broiled, sandwiches that are guaranteed mouth-stretchers, salads dramatically reposing in pineapple shells, coconut-dipped shrimp, burgers, and beef as fancy as filet mignon with *béarnaise*. There's a raw bar and no fewer than three other bars, usually elbow-to-elbow during the season. On Sunday, there's a steel band and special egg dishes, and at all times a wonderful waterfront seat for watching all the action on the Intracoastal Waterway.

*Price: About $20 per person*
*Open daily for lunch and dinner*
*Accepts all major credit cards*

# BUSCH'S

## 5855 North Ocean Boulevard, Delray Beach (Ocean Ridge)
### 905-732-8470

If you arrive here on a Thursday, you'll be able to order that pride of Charleston, she-crab soup; but on any day there are excellent seafood and soups to be had. At the right time of the year, there are soft-shell crabs from the Chesapeake, dolphin given a dousing of *sauce mornay* and rested on a bed of freshly made spinach, perfectly grilled swordfish; but always scallops, shrimp, oysters, and clams on the half shell, and a special lobster Savannah. The bar-lounge is an inviting staging area, with piano music and song, and the dining room gives you the feeling of being somewhere traditional and uncomplicated in the Midwest.

*Price: About $20 per person*
*Open Tues.–Sun. for dinner only; closed Mon.*
*Accepts all major credit cards*

# CAFÉ L'EUROPE
## 150 Worth Avenue (Esplanade), Palm Beach
### 305-655-4020

In the new, eastern reaches of fabulous Worth Avenue, with its anchor of Sak's department store and numerous other shopping extravaganzas, this elegantly outfitted café presides like a jewel in the crown—brick, brass, polished woods, intricate placement of mirrors and stunning positioning of flowers, watched over by a formal staff and introduced by a beautiful bar, the penultimate place to start or end an affair, to see and be seen—and to drink and dine extremely well. Start with something as hearty as French onion soup or a slice of the duck *terrine* with pistachios. At noontime—and this is a very popular retreat for shoppers and sightseers alike at lunch—there are *croissant* sandwiches and freshly assembled salads. Night brings such delights as grilled veal chop or poached salmon surrounded by a julienne of crisp vegetables, duck braced with a peppery sauce, chicken in tarragon cream. For finishers, there's the trendy chestnut ice cream but also such Escoffier standbys as peach Melba. The wine list has been carefully assembled and the captains are knowledgeable about that list.

*Price: About $35 per person*
*Open Mon.–Sat. for lunch and dinner; closed Sun.*
*Accepts all major credit cards*

# CAFÉ PALMIERS
## In the Hyatt Palm Beaches, 630 Clearwater Park Road, West Palm Beach
### 305-833-1234

A brilliant demonstration of what has happened in the grand hotels of this country, another confirmation that in the so-called signature rooms of our best hostelries, the level of dining has reached new heights. This is a splendiferous place, with the palm motif everywhere, accenting the soft grays and peach, reflected quietly in mirrors above ultra-comfortable banquettes. Table appointments are contemporary, the black-stem goblets unusual, standing out in a sea of pastel. Service is properly formal and informed, and the chefs prove again and again that taste did not depart with the decorator. No one does a better *carpaccio:* the razor-thin slices of dried sirloin are sprinkled with Parmesan and black pepper and served with a palate-tingling mustard sauce. The snails are deep-fried in a thin pastry with companions of cream cheese and crab spiked with just the right touch of garlic; the freshly-cooked *fettuccine* is tangled with pink strips of smoked salmon bathed in a fine cream sauce; the rack of lamb, one of their most popular dishes, is first rolled in lightly herbed crumbs and then christened with hollandaise boasting a hint of mint. The wine list complements such performance with intelligence. On Sundays there is a sensational brunch—another development in modern hotel-keeping we should all be grateful for.

*Price: About $35 per person*
*Open Mon.–Sat. for dinner only; closed Sun.*
*Accepts all major credit cards*

---

# THE EPICUREAN
## 331 South County Road, Palm Beach
### 305-659-2005

Mitch Susnar, a former actor, is the owner-operator-designer of this tribute to and reflection of the best of Palm Beach. The white-aproned black-vested staff moves professionally and proudly through the formally-appointed center room, with its stiff napery and the up-front lounge graced with mirrors and oversized French doors—their heavy brass hardware gleaming—overlooking the Palm Beach passing parade. The café, with its unobtrusive bar (typically, the bottles are out of sight), is the setting for five-to-eight-o'clock sessions of caviar, champagne, and jazz.

The kitchen measures up to the high standards of the setting, providing a limited menu noon and night, and then daily specials reflecting the vagaries of market supply and the whims of the chefs. Among the regular offerings to remember are the snail tartlets with goat cheese, the lobster strudel, the Italian water buffalo *mozzarella* layered with slices of thick, red tomatoes heightened with a splendid basil vinaigrette and sprigs of fresh basil. Entrées that helped establish The Epicurean, opened in January 1985, as one of the best of the best, include swordfish grilled with a pineapple-pepper *salsa,* capon breast saluted with a *chiffonade* of leeks, and *mignonettes* of lamb dolloped with hot pear chutney. The wine list is highly select. Reservations in season are a must.

*Price: About $40 per person*
*Open daily for breakfast, lunch, and dinner*
*Accepts all major credit cards*

# FENG LIN
## 1725 South Federal Highway, Delray Beach
### 305-278-8326

A trio of brothers, the Changs, have joined forces in this storefront hideaway, one with a parade of booths and a non-Chinese red decor. The Hunan and Szechuan cheffing here is worthy of a palace. From the first bite of the made-out-back crispy noodles to the last morsel of such Occidental desserts as strawberries in a crunchy almond basket, meals in this simple spot are indeed memorable. Feng Lin—which means "maple forest"—is a marvel, clearly the best of the many Chinese restaurants in the county.

*Price: About $15 per person*
*Open daily for lunch and dinner*
*Accepts all major credit cards*

# FUGI
## Del Mar Shopping Village, Palmetto Park Road and Powerline Road, Boca Raton
### 305-392-8778

For those enraptured by the raw fish and burning mustard approach to dining or dieting, this neat and colorful storefront operation is the place to go. The talented chef-owners work behind a long, comfortable, and low-slung *sushi* bar, doing their slicing and artistic arranging under a parade of pennants and banners overhead. While ceiling fans lazily turn and the soft sounds of Japanese music lull you into the Far East, settle on one of the *tatami* mats or sit upright at a table, following the *sushi* and *sashimi* with *sukiyaki,* the do-it-yourself *shabu shabu,* something subjected to the *tempura* treatment, chicken bedded down with vegetables, or carefully grilled fish. There's *sake* and Japanese beer to accompany it all, and for desserts fresh fruit or an interesting red bean ice cream.

*Price: About $15 per person*
*Open Mon.–Sat. for lunch and dinner; open Sun. for dinner only*
*Accepts all major credit cards*

# GAZEBO CAFÉ
## 4199 North Federal Highway, Boca Raton
### 305-395-6033

Hidden behind some greenery in front of a Grand Union shopping complex, this is the best show in town: Chef-owner Bill Sallas and his kitchen crew are in full view behind the see-it-all counter. There they assemble luncheon salads and sandwiches and the evening entrées of fresh fish, the best vichyssoise on the Gold Coast, shrimp given the butter-garlic scampi routine but with the addition of tomatoes and mushrooms, and chunks of beef dolloped with a good *béarnaise*. The wine list is small but acceptable. If you don't want to watch your meal being prepared, there are tables removed from all the action.

*Price: About $15 per person*
*Open Mon.–Fri. for lunch and dinner; open Sat. for dinner only; closed Sun.;*
*closed late summer*
*Accepts Visa and MasterCard*

# HAMBURGER HEAVEN
## 314 South County Road, Palm Beach
### 305-655-5277

A place to flee from all the high-flying, high-priced restaurants in the Worth Avenue area. The burgers are bountiful and the pies and cakes beautiful.

*Price: Under $10 per person*
*Open Mon.–Sat. for lunch and dinner; closed Sun.; closed Aug. 1–Sept. 15*
*No credit cards accepted*

# IL GIRASOLE
## 1911 South Federal Highway, Delray Beach
### 305-272-3566

Charles is the front man and Luigi is behind the burners. Together they spun off this sunflower from a local restaurant landmark called Vittorio, in 1981. The storefront setting, sandwiched into a string of shops off the road, is small enough for the pair to handle their legion of fans with considerable pampering, providing them with superb soups, reliable veal creations, whatever they can find fresh from the sea, desserts definitely worth the extra calories, and a parade of nightly specials.

*Price: About $20 per person*
*Open Tues.–Sun. for dinner only; closed Mon.*
*Accepts Visa and MasterCard*

---

## JOE MUER SEA FOOD
### 6450 North Federal Highway, Boca Raton
**305-997-6688**

Michiganders know—and honor—the name. In Detroit, the Muers have been serving seafood since the 1920s, and in Boca they do it the same way, insisting on freshness and quality, starting all meals with a dish of navy beans marinated with vinegar flecked with onion and parsley. There are chicken-lamb chop-prime steak alternatives for land-locked palates, but seafood is the best seller, and they prepare everything from finnan haddie to soft-shell crabs, swordfish to shrimp and smelts. The dining area was completely refurbished—beautifully—in 1984, making Muer's Southern mission the best-dressed fish house in the state, along with Miami's Fish Market in the Omni Hotel.

*Price: About $20 per person*
*Open daily for lunch and dinner; closed Sun., June–November*
*Accepts all major credit cards*

---

## LA VIEILLE MAISON
### 770 East Palmetto Park Road, Boca Raton
**305-391-6701**

By South Florida standards, this really is an "old house," a leftover of Boca's first real estate boom in the 1920s, built by an engineer working for that architect to the affluent, Addison Mizner, and artfully transformed into a mansion of Mediterranean magnificence by the same partnership that made such a success out of Lauderdale's Down Under and then moved on to another old house challenge, Casa Vecchia (see page 295). There's heavy emphasis on antiques and artifacts, highly artistic accent pieces, and dramatic arrays of flowers. And on the food and wines. This highly touted home possesses one of the best wine lists in the country, and while some argue the exorbitance of the fixed-price menu and the formality of the service, I have no argument with either. The food, from poached snails served on a julienne of vegetables or superb "maisonmade" sausage peppered with pistachios and served with a truffle-speckled sauce, on through the exquisitely fresh salads, and entrées of pompano with pecans, fresh trout with capers, venison, quail with grapes, duckling with turnips, is strictly superior. The best cheese tray in the South follows, along with something sweet. There are nearly two dozen entrées and numerous possibilities for starters and finishers. And, if your party is large enough (and wealthy enough), there's the wine room to reserve.

*Price: About $45 per person*
*Open daily for dinner only*
*Accepts all major credit cards*

## LE MONEGASQUE
### 2505 South Ocean Boulevard, Palm Beach
#### 305-585-0071

French dining in the pre-*nouvelle* manner, but with the slight twist, in that almost everything on the menu, and most of the decor, is keyed to owner Aldo Rinero's native Monaco. Thus the sweetbreads are *du Palais,* the filet mignon Princess, the pompano Grimaldi. Why not? Aldo loves his land and his kitchen here has all the right kind of expertise to produce superior food, from the coarse-grained *pâté* to *bouillabaisse* to *cassoulet.* The dessert cart follows similarly traditional lines; the wine list is limited.

In season, reservations are mandatory, but residents of the condominium above this touch of Monaco have priority so make sure of your timing. Also, Rinero returns home every summer, closing his restaurant from July through sometime in October.

*Price: About $30 per person*
*Open Tues.–Sun. for dinner only; closed Mon. and July–mid-October*
*Accepts all major credit cards*

## OAR HOUSE
### 3108 South Congress Avenue, Lake Worth (*north of Tenth Avenue*)
#### 305-965-9724

Classic fish house setting: rugged and uncomplicated with a parade of barrel stools clinging to the bar, leading to the dining room out back. The seafood is fresh and uncluttered by fancy sauces, thick breading, or high prices. Conch fritters, clam chowder, the blue and Dungeness crab, rock shrimp, and more than seventy different beers to set it all awash are among the highlights of Elsie and Ed Mulvihill's friendly home of happy informality.

*Price: About $10 per person*
*Open Mon.–Sat. for lunch and dinner; closed Sun.*
*Accepts Visa and MasterCard*

---

## OFF BROADWAY

In the Village Square Shopping Center, 21154 St. Andrews
Boulevard, Boca Raton
### 305-368-2622

A spotless statement that represents all that's great about delis—close to 200 menu items, outrageously oversize desserts, perfect potato pancakes, smoked fish platters, blintzes and bagels, pastrami and pickles, and budget-pleasing prices.

*Price: About $12 per person*
*Open daily for breakfast, lunch, and dinner*
*No credit cards accepted*

---

## THE ORIGINAL PANCAKE HOUSE

1715 South Federal Highway, Delray Beach
### 305-276-0769

When it started in Portland, Oregon, the late James Beard declared it to be one of the best restaurants in the country, and today, half a hundred links later, it's a nationwide chain with two other outlets in Florida, in Fort Lauderdale and Kendall in South Miami. And it's still one of the best. Because no one assembles a better German pancake, or the smaller Dutch version, or that mélange of sherry-mushroom-spiked cream sauce on biscuits layered with wonderful sausage.

*Price: Under $10 per person*
*Open daily for breakfast, lunch, and dinner*
*No credit cards accepted*

# PETITE MARMITE
## 309½ Worth Avenue, Palm Beach
### 305-655-0550

Constanzo "Gus" Pucillo and wife Geraldine are no longer in charge of this landmark they nurtured to international fame, but new owner Tommy Shiroyan, representative of a new breed on the avenue, is keeping alive the traditions, improving on the recipes, supervising the international staff. The mix-and-match Mediterranean setting of brick and tile with colorful plantings here and there has been spruced up. The Ricardo Room, named for a Florentine painter whose works grace the walls, is a delight, and there's no finer evocation of the French Riviera in Florida than the Garden Room with its skylight and hanging lush greenery. Among the outstanding creations of the kitchen are the lobster bisque, the chicken-okra soup, eggs Florentine, eggplant *Provençale, filet de sole Véronique,* chicken Mascotte, and a whole duck given the *bigarade* orange treatment. Desserts are still being rolled past guests with considerable pride: the pastries, cakes, chocolate *mousse,* the special orange cake, and *gâteau St. Honoré.* The adjoining lounge is a popular watering hole, and there's an ample supply of carefully selected wines.

*Price: About $30 per person*
*Open daily for lunch and dinner*
*Accepts all major credit cards*

# RAFFAELLO'S
## 725 East Palmetto Park Road, Boca Raton
### 305-392-4855

Clearly one of the outstanding Italian restaurants in Florida, professionally served and immaculately maintained with handsome table appointments, a general air of gentility, and much pride in the preparation of the food. Diners are greeted after apéritif time by a display of the night's specials: the pasta, seafood, and meats, along with a verbal recital. Those few minutes represent chef-owner Raffaello's success in the marketplace that day. All his farinaceous fare is freshly made on the premises—or next door where he runs a takeout pasta shop—and the regular menu lists more than a dozen possibilities. Along with his fine treatment of veal, of seafood, his lobster creations are especially noteworthy. And no one in the state or the South serves such incredible mussels. Eighteen giants comprise an appetizer course—for one—and they are beautifully blessed with the lightest of sauces, built around tomato, onion, garlic. There's a good selection of wines, including an excellent house-label Bordeaux.

*Price: About $25 per person*
*Open Mon.–Sat. for dinner only; closed Sun.*
*Accepts all major credit cards*

---

## SIAM GARDEN
### 680 Glades Road (Oaks Plaza), Boca Raton
### 305-368-9013

The menu is filled with Cantonese specialties as well as such Thai temptations as *satay,* that do-it-yourself starter course of lanced strips of meat that arrive with your very own mini-hibachi. Try also the sweet-and-sour crispy noodles, curries made with shrimp, pork, or beef that cooked in coconut milk, the hot and spicy *labb* (ground meat patties whose memory lingers long after the fire is stilled with some beer or wine). The setting is loyal to the name: There's a profusion of potted greens, turned-wood pillar-partitions, and an interior kind of a courtyard for sitting and slouching on comfortable cushions—Japanese style.

*Price: About $15 per person*
*Open daily for lunch and dinner*
*Accepts all major credit cards*

---

## TOM'S PLACE
### 1198 North Dixie Highway, Boca Raton
### 305-392-9504

Tom Wright is in charge here and he has most of his family on the payroll (except son Tom, Jr., who has his own Rib Heaven up Dixie Highway a few miles, in Delray Beach). The ribs are indeed finger lickin' good; the side dishes, the collard greens, cornmeal muffins, and warm potato salad are incredible. On weekends there's conch fritters, catfish, and hush puppies to be had.

*Price: About $12 per person*
*Open Wed.–Sat. for lunch and dinner; closed Sun.–Tues.*
*No credit cards accepted*

# FORT LAUDERDALE
# AND ENVIRONS

## AMBROSIA
### 1201 South Federal Highway, Pompano Beach
### 305-782-1111

*Opa!* Here is the best Greek restaurant in South Florida, loyal in every way to its name, which my Webster tells me means "anything exquisitely gratifying in taste or scent." But add sights as well. And sound. There's a *bouzouki* player and a piano but no navel maneuvers plague this place, which is designed with great restraint: a few decorative Greek handicrafts on the walls and a gallery of paintings by Greek-Mexican artist Phina Barzilai. There's equally commendable command in the kitchen, where the chefs produce marvelous marinated octopus and *garides Mykonos,* a small school of shrimp swimming in a tomato and pepper sauce, sprinkled with feta, and heightened with wine and herbs. Favorites among the dozen entrées include the veal chop, baby lamb chops, grilled *souvlaki* with onions, peppers, and tomatoes, and the pound-and-a-half fresh snapper, brought to the table whole in an eye-pleasing presentation. The wine list is limited, but there are a few Greek bottles available. And for desserts, of course there is *baklava,* and that other layered *filo* sweetie known as *galatoboureko.*

*Price: About $20 per person*
*Open daily for dinner only*
*Accepts all major credit cards*

## BRAUHAUS
### 1701 East Sunrise Boulevard, Fort Lauderdale
### 305-764-4104

This is as close as one gets to a *gumütlich* Bavarian beer hall on the Gold Coast. All the elements are there: An oompah band, shoe-slapping dancers, cuckoo clocks, and other mementos of the Old Country and a *Wunderbar* menu with all the classics—*würst* by the mile, tons of *kraut* and red cabbage, smoked pork, *sauerbraten,* and a good selection of German wine and beers.

*Price: About $15 per person*
*Open Tues.–Sun. for dinner; closed Mon.*
*Accepts all major credit cards*

# BROOKS
## 500 South Federal Highway, Deerfield Beach
### 305-427-9302

Bernard Perron, a Frenchman of energetic dedication who started his culinary career at the age of fourteen as *pâtissier,* is the always-gracious genius responsible for this ultra-elegant slice of fine dining. His pastry background shows: He makes one of the best pecan pies in the South. He also competes for title for best conch chowder, but then he spent many years working in and running class acts in the islands. His menu is always changing, reflecting the influences of market supply and food trends, and his own tireless determination to keep his customers happy—and coming back. His wine list is excellent, with many offerings by the glass. He has recruited a staff that reflects his own philosophy of providing friendly, yet formal and professional service. His family also gets into the act: wife, daughter out front and in the office, a son behind the burners, taking his licks just as father did years ago in France.

*Price: About $25 per person*
*Open daily for dinner; lunch, tea, and late-night supper only during the season*
*Accepts all major credit cards*

# CAFÉ DE GENEVE
## 1519 South Andrews Avenue, Fort Lauderdale
### 305-522-8928

George Wales, who started this regional slice of Switzerland in the early 1970s, sold the place in 1984, but to a fellow Swiss who is just as determined as the founder to keep the same menu and ensure that service and setting remain as chalet-cozy. That means the fun of fondues and such reliably prepared fare as veal in a rich, mushroom-dotted cream sauce, veal kidneys in a fine Madeira-blessed sauce, *coq au vin, cannelloni,* and crisp roast duck. The dessert cart is also a temptation and the *napoleons* are among the finest to be found anywhere. There are also several Swiss wines on the limited, but select, list.

*Price: About $20 per person*
*Open Mon.–Fri. for lunch; dinner daily*
*Accepts all major credit cards*

# CAFÉ MAX
## 2601 East Atlantic Boulevard, Pompano Beach
### 305-782-0606

Californian Dennis Max has brought the fresh breezes from his native state clear across the land to this intimate café awash with a touch of contemporary tempered by Art Deco. With his strikingly attractive wife, he oversees an intensely personal creation, one in which the food of the night is on view and described on an overhead blackboard. The kitchen staff is partially on view as well, and their performance and the presence of all that freshness on display guarantee a certain quality of food. Goat cheese is a common ingredient here, as is the mesquite used for grilling. The slabs of fish committed to those mesquite coals are treated to a slight christening of caper-flecked lime butter. Tuna is another favorite, as is the veal chop. And with a wine bar off to one side, there's another guarantee: the availability of top-quality California wines by the glass.

*Price: About $25 per person*
*Open daily for dinner only*
*Accepts all major credit cards*

# CAFÉ SEPTEMBER
## 2975 North Federal Highway, Fort Lauderdale
### 305-563-4331

Don't be led astray or become unduly concerned when entering what looks like another upscale Gold Coast disco. Proceed without delay to the "Sanctum Sanctoris," the inner sanctum where only forty fortunate guests can be seated. In a multi-level setting of brick, wood, and mirrors, accented with Mirós on the wall and glistening gold, silver, and crystal on the glass-top tables, it's the perfect size for a chef to display a full range of culinary wizardry, and, in this café, he's been given the necessary support to buy only the best, only the freshest, to work with. There are nightly specials on a constantly changing bill of fare, but superlative seafood *terrines,* coarse-grain *pâtés,* herb-coated steaks, rack of lamb, and venison are regulars. The wine list is acceptable and the desserts as individually tailored and varied as the rest of the menu.

*Price: About $35 per person*
*Open daily for dinner only*
*Accepts all major credit cards*

# CAP'S PLACE
## Cap's Dock, 2765 Northeast Court, Lighthouse Point
### 305-941-0418

A unique Florida experience: reachable only by boat on regular ferry service. It's a real blast from the past with the kind of rugged bar where one expects to find a belching Charles Laughton or an unshaven Bogie slouched over in a corner. The dining rooms are equally rustic, with historical mementos on the walls, and with a young, spiffy staff bringing the fresh fish, the fresh hearts of palm salads, and the best French fries in the state, cut from Idahos and brought to the table hotter than hot.

*Price: About $20 per person*
*Open daily for dinner*
*Accepts all major credit cards*

# CASA VECCHIA
## 209 North Birch Road, Fort Lauderdale
### 305-463-7575

In a Waterway-hugging home that was built for those made wealthy by Pond's cold cream, the team responsible for Boca's La Vieille Maison, another old house, has installed an interesting array of antiques and collectibles, fanning them out from terrace and patio, spreading them across two floors (avoid the second-floor rooms), creating in the process a mini-palazzo. Service is properly formal and the food preparation—Northern Italian naturally—is superb. Pasta is made on the premises, as are the *sorbets;* some of the herbs are grown in their own gardens between restaurant and water. There are a few French touches in the kitchen, but that's all to the good. And there's a lot of California in the wine list, especially among the cabernets. Italian wines should be better represented.

*Price: About $40 per person*
*Open daily for dinner*
*Accepts all major credit cards*

# CELEBRITY ROOM
In the Diplomat Hotel, 3515 South Ocean Drive, Hollywood
### 305-457-8111

Revitalized, refurbished, redecorated, and reborn in 1985, and still proud of its reputation as the best restaurant—and certainly the most expensive—in Hollywood, this is a room for the high-fliers and the expense accounts with no limits. But then what price Dover sole flown in fresh? Or fiddleheads and venison or some of the best veal creations to be found in the county? The Caesar salad reaches new heights in the hands of the competent captains, and, when dessert time rolls around, there's a stunning array of *crêpes,* tarts, and those multi-flowered *nouvelle cuisine* concoctions that are so pleasing to the eye as well as the sweet tooth. The wine list marches along but is not a gouger. The elegance of the setting matches the level of service and caliber of food. In season, reservations are required.

*Price: About $40 per person*
*Open daily for dinner only*
*Accepts all major credit cards*

# CHRISTINE LEE'S NORTHGATE
6191 Rock Island Road, Fort Lauderdale
### 305-726-0430

The same charming lady responsible for Miami's best Chinese restaurant (see the listing under the same name on page 265) repeated her success by cloning the non-Chinese decor, installing a front room of accommodating servers, and a kitchen that turns out the same reliable fare—the best Hunan, Szechuan, Cantonese food in Broward County—along with good prime steaks.

*Price: About $25 per person*
*Open daily for dinner*
*Accepts all major credit cards*

# CRAB POT CAFÉ

## 4480 North Federal Highway, Lighthouse Point
### 305-941-2722

Marylander Wayne Cordero, whose family hails from Chesapeake Bay well into the last century, opened this capstone of his mini-chain of Crab Pots in 1984. The café is a bit more pretentious in its menu aspirations than in some of the others, but the crab Imperial, oysters Rockefeller, and Dungeness crab succeed admirably. All the food is delivered by bright-eyed waitresses known as the "corps of crabettes."

*Price: About $20 per person*
*Open daily for dinner*
*Accepts all major credit cards*

# ERNIE'S BAR-B-QUE

## 1843 South Federal Highway, Fort Lauderdale
### 305-523-8636

Strictly informal and serving from early to late, noon and night. Don't miss the conch chowder before laying in to that slab of barbecue meat on the Bimini bread. And, if you want to munch *al fresco,* head for the high ground —on the second floor porch.

*Price: Under $10 per person*
*Open daily for lunch and dinner*
*No credit cards accepted*

# 15TH STREET FISHERIES AND BOAT HOUSE

## 1900 S.E. Fifteenth Street, Fort Lauderdale
### 305-763-2777

The setting on the Intracoastal is super; the service staff is smiling; the food is fresh and carefully prepared. In short, this is a not-to-be-missed Gold Coast experience. Owner-operator Mike Hurst, director of the National Restaurant Association, professor at the Hotel & Restaurant School of Florida International University, and an important force in the field, is an experienced professional, one who knows how to attract a crowd all year long. And how to amuse them: First he got alligator tail on menus across the state, and now he's importing "bugs"—Australian sand spiders that taste like a cross between lobster and shrimp. For less exotic fare, try his steaming Florida seafood answer to *bouillabaisse,* or a slab of whatever is promised to be fresh from the sea. And enjoy those special breads and the wines.

*Price: About $20 per person*
*Open daily for lunch and dinner*
*Accepts all major credit cards*

---

## FRENCH QUARTER
### 463 S.E. Eighth Avenue, Fort Lauderdale
#### 305-463-8000

The same Louis Flemati who blessed the Lauderdale landscape with Café de Paris converted this classic 1920s Spanish-style home into a New Orleans touch of France. Louis has the greenest thumb in the restaurant whirl: His pair of restaurants are lush and well loved, as are the dessert creations, the lobster salads for lunch, the duckling, curried scallops, pheasant, and Creole concoctions for dinner. Upstairs is a fine little lounge, as artistically arranged as everything else Flemati touches.

*Price: About $25 per person*
*Open Mon.–Fri. for lunch and dinner; Sat. dinner only; closed Sun.*
*Accepts all major credit cards*

---

## GERD MUELLER'S AMBRY
### 3016 East Commercial Boulevard, Fort Lauderdale
#### 305-771-7342

Soccer fans will recognize the name of this world-class athlete who now runs a restaurant with his wife. Mueller scored more points than any other player in World Cup competition. And now he's scoring points with his Ambry, tending bar in a gathering place for the local German community, overseeing an on-stage grill where reliable steaks are prepared, and a kitchen that churns out such German classics as calf's liver *nach Berliner Art* (with apple and onion).

*Price: About $20 per person*
*Open Mon.–Sat. for dinner; closed Sun.*
*Accepts all major credit cards*

# GIBBY'S

## 2900 N.E. Twelfth Terrace, Fort Lauderdale (Oakland Park)
### 305-565-2929

The original Gibby's started years ago in Montreal, in an ancient stable of historic importance. In the sunny South, they converted a fine old building into a country club of a place, one with a fine bar and lounge off to one side. The menu is not complicated; nor is it overpriced at noon or night. The fish is guaranteed fresh, the meats select, and the dessert portions gigantic. A favorite here is the *St. Honoré* creation, a perfect *coup de grâce* enjoyed with a flaming coffee.

*Price: About $20 per person*
*Open daily for lunch and dinner*
*Accepts all major credit cards*

---

# LA BONNE CRÊPE

## 815 East Las Olas Boulevard, Fort Lauderdale
### 305-761-1515

The lucky Pierre responsible for this splendid addition to the town's street of streets is a native of Brittany, where *crêpes* originated, and he is a highly skilled practitioner of the art of stuffing sweets and savouries into the thin pancakes. Salads and soups are also commendable and when he makes a *napoleon,* he approaches the Platonic ideal.

*Price: Under $10 per person*
*Open Mon.–Sat. for lunch and dinner; closed Sundays*
*Accepts Visa and MasterCard*

---

# LA FERME

## 1601 East Sunrise Boulevard, Fort Lauderdale
### 305-764-0987

The Terriers, Henri behind the burners and Marie-Paule out front, are now in their second decade of residency on the summit of local French culinary consistency. Doubled in size in 1984 and again refurbished, their still-intimate little farm is a joy—better than ever. The *pâtés* and soups are freshly assembled; the liver softly bathed in raspberry vinegar is superb, the poached salmon ever so delicate, the dessert chariot an eye-popping delight, and the *soufflés* puffed to perfection. The wine list, once a weak point, has been greatly expanded in recent years. The service is as pleasant as any restaurant in Florida—but then the staff takes their guidance, their inspiration, from the petite, effervescent lady in charge.

*Price: About $20 per person*
*Open Tues.–Sun. for dinner; closed Mon. and August–September*
*Accepts all major credit cards*

## LAGNIAPPE CAJUN HOUSE
### 230 East Las Olas Boulevard, Fort Lauderdale
#### 305-467-7500

Dave Rea and Ron Morrison, owners of this felicitous rendering of New Orleans in both spirit and substance, are not really good ole boys from bayou country, but they do know their craft and they do love Louisiana. It shows: in the *Sazeracs,* in the brewing of Community Coffee, the serving of shrimp *rémoulade,* the blackened fish Paul Prudhomme style, the presentation of those outsize sausages, and the preparation of crawfish. A final fillip: On the weekends they have Dixieland and New Orleans jazz sessions for breakfast and brunch. And at all times special corn muffins with the zing of hot peppers.

*Price: About $15 per person*
*Open Mon.–Fri. for lunch and dinner; Sat. and Sun. for dinner only*
*Accepts all major credit cards*

## LE CAFÉ DE PARIS
### 715 East Las Olas Boulevard, Fort Lauderdale
#### 305-467-2900

Ever since Swiss-born Louis Flemati took over what was then one of two or three French restaurants in the area, this café on Lauderdale's special street has blossomed. That was in 1970; today the café is better than ever. It's a bustling place at noon, but one can still find a sheltered, romantic corner (ask for the Montmartre Room). During the season the café is always filled at night, but reservations are honored and the place is so efficiently run there's no problem being accommodated. The wines are well selected, the bar is a super rallying point before and after dinner, and the menu runs a full gamut of Gallic café food, from superb luncheon omelets to dinner entrées of *sole à la meunière,* lobster, steaks and chops, sweetbreads, and duckling. The vegetables are crisp, the food delivered hot, and the bread, rolls, and pastries all prepared on the premises. An added plus is the music, a strolling violin and accordion duo that has been pleasing patrons almost as long as Louis has.

*Price: About $20 per person*
*Open daily for lunch and dinner*
*Accepts all major credit cards*

# THE LEFT BANK
214 S.E. Sixth Avenue, Fort Lauderdale
### 305-462-5376

Chef-owner Jean-Pierre Brehier is one of those indefatigable individuals who never cease trying to improve his performance and inspire his guests. He has a monthly newsletter which goes out to some 10,000 regular customers; he's always on the search for outstanding wines (he used to own a nearby wine store) and he regularly shifts menus to reflect the compatible marriages he makes between fresh Florida produce and French techniques of preparation. His vegetable *pâté* is a colorful tribute to the harvest and is served with a tomato-basil *coulis;* his marinated scallops are dressed with coconut and ginger and the Gulf shrimp with a lime-mustard sauce. A breast of chicken is coated with a grapefruit-lime *beurre blanc,* lamb chops with orange and kiwi suspended in a honey-mustard sauce, and there are liberal chunks of citrus in the luncheon spinach salad. Jean-Pierre is still a believer in the tableside pyromaniacal performances, flashing and flaming with a good deal of finesse. His veal creations keep getting better and better. Especially notable is the *plume de veau scallopine* he sautés in a flavorful mélange of herbs and spices and a school of baby shrimp and mushrooms swimming in sherry and Madeira. For starters there's the *bouillabaisse* custard with a saffron sauce or *carpaccio* or the *fettuccine* with smoked salmon slices or an excellent duckling *consommé.*

*Price: About $35 per person*
*Open daily for dinner*
*Accepts all major credit cards*

# MAI-KAI
3599 North Federal Highway, Fort Lauderdale
### 305-563-3272

This is one of our country's quintessential Polynesian playgrounds. Lushly landscaped, furnished with authentic island artifacts, staffed by torch- and sword-twirling Samoans and hip-swinging lovelies from wherever, it features an endless parade of specialty drinks (order the "Mystery Drink" if you want a real show) and the kind of food Trader Vic decreed was Polynesian years ago. The meats prepared in the Chinese wood-burning ovens are outstanding.

*Price: About $20 (added cover charge for show)*
*Open daily for dinner*
*Accepts all major credit cards*

## NADA'S DUBROVNIK
### 3433 Griffin Road, Davie
**305-981-5343**

The setting is storefront simple and the decor is provided by the patrons, but the food is as hearty and expansive as the Austro–Hungarian Empire. The soups are super, the lamb shanks sensational, and the *strudel*—Oh, the *strudel!* You can get apple and cheese and they're good enough for the Emperor.

*Price: About $10 per person*
*Open daily for dinner*
*No credit cards accepted*

## NOBI
### 3020 North Federal Highway, Fort Lauderdale
**305-561-3686**

In this vest pocket of a place, ambidextrous Japanese chefs manage to slice their fresh fish and put on a show while the corps of kimono-clad waitresses deliver to counter and booths luncheon servings of swiftly deep-fried pork or shrimp, mingled with vegetables and parsley, and dinners revolving around appetizers of artfully-presented *sushi* and *sashimi* and entrées of *teriyaki, sukiyaki,* and slices of abalone layered with a soybean paste. *Sake* and Japanese beer are available as proper complements to this authentic fare.

*Price: About $15 per person*
*Open Mon.–Fri. for lunch; daily for dinner*
*Accepts all major credit cards*

## OLD FLORIDA SEAFOOD HOUSE
### 1414 North Twenty-sixth Street, Fort Lauderdale (*Wilton Manors*)
**305-566-1044**

On one side is a large raw bar where the luscious bivalves are shucked before your very eyes; on the other is the room of booths and in the back a small private room for the regulars. The staff is smiling and friendly, the fish reliably fresh (except for the fish 'n' chips which the waitress will explain is frozen cod from Iceland), and the salads far better than the norm. There are also a couple of veal dishes that are alone worth the trip.

*Price: About $15 per person*
*Open daily for dinner*
*Accepts Visa and MasterCard*

---

## PAESANO
### 1301 East Las Olas Boulevard, Fort Lauderdale
#### 305-467-3266

An encapsulation of all things Italian—*tutto Italiano,* trattoria style. The walls are a wonder to behold, the tables, yes, with red-and-white checkered cloths with white napery on top, and there's similar dressing up of what trattorias routinely offer their fans. Here the cheffing is strictly first class and the serving staff extremely competent. The result is a happy, happy place, one with good Italian wines, along with bottlings from other countries. Pasta is homemade, the fish brought in fresh (zero in on the red snapper sautéed in white wine and then sprinkled with chopped olives and mushrooms), and the veal complemented with cheese stuffing and a pastry wrap.

*Price: About $20 per person*
*Open daily for dinner*
*Accepts all major credit cards*

---

## PAL'S CAPTAIN'S TABLE
### Cove Yacht Basin, Deerfield Beach
#### 305-427-4000

Joe Muer of Detroit and Boca Raton fish house fame bought this extremely successful, high-volume establishment for a few million dollars in 1984 and wisely kept on almost all of the staff. That means a continuation of that incredible treasure chest of two dozen desserts, the live entertainment, the carefully prepared fish entrées, the special luncheons, and a non-buffet Sunday brunch. And, of course, the same splendid waterfront setting, smack on the Intracoastal Waterway. Watch the boaters arrive in class for their meals and, if you want to join them outside, go next door to the wide wrap-around porch of the Cove for your pre- or post-drink.

*Price: About $20 per person*
*Open daily for lunch and dinner*
*Accepts all major credit cards*

# PIZZERIA UNO
## 6201 North Federal Highway, Fort Lauderdale
### 305-776-7825

What Ike Sewall and Ric Riccardo made famous in Chicago in the 1940s—deep-dish pizza—is now franchised elsewhere in the land, including Lauderdale, and it's authentic, right down to the special salad dressing. There is a splendid bar in this wood and brass setting.

*Price: Under $10 per person*
*Open daily for lunch and dinner*
*Accepts all major credit cards*

---

# RUTH'S CHRIS STEAK HOUSE
## 2525 North Federal Highway, Fort Lauderdale
### 305-565-2338

It's not Peter Luger's in Brooklyn, Palm in Manhattan or Miami or L.A.; it's a new link in a mini-chain that got its start in New Orleans. But it is good, very good. The server boldly proclaims it's the "Home of *Serious* Steaks," all of them prime, delivered to the table sizzling in pools of butter. There are salmon fillets, live Maine lobster, and Alaskan king crab legs on the menu, but they too arrive in a buttery state. This is not a place for cholesterol-watchers, but it's Mecca for All-American beef lovers. Delmonicos, New York strips, and a show-stopper of a porterhouse (ordered for two, three, or four), are the main attractions, cut off corn-fed Midwest cattle. Build up appetites with an order of the blackened tuna or the shrimp *rémoulade*. Both are loyal to their New Orleans origins.

This is not a stop on the budget trail: Everything, even the salad and baked potato, is *à la carte*. The wine list is extensive, and the presence of the bottles, tucked neatly into arched alcoves along the walls, adds to the ambiance of a setting that is extremely well illuminated in a soft, sophisticated manner. Reservations are mandatory on the weekends.

*Price: About $30 per person*
*Open Mon.–Fri. for lunch and dinner; Sat. and Sun. for dinner only*
*Accepts all major credit cards*

# WINDOWS ON THE GREEN

Pier 66, 2301 S.E. Seventeenth Street Causeway, Fort
Lauderdale
305-524-0611

An evening at this happily revitalized dining room must begin in the clouds
—in the revolving lounge, there for you to appreciate the Lauderdale landscape. Return there for late night dancing, but in between, settle into this
highly sophisticated setting with formal service and a kitchen that dazzles with
its *nouvelle* creations, starting with the display of the specials—in the manner
of a Le Français in Wheeling, Illinois—dramatically brought to the table
while violin music plays softly in the background. The introductory *galantine*
of seafood is striking and the poached turbot superb, as is the breast of duckling
stuffed with pecans, the *médaillons* of veal swimming in a wine-enhanced pear
sauce, and the salmon with fennel butter. Desserts are in the same eye-pleasing
category, presented with multi-hued ripples and spirals. The wine list is select,
but definitely on the expensive side.

*Price: About $35 per person*
*Open Mon.–Sat. for dinner only; closed Sun.*
*Accepts all major credit cards*

# WINE CELLAR

199 East Oakland Park Boulevard, Fort Lauderdale (*Oakland
Park*)
305-565-9021

Since 1984 this little jewel has had a new home, and it's even a happier abode
than the first Wine Cellar, filled with the trappings appropriate to the name,
and served by some of the friendliest faces in town—starting with owner-
maître d' Achim Samtlebe. He puts all his experience to good use: in making
the pastries, in greeting the guests, in supervising a motivated staff. And his
partner, chef Franz, does his thing: blending those fruit soups, saucing the
scallops (nobody does a better scallop appetizer), stuffing the veal with a
wonderful mélange of mustard, Madeira, mushrooms, cream cheese, and scallions. The wine list is excellent.

*Price: About $20 per person*
*Open Mon.–Fri. for lunch and dinner; Sat. for dinner only; closed Sun.*
*Accepts all major credit cards*

# YESTERDAY'S
### 3001 East Oakland Park Boulevard, Fort Lauderdale
#### 305-561-4400

This handsomely designed structure on the waterway has an extremely popular disco and, separated by sound-proof walls, a sophisticated, upscale, and very expensive place called The Plum Room, upstairs. Downstairs the dining rooms with Art Nouveau etched-glass ramble along the water. It's a grand place for a leisurely lunch, while watching the passing boat parade, or for dinner at night, when all is atwinkle. On Sundays there's a special brunch—the best in Broward County. Supervision here is highly professional, and the serving staff reflects it.

*Price: About $25 per person*
*Open daily for lunch and dinner*
*Accepts all major credit cards*

# YUM YUM OF SIAM
### 3856 North University Drive (*Mercede Americana Plaza*), Fort Lauderdale (*Sunrise*)
#### 305-742-0001

One of the older and more established of the nearly forty Thai restaurants that grace the landscape, this is a Western outpost of freshly-prepared food with names out of the Mysterious East—all the *pad* and *prigs, satays, toms,* and *gais,* which spell lightly spiced, stir-fried freshness with coconut milk, peanuts, and special rice much in evidence. Yum Yum also stocks a good supply of beer from the Far East.

*Price: About $12 per person*
*Open Tues.–Fri. for lunch and dinner; Sat. and Sun. for dinner only*
*Accepts all major credit cards*

## BERN'S STEAK HOUSE
1208 South Howard Street, Tampa
### 813-251-2421

With half a hundred available cuts of beef, organically grown vegetables (on Bern's own farm), house-made ice cream and sherbet, freshly brewed and ground coffee, and one of the largest collections of wines ever assembled by any restaurant in the history of the world, Bern Laxer is in command of what many critics consider to be the best steak house in the country. The seven-and-a-half-pound wine list, larger than the Manhattan telephone directory, lists 6,000 labels. It's also a splendidly useful guidebook, loaded with maps, photos, and specific directions on the location of wineries in this country and abroad.

If ever there was a perfectionist in this most trying of trades, it is Bern— omnipresent, grilling the meats himself or watching the several rooms from his office filled with closed-circuit television sets, making sure of the top quality of all his ingredients, searching out still more wines for his air-conditioned cellar/warehouses, wondering and worrying how he can improve his operation. His menu is already a crash course in the fine art of selecting, aging, and cutting beef, but he also serves superlative lamb and fantastically good chicken, sautéed in butter and showered with sesame seeds.

*Price: About $30 per person*
*Open daily for dinner only*
*Accepts all major credit cards*

## COLUMBIA
2117 East Seventh Avenue (*Ybor City*), Tampa
### 813-248-4961

A block-long happening, which started as a coffee house/café in 1905, this landmark is the oldest restaurant in the state—and it's been in the same family since its founding. The rooms go on forever, but begin an evening here at the cushy little bar near the entrance; then retire to the main cavern for the floor show—after working through the splendid 1905 salad and something special, such as snapper swimming with shrimp wrapped in bacon, onions, peppers, and eggplant, redolent of good olive oil flecked with garlic and enhanced by Sauternes. On stage will be flamenco and good music for dancing, plus the one-of-a-kind violinist doing his dramatic best to woo the audience and please his patrons. That's Cesar Gonzmart and with his sons he has successfully ensured that the family will continue the Columbia history. They also operate smaller clones in Sarasota on St. Armand's Circle and in St. Augustine in the heart of the historic district.

*Price: About $25 per person*
*Open daily for lunch and dinner*
*Accepts all major credit cards*

## CYPRESS ROOM
### In the Saddlebrook Golf and Tennis Club, Wesley Chapel
*(one mile east—exit 58—of I-75 on State Road 54)*
813-973-1111

There's an air of Arizona upscale resort about this giant dining room, one with a center-stage seafood buffet on Friday nights and another table-groaner of a brunch on Sundays, best in the Bay area. The desserts are remarkable at any time. The chefs here are always searching for innovative dishes, and in 1984 they installed a monster smoker in a smaller, clubbier restaurant across the courtyard—and there they smoke everything but the chef! Come early and walk the grounds of the country-club surroundings and remember to make reservations in season. Jackets are required for the men.

*Price: About $25 per person*
*Open daily for breakfast, lunch, and dinner*
*Accepts all major credit cards*

## DONATELLO
### 232 North Dale Mabry, Tampa
813-875-6660

The west coast of Florida has never been blessed with more than a scant few Italian restaurants that rise above the cliché-ridden routines familiar to all who eat out at the mom-and-pop operations in our major cities. But then came Cesare Tini with his Christmas 1985 gift to Tampa, a converted Chinese eatery that's a super slice of sophistication on a street of fast feeders. Service is black-suited and formal, soft lighting bounces off the glistening table appointments set on islands of pink highlighted by a profusion of pink roses, and the kitchen matches the high standards of that setting. All the farinaceous fare is made on the premises—daily—as are the desserts, and the menu is a lengthy one. Start with the *mozzarella bella,* a generous serving of crisply fried cheese embellished with anchovies and garlic, or the mussels in garlic and wine, the *ostriche gratinate,* freshly shucked oysters sizzling in shells filled with garlic butter dotted with bits of bread crumbs and parsley. Then order the veal Donatello, named for the place, which in turn honors the great sculptor: It's sautéed in a sea of wine-lemon butter, swimming with artichokes, fresh mushrooms, zucchini. Or try their version of the classic *osso buco,* delivered on a bed of saffron rice. Desserts are excellent and the list of Italian wines good.

*Price: About $25 per person*
*Open Mon.–Fri. for lunch and dinner; Sat. and Sun. for dinner only*
*Accepts all major credit cards*

---

## DON QUIJOTE
### 1536 East Seventh Avenue (*Ybor City*), Tampa
#### 813-247-9454

A midget feedery when stacked against Columbia (see page 307) but typical of the many little budget-stretching cafés in and around Ybor City, Tampa's century-old Spanish settlement. This one is operated by more recent arrivals, the Zapicos from Asturias. The *madre* is behind the burners, and *padre* runs the front room, which is a high-ceiling memory bank: It used to be the game room of El Centro Español.

*Price: About $10 per person*
*Open Mon.–Sat. for lunch and dinner; closed Sun.*
*No credit cards accepted*

---

## EL MADRID
### 415 Cleveland Street, Clearwater
#### 813-447-2211

There's considerable competition for the Spanish dining-out dollar in Tampa Bay, but the owners of this new (opened in November 1984) contender, Tito Vicente and Benny Perez, are doing their best to break the *arroz con pollo* ho-hums. Scallops are bathed in a Galician green sauce aglow with garlic; the *gazpacho* is presented with last-minute showers of croutons and cucumber; broiled prime rib is blessed with a red wine sauce, sole with bananas; and a creation named for the village in which Salvador Dali was born, Cadaques, features liberal portions of lobster and chicken coated with a flavorful seafood sauce spiked with Pernod and brandy. In addition to the usual *flan* for dessert, there's a fine bread pudding. The wine cellar, handsomely displayed by the entrance, has many of the better Spanish labels.

*Price: About $20 per person*
*Open Mon.–Fri. for lunch and dinner; Sat. for dinner only*
*Accepts all major credit cards*

---

# HEILMAN'S BEACHCOMBER
## 447 Mandalay Avenue, Clearwater Beach
### 813-442-4144

An all-American beachfront classic that's been doing things right since 1948. Another Heilman generation has moved into place and has maintained the standards—beautifully. The decor is strictly 1940s restaurant, and the staff smilingly reminds diners how pleasant people really can be in this business. The menu is predictably American, with liver and onions, prime rib, roast lamb, broiled snapper, steaks, chops, and the headliner, a back-to-the-farm fried chicken, with all the trimmings—from relish tray to muffins and banana bread, mashed potatoes to apple pie.

*Price: About $20 per person*
*Open daily for lunch and dinner*
*Accepts all major credit cards*

---

# J. FITZGERALD'S
## In the Lincoln Hotel, 4860 West Kennedy Boulevard, Tampa
### 813-875-6565

A raspberry rich retreat with lots of mahogany in evidence, some art on the walls, a highly intelligent level of illumination, and a staff that has worked out the start-up problems evident in early 1985. The kitchen has never faltered, however, and it's given local gourmands just cause to celebrate—crowning the bisque of rich lobster with a delicate pastry crust, flaming a freshly assembled mélange of shrimp and scallops in Cognac, layering superlative *médaillons* of veal with a lobster *mousse* insulated with spinach, serving steamed salmon with dollops of caviar, and treating trout to a bath of pecan butter. The wine list reflects intelligence, and the best way to start an evening of such seductive sensations is to share a bottle of Cristal champagne in the lobby lounge, watching the people parade in that smashing atrium of an architectural triumph.

*Price: About $30 per person*
*Open daily for lunch and dinner*
*Accepts all major credit cards*

# LAURO RISTORANTE
## 4010 West Waters Avenue, Tampa
### 813-884-4366

Named for and owned by the same Lauro who used to be in charge of the menu at Miami's Tiberio (see page 278). On this coast he immediately soared to the summit of Northern Italian establishments. He recruited a superb serving staff, collected some good Italian wines, and went to work creating such winners as Tiberio fans remember with pleasure: *agnolotti,* little *ravioli* (freshly made) filled with a judicious blend of spinach and *ricotta* and dolloped with a rich smooth cream sauce. Lauro's veal presentations are faultless, his fish fresh, and his desserts a delight.

*Price: About $25 per person*
*Open Mon.–Fri. for lunch and dinner; open Sat. for dinner only*
*Accepts all major credit cards*

# LOBSTER POT
## 17814 Gulf Boulevard, Redington Shores
### 813-391-8592

Owner-operator Eugen Fuhrmann is in charge of this intimate seafood server, and he obviously believes in restraint: in his flower-filled decor, in his sauces, in the pleasant manners of his staff of happy servers. The namesake lobster is always a reliable performance and his chefs do five glorious things to grouper; that is, when they're not brewing a marvelous Bermudian fish chowder, a real blast from the islands. Or giving *escargots* a curry bath, poaching salmon in white wine, and making excellent fritters which are the perfect finale to an evening here. The wine list is a pleasant surprise. Reservations are a must.

*Price: About $25 per person*
*Open daily for dinner only*
*Accepts all major credit cards*

# LOUIS PAPPAS
## 10 West Dodecanese Street, Tarpon Springs
### 813-937-5101

The trip north of St. Petersburg is worth it for anyone who wants to experience an important piece of Florida history—the Greek sponge divers and those who served them. Such as Louis M. Pappamichalopoulos, a Spartan who arrived in this country in 1904, and twenty years later opened a simple little café. Today it's as large as a Greek village and filled with memories. Forget the fact that the Greek salad is like nothing you ever ate in the Old Country, or that the place is a volume operation. It's fun and the food is good. The supervision, by the present members of the clan, is professional. And through the many windows are the famous sponge docks and enough souvenir shops to fill a few blocks in Athens.

*Price: About $20 per person*
*Open daily for lunch and dinner*
*Accepts all major credit cards*

# MILLER'S SEAFOOD CENTER
## 2315 West Linebaugh Road, Tampa
### 813-935-4793

Max Miller, who comes from Maine, opened this seafood shack in 1977, and he's never served a frozen fish since. The raw bar is probably the largest in the state—it seats some 65 hungry patrons—and he's found someone to produce the best Key lime pie on the west coast. But before that, dig into a Maine lobster, spoon some of that superb crab soup, or tear into a smoked mullet or a thick fillet of red snapper.

*Price: About $15 per person*
*Open Tues.–Sun. for dinner only; closed Mon.*
*No credit cards accepted*

# PASQUET
## 6730 Twenty-second Avenue North, St. Petersburg
### 813-384-0555

Convenient for ladies who love to linger over lunch after a go-around at the nearby Tyrone Mall, this dining room is an all-blue class act, the likes of which is seldom seen in St. Pete. The noontime buffets are close to exquisite, avoiding the let-it-all-hang-out approach, and the evenings romantic with soft lighting, good wines, music, and fine fare. After the innovative, complimentary, fluffy egg-taste tickler, try the oysters poached in champagne, the smoked salmon on *blinis,* and onward, ever onward, to a fillet of sole embellished with salmon *mousseline* in a Scotch whiskey sauce, the ultra-tender *médaillons* of veal in basil butter. The talents of this little gem approach the Platonic. And they have a fine selection of wines to march right along.

*Price: About $25 per person*
*Open Tues.–Sat. for lunch and dinner; open Sun. for dinner only*
*Accepts all major credit cards*

---

## PEPIN'S
### 4125 Fourth Street, St. Petersburg
#### 813-821-3773

A perfect place for a power lunch as well as a popular spot at night for a wide, interesting variety of locals and a few other fortunate souls who have discovered the merits and the absolute consistency of this reliable retreat. Country inn—Spanish *parador* style—in decor and staffed by a very friendly, knowledgeable crew of waiters, this solid performer has a good selection of reasonably priced wines and some of the best food to be found in Florida: fresh red snapper swimming in a fine *béchamel* sauce freckled with chunks of clam and shrimp and delivered with asparagus, pimientos, and peas; pompano baked whole in its own bed of rock salt; and steaks surely on a par with the best to be found at Bern's (see page 307).

*Price: About $20 per person*
*Open Tues.–Sun. for lunch and dinner*
*Accepts all major credit cards*

---

## RG'S NORTH
### 3807 Northdale Boulevard, Tampa
#### 813-963-2356

The letters stand for sparkplug Rusty Grimm, who, with partner Ron Ryan, is responsible for this thoroughly charming, quietly sophisticated hideaway, all rosy and blue and fussed over by a caring staff. The menu is not elaborate, but it is executed to perfection: There are nightly specials along with featured wines of the month. Among the triumphs to watch for are the scallop *mousse,* the shrimp *de Jonghe,* the salads assembled from impeccably fresh romaine and presented with apple and tomato, the duckling given a final char-grilling after roasting to crispify before letting it repose on a zesty peach sauce, and finally, the finishing course of an incomparable chocolate-pecan-toffee *mousse.*

*Price: About $25 per person*
*Open Mon.–Sat. for dinner only; closed Sun.*
*Accepts all major credit cards*

---

## SABALS
### 315 Main Street, Dunedin
**813-734-DINE**

A simply decorated storefront on an otherwise undistinguished street, this trendy—at least for these parts—almost Art Deco discovery is staffed by an enthusiastic crew, four of whom put it all together. There's a do-it-yourself feeling that survived their decorating and rehab efforts, but it's all fun. And so are the menu and carefully selected wine list. There's a wealth of nightly specials and the bill of fare is always changing, but among the fairly regular items to recommend with enthusiasm are the chilled shrimp, served with a spicy tomato sauce spiked with horseradish and sprinkled with golden raisins; the hot shrimp in a dark curry sauce; the *médaillons* of superbly tender veal sautéed with garlic and chopped shallots, finished with a rice wine vinegar cream and garnished with dried lily flowers and lotus seeds. The veggies here are admirable and such desserts as Italian cake with walnuts and the pecan pie with chocolate crust are real winners.

*Price: About $20 per person*
*Open Tues.–Sun. for dinner only; closed Mon.*
*Accepts all major credit cards*

---

## SELENA'S
### 1623 Snow Avenue, Tampa
**813-251-2116**

The Italian side of this split personality of a place is strictly Sicilian. Boldly so: When was the last time a restaurant opened and did not emphasize it was "Northern Italian"? And Sicilian means luscious *lasagne,* thickly breaded Parmesan dishes, and spicy, thick tomato sauces. From the Gulf of Mexico come the gumbo, the shrimp *rémoulade,* and the crab and shrimp in a Creole sauce. The wine list is good. There's an adjoining lounge with live entertainment and everywhere is the air of a revitalized Victorian escape, a vintage reflection of the reborn Hyde Park neighborhood that surrounds it.

*Price: About $20 per person*
*Open Mon.–Fri. for lunch and dinner; open Sat.–Sun. for dinner only*
*Accepts all major credit cards*

# SIPLE'S GARDEN SEAT
## 1234 Druid Road South, Clearwater
### 813-442-9681

A long-standing favorite of those genteel diners who like a country club setting for their lunches and dinners, a place that is immaculately maintained, and one with a grand view of sunsets over the water. Caressed by a grove of giant trees, this transformed mansion has been in the same family—and serving the public—since 1920. There's nothing French or fancy on the extensive menu, but freshness and the high quality of ingredients are always emphasized. The Cornish game hen, the duckling, the New England clam chowder, and the baked shrimp are only a few of the dishes to seek out while luxuriating in the comfort of a caring retreat. The wine list is not extensive, but there's a cozy little up-front lounge serving bountiful cocktails.

*Price: About $15 per person*
*Open daily for lunch and dinner*
*Accepts all major credit cards*

# SUKHOTHAI
## 8201 North Dale Mabry, Tampa
### 813-933-7990

Without question, this is the best of the Oriental restaurants along the Bay even though it is strictly Thai in its inspiration and execution. The fiery sauces are blended with diligence, the curry preparations superior, the serving of shrimp and crab, especially when married in a foil-wrap heady with some kind of magic, is sensational. There's a better wine list than usually encountered in Oriental restaurants and their beer is imported from Bangkok.

*Price: About $12 per person*
*Open Mon.–Fri. for lunch and dinner; open Sat.–Sun. for dinner only*
*Accepts all major credit cards*

# TIO PEPE
## 2930 Gulf-to-Bay Boulevard, Clearwater
### 813-725-3082

This "Uncle Pete" started his meteorically successful restauranting career with the unique Café Pepe on Tampa's West Kennedy Boulevard, and then converted an old mansion into a replication of dining rooms in Andalucia, or Galicia, Catalonia. The tiles are beautiful, the entryway bar, across from the baker, a good staging area. The smell of fresh-baked bread permeates the place. As does the noise of the satisfied guests who marvel at the consistency of a restaurant where the bean soup is always superior, the bacon-wrapped shrimp special, and the large slabs of meat and fish of prime quality. Spanish wines fill Tio Pepe's cellar, and if you want the better of the two *sangría* selections, order the one spiked with imported Spanish brandy.

*Price: About $15 per person*
*Open Tues.–Fri. for lunch and dinner; open Sat.–Sun. for dinner only*
*Accepts all major credit cards*

# THE VERANDAH
## 5250 West Kennedy Boulevard, Tampa
### 813-876-0168

Classy, brassy Old South setting with an appealing, popular lounge, an extensive wine bar, formal service, and interesting creations on the menu. Among the dishes to recommend are the almond-coated deep-fried shrimp, the prime rib, the ginger and elderberry-covered duckling, the grouper *en croûte* with its wild contrasts of textures and tastes—*duxelle* of mushroom and scallop *mousse,* curry, and dill. The wine list is extensive if a mite too expensive.

*Price: About $30 per person*
*Open Mon.–Fri. for lunch and dinner; open Sat. for dinner only*
*Accepts all major credit cards*

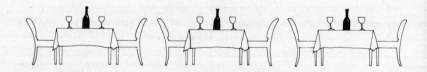

# THE WINE CELLAR
## 17307 Gulf Boulevard, North Redington Beach
### 813-393-3491

A trio of Germans are in charge here, and despite all the bustle, the private parties (often with an off-putting strolling accordion player), and the volume of the operation, the food is consistently good. Each of the main dining rooms is decorated in a different country style: My favorite refuges are a quiet corner in the French room or in the Swiss room, with its splendid painting of one of my favorite inns of the Emmenthal. There's a delicious Swiss cheese soup laced with a splash of kirsch. The Hungarians get into the act in the bountiful serving of *gulyás,* but we have to thank the Berliners for this cellar's treatment of calf's liver, dressing it up with apples and onions in a fine natural sauce. The wine list is extensive and the service efficient.

*Price: About $25 per person*
*Open daily for dinner only*
*Accepts all major credit cards*

# HAWAII

## *By Tom Horton*

**BRUNCH**
  Michel's at the Colony Surf
    (Oahu)

**CHINESE**
  King Tsin (Oahu)

**CONTINENTAL**
  Bagwells 2424 (Oahu)
  Edelweiss (Hawaii)
  Michel's at the Colony Surf
    (Oahu)
  The Willows (Oahu)

**FRENCH**
  Bon Appétit (Oahu)
  Chez Michel (Oahu)
  Chez Paul (Maui)
  Gerard's (Maui)
  La Mer (Oahu)

**GERMAN**
  Edelweiss (Hawaii)

**HAWAIIAN**
  The Willows (Oahu)

**ITALIAN**
  Longhi's (Maui)

**JAPANESE**
  Restaurant Suntory (Oahu)

**SEAFOOD**
  John Dominis (Oahu)
  Mama's Fish House (Maui)

**THAI**
  Keo's Thai Cuisine (Oahu)

Restaurants in Hawaii can no longer be accurately stereotyped as tourist traps serving frozen "mahimahi almondine" and "mile-high" coconut cream pie. There is now a great variety of fine restaurants dishing up everything from classic French cuisine to authentic meals of every kind of ethnic food imaginable.

As elsewhere in the United States, there is a strong emphasis on using the freshest local ingredients available. In Hawaii, this means excellent island fish: *ono, opakapaka, ahi, aku,* and fresh *mahimahi,* as opposed to the frozen species imported from Taiwan by the ton. Wonderful fruits and vegetables are also grown throughout the islands year-round, and the best restaurants take maximum advantage of this availability. The worst restaurants still take advantage of ocean views while charging tourists high prices for mediocre food.

The fresh fish, most of it of the deep-sea tuna, snapper, and dolphin variety, is the best of the foods produced locally. Authentic Hawaiian food—the kind you find in tiny neighborhood cafés, not at hotel luaus—is usually an acquired taste for the average Mainlander. However, the islands' multi-ethnic society is well represented in the wealth of good ethnic restaurants. Japanese and Chinese dominate, but there are also small, relatively inexpensive places serving tasty Korean, Filipino, and Thai food.

The number of restaurants with first-rate European cooking has also grown considerably, from the high-priced luxury hotels to the smaller places where the chef may also be the owner. While the posh rooms in the big resort hotels are invariably among the most expensive places to dine, it should also be stated that in Hawaii, unlike in most American cities, many of the best restaurants are found inside the hotels.

Unfortunately, the choice in dining falls off rapidly as you move from island to island. Waikiki and the rest of the island of Oahu offer a tremendous variety of quality restaurants. Maui, though it has always been weak on ethnic variety, continues to improve in both quality and versatility and is, by far, the best dining island after Oahu. Choices on Kauai and the Big Island of Hawaii are much less exciting.

Be prepared for generally high prices wherever you eat in Hawaii and brace yourself for a rude shock at the wine prices. Hawaii is one of the last states that applies a ridiculous *ad valorem* tax (20 percent) on all imported alcoholic beverages, including California as well as European wines. Most of the better restaurants make the situation worse by adding an unreasonable markup on their wines, resulting in high prices for ordinary bottles and outlandish prices for select vintages.

*Tom Horton is co-author, with wife Karen Horton, of* The Dolphin Guide to Hawaii, *published in 1985 by Doubleday. He has been the editor of* Spirit of Aloha, *the Aloha Airlines in-flight magazine, since 1977, has written extensively about island restaurants for a number of national publications, and is the author of several of* Honolulu *magazine's annual all-island restaurant guides.*

## BAGWELLS 2424
### In the Hyatt Regency Waikiki, 2424 Kalakaua Avenue
#### 808-922-9292

Plush burgundy-colored booths and a lavishly decorated room filled with fresh flowers and greenery, with tiny lights twinkling among the indoor tree branches, make Bagwells 2424 one of Waikiki's most glamorous settings for fine dining. Service is excellent and the kitchen has long been one of the most creative on the island, raising Bagwells well above the norm in hotel dining rooms. Fresh island fish is accorded wonderful treatment, such as the *opakapaka* with watercress and ginger. Specialties, such as breast of duckling with orange and black currants, the lobster and scallop casserole with truffles, and the braised breast of pheasant, are representative of the extensive menu of fish, fowl, beef, lamb, and veal. Each dish arrives at the table as a visual work of culinary art. The wine list is the most impressive in Hawaii in its depth of vintages and varietals from Europe and California, and numerous fine wines are available by the glass, but Bagwells is top-heavy on expensive bottlings and short on moderately priced wines.

*Price: About $35 per person*
*Open daily for dinner only*
*Accepts all major credit cards*

# BON APPÉTIT

In the Discovery Bay condominium building, 1778 Ala
Moana Boulevard (*across from Ilikai Hotel*)
**808-942-3837**

Owner-chef Guy Banal, at one time the executive chef at Bagwells 2424, took
over this tiny space in an unfavorable location on the ground floor of a massive
high-rise condominium and transformed it into possibly the best place for
French food in Hawaii, at prices below what is charged in the fancier Waikiki
hotel restaurants. The intimate room has been artfully arranged for maximum
seating that is still comfortable and elegantly stylish, with fresh roses accenting
the pink linen. Sliced breast of duck in a green peppercorn sauce is one of chef
Banal's finest works. Others include scallop *mousse* with caviar, sliced roasted
lobster tail, and fresh Hawaiian fish turned out with a French flair. The wine
list is short but wisely chosen. Bon Appétit's fixed-price dinners are exceptional bargains.

*Price: About $25 per person; four-course fixed-price dinners about $22*
*Open Mon.–Sat. for dinner only; closed Sun.*
*Accepts all major credit cards*

# CHEZ MICHEL

Eaton Square, 444 Hobron Lane
**808-955-7866**

Michel Martin is the best-known name connected to French food and enjoyable restaurants in Hawaii, and has been for some forty years. He was the
founder of Michel's at the Colony Surf and was the owner-operator of Chez
Michel for many years until he sold it to a man from Belgium in 1984.
However, Michel still keeps a hand in the business and the restaurant still
reflects his buoyant spirit. The garden-like atmosphere here makes it one of
the best choices in Waikiki for a first-rate lunch (and good lunch places are
limited in Waikiki), although the menu is much more extensive at dinner.
Daily specials, such as braised short ribs *jardinière* or fresh trout *grenobloise,*
highlight the lunch selections. Dinner brings fresh island fish, prepared *grenobloise* or *véronique,* outstanding sweetbreads, roasted duck, and a number of
good veal, lamb, and beef dishes. Chez Michel's one great weakness has always

been the founder's stubborn chauvinism in favoring French wines over California vintages, an attitude that's quite out of date even for a French restaurant.

*Price: About $30 per person; about $20 at lunch*
*Open Mon.–Fri. for lunch and dinner; Sat. and Sun. for dinner only*
*Accepts all major credit cards*

---

# CHEZ PAUL
## Highway 30 in Olowalu (*six miles south of Lahaina*)
### 808-661-3843

For a hundred and seventy-eighty years Olowalu was infamous as the site of the 1790 Olowalu Massacre, involving the enraged captain of an American trading ship who retaliated for the theft of a small boat by luring Hawaiians offshore and then opening fire on their canoes with the ship's cannons, slaughtering more than a hundred of the Hawaiians. But since 1968 the little village with the tragic history has been famous in a better light as the site of Chez Paul, the first restaurant of any consequence on Maui and still one of the best. Founder Paul Kirk, one of the great characters of Lahaina, has passed on, but the Chez Paul tradition has been faithfully upheld and even enhanced by owner Lucien Charbonnier. The country storefront beside the highway conceals a casually elegant French restaurant that is tiny in size but leaves a large impression on fanciers of French cuisine (alas, the bill also strikes a very high note). Chez Paul serves a delicious *scampi maison* and veal dishes that are distinguished by superb sauces. There's also fresh Maui fish, good duck and beef, and a first-rate, if all too expensive, list of wines. Reservations are a must during peak tourist seasons.

*Price: About $35 per person*
*Open daily for dinner only*
*Accepts all major credit cards*

---

# EDELWEISS
## Highway 19 in Waimea
### 808-885-6800

Hans-Peter Hager, owner and chef, is a young veteran of some famous kitchens throughout Hawaii and far beyond. He was executive chef when the opulent Mauna Lani Bay Hotel opened on the nearby Kohala Coast, and previously had a long career that included stops at the Mauna Kea Beach Hotel, the Kapalua Bay Hotel on Maui, and other world-class Rockresorts properties. In

1983 he put hotel kitchens behind him and bought this rustic roadside restaurant in misty Waimea, the headquarters town for the vast Parker Ranch cattle empire. Overnight Edelweiss became the best place to eat—and eat at a reasonable cost—on the island. The roughhewn wood building with open-beamed ceilings has room for just fifteen tables and they're usually occupied every night, especially during peak tourist seasons. This means you should be prepared to wait because Edelweiss does not take reservations. The waiting is worthwhile. Hans-Peter does all the cooking, lunch and dinner, and while the standing menu may feature some German classics along with Continental-style offerings, such as rack of lamb, the talk of the island is Hans-Peter's specials. He features an amazing number of specials each evening, using the freshest Big Island ingredients available (but not, thankfully, Big Island beef) and complements them with fine veal and other imports. There might also be venison from the Hawaiian island of Molokai, wild boar from the Big Island, fresh island fish, and such bountiful originals as the veal and scallops combination or the Big Island papaya stuffed with veal Stroganoff and covered with poached scallops. Prices are remarkably low for the quality and generous portions of the complete dinners. Whether you're staying on the Kohala Coast (that's about twenty to thirty minutes down the hill from Waimea) or further away in Kailua-Kona, it's worth the scenic drive to experience this cowtown restaurant with uptown cuisine.

*Price: About $23 per person*
*Open Tues.–Sun. for lunch and dinner; closed Mon.*
*Accepts all major credit cards*

---

# GERARD'S
## In Lahaina Market Place, corner of Front Street and Lahainaluna Road
### 808-661-8939

Gerard Reversade is one of Hawaii's most traveled French chefs, having labored with distinction in several notable restaurants on Oahu and Maui during the last fifteen years. Finally he has his own place and he has made the most of it, firmly establishing Gerard's as the first choice for full-fledged dining in Lahaina, where surf-and-turf-*cum*-salad-bar is more the norm. The restaurant is small, in the breezy style of a casual Parisian café, and pleasant when the temperatures are likewise and the tradewinds are blowing, but less pleasant if the trades die and Lahaina turns muggy. The menu changes regularly, but certain Gerard trademarks are usually in evidence: his famous duck *confit* that is deliciously crispy, and the sautéed frogs' legs that are the best in the islands. Fresh island fish reach new heights of flavor in the company of delicate sauces, and there's always a choice of interesting seafood, veal, beef, lamb, and chicken dishes. Desserts are made fresh daily and they are irresistible.

*Price: About $32 per person; considerably less at lunch*
*Open daily for lunch and dinner*
*Accepts all major credit cards*

---

# JOHN DOMINIS
## 43 Ahui Street (*off Ala Moana Boulevard near Kewalo Basin*)
### 523-0955

Nothing in Hawaii compares to John Dominis as the ultimate seafood restaurant. Honolulu political figure Andy Anderson, the man who would be mayor or governor but has failed to win either office, was far more successful when he spent $2.5 million to erect this huge fish emporium on a rocky point overlooking the channel used by fishing and pleasure boats cruising out of Kewalo Basin. John Dominis' prime vantage point allows views of the marine traffic, sunset surfers riding the big waves, and the sparkling skyline of Waikiki all the way to Diamond Head. The restaurant itself is a match for its setting: At the center of the sprawling dining room is a beautiful teakwood kiosk where the varieties of fresh fish are exhibited on beds of crushed ice, with a modest indoor lagoon accommodating a finny population that is still very much alive. John Dominis invariably has the island's largest variety of fresh Hawaiian fish, as well as numerous species flown in from the Mainland, and the kitchen excels in preparing seafood a number of interesting ways. Be adventurous and try some of the *ono, mahimahi,* or *opakapaka,* steamed Hawaiian or Oriental style. Be forwarned, however, that the prices for all this are very high and you should be particularly cautious about ordering any off-the-menu specials without first determining the price. (As at most restaurants throughout Hawaii, fresh island fish is priced according to the current market cost, so don't expect to see the price on the menu.) The size and popularity of John Dominis results in an unpredictable standard of service, but it remains the type of restaurant most visitors want for a seafood dinner. The wine list is undistinguished.

*Price: About $35 per person*
*Open daily for dinner only*
*Accepts all major credit cards*

# KEO'S THAI CUISINE
## 625 Kapahulu Avenue
### 808-737-8240

Keo Sananikone and his family started with a tiny restaurant called Mekong in a vintage Honolulu neighborhood in the 1970s. The place soon became one of the most successful ethnic food enterprises on the island. (The original Mekong, joined by a Mekong II, is still in business.) But Keo's has become a more elaborate showcase for the family's vaunted skills at producing traditional Thai dishes, as well as creating new ones of their own. Keo's, on the eastern boundaries of Waikiki, is now one of Honolulu's most celebrated restaurants, outshining larger, fancier, and more expensive establishments in the number of visiting celebrities and resident notables who are regular customers. The dining room is festively decorated with Thai art and antiques to set the mood for memorable feasts of garlic shrimp, spicy chicken soup, and such Keo's originals as the "evil jungle prince." Prices are most reasonable, and you can instruct your waiter on just how spicy you prefer your Thai food —mild, medium, hot, or volcanic. A cool way to begin is with a mango daiquiri.

*Price: About $15 per person*
*Open daily for dinner only*
*Accepts all major credit cards*

# KING TSIN
## 1486 South King Street
### 808-946-3273

The interior of this small restaurant may be quite plain and the location may be in the ordinary commercial district of one of Honolulu's older neighborhoods, but King Tsin has for some years been the best all-around Chinese restaurant on the island. The finest of spicy Northern China cooking is presented here, with wonderful examples of Hunan, Szechuan, Peking, and Shanghai specialties on the long and reasonably priced menu. There are hot Hunan prawns, shrimp in a rich black bean sauce, Szechuan steamed "five-piece duck," peppery Mongolian beef, and King Tsin's delightful beggar's chicken baked in a clay pot.

*Price: About $12 per person*
*Open daily for lunch and dinner*
*Accepts all major credit cards*

# LA MER

In the Halekulani Hotel, 2199 Kailia Road

808-923-2311

This is Waikiki's newest, most impressive, most expensive restaurant. Occupying the second level of the historic Halekulani's original main building facing Waikiki Beach (the old Halekulani was the last low-rise on the beach before it was torn down and replaced by a high-rise), La Mer is tastefully designed in understated browns and beiges. This permits the marvelous views to command center stage at Le Mer, where the dining room opens to views across Waikiki Beach and the night lights of Waikiki with the shadowy profile of Diamond Head rising in the distance. The menu changes regularly, but you can count on some memorable creations: perhaps a salad of cooked spinach with truffle juice, prawns with chervil and lemon rind, or beef tenderloin with cream of sweet peppers. Service and wines are all of the same elegant quality as the food, and once a week there is the chance to splurge on a five-course fixed-priced dinner that includes four different wines.

*Price: About $40 per person; five-course fixed-price menu, including four wines,*
*about $65 per person (featured weekly, call to confirm dates)*
*Open daily for dinner only*
*Accepts all major credit cards*

# LONGHI'S

888 Front Street in Lahaina

808-667-2288

Longhi's is the best-known and most successful restaurant in restaurant-clogged Lahaina, and it defies normal categorization. It exudes the casual, open-air personality of a sidewalk café, feeds on the flavor of a neighborhood Italian restaurant, occasionally jumps to the music of contemporary jazz, and has a specialized appeal to people just looking for a place to eat an out-of-the-ordinary breakfast or splurge on sinful desserts. There is a little of everything at Longhi's—except a menu. There isn't even a blackboard with daily specials posted. Breakfast, lunch, or dinner, the waiter will pull up a chair next to your table, seat himself and begin what amounts to a lecture on the food of the day. Although the food itself is somewhat overrated by people swept up in the campy performances of the waiters, you can rely on the freshest ingredients, hearty portions, and intriguing dishes from a kitchen that leans toward Italian flavoring. Longhi's produces the most high-tone breakfasts in Lahaina, enormous hot sandwiches, freshly made pastas, fresh island fish, veal, steak, chicken, and anything else that strikes the fancy of the kitchen or owner Bob Longhi. Desserts are sensational. All of this is carried on inside an informal, open-air, *bistro*-like environment, with black-and-white tile floors, on a part of Front Street which is elbow-to-elbow with strolling tourists. There's also a room upstairs for evening dining and there's often after-dinner jazz. Longhi's does not take reservations and is almost always filled during customary meal hours.

*Price: Dinner, about $25 per person; lunch, about $12 per person; breakfast, about $8 per person*
*Open daily for breakfast, lunch, and dinner*
*Accepts all major credit cards*

---

## MAMA'S FISH HOUSE
### One-and-a-half miles past Paia town
**808-579-9672**

Only a restaurant with something special to offer could succeed in this location far from the center of Maui tourism traffic (nearly an hour's drive from Lahaina-Kaanapali). Mama's Fish House has prospered for more than a decade because of its romantic setting overlooking Kua Cove, giving diners a balmy view of sunsets and ocean waves from the open-air dining room. Additionally, there is a genuine feeling of visiting an old island beach home for dinner, a feeling carried out by Mama's homemade honey bread, herbs from Mama's gardens, and fresh produce from neighboring Maui farms. Fresh island fish is smoked over kiawe wood or poached in cream with fresh mushrooms. There are many Mama's originals: papaya-seed salad dressing, Polynesian lobster with macadamia nuts, chilled papaya-coconut soup, *teriyaki* ginger fish that's made with fresh Hana ginger. It's worth the drive if you want to escape the crowded West Maui tourist scene for a few idyllic hours.

Look for the yellow blinking light and turn left at the ship's flagpole and angelfish sign.

*Price: About $25 per person*
*Open daily for dinner only*
*Accepts all major credit cards*

# MICHEL'S AT THE COLONY SURF

In the Colony Surf Condominium-Hotel, 2895 Kalakaua
Avenue (*across from Kapiolani Park*)

808-923-6552

The luxurious refinement of pastel-colored brocade furnishings, chandeliers, and tuxedoed waiters gives Michel's the feeling of a formal French restaurant one might come upon in San Francisco or New York, but the star attraction here is what lies outside the gilded dining rooms. Michel's sits right on a sandy beach and one whole side of the restaurant is open to the sea, allowing unobstructed views of the rolling surf, sparkling ocean waters, sailboats, and distant green mountains during the day, followed by spectacular sunsets and the glittering night lights of high-rise Waikiki. French dishes are featured on a menu that is more Continental in style. The food, though it can be inconsistent in quality when volume overwhelms attention to detail, is still far above what is customarily found at restaurants with great views and a high number of tourists. *Opakapaka bonne femme* stands out among Michel's Hawaiian seafood selections, and the roast loin of veal with cream and Cognac sauce is excellent. Dinner at Michel's is usually crowded with tourists (reservations are a must), but lunch can be a calmer experience that is no less elegant, and the sunny views are always thoroughly tranquilizing. A little-known fact is that in addition to the popular Sunday brunch, Michel's also serves breakfast during the week. The wines, as in most high-class Oahu restaurants, are overpriced and the list too short on California's best values.

*Price: About $35 per person*
*Open daily for lunch and dinner*
*Accepts all major credit cards*

# RESTAURANT SUNTORY

In the Royal Hawaiian Shopping Center, third floor, 2233
Kalakaua Avenue

808-922-5511

The Suntory Company of Japan has signature restaurants in many of the world's major cities, and the company spent lavishly on this Waikiki entry to create the most elegant Japanese restaurant in Hawaii. From the deep carpets and etched glass of the gracious cocktail lounge to the distinctive dining rooms decorated with Japanese art, Restaurant Suntory is a thoroughly soothing environment. While there are many good Japanese restaurants on Oahu specializing in specific styles of cooking, this one offers just about all of the most popular forms, each featured in a separate dining room. Most American tourists head directly for the *teppan* room, where the theatrics of the slicing-and-dicing chefs with the flashing long knives is the main attraction, to say nothing of the food (beef, chicken, and shrimp) that the cautious diner may watch sizzling on the grill, and be assured there's no danger of being served something raw. But there's also a *shabu shabu* room and, for those in search of more authentic Japanese food, a traditional Japanese room with *tatami* seating and an outstanding *sushi* bar.

*Price: About $22 per person*
*Open daily for lunch and dinner*
*Accepts all major credit cards*

---

# THE WILLOWS
## 901 Hausten Street
### 808-946-4808

The Willows is a throwback to the Honolulu of an earlier era, before jet airplanes began bringing millions to the islands. The restaurant has operated in the same modest residential neighborhood (ten minutes from Waikiki) since 1944. But it was virtually born again in 1980 when Randy Lee, longtime manager of the Halekulani Hotel when it was a beloved low-rise on Waikiki Beach, bought The Willows and set out to make it a devotional to food, music, and hospitality in the best Hawaiian tradition. He has succeeded. You can choose between the open-air, thatched-roof pavilions overlooking the tropical lagoons or the central courtyard's thatched-umbrella tables. In the evening, there is serenading by strolling Hawaiian musicians. The versatile menu features the Willows' famous Hawaiian curries, a number of authentic Hawaiian foods, fresh island fish, wok specialties, and a well-prepared list of lamb, veal, and beef. The Willows' executive chef Kusuma Cooray is a native of Sri Lanka and a graduate of London's Cordon Bleu School who first came to Hawaii to serve as the personal chef to heiress Doris Duke at her Diamond Head estate. There is more. The Kamaaina Suite at the Willows, an intimate second-level room overlooking the koi pond and the gardens, offers a fancier style of cuisine at a fancier price. And one of the most entertaining events on the island is the Willows' weekly Thursday *poi* luncheon, featuring authentic Hawaiian food and genuine old-fashioned Hawaiian entertainment of the kind you will not see in the Waikiki showrooms. (Get good directions before you go, because it's not easy to find if you're unfamiliar with the neighborhood.)

*Price: About $25 per person; considerably less at lunch; Kamaaina Suite*
*six-course fixed-price dinner about $45 per person*
*Open daily for lunch and dinner*
*Accepts all major credit cards*

# HOUSTON

## *By Teresa Byrne-Dodge*

**AMERICAN**
  The Womack's House

**BAR**
  La Carafe
  Marfreless
  Munchie's Classic Café

**BARBECUE**
  County Line
  Goode Company
  Otto's Barbecue
  W.T. Holt's

**BREAKFAST**
  Buffalo Grill
  Hampton's
  Merida

**CHINESE**
  Cloisonné
  Dong Ting
  Peng's
  Uncle Tai's Hunan Yuan

**CONTINENTAL/
INTERNATIONAL**
  Charley T's
  Cleo's 21

**CONTINENTAL/
INTERNATIONAL**
  Gerard's
  Harry's Kenya
  The Lancaster Grille
  Rainbow Lodge
  Tony's

**CREOLE/CAJUN**
  Atchafalaya River Café
  Bayou City Oyster Company
  Brennan's of Houston
  Magnolia Bar & Grill
  Mr. A's Uptown
  Willie G's

**ECLECTIC**
  Brennan's of Houston
  Café Annie
  Charley's 517
  Ouisie's Table
  The Remington
  SRO Bar & Grill

**DELICATESSEN**
  Butera's on Montrose
  Café Express

## FRENCH
Chez Nous
La Colombe d'Or
La Réserve
Le Restaurant de France
Ma Maison

## HAMBURGERS/HOT DOGS
Fuddrucker's
Goode Company Hamburgers &
  Taqueria
Hampton's
Otto's

## HEALTH FOOD
Chez Eddy

## HOTEL DINING ROOM
La Colombe D'Or
La Réserve
The Lancaster Grille
The Remington
Le Restaurant de France

## INDIAN
India's

## INDONESIAN
Mata Hari

## ITALIAN
Damian's Cucina Italiana
D'Amico Ristorante Italiano
The Lasagne Restaurant
Montesano

## JAPANESE
Fuji
Minato

## LEBANESE
Sammy's Lebanese Restaurant

## MEXICAN
Merida
Ninfa's
Spanish Village
Tila's Cantina & Taqueria

## PANORAMA
Cody's
Rainbow Lodge
Vargo's

## SEAFOOD
Bayou City Oyster Company
Captain Benny's Half Shell
Gaido's
Landry's Seafood Inn and
  Oyster Bar
Lavaca Bay
Mr. A's Uptown

## SPANISH
Mallorca's

## STEAKS AND CHOPS
Del Frisco's Steakhouse
River Oaks Grill
Rotisserie for Beef and Bird

## SUBURBAN
Chez Nous (Humble)
Gaido's (Galveston)
Landry's Seafood Inn and
  Oyster Bar (Katy)
Mallorca's (Kemah)
The Womack's House (Fulshear)

## THAI
The Golden Room
Renu's

## UNIQUE PROPERTIES
Hilltop Herb Farm

## VIETNAMESE
Kim Son

There was a time—and not all that long ago—when Houstonians had a choice of going out to eat steak . . . or steak. This was, after all, cattle country. But along with its swelling population, the city's culinary tradition has also grown much more cosmopolitan. Today Houston is an eater's town: seafood, Southern and country, Tex–Mex and Mex–Mex, barbecue, *nouvelle cuisine,* soul food, deli, New American cuisine, Cajun, Creole, and just about every imported ethnic edible, including Vietnamese, Thai, Chinese, Italian, French, Indian, Lebanese, Japanese, Indonesian, and Anglo-Irish. If not many people seem to realize this, it's only because the reputation has not yet caught up with the reality. Houstonians should be thankful, for eating in restaurants here has still escaped the compulsive earnestness that plagues it—and is becoming a bore—in some other cities.

Houston's food history is an ethnic stew of Old and New Worlds. To the north and west, the Germans who settled in the Hill Country contributed sausage, chicken-fried steak (a bunkhouse version of *Wiener Schnitzel*), and barbecue. The country Cajuns and citified Creoles to the east of the Sabine River sent over crawfish (never pronounced "crayfish" in this part of the country), gumbo, and rice-based dishes. A chili obsession crept up from the Southwest, bringing along *tortillas,* pinto and black beans, *tomatillos,* and giving birth to the idiosyncratic Tex–Mex. What's more, Houston chefs have access to a surfeit of indigenous food products, such as game (deer, javelina, quail), Gulf Coast riches (including oysters, crabs, enormous shrimp, and sweet-fleshed redfish), and the nuisance mesquite trees that provide such an ideal fire for cooking all of the above.

If one can make a general statement about food in Houston—and it's risky, for in the nation's fourth largest city there are hundreds of exceptions to any such pronouncement—it's that the food here is not necessarily hot, but intensely flavored. There is a lavish use of fresh ingredients, which are allowed to speak for themselves. Food handling is quick, subtle, and frying and grilling are very important. Pastas are also widely served in Houston restaurants. Chefs make their own, not just from wheat and eggs, but from chilies and squashes. Food presentation, often post-*nouvelle,* is following the trend set by the new, exquisitely understated restaurant settings; that is, toward a leaner, more self-conscious style, executed in a palette of earth tones.

You can still get a down-home chicken-fried steak with cream gravy in Houston and a mean bowl of "red"—chili so hot it can induce hallucinations—but generally chefs are cooking to please a sophisticated young population that has traveled and tasted extensively. *Nouvelle* cowboy? Forget it!

*Teresa Byrne-Dodge is the restaurant critic for* The Magazine *of* The Houston Post *and writes frequently on food and restaurants for national publications.*

---

## ATCHAFALAYA RIVER CAFÉ
### 8816 Westheimer Road (*near Fondren Road*)
#### 713-975-7873

If the Magnolia is genteel, then the Atchafalaya River Café is a raucous Cajun eatery, noisy and bright, featuring spicy south-Louisiana standards. There are bawdy stickers on the front door, old oak tables and mismatched straight chairs, a pressed-tin ceiling, Dixieland jazz, and plenty of white tile and neon. Live crawfish are sometimes allowed to roam on the bar for the customers' amusement.

Recommended dishes include cold boiled crawfish, the terrific fried catfish, stuffed flounder, spicy crawfish *etouffée,* and blackened redfish. For an appetizer, order the "mojo basket," a combination of steamed crawfish and clams, fried crab fingers, and oysters brochette. For dessert, try the *beignets* and *café au lait.* The Atchafalaya draws big crowds, so come prepared to wait for a table.

*Price: About $15 per person*
*Open daily for lunch and dinner*
*Accepts American Express, Visa, and MasterCard*

---

## BAYOU CITY OYSTER COMPANY
### 2171 Richmond Avenue (*at Greenbriar Street*)
#### 713-523-6640

Scalded in a buttery stew is nice, fried is better, and raw is best of all. The Bayou City Oyster Company does all manner of oysters, most of them beautifully. Nevertheless, a few experimental versions need to be sent back to the drawing table. (For example, the oysters *nacho,* loaded with cheese, *guacamole,* sour cream, and *jalapeños,* are awful.) Here's what you should come for: raw, mild-flavored oysters served ice cold with cocktail sauce, horseradish, and lemon wedges. These Southern oysters are softer-bodied than their cold-water counterparts. Fried oysters are plump and bursting with sea juice inside the crisp cornmeal crust. BCOC's oyster-full gumbo is good, too. Paradise shrimp

—split, charred in their shell, and seasoned with garlic-lemon butter—is also worthy. Otherwise, stick with the oyster dishes. The enormous cannery setting is really three restaurants in one. In fine weather, dine outside in the charming rooftop garden.

*Price: Under $12 per person*
*Open daily for lunch and dinner*
*Accepts all major credit cards*

---

# BRENNAN'S OF HOUSTON
### 3300 Smith Street (*just south of downtown*)
### 713-522-9711

Owned by New Orleans' Ella Brennan and run by her son, Alex Brennan-Martin, Brennan's of Houston provides the same excellent American food (including Creole specialties) and attentive service. Eat inside, in the lovely 1929 brick building, or outside in the shady courtyard.

You'll find the expected Creole gumbo and sherry-spiked turtle soup here, but the young kitchen staff has created many trend-setting game dishes as well: mesquite-grilled venison hash, Texas jackrabbit with fiddlehead ferns, and layered, smoked duck breast and fresh duck liver with sherry dressing. Try also the shrimp *rémoulade,* crab cakes, seafood-stuffed leg of capon, a faultless sautéed redfish topped with crab meat, and the shrimp-and-smoked-mushroom combo with buttery sauce and a bit of tomato. Count on fine desserts, including the renowned bananas Foster.

*Price: About $40 per person*
*Open daily for lunch and dinner*
*Accepts all major credit cards*

---

# BUFFALO GRILL
### 3116 Bissonnet Street (*at Buffalo Speedway*)
### 713-661-3663

The Buffalo Grill serves up soul food during the day, including meat loaf and pork chops with side dishes of boiled beans and greens. But come here for breakfast, when the watering hole attracts professionals and students starting the day with cheese grits, peppery pecan-smoked bacon, *huevos rancheros,* and/or fruit pancakes. Eggs can be ordered any way you like them. Try the popular "green and white," which has them soft scrambled with chopped scallions and sour cream. Serve yourself at the walk-up counter, then enjoy yourself seated at one of the old-fashioned oak tables.

*Price: About $3–$5 per person for breakfast*
*Open Mon.–Sat. for breakfast, lunch, and dinner; Sun. for lunch and dinner only*
*Accepts American Express, Visa, and MasterCard*

## BUTERA'S ON MONTROSE
### 5019 Montrose Boulevard (*north of Bissonnet Street*)
### 713-523-0722

Butera's is essentially like the good old-fashioned delis you'd find in New York or Chicago. There are always a couple of soup choices and *quiches,* excellent pecan-topped chicken-liver *pâté,* and dozens of salads and sandwich combinations (including Italian sausage and/or meatballs) listed on the chalkboard and, perhaps, 100 different brands of beer, most of them imports. The small deli is within a five-minute walk of the Museum of Modern Art and the Contemporary Arts Museum. The sidewalk dining provides excellent people-watching. The noontime crowds can be discouraging; evenings are more leisurely.

*Price: Under $10 per person*
*Open daily for lunch and dinner*
*Accepts all major credit cards*

## CAFÉ ANNIE
### 5860 Westheimer Road (*near Augusta Street*)
### 713-780-1522

Don't be misled by its gingham-and-cotton-eyelet name. This is an intimate European-style bistro where the chef—he has a Ph.D in biochemistry—turns out the city's most creative New American cuisine. Owner-chef Robert Del Grande is a local media darling besides, but his fame is more than justified: *pâtés* made from game, cured salmon with herbs and Scotch whiskey, chilled pasta salad studded with shrimp and mussels, pheasant with wild mushroom sauce, grilled shrimp with basil oil and *ancho* pepper preserve, and lamb chops with an onion ragout. Other highlights include a mixed salad of romaine and *radicchio* with grated Parmesan and olive oil, grilled sweetbreads with ginger and mint, an aristocratic veal chop, and the warmed semolina cake topped with three cheeses, liberally soaked with fragrant olive oil and colored with sweet pepper and scallion confetti. The wine list is of modest length and full of possibilities.

Mimi Del Grande is the gracious hostess in the front of the house. The restaurant consists of a romantic little bar near the entrance and a classically simple dining room, with pecan paneling, etched-glass dividers, and mauve accents. Crisp white linens and small arrangements of fresh flowers grace the tables, altogether making this the most urbane spot in town. Reservations are recommended.

*Price: About $35 per person*
*Open Tues.–Fri. for lunch and dinner; Sat. and Sun. for dinner only; closed Sun. and Mon.*
*Accepts all major credit cards*

---

# CAFÉ EXPRESS
## 1415 South Post Oak Lane (*just north of San Felipe Road*)
### 713-963-9777

Eat in or take out at this Art Deco-styled food emporium in the glitzy Galleria area. The 100-item menu is broken down into nine categories: soups, salads, sandwiches, deli plates, low-calorie offerings, pizza, *quiches,* chili, and desserts. Among the highlights are shrimp salad with fresh shrimp and bits of new potato folded into mayonnaise with fresh dill, saffron noodles with bay scallops and sweet peppers, a sandwich of smoked salmon on sourdough with cream cheese and raspberry preserves, cold roasted leg of lamb, and cold poached lobster with julienne salad. Daily pizza specials might include such diverse toppings as *chorizo,* cactus, sun-dried tomatoes, chèvre, and sweet peppers. Chili is based on either beef or venison. Desserts are among the best in the city.

Café Express serves a big lunchtime crowd of businessmen, joggers, Galleria shoppers, Yuppies, and housewives. Try evenings or Saturday afternoon for a slack time to linger over a meal and glass of wine. Delivery to nearby office buildings is also available.

*Price: About $10 per person*
*Open daily for lunch and dinner*
*Accepts all major credit cards*

# CAPTAIN BENNY'S HALF SHELL

7409 South Main Street (*near the Astrodome*), and other
locations
**713-795-9051**

Captain Benny's motto: Keep it simple, keep it fresh. And Houston seafood
lovers—including corporate bosses, professional football players, and journalists—have beaten a path to these landlocked boats to stand at the oyster bar
and keep the shuckers busy. You can also get cornmeal-coated fried shrimp,
catfish, and oysters and a dark, rich bowl of gumbo.

*Price: Under $10 per person*
*Open Mon.–Sat. for lunch and dinner; closed Sun.*
*No credit cards accepted*

# CHARLEY'S 517

517 Louisiana Street (*downtown near the Alley Theatre and
Jones Hall*)
**713-224-4438**

Charley's 517 might be likened to a Houston version of Sardi's: It is directly
across the street from Jones Hall and the Alley Theatre. The staff is trained
to accommodate theatergoers, even going so far as to fetch tickets from the
box office for tardy diners. This is an excellent choice to start a special evening,
with a classy, flower-bedecked, traditionally formal dining room.

The menu, ever evolving and shifting, is always on the cutting edge of New
American cuisine and emphasizes regional products, including game. Among
the local favorites are veal scallopine with sautéed apples in Calvados sauce,
grilled quail Flanagan marinated with juniper, wild boar grilled over apple,
hickory, and mesquite wood, venison *carpaccio* served with *tomatillo* relish and
*ancho chile* mayonnaise, and poached salmon with red wine butter, scallops,
and mussels. For dessert, order the aptly named "chocolate intemperance," a
wedge of dense chocolate—almost fudge—that might easily serve two more
temperate persons. The restaurant's managing director, oenophile Clive Berkman,
also has put together an award-winning wine list that boasts 755 varieties.
The collection has been ranked in the country's top 100 by *The Wine Spectator*
newspaper for several consecutive years. The extraordinary wine cellar (available
for special dinners) houses some 30,000 bottles. Many of the Southwest's

wine connoisseurs keep their favorite vintages in private bins in the bricked catacombs underground.

*Price: About $40 per person*
*Open Mon.–Fri. for lunch and dinner; Sat. for dinner only; closed Sun.*
*Accepts all major credit cards*

---

## CHARLEY T'S
### In Greenway Plaza, 3700 Buffalo Speedway
### 713-960-9711

Polished brass and woodwork and *New Yorker* prints on the wall make Charley T's feel like a little slice of the Big Apple. It's located in the office-residential community of Greenway Plaza, within dribbling distance of The Summit, home of the Houston Rockets.

Complimentary fried zucchini, dusted with grated Parmesan, is a delicious way to start. Entrées include stuffed shrimp with artichokes and fresh pasta, a variety of grilled fresh fish, steaks (including an excellent oyster-stuffed carpetbag steak), and lamb chops. For lighter appetites, the menu offers fresh seafood pasta and a stir-fried vegetable plate.

*Price: About $25 per person*
*Open Mon.–Fri. for lunch and dinner; Sat. for dinner only; closed Sun.*
*Accepts all major credit cards*

---

## CHEZ EDDY
### 6560 Fannin Street (*on the fourth floor of the Scurlock Tower in the Medical Center*)
### 713-790-6474

Wait! Don't take the "health food" heading as a reason to skip over Chez Eddy. This is health food that has died and gone to heaven. The gimmick is that Chez Eddy emphasizes food that is low in salt, calories, and animal fat. The happy news is that it's not the least bit dreary. Seasoning is provided by herbs, nuts, and fruit, and seafood (naturally) is the kitchen's big winner. Lump crab meat, for example, is dressed with a tarragon-kissed vinaigrette and nestles in an arrangement of crisply undercooked baby asparagus spears. Tiny oysters Rockefeller are decorated with little crisps of smoked boar and scented with Pernod. Fresh fish is grilled, and scallops of lean venison are pan-fried and served with a reduction of pan juices, brandy, walnuts, and maple syrup. A "lite" version of a carpetbagger's filet has the beef tenderloin stuffed with spinach, mushrooms, and oysters. The wine list is surprisingly reasonable, with several decent selections under $15.

The Sid Richardson Institute for Preventive Medicine is the underwriter for this sleekly modern and surprisingly sophisticated eatery. The service staff resembles a mini-U.N., with members hailing from all over the world, including the Middle East and Africa. Any language problems aside, they work together apparently seamlessly.

*Price: About $30 per person*
*Open Mon.–Fri. for lunch and dinner; Sat. for dinner only; closed Sun.*
*Accepts all major credit cards*

---

## CHEZ NOUS
### 217 South Avenue G, Humble
#### 713-446-6717

Someday people will forget that Humble's namesake was one of the world's major oil barons or that this little Houston footnote became the first Texas outpost for Macy's. Instead, all they will talk about is the wonderful classic French restaurant that thrives here in a modest middle-class neighborhood. This former Pentecostal church—between lives as house of prayer and house of food, it was an antique shop—may still be undergoing small renovational projects. Yet there is charm here: the dainty wallpaper, imposing wine rack, and a standard of food that would do honor to a Continental bistro in any sophisticated city. Most of the menu's offerings are classic, sturdy dishes with good sauces: *coq au vin,* steak *au poivre,* a *velouté* of shrimp and bay scallops, grilled lamb chops basted with olive oil and herbs. There are also a fine house *pâté,* onion soup, shrimps Provençale, and a tenderloin of beef that is served with an intricate sauce of Cognac, red wine, marrow, and mushrooms.

*Price: About $20–$25 per person*
*Open Mon.–Fri. for lunch and dinner; Sat. for dinner only; closed Sun.*
*Accepts all major credit cards*

---

## CLEO'S 21
### 1947 West Gray Street (*at Driscoll Street*)
#### 713-521-9209

When Cleo's 21 opened in 1985, it became a local restaurant phenomenon, instantly attracting Houston's café society. The soft-peach decor, punctuated with deep-green banquettes, and the salon setting are deliberately designed for table-hopping. In the adjoining bar, musicians provide show tunes and cabaret songs. Appetizers include a game *pâté* of the season, *médaillons* of fresh duck liver on a bed of spinach, and angel's hair pasta with marinated shellfish. Follow with the fisherman's chowder under a garlic-scented pastry dome and then an entrée of red snapper infused with fennel and lime, lobster and shellfish ragout, grilled rack of lamb with wild herbs, or boneless breast of Long Island duckling. Owner Marti Shlenker also thoughtfully lists several *cuisine minceur* selections, such as grilled salmon with sautéed spinach and tomato and a veal chop with basil *en papillote*. There is an engaging wine list, as well as a wide selection of port, brandy, Cognac, and Armagnac. Cleo's 21 is a good choice for a business dinner, better yet for romance.

*Price: About $30 per person*
*Open Mon.–Fri. for lunch and dinner; Sat. for dinner only; closed Sun.*
*Accepts all major credit cards*

---

# CLOISONNÉ

## In The Village, 6140 Village Parkway (*between Times Boulevard and Amherst Street*)
### 713-521-3020

Anyone who has visited Chinois on Main will recognize the influence of Wolfgang Puck on Jimmy Lynn's Chinese-Japanese-French café, right down to the *cloisonné* cranes. Lynn freely acknowledges his sources, and so far as knock-offs go this is a fine one. The intelligent menu lists concepts rather than specifics, which leaves the chef room to maneuver from day to day, depending on available fresh ingredients. Start with a bowl of wild mushroom soup, creamy and dense with slivers of pungent mushrooms and pieces of dried lily. Seafood dumplings may be shared by two or three persons. A hot salad of stir-fried bean curd and chunked shrimp makes a satisfying entrée, as do the sizzling fish in a "twice spicy" shrimp sauce, hacked beef salad, steeped redfish on fried rice with roasted shallots and Chardonnay sauce, and the lobster dressed with a winy, shrimp-scented cream sauce. There are also several inexpensive fried rice and vegetable dishes. The best dessert: three tiny custard cups of *crème brûlée*—mint, Mandarin orange, and ginger—each with a crackly, glazed crust of smoky burnt sugar.

Chinese-inspired though the food may be, the decor is light-years from "The Road to Pago-Pago"-style we have come to dread in many Chinese restaurants. The dining room-bar-kitchen are all in one long open room. The setting is minimalist Oriental, with a stunningly simple bar of split bamboo and gleaming black lacquer. Casual but striking.

*Price: About $12–$20 per person*
*Open Mon.–Fri. for lunch and dinner; Sat. and Sun. for dinner only*
*Accepts all major credit cards*

---

## CODY'S

3400 Montrose Boulevard, 10th floor (*between Alabama Street and Westheimer Road*)
**713-522-9747**

Because Cody's is located on the top floor of a building in a generally low-rise neighborhood, guests have an excellent view of the downtown skyline, a view as decidedly urban as the sleek charcoal gray-and-mauve decor inside. Look west for the glorious sunsets that put the Transco Tower and other Galleria-area giants in silhouette.

Happy hour is a major draw here, and the single professionals line up for complimentary munchies. At dinner, the cuisine is Gulf Coast contemporary, featuring crab- and shrimp-stuffed snapper Pontchartrain, bacon-wrapped char-broiled shrimp, and grilled quail. After dinner, there's live jazz.

*Price: About $20 per person*
*Open Mon.–Sat. for dinner only; closed Sun.*
*Accepts all major credit cards*

---

## COUNTY LINE

13850 Cutten Road (*north of FM 1960 West*)
**713-537-2454**

This far-north Houston restaurant—it's set in a handsome country lodge in the piney woods—is the first Houston outpost of an Austin-based barbecue chain. There's just barbecue here, no hamburgers or *fajitas*. Smoked prime rib is buttery tender (not mushy) with a crust of crisped fat. Sliced brisket is fork-tender. Chicken, sausage, and big ribs are all good, too. But if you can have only one thing, make it the smoked duck. Half a bird arrives with crisp, blackened skin. Inside, the meat—reddened from the twenty hours of smoking—is juicy, robust, and superb. Baked potatoes, slaw, beans, and homemade bread finish out the menu.

*Price: About $10–$15 per person*
*Open Sun.–Fri. for lunch; daily for dinner*
*Accepts all major credit cards*

# DAMIAN'S CUCINA ITALIANA
## 3011 Smith Street
### 713-522-0439

Careening down Smith Street toward the freeway access, you may easily overlook Damian's, so watch carefully. Inside, the softly glowing, countrified dining room is warm and inviting, with salmon walls and school-marm oak chairs. No spaghetti and meatballs here. Owner Damian Mandola subscribes to the *nuova cucina* school of cooking. Every meal starts with the kitchen's sultry *caponata,* which arrives with freshly made toast as the management's small gift to diners looking for a fine, medium-priced Italian meal. Classic pasta dishes, available as appetizers or entrées, follow. The *spaghetti alla carbonara* is, perhaps, the city's best version of this dish. The same menu at lunch and dinner includes entrées of charcoal-grilled shrimp, broiled trout with *pesto* and tomato, rosemary-scented grilled chicken, veal *piccata,* and chicken breasts stuffed with sausage and spinach. A dessert cart, shown tableside, features *cannoli, zabaglione, cappuccino* cake, and rum-soaked *cassata.*

*Price: About $20 per person*
*Open Mon.–Fri. for lunch and dinner; Sat. for dinner only; closed Sun.*
*Accepts all major credit cards*

---

# D'AMICO RISTORANTE ITALIANO
## 2407 Westheimer (*near Kirby Drive*)
### 713-524-5551

D'Amico's has its ups and downs, but when everything clicks it's superb: the courtly service, tender fresh pasta, enchanting surroundings with fringed lamps, and lace curtains. It has recently become the godfather to several area offspring, including the above-noted Damian's, Rocco's Pasta House, and Nash D'Amico's Pasta & Clam Bar.

The original family homestead continues to bear up well and still emphasizes Northern Italian favorites: angel's hair pasta with mussels and shrimp in white wine sauce, veal with Marsala and mushrooms, a thick grilled veal chop with garlic-butter sauce, and *fettuccine* bathed in fresh spinach sauce. Desserts are always memorable, especially the pastries.

*Price: About $25–$30 per person*
*Open Mon.–Fri. for lunch and dinner; Sat. for dinner only; closed Sun.*
*Accepts all major credit cards*

# DEL FRISCO'S STEAKHOUSE
In Oak Creek Village Plaza, 14641 Gladebrook Court
### 713-893-3339

This Gretna, Louisiana, import survived its transplant to Houston's 1960 area nicely and is feeding beef-eating suburbanites some of the best red meat in the city. The generous filet mignons, prime ribs, sirloins, and rib eyes are all cut to order in the kitchen, often by the owner himself. The lobsters, lamb chops, and shrimp are also served in macho portions. Other accoutrements receive just as much attention: Bread is a huge, crusty, braided loaf, loaded with sesame seeds, homemade and hot from the oven. If you finish it, the waiter will bring another. The house salad features mixed greens and fresh flowerets of broccoli and cauliflower. Potatoes and other extras must be ordered separately. Skip the potato and order instead the seductive spinach au gratin—lightly creamed and topped with a bubbling brown crust of melted cheese—or the excellent *fettuccine all' Alfredo*. The staff is young but briskly effective. Desserts are ho-hum, but you probably won't have room to try them anyway.

The dining room is small and plain with paneled walls and Western art prints. There are the prerequisite dim lights, white linen tablecloths, and balloon wineglasses. Reservations are recommended.

*Price: About $30 per person*
*Open Mon.–Sat. for dinner only; closed Sun.*
*Accepts all major credit cards*

# DONG TING
611 Stuart Street (*between Smith and Louisiana streets*)
### 713-527-0005

San Hwang's refined Dong Ting has married Chinese provincial cooking with the current thinking that less is more. The result might be best described as *nouvelle chinoise*, for the offerings are carefully choreographed from an overall menu based on earthy Hunan country classics.

Don't miss the lamb dumplings, which are gently steamed and brought to the table in their bamboo steamers with a side of hot chili paste. Other house specialties include smoked meats and clay pot entrées, which are slow-cooked for hours. Try the chunk pork or lion's head (crab and pork meatballs with mushrooms and Chinese cabbage). Somehow they don't fall apart until they are sitting on your plate. Spicy squids, a fragrant toss of trout with garlic,

chilies, coriander, ginger, and sesame oil, and the unexpected crab meat and
Chinese cabbage simmered in cream sauce are also remarkable.

*Price: About $18 per person*
*Open daily for lunch and dinner*
*Accepts all major credit cards*

---

# FUDDRUCKERS
## 1300 Chimney Rock (*and other Houston area locations*)
### 713-780-7080

More than one wit has observed that Fuddruckers is as much a miracle of
marketing as it is of hamburger grilling. So be it. Sure, the chain has a
pocketful of gimmicks: a glassed-in butcher shop so customers can watch the
steak being cut and ground, an on-premises bakery where the buns are made
daily, and a long condiment stand—inspiration to hundreds of other restaurants—that displays stunning tomatoes, lettuce, onions, etc. You serve yourself, moving through a cafeteria-style line. Grab a couple of beers, stroll on
out into the beer garden, and proceed to get your hands and face greasy.

*Price: Under $10 per person*
*Open Mon.–Sat. for lunch and dinner; closed Sun.*
*Accepts all major credit cards*

---

# FUJI
## 11124 Westheimer (*at Wilcrest Drive*)
### 713-789-9055

Fuji is home to a fine *sushi* bar—and much more. There is an appetizer of
baked king crab claw that is served absolutely plain in its slightly singed shell.
Pull it apart and find a surfeit of steaming, rich white crab meat. The *miso*
soup is a deluxe edition with chunks of tofu and—surprise—a couple of
cherrystone clams. Shrimp salad and crab salad both offer generous servings
of the cooked and chilled seafood with tissue-thin slices of tiny cucumber.
Complete dinners might be based on *sukiyaki, teriyaki* beef or chicken, seafood
*shabu-shabu,* or *tempura.* And the *sushi,* of course: exquisitely fresh, delightfully ingenious bundles of raw fish, vegetables, and vinegared rice wrapped
in papery-dry seaweed.

*Price: About $20 per person*
*Open Tues.–Fri. for lunch and dinner; Sat. and Sun. for dinner only;*
*closed Mon.*
*Accepts all major credit cards*

# GAIDO'S

## 3028 Seawall Boulevard, Galveston
### 409-762-0115; toll-free from Houston: 488-7005

To many visitors, Gaido's is Galveston, for the restaurant has been serving some of the best food on the island for three quarters of a century. Lately, the restaurant has gotten some competition from several new entries, including the Wentletrap, an upscale Continental restaurant situated in the historic Strand district and the hotel dining room at the luxurious San Luis, just up the seawall toward the west end.

But there will always be a Gaido's, where the fish is sparkling fresh and the service starchy. The menu resembles that at the Oyster Bar in New York City in its thoroughness. From cold appetizers to hot entrées, there are at least thirty different variations of shrimp and crab. Char-broiling is the best choice for preparation, be it shrimp, grouper, salmon, flounder, or red snapper. Any of the fish can also be stuffed with crab meat, served amondine, or napped with *bordelaise* sauce. There are also some fifteen choices of oysters, plus frogs' legs, scallops, lobster tails, beef, pork, and chicken. No reservations are accepted, so go prepared to wait perhaps as long as an hour. You can spend the time browsing in the adjoining gift shop.

*Price: About $15–$20 per person; Senior Dinner at lower rates for*
*guests over 65*
*Open Tues.–Sun. for lunch and dinner; closed Mon.*
*Accepts all major credit cards*

# GERARD'S

## 2300 Richton Street (*near Kirby Drive*)
### 713-524-3354

This elegant and strangely underrated restaurant serves ambitious Continental cuisine in a soothing, classic setting. Appetizers range from the expected, such as a cold steamed artichoke with creamy vinaigrette, to rarer offerings, such as oysters poached in champagne and *crêpes grand duc* filled with scallops, shrimp, crab, and mushrooms and glazed with hollandaise *mousseline*. A half-dozen *escargots* are served in individual porcelain cups, each sizzling in garlicky herbed butter and wearing a cap of puff pastry no larger than a quarter. Soups change daily—shrimp bisque and cream of watercress among them—and are consistently excellent. Recommended entrées include saffron-scented *coquilles Saint Jacques Marseillaise,* fresh flounder poached in vermouth with shellfish and glazed with cream sauce, roast duck in a delicate sauce based on hazelnuts, filet mignon stuffed with truffled *pâté,* and sirloin steak with green peppercorn sauce finished with brandy.

Those who have no shame may order a dessert sampler that highlights all the evening's offerings. But even if you don't order any dessert at all, the waiter will bring a giant ripe strawberry, twice dipped in white and dark chocolate, to have with coffee.

*Price: About $40 per person*
*Open Mon.–Fri. for lunch and dinner; Sat. for dinner only; closed Sun.*
*Accepts all major credit cards*

---

# THE GOLDEN ROOM
## 1209 Montrose Boulevard (*between Gray and Dallas streets*)
### 713-524-9614

In terms of sheer numbers, Houston's Thai population is quite small—only about 2,000 by a recent count. Yet their presence in the restaurant business is prominent. The city has at least a dozen good Thai restaurants, ranging from tiny mousy, converted houses to elegant cafés. The Golden Room is one of the former. But don't let the humble setting fool you. Owner Kay Soodjai and her cousin Supatra Yooto turn out memorable versions of *tom yum goong* (peppery shrimp and mushroom soup headily braced with lemon grass), *goong ten* (butterflied shrimp char-broiled with a spicy sauce), *ka-prao-nuah* (sliced beef stir-fried with sliced onions, hot peppers, and wilted basil), and the rich and chewy *ba-me-moo-dang* (barbecued pork slices, fried wonton, bean sprouts, and fish balls). All the standards are here, too: *pad thai* (fried rice noodles with bits of egg, ground peanuts, bean sprouts, and your choice of meat), grilled *satay* and *mee krob* (fried rice noodles drizzled with a light dressing and served with bean sprouts, chunks of scrambled egg, and sliced scallions).

*Price: Under $12 per person*
*Open Tues.–Fri. for lunch and dinner; Sat. and Sun. for dinner only;*
*closed Mon.*
*Accepts all major credit cards*

---

# GOODE COMPANY BARBECUE
## 5109 Kirby Drive (*near Bissonnet Street*)
### 713-522-2530

Barbecue and all the trimmings are served in this small woodsmoke-scented restaurant crowded with outlandish Texana. Moist and tender barbecued chicken is famous locally, as are the hot-sweet sausage links. Lean beef and

ham, overloaded baked potatoes, and homemade pecan pie are all prime, too.
It's a serve-yourself establishment. Eat on old tractor seats at community tables
—or step outside on the slab of concrete that serves as veranda.

*Price: Under $10 per person*
*Open daily for lunch and dinner*
*No credit cards accepted*

---

# GOODE COMPANY HAMBURGERS & TAQUERIA
### 4902 Kirby Drive (*south of U.S. 59*)
### 713-520-0197

This is the offshoot of the Goode Company Barbecue Company just across
the street, and it lives up to its progenitor's reputation. The menu is brief and
is dominated by mesquite-grilled burgers and Nathan's hot dogs. Toppings
that may be ordered extra include chili, *guacamole,* bacon, and cheese. Then
make your way to the condiment bar, where you pile on the sliced tomatoes,
onions, lettuce, *pico de gallo,* and such. A handful of Tex–Mex selections, such
as grilled chicken, *fajitas,* and *flautas,* plus strange-looking waffle-cut fries and
onion rings finish out the menu. The perfect foil, of course, is a sweating bottle
of American or Mexican beer pulled from the nearby crushed-ice-filled cooler.
Eat outside on the covered patio, where kitschy neon lighting gives a funky
street-fair feel at night.

*Price: Under $10 per person*
*Open daily for lunch and dinner*
*No credit cards accepted*

---

# HAMPTON'S
### 213 Milam Street (*at Congress Street, on Old Market Square*)
### 713-222-1661

This breezy downtown hamburgery is a favorite among the attorneys and
court personnel, bankers, architects, and sales people in the nearby office
buildings. They come here for man-sized hamburgers (the bun, by the way,
is a masterpiece), enormous platters of excellent meat-and-bean *nachos,* and a
couple varieties of sandwiches. Service is serve yourself; refill your soda or
iced-tea glass as often as you like. There is also canned beer (cases of it act
as door stops). Early in the morning—Hampton's opens at 6:30 A.M.—there

are omelets, pancakes, and Mexican-style breakfasts. The daily hours are clearly designed with commuters in mind, and the management closes at 2:30 P.M.

*Price: Under $10 per person*
*Open Mon.–Fri. for breakfast and lunch; closed Sat. and Sun.*
*No credit cards accepted*

---

## HARRY'S KENYA
### 1160 Smith Street (*at Dallas Street*)
### 713-650-1980

Harry's Kenya is almost too beautiful for its own good. One might mistakenly assume that a restaurant with such a striking exterior—an imaginative brass and copper animal-scape on the downtown office building walls—was overloaded with gimmickry inside. Indeed, no.

This terrific Continental restaurant (named for big-game hunter Harry Selby) lives up to virtually every demand: cunning appetizers, virtuoso soups, dramatic main courses, decadent desserts. The basically traditional surroundings are full of exotica, such as big-game trophies and evocative photography, altogether providing a feast for the eye as well as the stomach. With the fresh flowers, candlelight, and gentle piano music, Harry's Kenya is romantic, but its first calling is probably as a backdrop for power lunching. What could better enhance an executive's image than dining in the company of Africa's great prey?

The tariffs are high here, but worth it. Both lunch and dinner menus include many Continental classics, such as veal Oscar, *sole à la meunière*, grilled salmon, steak Diane, beef Wellington, lamb chops, and lobster thermidor. There are always several game offerings, too: antelope, wild boar, venison, duck, quail, goose. The Caesar salad is among the best in the city. The service is masterful.

*Price: About $40 per person*
*Open Mon.–Fri. for lunch and dinner; Sat. for dinner only; closed Sun.*
*Accepts all major credit cards*

---

## HILLTOP HERB FARM
### In the Carillon Shopping Village, 10001 Westheimer
### 713-784-5524

How can you keep them down on the farm after they've seen the city? Easy, bring the farm to the city. Which is what the mother-daughter team of Madalene Hill and Gwen Barclay did in 1984 when they built a big-city version of their beloved Hilltop Herb Farm, which has drawn gourmands and gardeners out to the country near Cleveland, Texas, since 1957. The Houston offshoot is a plant-filled greenhouse restaurant-cum-country store, where the women also sell their fresh and dried herbs, salad dressings, chutneys, *jalapeño* jelly, and teas.

Typically, there are only three entrée choices at lunch and about twice that many at dinner. Herbs, of course, are used extensively in all the courses. Entrées might be roast duck with star anise and Hilltop's herb jelly, roasted chicken with blueberry chutney and pecans, a pan-fried rib eye with red wine, rosemary, and fresh mushrooms, or fillet of fish with *cilantro* sauce. Call ahead to check the daily offerings. Look for the warmed holiday seed cake served with lemon curd among the desserts.

*Price: About $30 per person*
*Open Tues.–Sun. for lunch and dinner; closed Mon.*
*Accepts all major credit cards*

---

# INDIA'S
## 5704 Richmond Avenue (*near Chimney Rock*)
### 713-266-0131

No curry parlor this, India's offers a classic Continental setting for sampling the city's best Indian cuisine. It's also a good starting place for those who are intimidated by too much ethnicity in a new restaurant. India's doesn't have exotic travel murals on the wall or any alarming choices on the menu. The white linen tablecloths, discreet potted plants, and clearly spelled-out menu offerings are reassuring to dining-room-chair adventurers.

It's hard to imagine any meat-eater not liking the *tandoori* dishes here. Moist chicken is served with sliced onions and lemon wedges. Fish *tikka* is fillets of firm, smoky whitefish. The richest offering is *tandoori* prawn, reddened on the outside but whitely succulent inside. There are also numerous versions of the searing *vindaloo* curries, plus *aloo gobhi masala* (cauliflower and potatoes cooked dry with onions, tomatoes, and herbs), *biriyani* (seasoned rice), and an excellent rendition of *saag paneer,* spinach creamed to the texture of baby food and enriched with chunks of fresh homemade white cheese. Don't pass up the buttery chicken *tikki masala,* delicious hot Indian breads, or the strange but good *rasmalai* (small balls of homemade cream cheese bobbing in a bowl of reduced milk, almonds, and pistachios) for dessert. There is no beef or pork on the menu, but you probably won't even notice.

*Price: About $15–$20 per person*
*Open daily for lunch and dinner*
*Accepts all major credit cards*

# KIM SON
## 1801 St. Emanual Street (*at Jefferson Street*)
### 713-222-2461

Houston's Vietnamese population is second in size only to that of Los Angeles. Many refugees came here to resume a fishing or farming life, others to take up a professional trade or become teachers. And some, thank goodness, opened restaurants. None, yet, borders on greatness. Most dish up big and inexpensive meals to a predominantly Asian clientele; for the Americans, there are also several Chinese dishes, often served all-you-can-eat buffet style.

Kim Son—bustling, noisy, and a little grungy—is like that, too. If you are handed the Chinese menu, hand it back and ask for the Vietnamese menu, which lists nearly 200 dishes. Try the summer rolls in translucent rice paper wrappers, *banh zeo* (the menu calls it a Vietnamese pizza, but it's more like a vegetable-filled omelet), spring rolls with shatteringly brittle outsides and tender pork-and-seafood filling, and any of the soups, noodle dishes, and hot pots. Stop by late—Kim Son is often open after midnight—when philosophical discussions heat up among the university students who drop in.

*Price: Under $10 per person*
*Open daily for breakfast, lunch, and dinner*
*Accepts all major credit cards*

---

# LA CARAFE
## 813 Congress Street (*across from Old Market Square*)
### 713-229-9399

La Carafe is a second home for many professional types who like to get funky. No hard liquor is served, just wine and beer. The classic jukebox plays hits spanning the past sixty years, including standards by Tony Bennett, Judy Garland, Frank Sinatra, and Nat King Cole. The landmark building is a little musty, but that only adds to the charm. A good place for conversation with old and new friends.

*Price: Under $10 per person*
*Open daily*
*No credit cards accepted*

# LA COLOMBE D'OR

## 3410 Montrose Boulevard (*near Westheimer*)
### 713-524-7999

In a state known for its infatuation with things large, La Colombe d'Or has the distinction of being the smallest luxury hotel in Texas. Fewer than half a dozen suites, each hung with art from owner Steve Zimmerman's collection, occupy the two floors above the beautifully restored first-floor sitting room-bar-restaurant. The tiny, elegant dining room is the gathering place for many of Houston's best fed, as well as celebrity guests staying in the exclusive hotel. A splendid rack of lamb is among the kitchen's touted specialties, as is pasta Portofino, a homemade pasta dish topped with fresh lobster, crab meat, and caviar. If the weather is chilly and wet when you arrive, warm up before dinner with cocktails in front of the fireplace in the cozy bar. Reservations are recommended.

*Price: About $35 per person*
*Open Mon.–Fri. for lunch and dinner; Sat. for dinner only; closed Sun.*
*Accepts all major credit cards*

# THE LANCASTER GRILLE

## 701 Texas Avenue (*at Louisiana Street*)
### 713-228-9500

The Lancaster is a small, European-style hotel in downtown Houston, very British and masculine, like a gentleman's club, with hunting art and polo paraphernalia on the hunter-green walls. As does the nearby Charley's 517, the Lancaster Grille draws the performing arts crowd for dinner and after-theater drinks. At lunch, the Grille plays to a packed business crowd most days (reservations are necessary).

Among the perennial favorites are the apple brandy-laced onion soup served in a large, hollowed out *boule,* steak and oyster pie, grilled Cornish hens, salmon *mousse* poached in white wine with crawfish butter, Gulf red snapper baked in parchment with apples, bananas, almonds, and white wine, sautéed *médaillons* of fresh goose liver, and any number of grilled fish, steaks, and chops. Omelets and sandwiches are always available, too.

*Price: About $35 per person*
*Open daily for breakfast, lunch, and dinner*
*Accepts all major credit cards*

# LANDRY'S SEAFOOD INN AND OYSTER BAR

## 22215 Katy Freeway, Katy
### 713-392-0452

Good things do come in strange places. Follow Interstate 10 west of Houston for about 20 miles to the small bedroom community of Katy. On the south side of the freeway, in a nondescript shopping center, Landry's is a tiny, landlocked Cajun outpost. It's deliberately rough around the edges, with a U-shaped bar square in the middle of the room and a strictly roadside-diner ambience. This is a place where you can wear your cowboy hat and oversized belt buckle and no one will think twice. It's also a great place to take kids; the highchairs come stocked with crayons and printed pictures to color. The jukebox is free and pours out non-stop C&W.

Order a tray or two of boiled crawfish to start. These succulent little shellfish are cooked in loads of cayenne pepper, and your lips will soon begin to swell. A couple of longneck beers will help. Fresh Louisiana oysters can be ordered raw or fried. Follow with whole fried catfish, bayou-style frogs' legs, fried crab claws, broiled fish or shrimp, stuffed trout, or (if you must) a steak.

*Price: About $12–$15 per person*
*Open daily for dinner only*
*Accepts all major credit cards*

# LA RÉSERVE

## In the Inn on the Park, 4 Riverway Drive (*just off Woodway Drive*)
### 713-871-8177

Traditional Continental cuisine in a rich, clubby setting awaits lucky hotel guests—or anyone with a fat wallet. The young chef likes to use game, and his old-style creamed rabbit soup is pure earthiness. The fillet of lamb tenderloin with truffle butter sauce awards judicious diners with a platter of bright pink ovals of lamb, absolutely free of fat, arranged daisy-like around yet more lamb *médaillons.* Consider also the Dover sole with caviar butter, venison with pistachio sauce, a sauté of snails with noodles and *pesto,* lobster ragout, and crawfish *cassolette* with lobster sauce. Presentation is beautiful and witty.

As a member of the Four Seasons hotel chain, the restaurant also features several set low-calorie offerings. The three-course dinner is guaranteed to come in under 650 calories, while the two-course lunch promises no more than

500. The chef's savvy food choices mean you will never know you are eating diet food. If the above mention is irrelevant, then consider La Réserve's fabulous desserts, especially a stunning, made-to-order apple tart. So simple— but why can't more restaurants do it?

*Price: About $40 per person*
*Open Mon.–Fri. for lunch and dinner; Sat. for dinner only; closed Sun.*
*Accepts all major credit cards*

---

## THE LASAGNE RESTAURANT
3040 Farm Road 1960 East *(at Aldine-Westfield Road)*
**713-821-0110**

Skip the appetizers, forget the house salad, and refuse the desserts. But do come to The Lasagne Restaurant for the homemade pasta. The kitchen skips all over the map of Italy for inspiration, from the Genovese *linguine al pesto* to the Florentine dish of *spaghetti alla puttanesca* to the Sicilian-style *spaghetti alla vongole* with its stew of baby clams, garlic, and parsley in white or red sauce. Share an order of *ravioli* with a forcemeat of chicken, pork, ham, eggs, and Parmesan or ham-studded *spaghetti alla carbonara*. There are also complete dinners, such as veal *parmigiana,* chicken *cacciatore,* and *braciola* (a sautéed beef roll stuffed with ham, mozzarella, and herbs). This temple of comprehensive pasta is in a suburban shopping center in far northeast Houston, probably 45 minutes from downtown (on a good day), but reasonably close to Intercontinental Airport. The service is motherly. Reservations are generally unnecessary.

*Price: Under $10 per person*
*Open Tues.–Sun. for lunch and dinner; closed Mon.*
*Accepts all major credit cards*

---

## LAVACA BAY
474 South Highway 6 *( just south of Interstate 10)*
**713-558-0600**

Lavaca Bay—the name comes from the coastal bend of Texas—has staked its reputation on beef and seafood cooked in the style of the Corpus Christi-Port Lavaca area. There's nothing exotic in that frankly, but the standards of preparation here are high. Fried foods, such as the fat fingers of cheese, are delicate and grease-free. The house's special crab meat-stuffed peppers—a la-di-da version of *chiles rellenos*—are battered and quickly fried perfectly. ( Just beware of the killer red sauce that accompanies them.) Breaded and fried soft-shell crabs are feathery light. Grilled swordfish, frequently a daily special, is served with a wine sauce and a *rémoulade*. Soups are always fine, too.

The setting provides a much-needed aesthetic relief on this bustling commercial stretch of Texas Highway 6. Surf-white clapboards cover a three-story hexagonal gingerbread structure that was inspired by Matagorda Bay's old Half-Moon Reef Lighthouse. Inside, a graceful double stairway connects the first floor and mezzanine under the soaring, exposed-beam ceiling. Mounted trophies representing the various cattle breeds raised along the Texas coast line the wall.

*Price: About $15 per person*
*Open Sun.–Fri. for lunch and dinner; Sat. for dinner only*
*Accepts all major credit cards*

## LE RESTAURANT DE FRANCE
### In the Meridien Hotel, 400 Dallas Street (*at Bagby Street*)
### 713-759-0202

Le Restaurant de France, the house dining room of the Meridien Hotel, is clearly inspired by Paul Bocuse. The elegant, traditional dining room, fronted by a display of French country china, is a cool respite from the downtown workaday world outside.

The menu reflects seasonal fish and produce and may include *médaillons* of trout with a light lobster *mousse* on a bed of spinach, *suprême* of duck stuffed with goose liver, a complex lobster salad, roast rack of lamb, veal fillet with wild mushrooms, and pigeon served on a bed of wine-poached pears. Presentation is exquisitely detailed. Desserts are sensational. There is a very good wine list.

*Price: À la carte about $50 per person; fixed-price lunch and dinner*
*menus reasonable*
*Open Mon.–Fri. for lunch and dinner; Sat. for dinner only; closed Sun.*
*Accepts all major credit cards*

## MAGNOLIA BAR & GRILL
### 6000 Richmond Avenue (*near Chimney Rock*)
### 713-781-6207

A gracious plantation setting complete with shutters, slow-turning ceiling fans, and fresh greenery is the place to go for Cajun favorites: oyster po' boys, crawfish *etouffée,* silver-dollar-sized soft-shell crabs, and gumbo. The soups, in fact, may be Magnolia's *coup de grâce.* Both the seafood gumbo and crawfish bisque have become local standards against which other renditions may be measured. Also recommended are the shrimp salad, broiled flounder stuffed with a rich crab dressing, crab meat sauté, fried catfish, fried chicken wings, and shrimp Creole.

Sunday brunch is a stupendous Cajun feast, with a whole roast pig laid out on the enormous antique bar for your inspection, made-to-order omelets with crab or crawfish, all the oysters Rockefeller you can eat, delicious giblet-studded "dirty rice," and much more.

*Price: About $18 per person*
*Open daily for lunch and dinner*
*Accepts all major credit cards*

## MALLORCA'S
### At the Watergate Yachting Center, 1500 Farm Road 2094, Kemah
**713-334-2584**

The country club-like dining room would not be remarkable except for the fact that it overlooks the docks of one of the Gulf Coast's largest, most exclusive marinas. Mallorca's, which is open to the public, is accessible by water, of course, as well as helicopter (should you prefer to leave your yacht in deeper water). From downtown Houston, it's about an hour's drive. Owner-chef Jaime Duran is a native of Mallorca and offers a tempting selection of classic Spanish dishes, as well as a few French items. Be sure to order *gambas al ajillo* (shrimp quick-sizzled in garlicky olive oil), either as an appetizer or entrée. The *pâté maison* is headily seasoned, and grilled seafood is always dependable. There is also a seafood *paella* rampant with chicken, pork, shrimp, clams, and flounder. Have cocktails seated outside, catching a salty breeze.

*Price: About $20 per person*
*Open daily for lunch and dinner*
*Accepts all major credit cards*

## MA MAISON
### 1515 South Post Oak Lane (*off San Felipe Road*)
**713-840-0303**

On a rainy night in 1979 restaurateur Michael Lakhdar spotted this fine old house, shuttered and waiting to be dismantled, on the soon-to-be construction site of a high-rise development called Four Oaks Place. He convinced the developer to let him turn the former country lodge into the exclusive French restaurant that he subsequently dubbed Ma Maison. With extensive renovation and enlargement, Ma Maison now provides a rare link between old and new

Houston. Its simple lines and chaste façade contrast strikingly with the brazen glass skyscrapers that stand guard all around. Inside, the vaulted Tudor-style hall contains the refined main dining room, which intersects a sunny, plant-filled garden room. For private parties, there are also the informal bay room and a cool, understated wine room, with a wall of wine racks, working fireplace, and separate entrance from the outside for discreet comings and goings.

The culinary emphasis here is on traditional French country cooking; Lakhdar shies away from food trends. The chef's *pâté,* garlicky broiled snails, and scallop salad are all fine beginners. *Carpaccio,* napped with velvety herbed mayonnaise, is usually dependable, too. At lunch, there are many salads and omelets, as well as grilled fish. Sturdier dinner entrées include sweetbreads in port wine sauce, the house's *cassoulet,* roast duck in apple and green peppercorn sauce, trout and lump crab meat in brown butter, and several beef selections. Desserts are a mix of frou-frou and good sense: chocolate *mousse* and sweetened cream, *oeufs à la neige,* and apple tarts, or cheese and fruit.

*Price: About $35 per person*
*Open Mon.–Fri. for lunch and dinner; Sat. for dinner only; closed Sun.*
*Accepts all major credit cards*

---

## MARFRELESS
### 2006 Peden Street (*behind the River Oaks Theatre*)
### 713-528-0083

Some very private nooks upstairs, furnished with overstuffed couches, and Houston's most discreet waitresses make Marfreless the perfect setting for a budding romance. It's also very dark, with soft classical music. Sort of a tunnel of love for grown-ups. The clientele ranges from suit-and-ties to casual film buffs stopping in for a post-movie drink. The trick for newcomers is finding the entrance, which is unmarked.

*Price: Under $10 per person*
*Open daily*
*Accepts all major credit cards*

---

## MATA HARI
### In Carillon Shopping Village, 10001 Westheimer
### 713-977-4317

The name means "eye of the sun" or "dawn," and the food is unlike anything else in Houston. Mata Hari's comfortably exotic dining room makes broad use of Indonesia's famed batik fabrics in the drapes, tableclothes, and napkins. The traditional puppets, which played such a symbolic role in the film *The Year of Living Dangerously,* hang on the wall. The waiters are gracious and seem not to mind endlessly explaining the various dishes on the menu, such as *satay* (ribbons of marinated beef, pork, and chicken that are broiled and served with a spicy peanut sauce), *soto ayam* (a deluxe version of chicken soup with bean sprouts, potatoes, noodles, and sliced, hard-boiled egg), *gado-gado* (a sort of vegetable salad served with the ubiquitous hot-sweet peanut sauce), *rendang* (slow-cooked, meltingly tender beef in a curry-and-coconut-milk sauce), and *bahmie goreng* (sweetish noodles stir-fried with onions, garlic, spices, and shrimp). The restaurant's best bargain is the *rijstaffel* ("rice table"), which is a fabulous sampling of almost everything on the menu.

*Price: About $15 per person*
*Open Mon.–Fri. for lunch and dinner; Sat. for dinner only; closed Sun.*
*Accepts all major credit cards*

---

# MERIDA
## 250 Navigation Road (*and other locations*)
### 713-227-0260

Though only a block or two from the celebrity-plagued Ninfa's, Merida is distinctly unglamorous. This is where the local barrio neighbors choose to eat, as do university students and other Houstonians who want hearty Tex–Mex and Yucatan specialties: *Panuchos* (homemade corn *tortillas* filled with black beans, topped with marinated roast pork, lettuce, tomatoes, and pickled onions) are filling fare, as are the overstuffed, deep-fried *empanadas,* chicken- or beef-stuffed *flautas,* and *carne guisada.* With its scuffed linoleum floor, no-nonsense tile walls, and bottomless coffeepot, Merida is also the setting for many a weekend breakfast. Try the *chilaquiles* (eggs scrambled with *jalapeños,* onions, and bits of corn *tortilla*) covered with cheese and eaten with flour *tortillas* and warm *salsa* or *huevos a la Motulena* (fried eggs on a corn *tortilla* topped with cheese and green peas and served with black beans and Mexican sausage).

*Price: Under $10 per person*
*Open daily for breakfast, lunch, and dinner*
*Accepts all major credit cards*

# MINATO
## 10842 Westheimer (*near Wilcrest Drive*)
### 713-783-4790

Minato may be Houston's only Japanese–Korean restaurant. It certainly is the only one with a lady *sushi* chef (on Sunday only). Besides innumerable *sushi* and *sashimi* variations, Minato serves generous-sized dinners featuring chicken *teriyaki,* the house's deluxe *sukiyaki,* grilled salmon steak, and such that come with salad, vegetable *tempura,* boiled rice, and a couple of "chef's surprises" (grilled chicken wing and fried fish are likely possibilities). Korean entrées include *bool kal bi* (lean, barbecued beef) and *kalbee* (beef spare ribs). Just let the waitress know if you would like a bowl of *kim chee* (spicy pickled vegetables) on the side. The best news is the tariff: Minato can boast the city's best bargain among Japanese restaurants.

Decor is typical Japanese restaurant, with low, blond-wood, uncomfortable tables and chairs, a small *sushi* bar, and charming tatami room. The management keeps the restaurant open late—to 2 A.M.—and screens Japanese videos in the evening.

*Price: About $10–$15 per person*
*Open Mon.–Sat. for lunch and dinner; Sun. for dinner only*
*Accepts all major credit cards*

# MONTESANO
## 6009 Beverly Hill Lane (*near Fountainview Drive*)
### 713-977-4565

Restaurateur Antonio Mingalone opened his *nuova cucina* in 1984 during the depths of Houston's recession. The fact that he's done very well since the first month is probably the best testament to his handsomely designed Roman-style restaurant. The setting includes pillars, trickling fountain, and two wine rooms for private parties. For shy lovers, there is also a tiny draped cubbyhole for intimate suppers.

Of course, it never hurts to have your mother in the kitchen: Anna Montesano Mingalone, brought over from Southern Italy, is the co-genius behind the sophisticated menu. Together, mother and son have made Montesano a favorite retreat for the affluent and the astute. Try the kitchen's *scampi* specialty, any pasta-and-seafood combination, the *carpaccio Montesano,* or a veal dish. Save enough appetite for a selection from the dessert table.

*Price: About $25 per person*
*Open daily for lunch and dinner*
*Accepts all major credit cards*

# MR. A'S UPTOWN
## 6396 Richmond Avenue (*between Hillcroft and Fountainview streets*)
### 713-780-0993

Mr. A's Uptown is not located uptown (or even downtown) at all, but in southwest Houston in the heart of the nightclub district. This neon-bedazzled speakeasy (see it at night for the full effect) has been opened up inside to provide just one enormous L-shaped dining room that feels like a cool New Orleans–style restaurant-club, circa late 1950s. The small leg of the L is intimate and little trafficked, while the much larger main section is like one long runway trod by attractive guests (many taking a breather from the area's discos) making their self-conscious entrances and exits. Half-moon booths along the sides of the room provide a full view of the parade. The walls, exposed ceiling, and whirring ceiling fans are all painted deep black-green, against which orange lamps glow dully. The place cries out for a jazz band, and the management accommodates with regular bookings.

The menu is half Italian, half Louisiana: gumbo, "dirty" rice, oyster po' boys, fried crab fingers. Tender oysters *de Jonghe* are quick-baked in a butter-and-garlic brew. Broiled redfish is succulent and sweet. There is also a tile-faced pasta bar where customers can belly-up and observe fresh pasta being made and prepared with various Italian and Creole sauces.

*Price: About $16 per person*
*Open daily for lunch and dinner*
*Accepts all major credit cards*

# MUNCHIES CLASSIC CAFÉ
## 2349 Bissonnet Street (*at Morningside Drive*)
### 713-528-3545

The draw here, live classical music most nights, except when there is folk music or literary readings, makes Munchies Houston's most high-tone ex-icehouse. The owner is the principal French horn player for the Houston Symphony, and he often has friends and students in for a little tooting. Ambitious snacks —salmon *mousse,* fried Brie with fresh fruit, curried chicken salad, and such —will satisfy all but the most profound hungers. Don't overlook the neat ranks of cold imported beers in the cooler by the front door. Just pick out what you want, and the bartender will open it for you. There is no cover charge for the music.

*Price: Under $10 per person*
*Open Tues.–Sun. for dinner; closed Mon.*
*Accepts all major credit cards*

# NINFA'S
## 2704 Navigation Road (*and several other locations*)
### 713-228-1175

Restaurateur Ninfa Laurenzo—she is a minor local legend and was even the subject of a locally produced musical some years back—oversees this small chain of Tex–Mex restaurants. The cramped Navigation restaurant is the original location and the one to visit to spot celebrities. The other outposts are big noisy stadiums, where one's name is announced over the p.a. system when a table is finally ready. In all honesty, the food is pretty much the same at all the locations, and that's not bad. The green avocado-*cilantro* sauce that is served *gratis* with chips at every meal is easily the best of its kind in the entire state of Texas, and the chips are always fresh. *Tacos al carbon*—chunks of grilled beef rolled in soft warm flour *tortillas*—never fail to please meat-eaters. Grilled marinated chicken, pork *carnitas,* grilled shrimp, and *queso a la parilla* are all good choices, too. Finish up with puffy hot *sopapillas,* dusted with cinnamon and sugar and drizzled with honey.

*Price: About $10 per person*
*Open daily for lunch and dinner*
*Accepts all major credit cards*

# OTTO'S
## 5502 Memorial Drive (*near Westcott Street, just east of Memorial Park*)
### 713-864-2573

Otto's has a split personality: One side of the restaurant serves big juicy burgers and the other is a contender for the best barbecue among the spareribs-for-lunch bunch. If you can't decide, have both, along with generous portions of coleslaw, onions, and beer.

*Price: Under $10 per person*
*Open Mon.–Sat. for lunch and dinner; closed Sun.*
*No credit cards accepted*

# OUISIE'S TABLE

## 1708 Sunset Boulevard (*west of Main Street*)
### 713-528-2264

Blackboard specials change twice daily to complement seasonal availability at this quirky, comfortable Rice University-area restaurant. From time to time, expect to find such selections as *linguine* with shrimp *pesto,* the curry of the day, trout Provençale with zucchini, black bean soup, a Friday duck special, vegetable *lasagne,* and city-style chicken-fried steak.

Proprietress Elouise Cooper has no formal chef training but fabulous instincts, and one can always count on the fresh pasta, made by her son Tucker.

Ouisie's draws an artsy, professorial crowd. A "share" table is available for those who arrive at the restaurant alone but do not wish to remain so.

*Price: About $15–$20 per person*
*Open Tues.–Sat. for lunch and dinner; closed Sun. and Mon.*
*Accepts all major credit cards*

# PENG'S

## 5923 Westheimer
### 713-266-1825

The Peng family owns six restaurants in Taiwan, as well as this location in Houston. The food—mostly Hunan, some Cantonese—is always very good, sometimes excellent, and the food decoration and presentation are unlike anything usually seen: intricate, stretchable nets cut from a single carrot, tiny animals carved from radishes, good-luck Chinese characters tucked under the green garniture. There are no real surprises on the menu, but many welcome familiar faces: prawns in hot sauce, cold hacked chicken with sesame oiled noodles, broccoli in garlic sauce, steamed meat-filled dumplings, hot and sour soup, orangey sweet and sour shrimp. Don't miss the grainy, pungent squab soup served in lengths of bamboo. All this in a slightly schizophrenic dining room, with fountains, crystal chandeliers, and piano.

*Price: About $20 per person*
*Open daily for lunch and dinner*
*Accepts all major credit cards*

# RAINBOW LODGE
## 1 Birdsall Street (*off Memorial Drive*)
### 713-861-8666

Set on the steep bank of the Buffalo Bayou very near the museum estate of the late Miss Ima Hogg, Rainbow Lodge is an ersatz Bavarian hunting lodge, complete with gazebo and a topiary zoo. The interior has been likened to a Victorian brothel, with its fringy, cluttery bric-a-brac. The view of the bayou from the restaurant windows is lush and soothing.

The food is not always quite as wonderful as the setting, but it can occasionally astonish. Cool, mild smoked salmon, the chicken liver-based house *pâté,* French onion soup, pan-fried veal liver, stuffed trout, lamb filet wrapped in puff pastry, and fried quail have all proven good choices. The warm, yeasty rolls served with herb butter are addictive. Without fail, the desserts are extraordinary, especially the house's enriched walnut pie and a gooey confection of walnut-studded caramel nestled in a shortbread chamber coated with brittle chocolate. Sunday brunch, usually with a harpist and flutist providing background music, is also a favorite among Houstonians.

*Price: About $25 per person*
*Open Tues.–Fri. for lunch and dinner; Sat. and Sun. for dinner only; closed Mon.*
*Accepts all major credit cards*

# THE REMINGTON
## 1919 Briar Oaks Lane (*off San Felipe Road, near Loop 610 West*)
### 713-840-7621

If you know that the Remington Hotel was built by the same Rosewood Hotels, Inc., that built Dallas' Mansion on Turtle Creek and the Bel Air Hotel in Los Angeles, then you have a good idea of what to expect here: unabashed luxury, personalized service, privacy, and exquisite food.

The dining facilities include The Conservatory and the Garden Room (overlooking the 11-acre Post Oak Park), as well as the clubby and masculine Bar, where food is also served. The *nouvelliste* menus emphasize American and Southwestern cuisine, such as seared red snapper with crawfish and *picante* sauce, lamb loin with mustard and wild mushrooms, buffalo rib-eye with smoked corn salad, and grilled beef filet with duck liver. There are very good wines to complement the food.

*Price: About $35 per person*
*Open daily for lunch and dinner*
*Accepts all major credit cards*

# RENU'S

## 1230 Westheimer (*near Montrose Boulevard*)
### 713-528-6998

It's possible that Renu's is not Houston's oldest Thai restaurant, but it is the one that first became immensely popular and made it possible for all the others that have followed. It's located in a dingy strip shopping center in the heart of Montrose, Houston's version of Greenwich Village or San Francisco's North Beach. Regular customers all have their favorite dishes: curried squid, crunchy *mee krob,* stuffed chicken wings, the crusty-skinned and flamboyantly spiced Delighted Fish, and the brilliantly simple Tiger Cries (rare sliced steak served with a dazzlingly hot green sauce).

*Price: About $10 per person*
*Open Tues.–Fri. for lunch and dinner; Sat. and Sun. for dinner only; closed Mon.*
*Accepts all major credit cards*

# RIVER OAKS GRILL

## 2630 Westheimer (*at Kirby Drive*)
### 713-520-1738

River Oaks Grill is a cozy and handsome restaurant, all dark wood and brass with lattice work and hunting trophies on the wall. A "power bar" provides patrons with an overview of the dining area. The menu is limited, but that only allows the kitchen the time to prepare the seafood, steaks, and chops beautifully. No sauces, nothing redundant, just honest, well-conceived food in a clubby setting. French fried onion shreds and julienne strips of zucchini —you can get a half-and-half order—are delicious. If you are a hunter, the ROG kitchen will prepare your game for you.

*Price: About $15–$20 per person*
*Open Mon.–Sat. for dinner only; closed Sun.*
*Accepts all major credit cards*

# ROTISSERIE FOR BEEF AND BIRD
## 2200 Wilcrest Drive
### 713-977-9524

Rotisserie for Beef and Bird is a local favorite for the well-to-do professional crowd that comes here for the always dependable game, seafood, and beef prepared simply and well. Begin with an enormous bowl of steamed mussels and, perhaps, the cream of pheasant soup with dumplings. Entrées include pan-fried quail with smoked venison sausage, broiled and stuffed lobsters, a mixed grill of lamb chop, beef filet, and sausage, roasted goose, roasted pheasant, red snapper sautéed in brown butter, and filet mignon. The charcoal grilling is done in full view of guests, as the restaurant is built around an elaborate rotisserie and grill. The smooth service and owner Joe Mannke's upscale country inn setting make this one of Houston's most sought-after reservations. Excellent choice for a business meal or a romantic evening.

*Price: About $25–$30 per person*
*Open Mon.–Fri. for lunch and dinner; Sat. for dinner only; closed Sun.*
*Accepts all major credit cards*

---

# SAMMY'S LEBANESE RESTAURANT
## 5825 Richmond Avenue (*near Chimney Rock*)
### 713-780-0065

Set in a renovated house in southwest Houston, Sammy's is among the city's best restaurant bargains. The brown-wren setting won't impress you, but the service is very sweet and the kitchen competently prepares many of the traditional foods from across the Middle East: *falafel* (golf ball-sized pieces of deep-fried chick-pea batter that are crisp on the outside and slightly moist and crumbly on the inside), raw or baked *kibbie* (ground lamb mixed with bulghur wheat, onions, and spices), the cracked-wheat salad called *tabouli, baba ghanouj* (an oil-slickened dip of roasted and mashed eggplant, lemon juice, garlic, and ground sesame seeds), *shawarma* (Lebanese-style sliced beef), and *hummus* (a dip made of mashed chickpeas). *Shish kebab, gyros,* and leg of lamb are also very good, as are the barbecued chicken wings served with a wickedly garlicked potato purée. Avoid the leaden and too-cold stuffed grape leaves. For dessert there is an achingly sweet *baklava* or homemade yogurt with fresh strawberries.

*Price: Under $10 per person*
*Open daily for lunch and dinner*
*Accepts all major credit cards*

## SPANISH VILLAGE
### 4720 Almeda Road (*near Hermann Park*)
### 713-523-1727

The best margaritas in town and funky enclosed patio setting with year-round Christmas lights make the standard Tex–Mex combo plates taste even better. Look for *enchiladas, tacos, burritos,* and *nachos.* Spanish Village isn't fancy, but given the proper mind-set, it can be vastly entertaining.

*Price: Under $10 per person*
*Open Tues.–Sat. for lunch and dinner; closed Sun. and Mon.*
*Accepts all major credit cards*

## SRO BAR & GRILL
### 1800 South Post Oak Boulevard (*near San Felipe Road*)
### 713-626-7143

California cuisine has crept eastward to Houston, and SRO is one of its prime outposts. Unusual ingredients and surprising juxtapositions of flavors, textures, and sometimes temperatures are among the kitchen's trademarks. Specialties include warm *foie gras* salad with candied ginger, lobster *ravioli* with spaghetti of vegetables, spicy pasta with crawfish, grilled chicken with garlic and tequila butter, and thick, moist grilled veal liver with honey vinegar and onion marmalade. There are also some Deep-South-goes-*nouvelle* experiments, such as a whole deep-fried catfish laced with slivers of ginger and *nouveau* pizzas with topping combinations such as shrimp, leeks, wild mushrooms, and thyme.

SRO's casual-chic interior teams earthy textures with sienna tones. Note artist Karen Kirby's fabulous layered walls, executed in *"haute"* papier-mâché, with more than 100 transparent color washes added layer upon layer to produce a soft glow. The warm terra-cotta and midnight-blue room is hung with R. C. Gorman prints, for a relaxed Santa Fe feel. The beautiful people come here—it's adjacent to the private disco Boccaccio—and reservations are required.

*Price: About $30 per person*
*Open Mon.–Fri. for lunch and dinner; Sat. for dinner only; closed Sun.*
*Accepts all major credit cards*

# TILA'S CANTINA & TAQUERIA
### 616 Westheimer (*near Montrose Boulevard*)
### 713-520-6315

If French and American food may be termed "New," why not Mexican? Tila's takes some chances messing with Houstonians' much-loved ethnic cuisine—and succeeds wonderfully. Owner Clive DuVal presents a minimalist New Wave–postmodern diner in stark black and white where the color is provided by the diversified patrons and the flamboyant plates of food. The waitresses wear fifties-style nurses' uniforms and bizarre earrings. Outside the tinted picture windows, the throbbing Montrose-area street scene is worth the price of the meal itself.

The red *salsa* that accompanies the fresh thick corn chips seems, at first taste, no big deal. But the aftertaste and subsequent bites—once you've primed your mouth, so to speak—grow increasingly complex. Follow with a heap of gooey *nachos bandelier,* set off with refried black beans, buttery-ripe avocado crescents, white cheese, *pico de gallo,* and your choice of *fajita* strips or grilled chicken. The kitchen handles fresh seafood well; the crab *enchiladas* are a must. There are also roll-your-own *tacos,* mesquite-grilled chicken breast *burritos, quesadillas,* and a layered casserole of chicken, sour cream, cheese, and a red sauce called *chilaquiles.* For dessert, have a frozen fruit pop—mango, creamy coconut, watermelon, or cantaloupe.

*Price: Under $12 per person*
*Open daily for lunch and dinner*
*Accepts all major credit cards*

# TONY'S
### 1801 Post Oak Boulevard (*between Westheimer and San Felipe Road*)
### 713-622-6778

In Houston, Tony's is still the place to see celebrities and to be seen. For more than a decade, the rich, royal, and renowned have come to this plushly appointed restaurant in an unpretentious shopping center near the Galleria. The regular clientele finds nothing remarkable in millionaires arriving by helicopter in the parking lot out front, and entertainment superstars barely rate a second glance from the sophisticated diners. The cherub-faced owner, Tony Vallone, is the favorite host of pre-eminent gossip columnist Maxine Mesinger, who regularly chronicles the comings and goings of jetsetters from his restaurant. Perhaps most telling, Vallone has created a favorite sanctuary for "ladies who lunch," *de rigueur* in a city where society matrons wield enormous influence. Continental offerings include *tortellini* with *mascarpone* sauce and roasted pine nuts, *linguine pescatore,* veal chop with a vermouth and Fontina cheese sauce, *capellini* topped with fresh seafood and *beurre blanc,* squab with fig sauce, and seafood *gazpacho* filled with crab meat. There is also a glorious dessert cart in addition to the mountain of fresh fruit presented—*gratis*—to each table.

Tony's wine cellar, available for private parties, is probably the most famous subterranean retreat in the city, holding more than 100,000 bottles of wine.

*Price: About $40 per person*
*Open Mon.–Fri. for lunch and dinner; Sat. for dinner only; closed Sun.*
*Accepts all major credit cards*

---

# UNCLE TAI'S HUNAN YUAN
In Post Oak Central Shopping/Business Complex,
1980 South Post Oak Boulevard
### 713-960-8000

Quite simply, Uncle Tai's is Houston's best Oriental restaurant. The *haute chinoise* menu is extensive and frequently updated, and the kitchen's perennial winners include diced boneless squab packages, crisp honey-glazed walnuts, sliced prawns with garlic sauce, spicy bean curd, dry-sautéed shredded beef, Uncle Tai's tri-color lobster, pork, and shrimp with cashews, and boneless frogs' legs with eggplant. In addition, there is a magnificent crysanthemum hot pot served for four persons (order in advance), and Uncle has recently begun cooking game. For dessert, the sesame banana—a batter-dipped and fried chunk of banana that turns into a *beignet-*like puff, then dusted with sugar —is scrumptious.

Since packing up his wok and coming to Houston from New York in the late 1970s, W. D. Tai has also set a new local standard in Chinese restaurant decor. His dining room is cool, plain, and elegantly understated. On Sunday afternoons, Uncle and his staff open the kitchens to the public for cooking demonstrations. Reservations are always recommended.

*Price: About $25 per person*
*Open daily for lunch and dinner*
*Accepts all major credit cards*

# VARGO'S
## 2401 Fondren Road (*off Westheimer*)
### 713-782-3888

If your vision of Houston is one in which the landscape is flat, boring, treeless, and mostly concrete, you'll find a surprise at Vargo's. Here is a man-made paradise on twelve acres, filled with azaleas, crape myrtles, and mature, heavy-headed trees. Take cocktails and snacks out back on the veranda overlooking the rolling hills and a lake lively with swans and flamingos. Tame geese, ducks, and peacocks will come around begging for handouts. When it's time for dinner, you'll note the atrium-style dining room is built around a huge cedar tree and the two-story glass wall provides a sweeping view of the grounds. With such natural splendors, it shouldn't be surprising to learn that Vargo's has long been a favorite for local weddings and receptions.

The food? Mostly middling American selections, such as roast duckling, lamb chops, seafood Newburg, beef, and chicken. It should be better, but the incredible surroundings make up for many culinary gaps.

*Price: About $20 per person*
*Open Mon.–Fri. for lunch and dinner; Sat. and Sun. for dinner only*
*Accepts all major credit cards*

---

# WILLIE G'S
## 1605 South Post Oak Boulevard (*near San Felipe Road*)
### 713-840-7190

It's loud and it's crowded—and you must crunch across an oyster-shell-covered parking lot to get in the door—but this is the place for home-style Louisiana cooking. Roustabouts passing through town, graduate students, and CEO's stand cheek to jowl at Willie G's bar. During crawfish season (October through April), order a huge platter of the so-called mud bugs. You can peel them yourself, snapping the tail off the body and squeezing the meat into your mouth. Don't forget to "suck head" as the Cajuns do, by slurping the flavorful elixir from the creature's thorax. If you would rather not work so hard, choose then the crawfish *etouffée* or fried crawfish tails. Oysters, too, from Louisiana's Barataria Bay are served by the dozen. A house specialty is the seafood platter featuring a stuffed crab, whole catfish, fried shrimp, fried frogs' legs, oysters, and French fries.

*Price: About $15 per person*
*Open Mon.–Fri. for lunch and dinner; Sat. and Sun. for dinner only*
*Accepts all major credit cards*

# THE WOMACK'S HOUSE
## Farm Road 1093 (*just east of the town of Fulshear*)
### 713-346-1478

This is the kind of food from whence ersatz "home-cooking" restaurant chains must have taken their original inspiration. The Womack's House—and it is a rambling country home—is located straight west of Houston. It's homey and familiar. The management even sends out a newsletter to regular customers, notifying them of local happenings. Country-style dinners only are served in sweet dining rooms with oak tables and ladderback chairs set on wide-planked wood floors. The walls are papered with a genteel pattern, and ruffled white curtains hang at the windows. Even the toddlers' highchairs are graceful reproductions from another era. You choose the meat entrée from about a dozen selections, such as chicken-fried steak, fried chicken, livers and gizzards, grilled pork chops, fried shrimp, and meat loaf. Individual entrées are brought and served family style, along with a kettle of the day's soup, black-eyed peas cooked with pork, mashed potatoes and cream gravy, okra and stewed tomatoes, green beans, and a bucket of hot biscuits and cornbread.

The young waitresses and busboys try hard to please, and they're generally successful. Recently observed: The aproned waitress took a cranky toddler outside on the front porch to see a new litter of kittens, leaving her grateful parents a restful interlude to finish their meal. Reservations not accepted.

*Price: Adults, less than $12; children, less than $5*
*Open Wed.–Sun. for dinner only; Sun. for lunch and dinner; closed Mon.*
*and Tues.*
*Accepts all major credit cards*

# INDIANAPOLIS

## *By Donna Segal*

**AMERICAN**
Adam's Rib
Deeter's Nasch & Nip
Dodd's Town House
Hollyhock Hill Restaurant
Nashville House

**BREAKFAST**
Brother Juniper's Restaurant

**BRUNCH**
Keystone Café
Marker Restaurant

**CHINESE**
The Forbidden City
Great Wall Restaurant

**CONTINENTAL**
Crystal Room
Glass Chimney
King Cole Restaurant
The Restaurant in the
    Canterbury Hotel

**DELICATESSEN**
Shapiro's Delicatessen Cafeteria

**ECLECTIC**
Fletcher's American Grill &
    Café

**FAMILY**
Dodd's Town House
Hollyhock Hill Restaurant
Shaffers'

**FRENCH**
Chez Jean Restaurant Français

**GREEK**
Greco's Greek Restaurant

**ITALIAN**
Maxi
Milano Inn
Salvatore's Ristorante

**JAPANESE**
Daruma Restaurant

## PIZZA
The Ale Emporium
Iaria's Italian
  Restaurant
Union Jack Pub

## SEAFOOD
Majestic Oyster Bar &
  Grill

## SUBURBAN
Adam's Rib (Zionsville)
Chez Jean Restaurant Français
  (Mooresville)
Deeters Nasch & Nip (Carmel)
Glass Chimney (Carmel)
Nashville House (Nashville)

## UNIQUE PROPERTY
City Market

Indianapolis is a nice place to visit—and a nice place to live. First-time travelers to the city will like what they see, and those returning after a few years away will be pleasantly surprised with the changes they see.

The city has rapidly gained the reputation as a fun place to be, no longer dubbed "Indynoplace" by the natives. Instead, city leaders, business men and women, residents, and visitors are eager to boast of the city's merits.

The city's aim is to be known as the sports center of the country. There now is professional basketball, football, and hockey, and the Pan American games will be played here in 1987.

With these sports come many new restaurants and night spots in the downtown area. The longtime favorites, like the King Cole and Glass Chimney, still are here and still are good, but they are joined by other exciting restaurants that offer the diner a wide choice.

Within walking distance of the new Hoosier Dome, an outstanding sports and convention facility, there are new restaurants, grills, and bars that offer everything from burgers and milk shakes served in a fifties atmosphere to *haute cuisine*. Union Station, a restored train station, is scheduled to open this spring with a seafood restaurant, family restaurant, food court, and innumerable shops. The Shops At The Claypool also have new restaurants opening with several unique and locally owned restaurants in the food court.

A word of caution about most of the new places, if anyone in your party is under 21: Under Indiana law, persons under 21 may not enter an establishment that has a bar in view of the minor. At some places, those under 18 and accompanied by someone 21 or over are admitted. If there are minors in your group, check the status of the restaurant when making reservations.

*Donna Segal has for fifteen years covered all aspects of food and restaurants as food editor of* The Indianapolis Star.

---

# ADAM'S RIB
## 40 South Main Street, Zionsville
### 317-873-3301

Call ahead for reservations, as this place is a favorite with residents of Zionsville and neighboring Indianapolis. The regulars prefer dinner in the bar area, but families and newcomers usually ask for the dining room. The rustic surroundings add to the casual atmosphere that suits every occasion, whether it's a quick dinner after work or a leisurely anniversary celebration. There's always a selection of fresh fish, prime rib, and barbecued beef or pork ribs. Just check the board to see what specials are available. And don't be surprised to see game meats and even something as exotic as alligator. The selection at the salad bar is huge and can be a complete meal.

*Price: Under $25 per person*
*Open Mon.–Sat. for lunch and dinner; closed Sun.*
*Accepts all major credit cards*

---

# THE ALE EMPORIUM
## 8617 Allisonville Road (*tucked in the corner of the Castle Creek Plaza behind Castleton Square*)
### 317-842-1333

This neighborhood pub is always crowded. That's because the food is good, and the deep-dish pizza is superb. For a full meal, order a spinach salad with the pizza.

*Price: About $10 for a cheese or vegetarian pizza*
*Open daily for lunch and dinner*
*Accepts all major credit cards*

# BROTHER JUNIPER'S RESTAURANT
## 44 West Washington   317-636-2226
## 339 Massachusetts Avenue   317-636-3115
## 150 East 16 Street   317-924-9529

This is the place for a hearty, delicious, and inexpensive breakfast. You may be sitting next to a wino or a top business executive in this casual restaurant, as many of the downtown crowd stop here for breakfast. The reason is simple. The pancakes are so light, you'll wish you'd ordered a long rather than short stack. The omelets are huge and filled with your choice of fresh ingredients. Breads are homemade and great for French toast.

*Price: $3 or less*
*Open Mon.–Sat. for breakfast and lunch; closed Sun.*
*No credit cards accepted*

# CHEZ JEAN RESTAURANT FRANÇAIS
## Mooresville, Indiana
### 317-831-0870

Visitors are surprised to find this French countryside inn in the middle of farmland. But once inside, you'll think you're in France. And if you have the time, plan to spend the night in the Chez Jean Inn that adjoins the restaurant. It's complete with period furniture, down pillows, and comfort. The duck with orange sauce will make you want to use a spoon to savor every bit of the sauce. The wine list is very good. Service is pretentious at times, but very good. (About 30 minutes from downtown Indianapolis. Take State Road 67 to Mooresville.)

*Price: About $40 per person*
*Open Tues.–Sat. for dinner; closed Sun.*
*Accepts all major credit cards*

# CITY MARKET
## 222 East Market
### 317-633-3209

A visit to Indianapolis is not complete without lunch at one of the stands in the City Market. One step inside the building and you feel as if you're in an international village. The tantalizing aromas from the various stands will have you wondering which way to go first. Let your nose be your guide as to where to eat.

You'll find everything here. Try hot stew, a Polish sausage, Chinese, Philippine, or Southern fare. Or get a kosher-style hot dog, overstuffed beef sandwich topped with horseradish sauce, baked potato, shrimp cocktail, or African meat pie and head for a sunny spot in the surrounding mall during warm weather or sit upstairs along the balcony and listen to the entertainment that usually plays during the lunch hour.

And it's tradition before you head back to work to get a hot chocolate-chip cookie, fried fruit pie, dish of yogurt, piece of fresh fruit, or a gooey pastry to eat on the way.

*Price: Inexpensive*
*Most food stands are open only until 2 P.M.; closed on Sun.*
*No credit cards accepted*

---

# CRYSTAL ROOM
## In the Mariott, 2625 North Meridian Street
### 317-925-9512

You know it's going to be a special evening the minute the doorman opens the car door, gives you a smile, a warm greeting, and escorts you up the stairs to the main lobby. The crystal chandeliers, subdued mauve-and-gray decor, and stately marble columns set the mood for sheer elegance—and without false haughtiness.

Most of the entrées here are standard classic fare, but prepared so well that they indeed are special. The *pâté* of duck is not to be missed, and the lobster soup is equally good. Entrées are beautifully presented with an array of fresh vegetables and sculptured potatoes. The wine list is limited, but quite satisfactory.

*Price: About $35–$40 per person*
*Open Tues.–Sat. for dinner only; closed Sun. and Mon.*
*Accepts all major credit cards*

---

# DARUMA RESTAURANT
## 8130 East 21 Street (*in a shopping center strip near 21 Street and Franklin Road*)
### 317-899-3454

If you're lucky, you'll get a seat at the *sushi* bar of this authentic Japanese restaurant. But if it's crowded, which it is most of the time, you'll be seated in the dining room—on the floor. But don't worry, there's a pit for your legs to hang down, and the cushions are very comfortable for floor seating. This is the place for real comfort, because shoes are left at the entrance of the dining room, and the low tables and Oriental privacy screens are most conducive to a leisurely dinner and long conversations.

The *sushi* and *sashimi* are as artfully presented as they are pleasing to the palate. But don't just stick to *sushi*. Be sure to try the *yakitori* (grilled chicken on a skewer). There are also *sukiyaki, tempura,* and *teriyaki* dishes, but be sure to leave room for dessert. The *tempura* ice cream (ice cream dipped in *tempura* batter and fried) is unusual and refreshing.

The outside of the restaurant tends to look uninviting, but don't let that deter you from the good food inside.

*Price: Under $20 a person*
*Open Tues.–Sun. for dinner only; closed Mon.*
*Accepts all major credit cards*

# DEETERS NASCH & NIP
## 12901 North Meridian Street, Carmel
### 317-844-8500

Deeters is the place to unwind after a busy day. Order wine by the glass, from a list of bottles opened that night, and then select from a menu that offers simple but exquisitely prepared food. There is nothing fancy here, just the wonderful peasant-type food that you're likely to find in a small European countryside restaurant. The paneling and booths give an almost pub-type atmosphere, although the bar is tucked away from view.

The chicken is expertly roasted, the ribs will have you licking your fingers, and the fish is always excellent. The waitresses will do a good job convincing you to order the soup or vegetable of the day, and you won't be sorry if you do. The soups and vegetables are always excellent. Owner Dieter Puska oversees the food preparation as he does for the adjoining Glass Chimney. Service is friendly and everyone feels so welcome that sometimes it gets quite noisy. Reservations are essential.

*Price: Under $20 per person*
*Open Mon.–Sat. for dinner only; closed Sun.*
*All major credit cards accepted*

# DODD'S TOWN HOUSE
## 5694 North Meridian Street
### 317-255-0872

You may think you're lost as you wend your way to this old-time favorite: It's right in the center of a well-to-do residential neighborhood. But, as it's an old house, the restaurant fits right in.

Casual is the name of the game: There are no pretentions here, just good homey food. It's the place to get aged steaks pan fried to sear in the juices and retain the flavor and goodness of the meat.

Little has changed here over the years. It's not fancy, but the food is well prepared. Try the fish—broiled or fried—or opt for a sandwich and cup of homemade soup. The pies are not to be missed: If you're lucky, you'll be there on chocolate pie day.

And if there's no room for dessert, take a piece home or even a whole pie to go. No liquor is served.

*Price: Under $15 per person*
*Open Tues.–Sun. for dinner only; closed Mon.*
*Accepts all major credit cards*

# FLETCHER'S AMERICAN GRILL & CAFÉ
## 107 South Pennsylvania Street
### 317-632-2500

The café offers more formal dining downstairs, while the grill joins the bar on the street level. See what fish of the day is grilled over mesquite or try the unusual pizza and a salad with a choice of excellent salad dressings. Waiters and waitresses tend to be somewhat brusque, but ignore that, as the food is good.

*Price: About $20–$25 for the grill*
*Open Mon.–Sat. for lunch and dinner; closed Sun.*
*Accepts all major credit cards*

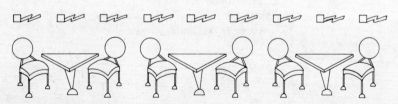

# THE FORBIDDEN CITY
### Glen Lake Plaza, 65 Street at Keystone Avenue
### 317-257-7388

This is the place for Peking duck with no wait. Order it when you arrive or when you call for reservations rather than the day before as most restaurants require. The restaurant also offers Hunan, Szechuan, and Mandarin cuisines in a formal setting.

*Price: $20 for two for duck*
*Open daily for lunch and dinner*
*Accepts all major credit cards*

# GLASS CHIMNEY
### 12901 North Meridian Street, Carmel
### 317-844-0921

Fine Continental dining in a relaxed atmosphere is available every night but Sunday. Here you'll find the classic dishes prepared in true European style. Several dishes are prepared tableside. Boneless duck is a specialty, as are the soups—especially the *bouillabaisse*. Owner-chef Dieter Puska also does an excellent job with fresh fish. About 40 minutes' drive from downtown.

*Price: About $35–$40 per person*
*Open Mon.–Sat. for dinner only; closed Sun.*
*Accepts all major credit cards*

# GREAT WALL RESTAURANT
### In the Castleton Corner Plaza Shopping Center at I-465 and
### Allisonville Road, 8528 Castleton Corner Drive
### 317-849-2218

The attractive shades of mauve-and-gray upholstered chairs, tablecloths, and wall hangings make for a very pleasant and surprising atmosphere for a Chinese restaurant. Ask for a roomy booth when making reservations, and when you arrive ask if owner Walter Lee is there. If so, let him help you order or request his suggestion for the day. He is happy to prepare dishes on request if the ingredients are available. The restaurant specializes in low-calorie, low-cholesterol, and low-sodium dishes. Seasonal marinated vegetables arrive with the menu to ward off hunger. Szechuan, Hunan, and Cantonese dishes are available.

*Price: Under $12 per person*
*Open daily for lunch and dinner*
*Accepts all major credit cards*

---

## GRECO'S GREEK RESTAURANT
### 3849 Georgetown Road in the Lafayette Shoppes (*across the street from the Lafayette Shopping Center*)
### 317-299-5533

*"Opa!"* the waitress shouts as she ignites the cheese and in a flash douses the flame with a squeeze of lemon juice. *Saganaki,* a traditional flaming cheese appetizer, is just one of the many authentic appetizers on the Greek menu. Order, then clap your hands, tap your foot, and sing along with the piped-in Greek music, as you sip wine and wait for a little bit of Greece to come your way.

*Price: Under $15 per person*
*Open Tues.–Sun. for lunch and dinner; closed Mon.*
*Accepts all major credit cards*

---

## HOLLYHOCK HILL RESTAURANT
### 8110 North College Avenue
### 317-251-2294

Pan-fried chicken is the specialty here, and there is plenty of it served up family style, with fluffy mashed potatoes, corn, green beans, and plenty of warm rolls. Steaks and fish also are on the menu, but most people come for the chicken. Also in a converted home and residential area, this charming place is a favorite for family celebrations.

*Price: About $10 for chicken dinners; there is a child's menu*
*Open Tues.–Sat. for dinner only; Sun. for lunch and dinner; closed Mon.*
*Accepts all major credit cards*

# IARIA'S ITALIAN RESTAURANT
## 317 South College Avenue
### 317-638-7706

Few people know about it, but those who do rave about the pizza. It has real flavor in the sauce, a crust that is delectable, and a generous amount of toppings.

*Price: About $7 for a large pepperoni pizza*
*Open Mon.–Sat. for lunch and dinner; closed Sun.*
*Accepts Visa and MasterCard*

# KEYSTONE CAFÉ IN THE RADISSON PLAZA
## In the Keystone at the Crossing Shopping Center (*enter from 86 Street just east of Keystone*)
### 317-846-2700

This Sunday buffet is so large it takes up most of the hotel lobby. Peel-and-eat shrimp, oysters on the half shell, and a pasta bar are featured along with a carving station for roast beef and an omelet station. The dessert bar is huge, and lets you be a child again as you build your own sundae.

*Price: $12.75 per person*
*Buffet served Sun. from 10:30 A.M. to 2:30 P.M*
*Accepts all major credit cards*

# KING COLE RESTAURANT
## 7 North Meridian Street
### 317-638-5588

"Don't mess with a good thing" could well be the King Cole's motto. This old-timer in the midst of a changing restaurant scene in Indianapolis still does a good job of holding its own. The reason is simple. The Continental food is good, the service satisfactory, and the decor most conducive to fine dining. Take time to admire the many original seventeenth- and eighteenth-century paintings hung throughout the dining room before being seated. Included in the collection are two original Gainsborough paintings.

Although not known as a seafood house, the fresh seafood of the day cannot be beat. It is a popular offering for both lunch and dinner, especially when the catch is red snapper. Other favorites of regulars are the roast rack of lamb and prime rib of beef. Two items are featured daily as the Gourmet Special which includes an appetizer, entrée, and dessert for $15.95. Be careful you don't fill up on the homemade rolls and complimentary liver *pâté,* corn relish, and cheese before the entrée arrives.

*Price: About $25–$35 per person*
*Open Mon.–Sat. for lunch and dinner; closed Sun.*
*Accepts all major credit cards*

## MAJESTIC OYSTER BAR & GRILL
### 47 South Pennsylvania Street
### 317-636-5418

There's more than oysters at this attractive seafood restaurant located on the first floor of the historic Majestic Building. Much of the beauty of the gracious building was preserved during the restoration, including the marble supporting pillars and the balcony that overlooks the dining room and provides space for private parties. An upbeat green-and-white tile floor adds a striking contrast to the formality of the white linen tablecloths, stately maroon chairs, and Austrian shades on the spacious windows.

At lunch try the fried shrimp sandwiches with homemade crispy potato chips, or one of the fresh fish choices. For dinner start with shucked oysters or fish chowder followed by grilled scallops, shark, yellowfin tuna, or one of the evening specials.

*Price: About $25 per person*
*Open daily for lunch and dinner*
*Accepts all major credit cards*

## MARKER RESTAURANT
### In the Adams Mark Hotel, 2544 Executive Drive (*near the airport*)
### 317-248-8182

Come with an appetite for this bountiful buffet that features omelets and waffles made to order, and a wide selection of breakfast and dinner fare. Ice carvings are the centerpieces on the main table, where several different entrées are featured each week.

*Price: About $12 for adults; $4.95 for children five to twelve (under five are free)*
*Open Sundays 10:30 A.M. to 2:00 P.M.*
*Accepts all major credit cards*

# MAXI

In the Century Building, 36 South Pennsylvania Street
### 317-631-6294

There's more than pasta at this formal restaurant specializing in Northern Italian and Continental fare. Originally an Italian restaurant, the menu now sports selections any world traveler will recognize. Prices are steep, so you may want to share a superb *tortellini* or *fettuccine* dish before choosing one of several veal entrées.

There's an equally good menu at lunch at much lower prices. Before dinner, visit the champagne bar or opt to have a *cappuccino* there after dinner.

*Price: About $40 per person*
*Open Mon.–Sat. for lunch and dinner; closed Sun.*
*Accepts all major credit cards*

# MILANO INN

231 South College Avenue
### 317-632-8834

When this small southside restaurant, situated near a longtime Italian neighborhood, was extensively remodeled, something was lost in the transition— in the dining room, that is, not the kitchen. The homemade sauces still simmer in a large vat on the stove, but the look of a modest mom-and-pop operation in the dining room has given way to a spiral staircase in the foyer, new booths, and a lavish carved wood and mirrored bar. The food still is good Southern Italian fare, but now served in spiffed-up surroundings.

Try the noontime specials, and, if you're lucky, it'll be the day that homemade cheese *ravioli* is on the menu.

*Price: Lunch, under $5; dinner, about $12–$15*
*Open Mon.–Sat. for lunch and dinner; Sun. for dinner only*
*Accepts all major credit cards*

# NASHVILLE HOUSE

Main Street at Van Buren Street, Nashville
### 812-988-4554

If you're looking for typical Indiana fare, you'll find it here. People stand in line for hours waiting to sink their teeth into the famous Brown County hot fried biscuits served with homemade baked apple butter. Call ahead to make reservations, or put your name in at the desk and then browse around the town of Nashville visiting the shops and art exhibits while waiting.

Fried chicken, ham, and roast turkey are the specialties that make this Hoosier fare so popular. No liquor is served. And don't forget to buy some apple butter at the connecting general store when you leave. About a one-and-a-quarter hour's drive.

*Price: About $12 per person*
*Open Wed.–Mon. for lunch and dinner; closed Tues.*
*Accepts all major credit cards*

# THE RESTAURANT IN THE CANTERBURY HOTEL
## 123 South Illinois Street
### 317-634-3000

This newcomer is small in size but mighty in ability. Seating is limited, so reservations are advised. The dark paneling and upholstered chairs give a library appearance to the room that is conducive to quiet, leisurely dining. Service and food are excellent. California has a big influence in the menu, and the chef does a beautiful job of teaming fresh and unusual produce with fresh herbs and meats. Usually there are several fresh seafood offerings that are grilled or poached. Much of the fish and beef are grilled over mesquite. Artfully garnished plates, warm house-baked bread, and wine from a well-stocked reserve are the noticeable little touches that make the meal complete.

*Price: About $35–$40 per person*
*Open daily for lunch and dinner*
*Accepts all major credit cards*

# SALVATORE'S RISTORANTE
## In the Old Towne Shopping Center, 1268 West 86 Street
### 317-844-9144

This neighborhood restaurant is a pasta hunter's find. Most sauces and pasta are made to order and offer a flavorful marriage of seasonings unique to each dish. The mirrored walls, light wood paneling, and deep-green accents are most inducive for lingering, although the service is quick and very pleasant.

For an appetizer share the *panzerotti,* a fried pie stuffed with well-seasoned plum tomatoes, cheeses, and spices, or a gourmet pizza with a topping of artichokes, clams, Gorgonzola cheese, or *pesto.* The veal *campania* with a caper sauce is superb. A pasta bar is available for the lunch crowd. For evening it's best to make reservations.

*Price: $7–$12 per person*
*Open Mon.–Sat. for lunch and dinner; Sun. for dinner only*
*Accepts all major credit cards*

---

# SHAFFERS'

6125 Hillside Avenue (*off Keystone Avenue, enter the small shopping area directly across from the Keystone entrance to Glendale Mall*)
### 317-253-1404

From the minute you enter Shaffers', you know that you're welcome. The waiters and waitresses, many of whom are relatives and friends of the owners, are very friendly and will help you chose from the large menu.

They are known for their *fondues*—cheese, meat, and chocolate—but they also have a good reputation for their sandwiches, steaks, and fish.

Don't go alone if you plan to have *fondue*. The specialties are for two or more. And if you're not too hungry, ask to see the sandwich menu. Even though it's not offered at night, the sandwiches are available. And they are big —large enough for sharing. Share a sandwich and an order of crunchy munchies (fried vegetables), and then splurge on the chocolate *fondue*. It's so sinfully good that you'll be tempted to eat it with a spoon.

*Price: Under $20 per person*
*Open Mon.–Sat. for lunch and dinner; Sun. for dinner only*
*Accepts all major credit cards*

---

# SHAPIRO'S DELICATESSEN CAFETERIA

808 South Meridian Street    317-631-4041
2370 West 86 Street    317-872-7255

Decisions on what to get are difficult to make at this landmark deli that has people standing in line to get kosher-style hot corned beef sandwiches on fantastic rye bread (even New Yorkers buy it to take home), chopped liver like mother used to make, and creamy cheesecake topped with some of the largest strawberries you'll ever see.

The mouth-watering carrot cake, cheesecake, puddings, and fresh fruit are at the front of the line, so be careful you don't fill your tray before you get to the stuffed peppers, rolled cabbage, baked chicken, short ribs, mile-high sandwiches, or freshly prepared soups. If you're in the mood for breakfast food in the middle of the day, you can probably talk them into fixing you a lox and bagel platter or a salami omelet.

Be prepared for long lines at lunchtime, especially at the Meridian Street location. Everything on the menu is available at the takeout deli and bakery.

*Price: About $5 per person*
*Open daily for breakfast, lunch, and dinner*
*No credit cards accepted*

---

# UNION JACK PUB
## 924 Broad Ripple Avenue
### 317-257-4343

When this pub opened, their pizza business became so brisk that they had to open a separate entrance for the takeout trade.

*Price: About $11 for a large cheese and* pepperoni *pizza*
*Open daily for lunch and dinner*
*Accepts all major credit cards*

# KANSAS CITY

## *By Art Siemering*

**AMERICAN**
  The American Restaurant
  Leona Yarbrough Restaurant
  Pam Pam West
  Stephenson's Apple Farm
    Restaurant
  Stroud's

**BAR**
  Houlihan's Old Place

**BARBECUE**
  Arthur Bryant Barbeque
  Gates & Sons Bar-B-Q
  Richard's Famous Bar-B-Q
  Snead's Barbecue
  Zarda Bar-B-Q

**BREAKFAST**
  Sidney's Restaurant

**BRUNCH**
  The Prospect of Westport

**CHINESE**
  Princess Garden Restaurant

**CONTINENTAL**
  Fedora Café and Bar

**DELICATESSEN**
  Pumpernik's

**ECLECTIC**
  Café Allegro

**FAMILY RESTAURANT**
  Bishop's Buffet

**FAST FOOD**
  Winstead's

**FRENCH**
  La Mediterranée

**HOTEL DINING ROOM**
  Pam Pam West
  Skies

**ITALIAN**
  Italian Gardens Restaurant
  Jasper's
  Lombardo's

JAPANESE
  Jun's Authentic Japanese
    Restaurant

MEXICAN
  Acapulco Mexican Restaurant
  Dos Hombres

OPEN LATE
  The Granfalloon Bar & Grill

PANORAMA
  Skies

SEAFOOD
  Bristol Bar & Grill
  Savoy Grill

SOUL FOOD
  Ruby's Soul Food

STEAKS
  Hereford House
  Jess & Jim's Steak House

SUBURBAN
  Gates & Sons Bar-B-Q
    (Leawood, Kansas)
  Jess & Jim's Steak House
    (Martin City)
  Snead's Barbecue (Belton)
  Zarda Bar-B-Q (Lenexa,
    Kansas)

SWISS
  Andre's

UNIQUE PROPERTIES
  Stroud's

V isitors speeding southward from the airport soon catch their first glimpse of the Kansas City skyline, spread out before them like a well-stocked smorgasbord.

The comparison is particularly apt because the city has always ministered eagerly to the needs of a hungry clientele.

In that long-gone era when steers were the town's most obvious means of support, Kansas City lent its name to what would become a fabled steak, the K.C. strip—a short loin cut.

The railroads that herded cattle here also carried talented strangers who came to practice the art of barbecue. This is the place where Southern and Western styles of smoke cookery, which seemingly were so at odds, sat down and made peace.

Today, pork ribs and beef briskets cook side by side in venerable pits (the current count is roughly sixty) that collectively have felled whole forests of hickory trees.

When Calvin Trillin in *The New Yorker* called Arthur Bryant's barbecue place "the single best restaurant in the world," he wasn't merely being provocative. He was mirroring the mood of the city in which he was raised. People here are as likely to revere a doughnut shop like Lamar's or a drive-in like Winstead's as they are a place whose cooking is more complex. Good food, in other words, cuts a wide swath through the heart of this heartland city.

In an urban complex that covers all or part of seven counties in Missouri and Kansas and embraces 316 square miles, the citizens think nothing of crossing state lines, breaching municipal boundaries, or making themselves at home in neighborhoods that are completely foreign, all in pursuit of a better place to eat.

For the visitor, their trail should not prove too cold to follow. This list includes a few recent upstarts, but most of the restaurants are Kansas City institutions that have met the test of considerable time.

A handful of the city's best are scattered widely, but most are clustered in the center city belt that cinches downtown to the Country Club Plaza shopping district, about four miles due south.

*A note on Kansas liquor laws:* Liquor, including wine, can be served only in private clubs. Seating in the club sections of Kansas restaurants is limited to holders of current Kansas club cards, which require a $10 fee and a ten-day waiting period. Theoretically, you need a membership at each place you plan to visit, but most popular restaurants have a reciprocal acceptance of cards with each other.

*Art Siemering is food editor and restaurant critic for* The Kansas City Star. *Prior to that, he was editor of* Omaha *magazine and food editor for the* Daytona Beach News-Journal.

---

# ACAPULCO MEXICAN RESTAURANT
## 310 Admiral Boulevard
### 816-471-8989

Mexican food in this part of the country is fairly authentic but never adventuresome. Still, no one does the standard *antojitos* ("little whims") better than the Acapulco.

Chicken *enchiladas* are fat with coarsely shredded meat. *Chorizo enchiladas* are filled with a crumbled Mexican sausage spicy enough to bite back. Chili con carne contains cooked pork and vegetables in a thin, scarlet broth.

The sign out front is a work of classic neon art, but the dining room will never be mistaken for one of those palmy California places.

*Price: About $7 per person*
*Open Mon.–Sat. for lunch and dinner; closed Sun.*
*No credit cards accepted*

---

# THE AMERICAN RESTAURANT
## 200 East 25 Street (*atop Crown Center*)
### 816-471-8050

The American Restaurant stands at the forefront of serious interest in America's native cooking. The menu is a roll call of regional ingredients: crawfish, California snails, quail, spiny lobster, blue corn tortillas, Pacific salmon, and, of course, the Kansas City strip steak.

A recent menu addition is barbecued shrimp, served over a pilaf of Kansas wheat, a dish that was eagerly received at the 1985 Inaugural Taste of America.

The restaurant's signature dessert, Sugarbush Mountain maple *mousse,* is a must. California is heavily represented on an extensive wine list. The glittering, multi-leveled dining room is perched atop downtown's Crown Center complex. At sunset the shutters roll up to reveal a romantic panorama of the city that changes into starlight before dessert.

*Price: Under $30 per person*
*Open Mon.–Sat. for dinner only; closed Sun.*
*Accepts all major credit cards*

---

# ANDRE'S
## 5018 Main Street
### 816-561-3440

Midday meals are a simple, Swiss-accented affair in the tearoom at Andre's. Entrées, such as roast pork loin or fried fish, are complemented by a daily *quiche.*

The restaurant's prime attraction, as bountiful counters worthy of Zurich or Vienna will testify, are the pastries and candies.

Lunch is served in an Alpine lodge-like setting. Coffee and pastries are available until late in the afternoon. Reservations are a good idea unless you arrive early or late.

*Price: Under $8 per person*
*Open Tues.–Sat. for lunch only; closed Sun. and Mon.*
*No credit cards accepted*

# ARTHUR BRYANT BARBEQUE
## 1727 Brooklyn Avenue
### 816-231-1123

Just in case the late Arthur Bryant's reputation has not yet penetrated Inner Mongolia, let us affirm that it has rested all these years on an arguably unique sauce.

The thick, brick-red stuff that a practiced counterman slaps on pork ribs or beef brisket sandwiches is somewhat gritty and peppery hot. The secret is not out, but it's a fair guess that the formula includes plenty of dry spices— cayenne, paprika, and such.

The old "grease house," as Mr. Bryant used to call it, has been cleaned up a lot, but little on the menu has been allowed to slide. The beef is sliced more thinly now, the "brownies" (charred trimmings, free for the snatching) are seen less often these days, and the crisper French fries don't absorb so much lard, but the sainted sauce—thank heaven for great favors—remains the same.

Bryant's is located in a not-so-prosperous neighborhood little more than a mile due east of downtown ( just find 18 Street, follow it to Brooklyn Avenue and turn north).

*Price: Under $8 per person*
*Open daily for lunch and dinner*
*No credit cards accepted*


# BISHOP'S BUFFET
## In the Bannister Mall Shopping Center, Bannister Road and Interstate 435
### 816-765-3110

Bishop's, a popular regional chain of cafeterias, makes the most of simple fare, such as fried chicken, broiled fish, and Swiss steak. Breads and desserts are baked on the premises. Chocolate ambrosia and coconut cream pies are not to be missed.

The menu offers lots of choices for children, who will get a balloon as they leave. The surroundings are always clean and attractive. Service is stressed, but no tipping is allowed.

*Price: Under $7 per person*
*Open daily for lunch and dinner*
*No credit cards accepted*

# BRISTOL BAR & GRILL
## 4740 Jefferson Street
### 816-756-0606

The Bristol delivers the mesquite-grilled goods in flamboyant fashion. Air-expressed seafood offerings run to twenty or more on any given day. Choicest seats are in the back room, under an imposing stained-glass dome.

Reservations are a smart idea, but the upfront bar provides an inviting place to wait. If you're detained there too long, the seafood appetizer bar may convince you that dinner is unnecessary.

*Price: Under $25 per person*
*Open Mon.–Sat. for lunch and dinner; Sun. for dinner only*
*Accepts all major credit cards*

# CAFÉ ALLEGRO
## 1815 West 39 Street
### 816-561-3663

Café Allegro can't easily be pigeonholed, except to say that its cross-cultural cooking is strictly *au courant*.

The restaurant goes outside the usual supply lines for fresh local ingredients, such as wild greens and free-range chickens. The fresh pasta of the day is always a good bet. Peppered filet mignon over Maytag blue cheese sauce exposes an old Midwestern staple to a whole new point of view.

The wine list offers a wide range of choices (and prices) among California cabernets and chardonnays. Reservations for lunch or dinner are a must.

*Price: Under $25 per person*
*Open Mon.–Fri. for lunch and dinner; Sat. for dinner only; closed Sun.*
*Accepts all major credit cards*

# DOS HOMBRES

6318 Brookside Plaza    816-523-5462
760 East 88 Street    816-765-0980
13035 Holmes Street    816-942-9400
410 Armour Road, North Kansas City    816-472-5947
10000 West 63 Street, Shawnee, Kansas    913-236-9524

If you're willing to sacrifice a little ethnic flair for the sake of convenience, you'll do no better than at this locally owned chain. Sparks of originality make the menu especially interesting.

Just brush the ferns aside and relax over a respectable margarita and perhaps a "torpedo *burrito*," whose ominous name is belied by a savory filling of beef, egg, vegetables, cheese, and seasonings. If you're a connoisseur of tequilas, you'll find a notable collection to choose from. The restaurant's original outlet is in a charming urban neighborhood; four other locations are scattered citywide.

*Price: Under $10 per person*
*Open daily for lunch and dinner*
*Accepts all major credit cards*

# FEDORA CAFÉ AND BAR

210 West 47 Street
**816-561-6565**

Fedora is an endearingly brassy bistro. Its trendy specialties take a bi-Continental approach in which European cooking techniques are matched with impeccable American ingredients.

Among the best examples are spit-roasted duck and fresh fish cooked on a wood-burning grill or blackened in an iron skillet, Cajun-style. California pizzas vie with East Coast *calzones.* Pastas are all freshly made. Pick hit among desserts is a white-on-white chocolate *tartufo,* served with hot fudge sauce. A well-balanced wine list gives Italy and Germany their due.

If looks could kill, a fleet of five-door Cadillacs would have to be summoned each night the place is open. Fedora's knock-em-dead decor draws on dividers of curvaceous carved mahogany and etched glass, gray herringbone banquettes, and scallop-backed chairs set off by apricot walls.

*Price: Under $25 per person*
*Open Mon.–Sat. for lunch and dinner; Sun. for brunch and dinner*
*Accepts all major credit cards*

# GATES & SON'S BAR-B-Q

## 1411 Swope Parkway    816-921-0409
## 2001 West 103 Terrace, Leawood, Kansas    913-383-1752

If it weren't for Arthur Bryant's barbecue (and the similar stuff turned out by the late master's protégé, Richard France, see page 399), the Gates chain's handiwork would probably be the critics' choice.

It may be the people's choice at that. Gates' food is far less polarizing; Bryant's sauce, for example, has always had its detractors. The Gates potion is quite peppery and tart (although a milder version is available as well). The ribs are thoroughly smoked and nicely charred. The beef has a juicy quality whose secret other cooks surely envy.

Ollie Gates, with forty years of experience behind him, has expanded his original inner city operation to include clean, efficient outposts throughout the metro area. The Swope Parkway location is most convenient to midtown hotels; the Leawood restaurant is close to hotels in suburban Overland Park.

*Price: About $8 per person*
*Open daily for lunch and dinner*
*No credit cards accepted*

---

# THE GRANFALLOON BAR & GRILL

## 621 West 48 Street
### 816-753-7850

This glossy gathering place on the Country Club Plaza mounts the city's most engaging late, late show.

Except on Sundays, when the grill is turned off at 11 P.M., food that may be ordered into the wee hours ranges from omelets and burgers to a decent K.C. strip steak. A quarter-pound smoked sausage smothered in chili is a far cry from your commonplace intestinal percussion device.

*Price: About $10 per person (unless you splurge on steaks or chops)*
*Open daily for lunch and dinner*
*Accepts all major credit cards*

# HEREFORD HOUSE
2 East 20 Street (*at Main Street*)
816-842-1080

The Kansas City steak is more likely to be a Kansas steak these days. Packing plants have moved closer to the source, and their output arrives in town as primal cuts in plastic bags. In spite of that, the steaks still taste fine.

The great schism among steak fanciers pits those knowing folks who insist on charcoal broiling against others who are willing to settle for fried.

Happily, the Hereford House falls in with the broiler crowd. That, coupled with an admirable respect for quality, makes it the best steak house in town.

The place is a sensual delight. You can smell steak a block away. Once inside, you can watch the steaks acquire their deep brown finish in an open kitchen (the Hereford House had theirs long before the idea was promoted by California's Wolfgang Puck).

The beautifully turned-out end results—eight cuts ranging from an 8-ounce top sirloin to a 16-ounce T-bone—will confirm your earlier instincts.

The steaks leave little reason to order anything else, but if you prefer something lighter at lunch, consider a hamburger ground from steak trimmings or an honest-to-Custer buffalo burger. The restaurant accepts no reservations.

*Price: Under $20 per person for steaks*
*Open Mon.–Fri. for lunch and dinner; Sat. for dinner only; closed Sun.*
*Accepts all major credit cards*

# HOULIHAN'S OLD PLACE
4743 Pennsylvania Avenue
816-561-3141

Houlihan's, the original model for many namesakes nationwide, is as busy as any bar in town. This classy Plaza establishment makes the most of antique-store decor and a grab-bag menu.

Burgers and salads are longtime staples. A line of lighter entrées complements sturdier beef and poultry dishes.

The wine list is short but well rounded; several premium wines are sold by the glass. Except at off hours, reservations are advisable.

*Price: Under $15 per person*
*Open daily for lunch and dinner*
*Accepts all major credit cards*

# ITALIAN GARDENS RESTAURANT
## 1110 Baltimore Avenue
### 816-221-9311

In an age when some diners are addicted to restaurant roulette, tradition still has its following, too. So it does at Italian Gardens, a downtown restaurant that has stayed put since 1930. Things are a little quiet there at night, but at noon they're as busy as ever.

Traditional luncheon specials—liver and onions, baked chicken and dressing, and short ribs of beef—are the big midday attraction, although the menu carries a large complement of Italian-American steak house fare.

In the dark, comfortable main dining room, family portraits jockey for wall space with years' worth of autographed photos left by show biz visitors.

*Price: Under $8 per person at lunch*
*Open Mon.–Sat. for lunch and dinner; closed Sun.*
*Accepts all major credit cards*

# JASPER'S
## 405 West 75 Street
### 816-363-3003

Jasper's, the city's most honored restaurant over the years, has never stopped to rest on its laurels.

The Continental menu speaks with a pronounced Northern Italian accent. Among its superb trademarks are lobster *Livornese con risotto* and veal scallopine *Don Salvatore,* cooked with artichoke hearts and *bordelaise* sauce and served over wild rice.

Dining rooms, done in extravagant style, are awash in velvet, mirrors, crystal chandeliers, and candelabras.

The restaurant's solid wine list includes an extraordinary number of good Italian bottles. A supplemental list of rare French wines, some priced in four figures, is mainly for window shoppers.

*Price: Under $30 per person*
*Open Mon.–Sat. for lunch and dinner; closed Sun.*
*Accepts all major credit cards*

# JESS & JIM'S STEAK HOUSE
## 135 and Locust streets, Martin City
### 816-942-9909

A toothsome display of raw materials in a cold case near the cashier's desk will set the steak lover's mouth watering long before he's seated. Although Jess & Jim's opts for frying steaks on a griddle, the tender end results speak for themselves.

Foremost among the offerings is the 25-ounce boneless Playboy strip, a monster version of the premium-quality short loin steak that is more widely known as a K.C. strip steak. Although a platter-overlapping porterhouse weighs in at 30 ounces, the lighter eater should not be discouraged. The menu's smallest cut is an 8-ounce filet mignon. Side dishes included in each meal's price are mostly forgettable. An exception is a big twice-baked potato whose center is mashed and fluffed before it comes to the table.

Jess & Jim's, which looks a little like your average Elks Club, is one of several home-owned eateries in the tiny south suburban community of Martin City. If the wait there proves too long, you can choose among two barbecue joints, a chicken place, and restaurants that serve Italian or Mexican food.

Plan on a 45-minute drive from downtown. The restaurant accepts no reservations.

*Price: About $15 per person for steaks*
*Open Mon.–Sat. for lunch and dinner; closed Sun.*
*No credit cards accepted*

# JUN'S AUTHENTIC JAPANESE RESTAURANT
## 516 West 103 Street
### 816-942-7263

Jun's, a fine, family-run concern, forgos the *teppan* tables in favor of a worthy *sushi* bar. Diners can sit at a counter and watch the *sushi* chef at work or have the bite-sized delicacies brought to their table. Either way, it's an enlightening experience enhanced by a variety of Japanese specialties, including *shabu-shabu* (beef and vegetables cooked in broth), *sukiyaki,* and *yakitori.*

Conventional American dinette seating is augmented by several *tatami* (straw mat) booths. Reservations are usually unnecessary.

*Price: About $15 per person*
*Open Tues.–Sat. for lunch and dinner; Sun. for dinner only; closed Mon.*
*Accepts all major credit cards*

# LA MEDITERRANÉE
## 4742 Pennsylvania Avenue
### 816-561-2916

Kansas City's bastion of classic French cooking is centrally located on the Country Club Plaza. Gilbert Jahier, the restaurant's chef-owner, is a creative fellow whose fondness for fish (24 seafood entrées, including such European specimens as sea bream and John Dory) and game (pheasant, boar, and partridge) have served his clientele well.

La Med's formidable wine list runs to more than 200 bottlings. The dining rooms are elegant but decidedly home-like.

*Price: Under $30 per person*
*Open Mon.–Fri. for lunch and dinner; Sat. for dinner only; closed Sun.*
*Accepts all major credit cards*

---

# LEONA YARBROUGH RESTAURANT
## 2800 West 53 Street, Fairway, Kansas
### 913-722-4800

Leona Yarbrough's is this city's citadel of the square meal. Chicken is fried to order in a skillet. Short ribs of beef are served in a piquant, horseradish-sparked brown gravy. Fried sweetbreads are delicate and devoid of grease.

The place has a Danish heritage, although *frikadeller* (Danish meatballs) are the menu's only hint of it. Breads and desserts are baked on the premises. Dinner prices are all-inclusive, from appetizer to dessert. Diners write up their own orders as they might on a train. Aside from that, table service is strictly traditional.

The decor is well-aged but rather grand in its way. Table linens are crisp and immaculate. Peacock-blue banquettes are as pleasing to the eye as they are to the seat. No liquor is served; cranberry juice is the strongest drink to be had. The restaurant accepts no reservations.

*Price: Under $7 per person*
*Open Tues.–Sun. for lunch and dinner; closed Mon.*
*No credit cards accepted*

# LOMBARDO'S
## 3550 Broadway
### 816-931-3200

Conjure up the perfect restaurateur and surely he (or she) will be one who's usually on the premises checking the tables, conferring in the kitchen, and greeting seated customers.

Such a host is John Lombardo, who left the hotel business to concentrate on something nearer to his roots. His menu's better specialties are equaled nowhere else in town.

*Fritto misto,* an assortment of fried vegetable appetizers, may be even lighter than Japanese *tempura. Saltimbocca* is strictly authentic, even to the sprig of sage employed as garnish. *Linguine tutto mare* tosses noodles in cream sauce with a lush array of seafood. Better-quality Italian bottles dot a respectable wine list.

*Price: Under $20 per person*
*Open Mon.–Fri. for lunch and dinner; Sat. for dinner only; closed Sun.*
*Accepts all major credit cards*

# PAM PAM WEST
## In the Alameda Plaza Hotel, Wornall Road at Ward Parkway
### 816-756-1500

In an age of standardization, great hotel coffee shops are as rare as a lost gold mine. Pam Pam West's link with tradition is an oversized menu that stresses mostly simple stuff—steaks, chops, fried seafood, and such—turned out with perfect integrity.

You can still have a satisfying hot beef sandwich or enjoy breakfast at any time of the day. Diet watchers will find a longer-than-customary list of choices.

The decor, designed to be trendy at the dawn of the seventies, seems quite dated today, but seating is supremely comfortable. Experienced waitresses display real personality, not the well-coached kind.

*Price: About $12 per person for full meals*
*Open daily for breakfast, lunch, and dinner*
*Accepts all major credit cards*

# PRINCESS GARDEN RESTAURANT
## 8906 Wornall Road
### 816-444-3709

Chinese menus tend to look a lot alike, but Orientally attuned taste buds are seldom confused. This town has a wealth of contenders in the Mandarin and Szechuan categories, but the Princess Garden's menu is in a class by itself.

Chef Chang (who is also the restaurant's owner) carves a peerless Peking duck at tableside, and from there on out, things hardly go downhill. Stir-fried shrimp served with tender broccoli in a tart-sweet wine sauce is another specialty of the house.

Clean, pared-down lines give the darkish dining room a modern look. Traditional fixtures, such as temple lamps, are used as accents.

Long weekend waits are not uncommon, but the Garden's bar lets you sit it out in comfort. There's a long list of exotic drinks—heavy on rum and pineapple juice but—mercifully—minus those little umbrellas.

*Price: Under $12 per person*
*Open Tues.–Sun. for lunch and dinner; closed Mon.*
*Accepts all major credit cards*

# THE PROSPECT OF WESTPORT
## 4109 Pennsylvania Avenue
### 816-753-2227

For a Sunday brunch that indulges wretched excess, head for almost any hotel in town. For one that goes its own way, consider the Prospect's perfect set piece, served graciously from a massive antique oak buffet.

The offerings, which rarely change, include almond-filled French toast, Welsh rarebit over bacon on an English muffin, and scrambled eggs with scallions and sautéed mushrooms. Sample them all if you like and make a second trip for more.

This Westport-area restaurant, a two-tiered, skylighted rain forest of hanging plants, offers lots of lovely vantage points. In good weather, you can opt for an adjacent courtyard. Reservations are optional.

*Price: About $6 per person*
*Open Mon.–Sat. for breakfast, lunch, and dinner; Sun. for lunch and dinner*
*Accepts all major credit cards*

# PUMPERNIK'S

## 3820 West 95 Street, Leawood
### 913-381-0061

Pumpernik's is not New York's Carnegie Delicatessen, but it's miles ahead of those glorified sandwich shops that like to label themselves as delis.

At any rate, it's the only place in town where you'll find such an array of Jewish specialties, from pastrami and tongue to knishes and blintzes. If you're searching for standouts, try the potato pancake sandwich, spread with horseradish sauce and thick with sliced brisket. Desserts, such as Boston cream pie and double layered chocolate chiffon pie, are singularly imaginative.

The surroundings have a cowboy feel, but what can you say? Pumpernik's is a fixture in the suburban Ranch Mart Shopping Center.

*Price: About $9 per person*
*Open daily for breakfast, lunch, and dinner*
*Accepts Visa and MasterCard*

# RICHARD'S FAMOUS BAR-B-Q

## 6201 Blue Parkway (*about a mile west of Interstate 435*)
### 816-921-9330

Richard France spent the best years of his life with Arthur Bryant (see page 389). The surest proof of what he learned lands with a slap on the plate as each customer files by the order window at Richard's own place.

His charred, coarsely sliced beef brisket, in particular, tastes more like Bryant's of the good old days than the thin-sliced stuff that others cook there now.

Richard's fiery orange lava is a duplicate of Bryant's barbecue sauce. Mr. France admits that he was often present when the master made his up. If prices at Richard's seem especially agreeable, perhaps it's because the appetizer is free. A tray of crisp burnt ends is kept within reach of anyone who is bold enough to grab some.

*Price: Under $8 per person*
*Open daily for lunch and dinner*
*No credit cards accepted*

# RUBY'S SOUL FOOD
## 1506 Brooklyn Avenue
### 816-421-8514

The building, just a few steps south of busy Truman Road, is painted a shocking shade of green, but the handiwork inside is as mellow as the corn whiskey that the McCormick Distillery makes a few miles up the Missouri River.

A typical midday menu at Ruby Johnson's place ranges from neckbones and chitterlings to Southern-fried steak and pork chops with dressing. The lady's cornbread and sweet potato pie are widely admired.

Dining at Ruby's is a down-home experience. Kitchen curtains grace the windows; tables are decked out in red-checkered cloths. Sassy slogans ("Slow down—you'll love longer") dot the walls. Ruby says everyone is welcome and she means it.

*Price: Under $7 per person at lunch*
*Open Tues. and Wed. for breakfast and lunch; Thurs. and Fri. for breakfast,*
*lunch, and dinner; closed Sun. and Mon.*
*No credit cards accepted*

# SAVOY GRILL
## Ninth and Central streets (*three blocks west of Main Street*)
### 816-842-3890

At the same address since 1903 and looking like some cattle baron's exclusive club is the scrupulously maintained Savoy Grill. Actually it's the front room and bar that has the real ring of old Kansas City, with its pillars, its high-backed booths, and its Western murals. The rest of the rooms are not quite so evocative.

Although steaks get their share of menu space, most locals see the Savoy as a seafood place. Among the enduring specialties are a broiled seafood casserole and a classic shrimp *de Jonghe.* Much emphasis is placed on lobster. The live ones, broiled or steamed, may be had in preparations such as Thermidor and Newburg, and there's a very good baked Downeast lobster pie.

The experienced waiters practice the gentlemanly strain of good service that has almost disappeared these days. The restaurant keeps a good and varied wine list.

*Price: Under $30 per person*
*Open Mon.–Sat. for lunch and dinner; Sun. for dinner only*
*Accepts all major credit cards*

# SIDNEY'S RESTAURANT
### 3623 Broadway
#### 816-531-2725

The conversation among early risers is as brisk as the service at Sidney's. Choice counter seats are usually seized by regulars who like to crack wise with the waitresses and watch a master short-order cook at work in his tightly organized, stainless steel kitchen.

Luckily, he hasn't learned to take shortcuts. Home fries are freshly diced in large wedges. Pancake batter is stirred from scratch. Scrambled eggs are whipped in a malt machine. Breakfast is served at all hours every day.

*Price: Under $4 per person*
*Open daily for breakfast all day*
*No credit cards accepted*

# SKIES
### In the Hyatt Regency Kansas City Hotel, 2345 McGee Street
#### 816-421-1234

Skies defies the old restaurant business axiom that quality goes down as the elevator goes up. The revolving rooftop restaurant matches a peerless view of the city with a highly respectable menu. The list pits certified Angus beef against a host of fresh seafoods.

Char-broiled duck wings—a dividend from the hotel's downstairs restaurant, which specializes in spit-roasted poultry—are a novel appetizer. The wine list is short but impeccable. Reservations are usually a must.

*Price: Under $25 per person*
*Open daily for dinner only*
*Accepts all major credit cards*

# SNEAD'S BARBECUE
## 171 Street and Holmes Road, Belton
### 816-331-7979

Bill Snead's place, planted in the middle of nowhere since 1955, has the city folks streaming in seven days a week. In a dining room that's as plain as any old country café's, platters full of smoked meats arrive dry, without so much as a drop of barbecue sauce.

Diners pour sauce on to taste, choosing between one that's dark brown and sweet (heavily laced with molasses) and a tomatoey one that leaves a pungent aftertaste. Crisp French fries are cut from fresh potatoes. The usual side dishes (barbecue beans, potato salad, and such) are of equal quality.

Smoked chicken is a welcome alternative for people who've had it with red meat. Allow about an hour to get to Snead's from downtown.

*Price: About $7 per person*
*Open Wed.–Sun. for lunch and dinner; closed Mon. and Tues.*
*Accepts Visa and MasterCard*

# STEPHENSON'S APPLE FARM RESTAURANT
## 16401 East 40 Highway
### 816-373-5400

This colorful country inn at the edge of an old apple orchard dotes on hickory smoked meats—pork ribs, beef brisket, ham, and chicken. Old-time home-made side dishes include apple fritters, apple butter, frozen fruit salad, corn relish, and a zucchini casserole with the consistency of corn pudding.

Those who would forgo the smoked stuff should consider baked chicken, a specialty that is smothered in butter and cream. Drinks with an apple theme include cider (you may sample it freely while waiting to be seated), Missouri-made wine, and the restaurant's "polished apple daiquiri."

Stephenson's is located about five miles east of the Truman Sports Complex. Reservations are nearly always a must.

*Price: Under $15 per person*
*Open daily for lunch and dinner*
*Accepts all major credit cards*

# STROUD'S
## 1015 East 85 Street
### 816-333-2132

Although it's now surrounded by the city, Stroud's still looks like the roadhouse it once was. Choicest parking spaces are at the very edge of a busy street; customers must walk in the road to reach the door. Once inside, they must run the gamut of a busy bar and navigate a wavy wooden floor to reach their tables.

Why do people put up with such discomfort? Because the skillet-fried chicken is a wondrous creation, better than Mother's best. Other entrées, particularly the catfish and chicken-fried steak, are just as good.

Pan gravy is flecked with pepper and browned bits. Freshly sliced cottage fries are a little bit of heaven, and the mashed potatoes are as honest as Washington and Lincoln put together.

A basket of cinnamon rolls comes with dinner. Groups are served family style, with bowls and platters to pass around. A doggie bag is delivered at meal's end whether anyone asks for one or not. Plan to come early or stand in line.

*Price: Under $10 per person*
*Open Fri.–Sun. for lunch and dinner; Mon.–Thurs. for dinner only*
*Accepts all major credit cards*

# WINSTEAD'S
## 101 Brush Creek Boulevard
### 816-753-2244

It's nothing more than a drive-in restaurant, with "curb service" and plenty of seats inside. The "steakburgers" are a little on the dry side, but the fountain treats can't be beat. Sodas are made the old-fashioned way. Regular malts (in seven flavors) are creamy smooth. The "special chocolate malt" is so thick that it must be eaten with a spoon.

Winstead's has four locations in all, but the original—still hanging in there on some very desirable real estate at the east edge of the Country Club Plaza —is the one to visit. Its glazed tile exterior looks much as it did in the 1940s; the dining room was freshened up a bit, sometime within the last twenty years or so.

*Price: Under $4 per person*
*Open daily for lunch and dinner*
*No credit cards accepted*

# ZARDA BAR-B-Q

11931 West 87 Street, Lenexa, Kansas (*just west of Interstate 35*)

**913-492-2330**

The powerful perfume of burning hickory wood should convince the visitor that this place does it right.

Succulent pork ribs are doused with Zarda's dark, smoky, only slightly biting sauce. Side dishes, save for barbecue beans, are entirely forgettable, as is the restaurant's "Howdy, Pard'ner!" decor.

*Price: About $8 per person*
*Open daily for lunch and dinner*
*Accepts Visa and MasterCard*

# LAS VEGAS, RENO, AND TAHOE

## BY ELLIOT S. KRANE

**BAKERY**
  Marie Callender's (Las Vegas)

**BAR**
  Elephant Bar (Las Vegas)

**BUFFET**
  Golden Nugget (Las Vegas)

**CHINESE**
  Chin's (Las Vegas)

**CONTINENTAL**
  Aristocrat (Las Vegas)
  Café Monique (Las Vegas)
  Elaine's (Las Vegas)
  Harrah's Summit (Lake Tahoe)
  Imperial Room (Las Vegas)
  Liberace's Tivoli Gardens (Las
    Vegas)
  Michael's (Las Vegas)
  Monte Carlo Room (Las Vegas)
  Sultan's Table (Las Vegas)
  Top of the Hilton (Reno)

**DELICATESSEN**
  New York Deli (Las Vegas)

**ENGLISH**
  The Barronshire (Las Vegas)

**FAST FOOD**
  Olde Philadelphia (Las Vegas)

**FRENCH**
  André's (Las Vegas)
  Café Gigi (Las Vegas)
  Gigi (Reno)
  Palace Court (Las Vegas)
  Pamplemousse (Las Vegas)
  Pegasus (Las Vegas)

**GREEK**
  Café Michelle (Las Vegas)

**HAMBURGERS/HOT DOGS**
  Bono's (Las Vegas)
  Huey's Saloon (Las Vegas)

## ITALIAN
Bootlegger (Las Vegas)
Chicago Joe's (Las Vegas)
Limelight (Las Vegas)
State Street (Las Vegas)
Venetian (Las Vegas)

## JAPANESE
Ginza Restaurant (Las Vegas)

## STEAKS AND CHOPS
Harrah's Steak House (Reno)

## SWISS
The Swiss Café (Las Vegas)

"We're coming to Las Vegas for a convention. Where can we find a small, out-of-the-way restaurant, away from the glitter of the Strip? Some place where we can get excellent service and superb food?"

These are the questions visitors to this twenty-four-hour-a-day city ask most often as they plan their trips to the Silver State. With more than 700 restaurants to choose from in Las Vegas, the visitor can, almost without exception, find the finest restaurants in the major hotels, which always have at least one gourmet room and sometimes as many as three.

Unlike hotel dining rooms across the country, the gourmet rooms in Las Vegas are used to attracting the high rollers who can afford (or get "comped" for) the best that money can buy. The competition is, therefore, keen between the hotel casinos to provide exacting service, varied and exotic foods, and wine lists that will keep these guests coming back again and again.

With this preponderance of gourmet restaurants, the single largest category is still Italian rather than French, for although Nevada was founded by Mormons, the gaming establishments were opened by Italians, and the owners and players at the casinos favor veal scallopine over sole *meunière*.

The hotel kitchens have provided the wellsprings of the local restaurant industry both in Las Vegas and Reno, and, almost without exception, that little out-of-the-way gem of a restaurant visitors seek is the enterprise of a chef or captain who recently broke away from his job at a hotel dining room.

Reno, nicknamed the "Biggest Little City in the West," was named after General Jesse Lee Reno, a Union officer and hero during the Civil War. The tradition of the Old West continues in its hotels, casinos, and restaurants with their informal, come-as-you-are dress and decor.

There are more than a hundred dining spots in Reno, ranging from family-style eateries to elegant gourmet restaurants, but a glance around the most posh room will find as many guests attired in Levis and plaid shirts, as in jackets or long gowns. The expression "laid back" may well have been coined in the Reno–Tahoe area. It's certainly practiced here.

*Elliot S. Krane is restaurant editor for the* Las Vegas Review-Journal *and publishes* Flight Paths, Sunworld International Airways' *in-flight magazine and dining guide. He also writes a weekly column for the* Atlantic City Press.

---

# ANDRÉ'S
## 401 South Sixth Street, Las Vegas
### 702-385-5016

Almost downtown, but located in an old home resembling a French country house, André's is a beautiful surprise, with dining carried out in several small rooms rather than one large one. Chef-owner André Rochat presides over a menu that includes a Belgian endive salad with smoked goose breast, watercress, goat cheese, and walnut dressing. The fresh poached salmon is a masterpiece, surrounded by fanned-out slices of celery. The cheesecake is one of the best desserts from the cart.

*Price: About $45 per person*
*Open nightly for dinner only*
*Accepts all major credit cards*

---

# ARISTOCRAT
## 850 South Rancho Drive, Las Vegas
### 702-870-1977

Founded by a former captain at Caesars Palace, the Aristocrat is now owned by a colleague who has maintained the restaurant's high standards. Located in the middle of a shopping center, this small, charming dining room provides personable service to the eighty-five customers it can accommodate at a seating. Four good soups—cream of broccoli, New England clam chowder, a French onion with bubbling cheese topping, and chicken broth with vegetables under puff pastry—are regularly on the menu. Two beef renditions—Stroganoff and Wellington—and a variety of fish, including red snapper, are all handsomely served, and the freshly made desserts like creamy chocolate *mousse* complete a delicious meal here.

*Price: About $30 per person*
*Open Mon.–Fri. for lunch and dinner; Sat. and Sun. for dinner only*
*Accepts all major credit cards*

# THE BARRONSHIRE

In the Las Vegas Hilton, 3000 Paradise Road, Las Vegas
702-732-5111

Prime rib served by a carver, Yorkshire pudding, and a dessert *soufflé* are featured here. The place resembles an English manor house, and the costumed servers give you a good sense of nineteenth-century dining.

*Price: About $15–$20 per person*
*Open nightly for dinner only*
*Accepts all major credit cards*

# BONO'S

402 East Charleston Boulevard, Las Vegas
702-382-9910

A seeded roll, a grilled Vienna sausage piled high with tomatoes, lettuce, relish, pickle, and assorted condiments make a meal at Bono's.

*Price: Under $10 per person*
*Open Mon.–Sat. for lunch and dinner; closed Sun.*
*No credit cards accepted*

# BOOTLEGGER

5025 Eastern Avenue, Las Vegas
702-736-4939

This family-run restaurant, opened in the 1940s, is still supervised by "Mama" Maria Perry, 69, who each morning oversees the making of the sauces. The homey cocktail lounge, complete with fireplace, is located just inside the entrance, and the whole place is covered with family photos from the Old Country and from the early days of Las Vegas history.

More than two dozen pastas are offered, and for an additional $3, you'll get soup, salad, and a basket of homemade bread. Seafood dishes, such as lobster *fra diavolo*, clams, and *calamari* (all served with a side order of *linguine*), come in portions so large that a takeout container is quite the norm here. The restaurant also offers a dieter's menu with items such as *fettuccine* with broccoli and *ricotta*.

*Price: About $20 per person*
*Open Tues.–Sat. for lunch and dinner; Sun. for dinner only; closed Mon.*
*Accepts all major credit cards*

# CAFÉ GIGI

In the MGM Grand Hotel, 3645 Las Vegas Boulevard South,
Las Vegas
702-739-4111

If Toulouse-Lautrec had enough money and the exchange rate was good, he might be a regular at the MGM Grand's Café Gigi, for the *fin-de-siècle* French decor and exquisite food are perfectly matched. Located in a crystal-chandeliered room with discreet booths lining both sides, the Gigi has a brigade of captains, waiters, and busboys eager to make your meal memorable. *Médaillons* of lobster with a caviar mayonnaise or smoked Scottish salmon with black bread are two very pleasant ways to start the meal. The oysters Rockefeller come on a bed of rock salt, while the *escargots à la bourguignonne* are served in their shell. The specialty of the Gigi is the *côte de veau nouveau Prince Orloff* —a baby veal chop sautéed with mushrooms and wine. The pastry cart, with its *petit fours,* and special fruits and coffee top off a splendid evening's dinner.

*Price: About $45 per person*
*Open nightly for dinner only*
*Accepts all major credit cards*

# CAFÉ MICHELLE

Mission Shopping Center, Flamingo Road, Las Vegas
702-735-8686

A favorite with local and visiting performers, Café Michelle has a sidewalk café commanding a view of the busy shopping center and the even busier Flamingo Road, so it's a pleasant place to sit in amiable weather. Because the restaurant caters to many entertainers, the menu includes a number of unusual start-the-day items. The omelets include asparagus, spinach, and a house *frittata* that consists of three eggs, potatoes, onions, and feta cheese, all served pancake style.

There is also a good spinach pie, eggs Laredo, eggs Benedict, and five types of *crêpes.* In the evening, braised calf's sweetbreads *financière* and *bouillabaisse* are good bets.

*Price: About $20 per person*
*Open Mon.–Sat. for lunch and dinner; Sun. for lunch only*
*Accepts all major credit cards*

# CAFÉ MONIQUE
## 3246 East Desert Inn Road, Las Vegas
### 702-733-7271

The former owner of the popular Café Michelle opened Café Monique in the fall of 1985 and is serving full houses every night. Nick Messologitis offers a Continental combination of dishes—Greek, Italian, French, New Orleans, and Spanish. His menu includes *capellini* Monte Carlo (angel's hair pasta with seafood), blackened sea bass with rice Creole, *paella Valenciana,* and *baklava* cheesecake for dessert.

*Price: About $22 per person*
*Open Mon.–Fri. for lunch and dinner; Sat. for dinner only; closed Sun.*
*Accepts all major credit cards*

# CHICAGO JOE'S
## 820 South 4 Street, Las Vegas
### 702-382-5246

Located in a small downtown house, this restaurant attracts a large lunch trade who come here especially for the Chicago-style meatball sandwiches on fresh rolls.

*Price: Under $10 per person*
*Open Mon.–Fri. for lunch and dinner; Sat. for dinner only; closed Sun.*
*Accepts Visa and Mastercard*

# CHIN'S
## 2800 East Desert Inn Road, Las Vegas
### 702-733-7764

Chin's has been called the "Chinese restaurant for people who don't like Chinese food," with several unique dishes sure to please the Occidental palate.

Owner Tola Chin was born in Hong Kong, and he is a master of stir-fry cooking that seals in the flavors of foods. Good appetizers include shrimp puffs, spring rolls, and a crackling salad made with fried chicken, while the best entrées would be Chin's beef and crystal shrimp. In season, he prepares an exquisite chicken with strawberries (a nice variation on lemon chicken), and his "crispy" pudding (served in a sugar shell) is always memorable. Chin is happy to show you through his small kitchen, so take him up on the offer.

*Price: About $30 per person*
*Open nightly for dinner only*
*Accepts all major credit cards*

# ELAINE'S

### In the Golden Nugget Hotel, 129 Fremont Street, Las Vegas
#### 702-385-7111

Having cost more than a million dollars to build, this intimate gourmet restaurant is the talk of the town. The main room, with Victorian decor, is lined with booths, covered with a domed ceiling, and has curtained entrances and exits to the kitchens, enhancing the quiet atmosphere of the dining area.

The restaurant is named for the owner's wife, Elaine Wynn, who also has a namesake dish—clams Elaine, made with horseradish, chopped hazelnuts, and sauce *Choron*. Snails are baked with garlic butter and Pernod in a casserole topped with puff pastry. Smirnoff salad is made with strips of chicken breast sautéed in olive oil and then flamed with vodka, deglazed with red wine vinegar, and served over Boston and romaine lettuce, watercress, and tomatoes, tossed with Dijon mustard and pine nuts. The apricot *soufflé* (which must be ordered at the start of the meal) is served with *crème Chantilly* and is exceptionally good.

*Price: About $50 per person*
*Open nightly for dinner only*
*Accepts all major credit cards*

# ELEPHANT BAR

### 2797 South Maryland Parkway, Las Vegas
#### 702-737-1586

A popular gathering place for the young and would-be-young. The bar itself is about the height of an elephant—eighteen feet—and mirrored and stacked with bottles full of exotic liquors.

*Price: Depends on what you order*
*Open daily for lunch and dinner*
*Accepts American Express, Visa, and MasterCard*

# GIGI

### In the MGM Grand Hotel, 2500 East Second Street, Reno
#### 702-789-2000

Gigi is a slightly larger version of the Café Gigi in Las Vegas (see above), and the manner is a bit grander. The management has set an innovation in pricing, with all entrées (fifteen of them) at $18, including breast of pheasant under glass, *tournedos* of beef, and steak Diane. The same idea is carried from *hors d'oeuvres* ($6), through soups ($3), salads ($4), and desserts ($3)—this last category listing *crêpes Suzette,* strawberries Romanoff, and cherries jubilee. The only exceptions to this price policy are the Maine lobster, the abalone, and the rotisserie platters of roasted saddle of veal, *chateaubriand bouquetière,* and rack of lamb.

*Price: About $35 per person*
*Open nightly for dinner only*
*Accepts all major credit cards*

---

## GINZA RESTAURANT
### 1000 East Sahara Avenue, Las Vegas
#### 702-732-3080

This small Japanese restaurant and *sushi* bar, run by Kay Takita, draws a local and international crowd to its dozen tables. Each entrée comes with a choice of *miso* or egg-flower soup, and the *yosenabe* (a kind of Japanese *bouillabaisse*) is a specialty, served in a stone bowl and packed with shrimp, crab, fish, and clams in a bubbling fish broth.

*Price: About $30 per person*
*Open nightly for dinner only*
*Accepts all major credit cards*

---

## GOLDEN NUGGET
### 129 East Fremont Street, Las Vegas
#### 702-385-7111

A buffet without equal in a city with more than three dozen buffets. The Golden Nugget offers a daily soup, a variety of entrées, including three from its gourmet Chinese restaurant, a grand salad bar, and a choice of many desserts, including a luscious bread pudding in a chafing dish.

*Price: $8.50 for dinner buffet*
*Open daily for breakfast, lunch, and dinner*
*Accepts all major credit cards*

# HARRAH'S STEAK HOUSE
## In Harrah's Hotel, Second and Center streets, Reno
### 702-786-3232

The late Bill Harrah established a tradition at his hotels and restaurants, demanding only the finest food and service be extended to his guests, a tradition that has been impeccably maintained at Harrah's Steak House, located one floor below the casino. The restaurant is decorated in classic Western style, but this is more than just a steak house kitchen: You'll enjoy scallops *Ste. Michelle,* frogs legs *provençal,* Caesar salad, veal Oscar, and filet of beef Wellington, in addition to excellent steaks cooked the way you want them to be. Harrah's chocolate cake, pine nut ice cream, and ice cream layer cake with chocolate *fondue* are happy endings to a meal here. There is an extensive list of imported and domestic wines.

*Price: About $45 per person*
*Open nightly for dinner only*
*Accepts all major credit cards*

# HUEY'S SALOON
## 3557 South Maryland Parkway, Las Vegas
### 702-732-8411

The burgers here are thick, cooked-to-order, and served on an onion roll with a special semisweet relish and all the fixings.

*Price: Under $10 per person*
*Open Mon.–Fri. for lunch and dinner; Sat. for dinner only; closed Sun.*
*Accepts American Express, Visa, and MasterCard*

# IMPERIAL ROOM
## At the Las Vegas Hilton, 3000 Paradise Road, Las Vegas
### 702-732-5111

The Hilton has several of its restaurants arranged around a court area, with the Imperial Room commanding the prime location. Inside the entrance of the Imperial is a plush cocktail area and a center-island display of replicas of England's crown jewels. Around this island are velvet-lined booths, which are the most sought after.

The most popular appetizers include smoked Scottish salmon and baked cherrystone clams. Entrées include abalone steak with almonds, filet mignon

Wellington, and beef Stroganoff. The specialty of the house is rack of lamb Imperial, served for two at $50. The chef is also happy to accommodate special requests: Bill Cosby once brought a plate of Philadelphia scrapple with him.

*Price: About $50 per person*
*Open nightly for dinner only*
*Accepts all major credit cards*

---

## LIBERACE'S TIVOLI GARDENS
### 1775 East Tropicana Avenue, Las Vegas
#### 702-739-8762

Anyone who has ever attended one of Liberace's extravagant stage shows might easily imagine this is the kind of place the performer would open—full of expensive antiques, flourishing plants, stained-glass windows, and ornate furnishings. For the ultimate in conspicuous consumption, you may sit in gilded chairs, dine on a superb English antique table, and then take the whole set home with you for $30,000—with dinner thrown in. An Arab emir bought the whole lot, and then added $5,000 worth of china.

This is a celebrity gathering place and it's often frequented by its famous owner, who might some night sit down at the lighted piano in the cocktail lounge.

*Price: About $40 per person*
*Open daily for lunch and dinner*
*Accepts all major credit cards*

---

## LIMELIGHT
### 2340 East Tropicana Road, Las Vegas
#### 702-739-1410

Luke Manfredi, his wife, son, and daughter moved to Las Vegas from Cleveland in 1980 and brought with them an extensive menu of Italian specialties. They now serve them up at welcome moderate prices. Dishes like avocado filled with baby shrimp, or a *frutti di mare* composed of squid, clams, and shrimp go for only $4.50. Seafood seems to dominate this Southern Italian restaurant, but there are some good chicken dishes too—*alla Angelo, al'limone,* and *alla parmigiana,* for instance. All entrées come with a house salad. Dessert may include a fancy trifle or a good homemade cheesecake.

*Price: About $14 per person*
*Open Mon.–Sat. for lunch and dinner; Sun. for dinner only*
*Accepts all major credit cards*

# MARIE CALLENDER'S
## 600 East Sahara Avenue, Las Vegas
### 702-734-6572

Fresh fruit pies with just a modicum of filler and a great flaky crust make Marie Callender's tops in town. The cherry pies are especially scrumptious.

*Price: According to what you order*
*Open Tues.–Sun.; closed Mon.*
*Accepts Visa and MasterCard*

# MICHAEL'S
## In the Barbary Coast Hotel, 3595 Las Vegas Boulevard South, Las Vegas
### 702-737-7111

The Barbary Coast, with just 125 rooms, sits in the middle of Las Vegas' version of Times Square, surrounded on all sides by two- and three-thousand-room hotel casinos. Yet this little hotel houses one of the finest restaurants in Nevada—Michael's, a little gem seating just sixty people on banquettes covered with Italian lace. The place is staffed by captains and waiters who once served at the famous Candlelight Room in the old Flamingo Hotel a decade ago.

The presentation of a relish tray tastefully arranged with miniature corn, cherry tomatoes, olives, cheese dip, kumquats, and Middle Eastern flatbread provides sustenance while you look over the menu. The shrimp cocktail on a frosted glass globe makes for a romantic starter, and the *escargots* served on slivers of artichoke hearts and covered with puff pastry is a delight. Entrées served with flair include veal *française*, rack of lamb *bouquetière*, and Maine lobster. Desserts include a complimentary bowl of fresh fruit (almost always out of season) and fruit slices dipped in both white and dark chocolate.

*Price: About $50 per person*
*Open nightly for dinner only*
*Accepts all major credit cards*

# MONTE CARLO ROOM

At the Desert Inn Hotel, 3145 Las Vegas Boulevard South,
Las Vegas
702-733-4444

Attractive double doors of oak and stained glass lead you into the elegant
Monte Carlo Room, just past the baccarat tables at the Desert Inn's casino.
Built in the 1950s, the hotel was completely refurbished when Howard
Hughes bought it, and when the Monte Carlo Room opened in 1964 it
established its reputation as one of the best dining rooms on the Strip.

Among the most popular appetizers are the shrimp, lobster, and seafood
(arranged on a cone of ice) and the shrimp *scampi* sautéed with garlic. Among
the international dishes on the menu, *grenadins de veau Prince Chimay, noisettes*
of baby lamb *bourgeois,* and *médaillons* of beef Monte Carlo are excellent. The
hobo steak, baked in rock salt, is unique to these parts.

Most diners start their meal with the spinach salad tossed tableside and end
the evening with bananas Foster flamed at the same spot.

*Price: About $50 per person*
*Open nightly for dinner only*
*Accepts all major credit cards*

# NEW YORK DELI

2585 East Flamingo Road, Las Vegas
702-733-9594

The best-stocked deli in the city, tripled in size this past year and still maintains
the personal service that has been its hallmark. Don't miss the matzo ball soup.

*Price: Under $10 per person*
*Open Mon.–Fri. for lunch and dinner; Sat. for dinner only; closed Sun.*
*Accepts Visa and MasterCard*

# OLDE PHILADELPHIA

3430 East Tropicana Avenue, Las Vegas
702-456-0864

Run by a graduate of Pat's, the famous creator of the Philadelphia cheese steak,
this small shop sells over 300,000 cheese steaks a year.

*Price: Under $10 per person*
*Open Mon.–Fri. for lunch and dinner; Sat. for dinner only; closed Sun.*
*No credit cards accepted*

# PALACE COURT

In Caesars Palace, 3570 Las Vegas Boulevard South, Las
Vegas

702-731-7547

Under a stained-glass dome, overlooking an Olympic-size swimming pool decorated with Italian marble, this Caesars Palace showplace serves elegant dinners to those lucky enough to snare a reservation long in advance for one of the eighty seats in the dining room. The tables are covered with lace, the flatware is vermeil, the china Lenox, the glassware crystal, and the waiters white-gloved. They will happily serve you caviar wheeled to your table on a massive carved cake of ice. The caviar (served with Russian vodka) goes for about $42 per ounce. Somewhat less pricey is the popular pike *mousse* appetizer, and the poached filet of Dover sole stuffed with lobster *mousse* is a superb entrée. You may also order *tournedos,* rack of lamb, lobster Thermidor, and floating island or kiwi tart for dessert. Allow at least two-and-a-half hours to dine here, and you'll love every minute.

*Price: About $40 per person*
*Open nightly for dinner only*
*Accepts all major credit cards*

# PAMPLEMOUSSE

400 East Sahara Avenue, Las Vegas

702-733-2066

Here's one of those out-of-the-way places visitors seek. It's located down the street from the Sahara Hotel and has the atmosphere of a French country restaurant. You'll be brought a large basket of vegetables with which to make your salad, and from then on owner Georges La Forge and his staff will explain the evening's entrées, which include fresh fish, capon, veal, duck, quail, and steaks. The selection of desserts includes *coupe à la maison, crème caramel,* and *poire belle Hélène.* Since the place seats only eighty people and is very popular, reservations are a must.

*Price: About $40 per person*
*Open Tues.–Sun. for dinner only; closed Mon.*
*Accepts all major credit cards*

# PEGASUS
In the Alexis Park Hotel on Harmon, 375 East Harmon
Avenue, Las Vegas
702-796-3300

The decorators and designers of Pegasus, opened in 1984, went all out to create an atmosphere of true elegance that includes gold flatware, Limoges china, Austrian crystal, chairs upholstered with French fabric that cost $700 a yard, silver platecovers, Cartier champagne stands, and custom-made chandeliers, all of which may explain why Pegasus is one of the city's most expensive restaurants. But, as with any lesser restaurant, the food is the real standard, and you won't be disappointed here with the *pâté* of pheasant and avocado, the grapefruit salad with chutney dressing, the baby squid sautéed with eggplant, tomatoes, and garlic, or the chicken with prawns and veal with kiwi.

*Price: About $65 per person*
*Open nightly for dinner only*
*Accepts all major credit cards*

# STATE STREET
2570 State Street, Las Vegas
702-733-0225

Everything at State Street is done with *brio.* The owner is Gianni Russo, who played in a number of Hollywood films, including *The Godfather,* and he maintains a stylish, all-night restaurant, lounge, sometimes-disco, and wait-till-dawn refuge with a large celebrity clientele. Russo, who often likes to sing for his guests' suppers, reports that the first item he ran out of on opening day was caviar.

I recommend the spinach and Caesar salads (both prepared tableside), the *linguine* with clam sauce (red or white), and the *pasta pesce alla Russo* (with seafood). There is a "nibblers'" late-night menu that includes fried *calamari* and zucchini.

The coffee *"diablo"* is showy, with flaming orange peel and liquors streaming down the cup, but the exhibition is worth the price.

*Price: About $30 per person*
*Open nightly for dinner only*
*Accepts all major credit cards*

# SULTAN'S TABLE

At the Dunes Hotel, 3650 Las Vegas Boulevard South,
Las Vegas
702-737-4110

Some may call it schmaltzy to have a dozen violinists in tails serenading you at your table. Add to this a revolving platform in the middle of the room where the pianist performs, an arrangement of pools and fountains between the tables, and you have the Sultan's Table—a place that gives you a good sense of the persistence of Las Vegas' legacy of glamor and romance from the sixties and seventies.

The Sultan's Table is a must-see dining room where the atmosphere exceeds the menu, but where you can eat well, too. After the dazzle of the decor, shrimp cocktail, Caesar salad, and *tournedos* of beef with *sauce périgourdine* may seem rather pedestrian, but they are well prepared. The dessert platter is impressive, however, whether you wish to order the cherries jubilee or the baked Alaska, or subsist on the chocolate-covered cherries, the cakes, and the *petit fours*.

*Price: About $40 per person*
*Open Wed.–Sun. for dinner only; closed Mon. and Tues.*
*Accepts all major credit cards*

# SUMMIT–HARRAH'S HOTEL

Lake Tahoe
702-588-6606

The electric blue of Lake Tahoe, the pristine snow-covered mountains, and an imaginative menu combine to make dining at the top of Harrah's Tahoe a truly memorable experience.

From appetizers such as bluepoint oysters and seafood *crêpes* to a Grand Marnier *soufflé* with chocolate rum sauce, each meal is a series of taste delights.

Our captain suggested Hawaiian salmon which was rolled in cornflakes and basted in *teriyaki* sauce. Other specials are the *tournedos* Alaska (served with crab meat) and red snapper Rockefeller.

The menu is changed four times a year to match the seasonal ingredients available.

Following the salad course, prior to the entrée, a complimentary *sorbet,* pineapple sherbet with champagne, is served.

The founder of the hotel, Bill Harrah, has passed away but his insistence on excellence and service is maintained, making this one of the best restaurants in the state.

*Price: About $50 per person*
*Open nightly for dinner only*
*Accepts all major credit cards*

---

## THE SWISS CAFÉ
### 1431 East Charleston Boulevard, Las Vegas
#### 702-382-6444

Hidden away in a small shopping center that boasts, ironically, a Weight Watchers office, is a jewel of a restaurant, the Swiss Café. With just thirty seats, the dining room is filled every night (except on Mondays, when it's closed) by locals who have taken this place to heart.

Despite the Swiss appellation, the current management is German and this is really a continental menu. Owners Wolfgang and Mary Haubold create unusual dishes for an ever-changing menu. For example, hearts of artichoke salad comes with sliced beefsteak tomatoes and a honey dressing. Every plate is brought from the kitchen with a lovely garniture: The shrimp *scampi* is served in a Riesling sauce and is arranged on the plate crisp with green strips of zucchini. Desserts include brandy ice cream, strawberry *mousse,* and chocolate-covered strawberries.

*Price: About $25 per person*
*Open Mon. for lunch only; Tues.–Fri. for lunch and dinner; Sat. for dinner only; closed Sun.*
*Accepts all major credit cards*

# TOP OF THE HILTON
### In the Reno Hilton, 225 North Sierra Street, Reno
#### 702-322-1111

The view of a sunset on the snow-covered Sierra Mountains provides a magnificent backdrop for the Top of the Hilton dining room. Dark brown woods and matching seat covers are enhanced by subtle lighting, all creating an ambiance of quiet comfort. The kitchen prides itself on its oysters Rockefeller and its *escargots à la bourguignonne,* and the house special salad is a mix of greens, beets, celery, tomatoes, and Marco Polo dressing. Tableside dishes, such as rack of lamb and *chateaubriand,* are expensive—$35 per person and served only for two. For early birds, however, there is not only that sunset but a special menu of salad, entrées, such as steak and shrimp, sherbet, and coffee for just $12.

*Price: About $40 per person*
*Open nightly for dinner only*
*Accepts all major credit cards*

# VENETIAN
### 3713 West Sahara Avenue, Las Vegas
#### 702-876-4190

Tangy, spicy pork neck bones are featured at the Venetian as a unique appetizer. Try the sautéed greens, with broccoli bits and spinach greens sautéed in fresh garlic and olive oil with lemon juice. Pasta dishes include *fettuccine al pesto,* pasta *pomodoro,* and *linguine* with shrimp sauce, among a selection of three dozen varieties. One of the oldest Italian restaurants in Las Vegas.

*Price: About $20 per person*
*Open Tues.–Sun. for lunch and dinner; closed Mon.*
*Accepts American Express, Visa, and MasterCard*

# LOS ANGELES

## *By Lois Dwan*

**AMERICAN**
  Colorado Café
  Cutters
  Pastel

**BAR**
  Tower
  Yamashiro Sky Room

**BREAKFAST**
  Geoffrey's
  Hotel Bel-Air
  West Beach Café

**CAJUN**
  Orleans

**CALIFORNIA CUISINE**
  Camelions
  Chinois on Main
  Michael's
  Saint Estephe
  Spago
  Trumps
  West Beach Café

**CHINESE**
  Diamond Seafood
  Green Jade
  Hunan Taste
  Madame Wu's Garden
  Mandarette
  The Mandarin
  Mon Kee's Seafood

**CRAB HOUSE**
  Maryland Crab House

**CREOLE**
  Homer and Edy's Bistro
  Orleans

**DELICATESSEN**
  Hugo's
  Nate 'N' Al's

**ENGLISH**
  Alexander's of London
  The Darwin
  Oscar's

**ETHIOPIAN**
  Ghion

## FRENCH
Bernard's
Bistango
La Toque
Le Dôme
L'Ermitage
L'Orangerie
Max au Triangle
Michael's

## GERMAN
Knoll's Black Forest Inn

## GREEK
Angie's
Papadakis Taverna

## HAMBURGERS
Cassel's
Hampton's
Nucleus Nuance

## HOTEL DINING ROOM
Bernard's
Ravel Sheraton Grande

## HUNGARIAN
Veronika

## INDIAN
Akbar
Gitanjali
Paru's Indian Vegetarian
  Restaurant
Paul Bhalla's Cuisine of India

## INTERNATIONAL
Café Le Monde
Chasen's
Chinois on Main
La Scala
Studio Grill
385 North
Trader Vic's
West Beach Café

## ITALIAN
Adriano's
Chianti
Emilio's Ristorante
Il Giardino
La Scala Presto
Peppone
Primi
Rex Il Ristorante
Valentino
Verdi Ristorante di Musica

## JAPANESE
A Thousand Cranes
Horikawa
Inagiku Restaurant
Katsu

## KOREAN
Korean Gardens

## KOSHER
Judy's La Petite Restaurant
The Kosher Nostra

## MEXICAN
Antonio's
Casablanca Mexican Seafood
El Cholo

## MOROCCAN
Dar Maghreb
Koutoubia

## NICARAGUAN
La Plancha

## OPEN LATE
Angie's
Antonio's
Bistango
Casablanca Mexican Seafood
Chianti
Chinois on Main
Chrystie's Bar & Grill
Colorado Café
Cutters
Darwin
Diamond Seafood
Ghion
Hugo's
Korean Gardens
Mandarette
Mischa's
La Scala
La Scala Presto
Le Dôme
L'Orangerie
Oscar's
Pacific Dining Car
Pastel
Primi
Saint Estephe
Siamese Princess
Spago
Studio Grill
Toledo
Trader Vic's
Trumps
Verdi Ristorante di Musica

## PANORAMA
Fiasco
Le Dôme
Tower
Yamashiro Sky Room

## POLISH
Warszawa

## POLYNESIAN
Trader Vic's

## RUMANIAN
Orza's

## RUSSIAN
Mischa's

## SEAFOOD
Chez Jay
Diamond Seafood

## SPANISH
Toledo Restaurant

## STEAKS AND CHOPS
Chrystie's Bar & Grill
Lawry's California Center
Lawry's the Prime Rib
Pacific Dining Car
Palm

## SUBURBAN/REGIONAL
Downey's (Santa Barbara)
The Ranch House (Ojai)
The Swiss Restaurant (Torrance)

## THAI
Siamese Princess
Talesai
Thai Gourmet

## TUNISIAN
Moun of Tunis

## VEGETARIAN

Meyera

Paru's Indian Vegetarian
Restaurant

## VIETNAMESE

Saigon Flavor Restaurant

Vinh Vietnamese Cuisine

## WEST AFRICAN

Rosalind's West African Cuisine

## WINE BAR/RESTAURANT

Wine Bistro and Café

These have been the most brilliant years in Los Angeles restaurant history. A concentration of young chefs who exploded on contact was one reason. They competed, compared, experimented, and established what in stabler times would be a school—the Impressionists, the Romanticists.

As elsewhere, this gastronomic phenomenon developed from the French *nouvelle cuisine,* out of favor, done to death by the extremists, but with the lasting value of freeing the chefs from exile in the kitchen, and giving their craft a dignity to attract uncommon young people.

It developed somewhat differently, perhaps more strongly, in Los Angeles because the great wealth of Southern California produce—existing or possible —provided the raw materials to fire imaginations. And because of the late, great Jean Bertranou, chef-owner of L'Ermitage, who knew when enough was enough and held the chefs on course.

Where we are now, halfway through the next decade, is not so clear. We may be deepening and consolidating. The creative energy may be seeping down from the star points. It may be scattering. We will not know for a while.

In preparing this chapter, however, I have been impressed by the number of fine restaurants I did not have room to include. That *is* a good sign.

*Lois Dwan recently retired as restaurant critic for the* Los Angeles Times. *She continues as a free-lance writer for the* Times *and other publications and is working on a book.*

# ADRIANO'S
## 2930 Beverly Glen Circle, West Los Angeles
### 213-475-9807

A smart little restaurant that ignores both its shopping-circle neighbors and the view from a mountaintop behind tall hedges around the patio. But it's nice in there, with a real elegance of polished wood and gleaming brass. The food might be called "international" in Italy, meaning from all parts of Italy. It is prepared with care and can be pretty special. The usuals—*vitello tonnato, tortellini* with chicken, *carpaccio*—are a bit more than expected. Others, not quite so familiar, such as *fettuccine Tre P (prosciutto, Parmigiano, peas), vitellina alla veronese* with capers and olives, and a duck roasted with olives, are fine. Some good Italian wines.

*Price: About $25 per person*
*Open Tues.–Sat. for lunch and dinner; Sat. for dinner only; closed Sun.*
*Accepts American Express, Visa, and MasterCard*

# AKBAR
## 590 Washington Street, Marina del Rey
### 213-822-4116

The sophisticated use of spices in this cool, dark place is evident upon entering. Trust your nose in an Indian restaurant. No two should smell alike, let alone taste alike. In spite of a somewhat off location, Akbar has held its own for a number of years. Some aficionados consider it the best in the city. We can recommend the chicken *vindaloo,* anything from the *tandoor,* and a particularly pleasing vegetarian meal. There is an adequate wine list.

*Price: About $20 per person*
*Open Mon.–Sat. for lunch and dinner; Sun. for dinner only*
*Accepts all major credit cards*

# ALEXANDER'S OF LONDON
## 8771 West Pico Boulevard (*near Robertson Boulevard*)
### 213-273-1166

This is a very English restaurant, although the three partners each came from different parts of Europe, and the menu is not English at all. But there was an Alexander's in London, and the acquired characteristics—courtesy, formality, and restraint—migrated intact. The immaculate tables shine with wineglasses and well-designed brass candlesticks. There is softening greenery against the white walls but no flowers, and plates are arranged for neatness, not for color or design. An all-white meal can arrive on an all-white plate, and does.

The menu is as reticent as the room. No rosebuds in the lentil soup. The chef is more important than the idea. In his hands, the dishes are not as familiar as they seem. *Pollo supreso* relates to chicken Kiev, with a copious run-off of butter and a nice dosage of garlic; calf's liver is magnificent with fresh sage and a reduction of wine, accompanied by thick wedges of crisp potatoes. Veal *paulignac* (wine, cream, and mushrooms), spinach *manicotti* and mushrooms *pitagora* with spinach and cheese can be recommended, as can the soups and a well-bred *pâté maison*. Oranges with anisette are a good finishing taste. There is a sketchy wine list.

*Price: About $20 per person*
*Open Mon.–Fri. for lunch and dinner; Sat. for dinner only; closed Sun.*
*Accepts American Express, Diners Club, Visa, and MasterCard*

---

# ANGIE'S
## 11700 Wilshire Boulevard (*near Barrington Avenue*), West Los Angeles
### 213-477-1517

Angie's is not entirely Greek—there are other things on the menu and, be warned, it is also a singles bar—but it is easing to Greek, adding one new dish from the family archives each time the menu is changed. The dining room is a tolerable distance from the mating game, plain but comfortable. The respected Anastasia (Ann) Pappas, having given dignity to coffee shops, is doing very well with this larger challenge. It is Greek as we know it, and treated with respect. *Moussaka* is smooth and light, incorporating *béchamel* instead of adding it as an unrelated Mont Bland. *Souvlaki* is tender, marinated in herbs, and finished rare. There is a splendid sandwich heaped with chopped sautéed spinach, enriched with feta cheese, a poached egg, and hollandaise, served open-face on *koulouri* (Greek bread). This can be dinner for a pittance, with very fresh, very crisp, fried *calamari* to begin and raspberries to end. Also recommended: veal Athenian, with shallots, mushrooms, and green peppers; simply finished fish; chicken soup with spinach; thin pasta with feta and brown butter, yogurt to add as wished. For the purpose, the wines are excellent. Open from 11 a.m. to midnight.

*Price: About $15 per person*
*Open Mon.–Fri. for lunch and dinner; Sat. and Sun. for dinner only*
*Accepts American Express, Visa, and MasterCard*

# ANTONIO'S
7472 Melrose Avenue (*near La Brea Avenue*), Hollywood
### 213-655-0480

Antonio Gutierrez announced his intentions with the formal decor of his restaurant and by extending the menu to include dishes of Central and Southern Mexico. They are openly listed as specials now, but it is still a good idea to ask Antonio to suggest. There may be chicken *yucateco,* for instance, made with forty ingredients, or any of a half dozen other ways with chicken: stewed in a *salsa verde* made of *tomatillos,* green pepper, and celery; or chicken *pipian,* with ground pumpkin and sunflower seeds in the chile-bright sauce; or pretty heavenly in an almond sauce. He may stew a veal shank or stuff a pepper with beef, apples, bananas, and *cilantro.* His *jícama* salad is a cool and lovely counterpoint to the generally controlled heat of the chilies. Surprisingly good list of wines. Mariachis.

*Price: About $20 per person*
*Open Tues.–Fri. for lunch and dinner; Sat. and Sun. from 3 P.M.; closed*
*Mondays*
*Accepts American Express, Visa, and MasterCard*

---

# A THOUSAND CRANES
In the New Otani Hotel, 120 South Los Angeles Street
### 213-629-1200

The essence of calm in the middle of the city. A garden spreads over a roof outside the windows, and there is the sound of water falling over rocks. I even thought I heard the peaceful croak of a frog. Waitresses are beautiful in their kimonos, soothing in their efficiency. Sometimes there is the sad, strange music of the *koto.* Even the menu is calming in its simplicity. There are the dishes prepared tableside to be eaten immediately—*shabu-shabu, sukiyaki,* and other elaborations—good *tempura* and excellent salmon *teriyaki. Uni* is served with great generosity. *Sushi* and *tempura* bars.

*Price: About $25 per person*
*Open Mon.–Fri. for breakfast, lunch, and dinner; Sat. and Sun. for dinner only*
*Accepts all major credit cards*

# BERNARD'S

## In the Biltmore Hotel, 515 South Olive Street
### 213-612-1580

Suave is the word for Bernard's, a quality almost belonging to another time, as does the massive luxury of the 63-year-old Biltmore itself. But Bernard's is no soothing dose of nostalgia. It makes good use of the fine oak paneling and great carved pillars, beautifully restored to their former luster, but sets Mies van der Rohe chairs at the tables, where black Rosenthal plates are set with the old silver of the hotel.

The kitchen is thoroughly contemporary—and respectfully classic. Seafood is emphasized, but not unduly. The chef may stew Pacific lobster in white wine, coddle salmon in champagne, serve sea trout in a reduction of red wine with truffles, add tarragon to the sauce for *noisettes* of lamb, or rouse a delicate sand dab with a scarlet banner of puréed red bell peppers. Desserts are quite splendid—white chocolate cake has become a classic. The wine list has been carefully compiled. Service is skilled and formal.

*Price: About $35 per person*
*Open Mon.–Fri. for lunch and dinner; Sat. for dinner only; closed Sun.*
*Accepts all major credit cards*

---

# BISTANGO

## 133 North La Cienega Boulevard *(near Wilshire Boulevard)*, Beverly Hills
### 213-652-7788

Bistango is French slang for *bistro* and, to that end, the kitchen serves pizza and other casual things in the reasonably removed café. Chef Claude Segal presides in the more serious dining room and, although he is having some trouble adjusting his master's stroke to the shallows of *bistro* cooking, he is the compelling reason to brave the paper placemats and noise of this otherwise handsome room. He does a knockout treatment of veal shank, cut from the bone, deeply flavored, richly sauced, with the contrast and sweetening of onions, carrots, peppers, and tiny sprigs of crisp celery leaves.

In the *bistro* tradition, he works with humble ingredients—the hind leg of a rabbit, or a combining of crisply finished kidneys, sweetbreads, and liver laid over leeks and onion—and very well. But whether he starts with a rabbit or a sow's ear, he does not seem to mind as long as he can make sauces. He plays with their tones, their colors, their infinite shadings of flavor. They shine on the plate. They unfold on the palate. No way are they *bistro* sauces. A deep

LOS ANGELES 429

brown wonder for *salmis de perdreaux;* conciliatory, with an almost vanilla taste for seafood *fettuccine.* Cocktails and good wines are served. Open to midnight. Café to 1 A.M.

*Price: About $20 per person*
*Open Sun.–Fri. for lunch and dinner; Sat. for dinner only*
*Accepts American Express, Visa, and MasterCard*

# CAFÉ LE MONDE

## 915 North Glendale Avenue (*near Ventura Freeway* [*134*]), Glendale
### 818-240-1621

A nicely disguised coffee shop, owned and completely staffed by the Guerrero family from Manila, serving a happy and confusing reconciliation of French, Spanish, Chinese, Malay, Indian, and Indonesian cooking—possibly resulting in Filipino, although it is hard to be sure. A French dish may finish with a Spanish sauce, or vice versa. *Suprême de volaille Le Monde* is stuffed chicken breast with Spanish sausage and a healthy dose of garlic, garnished with whole scallions in the Chinese manner and finished with a sherry sauce. *Bar* (sea bass) is fresh and French with a sorrel and lemon butter. Tongue is definitely Spanish with wine, tomatoes, mushrooms, capers, and olives—except for the Cognac. Some indisputably Filipino names appear: *lumpia, adobong manok, inihaw na baboy*—as well as *salade chinoise* and *coquilles Saint-Jacques au safran.* Their version of *tamale* begins with a *masa* of toasted rice and peanut butter, is filled with coconut, shrimp, and chicken and wrapped in banana leaves. A daughter plays classical piano. It may be bewildering, but it's happy. The wine list is exceptionally well selected and fairly priced.

*Price: About $17 per person*
*Open Tues.–Fri. for lunch and dinner; Sat. and Sun. for dinner only; closed Mon.*
*Accepts Visa and MasterCard*

# CAMELIONS

## 246 26 Street (*near San Vicente Boulevard*), Santa Monica
### 213-395-0746

Camelions arrived quietly, settled into a wonderful, rambling old building with iron gates and a patio (an interpretation of early California by John Byers), and quickly revealed itself as the ultimate small restaurant. The serenely competent Marsha Sands has made it friendly within well-bred limits that permit no lapses in proper ritual.

The chef is the amazingly young Elka Gilmore, who studied in Boston and France with chefs she respected. "My training keeps me from the bizarre," she says. She makes no attempt to astonish, but refuses to bore. She keeps her flavors clean and unmuddled, has a marvelous instinct for textures. Out of a thoroughly inadequate kitchen—the house is an historical landmark and cannot be remodeled—she sends forth dishes such as eggplant soup with roasted peppers; *aiguillettes* of squab circled in a wreath over the glossy green of barely warmed spinach; lovely little veal scallops with puréed peppers as a bright sauce; crisped *shiitake* mushrooms to contrast with voluptuous sweetbreads; a salad that sets warm chicken slices along points of endive with chopped limestone lettuce as a garnish. There is more. It's a changing menu of controlled and logical experiment. There is a short, but good, wine list.

*Price: About $25 per person*
*Open Mon.–Sat. for lunch and dinner; Sun. for dinner only*
*Accepts American Express, Visa, and MasterCard*

---

# CASABLANCA MEXICAN SEAFOOD
220 Lincoln Boulevard (*near Rose Avenue*), Venice
**213-392-5751**

Casablanca is bright with parrots painted on the wall and a barber chair installed with all the dignity of a throne. The food is Central Mexican—not a *taco* or an *enchilada* to be seen—and concentrates on seafood. Best are the several ways with *calamari*—steaks not tentacles—reminding me of abalone. Others for attention would include duck in *salsa verde* with *pipian*; a little number called "Play-It-Again-Carlos," which is a thin steak with a different *chiles relleno*; whole stuffed baby salmon; Pacific snapper *veracruzano*. Mariachis some nights. Open to 11 P.M.

*Price: About $25 per person*
*Open daily for lunch and dinner*
*Accepts Visa and MasterCard*

---

# CASSELL'S HAMBURGERS
3300 West Sixth Street (*near Vermont Avenue*)
**213-480-8668**

Prime beef is ground daily, broiled on a special grill, and presented on specially made buns with homemade mayonnaise, Roquefort, or other embellishments, as it pleases. Also splendid baked ham sandwiches. A plain, well-lighted place.

*Price: Under $10 per person*
*Open Mon.–Sat. 10 A.M. to 3 P.M.; closed Sun.*
*No credit cards accepted*

# CHASEN'S
## 9039 Beverly Boulevard (*near Doheny Drive*), Beverly Hills
### 213-271-2168

Although foodies profess disdain for Chasen's, there are those of us who love it, perhaps for its stubborn continuity as much as anything, the disdainful rejection of the new-is-always-better theory. "Sometimes I think people have forgotten what used to be good," said Maude Chasen, who has carried on and added on, but kept intact the restaurant credo of her late husband, Dave Chasen. Whatever, the restaurant is always crowded, celebrities are always present, and the scene at the entrance could be a full-page spread for the old *Vanity Fair*.

There are some good dishes on the lengthy menu, a heterogeneous range from beluga caviar, sweetbreads *financier* to deviled beef bones, and the Sunday night special of chicken pot pie. (The hobo steak, which can be glorious, is not listed. It is briefly baked in rock salt, then sliced and finished in butter at the table.) There are a couple of sentimental and excellent salads named Maude and Kay, a Caesar done with full ritual, superior thinly sliced calf's liver—and all sorts of things we have forgotten were so good—including an excellent hamburger. There are good, but expensive, wines.

*Price: About $40 per person*
*Open Tues.–Sun. for dinner; closed Mon.*
*No credit cards accepted*

# CHEZ JAY
## 1657 Ocean Avenue, Santa Monica
### 213-395-1741

The best seafood in Los Angeles will be found in the best restaurants. Seafood houses have yielded pride of place to the gastronomic stars, unable or unwilling to compete for rarities flown over the Pole or for even the best of the Pacific. Chez Jay is almost an exception. More a personality than a restaurant, done up in early seafaring dismay, it is the impossible-to-describe handiwork of Jay Fiondella, who dives for treasure, floats around in hot air balloons, and hunts for lost planes in Antarctica in his off hours. Beach bums are cheek-by-jowl with glamor in mufti, and there is a very special mood when the first icy martini is raised and the first peanut shell tossed to the floor. The fish is almost always well and simply prepared, accompanied by a pure Los Angeles mystery called "La Jolla potatoes," a *gratin* with bananas. Cocktails. Minimum wine list—mostly Jay's favorite Alsatian Riesling.

*Price: About $15 per person*
*Open Mon.–Sat. for lunch and dinner; Sun. for dinner only*
*Accepts all major credit cards*

---

# CHIANTI
## 7383 Melrose Avenue, Hollywood
### 213-653-8333

Probably as sentimental a restaurant as we have, excluding Musso's and Chasen's, Chianti was rescued and lovingly restored—but not changed—by a couple of romantic young men, Jerry Magnin and Larry Mindel (who went on to become a company creating other Italian restaurants, such as Prego and Harry's Bar). They left all the dark woods and the faded murals, replaced the beveled glass, and somehow gave it a new feeling of occasion. The food is more modern, and, although it does not leap far over the bounds of the accustomed, it is prepared with care and served with ceremony. There is good veal, fresh fish, an excellent grilled chicken, and pastas with lots of cream. Cocktails and a good wine list.

*Price: About $30 per person*
*Open Mon.–Sat. for lunch and dinner; Sun. for dinner only*
*Accepts American Express, Visa, and MasterCard*

---

# CHINOIS ON MAIN
## 2709 Main Street, Santa Monica
### 213-392-9025; 213-392-3037

It's not really Chinese, it's Wolfgang Puck, our midsummer night's beamish boy in his second brilliant attack on conformity. (The first is Spago.) The restaurant is small, noisy, crowded, and Chinese to the extent of a handsome gilded Buddha over the bar and two marvelous *cloisonné* cranes among the tables. A little Japanese *sashimi* does not fare as well as some American natives dishes, such as the fresh, sweet cockles, or the lovely fat mussels with roe, costumed with long tails of big chives. Catfish looks Chinese and tastes Chinese. Carp, prepared similarly, deep-fried in a wok, is even more persuasive. Cut from the bone when served, it mingles with the sauce of soy, coriander, and wine. Best is that Chinese fish, the turbot, steamed to perfection in a style more or less Cantonese.

There is sometimes a Chinese lilt to the crisp-skinned duck with plum sauce. Or, Mongolian lamb—forget that it is the rack—with a sauce of coriander, mint, and parsley in which thin slices of sautéed eggplant are luxuriously immersed. Mongolian beef—it's a rare New York steak—has Szechuan peppers in a sweetish sauce strewn with spinach leaves. Marvelous *crème brûlée.* What's in a name? It is beautiful food. There is a small, good list of wines.

*Price: About $30 per person*
*Open Wed.–Fri. for lunch; daily for dinner*
*Accepts American Express, Visa, and MasterCard*

---

## CHRYSTIE'S BAR & GRILL
### 8442 Wilshire Boulevard (*near La Cienega Boulevard*), Beverly Hills
### 213-655-8113

A nicely balanced return to the American equivalent of the European *bistro,* serving simple food in honorable fashion and welcoming the regulars at the bar. Broiled steaks, lamb chops, and chicken all have their good, charred virtues. They do well with calf's liver and fresh fish, and there is a first-rate chicken *nachos,* with cheese, chopped tomatoes, onions, and sour cream, and good *guacamole.* Cocktails and quite interesting wines. Open to 2 A.M.

*Price: About $20 per person*
*Open daily for lunch and dinner*
*Accepts all major credit cards*

---

## COLORADO CAFÉ
### In Colorado Place, 2425 Colorado Boulevard, Santa Monica
### 213-828-5057

At the garden edge of The Market with its varied foods in mini-restaurants, Colorado Café is light, airy, and comfortable. The key dish is a whole—or half—chicken roasted on a vertical spit ("spanek method") with herbs and no butter. Other things tend to the country cooking of Le Dôme (see page 450) —mussels sautéed in the Brussels fashion, a lamb burger, bratwurst with red cabbage, calf's liver with shallots, etc.—as well as lighter omelets, salads, and pastas. Good list of inexpensive wines.

*Price: About $15 per person*
*Open Mon.–Fri. for lunch and dinner; Sat. for dinner only; closed Sun.*
*Accepts all major credit cards*

# CUTTERS

In Colorado Place, 2425 Colorado Avenue, Santa Monica
### 213-453-3588

Cutters is a bite-your-tongue refutation of all the mean things ever said about chains. It has imagination, reasonable preparation, a room with clean lines, clear colors, windows, and outside tables. The enormous menu touches all bases from pizza and *calamari* through Hawaiian *ahi* to absolutely stunning Quilcene Bay oysters, Whidby Island mussels, and that rarest of the rare, Olympia oysters on the half shell. Add to that an exhaustive selection of about every liquor made and an intelligent list of wines, many by the glass. It is crowded and noisy, and preparation sometimes suffers from haste and the numbers to be served.

*Price: About $15 per person*
*Open daily for lunch and dinner*
*Accepts American Express, Visa, and MasterCard*

# DAR MAGHREB

7651 Sunset Boulevard (*near La Brea Avenue*), Hollywood
### 213-876-7651

Impressively beautiful with high ceilings, spacious rooms lavishly tiled and cushioned, a quiet pond under an open roof at the entrance. Dinners are the expected *harira,* salad, *couscous,* fruit or *baklava,* with lamb, pigeon, rabbit, or chicken for the climactic course. The food is generally quite acceptable, although there is inconsistency in both food and service. This is one for the atmosphere, which is pretty smashing.

*Price: About $25 per person*
*Open daily for dinner*
*Accepts Visa and MasterCard*

# THE DARWIN

312 Wilshire Boulevard, Santa Monica
### 213-458-4143

Charles Lamb could have dined with Coleridge at The Darwin, and neither would have noticed he was so far from the Inner Temple. It is dignified and decorous, paneled and wainscoted with fine polished wood. Ceilings are coffered. Banquettes are finished in a proper small pattern suggesting brocade.

That is the Café. Through another entrance and separate is the Pub, with people standing, people at the fine, long bar, people throwing darts, people making noise. The Café is quiet.

There can be no doubting the Britishness of the Cornish pasties, Yorkshire pudding, and the rest, all honorably prepared. The deep-fried meat shell of the Scotch egg is thick, crunchy, fresh, and good. Mushrooms, mild in their marinade, contrast pleasantly with crisp, pickled scallions. Hearty portions of steak and mushroom pie are filled to the brim, long-cooked to sturdy homogeny. There are steaks, rib chops, bacon, and sausage on the mixed grill, thinly cut, not rare. Bird's custard is trifle as it was when it began—pound cake soaked in sherry with a custardy sauce. The Pub is as convincing as the Café, with beer, ale, and stout on draught and in bottles. It is a right jolly place for the loner to have very good fish and chips with a pint of the best. Minimal wine list.

*Price: About $20 per person*
*Open daily for lunch and dinner*
*Accepts Visa and MasterCard*

---

## DIAMOND SEAFOOD
### 724 North Hill Street, #131 Food Center
#### 213-617-0666

A strong contender for the best of Chinese seafood honors, Diamond Seafood is neater, easier, and less crowded than some of the others. Fish and shellfish swim, crawl, or wiggle a claw in the tanks at the entrance, ready to make the supreme sacrifice for gastronomy's sweet sake. Indubitably, the fish is fresh.

Lobster is offered in various fashions, but my preference is for plain and untampered. Three sauces are served separately for those who prefer tampered —or don't like lobster. Also recommended: mixed seafood with assorted vegetables—those as fresh as the fish—with ginger, scallions, straw mushrooms, and small bites of fresh orange to brighten the plate; scallops pan-fried with croquettes of clear noodles; soups are generally fine. *Dim sum* served to 2:30 P.M.

*Price: About $20 per person*
*Open daily for lunch and dinner*
*Accepts American Express, Visa, and MasterCard*

# DOWNEY'S
## 1305 State Street, Santa Barbara
### 805-966-5006

John Downey combines an insatiable curiosity about Southern California products with a solid professional background that enables him to use them to their best advantage. His blackboard menu is an exploration of plenty, as though he had circled the hills and the waters finding things no one else knew were there. Tom Sheppard brings his tomatoes to the kitchen door, vine-ripe and bursting with flavor. They go on the menu as Tom Sheppard's tomatoes, with sweet red local onions and a basil-scented vinaigrette. Magnificent mussels are cultivated down the way, presented in the shell with mustard cream. There may be local prawns with Mission Canyon *chanterelles,* or fresh summer savory with delicate pea soup, or Ojai squab with *bok choy* sliding into a sauce of whole garlic and fresh thyme as easily as into love on a summer night. Sage made the inspired liaison between lentils and perfectly prepared pork one night. His *feuilletage* is light and lovely. His desserts are made with double chocolate, not to be missed. Cheeses are also exceptional. Some excellent wines at fair prices. It's about a two-hour drive from Los Angeles.

*Price: About $30 per person*
*Open Tues.–Fri. for lunch and dinner; Sat. for dinner only; closed Sun. and Mon.*
*Accepts Visa and MasterCard*

# EL CHOLO
## 1121 South Western Avenue (*near Olympic Boulevard*)
### 213-734-2773

Among its many crosses, Los Angeles must bear with the *misconcepcion* that its beloved Mexican food is no more than a bastard simplification of the "real Mexican" of Mexico City. Not true. The cooking of Mexico City is Spanish-influenced Aztec. Los Angeles Mexican comes from the Pueblo Indians, who, ignored in an isolated part of the country (now New Mexico, Arizona, Sonora, and Chihuahua), developed their own style of cooking. It has changed very little in becoming the second food of Los Angeles.

There are no "best" Mexican restaurants in L.A. Only a thousand favorites. El Cholo is an excellent example of that kind of attention to quality. It is the oldest continuing Mexican restaurant in the city, in the Borquez-Salisbury family, and has been at its present location, since 1927, growing into patios and large, comfortable rooms with fireplaces. I should think they were first with the menu we all know by heart: *enchilada, taco, chiles relleno,* green corn *tamale, tostada,* etc. And it is all first rate. Great margaritas.

*Price: About $10 per person*
*Open daily for lunch and dinner*
*Accepts American Express, Visa, and MasterCard*

---

## EMILIO'S RISTORANTE
### 6602 Melrose Avenue (*at Highland Avenue*), Hollywood
### 213-935-4922

Emilio Baglioni stays with the traditions of Italian cooking, strongly influenced by the ways of his native Abruzzo. It is sturdy fare, with the emphasis on well-tuned pastas with the rolling names—*puttanesca, chitarra, amatriciana, carbonara*—and hearty entrées, such as *osso buco* and *bollito misto*. Seafood is well handled: *calamari,* quickly cooked in white wine and oregano, or, perhaps, a whole barracuda baked in wine.

The restaurant sprawls in all directions, including one that leads to a fountain and seven pillars (for the seven hills of Rome). Baglioni even plays the concertina. It's all relaxed confusion, not for everyone, but a homey antidote to the esoteric. Some good wines.

*Price: About $25 per person*
*Open Thurs. and Fri. for lunch and dinner; Sat.–Wed. for dinner only*
*Accepts all major credit cards*

---

## FIASCO
### 4451 Admiralty Way, Marina del Rey
### 213-823-6395

For a long time Fiasco was almost the only restaurant on the Marina that did not require penance—poor food, a long wait, or both—for the privilege of watching the boats on the Marina. They took reservations, prepared the steaks and chops decently, served them with decorum. Recently they have acquired a new chef and are making tentative moves into L.A. contemporary. They have a way to go, but the steaks have been joined by dishes such as broiled chicken marinated in tamarind and lemon grass, smoked trout, a good *pâté,* a veal chop with wild mushrooms, and other dishes. A superior wine list.

*Price: About $20 per person*
*Open daily for lunch and dinner; Sat. and Sun. for brunch*
*Accepts all major credit cards*

# GEOFFREY'S
## 27400 Pacific Coast Highway, Malibu
### 213-457-1519

Holiday House is so beautifully situated on its cliff over the Pacific, it could be forgiven almost anything. Anything, that is, except a poor restaurant. Geoffrey's (pronounced Joffrey's) is the best and most promising in a long line of dull thuds. The room has been calmed and adjusted. There are big windows for the view, and an outside terrace winds around the cliff edge—heavenly on a moonlit night or for breakfast on a bright Sunday.

The kitchen is responsible and talented, but tentative, not yet strong enough to distract from the view. There is competent preparation of very good things, but not inspired preparation. No dull thuds, however, and quite satisfactory for breakfast or lunch. Careful listing of wines.

*Price: About $30 per person; breakfast or lunch is less*
*Open Mon.–Fri. for breakfast, lunch, and dinner; Sat. and Sun. for brunch and dinner*
*Accepts American Express, Visa, and MasterCard*

# GHION
## 10401 West Washington Boulevard (*near Overland Avenue*), Culver City
### 213-559-6214

The Ethiopians put various things together in a sort of stew called *wat,* usually highly, but carefully, spiced. Garlic, onions, green peppers, cumin, ginger, chilies, and others give flavor to beef, chicken, lentils, and some innards, such as liver and tripe. *Kitfo* is a spicy version of steak *tartare*. Salads, collard greens, and lentils are the usual accompaniments. The entire dinner will arrive on a large, damp, springy pancake-bread called *injera*. Pieces of *injera* are torn off and used as a sort of edible fork. Ghion is a plain and pleasant place, persuasive in the careful handling of this unfamiliar food.

*Price: About $10 per person*
*Open Tues.–Sun. for lunch and dinner; closed Mon.*
*Accepts American Express, Visa, and MasterCard*

# GITANJALI
414 North La Cienega Boulevard (*near Beverly Boulevard*),
West Hollywood
**213-657-2117**

Even in Los Angeles, an Indian facade on La Cienega can be a little off-putting, and waiters in costume are not necessarily reassuring. But owner Prem Chadha has proved his competence with the intricacies of Indian cooking and has gathered enough of a following to allow him to open the more formally beautiful Shanta in Santa Monica (502 Santa Monica Boulevard; 213-451-9691).

Recommended: Any of the *tandoori* specials, the *tikkas,* the chicken *vindaloo,* and the vegetable dishes. Good selection of imported beers and probably the most serious wine list of any Indian restaurant in the city.

*Price: About $20 per person*
*Open for Mon.–Fri. lunch; Sat. and Sun. for dinner only*
*Accepts all major credit cards*

---

# GREEN JADE
750 North Hill Street
**213-680-1528**

They love the wild pepper in Hunan as much as they do in Szechuan but seem to use it more precisely, more for its depth and drama than for its heat. Which may or may not be due to the efforts of Hom, a wealthy gourmand prime minister of China. He returned to Hunan with the best recipes of Peking, sought out the finest local chefs, and bade them improve on the originals. Or so they say. There is, for example, a minced chicken soup served in a bamboo cup. The delicately flavored chicken is made into a sort of dumpling with the contrasting texture of chopped water chestnuts that gradually disintegrates into the clear, strong broth with its edge of hotness. Purely wonderful.

The Green Jade is large, comfortable, and simply decorated. The hot-and-sour soup emerges as an unmuddled delicacy. Beef tendon is a surprising pleasure with spinach for color and texture contrast, flavor in the sauce, rich with the tamed peppers and anise. (One writer describes the sauces as "aristocratic mustiness.") Even the bean curd of Hunan is lighter, spongier, and more flavor-absorbing than elsewhere. Try Hom's bean curd. *Sah-go,* a casserole with rice noodles, is consistently fine. There is also the challenge of sea slugs; they love them in Hunan.

*Price: About $20 per person*
*Open daily for lunch and dinner*
*Accepts Visa and MasterCard*

---

# HAMPTON'S
## 1342 North Highland Avenue (*near Sunset Boulevard*), Hollywood
### 213-469-1090

An honorable burger—beef ground twice daily—with charm of place and some good wines. There are all sorts of embellishments to add as wished, as well as a thoughtful salad bar.

There's another Hampton's at 4301 Riverside Drive, Burbank (818-645-3009).

*Price: Under $10 per person*
*Open daily for lunch and dinner*
*Accepts American Express, Visa, and MasterCard*

---

# HOMER AND EDY'S BISTRO
## 2839 South Robertson Boulevard (*near the Santa Monica Freeway*)
### 213-559-5102

Homer and Edy were turning out estimable gumbos, *etouffées,* sweet potato pies, and the rest of the legend long before we all went mad over blackened redfish. They managed to achieve a homey charm in a patchwork building—continuing to expand into space that isn't there—and to ignore the difficult location, which will put no one in mind of the French Quarter. Homer is no longer active, but his skills (he was a chef on the Southern Pacific) and his recipes have been handed along to an able successor, who has the feel, Homer says. His gumbos—three on the menu—are dark depths of many flavors, hotness shimmering around them like the heat of a summer day. The oyster loaf is simply a hollowed bread filled with sautéed oysters and doused with spicy, clarified butter. The strangely named *court bouillon* is a small broiled fish laid over bread and sauced with an intricacy based on tomatoes. Jazz pianist most nights and a private jazz club (easily joined, I am told) keep things going from midnight to 4 A.M. Saturday nights. Adequate wines.

*Price: About $25 per person*
*Open Mon.–Fri. for lunch and dinner; Sat. for dinner only; closed Sun.*
*Accepts all major credit cards*

---

# HORIKAWA
## 111 South San Pedro Street
### 213-680-9355

Possibly a stroll through Little Tokyo, with particular attention to Weller Court and the Japanese Village Plaza, is the most pleasant way to discover the different styles of Japanese food. Many of the little shops specialize in only one—*sushi, sashimi, yakitori* (broiled "little things"), *teppan-yaki, yudo-mono* (noodles), *tempura,* and others.

Horikawa is at the far edge, down some steps in a bank building, offering most of the different methods. (The Japanese say that tasting something never tasted before will add days to your life.) It's large and handsome, sometimes prone to shortcuts in serving the classics, but one of two restaurants recommended for a *kaiseke* dinner—"as the chef wishes"—and the chef does well with all the flourishes and symbols. *Tatami* rooms for special dinners.

*Price: About $30 per person*
*Open Mon.–Fri. for lunch and dinner; Sat. for dinner only; closed Sun.*
*Accepts all major credit cards*

---

# HOTEL BEL-AIR
## 701 Stone Canyon Road, Bel-Air
### 213-472-1211

The Hotel Bel-Air has always been our bougainvillea-hung dream of life in Los Angeles, reassurance for ourselves as much as for visitors, well-kempt garden, sycamore trees, and swans swimming under a bridge. It has recently been carefully freshened and the menu moved into the twentieth century, not entirely wonderful for dinner, but pure bliss for Sunday breakfast. The menu is not astonishing, but dishes are carefully prepared and gracefully served. It is elegant stroking. We leave calmed for the world. Some good wines and cocktails.

*Price: About $25 per person for breakfast*
*Open daily for breakfast, lunch, and dinner*
*Accepts all major credit cards*

# HUGO'S

8401 Santa Monica Boulevard (*near La Cienega Boulevard*),
West Hollywood
213-654-3993; 213-654-4088

Hugo's is not really a deli, not really American, either—tending to Italian—but then it is hard to tell what Hugo's really is. A meat market with beautiful white veals; a specialty grocer with olive oils, vinegars, cheeses, and wines; a takeout, a deli, a quite extraordinary restaurant with all sorts of good things, such as sun-dried tomatoes, Santa Barbara prawns, baby zucchini, the white veal, chicken, baby corn, *pancetta,* buffalo *mozzarella,* and more, variously put together in salads or with pastas, or in other complicated and quite competent ways. Good wines. Open to midnight

*Price: About $22 per person*
*Open daily for breakfast, lunch, and dinner*
*Accepts American Express, Visa, and MasterCard*

# HUNAN TASTE

6031 West San Vicente Boulevard (*east of Fairfax Avenue and
Olympic Boulevard*)
213-936-5621

A personal favorite. In spite of the name of his pretty new restaurant, I think of Tom Yan as a Shanghai chef, mostly because of his extraordinary sautéed shrimp, which, in my opinion, only Shanghai chefs can manage. He does another Peking-styled velvet shrimp that is almost as good. Excellent hot and sour soup; an unusual Hunan beef with mandarin orange rind, rock sugar, and nuts; fine breast of duck, sliced thin and wok-fried with plum sauce and peppers. Wine and beer.

*Price: About $20 per person*
*Open daily for lunch and dinner*
*Accepts all major credit cards*

# IL GIARDINO

9235 West Third Street, Beverly Hills
213-275-5444

One hesitates to write of Il Giardino, but it must be written of, because if all is well when this book appears—if it still exists, even—it is as purely Italian as any in this land. No one speaks English, but what does that matter when they know so well what they are doing? Unaware of American prejudices, they delightedly show their extraordinary skills in a sort of greenhouse almost hidden in an odd, industrial part of Beverly Hills. Solidity is not a word that would apply to any aspect.

The food has the intellectual simplicity of Tuscany with added exuberance. They bring in their own fresh fish: true *scampi, orata, branzino, triglie,* the last a small redfish no one knew the English name for, boned at the table after a brief poaching in tomatoes, garlic, and tiny red pepper pods. They make a marvelous warm seafood salad and an equally fine seafood pasta. *Aragosta e fagioli*—also called "rich man-poor man"—is lobster being wonderfully congenial with fat, comforting beans, vinegar, olive oil, and thyme providing a frugal liaison. *Risotto bruno* is another amazing dish, the perfectly cooked rice enriched with a long-cooked brown sauce as it is served. *Pasta e fagioli* is a textbook example of its kind. A veal chop is served with big, crisped leaves of sage. The austere *cotoletta alla milanese* comes with a cheering sauce and two kinds of mushrooms. Remember, it may all be just a dream, gone with the day. Wines are adequate.

*Price: About $30 per person*
*Open Mon.–Sat. for lunch and dinner; closed Sun.*
*Accepts American Express, Visa, and MasterCard*

---

## INAGIKU RESTAURANT
### Bonaventure Hotel, Figueroa at Fifth Street
#### 213-614-0820

It's worth ascending to the eighth circle of the Bonaventure only for the *tempura,* which is probably as fine as it can be and what the Inagiku restaurants do best in Japan. Nothing else is worth the trip.

*Price: About $20 per person*
*Open Mon.–Fri. for lunch and dinner; Sat. and Sun. for dinner only*
*Accepts all major credit cards*

# JUDY'S LA PETITE RESTAURANT

## 129 North La Brea Avenue (*near Beverly Boulevard*)
### 213-936-7372

Judy's La Petite is *glatt* kosher, which means all the way, all rules observed. She has even managed to persuade her Chinese chef to make *glatt* kosher Chinese, as well as dishes such as beef Wellington, goulash, brisket of beef, roast chicken, and others. Kosher wines.

*Price: About $10 per person*
*Open daily for lunch and dinner*
*Accepts American Express, Visa, and MasterCard*

# KATSU

## 1972 Hillhurst Avenue (*near Los Feliz Boulevard*), Hollywood
### 213-665-1891

A smart, sleek, very modern little place, generally conceded to have the best, most imaginative *sushi* in town, and also serving highly satisfactory dinners structured around the very fresh fish. This is a place to ask for advice.

*Price: About $20 per person*
*Open Mon.–Fri. for lunch and dinner; Sat. and Sun. for dinner only*
*Accepts American Express, Visa, and MasterCard*

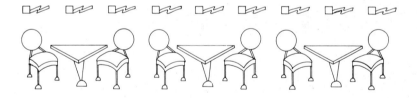

## KNOLL'S BLACK FOREST INN

2454 Wilshire Boulevard, Santa Monica
213-395-2212

Norbert and Hildegard Knoll recently celebrated a twenty-fifth anniversary in their new and much larger restaurant with different rooms for different moods, ranging from the formality of paneled walls and porcelain chandeliers to the leisure of a charming garden. Knoll has moved a little beyond the German–American standards, although they are still there—*sauerkraut* made with wine, *sauerbraten* with wonderfully crisp potato pancakes, sausages, herring, hot potato salad, excellent headcheese, etc. But he is from Stuttgart in Swabia and anxious to prove there can be a light hand in a German kitchen. Venison appears in its season, with *Pfifferlinge* (fresh from Washington), white wine, *demi-glace,* tomato, chervil, and tarragon.

The distinguishing specialty of Swabia is *spätzle,* the tiny squiggles made by pressing dough through a colander into boiling stock. *Mit Schinken und Käse* (ham and cheese cut to matching squiggles) they are delightful. There are also *Maultaschen,* pillows of noodle dough filled with meat and spinach, varied by sauces and garnishes, and sometimes the tiny dumpling called *Knöpfle.* A respectable listing of German wines.

*Price: About $25 per person*
*Open Mon.–Fri. for lunch and dinner; Sat. and Sun. for dinner only*
*Accepts American Express, Visa, and MasterCard*

## KOREAN GARDENS

950 South Vermont Avenue (*near Olympic Boulevard*)
213-388-3042

Korea Town takes shape in a small area not far from downtown L.A., serving more than 200,000 Koreans. Restaurants seem to open by the minute, all with fairly similar menus. Korean Gardens was an early contender, a little more elaborate, more settled, and with fewer communications problems. *Mandu-kuk,* a stout beef broth with dumplings, is brought immediately with *kim chee,* the pickled cabbage fired by the potent Korean chile pepper. The small brazier on the table is for cooking one's own thin slices of marinated beef *(bul-kogi)* and other meats or casseroles.

Recommended dishes would include *yuk hwe bibim bahp*—if only because it is such fun to say—a sort of steak tartare with vegetables and rice; *juk,* a marvelously comforting porridge of rice with abalone or pine nuts; either— or both—of the two festival dishes the Korean Gardens will do with advance notice. *Sinsullo* is an elaborate casserole, beautifully arranged and presented before hot broth is poured over and it is briefly cooked. *Kunjol pan* has eight heavenly vegetables in a compartmentalized tray, to be rolled in a *crêpe* and eaten with chopsticks—not without difficulty.

*Price: About $10 per person*
*Open daily for lunch and dinner*
*Accepts American Express, Visa, and MasterCard*

---

## THE KOSHER NOSTRA
### 365 South Fairfax Avenue (*near Third Street*)
### 213-655-1994

A nice, old-fashioned place with dark wooden tables and a lot of greenery. Howard Weiss is a former comedy writer who makes kosher *pizzas, lasagne, tacos, falafel,* egg creams, and jokes.

*Price: About $7 per person*
*Open Sun.–Fri. for lunch only; Thurs. and Sat. for dinner only*
*No credit cards accepted*

---

## KOUTOUBIA
### 2116 Westwood Boulevard (*south of Wilshire Boulevard*), Westwood
### 213-475-0729

Koutoubia is less than opulent under its tented ceiling, but probably the most personal of the city's Moroccan restaurants. Michel Obayon creates the proper atmosphere with all the proper rituals—low tables, pillows to sit on, cleansing water poured by a kneeling waiter. (One eats with the fingers, but only with the thumb and two first fingers of the right hand.)

Moreover, his menu is more extensive and more flexible than others. Besides the fixed-price dinners, there are several different treatments of *couscous,* chicken, lamb, etc., not only offering more flexibility, but lighter eating. The *b'stila,* at its best one of the great dishes of the world, has come close to that pinnacle here. A salad of eggplant purée and crisp vegetables is decidedly superior, and the chicken with wonderful olives and marinated lemon is worth a trip. Mint tea and a surprising selection of wines, priced somewhat whimsically.

*Price: About $20 per person*
*Open daily for dinner*
*Accepts all major credit cards*

# LA PLANCHA

## 2818 West Ninth Street *(near Vermont Avenue)*
### 213-383-1449

Make-do tropical with tiled floors, off-white walls, and scrolled wood, La Plancha is the personal labor of Milton Molina. What is important in Nicaraguan food? "First the rice. . . ." It must be cooked exactly, just until it is fluffy. It's a mild cuisine, he tells us, but flavorful, hence the rice is boiled with onions and bell peppers. Almost everything else is marinated in orange and lime juice with *achiote* and pepper—and it all has to be very fresh.

What should we order? The *empanada,* a sweet, ripe plantain stuffed with *cotija* cheese, deep-fried, served very hot; breast of chicken *(pechuga de pollo),* juicy, charred, responding to a bright, fresh *salsa* of green pepper, tomato, scallions, slashed with chile hotness. Also: a spectacular *albóndigas;* beef, boiled, then shredded, combined with rice and all sorts of other things *(carne desmenuzada);* broiled whole fish; two mysterious, custardy milk reductions—*atolillo* with rice and *torta de leche* with rum.

*Price: About $8 per person*
*Open Tues.–Sun. for lunch and dinner; closed Mon.*
*Accepts Visa and MasterCard*

# LA SCALA

## 9455 Santa Monica Boulevard, Beverly Hills
### 213-275-0579

Jean Leon has gone beyond the merely elaborate to the more difficult mastery of the simple. La Scala is a classic in Los Angeles, calmly holding its own amid the clamor of the new by understanding the drama required. The dining room is small yet, without an iota of congruity, manages to achieve a persuasive dignity. Straw-covered *fiaschi* of Chianti dangle above marvelous Italian urns filled with flowers. Booths are large, and seated in them will be the most distinguished profiles in town.

In these times of the forever new, the menu is also deceptive. Boring, say some. But La Scala has done its exploring and the talented chef, Emilio Nunez, has perfected its discoveries. Nor have they ceased their quiet experimenting. Recently, there were Chinese overtones to the Italian dishes. Basil was incorporated in the *fettuccine* paste, and the dish was finished with a beautifully controlled Gorgonzola sauce. Pasta as light as cobwebs was dressed with Santa Barbara shrimp, sweet pepper, and a flash of chili. Veals are superb. Seafood is sweet and fresh, prepared with magnificent simplicity. Extraordinary wines, including some from the Jean Leon vineyards in Spain.

*Price: About $50 per person*
*Open Mon.–Fri. for lunch and dinner; Sat. for dinner only; closed Sun.*
*Accepts all major credit cards*

---

# LA SCALA PRESTO
## 11740 San Vicente Boulevard, Brentwood
### 213-826-6100

Tidy is the word for this small trattoria, constructed around an open kitchen, a counter, some fine tiles, and framed caricatures on the walls. Essentially, it is a generous sampling of La Scala's (see page 448) menu, prepared without condescension. The same sensitively voluptuous pasta, the best roasted peppers in town, the exemplary *carpaccio,* pizza, salads, soups, and a couple of chicken dishes. A short list of Italian wines, and a good house wine.

*Price: About $15 per person*
*Open daily for lunch and dinner*
*Accepts American Express, Visa, and MasterCard*

---

# LA TOQUE
## 8171 Sunset Boulevard (*near Crescent Heights Boulevard*), Sunset Strip
### 213-656-7515

At night, his style is religiously French, says chef-owner Kenneth Frank, while his fixed-price lunch is California fun. Our first native-born star of the kitchen does not intend to be tossed into any general classification. His knowledge was hard-won in French kitchens, and he understands the true importance of *la nouvelle,* which is to free the chef to do his own thing. That he does.

Strongly dedicated to developing Los Angeles individuality, he uses Pacific lobster, salmon propagated by Indians in Washington, Pacific snapper, Santa Barbara shrimp, newly found local mushrooms, etc. He begins with French technique, but a sand dab is not a Dover sole, he says, so he plays with variations from the French premise, more anxious to convince than to surprise. There may be two ways with salmon and Barsac, another with Sauternes and ginger, a try with cabernet, before he finds what he wants. He sends forth beautiful arrangements. A pale cream bisque in a white plate, bejeweled with bright chips of vegetables and lobster, for instance. Angular shapes of green-skinned cucumbers dramatize the Saint-Pierre in its sauce of *oursins.* Rose petals and pea pods add color to a superb salmon trout *soufflé*.

The menu changes every day. The fixed-price lunch is a true bargain. Good cheeses and an unusual wine list.

*Price: About $35 per person*
*Open Mon.–Fri. for lunch and dinner; Sat. for dinner only; closed Sun.*
*Accepts all major credit cards*

---

## LAWRY'S CALIFORNIA CENTER
### 570 West Avenue 26 (*near Figueroa Street*)
### 213-224-6850

---

## LAWRY'S THE PRIME RIB
### 55 North La Cienega Boulevard
### 213-652-2827

Steaks and fresh fish are broiled over charcoal in a sumptuous formal garden, which is the real reason for going. There are suitable accompaniments, *mariachis, margaritas,* cocktails, and a well-stocked shop where wine may be selected at retail plus moderate corkage.

Lawry's The Prime Rib serves only roast beef, carved from a silver cart as wished. Also suitable accompaniments. Some wines and a pleasant bar.

*Price: About $20 per person*
*Lawry's California Center is open daily for lunch; Tues.–Sun. for dinner only;*
*Lawry's Prime Rib is open daily for dinner only*
*Accepts American Express, Visa, and MasterCard*

---

## LE DÔME
### 8720 Sunset Boulevard (*near La Cienega Boulevard*), Sunset Strip
### 213-659-6919

Le Dôme has recently found its original way. Planned to be elegant informality, serving anything, anytime, they were beguiled by the Pied Piper of the arty minimal (along with everyone else) and almost followed it to disaster. Raspberry vinegar and warm duck were not their thing, and they have returned to what they do best—country cooking, with some influence from Eddie Kirkhof's native Belgium.

They are happily back with the *boudins, choucroute garnie,* cold veal tongue, an *assiette de charcuterie* with a fine dark, salty ham, generally excellent *pâtés* and *terrines,* sometimes a superb *fromage du tête.* They marinate their own herring, handle fresh seafood with care, and were one of the first to recognize the virtues of fresh tuna. Salads are elaborate and desserts unabashed indulgence.

The elegance of a Grecian façade and an incomparable view make it an unhumble *bistro,* but it is easy, relaxed, and the circular bar under the dome is one of the happier gathering places. Excellent wine list.

*Price: About $25 per person*
*Open Mon.–Fri. for lunch and dinner; Sat. for dinner only; closed Sun.*
*Accepts all major credit cards*

---

# L'ERMITAGE
## 730 North La Cienega Boulevard (*near Melrose Avenue*)
### 213-652-5840

Jean Bertranou set the standards for the French restaurants of Los Angeles at L'Ermitage, guiding them through the shoals of *la nouvelle* to the heady challenge of creating their own distinction from whatever was here or could be here. When he died in 1980, there were fears things would fall apart, but L'Ermitage did not, thanks to Michel Blanchet, his longtime assistant. Blanchet has calmly continued what might be called Bertranou's principled derring-do, eschewing the trends, experimenting from reason—from the inside out—and within the rules. His immaculate technique is French and classical, entirely at ease in the world of the contemporary.

Anything encased in his superb *feuilletage* can be recommended, as can the *terrines*—recently it was crab, smooth as ivory, centered with spinach, dressed with one sauce green with cucumber and another red with tomato. His seafood is exemplary—perfectly poached salmon with two sauces swirled in a *yin-yang,* delicate as old lace on the plate. Or, Saint-Pierre, ethereal in a red wine sauce with marrow and *morels.* Lamb is fine, either roasted with herbs, or in a flaky *croûte.* A *mousseline* of veal may be wrapped in caul fat for its roasting. *Aiguilette de canard au St. Emilion* is a signature dish. The restaurant is austerely beautiful, with fine appointments, dramatic flower arrangements, and an impeccable display table for cheeses and pastries. It's coolly formal, intended for the contemplation and savoring of food, not for merriment, but the food is worth contemplating. Service is discreetly skillful. Wines are rare and highly priced.

*Price: About $45 per person*
*Open Mon.–Sat. for dinner only; closed Sun.*
*Accepts all major credit cards*

# L'ORANGERIE
## 903 North La Cienega Boulevard, West Hollywood
### 213-652-9770

Light is the theme and medium of this luminous restaurant, used with clear, direct colors, played with in mirrors, coaxed from narrow spaces, reflected from wineglasses. There is also the luxury of the *orangerie,* that status symbol of the princes of Europe from the sixteenth to eighteenth centuries—a massive arrangement of flowers in an Italian stone urn, two sexy French sphinxes, handsome tiles, fine tapestries, and tables set with Limoges.

It's as French and as beautiful as any restaurant in the city, and the food is quite equal to the challenge. Salads become almost a declaration of intent in the care for color, respect for vegetables, and atonal flavors. They appear in seemingly endlessly different combinations, dressed with dramatic correctness. Specialties will include whatever the fresh fish—sea bass turbaned over fresh, buttery spinach, finished in different sauces with sautéed cucumbers to bridge the flavors. Veal in all its fashions is sweet and delicate, even sauced with three mustards. Stars among the appetizers would include the extraordinary *terrine de lapin, rillettes de canard, soupe de poisson avec rouille.* Desserts, especially the pastries, especially the apple tart, are fine.

*Price: About $40 per person*
*Open daily for dinner only*
*Accepts all major credit cards*

# MADAME WU'S GARDEN
## 2201 Wilshire Boulevard, Santa Monica
### 213-828-5656

Madame Sylvia Wu has stayed bravely with the Cantonese while all about her were looking north for inspiration. That Cantonese food is highly regarded in China is a fact ignored by the foodies. Madame Wu is something of a legend, almost more important than her serenely beautiful restaurant. Wu's beef is a signature dish, Chinese chicken salad is one of the better versions, Peking duck with thousand-layer buns is excellent, and so is *go-ba* shrimp. Cocktails and some wines.

*Price: About $30 per person*
*Open Sun.–Fri. for lunch and dinner; Sat. for dinner only*
*Accepts all major credit cards*

# MANDARETTE

8386 Beverly Boulevard (*near La Cienega Boulevard*)
**213-655-6115**

Phillip Chiang, the capable manager of his mother's Beverly Hills Mandarin, has developed his own interpretation of Chinese fast food, or, more precisely, as he describes the *shiao-tsu,* as "small tastes on small plates." There is a fairly lengthy list of small tastes that can stop anywhere along the line, but will eventually be a completely satisfying meal.

*Price: About $15 per person*
*Open daily for lunch and dinner*
*Accepts Visa and MasterCard*

# THE MANDARIN

430 North Camden Drive, Beverly Hills
**213-272-0267**

Cecilia Chiang has created an aristocratic setting for her Beverly Hills Mandarin, with carved woods, silks embroidered in the forbidden stitch, jade and blue tiles, the true Chinese red in a coromandel screen. She grew up in the privileged Peking that existed before the Second World War, but she has dishes from all the provinces on her menu: the most beautifully presented Peking duck; Mongolian lamb; Szechuan shrimp with tell-tale hotness and inimitable flavor; shark-fin soup; beggar's chicken baked in clay. This is a responsible restaurant with a wider range than most—going as far as a hint of *nouvelle* Chinese. Cocktails and an exceptionally well-chosen wine list at fair prices.

*Price: About $30 per person*
*Open daily for lunch and dinner*
*Accepts all major credit cards*

# MARYLAND CRAB HOUSE
## 2424 West Pico Boulevard, Santa Monica
### 213-450-5555

The Chesapeake Bay crabs are dumped by the half-dozen on butcher paper, to be attacked with fingers, fork, and large wooden mallet. The spiced sauce in which they are traditionally cooked adds to the delightful messiness, although it does make it difficult to taste the crabs. Good crab cakes.

*Price: About $10 per person*
*Open Tues.–Sun. for lunch and dinner; closed Mon.*
*Accepts Carte Blanche, Diners Club, Visa, and MasterCard*

# MAX AU TRIANGLE
## 233 North Beverly Drive, Beverly Hills
### 213-550-8486

Whatever one thinks of the setting here—an airline terminal to some, magnificent state of the art to others—there is no denying the individual brilliance of chef Joachim Splichal. He is thoroughly contemporary in his willingness to experiment, with the palate and background—he apprenticed with Jacques Maximin at the Hôtel Négresco in Nice—to keep the experiments within the bounds of right reason. His dishes are fresh and original, but never unprincipled. He is somewhat uncontemporary in his attention to detail. "If I can serve a table where each detail is perfection," he says, "then I am happy. Even if no one understands."

Besides an extensive *à la carte* menu, there are six fixed-price dinners, including an almost irresistible vegetarian, another "where taste and dietetics join forces," one entirely of lobster. (Pay attention to the season. He loves freshness.)

He serves fresh truffles with warm potatoes and corn in walnut oil and wraps lamb and *chanterelles* in a spinach leaf, then in a *crêpe,* and serves it with a port wine sauce. He puts sweetbreads in a *strüdel* dough with an *haché* of *chanterelles,* presents it magnificently on a six-pointed star of greens with *batons* of mushrooms and a parsley sauce. He makes a ragout of cockscombs and stuffs *ravioli* with crab and leek, dressed with a sauce of sun-dried tomatoes. The dessert menu is as lengthy as the rest. Excellent wines.

*Price: About $40 per person*
*Open Mon.–Fri. for lunch and dinner; Sat. for dinner only; closed Sun.*
*Accepts all major credit cards*

# MEYERA

### 3009 Main Street, Santa Monica
### 213-399-1010

A vegetarian meal is no dutiful abstention in this calmly civilized place. Meyera gathers ideas where she may—Greek salad dressed with mint and yogurt; breaded *tofu* with broccoli and *mozzarella; spanakopita* in an elegant *filo*. She makes her own bread and pastries and offers a good selection of wines.

*Price: About $20 per person*
*Open daily for dinner only*
*Accepts Visa and MasterCard*

# MICHAEL'S

### 1147 Third Street, Santa Monica
### 213-451-0843

Michael's does not seem French, but Michael McCarty's training was thoroughly and soundly French, and there surely are French principles at work. But it's also purely Los Angeles contemporary, and, however categorized, an alert, assertive, finely tuned restaurant that would do well perhaps even in Paris.

It is sparely elegant with thick, rounded stucco walls, fine modern art, beveled-glass doors folding back to join the dining room to the terrace and the sunken garden. The food, says Michael, is ". . . simple, understated, each thing solid, fresh, and of the region. We pull out the natural tastes, then add a little punch." Which means many things grilled and many salads, with the punch in the sauce or the unexpected taste combination. There will be new things, such as tiny oysters from Washington in a vinegared *fumet* butter with equally tiny scallops, little *batons* of vegetables for color. Quality is solid. Duck, chicken, and squab come from special breeders, steelhead salmon— lovely with a simple *beurre blanc*—from Oregon. Methods vary. Scallops may be presented in red wine butter on a purée of watercress; veal may be dressed with caramelized lemon; lamb painted with red currant sauce. Excellent desserts and extraordinary wines. A service charge of 17 percent is added to your bill.

*Price: About $50 per person*
*Open Tues.–Fri. for lunch and dinner; Sat. and Sun. for dinner only;*
*closed Mon.*
*Accepts all major credit cards*

# MISCHA'S

7561 Sunset Boulevard (*near Fairfax Avenue*), Hollywood
### 213-874-3467

Mischa Markarian, grandson of a chef to the Czar, son of a chef mother and an Armenian restaurateur father, is determined to make his restaurant an Old Country way of life. He has covered the walls with giant Russian murals, bright as playing cards with their legends of Cossacks and courage. A guest may borrow a *balalaika* and join the small orchestra. Another may sing a sad Russian song. There may be a touring ballet company to perform. Or Mischa himself will dance the *gopak*.

The kitchen is equally intent on maintaining tradition. It's comfort for exiles and no place for experiment. There are *zakuski*—stuffed grape or cabbage leaves, smoked sausages and fish, salmon *pâté*, eggs or *blini* filled with salmon roe, eggplant *terrines*, and *pirozhki*. *Pelmeni* are fine, as are beef Stroganoff and *shashlyk*, and Mariam Markarian prepares a superb *sedlo* (lamb marinated in pomegranate juice). Mischa is serious about wines and has a good short list of interesting Californians.

*Price: About $20 per person*
*Open daily for dinner only*
*Accepts all major credit cards*

# MON KEE'S SEAFOOD

679 North Spring Street
### 213-628-6717

There are so many Chinese restaurants in Los Angeles—more than 1,000 at last estimate—that the best can be no more than the prize of a random sampling. Chefs who appear and disappear like disembodied spirits make it even more difficult.

Mon Kee may not be the best for Chinese seafood—although it has been best for me—but it was there at the beginning, and still glows with that first fine, careless rapture. The bliss served up at those plain tables was worth standing in line for, and still is, despite several lesser Mon Kee's scattered about the city. The menu seems to list almost every fish of every water, each prepared in about fifteen different ways, but it's hard to get past the ginger crab or the lobster with black bean sauce—messy as all get-out, but glory with every sticky bite. We can also recommend the seafood soup; a hot-pot combination; oysters from Oregon with a crispness reminding one of an unsweetened fortune cookie; squid in garlic and black bean sauce; clams in an almost jellied garlic and onion sauce. There will be a wait, and more than likely a table shared with strangers. Beer is best with this food.

*Price: About $20 per person*
*Open daily for lunch and dinner*
*Accepts American Express, Visa, and MasterCard*

---

# MOUN OF TUNIS
7445½ Sunset Boulevard (*near Gardner Street*), Hollywood
**213-874-3333**

It's down an alley that could almost be Tunis. There are low brass tables, rose water for the fingers, and the *brik,* that fine and drippy pastry folded over a soft-cooked egg and various other things. Tastes are combined in unexpected ways—carrots with orange blossoms; chicken with pickled lemon, almonds, and a touch of *h'risa,* which means hot; lamb with cumin and coriander. Belly dancers some nights. Tunisian wines.

*Price: About $20 per person*
*Open daily for dinner only*
*Accepts all major credit cards*

---

# NATE 'N' AL'S DELICATESSEN
414 North Beverly Drive, Beverly Hills
**213-274-0101**

A Los Angeles classic, where everybody stands in line and the waitresses are really sorry for the delay and immediately bring a comforting cup of coffee. It's brisk and plain, but the smells are right, the quality is high, and there are New Yorkers who swear they could not stand their exile without it. Many a big deal has been closed over breakfast at Nate 'N' Al's. Try *matzoh brie* or eggs scrambled with lox and onions, or the cheese blintzes, or a sturgeon sandwich. A few wines are available.

*Price: About $15 per person*
*Open daily for breakfast, lunch, and dinner*
*Accepts Carte Blanche and Diners Club*

# NUCLEUS NUANCE

7267 Melrose Avenue (*near La Brea Avenue*), Hollywood
### 213-939-8666

There is an "evolution burger" on the lunch menu, and "Ra, the untouchable" at dinner. Neither is your garden variety hamburger—Ra adds mushrooms, cheese, green peppers, and onions—but they are a nice change of taste. There are other pleasant things to eat at this congenial little place, with live jazz and space for dancing at night. Nice wine list.

*Price: About $20 per person*
*Open Mon.–Fri. for lunch and dinner; Sat. for dinner only; closed Sun.*
*Accepts all major credit cards*

# ORLEANS

11705 National Boulevard (*near Barrington Avenue*), West Los
Angeles
### 213-479-4187

According to the books, Cajun is country cooking developed by the French Acadians, while Creole is the more sophisticated amalgam of French, Spanish, African, and Choctaw Indian developed in the cities. However, distinctions tend to blur, and what we have at Orleans is from Paul Prudhomme, who calls his interpretation Louisiana cooking. He advised on the menu, instructed the chefs, and furnished the spices. Not quite Prudhomme, but a decent disciple.

It's a stripped-down room with bare floors and bare walls hung with antique patchwork quilts—relaxed, noisy, and friendly. They do well with the obligatory blackened redfish, almost as well with a blackened prime rib. Any flavor to the gumbo is lost to the hotness and salads are lackadaisical. But breads— variously made of fruit, nuts, *jalapeño* peppers, yeast, whole wheat—are fine. So is the "popcorn," morsels of fish (preferably crawfish), crisp and spicy in a cornmeal batter. Sunday afternoon jazz concerts. Adequate wine list.

*Price: About $20 per person*
*Open Tues.–Sun. for dinner only; closed Mon.*
*Accepts American Express, Visa, and MasterCard*

# ORZA'S
## 708 Valentino Place, Hollywood
### 213-465-4884

At Orza's, the Rumanian ways with food are shown to be simpler, subtler, leaner, lighter than others of Middle Europe, with an emphasis on *grillades* —meats broiled over charcoal. Sweetbreads are wonderful in this fashion, and so is *mititei,* a skinless sausage of beef and herbs. Beef, stewed and finished with browned onions, fresh tomatoes, green pepper, and a tang of vinegar, is splendid with *mamaliga* (cornmeal). There are marinated mushrooms, pilafs, *moussaka,* stuffed grape leaves, and other familiars—all a bit unfamiliar, but very good, and presented with friendliness. Rumanian wines.

*Price: About $12 per person*
*Open Mon.–Fri. for lunch and dinner; Sat. for dinner only; closed Sun.*
*Accepts Visa and MasterCard*

# OSCAR'S
## 8210 Sunset Boulevard (*near La Cienega Boulevard*), West Hollywood
### 213-654-3457

Oscar's has grown beyond its tiny wine-bar beginning, into a proper restaurant and all the available space in an old Hollywood building redolent with a lot of old Hollywood history. The menu offers all the homey stalwarts with the lovely names: bangers and mash, soused mackerel, shepherd's pie, treacle tart, kippers, smoked eel, trifle, steak and kidney pie, and the rest.

*Price: About $22 per person*
*Open Tues.–Fri. for lunch and dinner; Mon. and Sat. for dinner only; closed Sun.*
*Accepts Visa and MasterCard*

# PACIFIC DINING CAR
## 1310 West Sixth Street (*near Lucas Street, between Alvorado and Figueroa streets*)
### 213-483-6000

Into its third generation, a Los Angeles classic, the Dining Car grows a little shabby around the edges, but still hangs its own beef and broils the steaks over charcoal. They can also turn out one of the better Caesar salads. Some older wines on the list at almost fair prices.

*Price: About $30 per person*
*Open 24 hours a day*
*Accepts Visa and MasterCard*

---

# PALM
### 9001 Santa Monica Boulevard (*near Doheny Drive*), West Hollywood
### 213-550-8811

Styled after the New York original with bright lights, noise, cartoons on the walls, and waiters better trained to be taxi drivers, The Palm puts forth steaks of enormous size, cut from Eastern beef and aged in its own lockers. The steaks are well worth their startling price, as are the gigantic lobsters from the cold waters of Nova Scotia. Cottage-fried potatoes and cheesecake are unfamiliar Eastern versions deserving more attention in these parts. Other things are good enough, but just as good in less frantic places elsewhere.

*Price: About $35 per person*
*Open Mon.–Fri. for lunch and dinner; Sat. and Sun. for dinner only*
*Accepts all major credit cards*

---

# PAPADAKIS TAVERNA
### 301 West Sixth Street, San Pedro
### 213-548-1186

The Pacific is not the wine-dark Aegean, but it has its own blue-water fascination, and why not a Greek *taverna* in San Pedro where the fishing boats come in with their shining cargo? John Papadakis, who once played football for USC, says a *taverna* should be "bright, open, and energetic," and his is that. He follows his grandfather's rules and recipes—"buy only the best"—and keeps in shape by leading his waiters and anyone else in Greek dances down the narrow aisles.

The menu goes beyond the usual, by putting artichokes into crisp *filo* wrappers—although *tiropita* with feta and *kasseri* should not be missed. Lamb is fine, whether as the traditional *arni psito* (roasted), or chops, or charcoal-broiled saddle. The *moussaka* is one of the best. Ditto the *baklava*. A merry place and the food is first rate. Greek wines and a good selection of Californians. About a 30-minute drive from Los Angeles.

*Price: About $17 per person*
*Open Tues.–Sun. for dinner only; closed Mon.*
*Accepts Visa and MasterCard*

# PARU'S INDIAN VEGETARIAN RESTAURANT
## 5140 Sunset Boulevard, Hollywood
### 213-661-7600

Almost a secret behind a locked gate—it's necessary to ring a bell—Paru's serves the Southern Madras vegetarian dishes. Best of these and best reason for going is *masala dosa,* a large, thin, slightly crisp pancake made of fermented rice flour and black lentils rolled around a filling of potatoes tasting of tamarind, chutney, poppy seeds, and a few other things. It must be tried; it cannot be imagined.

*Price: About $10 per person*
*Open Tues.–Sun. for lunch and dinner; closed Mon.*
*Accepts Visa and MasterCard*

# PASTEL
## In the Rodeo Collection, 421 North Rodeo Drive, Beverly Hills
### 213-274-9775

The fine hand of those who run L'Orangerie (see page 452) shows most clearly in the appetizers at this bright, state-of-the-art place. Carefully constructed small tastes—chèvre melted on chicory with bright little mounds of chopped fresh tomatoes quartering the plate, excellent mussels in a reticent cream sauce, or smoked eel in a mini-*quiche.* These may change, but the main courses stay with roast beef, a superb prime rib steak, spit-roasted chicken, or fresh fish. A pleasant selection of desserts, coffee, and a half bottle of wine are included in the fixed price. Outside tables.

*Price: $25 per person*
*Open daily for lunch and dinner*
*Accepts American Express, Visa, and MasterCard*

# PAUL BHALLA'S CUISINE OF INDIA
## 10853 Lindbrook Drive, Westwood
### 213-208-8535

We begin to know Indian cooking as a complexity probably forever beyond our total comprehension, easier when we believed in Major Grey and yellow curry powder. Paul Bhalla was one of the first to introduce us to the tapestried fascination of spices and the virtues of the *tandoor*. He has furnished his restaurant with lovely old hand-wrought brass and enamel trays, *chanar* tables, and *angoori* screens from his home in the Punjab, and prepares dishes as authentic as squeamish American palates will allow. In the Punjab, lamb is king, and there is a superb *saag-wala-lela* with spinach. Also recommend: *murg* (chicken) *tandoori*—anything from the *tandoors* especially the *naan*—*murg tikka, vindaloo, makhni* (butter chicken), *korma* of beef or lamb, *biriani* presented with silver leaf, as is the pheasant *bhuna*.

*Price: About $17 per person*
*Open Tues.–Sun. for dinner only; closed Mon.*
*Accepts Visa and MasterCard*

---

# PEPPONE
## 11628 Barrington Court (*near Sunset Boulevard*), Brentwood
### 213-476-7379

The entrance is turbulent, with a wait in the bar where there is no room to wait, the room is dim, and the menu lists mostly familiar dishes. But owner Gianni Paoletti is a superb chef from Venice, therefore doing *fegato alla veneziana* better than anyone else, and adding extra integrity to the usuals. Fish is at its freshest and best. Sand dabs taste the way they should. *Spaghetti col tonno* is a Venetian dish with fresh tomatoes and a lingering taste of anchovies well worth asking for. Ask for the specials. Ask Gianni to advise. Exceptional wine list.

*Price: About $30 per person*
*Open Tues.–Fri. for lunch and dinner; Sat. for dinner only; closed Sun.*
*Accepts all major credit cards*

---

# PRIMI
## 10543 West Pico Boulevard (*near Beverly Glen Boulevard*), Rancho Park
### 213-475-9235; 213-475-9335

From Valentino (see page 473): Primi refers to *primi piatti,* the classic approach to first courses. With the stainless steel ceiling, the swatches of painted Thai silk on the wall, the patio, the open kitchen, and his crew of *bambini*—the very young chefs he searched out in Italy—Piero Selvaggio has brilliantly met the challenge of adding dignity to casual eating. He offers a great variety of first courses—*paninoteca* with different cheeses, *focaccia,* stuffed and folded with goat cheese, sun-dried tomatoes, etc.—including pasta and superb *risotti*.

The idea is to drop in for a glass of wine and a little something—although it is doubtful anyone will stop before the little somethings add up to a full meal. Excellent wines by the glass, as well as some special vintages by the bottle.

*Price: About $17 per person; Complete primi piatti dinner, $25*
*Open Mon.–Sat. for lunch and dinner; Sun. for dinner only*
*Accepts American Express and MasterCard*

## THE RANCH HOUSE
### 102 Besant Road, Meiners Oaks, Ojai
#### 805-646-2360

Alan Hooker was planting a garden with herbs, fruits, and vegetables a good quarter of a century before the rest of us discovered the limitations of the supermarkets. He was also experimenting with their best use, thereby developing not only a sensitive palate, but his own highly original and carefully controlled repertoire of dishes. He tried and erred with breads until they are now worth a trip from the moon. He discovered he could have the heavy onion soup he liked if he countered the sweetness with French sorrel. He tried several ways of making carrots more interesting, finally created a sauce by blending hot butter and seeds—poppy, sesame, and the rest—with a little red pepper. Worked fine with the carrots and also with broiled salmon. He makes his own vinegar from French Burgundies.

One year, he blended forty varieties of fragrant leaf geranium with lemon and mint in a salad dressing. There are more than seventy-five different herbs, as well as vegetables, fruits, trees, flowers, and shrubs in the garden surrounding the restaurant. Guests walk along paths, past a brook, and are surrounded by garden calm while they eat. There is an outside terrace and big windows in the dining room. A lovely place, well worth the 90-minute trip. Excellent wines.

*Price: About $30 per person*
*Open Wed.–Sat. for dinner only; Sun. for brunch and dinner; closed Mon. and Tues.*
*Accepts all major credit cards*

## RAVEL SHERATON GRANDE
### 333 South Figueroa Street
#### 213-617-1133

Sheraton has been the most sensible of any of the hotel chains in upgrading its restaurants and, at the moment, Ravel is their star in Los Angeles. Random blocks of desert colors, capricious floor levels, and etched-glass dividers disguise the straight lines of the room. Beautifully used spotlights somehow create privacy as they also transform the guests into part of the decor.

The kitchen is both courageous and inventive, sometimes a little too much so. But even the failures are interesting. Among the successes: oysters wrapped in two kinds of Chinese cabbage, poached and finished with a harmonious oyster sauce; *terrine* of wild boar with a Cumberland sauce sharpened with cranberries and red wine; *médaillons* of veal dressed with the essence of caper; an illogical but fine eye of lamb with chicken *mousse;* sea bass, beautifully finished in a rich, almost jellied, red wine sauce with *cilantro.* Service is a little shaky, and explanations are lengthy and boring. A special fixed-price dinner with two entrées costs less and is worth trying. Satisfactory wine list. Afternoon tea is served in the lobby and there is shuttle service to the Music Center.

*Price: About $30 per person*
*Open Mon.–Fri. for lunch and dinner; Sat. and Sun. for dinner only*
*Accepts all major credit cards*

---

# REX IL RISTORANTE
## 617 South Olive Street
### 213-799-0977

There is no other restaurant quite like it any place, not even in Italy whence the excitement emanates, but must be searched for in little towns between the big cities. Mauro Vincenti, scholar, artist, former cinematographer, and producer, presents his discoveries with a full panoply of luxuries. The restaurant is set in a 1930s haberdashery, marvelously restored with the elegance of Lalique glass, wrought iron, and marble. Great hand-hewn oak pillars anchor the balcony-framed room to a graceful sweep of stairs. The dramatic, mildly Art Deco furnishings are soft and sensuous in purples shading to pinks and grays. Tables are set with Ginori china, Murano glasses, and Ricci silver. Service is well-nigh impeccable, as is the food, a little *nuova cucina,* a little sixteenth-century influence, a little provincial Italian, and all of it brilliantly realized.

There may be *capelli d'angelo* black with the ink of squid, or *tagliolini* with vegetables and black truffles, or gossamer *ravioli* with sea bass. Chef Filippo Costa walks through the dining room, suggesting: "There is crayfish tonight, we have made *gnocchi,* the lamb is excellent . . ." The lamb may be an oval of sirloin laid on a clear, magnificently simple reduction of the meat's own juices with *porcini.* Veal may come as thin delicacies of *straccetti* with crisp slices of artichoke heart, or as fat *médaillons,* piled with sweetbreads, finished with the nutty depth of Vernaccia wine. Whatever, trust

Mauro, trust Filippo. Rex is a mood. Excellent wines. Cocktails and dancing in the mezzanine bar.

*Price: About $45 per person*
*Open Mon.–Fri. for lunch and dinner; Sat. for dinner only; closed Sun.*
*Accepts all major credit cards*

---

## ROSALIND'S WEST AFRICAN CUISINE
1941 South La Cienega Boulevard (*near Santa Monica*
*Freeway*)
213-559-8816

In this friendly restaurant, suggesting, rather than replicating Africa, Rosalind Lindquist of Liberia and her husband, Lyle, a former Peace Corps teacher, have put together a gastronomic tour of West Africa. Spinach and shrimp come together in the manner of Nigeria; eggplant is Ghanian-styled; collards are sautéed in peanut oil as in Liberia; a lemony lift to *yassa* (chicken) comes from Senegal, the beef from Sierra Leone. A ground-nut stew is particularly fine, whatever its origin. Appetizers include *ojojo* meatballs, plantain with ginger and cayenne, yam balls, lamb cakes, etc. It is a tour worth taking.

*Price: About $10 per person*
*Open Tues.–Fri. for lunch and dinner; Sat. and Sun. for dinner only; closed*
*Mon.*
*Accepts all major credit cards*

---

## SAIGON FLAVOR RESTAURANT
1044 South Fairfax Avenue (*near Olympic Boulevard*)
213-935-1564

Of all the Southeast Asian restaurants coming to town, the Vietnamese are the most elusive, easy to enjoy, hard to understand.

Saigon Flavor is a handsome restaurant, with murals extending the side walls and many plants in fine copper pots marching down the middle. Service can be somewhat indifferent, but the food is generally wonderful. Beguiling preparations, such as *chao tom,* shrimp paste broiled around sugar cane, then wrapped in lettuce and rice paper with mint, slices of apple, carrot, and cucumber. Or, *cang cua chien bao tom,* crab claws wrapped in shrimp paste and deep-fried. Or, the specialty of the house, *cua rang muoi,* which is marinated crab roasted with butter and garlic in a wok. There are also curries, stuffed grape leaves, and vegetarian dishes.

*Price: About $12 per person*
*Open Wed.–Mon. for lunch and dinner; closed Tues.*
*Accepts Visa and MasterCard*

---

# SAINT ESTEPHE
## 2640 North Sepulveda Boulevard, Manhattan Beach
### 213-545-1334

John Sedlar and Steve Garcia began with an estimable small restaurant in a shopping plaza, then turned their French thinking (Sedlar trained with the great Jean Bertranou) to making Southwest cooking acceptable to polite cuisine—something like making a lady of Eliza Doolittle. But Sedlar uses his chilies subtly, for flavor and brightness, not for hotness, and dishes come forth as meticulously groomed as Eliza dressed for the ball.

He serves blue corn tortillas with caviar, and they are as to the manor born. Lobster chunks are entirely compatible with *cilantro* and *calabacita* (corn and zucchini with chopped chiles) in *mille-feuille*. *Ravioli* are filled with pork and red chiles, cooled with goat cheese in a cream and garlic sauce. He weaves ribbons of sea bass and salmon to a lattice sparked with green Chimayo chilies in the sauce; accents lamb sweetbreads with *caribe* (red chile seeds). Chile also sharpens a pretty mix of gold and blue corn in a tiny pot and adds considerable spirit to a *soufflé*. There may be wild *quelite* greens in a sauce with *jalapeño* vinegar. Milder choices are offered the timid. The straight lines of shopping-center space have been softened with tall plants, given distinction with a Peruvian tapestry and Warhol studies of fruits. Good wines, priced high.

*Price: About $30 per person; tasting menu higher*
*Open Mon.–Fri. for lunch and dinner; Sat. for dinner only; closed Sun.*
*Accepts Visa and MasterCard*

---

# SIAMESE PRINCESS
## 8048 West Third Street (*near Fairfax Avenue*)
### 213-653-2643

Thai restaurants are scattered all over the city, most of them doing surprisingly well with an ancient and sophisticated way of cooking.

The Siamese Princess proclaims its royalty with photos of kings, queens, and princesses, and some right royal purple prose—"a festival of flavors and a feast for the eyes and the tum"—which should be ignored; the chef is serious. His *mee krob* is not so great, but another salad, *nam chim,* with green onions, *cilantro,* hot pork sausage, and peanuts, is fine. *Ka tong tong* is a splendid combination of scallops and mussels in a spicy coconut milk sauce, presented in an artichoke shell. Others would include: *mu wan,* glazed squid with *cilantro; ma haw* ("galloping horses"), a pleasant mix of ground peanuts, pork, *cilantro,* and spices, served on fresh pineapple. Wine and beer are available.

*Price: About $15 per person*
*Open daily for lunch and dinner*
*Accepts all major credit cards*

# SPAGO

1114 Horn Avenue (*near Sunset Boulevard*), West Hollywood
**213-652-4025**

Spago is Wolfgang Puck's direct hit on a target no one else knew was there —or could have come close to. His own explanation—"local products, freshness, simplicity, lower prices, less solemnity, no truffles"—leaves out the vital factor of his own beautifully honed talent. It may even be that dramatizing the simple was the best thing possible to be done with that talent.

His pizzas are as fine as pizzas can be, with goat cheese, sun-dried tomatoes, Santa Barbara shrimp, duck sausage, and fresh herbs. His pastas are equally fine and original. But he also goes on to the freshest fish he can find, grilled with the bone in, gilded with butter, garnished with sweet Maui onions. He marinates fresh tuna, serves it raw with onions and olive oil, or grills it with basil and chives. He makes one of the best fish soups around, redolent with saffron and fennel. A salad of *rucola, radicchio,* and *mâche* may be garnished with toasted goat cheese, or with a grilled duck leg. Chicken, duck, and squab are grilled, and sometimes arrive fragrant with juniper. Desserts are wondrous. The room is slightly incoherent, with splendid big flower arrangements, small tables, and uncomfortable chairs. The wine list and wine prices continue to improve. Open to midnight.

*Price: About $30 per person*
*Open daily for dinner*
*Accepts American Express, Visa, and MasterCard*

# STUDIO GRILL
*7321 Santa Monica Boulevard (near La Brea Avenue),*
Hollywood
213-874-9202

The Pepsi-Cola sign still hangs over the entrance, but within, the Studio Grill has evolved from off-beat adventure to a suggestion of elegance and a scholarly approach to food that keeps adventure disciplined. Pomegranates in a tin colander have been replaced by great bunches of flowers, and the walls are hung with paintings by owner Ardison Phillips. The chef and Phillips debonairly adapt from other countries, so there may be beef and black mushrooms in oyster sauce, *zarzuela* (a Spanish seafood stew), Italian *carpaccio* with capers and anchovies in the mayonnaise, shrimp marinated in lime and wrapped in ginger, snails with Pernod in the garlic butter, a goose roasted with *framboise,* and an elegant hamburger. They may not always convince, but they do not bore. Phillips' intense interest in wine has resulted in a remarkable list of both French and Californian, several available by the glass.

*Price: About $20 per person*
*Open Mon.–Fri. for lunch and dinner; Sat. for dinner only; closed Sun.*
*Accepts all major credit cards*

# THE SWISS RESTAURANT
In Hillside Village, 24590 Hawthorne Boulevard, Torrance
213-378-2686

Georges Tribelhorn is very clear about what is Swiss and what is not. *"Pasta, polenta, spätzle—*which we call *chnöpfli—*and, as everyone, we learned from the French. *Wiener Schnitzel* is not Swiss, although it is on the menu, but I drew the line at *sauerbraten."* Georges and Valerie Tribelhorn could not resist buying the restaurant next door to their well-regarded and definitely French Marengo. It already had the rough wood and beamed ceiling, needed only the banners of the cantons to turn it into a persuasive chalet.

There are some purely Swiss dishes on the menu. *Chas chüchli,* a small, delicate tart, crisply crusted, rich with cream and two cheeses; an admirable cheese *fondue;* and an ingenious adaptation of the *raclette* to the needs of a restaurant. The special cheese is sufficiently melted in slices, served over thick slices of potato. Whether they should be there or not, the various *Schnitzels* are nicely handled, bountifully garnished with warm red cabbage, spinach, and *chnöpfli* The desserts are not really Swiss, Tribelhorn says, but a hot apple crisp with raisins, nuts, and cinnamon must be close. Great *cappuccino*. Sensible selection of wines, sensibly priced. About a 30-minute drive from Los Angeles.

*Price: About $17 per person*
*Open Mon.–Sat. for lunch and dinner; Sun. for brunch only*
*Accepts all major credit cards*

# TALESAI

## 9043 Sunset Boulevard (*near Doheny Drive*), West Hollywood
### 213-275-9724

The most carefully realized of all our Thai restaurants, Talesai is stunning in its pure white simplicity with graphics and sculpture by Thai artist Komol Tassananchalee, the food equally complicated in its simplicity. Vilai Yenbamroong, who was a caterer in Bangkok, is the accomplished chef, and also the mother of young proprietor Prakas Yenbamroong.

The crisp noodle and shrimp dish called *mee krob,* on every Thai menu, is also so familiar it becomes a test, one nicely passed here. Soups are fine: *tohm khar gai* is chicken, coconut milk, and lemon grass, edged with hotness. Salads are equally fine: *Larb* has ground chicken with mint, lime, crisp red onions, and green chiles. There is a Talesai special of finely minced pork, shrimp, onions, and peanuts to be piled on little rice cakes that should not be missed. Also recommended: *gai hor,* chicken marinated in herbs, wrapped neatly in corn husks, sautéed, and served with a little sweetness in the sauce; *pad gra pow,* chicken with peppers cooled in mint and other herbs; a whole fish in a resounding dark, sweet chile sauce.

*Price: About $20 per person*
*Open Mon.–Fri. for lunch and dinner; Sat. and Sun. for dinner only*
*Accepts Visa and MasterCard*

# THAI GOURMET

## 8650 Reseda Boulevard (*near Roscoe Boulevard*), Northridge
### 818-701-5712

Difficult to find in a restaurant wasteland, Thai Gourmet is worth the trip and the search. It is distinguished by the fact that Monkgorn Kaiwsai—sometimes host, waiter, and chef—is from northeastern Thailand, where the cooking is closely related to the Laotian, and that he was a chef before he came to Los Angeles to study art. He makes only undamaging concessions to American prejudices—easy on the *nam pla* and careful inquiries as to chile tolerance. He has a remarkably precise judgment of taste balances.

His is one of the better *mee krobs* and the *saté* is fine. His curries are as baffling as any, but the flavors blend to be no more than a bolster to the principal taste. Salads perhaps come closer to basic Thai thinking. *Larb kai,* chicken bits with peanuts, *laos,* mint leaves, chile, and lime juice; *nuea nom toke,* beef salad with soy, scallions, lemon juice, and mint. Beef, marinated in wine and sesame seeds, achieves a dark taste edged with chile hotness and cooled with *cilantro.* Kaiwsai makes his own creamy, voluptuous ice cream with corn kernels, coconut milk, and jackfruit.

*Price: About $10 per person*
*Open Mon., Tues., Thurs., and Fri. for lunch and dinner; Sat. and Sun. for dinner only; closed Wed.*
*Accepts Visa and MasterCard*

---

# 385 NORTH
## 385 North La Cienega Boulevard, West Hollywood
### 213-657-3850

Roy Yamaguchi happily presides over a large and rambling space, finished in sobered rose, grays, and charcoals. It seats 180, which is a lot for Yamaguchi's meticulous style, but he finds it a simple problem of kitchen technology: "Delegate and produce . . . pre-planning as the Chinese do." He works toward harmony, putting small tastes together for their effect on each other and their value as a whole—rather like a mosaic. Peppered salmon in puff pastry with *ratatouille* in a parsley sauce, for example. Or the grilled, marinated duck leg with a *confit* of gizzards, endive and other greens, papaya, hazelnuts, walnut oil, and raspberry vinegar. It works, as does his use of aromatic vegetables, slivered and not quite raw, with a number of dishes.

His skill with flavors is evident in mussel soup, which becomes an augmented essence of mussels. He braises the same mussels for their texture contrast to slivered celery and Chinese long beans, with mustard and garlic. Chinese and Japanese ingredients show occasionally in Western dress, or as small things, such as *gyoza,* Japanese dumplings, stuffed with seafood. Desserts stray from the usual—a glazed pear incorporated in a square of cake and laid over a somehow essential caramel sauce. Short, well-chosen wine list, nicely priced.

*Price: About $25 per person*
*Open Mon.–Fri. for lunch and dinner; Sat. for dinner only; closed Sun.*
*Accepts American Express, Visa, and MasterCard*

# TOLEDO RESTAURANT

11613 Santa Monica Boulevard (*near Sawtelle Avenue*), West
Los Angeles
213-477-2400

Pedro Calle has braved a curious lack of curiosity over Hispanic cuisine in
this city of Spanish heritage with the first convincing Spanish restaurant in
some time. Toledo is small but true, with straw in the rough-plastered walls,
a winter's supply of wood piled for a non-working fireplace, hanging herbs,
and wine bottles binned up to the ceiling.

The tastes are right at Toledo. *Paella,* the undefinable dish, is fine with
squid, chicken, shrimp, saffron, and half a dozen other things united in a
fresh-tasting wonder. *Sopa de ajo,* the soup of the poor, is a pungent pottage
good enough for the rich. There is a fine, garlicky *pollo al ajilla,* excellent
treatments of seafood and beef that is often marinated and served with fresh
green sauces. Tripe here becomes urbane after a long processing with herbs,
saffron, sherry, and *chorizo* that manages to puff it up to a beguiling lightness.
There are some good Spanish wines in those bins.

*Price: About $20 per person*
*Open Tues.–Fri. for lunch and dinner; Sat. and Sun. for dinner only; closed
Mon.*
*Accepts American Express, Visa, and MasterCard*

---

# TOWER

In the Transamerica Center, 1150 South Olive Street
213-746-1554; 213-746-1825

The Tower was recently bought by Saga Corporation and, as of this writing,
intentions have not been made clear. However, the bar commands a dramatic
view of the city and on a clear day you can see Los Angeles. Sunsets are
beautiful and, after dark, the freeways flow with living light.

*Open Mon.–Fri. for lunch and dinner; Sat. for dinner only; closed Sun.*
*Accepts all major credit cards*

# TRADER VIC'S

In the Beverly Hilton Hotel, 9876 Wilshire Boulevard,
Beverly Hills
213-274-7777

The late Victor Bergeron built his reputation on a way of cooking nonexistent before he created it and artfully managed not to be trapped. He was so far ahead of his time that no one has yet caught up with him. Nor has anyone managed to duplicate his success with multiple restaurants. They were set to a formula, but not in concrete. It is a point that we never go to Trader Vic's without asking what's new, and that something always is.

That may be one aspect that will not continue without him. But the resilient organization he built carries on smoothly. Marvels still come from the Chinese ovens: beef with fine slinky noodles fragrant with *coriander;* rack of lamb and salmon at their very best. There are more things on that long menu than we will ever eat—the Chinese dishes, the things with *tofu*—a *tofu terrine* with chicken livers, garlic, mace, nutmeg. I once asked the Trader to explain his success. "It's easy. If you look at life the way it really is. . . . Quality is important. The people who work for us are important. The customers are important. If any of our restaurants starts making too much money by cutting down on quality, we close the goddamn place. That's the way the mop splashes." Have a mai-tai—the rum-based cocktail created by Vic.

*Price: About $40 per person*
*Open daily for dinner only*
*Accepts all major credit cards*

# TRUMPS

8764 Melrose Avenue (*near Robertson Boulevard*), West
Hollywood
213-855-1480

Trumps is raftered and skylighted, with the neutral, natural colors of concrete, raffia, rattan, wood, and sandstone as background for flowers on the bar and the brilliance of frequently changing paintings. It is relaxed, accommodating, and noisy. Michael Roberts has set his menu to the same sprung rhythm. He is dedicated to French technique, but few dishes appear without his own cadenza—such as Greek olives with sweetbreads.

One night we had only appetizers: fine fresh oysters, warmed, not cooked, with softened cheese and a little caviar; marinated raw tuna; sautéed shad roe with dill sauce; eggs lightly scrambled with truffle sauce. Roberts has the ability to add distinction, even glory, to the mundane, such as potato pancakes, crisp and delicate with warm goat cheese and sautéed apples; or the boarding-house taste of rutabaga become subtle as a cold cream soup patterned with *crème fraîche.* Veal stock and soy are homage to the dark flavors of oysters and *shiitake* mushrooms with *fettuccine.* He grills seafood, veal chops, and other meats over oak, plans vegetables to the dish. Best dessert—a fresh fruit *charlotte.* Thoughtful wine list. Tea every afternoon from 3:30 P.M.

*Price: About $35 per person*
*Open Mon.–Sat. for lunch and dinner; closed Sun.*
*Accepts American Express, Carte Blanche, Visa, and MasterCard*

---

# VALENTINO
## 3115 Pico Boulevard, Santa Monica
### 213-829-4313

Valentino is always a new experience. We take notes and never finish. We are never bored. Owner Piero Selvaggio is one of the few tuned to and in step with what is happening in Italy. Evolution, *aromi* (meaning aromatic), and, I think, love are the key words. Recently, he was blending seafood, herbs, or vegetables into the pasta itself, sea bass in *gnocchi,* for instance. There may be dishes as simple as *bruschetta,* bread, lightly toasted with a little garlic then dipped into olive oil, making clear the wonder of fine olive oil. What Selvaggio calls "the beloved paladin of Italian cooking," the *risotto,* is equally a revelation—he keeps a special chef for that alone. If white truffles are in season, *risotto* becomes the ultimate dish, "God's great porridge." *Porcini,* the fabulous, sensuous wild Italian mushrooms, are marinated with rosemary, garlic, and thyme before being broiled. Or braised with bay scallops and *radicchio,* or baked with eggplant and oregano. Truffles might be stuffed in a breast of chicken with spinach, wrapped in a lettuce leaf, and broiled. Whatever, it will be a brilliant, unpredictable, kaleidoscopic performance. Best idea is to ask Piero to plan the meal and choose the wine. The cellar is the most extensive in the city, as fine in Californian bottlings as it is in Italian.

*Price: About $35 per person*
*Open Mon.–Sat. for dinner; Fri. for lunch and dinner; closed Sun.*
*Accepts all major credit cards*

# VERDI RISTORANTE DI MUSICA
## 1519 Wilshire Boulevard, Santa Monica
### 213-393-0706

Verdi is a restaurant run by amateurs, giving equal billing to serious food and serious music, a concept any good restaurant critic would dismiss out of hand. Bernard and Sheila Segal trod a fine line, but kept their balance by relying on simplicity and flexibility—and a little serendipity along the way. The room is equally effective as theater or restaurant, changing like one of those paintings that can be cubes or pyramids or cones depending on the sight lines. While it is not the Met, the small repertory company holds to reasonable professional standards. The food is Tuscan, because, say the Segals, "it is lighter, a reflection of the future." Thin slices of raw beef ennobled with herbs and extra virgin olive oil; salmon trout with only a branch of sweet basil added to its own fine flavor; *shiitake* mushrooms marinated in the beautiful olive oil. Pastas are rich with cheeses, light with fresh tomatoes and basil; *cannelloni* and *lasagne* become delicacies. The classic chicken dish of Florence is made from a bird that is split, flattened, broiled, and primly laid over lemon slices with sprigs of rosemary for modesty. Veals are excellent and so is a redolent-with-herbs rack of lamb. Service stops during a performance, which can be disconcerting if only bread is on the table. Some good but expensive wines.

*Price: About $25 per person*
*Open Tues.–Sun. for dinner; Fri. for lunch and dinner; closed Mon.*
*Accepts all major credit cards*

# VERONIKA
## 8164 Third Street (*near Crescent Heights*)
### 213-656-9330

It's a small house set behind an immaculate, pebbled garden where they grow celery and Italian parsley. There are chandeliers with prisms and tiny silk shades, flowered voile curtains to match the flowered plates, and baby roses on the tables. A mynah bird whistles admiringly and sometimes flaunts his startling vocabulary. George Lampel handles the dining room. His wife, Veronika, is the chef.

Veronika has explosive feelings about Hungarian food as presented in this country; she writes her menu in French to make clear her disdain for the run-of-the-mill goulash and checked tablecloths. Her menu is probably more baroque than refined French, but the finesse of *le goulasche de boeuf* is clear, the beef lightly sautéed, its sauce little more than a concentration of its own juices with sweet Hungarian paprika. Chicken *paprikás* is equally a lesson in restraint with melted onions and sweet cream. There are flaky *bouchées,* an excellent *pâté en gelée,* careful salads, and dishes garnished with Brussels sprouts crisped in butter with outer leaves spread like petals. There are half a dozen *Torten* and the lovely *Salzburger nockerl.* Minimal wine list.

*Price: About $25 per person*
*Open Tues.–Sun. for dinner only; closed Mon.*
*Accepts all major credit cards*

---

# VINH VIETNAMESE CUISINE
18708 Ventura Boulevard (*near Reseda Boulevard*), Tarzana
**818-345-9123**

Forced to flee Vietnam, Tuan Nguyen, a lieutenant colonel in the army, and Le, his wife, a law student and dedicated non-cook, ended up with a restaurant in Patchogue, New York. It was declared successful by *The New York Times,* but they missed their own people, and so moved to California and opened Vinh, a calm and pretty place.

Le is the chef, with a subtle, highly persuasive interpretation of Vietnamese food. Tuan takes care of the dining room. Between them, they may have created the best Vietnamese restaurant in Southern California. Among the many dishes listed: a chicken salad with mint, lemon grass, *cilantro,* garlic, and onions; a whole rock cod *(ca xot dau)* roasted with ginger, garlic, and black bean sauce; duck in ginger and garlic; *banh xeo ga,* a crisp pancake filled with all sorts of things; and several really wonderful ways with shrimp. Le Nguyen uses *nuoc mam* sparingly, but Tuan Nguyen puts a bottle on the table for those who love it. Wine—with some good names—and beer.

*Price: About $15 per person*
*Open Tues.–Fri. for lunch and dinner; Sat. and Sun. for dinner only;*
*closed Mon.*
*Accepts all major credit cards*

# WARSZAWA
## 1414 Lincoln Boulevard, Santa Monica
### 213-393-8831

Warszawa offers Los Angeles about its only convincing evidence of the sophistication of Polish cuisine, evident in the use of stocks, meat glazes, and wines. There are the almost-familiar *pierogi,* noodle paste filled with meat, onions, mushrooms, and sometimes cheese, and served with sour cream. Or *zrazy,* or *bigos,* the hunter's stew of many meats, beef, bacon, ham hocks, sausages, layered with cabbage, *sauerkraut,* onions, and apples. Or *olabki,* cabbage stuffed with meat, rice, and onions, served with sour cream. Warszawa is in a small brown house covered with bougainvillea, its rooms hung with the marvelous theater posters Poland does better than anyone.

*Price: About $25 per person*
*Open Wed.–Mon. for dinner; closed Tues.*
*Accepts all major credit cards*

# WEST BEACH CAFÉ
## 60 North Venice Boulevard (*near Pacific Avenue*), Venice
### 213-823-5396

The West Beach began at the beginning, and therefore developed, rather than changed, which is as it should be. It's still small, arty, and casual, but it's efficiently casual with proper amenities, and is entirely assured in its way with food. The menu, which changes once a week, may offer a fat, herby seafood sausage; thin-sliced loin of veal raw, with chopped greens, nuts, and olive oil; a *taco* upgraded with filet mignon, the steak piled in juicy squares, wreathed with little mounds of refried beans, *cilantro, guacamole,* chopped onions, etc. *Tagliarini* is exalted by plump oysters. The always-fresh fish will be simply grilled or char-broiled with herby overtones. There may be an excellent *risotto* with baby asparagus, corn, and carefully controlled Gorgonzola. Desserts are more than usual temptations: a crisper, cleaner caramel nut cake, fruit warm in *sabayon,* a freshly baked fruit tart with whipped cream.

Sunday breakfast is splendid, starring a superb Belgian waffle and a Mexican plate built around velvety eggs scrambled with sweet peppers, *cilantro,* and a little chile hotness. The paintings are a changing exhibit, different each month. Good wines. Good brandies and liqueurs. Breakfast every morning.

*Price: About $24 per person*
*Open daily for breakfast, lunch, and dinner*
*Accepts Visa and MasterCard*

# WINE BISTRO AND CAFÉ

11915 Ventura Boulevard (*near Laurel Canyon Boulevard*),
Studio City
**818-766-6233**

Fine wines are available in a wine machine to be accompanied—or not—by *bistro* dishes, such as sausages, *terrines,* cheeses, pastas, and the like, carefully prepared by Alain Cuny, the well-regarded French chef and proprietor of Le Sanglier in Tarzana.

*Price: About $15 per person*
*Open Mon.–Fri. for lunch and dinner; Sat. for dinner only; closed Sun.*
*Accepts all major credit cards*

---

# YAMASHIRO SKY ROOM

1999 North Sycamore Avenue (*off Franklin Avenue, near La Brea Avenue*), Hollywood
**213-466-5125**

A hilltop pagoda offering a magical view of the city to set the mood for a romantic evening. Fine for cocktails, but do not be tempted to linger on for dinner.

*Price: About $12 per person*
*Open daily for lunch and dinner*
*Accepts American Express, Visa, and MasterCard*

# LOUISVILLE

## *By Elaine Corn*

**AMERICAN**
Captain's Quarters
Huber Family Farm and
    Restaurant
Mike Linnig's
Science Hill Inn

**BAKERY**
Parisian Pantry

**BARBECUE**
The Country Pit
Rib Café
Rib Tavern

**CHINESE**
Emperor of China Restaurant
    and Lounge
Empress of China Restaurant
    and Lounge

**ECLECTIC**
Afro–German Tearoom
Café Metro
Myra's Restaurant

**FAMILY**
Huber Family Farm and
    Restaurant
Rocky's Sub Pub
W. W. Cousins

**FAST FOOD**
Rocky's Sub Pub

**FRENCH**
Parisian Pantry

**HAMBURGERS**
Myra's Restaurant
W.W. Cousins

**ITALIAN**
Afro–German Tearoom
Casa Grisanti

**PIZZA**
Impellizzeri's
Rocky's Sub Pub

**STEAKS AND CHOPS**
Pat's Steak House

## SUBURBS/REGIONAL

Huber Family Farm and
  Restaurant (Starlight, Indiana)
Rocky's Sub Pub (Jeffersonville,
  Indiana)
Science Hill Inn (Shelbyville)

## UNIQUE PROPERTIES

The English Grill
J. Graham's

## WINE BAR

The Winery

The home of Kentucky Fried Chicken is at least shedding its old skin, batter included. An exciting culinary awakening has refined competition and brought a tempting sense of what's going to happen next to Louisville dining.

It's being done with food that grows right here—raspberries, blackberries, asparagus, Kentucky's native Bibb lettuce, country hams, and excellent lamb. Along a strip of Bardstown Road, there are more cute boutique restaurants than the upwardly mobile can aspire to in a single Volvo. What's more, the local thirst for hard liquor, namely the state's bourbon, is now being quenched more and more by good wines.

But if you've never eaten home-style cooking, rest assured there is no shortage of the almighty steak, catfish, grits, onion rings, hickory-smoked ribs, country ham, and our one eccentricity—the Hot Brown, the famous open-faced sandwich with cheese sauce created in the 1930s at the Brown Hotel kitchen (see Unique Properties) now found all over town.

When in Louisville, you won't be disappointed by the tradition of hospitality and low prices, and on-street parking is a nice bonus. As to the flaws, the management of even the better restaurants seems impervious to an aural state of obnoxiousness from lousy acoustics, hard surfaces, and amateurish live music. Glass-framed cliché poster art only causes the noise to ricochet and cheats the eye as well.

One word of caution: Never eat the Kentucky chili, unless you like spaghetti sauce with chili powder over noodles.

*Elaine Corn is the food editor of the* Louisville Courier-Journal.

# AFRO–GERMAN TEAROOM
## 639 South Shelby Street
### 502-585-3484

Named for the neighborhood not the cuisine, this 50-seat trattoria-style restaurant is the dream of Reverend Vernon Robertson, who was inspired during a trip to Rome by an order of women there who served fine food to raise money for missionary work. The Tearoom's money goes to inner-city Montessori schools. Most of the employees are volunteers.

Imagine a pretty coral-peach-olive room dotted with odd art, streaked in sunlight during the day, and lighted by candles during the evening.

The commandment here is, Thou shalt not conjure up casseroles and sauerkraut. Instead, the cooking is European and the staff dedicated, the food prepared as it's ordered (just as in Rome, says Father Robertson). There is an emphasis on fresh herbs and fish sautéed to a fine resiliency. Desserts are the kind confessions are made of. Presentations are breathtaking on colorful pottery from Vietri, Italy. The wine list is slim.

A little bit of heaven with an urban mission? For some the arrangement might give a peculiar perspective on the dining experience, in that when a priest asks you how you like the food—and he will—it's very difficult to lie. The restaurant is located in the back of St. Martin's church. There are two seatings on Saturday night.

*Price: About $12 per person*
*Open Mon.–Fri. for lunch only; Fri. and Sat. for dinner only; closed Sun.*
*No credit cards accepted*

# CAFÉ METRO
## 1700 Bardstown Road
### 502-458-4830

Since its 1981 opening, this neighborhood restaurant has drawn a crowd from all parts of the city and state. It was a media circus all its own during Louisville's publicity over heart implants, and national and international reporters drained expense accounts on veal sweetbreads and voluptuous desserts while enjoying the attention lavished on them by owners Nancy and David Shepherd.

The food might be judged to be "breakaway modern"—beautiful without being intimidating (sauces are served over, not under, the food). Flavors delight by their surprising combinations, such as swordfish with ginger, soy, and sesame. Notice how the entrées are printed in a subtle line-up, from the lightest fish first to the heaviest tenderloin last. Café Metro has one of the city's rare fixed-price menus, and it can get expensive if you also want soup and salad. But soup is particularly good here, especially if it's a day for tomato cream with Dubonnet or the crab bisque. Dessert has always been a problem here: Customers used to come for nothing but. Do so at your own risk, for dinner tables take precedence. If you like your whipped cream practically straight, there's a number called *gâteau ganache* that's pretty close. For chocophiles, there's Chocolate Seduction and Lenôtre's Concord, both made by bakers trained by David's mother. There is only a limited (though selective) wine list. No reservations are accepted. The dress is informal.

*Price: About $25 per person*
*Open daily for dinner only*
*Accepts American Express, Visa, and MasterCard*

---

## CAPTAIN'S QUARTERS
### 6222 Gutherie Beach Road at Harrods Creek
#### 502-228-1651; 502-228-8300

It's a nice drive up-river to this popular watering spot smack on the Ohio's banks. Recently purchased by former governor John Y. Brown, this old waystation at Mile 595.8 from Pittsburgh is now bedecked with enough wood terraces for everyone to get a good look at the water. Without the beautiful view to distract you, you might notice the food, which (except for the fried banana peppers) comes in third after a lawn chair and a beer. The menu is mostly hamburgers. Breathe deeply and watch the boats on the river. In winter go inside for Southern fried chicken or prime rib.

*Price: About $12 per person*
*Open daily for lunch and dinner*
*Accepts American Express, Visa, and MasterCard*

---

## CASA GRISANTI
### 1000 East Liberty Street
#### 502-584-4377

For many years Louisville's premier restaurant and host to local and out-of-town *glitterati,* Casa Grisanti endures as the standard of fine dining and discreet service in this region. Don't be misled by the shabby neighborhood. Dress to the nines and savor the dignity of the place. Let the valet park your car.

What's special about Casa is that there is a feeling of being perched along a great north-south axis of Italian cuisine.

Invent a dish, swap ingredients, consult with the chef. Waiters actually seem pleased when diners dare alter recipes. But be sure to read the menu before allowing off-the-menu suggestions, or you'll miss good reading if you don't. There is a fine *risotto con cozze* (saffron-scented rice with mussels) and *creste al boscaiolo,* a spinach and semolina pasta combination with *porcini* mushrooms and rosemary. Try anything with squid, especially those marinated in a cool salad. There is a separate list of Casa's classics, dishes regulars wouldn't do without. A new dish—and a true Casa happening—is *insalata con carciofi,* made with roasted red, green and yellow peppers, eggplant, and artichoke hearts delicately dressed with extra virgin olive oil.

Few items escape Casa's signature tableside flaming, not even dessert. Special-order hot *soufflés* are doused with liqueur and flamed not far from your elbows. Bar items and 250 selections from a wine list are priced to the max. Reservations are a must.

*Price: About $30 per person*
*Open Mon.–Sat. for dinner only; closed Sun.*
*Accepts all major credit cards*

---

# THE COUNTRY PIT
## 3400 Cane Run Road
### 502-772-2538

Housed in an abandoned hardware store, this place serves a spicy-hot, Southern-style pit barbecue. There are three sauces to choose from—hot, mild, and "southern" (Alabama-inspired, tangy, and hot). The hot sauce was once described as "creek sauce," because after you eating it, the nearby creek was the only place you could find relief. The peppery kick hits a few seconds after it's too late. Pork ribs and beef are meaty and tender and heaped generously by friendly employees and members of the Johnson family. Dinners have all the fixings—beans, slaw, and rolls. They also serve chicken wings, beef sandwiches, and potato salad. There's a beer garden, a drive-through window, and a dozen or so family tables in the front room. They also do catering. In the summer there's an outdoor Sunday buffet.

*Price: About $4.50 per person*
*Open Sun.–Thurs. for lunch and dinner; Fri. and Sat., from 11 A.M.*
*No credit cards or checks accepted*

# EMPRESS OF CHINA RESTAURANT AND LOUNGE

2249 Hikes Lane    502-451-2500

# EMPEROR OF CHINA RESTAURANT AND LOUNGE

210 Holiday Manor Shopping Center, at Brownsboro Road
502-426-1717

You won't find egg *foo yung* on the menus of these two family-run restaurants, not even if you ask. Some of the best dishes aren't on the menu at Empress of China either, even though regulars know what they are. When Ai-Ling Wang and her husband Jeffrey (the chef) created Emperor of China in late 1984, all the off-menu secrets at their original restaurant, Empress of China, became featured fare.

"Summer Special" (served all year round) is a gorgeous presentation of hot cellophane noodles in mustard sauce placed in the center of the plate, then mixed at the table with cold, perfectly cut shrimp, egg, and cucumber, with scallops set at the rim. (It's on Emperor's menu, but on request at Empress.) It is difficult not to be dazzled by the daily availability of jellyfish, sea cucumber, lettuce-wrapped chicken, veal with orange-rind flavor, chicken with watercress, and squid with dried chili peppers. The *tofu* is fresh and a standout in Eight Treasure *Tofu* (off the menu at both locations). Each site has a bar and exotic drinks with paper parasol garnishes. Take a whiff of Emperor's menu; it's scented. Reservations are appreciated.

*Price: About $15 per person*
*Open daily for lunch and dinner*
*Accepts all major credit cards*

# THE ENGLISH GRILL and J. GRAHAM'S

In the Brown Hotel, 4th Avenue Mall and Broadway
502-583-1234

You know the minute you walk in you're in Louisville's political vault. With its luxurious mahogany panels, ceiling gargoyles, and warming stained glass, the English Grill is a place where pols have blown a lot of smoke, a room where you can still feel the deals being sealed. The powerbrokers came here and drank bourbon and gin and drank and drank some more. Men stood at the bar.

These days the Grill is an elegant dining room owned by Hilton Hotels. It has white tablecloths, water goblets, and dessert carts. If only the Old Boys could see it now. The only thing they'd recognize would be the beloved Hot Brown, the famous dish accidentally created by chef Fred K. Schmidt in the 1930s. He took leftover turkey (*Note:* turkey, *not* chicken or ham!), laid it on toast points, smothered it with on-hand hollandaise, and a *Mornay* heavily enriched with Parmesan cheese, ran it under the broiler, garnished it with tomato and a crisscross of bacon, and served it bubbling hot in the dish in which it was cooked. The Hot Brown has outlived its permutations made with chicken and cling peaches, or suffocating under a yellow sheath of funny cheese. Many cooks in Kentucky can make this dish and make it right, but there is nothing so fine as a Hot Brown at the Brown itself. A ground-floor café, J. Graham's, also serves the dish. Reservations are advisable at the Grill but not taken at J. Graham's.

*Price: $5.95 for a Hot Brown; dinner at the English Grill, about $25 per person; at J. Graham's, about $8–$10 per person*
*Open daily for lunch and dinner*
*Accepts all major credit cards*

---

# HUBER FAMILY FARM AND RESTAURANT
## Scottsville Road, Starlight, Indiana
### 812-923-5255; 812-923-5597

Two years ago, Joe Huber stood on an empty spot on his vast U-Pick Farm and said he'd like to build a restaurant where he'd serve the food picked in his field. Six months later, he stood in front of his new restaurant and said he'd like some patio chairs, a few porch swings, some potted geraniums, a bandstand, and a pond.

It's all there, even the pond. The barn-like restaurant contains long rows of tables to seat multitudes, from infants to senior citizens. Seen from the windows is Huber's prized crop—red raspberries. Show up in June and the little jewels are in the restaurant's pie and cobbler. Come in May, you get strawberries in shortcake and jam. In mid-summer, sink your teeth into blackberries, then fresh squash and eggplant, and autumn's pumpkin pie.

Hot fried biscuits with apple butter in a squirt bottle come with fried chicken, farm catfish, pork chops, country ham, or the sweet Amish ham from a nearby Amish village. A vegetable plate of seasonal bounty is always available. You'll want to take home a jug of Huber's homemade apple cider. You might want to set aside some time for picking.

It helps to have a reservation, although the restaurant seats 260 inside, 150 on the patio, and 160 in a picnic area. There is a takeout window and a full bar.

*Directions:* Take Interstate 64 west to the Greenville–Paoli exit, Highway 150; follow the hand-lettered signs to Huber's. It's a nice 30-minute drive.

*Price: From $3–$10 per person; children under three eat free of charge*
*Open Mon.–Sat. for lunch and dinner; Sun. 11 A.M.–6 P.M.*
*No credit cards accepted*

---

# IMPELLIZZERI'S PIZZA
## 2306 Bardstown Road
### 502-451-7177

Impellizzeri's Pizza crusts are so thick they practically breathe. The fennel sausage is homemade, the tomato sauce dark red, and the cheese thick as a sidewalk. I once tipped a kid $15 to deliver one of these pizzas to my office —in spite of Impellizzeri's no-delivery policy. Extra dough is shaped into bread sticks easy to mistake for Louisville Sluggers—if it weren't for all the garlic butter.

The atmosphere is Naked Bulb, the confines small. The mayhem makes a Bruce Springsteen concert look like a church meeting. Depending on what you consider lucky, you can pick up your order after calling ahead or you'll just try to grab a seat and order on the premises. The phone is always blasting. Imagine working in this chaos and getting a call from ten stoned people who can't agree on anchovies or *pepperoni* for a topping. The line forms at 4 P.M. A "small" to the untrained eye is really large. Best thing to do is to order takeout, drive a few blocks away to beautiful Cherokee Park, and enjoy your pizza there.

*Price: From $6.95 to $22.95 for various pizzas*
*Open Tues.–Sun. for dinner only; closed Mon.*
*No credit cards accepted*

---

# MIKE LINNIG'S
## 9308 Cane Run Road
### 502-937-9888

This place doesn't serve seafood, it serves pond food, for this is where you go for catfish, frogs legs, and turtle soup. A fine meal batter with the flavor of corn is made right here, and just about everything that fries gets dusted with it. Shoot, given the chance they'd fry the salad. Onion rings done in that same batter are like bracelets for elephants. Get one order per table.

Sit under a vast grove of trees at concrete picnic tables. Waiters take your order sometimes without writing it down, and the mood is "good-ole-boy" on its best behavior. It is the custom between ordering and waiting to walk the path to the Ohio River and back. By that time (it never fails) your food is five minutes away. What appears to be outhouses are where you get your beer. There are swings for the children. They also offer takeout service.

*Directions:* About 25 minutes from downtown. Take I-264 west to Cane Run Road South. Go five miles and turn right at Greenwood. Go to the blinking light, turn left, and go two miles. The restaurant will be on your right.

*Price: About $5 per person*
*Open Tues.–Sun. for lunch and dinner; closed Mon.*
*No credit cards or personal checks accepted*

---

# MYRA'S RESTAURANT
## 2420 Grinstead Drive
### 502-454-5250

Hard to classify, but sophisticated and easy to like. The management claims no Americanization. But in spite of delicate *carpaccio,* lamb chops with feta and mint, and *linguine con vongole,* you could sure get fooled by that prime ground chuck cooked to order on a buttered onion roll with tomato, onion, and lettuce. No ordinary dish, this is Louisville's ultra-burger, the one served with Myra's zesty "Famous Sauce" that owner Tim Barnes generously shares with anyone who asks.

You'll also like the chicken curry and a winning Cajun shrimp dish whose recipe is credited to K-Paul's Louisiana Kitchen in New Orleans. This goes great with a *jalapeño-*laced Cajun martini. Try also the soft-shell crabs in season and the steak of the day, which might feature spicy mushrooms, oyster sauce, or fresh horseradish-brandy cream. Also, omelets of the day and eggs Benedict are close to perfection.

The best part about Myra's is that its pricing and food appeal nestle nicely in anyone's budget and any gastronomic urge. You'd be happy if you only order a "Zebra Brownie"—those double-rich chocolate brownies with the cheesecake filling with whipped cream and shaved chocolate. If you feel like everybody knows everybody else, you're right. The neighborhood, in a pretty part of town, clings tightly, and the bar is positively a hangout for locals. The place can get loud with or without the lounge piano. All wine is available by the bottle or the glass. Reservations are not accepted.

*Price: About $10–$12 per person*
*Open Mon.–Fri. for lunch and dinner; Sat. and Sun. for dinner only*
*Accepts American Express, Visa, and MasterCard*

# PARISIAN PANTRY
## 1582 Bardstown Road at Bonnycastle Avenue
### 502-452-6326

The one thing the Parisian Pantry can always be counted on to do well is bake. And they do it all day and most of the night, making this the best combination of France and Louisville since Louis XIV lent us his name.

Come at sunrise for *cappuccino,* sit at an antique oak table and watch this neighborhood come alive. Behind a glass display is the restaurant's best import, Yvette Bowers, with whom locals practice their French. The kitchen serves *croissants* (plain, cinnamon, and almond), softball-size *pain aux raisins; baguettes, boule,* and *pain brioche.* Linger through lunch with savory *croissants* stuffed with ham and Gruyère cheese. Arrive late for *pâte à chou* filled with caramel, coffee cream, and *mousse.*

There is an airy atmosphere downstairs with monthly art exhibits. Upstairs, there are a number of rooms (with original fireplaces) in country French motifs for both private and public dining. There are about forty French wines and a few California bottlings offered.

*Price: About $2 for pastry and beverage; $12–$15 per person for full meals*
*Open Tues.–Sun. for breakfast, lunch, and dinner; closed Mon.*
*Accepts Visa and MasterCard*

---

# PAT'S (FORMERLY MIN'S) STEAK HOUSE
## 2437 Brownsboro Road
### 502-896-9234; 502-893-2062

Go back in time to the meat-and-potatoes era where middle-aged black waiters serve in the Southern tradition—green jackets, no chitchat, impeccable service —and sink your chopper into hunks of hide that would horrify anyone but a rancher. Pat's (the logo's apostrophe is actually a shamrock) is an Irish legacy of thirty years' standing. It's a saloon-y place with lots of pine-paneled walls you wish could talk, for it's long been a favorite hangout for politicians. It is not unusual to see a fleet of silver Lincoln Continentals parked by the lawn jockey out front—a sure signal former governor John Y. Brown and his entourage are in town.

If you've been eating lightly lately, the laminated menu promises a welcome flourish of hand-cut flesh. Lest you under-order, the menu lists steaks in ounces, starting with the 8- to 9-ounce Lady Filet Mignon and ending with Pat's Aged New York Strip, weighing in at 22 ounces. Locals also love the frogs legs, chicken livers, and pan-fried oysters. Dress up the lackluster head of lettuce by ordering the toothsome homemade blue cheese dressing. Don't forget your lima beans, your creamed cauliflower, and, of course, your potatoes. Nothing fancy, just food the way it's always been in these parts. Dress is casual.

*Price: About $15–$25 per person*
*Open Mon.–Sat. for dinner only; closed Sun.*
*No credit cards accepted*

---

## RIB CAFÉ
### 3940 DuPont Circle
### 502-897-7427

This is the haughty child of the Rib Tavern parent (see below) with pretty much the same menu. But here the ribs are served in a room with ceiling fans, video screens the size of garages, hot music, and white tablecloths. They even serve pasta. It's the kind of barbecue that wants to be a millionaire by the time it's thirty. The Café resides in a slick, peachy building. Families may be seated in a room to the side of a hectic bar. Servers dress a little less outrageously than the customers, though the women still show a lot of leg. At 10 P.M. on Saturday, bones aren't the only thing getting picked up: The opposite end of the restaurant becomes a pulsating nightclub with a $2 cover. If the term "meat market" comes to mind, remember that this is a barbecue place, one that manages to control all its elements with a "G" rating, and there is a children's menu. No reservations taken and waiting can be long.

*Price: About $8 per person for barbecue*
*Open Mon.–Sat. for lunch and dinner; Sun. for dinner only*
*Accepts all major credit cards; no checks accepted*

---

## RIB TAVERN
### 4157 Bardstown Road
### 502-499-1515

Voted the most popular restaurant in Louisville in a 1984 *Louisville Courier-Journal* poll, this is where barbecue connoisseurs come to live out fantasies of unbridled rib lust and to listen to music in an atmosphere that can only be described as Upscale Beer Lodge, with eclectic decor and stained glass. What you really come for is the food, the tenderest meat this side of your knife. Huge slabs of baby back ribs exude fire and smoke from hours spent over hickory. Tour the world of barbecue with combination plates of chicken, ribs, and sausage. The notorious onion ring loaf overfeeds any table, no matter how many in your party. Start with fried appetizers that are fat-free and crisp. Also try the fish.

If you can find a moment to glance up from your carnivorous frenzy, it will be difficult not to notice the waitresses, whose short outfits reveal frilly, peek-a-boo underpants that outrage women customers and delight the men. This is a folksy place, and you'll feel just as comfortable in shorts or a suit. The bar is loud, but has a good beer selection. No reservations are accepted, and there's often a long wait.

*Directions:* Take Bardstown Road south beyond Watterson Expressway and just over Beuchel By-pass. The Rib Tavern is on your left. Ample parking.

*Price: About $10 per person for ribs*
*Open daily for lunch and dinner*
*Accepts all major credit cards*

---

# ROCKY'S SUB PUB
## 1207 East Market Street, Jeffersonville, Indiana
### 812-282-3844

Rocky's was opened in 1978 by a New York Italian who titled his sandwich spot after the long-suffering movie character of the same name. Now a full-course restaurant, Rocky's has absorbed its popularity with recent expansion. Pass the time reading the eight-page menu, from *mozzarella* sticks to *calzones* and homemade *cannoli*. Pizzas come to the red-checkered tablecloths as spinning showpieces on what look like metal cake stands. The big attraction is whole wheat pizza, which owner John Fondrisi says his mother used to make for him long before the 1960s' grain drain. On the classy end are *prosciutto* bread, veal Milano with olive oil, garlic, and wine. But don't forget why this place exists—five-inch-high subs.

With 33 imported beers, you can bet the Red Stripe you remember from your vacation to Jamaica is here. A surprising number of French and American wines (unnecessary to match up with this food) are much appreciated. Rocky's is lots of fun. Bring the kids. Everything on the menu may be taken out or delivered.

*Directions:* About a 10-minute drive from downtown. Take I-65 north over the Ohio River to the Jeffersonville, Indiana, exit. Turn right at Court Street and go one block to Mulberry. Turn right and go three blocks to Market Street. Turn left and drive one mile to Rocky's on your left.

*Price: About $6 per person, less for pizza*
*Open Mon.–Sat. for lunch and dinner; Sun. for dinner only*
*Accepts Visa and MasterCard*

# SCIENCE HILL INN
## 525 Washington Street, Shelbyville
### 502-633-2825

For exquisite luncheons of regional cuisine in a resplendent setting, make this drive through horse country to Shelby County. The Georgian Room, circa 1790, is what one can only suppose is a vast Southern parlor frozen in time. Chandeliers hang clink-to-clink and twinkle on priceless silver antiques holding grits. (These antiques are on loan from the Wakefield-Scearce Galleries next door.)

You'll find fine country ham, fried chicken, and trout, all prepared with finesse. Chef Donna Gill has taken Southern food and cleaned up the rough, greasy edges. Salad is a proud display of Kentucky Bibb. An old favorite, tomato pudding, is cooked a little less and with more freshness than the way Grandma did it. Trout here never hits the ice.

A substantial Sunday brunch features grits, cornbread made the hot-water way, and bread pudding made of yesterday's biscuits soaked in a bourbon sauce that leaves no doubt about its main ingredient. There is a small wine list.

*Directions:* Take I-64 east to first Shelbyville exit. Turn left and go to first light, then turn right on U.S. 60. Drive about 1½ miles through town to Fifth Street; turn left, go to Washington Street, and turn left. About half an hour's drive.

*Price: About $8 per person*
*Open Tues.–Sat. for lunch only; Sun. for brunch; closed Mon.*
*Accepts American Express, Visa, and MasterCard*

# THE WINERY
## 1574 Bardstown Road
### 502-458-2783

Louisville's first wine bar, formal enough for the town's theatergoers but casual enough so that servers don't wear black-tie, has an iconoclasm that puts green with purple, wine with Louisvillians (who take their bourbon with branch water), and a culinary bandit (who actually looks a bit like Waylon Jennings) behind the stove who follows his own nose instead of the dictates of the orthodoxy.

Forty wines attached to a nitrogen-displacement system allow you to taste by the glass from the low and high ends of the selection, and you may interchange wines in groups for a tasting of several wines at a time. Wine is available by the bottle too, of course.

In the kitchen the culinary outlaws make the marriage of wine and food more like an elopement. They're back there getting lusty with puréed sun-dried tomatoes and jumbo shrimp, but also find room for deep-dish oyster pie or chicken salad with roasted peppers and chili mayonnaise. Required desserts will remind you of the excesses of a Rubens painting.

The entrance is in the rear of the building. Inside the walls are bare except for sparse, contemporary poster art. The dining room is loud when full, and the pianist is usually going strong. Reservations taken for parties of six or more only.

*Price: About $20 per person*
*Open Mon.–Sat. for dinner only; closed Sun.*
*Accepts all major credit cards*

---

# W. W. COUSINS
## 900 DuPont Road at Breckinridge Lane
### 502-897-9684

Except for the meat itself, you have no one to blame for the outcome of your hamburger here. They cook it, you build it. Fresh meat—as much as half a pound—obviously ground from the sides of the steer visibly hanging from meat hooks, is cooked to order and placed on a yeasty bun made right on the premises. About forty fixings lie before you—including homemade steak sauce, semisweet mustard sauce, and horseradish, plus pizza sauce, fresh banana peppers, the ubiquitous bean sprouts, sweet and dill relishes, coconut, and peanuts, and, yes, a choice between real mayonnaise or Miracle Whip. If you're slow, the line behind you lengthens. Believe me, you will brighten at the sight of the ketchup and mustard. Beer, soft drinks, on-premises-baked brownies, ice cream cones, and chocolate chip cookies are also sold.

*Price: About $5 for adults; $2 for children*
*Open daily for lunch and dinner*
*Accepts most major credit cards*

# MEMPHIS

## By Tom Martin

**AMERICAN**
Café Meridien
Dux

**BARBECUE**
Charlie Vergos The
  Rendezvous
John Wills' Barbecue Pit
Leonard's
Smokey Ridge
Willingham's

**CHINESE**
Formosa
Jimmy Tin's Port Shanghai
Wang's Mandarin House

**FRENCH**
Chervil's
Chez Philippe
La Tourelle
Vieux Chalet

**GERMAN**
Erika's

**GREEK**
Melos Taverna
Zorba's

**HEALTH FOOD**
La Montagne

**HOTEL DINING ROOM**
Chervil's
Chez Philippe
Dux

**ITALIAN**
The Palm Court

**MEXICAN**
Gonzales' and Gertrudes'
Molly's La Casita

**SEAFOOD**
Captain Bilbo's River
  Restaurant

**SOUL FOOD**
Four Way Grill

**VIETNAMESE**
Lotus

Memphis restaurants, like the city's reputation, have come a long way in the last few years. In the late 1960s and early 1970s, the city lived under the cloud of the Martin Luther King, Jr. assassination, fire and police strikes, and the slow decay of the downtown area. But that began to change in the early 1980s. Downtown redevelopment caught fire with the reopening of The Peabody in 1981, once again one of the South's grand hotels. The 1980s have also witnessed the rebirth of the blues on Beale Street with the opening of a bright and brassy shopping and entertainment district on the famous street. A $65-million attraction with the unlikely name of Mud Island has transformed a grassy island just off the riverfront into a recreational and educational playland connected to downtown by a Swiss monorail. With all this activity, festivals like Memphis-in-May have grown in popularity since the late 1970s, and are now attracting more than a million people downtown in the spring and summer months.

This quickening pace has brought with it a plethora of new restaurants. Prior to 1967, Memphis nightlife had stifled under stiff liquor laws that prevented restaurants and night spots from serving liquor by the drink and forced patrons to "brown bag" it. Once these restrictions were lifted, dozens of new restaurants and clubs opened. A midtown entertainment district called Overton Square served as one focal point for this flurry of new activity, and the downtown development ten years later provided a needed second focus.

The city's selection of fine restaurants is admittedly not extensive, especially for a city approaching the million mark in metropolitan population. Memphis is particularly lacking in good ethnic restaurants. You won't find an Indian restaurant here, for instance, or a Middle Eastern one. And there are but a handful of German, Greek, and Italian restaurants. The only ethnic category well-represented is Chinese, with close to twenty good restaurants offering a nice variety of Mandarin, Hunan, Szechuan, and Cantonese dishes.

This relative lack of ethnic restaurants can be tied, in part, to a series of yellow fever epidemics that almost wiped out Memphis in the 1870s. Huge segments of the city's immigrant population—the Germans, Italians, and others—left the city never to return. As a result, Memphis has a much more homogeneous ethnic makeup than St. Louis to the north or New Orleans to the south; only in the last twenty years has the population become more diverse.

If there is one specialty for which Memphis is famous it is barbecued pork. Memphis has been called the "pork barbecue capital of the world," and with over sixty barbecue restaurants for you to choose from, the title seems appropriate. Since 1978, Memphis has hosted the "Memphis in May International Barbecue Cooking Contest," and it now attracts 200 teams and more than 250,000 spectators over a two-day period to Tom Lee Park on the waterfront.

But barbecue isn't the only culinary offering you'll find in Memphis. A new interest in fine food and wine has spawned several imaginative restaurants in the last few years. In 1984, Le Maison Meridien, the Memphis Culinary Academy, began training professional chefs in the region, becoming one of only a handful of such institutions in the country. The school's presence should also help improve food quality and presentation in the area.

Memphis may not be able to attract tourists solely on the basis of its culinary reputation, but those who enjoy fine dining certainly shouldn't dread coming here any longer. With reasonable representatives of Vietnamese, Greek, German, and Italian cooking, and several excellent restaurants serving Chinese, traditional French, and New American cuisine, the capital of the Mid-South need not apologize at all for its array of restaurants. And if it's barbecue for which you've a hankering, you have indeed come to the right place.

*Tom Martin is restaurant critic for* Memphis *magazine.*

---

## CAFÉ MERIDIEN
In Victorian Village historic district, 680 Adams Avenue
**901-525-1170**

This restaurant is unique in many ways. It is the only Memphis restaurant housed in a pair of carriage houses that date back to 1870. It is also one of a handful of restaurants in the country staffed by advanced students associated with the Memphis Culinary Academy, the South's only professional training school for chefs. The students work under the watchful eye of Joseph Carey, the head of the school and part-owner of the restaurant. The food style is New American, and Carey himself was part of the birth of this approach to cooking in San Francisco. The restaurant showcases fresh ingredients and simple preparations in such dishes as filet of Ozark smoked trout and sassafras-smoked ham, both available as appetizers. Several Creole and Cajun dishes are also offered (Carey is a native of New Orleans), including gumbo filé, jambalaya, and shrimp *rémoulade.* Rounding out the selection are several creative combinations, among them: hickory-and-sassafras-smoked pork loin, catfish *doré,* mesquite-grilled quail, and boneless leg of lamb with a raspberry-zinfandel sauce.

*Price: About $30 per person*
*Open Mon.–Fri. for lunch and dinner; Sat. for dinner only; closed Sun.*
*Accepts all major credit cards*

# CAPTAIN BILBO'S RIVER RESTAURANT
## 263 Wagner Place (*near Beale Street*)
### 901-526-1966

Captain Bilbo's began as an ambitious experiment a few years ago on Wagner Place, where Beale Street meets the Mississippi River. Its owners gambled on the chancy notion that they could attract enough locals and tourists to fill up a 600-seat seafood restaurant and music bar often enough to make money. In retrospect, their only mistake may have been in making the restaurant too small. Captain Bilbo's has become Memphis' busiest night spot, and one of the busiest in the country. On a good Saturday night, more than 1,000 diners will be served in the 316-seat dining room, and hundreds more will pack the boisterous lounge, where the wait for a seat in the restaurant may take over two hours. But go anyway. The music is good and the time passes quickly. Once seated, you'll have a shot at one of the most complete seafood menus in town. And, while the volume limits the complexity and presentation of the dishes, they are consistently well prepared. Among the better items are shrimp Cadwallader (in a brown butter sauce), flounder Gasconade with shrimp and crab meat, and for those who like fried items, all the seafood at Captain Bilbo's is hand-breaded and expertly fried.

*Price: About $20 per person*
*Open daily for dinner only*
*Accepts all major credit cards*

# CHARLIE VERGOS THE RENDEZVOUS
## In General Washburn Alley, 52 South Second Street
### 901-523-2746

If Memphis ever appoints an ambassador of barbecue, count on Charlie Vergos, the owner of The Rendezvous, to get the most votes. The longtime restaurateur has introduced many a visitor to the finer points of barbecued ribs at The Rendezvous, his downtown cavern just off Union Avenue. Now he's even shipping his ribs via Federal Express all over the country, fully cooked and ready to enjoy. The atmosphere at The Rendezvous is nothing short of spectacular. No other Memphis restaurant even approaches The Rendezvous in making the most of memorabilia, bric-a-brac, and paraphernalia from an age gone by. From Essolene gas signs to gun racks to old cartoons from the *Memphis Commercial Appeal,* the walls are covered like a museum that takes kitsch to a whole new dimension. But Vergos doesn't pack them in practically every night he's open just because of the scenery. The food is good, from the smoked-sausage-and-cheese appetizer plates to the ribs and pork loin for which the restaurant's become famous. Some will say The Rendezvous' preparation leaves the ribs too dry, since a dry seasoning is used as the major flavor ingredient, and the ribs aren't as well-sauced as some in town. But I've always found the meat tender and moist enough, and a spicy liquid sauce available at the table is perfect for those who want a wetter rib. Don't overlook the pork loin plate, either—two thick slices of loin chop cooked in barbecue sauce until they're fork-tender. The Rendezvous is one of the few places in town serving this cut, which is surprising since it's so good. The Rendezvous' reputation for showing diners a good time in a carnival-like atmosphere is clearly well deserved.

*Price: About $15 per person*
*Open Fri. and Sat. for lunch and dinner; Tues.—Thurs. for dinner only; closed Sun. and Mon.*
*Accepts all major credit cards*

---

# CHERVIL'S
## In the Holiday Inn Crowne Plaza Hotel, 250 North Main Street
### 901-527-7300

If you picture Holiday Inn restaurants as predictable and boring, Chervil's will be a delightful surprise. The Crowne Plaza group is the hotel chain's venture into upscale all-suite hotels, and if the Memphis version is any indication, they're doing a nice job of changing their image. Chervil's is the top-of-the-line restaurant at the Crowne Plaza, and it lives up to that distinction in many ways. The menu is filled with such delights as bay scallops with warmed kiwi in puff pastry, lobster *ravioli* with saffron, dilled *gravlax,* and warmed duck breast on a nest of *radicchio* and endive. And that's just for starters. The entrée selection includes such creations as lobster fricassee *primavera,* breast of duck with cranberry-orange sauce, and veal *forestière* with *chanterelle* mushrooms. The meal will include little extras like a bit of seafood *terrine* with caviar or a small slice of *pâté* as you scan the menu; later a serving of *sorbet* in a graceful porcelain swan between courses. Service is refined and attentive. Some may be disappointed with the dessert selections, which are a bit limited, but the restaurant is still young and this should improve with time.

*Price: About $50 per person*
*Open Mon.—Fri. for lunch; Mon.—Sat. for dinner; closed Sun.*
*Accepts all major credit cards*

# CHEZ PHILIPPE
## In The Peabody Hotel, 149 Union Avenue
### 901-529-4188

This is, to my mind, the very best Memphis has to offer. Though it got off to a bumpy start when it first opened in 1982, Chez Philippe is now firmly established as the region's most competent, imaginative restaurant. From the moment one steps between the panels of frosted glass that separate Chez Philippe from The Peabody's famous lobby (you may have heard of the ducks that waddle in each day to the strains of a John Philip Sousa march), it is clear the occasion will be memorable. The decor is splendid: crisp pink linens, hand-painted murals of a masquerade, dramatic high ceilings, with live harp music adding an ethereal touch. But the food is the star attraction: Chef Jose Gutierrez has created a *nouvelle* menu that includes such delights as lobster salad with warm truffle butter dressing, breast of squab on a bed of pink pears, and *médaillons* of venison in Pommard wine. The dishes imaginatively match diverse colors, textures, and flavors in combinations that are fresh and tantalizing to the eye and palate. The presentation of the check may bring a tightening in the chest (it is the city's most expensive restaurant), but considering the quality of the ingredients, the skill of preparation, and the overall sense of celebration that practically spills out of the kitchen, it's worth every penny.

*Price: About $50 per person*
*Open Mon.–Sat. for dinner only; closed Sun.*
*Accepts all major credit cards*

# DUX
## In the Peabody Hotel, 149 Union Avenue
### 901-529-4199

This restaurant, which features American cuisine exclusively, changes its menu with the seasons so it can use only the freshest available ingredients. The result is a selection of outstanding dishes in both concept and execution. The restaurant is classy, with stark black, white, and maroon colors. Being The Peabody's medium-priced restaurant, Dux has to be affordable enough for the hotel guests, yet interesting enough to attract local diners, and it strikes this middle ground surprisingly well. Typical of the changing selections is smoked catfish fillet, a flavorful first course served with coriander sauce. A ragout of mussels and clams served over garlic toast points is another. Other excellent items are the sliced pork tenderloin stuffed with sausage served with a Dijon mustard sauce, mesquite-grilled shrimp and scallops with spicy red pepper, and sautéed veal scallops with mustard cream. Several desserts are excellent, such as bread pudding with whiskey sauce and the marvelous creations from The Peabody's superb pastry kitchen.

*Price: About $35 per person*
*Open daily for breakfast, lunch, and dinner*
*Accepts all major credit cards*

---

## ERIKA'S
### 52 South Second Street
### 901-526-5522

This downtown fixture is reminiscent of many family-style restaurants throughout Germany: The menu is typed out on plain white paper, the waitresses are friendly and efficient, and the food is simple, substantial, and satisfying. You won't find *deluxe cuisine* here, but then you rarely find that in the Germanic countries either. What you will find are hearty bowls of goulash soup, herring in sour cream, *leberknodel* (liver dumplings), *sauerbraten* (beef pot roast), *schweinebraten* (pork loin roast), and *Wiener Schnitzel,* served in four varieties. The accompaniments for these traditional dishes are similarly unpretentious: creamed potatoes, sauerkraut, red cabbage, pan-fried potatoes, and potato pancakes. But what makes Erika's so popular (try getting a table there at noontime and you may have to wait) is that these unrefined dishes are so well prepared. The *schnitzel* is never greasy, the goulash always thick with meat, the *schweinebraten* fork-tender. If you want something special for dessert, call ahead of time and try to talk Erika into making a Black Forest torte. And even if you aren't successful, the apple *strudel* is a fine substitute.

*Price: About $15 per person*
*Open Mon.–Thurs. for lunch and dinner; Fri. and Sat. for dinner only; closed Sun.*
*Accepts all major credit cards*

---

## FORMOSA
### 3735 Summer Avenue
### 901-323-4819

This restaurant is the favorite of a great many diehard aficionados of Oriental food, and it was one of the first in Memphis to feature hot, spicy fare. The atmosphere is crowded, noisy, and a bit garish, and one can generally expect to wait 30 minutes or more for an empty table, especially on weekends. The reason for the hubbub is the food. Fried wontons are better than average, light, airy, and not at all greasy. The Chinese sausage is a must for starters: crisp, thinly sliced, smoky, and served with slivered scallions. The hundred flower chicken—*cha pai hua chi*—is also excellent, with tender breast pieces lightly fried and topped with sesame seeds on a bed of crisp noodles. The hot-and-sour soup sets the standard for Memphis, the tartness of vinegar and the fire of the pepper blending well with chicken stock, bamboo shoots, pork, dried mushrooms, and bean curd. Those who like it hot will like it here, and the source of the spiciness varies with each dish. Mongolian beef derives its fieriness from hot sesame oil and ginger; *kung pao* scallops are flavored with whole dried chilies, also used in the onion-pepper chicken. Some may be put off by Formosa's frenetic atmosphere, but the regulars have learned to tune it out as they savor each dish.

*Price: About $10 per person*
*Open Tues.–Sun. for dinner only; closed Mon.*
*Accepts Visa and MasterCard*

## FOUR WAY GRILL
### 998 Mississippi Boulevard
#### 901-775-2351

This Memphis institution has been serving up some of the best fried chicken, cornbread, vegetables, and cobblers for years. The waitresses are as friendly as they come, the decor is simple (oilcloths on the tables and a jukebox in the corner), and on every table you'll find bottles of pepper sauce and Louisiana hot sauce. The cobblers are truly memorable: extremely flaky crusts (and there's always the right mixture of fruit and crust in each serving) and hot syrupy filling that changes daily. In the summertime the peach is especially good.

*Price: About $7.50 per person*
*Open daily for breakfast, lunch, and dinner*
*No credit cards accepted*

## GONZALES' AND GERTRUDES'
### In Overton Square, 35 South Cooper Street
#### 901-725-0005

Hardcore Mexican food fanatics—those who like the food so hot it leaves timid souls gasping—may find the food here too tame, but the selection is imaginative and the ingredients always fresh. The margaritas at G&G's are a perfect balance of tartness and sweetness. They go well with the *quesadilla de la casa:* two flour *tortillas* filled with beef or chicken and topped with cheese, chilies, and sour cream. The *salsa* has a nice flavoring of *cilantro,* though it needs a little more *jalapeño.* Other good starters are the *sopa de albóndigas* (a meatball soup) and the *taquitos rancheros.* In addition to the usual *chimichangas, enchiladas,* and *burritos,* G&G's offers steak *picado,* bits of top sirloin cooked with green peppers, tomatoes, and herbs, and *puerco asada,* a plate of well-seasoned pork loin served with flour *tortillas,* and a fiery *jalapeño*-based relish called *pico de gallo.* The *arroz con camarones* (shrimp and rice with onions, peppers, and tomatoes) is also quite good. If you simply want to be blown away by the chilies, you may be disappointed, but if you like to taste what you're eating, G&G's should satisfy.

*Price: About $15 per person*
*Open daily for lunch and dinner*
*Accepts all major credit cards*

---

# JIMMY TIN'S PORT SHANGHAI
## 2725 South Mendenhall Avenue
### 901-794-4134

This East Memphis establishment suffers somewhat from a low visibility location in a shopping center, but loyal patrons who have made it a point to search out Jimmy Tin's have been rewarded with excellent food and gracious service. While decor may be of only minimal interest to those in search of a Chinese meal, Port Shanghai is truly a cut above in that department. You won't find cheap bric-a-brac here; instead, the dining rooms are divided by rich silk panels, the lighting is soft, and the round tables are covered in subdued coral-colored cloths. Appetizers and soups are fairly predictable, but a number of entrées are outstanding. Sardai beef is a dish of Malaysian origin, similar to Thai satays, with flavorings of onions, ginger, and curry. Pork plum blossom Shanghai is also nice, as is the Mandarin chicken, and the pepper shrimp. The *mu shu* pork is also well prepared at Jimmy Tin's, with thin Chinese *crêpes* coated with *hoisin* sauce and filled with pork loin, bean sprouts, bok choy, and scallions. With the fresh, well-seasoned, and well-presented fare at Jimmy Tin's, the faithful clientele is easy to understand.

*Price: About $15 per person*
*Open Mon.–Fri. for lunch and dinner; Sat. and Sun. for dinner only*
*Accepts all major credit cards*

# JOHN WILLS' BARBECUE PIT
## 2450 Central Avenue
### 901-274-8000

John Wills was catapulted from winning the championship of the Memphis-in-May barbecue contest to owning a successful barbecue restaurant, opened in 1983, which immediately became one of the most popular spots in town. You may have a wait on a Saturday night; try to go instead on a weeknight, when you can take time to savor the superb ribs and shoulder that have made John Wills famous. It's an attractive restaurant, with green painted tables, abundant use of natural wood, and clever photos of hogs adorning the walls. The selection of barbecue includes beef and pork ribs, pork shoulder, beef brisket, and sausage. The pork shoulder is cut in medium-to-large chunks and is quite tender. You won't find much fat, and very little sauce is served directly on the meat, which allows you to add the amount you prefer. The regular sauce is a little tame, but the hot sauce served in glass shaker bottles more than makes up for it. Wills' ribs are also terrific, very meaty, cooked until the meat falls quite easily from the bones, and brushed with sauce so that a somewhat crusty layer of it coats the meat. The ribs aren't dusted with powdery spices like some you'll find in Memphis. The barbecue beans are highly spiced, full of meat, and thick enough to indicate long, slow simmering. The coleslaw is also highly seasoned with mustard and vinegar in a slightly sweet sauce. All in all, John Wills is a championship restaurant in a barbecue-crazy town.

*Price: About $12 per person*
*Open daily for lunch and dinner*
*Accepts all major credit cards*

# JUSTINE'S
## 919 Coward Place
### 901-527-3815

This is the *grande dame* of Memphis restaurants, a genteel dining room that's been at it for over thirty years. The restaurant is housed in Coward Place, a restored mansion built in 1843, and the setting is grand. The tables are always adorned with fresh roses, in the summer months from the restaurant's own gardens, and lilting live piano music fills the house from the foyer. Don't go to Justine's if you're looking for innovation; the menu never changes and some of the dishes lack imagination. Justine's is a restaurant steeped in the traditions of New Orleans, with dependable seafood specialties and steaks grilled over real charcoal. Some of the better dishes are *crabes* Justine, vichyssoise, pompano

Claudet, *tournedos béarnaise,* and trout Marguery. The rum-cream pie that Craig Claiborne extolled in a 1966 column is still there, and still delightful.

*Price: About $35 per person*
*Open Mon.–Sat. for dinner only; closed Sun.*
*Accepts all major credit cards*

---

# LA MONTAGNE
## 3550 Park Avenue
### 901-458-1060

This natural foods restaurant is much more than a health food headquarters. While many of the dishes feature bean sprouts, bulgur, whole wheat breads, and sesame seeds, you'll also find excellent seafood entrées which change daily: sautéed shrimp, chicken *teriyaki,* and—lo and behold—even filet mignon. What makes the restaurant so pleasant for faddists and middle-of-the-roaders alike is the freshness of the ingredients and the simplicity and care with which they are prepared. Add to that pleasant and polished surroundings and a gracious serving staff, and you have a worthwhile attraction.

*Price: About $15 per person*
*Open Sun. for breakfast, lunch, and dinner; Mon.–Sat. for lunch and dinner only*
*Accepts all major credit cards*

---

# LA TOURELLE
## 2146 Monroe Avenue (*near Overton Square*)
### 901-726-5771

This charming restaurant in the Overton Square entertainment district features a French menu that changes monthly, and shows just a shade of influence from the New American cooking style. The peach-colored walls, white and green linens, lace curtains, and tulip-shaded light fixtures give the feel of a small French inn, and the food enhances that feeling. While the menu is constantly changing, some dishes are carried over from month to month. A typical sampling might include cream of mussel soup in an orange-flavored stock, scallop *mousseline* with tomato sauce, shrimp *quenelles* with shallots, salmon steaks with basil butter, and Kahlùa *mousse.* La Tourelle has become known for its Queen Mother cake, a triple chocolate blockbuster that is not for the weak-hearted. Though not a flawless restaurant, La Tourelle is unpretentious, distinctive, and compelling. With such a combination, it's no wonder the small restaurant has welcomed Memphis diners for longer than many of the city's better restaurants have been in business.

*Price: About $25 per person; fixed-price dinners under $20 also available*
*Open Tues.–Sat. for dinner only; closed Sun. and Mon.*
*Accepts all major credit cards*

## LEONARD'S
### 1140 South Bellevue Boulevard
#### 901-948-1581

Since 1932, Leonard's neon pig has beckoned those in need of a hickory fix to the simple booths and plain tables where smiling waitresses pile on the plates of ribs and pork shoulder daily. In the halcyon days of post-Second World War America, Leonard's became famous as the world's largest drive-in restaurant, and though the curbside service is no longer a feature, Leonard's still gets an occasional mention in the national press. Happily, the years have been kind to Leonard's, and its success hasn't spoiled the quality of the food. Though it has opened two suburban outlets, they don't hold a candle to the original location for sheer style. Leonard's ribs are meaty and lean, with a good smoked flavor and not too much sauce. Pork shoulder is chopped in large chunks and served covered with a fairly mild sauce. You can add some punch with a red pepper sauce at the table. Don't miss trying the onion rings, huge, golden-battered rings of sweet onion fried to a crisp texture. You might find them too large, but they're a pleasant change from the uniform frozen variety. The lemon ice box pie is also a must, tart and creamy and a perfect end to the trip down Memory Lane.

*Price: About $10 per person*
*Open daily for lunch and dinner*
*Accepts Visa and MasterCard*

## LOTUS
### 4970 Summer Avenue
#### 901-682-1151

Though its setting may be somewhat humble, the food at Lotus is the attraction, and many of the Vietnamese dishes served there are available at no other Memphis restaurant. Skip the traditional appetizers and move down the menu to the special house selections. Both the *banh cuon* and the *bang xeo* are delicious. *Banh cuon* are dumplings made with rice flour and filled with a ground pork and mushroom mixture. They're served with a four-alarm chilie paste, and garnished with cucumber, crisp fried onion, and bean sprouts. The *banh xeo,* or golden salty cake, is like an omelet made with rice flour batter and folded over pork, shrimp, and bean sprouts, then served on a bed of lettuce, with a bit of shredded carrot for color. Chicken Lotus style is an original dish, with crisp-roasted chicken pieces with a slightly barbecued flavor, served with celery, onions, and a thick sesame sauce. Another house specialty well worth trying is the Vietnamese style *vermicelli,* thin noodles tossed with shrimp, green peppers, and bean sprouts, then laced with hot curry sauce and chili peppers; this dish is not for the meek. Also good are salty shrimp Lotus style (not salty at all), stuffed bean curd, and the rice-noodle combination. Finish a meal there with banana fritters, chunks of banana coated in batter and quick-fried, topped with a toffee sauce, and served with ice cream. Heavy, perhaps, but delicious just the same.

*Price: About $10 per person*
*Open Mon.–Fri. for lunch and dinner; Sat. and Sun. for dinner only*
*Accepts Visa and MasterCard*

---

# MELOS TAVERNA
## In Overton Square, 2021 Madison Avenue
### 901-725-1863

Tom and Sophia Stergios opened Melos Taverna (*melos* is Greek for "windmill") in 1982. It's a simple family-run restaurant with a lighthearted, festive atmosphere and a competent selection of Greek standards. The menu may lack a little in imagination, but you can easily put together an interesting meal. Start with *zajiki* salad, a cool mixture of yogurt, cucumber, and garlic, or the *melijonasalata,* a thick purée of cooked eggplant, olive oil, herbs, and garlic. The *horatiki,* a country salad, is just like the ones you get in Greece: sliced tomatoes and cucumbers with crumbled feta cheese, salty Greek olives, and rich olive oil. Chicken *riganato,* simply roasted with oregano, lemon juice, and garlic, is quite flavorful, but watch out for the lamb, which is usually over-cooked. The traditional dishes are worth trying, including *moussaka,* *spanakopita* (spinach pie with feta and dill), and *tiropita* (cheese-filled *filo* pastry).

*Price: About $15 per person*
*Open Tues.–Sat. for dinner only; closed Sun. and Mon.*
*Accepts all major credit cards*

# MOLLY'S LA CASITA

2006 Madison Avenue   901-726-1873
4972 Park Avenue   901-685-1616

Molly Gonzales opened her original La Casita in a humble place on Lamar Avenue, and while the surroundings may have been unimpressive, Molly's food won her a legion of fans. She's come a long way from Lamar Avenue, having opened two nicely decorated restaurants in the last few years. While she no longer does the cooking, her influence is still felt. From the first taste of *salsa*, the dishes are well spiced, hot enough to bring a bit of perspiration just below the eyes. Some of the best entrées are the *chilies rellenos*, two *posia* peppers, blackened and stuffed with cheese or meat, then coated in egg batter and fried. *Tacos al carbon* is also excellent: three flour *tortillas* stuffed with thin sliced steak and garnished with *pico de gallo* and *guacamole*. Molly's also serves the traditional *burritos, enchiladas,* and a very good plate of *tamales* with a choice of *mole* sauce, *salsa verde*, chili gravy, or cheese sauce. For those who can take this kind of food early in the day, the restaurant offers Mexican omelets and *huevos rancheros* from 11:00 A.M. to 4:00 P.M. daily.

*Price: About $12 per person*
*Open daily for lunch and dinner*
*Accepts all major credit cards*

# PALM COURT

2101 Overton Square Lane
901-725-6797

Michael Cahhal, chef and principal owner of The Palm Court, has become one of the most visible personalities in the Memphis food world since his arrival a few short years ago. But despite the many demands on his time for cooking classes, he has managed to create an altogether satisfying Northern Italian restaurant. It is set in a large atrium that once housed an ice skating rink. Gathered fabric canopies along with huge potted palms have been added to give the large room a more intimate feel. The menu includes classics from the Piedmont, Lombardy, Emilia-Romagna, and other northern regions of Italy. Some of the better dishes are *gnochetti* in cream, braised mussels and clams, sautéed snails in angel's hair pasta, *fettuccine Portofino, fettuccine Alfredo*, and lobster *fra diavolo*. The *cioppino*, with clams, mussels, lobster, and shrimp, is also quite respectable. One of the better desserts is the traditional *zabaglione*, especially when it's served over fresh raspberries in season.

*Price: About $30 per person*
*Open Tues.–Sun. for dinner only; closed Mon.*
*Accepts all major credit cards*

# SMOKEY RIDGE
### 3333 Winchester Road
### 901-795-7534

This friendly place near Memphis International Airport describes its offerings as "real old-fashioned hickory-smoked barbecue." From the scent of the smoke in the parking lot, you can sense the claim is legitimate. When the barbecue appears in front of you, you're assured. The large pieces pulled from the shoulder are nicely smoked, with the most pungent taste of hickory in town. The meat is tender and served with just a bit of sauce. Three sauces—mild, hot, and extra hot—are available. Ask for the extra hot (they usually keep it behind the counter in a yellow squeeze bottle); it's as incendiary as any you'll find and a little goes a long way. Smokey Ridge's ribs are meaty, with the same well-smoked flavor, though at times they can be a little chewy. The log-cabin atmosphere is quite comfortable, the waitresses go out of their way to be friendly and accommodating, and the barbecue is first rate.

*Price: About $12 per person*
*Open Mon.–Sat. for lunch and dinner; closed Sun.*
*Accepts all major credit cards*

---

# VIEUX CHALET
### 3264 Summer Avenue (*near Highland Avenue*)
### 901-452-6211

This restaurant, like Justine's, has borrowed heavily from New Orleans for its cuisine and style. The food is always dependable and well prepared; the service refined, yet friendly. But Vieux Chalet's main attribute is that the place is so downright comfortable. All oyster dishes are good, as well as the shrimp with *rémoulade* sauce. Bypass the onion soup for a shot at the gumbo Creole or turtle soup with sherry. The beef is well aged, truly prime, and served with several excellent sauces, among them an oyster sauce that's a nice change of pace. The *poisson grand père* is always quite fresh, with the type of fish changing daily. The appropriate finale for a dinner at Vieux Chalet is bananas Foster, flamed tableside. With just a little imagination, you can close your eyes and pretend you're another 300 miles downriver. Reservations are required.

*Price: About $30 per person*
*Open Tues.–Sat. for dinner only; closed Sun. and Mon.*
*Accepts all major credit cards*

# WANG'S MANDARIN HOUSE
## 1183 Park Place Mall
### 901-767-0354

Wang's Mandarin House only opened in 1984, but it has quickly established itself as a local favorite, especially among those who favor highly spiced Szechuan and Mandarin fare. The decor is subdued, with burnt-orange wall coverings, brown linens, and natural wood-and-glass partitions that divide the room into smaller sections. The real color is saved for the dishes themselves, a marvelous array of Hunan, Mandarin, and Szechuan dishes. Excellent first courses include cold noodles with sesame sauce, crisp spring rolls with chili sauce, marinated beef on skewers, fiery hot-and-sour soup, and the house special soup, a flavorful blend of pork, snow peas, shrimp, scallions, and mushrooms. Among the entrées, standouts are the crispy orange-flavor beef, the "Mandarin flower basket," harvest lamb Hunan style, General Tsao's chicken, crisp whole fish, and the house special prawns with walnuts. Finish the evening with a fresh fruit plate, a feast for the eyes with fruit carved into a variety of shapes, some suggesting birds, others flowers. The dish is indicative of the entire dining experience at the Mandarin House—fresh and colorful.

*Price: About $15 per person*
*Open daily for lunch and dinner*
*Accepts all major credit cards*

# WILLINGHAM'S
## 150 Highway 72 East, Collierville, Tennessee
### 901-853-1222

Near the entrance to Willingham's sits a large cast-iron monstrosity called a Turbo-Wham cooker. It's the invention of John Willingham, the restaurant's owner and the winner of the Memphis-in-May barbecue contest in 1983 and 1984. In the Wham cooker (a shortened version of Willingham), several racks of ribs and pork shoulders hang from a rotating spit. Instead of cooking over an open flame, the meat is seared with indirect heat, which holds in the natural juices and prevents ash and soot from covering the pork's surface. According to Willingham, the Wham is the magic behind his championship performance at every cooking contest he's entered. Can the Wham turn out decent ribs and shoulder? And how! The ribs are the best I've had in any restaurant, and in Memphis that takes in a lot of real estate. What makes them unique is the clean quality of the preparation. You won't find them covered with any sticky sauce; the ribs are coated before cooking with Willingham's secret seasoning mix, and during the cooking the flavors permeate the meat, the ribs stay juicy, and the meat comes out perfectly tender. The shoulder is equally good, large pieces pulled from the bones, smoky in flavor, devoid of fat. The Wham cooker may just prove that high technology can even work its way into a corner of the barbecuing kitchen.

*Price: About $10 per person*
*Open daily for lunch and dinner*
*Accepts Visa and MasterCard*

---

# ZORBA'S
## In Park Place Mall, 1211 Park Place Center
### 901-685-6955

This small, pleasant restaurant, with tile floors, arched passageways, and a sprinkling of Greek posters and artifacts, features a varied and interesting menu. In addition to the more expected Greek standards, such as *souvlakia* and *baklava,* Zorba's offers some surprises: char-broiled red snapper and chicken breast stuffed with feta cheese. One of the better appetizers is *saganaki,* a large rectangle of *kasseri* cheese fried in butter and lemon juice. The *psari tis skaras,* char-broiled red snapper, is nicely grilled and served with a fresh-tasting tomato sauce. The *moussaka* is very moist, with the flavors of cinnamon-laced ground lamb, sliced eggplant, and *béchamel* sauce nicely blended. *Kotopita,* breast of chicken baked in a crisp, light filo pastry shell, is also recommended. Don't let the excellent *baklava* distract from some of the other dessert special-ties: *loukoumathes,* deep-fried puffs filled with yogurt and served warm with honey, or the *galaktoboureko,* a delicious rectangle of filo filled with sweet custard and served in syrup. The sticky desserts are perfect with tiny cups of thick Greek coffee.

*Price: About $15 per person*
*Open Mon.–Sat. for lunch and dinner; closed Sun.*
*Accepts all major credit cards*

# MILWAUKEE

## BY CONSTANCE DANIELL

**CONTINENTAL**
Boulevard Inn
The English Room
Grenadier's Restaurant
John Byron's
Mike & Anna's

**GERMAN**
Boulevard Inn
Karl Ratzsch's Restaurant

**HOTEL DINING ROOM**
The English Room

**ITALIAN**
Café Siciliano

**SEAFOOD**
River Lane Inn

**SERBIAN**
Three Brothers Bar &
Restaurant

**STEAKS AND CHOPS**
Sally's Steak House

It's hard to get a bad meal in Milwaukee. That may sound provincial, but happily it's true.

This is a town where the Friday night fish fry dates back more than fifty years. Where almost every corner tavern offers a respectable steak sandwich or hamburger for a very reasonable price. And where visitors are often overwhelmed by the generous portions served in restaurants—probably a throwback to a tradition of hearty, wholesome meals established by the German immigrants who were the city's first settlers.

At the same time, visitors are almost always pleasantly surprised at the warmth and friendliness they encounter here. If it's hard to get a bad meal in Milwaukee, it's nearly impossible to be treated rudely by a headwaiter.

Be that as it may, the following is a list of some of this city's fine eating establishments. In all cases, the price ranges at the high end do not include the cost of lobster or lobster tails, both of which are usually printed as "market price" on the menu.

A word about Milwaukee's Downtown. Unlike many cities, Milwaukee does not have an uptown or midtown, just, by some peculiar reasoning, a Downtown, which is located in the central, easternmost area of the city adjoining Lake Michigan.

It's the area in which most of the major hotels, stores, businesses, and restaurants are clustered. In Milwaukee's Downtown, EVERYTHING is within walking distance.

And the distances given for restaurants outside the Downtown area are not conservative estimates. In many respects, Milwaukee is very much a small town. Traffic jams are practically unheard of and it's very easy to get around using the efficient expressway system.

*Constance Daniell is a food writer and columnist for* The Milwaukee Journal.

## BOULEVARD INN
### 4300 West Lloyd Street
#### 414-445-4221

This is another of Milwaukee's beloved family restaurants, managed by brothers Gary and Mark Strothmann, youthful grandsons of the founder.

Although it's only a 12-minute drive west from Downtown Milwaukee, the restaurant manages to convey the serenity of a country inn. Large windows overlook the rolling lawns of an adjacent park and a broad boulevard. The decor is tasteful: thick carpeting, white sheers at the windows, a striking navy-and-salmon color scheme, and fresh flowers at each table create a gracious atmosphere for relaxed family dining.

The cuisine is continental plus "as much German food as Milwaukee demands," remarked Gary Strothmann. "We took off the *sauerbraten* and so many people screamed we had to put it back."

Each night there are five to six fresh fish and seafood entrées, including bay scallops and blackened redfish. Veal sweetbreads with mushrooms and shallots in champagne are a regular and popular item, as is duckling with wild rice and red cabbage. All vegetables are fresh, everything is in season. There is pleasant piano music each evening. All breads, rolls, and desserts are homemade. Don't miss Suzy's cream cheese cheesecake. Made by Mark Strothmann's wife, Suzy, the cheesecake became so popular it has taken off as a separate business.

*Price: About $10–$15 per person*
*Open daily for lunch and dinner*
*Accepts all major credit cards*

## CAFÉ SICILIANO
### In the Fox Point Shopping Center,
### 6904 North Santa Monica Boulevard
#### 414-352-5757

Back in the early thirties, right after Prohibition ended, Pop Maniaci's was a popular gathering spot for aficionados of Italian food. The restaurant, alas, along with a good part of the Third Ward, the heart of Milwaukee's Italian community, was razed some years ago to make way for an expressway. The good news is that the Maniaci family tradition continues today at Café Siciliano under the aegis of Pop's son Arthur and his wife, Rose.

Arthur mans the kitchen with the help of longtime associate chef Elaine Wofford. Together they turn out superb veal dishes, seafood, chicken *cac-*

*ciatore,* and other fine entrées in full-course meals that include *antipasto,* soup, salad, potato or pasta, Italian bread, butter, and coffee.

Recipes for the chicken *cacciatore, cannoli,* and many other Italian specialties have been retained from the days when Arthur's mother did the cooking at the old stand. Arthur Maniaci has supplemented them with fine pastas and seafood creations, such as shrimp Michelle, named for the youngest of his and Rose's eight children. (The shrimp are wrapped in *prosciutto* and baked with butter, lemon, garlic, and Italian seasonings, and served on rice or pasta.) All desserts are homemade.

A smiling Rose Maniaci acts as hostess, greeter, and waitress and fills in capably at whatever other jobs need to be done. She makes everyone—regular customers or first arrivals—feel as if they've been here before.

Designed to resemble an Italian courtyard with white stucco walls, ceramic-tile floor, and softly glowing lamplights, the restaurant has an easy, relaxed ambience. The café is a 20-minute drive from downtown. Reservations are recommended.

*Price: About $9.25–$15 per person*
*Open Mon.–Sat. for dinner only; closed Sun.*
*Accepts all major credit cards*

---

# THE ENGLISH ROOM
In the Hotel Pfister, 424 East Wisconsin Avenue
### 414-273-8222

A formal English decor with frosted glass panels, softly lit chandeliers, and tapestry-covered dining chairs create the perfect setting for the Continental cuisine and elegant service to be found here.

Dramatic tableside cooking is a hallmark, and on nights when it isn't too busy, genial and imposing maître d'hotel Frank Bonfiglio will arrive at your table at dessert time to prepare his famous *sabayon.*

Sweetbreads, rack of lamb, and a variety of veal, fresh seafood, and fish dishes are regularly featured. One or two specials are offered daily. Fresh vegetables are prepared to perfection. The wine list is exceptional, with more than 400 fine labels from which to choose. Also available are selections approved for Heart Healthy Dining by the American Heart Association. Reservations are recommended.

*Price: About $14–$22 per person*
*Open daily for lunch and dinner*
*Accepts all major credit cards*

# GRENADIER'S RESTAURANT
## 747 North Broadway
### 414-276-0747

The Grenadier's French-style dining room, lit by a replica of the glittering crystal chandelier in Empress Josephine's boudoir, affords Continental dining at its most elegant. Less formal, but equally attractive, are the glass-walled Garden Room and the Grill.

Chef-owner Knut Apitz, German born and trained, delights in creating selections tailored to diners' individual tastes. Most evenings he visits each table personally to talk with patrons about their special food interests. Visit here one year and return the next, and most likely he'll greet you by name.

Diners, in turn, are usually delighted by Apitz's culinary expertise and amiable sense of humor. "We accept all credit cards," he says, a slight smile playing on his lips, "except Sears and Penney's." Specialties are seafood—flown in from the East and West coasts and Europe—prepared along with local freshwater fish. Desserts are made in the Grenadier's kitchen.

The menu varies according to what's fresh and in season: One night it might include sautéed soft-shell crabs, delicately flavored *poussin* with *morels,* or breast of veal dressed in a raspberry sauce with fiddlehead ferns.

The restaurant's waiters have been credited by local critics as providing the best service in town. Grenadier's has a discriminating selection of nearly 100 French, German, and Italian wines. There is piano music, evenings, in the grill.

*Price: About $13–$18 per person;* dégustation *dinners to order with one or two day's notice*
*Open Mon.–Fri. for lunch and dinner; Sat. for dinner only; closed Sun.*
*Accepts all major credit cards*

# JOHN BYRON'S
## 777 East Michigan Street (*on the Galleria level of First Wisconsin Center*)
### 414-291-5220

In the eight years since it opened, John Byron's, with its spacious dining room and a view of Lake Michigan, has earned accolades from reviewers and patrons alike. Credit goes to owner John Burns and Chef Sandy D'Amato, two young, enthusiastic men who collaborate to keep the Continental menu innovative and ever-changing. Fresh seafood flown in daily ranges from salmon, sturgeon, and sole to tuna, swordfish, and shark, always prepared imaginatively by the creative D'Amato. Sauces utilizing *cèpes, morels, chanterelles,* and other exotic mushrooms in season enhance the seafood entrées and other daily specials, such as rack of lamb, fresh pheasant, and marinated grilled duck breast.

Included in *The Wine Spectator* newspaper as one of this country's Top 100 wine lists, the restaurant's wine cellar offers more than 180 wines, priced just a dollar or two above retail costs to encourage patrons to drink wine with their meals. A classical music quartet—harp, violin, flute, and guitar—provides pleasant background music through the dinner hours. Reservations are recommended.

*Price: About $14–$20 per person*
*Open Mon.–Fri. for lunch; Mon.–Sat. for dinner; closed Sun.*
*Accepts all major credit cards*

---

# KARL RATZSCH'S RESTAURANT
## 320 East Mason Street
### 414-276-2720

"Milwaukee's Famous Old World Restaurant" is the slogan of this fine old enterprise that specializes in German–Hungarian cuisine. The Hungarian influence stems from Mama Ratzsch, as she was fondly known, who, with her husband, opened the restaurant in the late twenties.

The restaurant boasts a courtly charm, enhanced by burnished wood paneling and a collection of handpainted plates and sparkling antique glassware and beer steins, displayed throughout the dining rooms. A string trio plies diners with Viennese melodies every evening. Schmaltzy, but in this setting, delightful. Currently managed by the personable Kelly Ratzsch (Karl August Ratzsch III), grandson of the founders, the restaurant offers a wide selection of hearty German favorites. There's *Wiener Schnitzel,* of course, but my personal preferences are goose shanks with dressing and a marvelous dark brown gravy and planked whitefish piped with snowy mashed potatoes. For a light, after-the-theater supper, try the wonderful, puffy German pancake sprinkled with powdered sugar and served with applesauce.

Apple *strudel* and Viennese chocolate torte, made from the recipes of Mama Ratzsch, are popular desserts.

The wine list is extensive—some 350 labels including a very good selection of German and French wines, and some good American wines as well.

*Price: About $12–$20 per person*
*Open daily for lunch and dinner*
*Accepts all major credit cards*

# MIKE & ANNA'S
## 1978 South 8 Street
### 414-643-0072

This small, trendy dining spot in an unpretentious white frame building on Milwaukee's near South Side (7 minutes from Downtown) opened to critical raves four years ago. The applause hasn't stopped yet.

Owner Anthony Harvey, who grew up on the East Coast and served his food apprenticeship in restaurants there, describes the menu as "California cuisine with a bit of *nouvelle.*"

Sample entrées: rack of lamb *en croûte* suffed with *morels, shiitake* and *chanterelles,* served with *sauce Choron;* duck breast with hazelnut-raspberry sauce; and fresh tuna, sautéed lightly and dressed with a *beurre rouge.* About half the menu is fish or shellfish. Breast of pheasant, quail, and other game birds are offered when available.

Sourdough bread and desserts are made fresh daily on the premises. Chocolate decadence, a flourless chocolate cake, and chocolate cheesecake are two popular selections.

The color scheme is maroon and silver. Maroon tablecloths are covered with sheets of white drawing paper accompanied by a box of crayons so patrons can color as they cocktail. The wine list is extensive, with lots of California labels, a good number of French, and a few German. Ten varietals can be ordered by the glass. Reservations are recommended.

*Price: About $9–$17 per person*
*Open daily for dinner only*
*Accepts all major credit cards*

# RIVER LANE INN
## 4313 West River Lane
### 414-354-1995

The menu at the River Lane Inn is chalked on a blackboard, enabling the chef to utilize whatever fresh ingredients are available at this restaurant known almost exclusively for its fine seafood and fish selections. Creole–Cajun cooking is also featured, resulting in a blackened blackfish so popular it has become a permanent offering.

Owner Jim Marks describes his restaurant's cooking style as "basically good American cuisine with an emphasis on seafood." There's a lobster boil on Wednesday nights: whole live Maine lobster, salad, roll, vegetable, and potato. On Wednesday nights, understandably, the place is jammed.

There's a nice selection of wines by the glass, both varietal and generic, with emphasis, given the restaurant's focus on seafood, on the dry whites.

*Price: About $10–$15 per person*
*Open Mon.–Fri. for lunch and dinner; Sat. for dinner only; closed Sun.*
*Accepts all major credit cards*

---

# SALLY'S STEAK HOUSE
## In the Knickerbocker Hotel, 1028 East Juneau Avenue
### 414-272-5363

Actor Paul Newman comes here when he's in town. So do racecar driver Mario Andretti, actress Shelley Winters, local sports figures and visiting coaches, managers, and players. They come here for the same reasons that the less famous do: The food is terrific, the drinks are hefty (at least 2 ounces of spirits each), the prices are right, and the place swings. It's fun.

In the latter respect the atmosphere reflects the vivacious personality of owner Sally Papia, who started the restaurant twenty-three years ago as a prime steak and chop house. A whopping 26-ounce porterhouse, buried under a mound of Sally's famous French fried onion rings, is still a popular entrée.

As times and food tastes changed, so did Sally, introducing a variety of seafood dishes and such Italian specialties as a 4½-pound duck stuffed with chestnuts and Italian sausage. Other popular items: Sicilian steaks, chicken *Vesuvio,* and *spiedini.* The fish fry on Friday nights is a terrific bargain: homemade Italian soup or clam chowder, fried perch or cod, salad, dessert and bread and butter, for $5.95.

The atmosphere is warm and friendly. Beribboned bouquets of pink- and rose-colored silk flowers are everywhere, providing a bright foil for vaulted leaded-glass windows and gleaming wine racks. California and imported premium house wines are available by the glass or carafe.

*Price: About $6–$17 per person*
*Open Mon.–Fri. for lunch and dinner; Sat. for dinner only; closed Sun.*
*Accepts all major credit cards*

# THREE BROTHERS BAR & RESTAURANT
## 2414 South St. Clair Street
### 414-481-7530

Don't let the linoleum tile floors, jukebox, and chrome tables fool you; Three Brothers offers as fine a Serbian cuisine as can be found anywhere. And the prices are extremely reasonable. Housed in a Victorian landmark building (it's on the National Register of Historic Places) the restaurant looks just as it must have when it was built by the Jos. Schlitz Brewing Co. as a family saloon back in 1897.

Purchased in the mid-fifties by Serbian immigrants Milun Radicevich and his wife, Milunka, who turned it into a restaurant, the enterprise is now in the capable hands of Branko Radicevich, one of the founders' three sons for whom the restaurant is named. Branko Radicevich has wisely retained the unspoiled Serbian flavor of the restaurant, along with all the family recipes his mother brought from her village.

Hers is the recipe used for *burek*—a layered creation of feather-light, paper-thin pastry baked with spinach, beef, or cheese fillings, as well as the recipes for roast suckling pig, stuffed veal breast, and a host of other Serbian delights. And hers, most assuredly, are the recipes for homemade desserts of strudel, *palachinka* (Serbian *crêpes*), and chocolate-walnut torte. A specialty is homemade bread with a goat's milk spread that is similar to Boursin cheese but contains less cholesterol.

There's a modest wine list of good, not great, wines. About 10 minutes from downtown Milwaukee on the city's near South Side, but call for reservations and directions: The location is out of the way and somewhat hard to find.

*Price: About $8.50–$10.50 per person*
*Open Tues.–Sun. for dinner only; closed Mon.*
*No credit cards accepted*

# MINNEAPOLIS/ ST. PAUL

## By Jeremy Iggers and Karin Winegar

**AMERICAN**
Peter's Grill

**BARBECUE**
Rudolph's Bar-B-Que

**CAMBODIAN**
Angkor

**ECLECTIC**
Faegre's
The Fifth Season
The Harbor View Café
Primavera
Rupert's American Café and
Nightclub

**FRENCH**
The 510 Restaurant
The New French Café

**GERMAN**
Black Forest Inn

**INDIAN/AFGHAN**
Caravan Serai (St. Paul)

**ITALIAN**
Coco Lezzone

**OPEN LATE**
Rudolph's Bar-B-Que

**SCANDINAVIAN**
Ernie's Scandinavian Restaurant

**SEAFOOD**
Café Kardamena

**SRI LANKAN**
Sri Lanka Curry House

**SUBURBAN**
The Harbor View Café (Pepin)

**VEGETARIAN**
Café Kardamena

**VIETNAMESE**
Matin

In spite of Minnesota's strong Scandinavian heritage, real Scandinavian cuisine is a rarity in these parts. Most Minnesotans seem more partial to trendy eateries like T.G.I. Friday's, mass-produced "Mexican" food like El Torito's, or Americanized versions of Italian. In this respect, they are probably no different from most of their fellow Americans, coast-to-coast. Szechuan made some inroads, but hot spice is anathema to most Minnesotans, who prefer such old-time Cantonese restaurants as The Nankin, a downtown Minneapolis institution. This is still meat and potatoes country, by and large, and for steak lovers, the top spots include the very elegant Murray's Restaurant and Lounge (26 South 6th Street, 612-339-0909), and the less-elegant Lindey's Prime Steak House (3610 Snelling Avenue North, Arden Hills, 612-633-9813).

On the other hand, the Twin Cities do have a substantial nucleus of more adventuresome diners, who patronize the growing number of ethnic restaurants. Minnesota's collection of exotic restaurants by now includes no less than seventeen Vietnamese restaurants, plus at least three Thai establishments, one Afghan, one Rumanian, one Czech, one Polish, one West Indian, two East Indian, two Ethiopian, one Sri Lankan (reportedly the only one in the United States), one Laotian, and one Cambodian. And in the last few years, a new generation of very stylish Yuppie restaurants have sprung up, offering a creative and eclectic blend of French, Italian, and *nouvelle* American cuisine.

*Jeremy Iggers is restaurant critic for the* Minneapolis Star and Tribune *and author of* The Joy of Cheesecake. *Karin Winegar is former restaurant critic for the* Minneapolis Star and Tribune, *where she is currently a feature writer. She is also author of* Let's Eat Out, A Twin Cities Restaurant Guide *(1983).*

---

# ANGKOR
## 2219 Central Avenue, N.E., Minneapolis
### 612-781-3116

Cambodian cuisine bears a strong resemblance to Vietnamese. You can probably find better renditions of Southeast Asian cooking elsewhere in the area, but Angkor's cooking is good enough to be enjoyable, and there are a few items on the menu that you probably can't find anywhere else in America.

Stick to items on the Cambodian side of the menu—a single page offering spring rolls, noodle and rice dishes—the rest is modified, unimpressive Chinese stuff. But what makes Angkor worth a visit is the hauntingly beautiful Cambodian music, performed live on Friday and Saturday nights before a *trompe l'oeil* backdrop of Angkor Wat itself.

*Price: About $10 per person*
*Open Mon.–Sat. for lunch and dinner; closed Sun.*
*Accepts Visa and MasterCard*

## BLACK FOREST INN
### 1 East 26 Street, Minneapolis
### 612-872-0812

The Black Forest is rightfully renowned for hefty portions of heavy German food and its pleasant, popular outdoor courtyard. Sitting around the fountain, under the grape arbor, over glass steins of beer is one of the best ways to while away a Minnesota summer's night.

Gigantic servings of onion rings are a favorite, and the *Wiener Schnitzel* with applesauce and potato pancakes, *bratwurst,* smoked pork chops, deep-fried sauerkraut, cheese balls, and outsized portions of hot apple *strudel* with ice cream are recommended.

The Black Forest is virtually the school cafeteria for students and artists from the neighboring Minneapolis Institute of Art and Minneapolis College of Art and Design. The waitresses are some of the best in the trade; warm and efficient and a tad artsy themselves, but not intrusive about it.

*Price: About $12 per person*
*Open daily for lunch and dinner*
*Accepts all major credit cards*

## CAFÉ KARDAMENA
### 300 First Avenue North, Minneapolis
### 612-342-9230

Imagine a Japanese-vegetarian-Greek-macrobiotic menu interlaced with New Wave sensibilities and you have the odd little Café Kardamena. Descendant of an early seventies cooperative, it is now the Twin Cities' answer to Greens, San Francisco's chic vegetarian haven. It is also the answer to where the leaders of the holistic health community and its practitioners eat: Rolfers, chiropractors, artists, musicians, writers, filmmakers, the well-traveled, the well-heeled, and those with high dietary principles all gather in this one-room café.

Service has improved over the years, rising from petulant and crabby to merely silent and a bit slow. The decor is as always, simply natural brick, a big window, pressed metal ceiling, and fresh flowers on the table.

But the food is the draw: smoked fish and pasta salad, fresh rainbow trout prepared different ways daily, *soba* noodle salad with spicy ginger *tahini* sauce, Indian cold salad plate, Vietnamese-style fresh halibut, black bean soup, wild rice vegetable soup, chilled beet orange soup, Greek salad, *miso pâté,* and *tofu* croquettes. Even the desserts are healthy but tasty: tarts, apple-almond *kanten,* and chocolate carrot cake. Fruit juices, herbal teas, and decaffeinated coffees are offered as well as a few wines—California, French, and Minnesota—and beer. The cobble-floored outdoor patio to the rear is ideal for summer dining.

*Price: About $10 per person*
*Open Mon.–Sat. for lunch and dinner; closed Sun.*
*No credit cards accepted*

---

# CARAVAN SERAI
## 2046 Pinehurst Avenue, St. Paul
### 612-690-1935

The Caravan Serai is renowned for the homey quality of its cuisine and the cordiality of its owner, Abdul Khayoum, who introduced the cooking of his native Afghanistan to the Twin Cities over a decade ago.

The Afghan appetizer assortment contains a memorable mix of flavors, textures, and tastes—mint, eggplant, yogurt, minced pork, and crisp pastry. And the hearty Afghan-style bean-and-noodle soup. The entrées are divided among Indian and Afghan foods, including *tandoori* chicken, curried shrimp, *rotis, nan, morgh kabob,* and lamb with pomegranate sauce.

Seating is at tables or on cushions on the floor. There are limited wine and beer choices, but the best beverage (not on the menu) is *sheer chai*—a blend of cardamom, tea, honey, and steamed milk.

*Price: About $10 per person*
*Open Mon.–Fri. for lunch and dinner; Sat. and Sun. for dinner only*
*Accepts all major credit cards*

# COCOLEZZONE
## 5410 Wayzata Boulevard, Golden Valley
### 612-544-4014

CocoLezzone (Italian for "cook" and "person of filthy habits") is handsome, affordable, accessible from downtown, and one of the more authentic attempts at Italian cuisine to be found in these parts. This is not truckdriver Italian with great mounds of red sauce and warty-looking meatballs, but rather *nuova cucina:* clean, simple, and light. Go for the appetizer tray, the melon with *prosciutto,* small pizzas grilled in a wood-burning oven (especially recommended are those with wild mushrooms, four different cheeses, or fresh *mozzarella* and basil), chicken breast grilled with basil, *pesto, sorbetto,* and *gelato,* as well as classic Italian pastries. Linger in the tasteful, bright room where marble floors flow naturally beneath Hundertwasser prints, silk flowers, and brass fixtures.

*Price: About $15 per person*
*Open Mon.–Fri. for lunch and dinner; Sat. for dinner only; closed Sun.*
*Accepts all major credit cards*

# ERNIE'S SCANDINAVIAN RESTAURANT
## 5200 Minnehaha Avenue, Minneapolis
### 612-721-3610

Ya, you betcha. Ernie Skage, formerly of Trondheim, Norway, finally realized his boyhood dream—to come to America and open a Scandinavian restaurant. This is not Scandinavian cuisine in the grand style of the Grand Hotel in Oslo—Ernie has been known to pile up his open-faced sandwiches on Wonder bread—but it's a lot of fun. Ernie has a villainous waxed mustache and a musical Nörsk accent, and when he's in a good mood, he performs magic tricks for the customers. His pickled herring is first rate, and so is the lobster bisque. Sundays, Ernie puts out a big brunch spread with nearly everything on the menu, including Swedish meatballs and roast lamb, several different kinds of herring, prepared salads, and more. On Friday nights, when the weather allows, Ernie puts out a Viking feast complete with roast pig, roast lamb, *lefser* (Norwegian potato *tortillas*), homemade ice cream, and more. Be sure to take note of the decor: The walls are lined with orange shag carpeting and there's a wonderful mural of a fjord on the way to the basement restrooms.

*Price: About $12 per person*
*Open Mon.–Sat. for lunch and dinner; Sunday for brunch only*
*No credit cards accepted*

# FAEGRE'S
### 430 First Avenue North, Minneapolis
#### 612-332-3515

Faegre's perches on a corner opposite the Loon Café, the Twin Cities' hottest downtown singles bar, and the traffic between the two on a weekend night is furious. The knowledgeable will eat at Faegre's, where the chefs know from seasoning and offer an inventive menu of New American cuisine, and then adjourn to the Loon afterwards.

Floor-to-ceiling window glass allows a view of the passing parade; otherwise Faegre's only notable physical features are a custom porcelain tile bar front and the works of local artists on the walls. The hard surfaces make the room noisy, the seating is a bit cramped, and the floor plan is awkward.

Regulars return for the fish soup with *rouille,* Caesar salads in two sizes, mounds of thin, elegant French fries with *béarnaise* sauce, Brazilian black bean soup, chicken and shrimp bisque, assorted *pâtés,* chicken liver and apple *mousse, fritto misto* with tomato and herb sauce, Chinese chicken salad, crab with lime and *cilantro* mayonnaise, *fettuccine, osso buco,* halibut baked in olive oil, garlic, chilies, and oregano, *gâteau marjolaine,* and homemade strawberry ice cream.

*Price: About $15 per person*
*Open Mon.–Sat. for lunch and dinner; Sun. for dinner only*
*Accepts all major credit cards*

# THE FIFTH SEASON
### In the Amfac Hotel, 30 South 7 Street, Minneapolis
#### 612-349-4022

Dinner at the Season is a bit like dining in a plush greenhouse: A sweep of skylight floods the south side of the room with light; the fresh flowers, floral-painted china, and fern-print carpet add to the effect. Because of its location, price, and lack of visibility from the street, customers tend to be guests at the hotel or businessfolk on an expense account.

It's always the season for regional American cuisine at the Fifth Season: meaning *ballotine* of Maine lobster, an appetizer salad concocted with mixed greens and frogs legs bathed in vinaigrette, cream of mussel soup with saffron, Colorado rack of lamb, salmon fillet with *morel* sauce, Wisconsin veal chop in *morel* sauce, and an artfully assembled appetizer—breast of Wisconsin duckling in raspberry *mousse* garnished with gem-like bits of orange and strawberries. More attention is given to visual beauty than substance among the desserts, where only the chocolate rum torte shines.

*Price: About $30 per person*
*Open Mon.–Fri. for lunch and dinner; Sat. for dinner only; closed Sun.*
*Accepts all major credit cards*

---

## THE 510 RESTAURANT
### 510 Groveland Avenue, Minneapolis
#### 612-874-6440

Located in the stately hushed banquet room of an old grande dame of an apartment building near the Guthrie Theatre and Walker Art Center, The 510 is still the Twin Cities' chief claim to gourmet dining.

It's a dignified, even a bit intimidating, setting, with textiles and carpets of soothing grays and ivories, fresh flowers, and Chippendale chairs. Slim, knowledgeable young waiters glide among the tables dealing out a feast whose only fault is a tendency to be overly rich: wild mushroom tart with walnut brandy sauce, assorted *terrines,* grilled breast of chicken with cucumbers, sorrel, and *crème fraîche,* rack of lamb with roast garlic sauce, *médaillons* of pork tenderloin, and roast sliced loin of veal in tomato-and-marjoram *beurre blanc.* The dessert *soufflés* (Grand Marnier, chocolate, or fresh fruit) are a house specialty and the homemade ice creams and *sorbets* are whipped up in some novel flavors.

Owner Gordon Schutte, who owns more one-of-a-kind restaurants than any other restaurateur in town, has a passion for fine wines. As a result, The 510 boasts one of the largest wine lists in the state, with emphasis on California vintages.

Clientele includes Old Money, new but tasteful money, local author Judith Guest, members of the Pillsbury clan, world-class musicians, such as Neville Mariner and Henry Charles Smith, and couples who have scrimped to go somewhere special on their anniversaries.

*Price: About $30 per person*
*Open Mon.–Fri. for lunch and dinner; Sat. for dinner only; closed Sun.*
*Accepts all major credit cards*

---

## THE HARBOR VIEW CAFÉ
### First and Main streets, Pepin, Wisconsin
#### 715-442-3893

Although the Harbor View lies 80 miles south of the Twin Cities along the bluffs of Lake Pepin, the food is worth the drive, and, on a spring, summer, or fall day, so is the drive. Roll down on the Minnesota side of the Mississippi River and return on the Wisconsin farmland side or vice versa.

The cuisine is as honest, fresh, and enjoyable as its setting, an 1858 clapboard storefront tavern (facing the Pepin yacht marina) with tin ceiling and pine front bar, ceiling fans, seven booths with odd-lot chairs, and a plate rail packed with old books.

The menu posted on blackboard behind the bar lists such pleasures as *cioppino,* baby coho salmon stuffed with scallops or shrimp and baked *en papillote,* broiled shark, *lasagne San Marco,* fresh squid stuffed with pistachio *pesto,* Singapore noodles, *fettuccine Papalina,* and Hunan pork with Chinese pickles. There's a surprisingly good wine list. Desserts are equally good, if a bit on the rich side. Look for Georgia walnut pie, caramel *flan,* chocolate buttercream pie, hazelnut cheesecake, bittersweet chocolate torte, and strawberry amaretto torte. Arrive early, say before 6 P.M., or face a line of middle-aged motorboaters and houseboaters who make it white-shoes-and-matching-belt heaven at twilight.

*Price: About $15 per person*
*Open Thurs.–Mon. for lunch and dinner; closed Tues. and Wed. and from*
*sometime in December until March*
*No credit cards accepted*

---

# MATIN
## 416 First Avenue North, Minneapolis
### 612-340-0150

It's hard to pick a favorite Vietnamese restaurant; there are a lot of very good ones in the Twin Cities. But Matin offers a more extensive menu than most, plus a wine-and-beer license, and its warehouse district location is within walking distance of the downtown hotels. Be sure to order the superb egg rolls Imperial, made of rice paper stuffed with pork, rice noodles, and shreds of carrot, and served with a dipping sauce made with *nuoc mam,* the salty fish-based sauce that the Vietnamese use in place of soy sauce. Other best bets include the very spicy Imperial chicken and the curried beef in spicy coconut gravy. Evenings only Matin serves a Vietnamese beef *fondue* cooked at table-side.

*Price: About $10 per person*
*Open Mon.–Fri. for lunch and dinner; Sat. for dinner only; closed Sun.*
*Accepts Visa and MasterCard*

# THE NEW FRENCH CAFÉ
## 128 North 4 Street, Minneapolis
### 612-338-3790

The earliest outpost of *nouvelle cuisine* in the Twin Cities, The New French has an intelligent wine list, sophisticated cookery, and a power (in the arts world, in particular) lunch clientele.

Breakfast is overpriced; the café's minimalist decor—white, flat surfaces—gives the room a case of bad acoustics, and the service can be chilly. But the café redeems itself by the splendid execution of meals such as lamb chops in green peppercorn sauce, filet of fresh salmon in white wine and cream, shallots, and saffron, rack of lamb with zinfandel sauce and baby vegetables, salmon with pomegranate cream sauce, fresh game specials, halibut poached with vermouth-lime-cream sauce, homemade *terrines* and *pâtés,* a wild mushroom appetizer, raspberry Bavarian creams, plum tart, and *reine de Saba,* puff pastry filled with blackberries and whipped cream. The New French makes its own ice creams and *sorbets* with stellar examples in their *espresso*–chocolate chip ice cream and mango *sorbet.*

The wine list, which strongly favors California and France, changes four times a year. Some of the best bar wines by the glass can be found here.
*Price: About $25–$30 per person for the four-course price-fixed meal; $35 for* à la carte; *reduced-choice and -price late-night menu is available Fri. and Sat.*
*night from 9:30 P.M. to midnight*
*Open daily for lunch and dinner*
*Accepts all major credit cards*

# PETER'S GRILL
## 116 South 9 Street (*in the Foshay Tower*), Minneapolis
### 612-333-1981

After 66 years in the same location, Minneapolis' oldest restaurant recently moved across the street, to the Foshay Tower, but the menu and Art Deco interior have been faithfully preserved. Only the prices have changed, but not much. Peter's is one of the few outposts of old-fashioned American cooking here in the Heartland—excellent homemade vegetable soup, roast chicken with stuffing and real whipped potatoes, and a world-class green apple pie. Last time we checked, the Wednesday night chicken dinner special was $2.25. At lunchtime, you'll be lucky to find a booth or a seat at the counter.
*Price: About $5 per person*
*Open Mon.–Sat. for lunch and dinner; closed Sun.*
*No credit cards accepted*

# PRIMAVERA
International Market Square, 275 Market Street, Minneapolis
**612-339-8000**

The former Munsingwear factory and warehouse has been stylishly remodeled to a design wholesalers' headquarters, and Primavera occupies its airy atrium. The cuisine is light, sensuous, and surprisingly affordable, given the ingredients, formal service, and setting: Some of the dishes include delicate shrimp *flan* with carrots and leeks, sautéed duck livers with poached pear, port wine, and shallot sauce, grilled lobster salad with avocado, papaya, and lime and mint vinaigrette, smoked chicken breast with tomato-basil vinaigrette, Wisconsin veal stuffed with Minnesota *morels* and spinach in rosemary-butter sauce, broiled salmon with ginger butter and lime butter sauce, grilled sea scallops on braised spinach with cabernet butter sauce, puff pastry stuffed with white chocolate *mousse* in raspberry *coulis,* and hazelnut meringue with fruit *gelati* and fruit purée. The clientele leans heavily toward decorators and designers —all dressed to perfection. Service is often unnecessarily slow. Primavera is, unfortunately, open for lunch only on weekdays, while reserving each evening for private group dinners.

*Price: About $12 per person*
*Open Mon.–Fri. for lunch only; closed Sat. and Sun.*
*Accepts all major credit cards*

# RUDOLPH'S BAR-B-QUE
1933 Lyndale Avenue South, Minneapolis
**612-871-8969**

No greasy rib joint this. Rudolph's 1920s Art Deco design and copious hot ribs have them standing in lines down the block. Well they should: Rudolph's has won first prize for "Best Ribs in America" two years out of three at the National Rib Cook-Off in Cleveland, Ohio (1983 and 1985). Menu items take their names from movie stars of the twenties and thirties—John Wayne, Theda Bara, and Rudolph Valentino—but the attractions at the tables are the chewy, hickory-smoked ribs and chicken, coarse, oniony coleslaw, French fries, and watery corn on the cob. Open late every night.

*Price: About $10 per person*
*Open daily for lunch and dinner*
*No credit cards accepted*

# RUPERT'S AMERICAN CAFÉ AND NIGHTCLUB

## 5410 Wayzata Boulevard, Golden Valley
### 612-544-4993

Mesquite grilling and Art Nouveau decor are fads all over, but Rupert's offers much-better-than-average renditions of both. And the kitchen is a solid one: The assorted steaks, chops, and nightly fish specials all seem to have a little more flavor and character than the usual, as do the barbecued offerings, which are slow-cooked in an oakwood smoker. That's all pretty basic stuff, but the kitchen also turns out some more ambitious offerings, such as smoked scallops with *fettuccine,* cream, garlic, fresh basil, and golden caviar and a spicy Mott Street chicken. The adjoining dress-up nightclub draws big crowds, especially on weekends, so dinner reservations are strongly recommended.

*Price: About $25 per person*
*Open daily for breakfast, lunch, and dinner*
*Accepts American Express, Visa, and MasterCard*

# SRI LANKA CURRY HOUSE

## 2821 Hennepin Avenue, Minneapolis
### 612-871-2400

The presiding genius here is owner-chef-entertainer-beauty Heather Balasuriya, who brought her spicy hot native cuisine to Minnesota almost a decade ago.

To be a customer is to become an addict and inevitably a friend: On weekends, chef Balasuriya pops out of the kitchen between dishes to grab a microphone and to join the duo on the small stage. On weekdays, she likes to greet guests and spend a minute at their tables.

Warning! Order mild the first time and medium on the second visit only if you dare. Curried chicken wings, vegetable *roti* with shrimp, beef *mallung,* whole curried lobster, curried shrimp or fresh fish, both combination platters —in fact, everything on the menu, *except* the meat curry at the bottom of the menu—are recommended. Superb, rich woodapple, mango, or jackfruit creams for dessert.

*Price: About $12 per person*
*Open Tues.–Fri. for lunch and dinner; Sat. and Sun. for dinner only;*
*closed Mon.*
*Accepts all major credit cards*

# NEW ORLEANS

## BY THOMAS G. FITZMORRIS

**BREAKFAST**
　Café du Monde
　Morning Call
　Mother's

**BRUNCH**
　Brennan's

**CAFÉ**
　Café du Monde
　Morning Call

**CHINESE**
　Fortune Gardens
　Peking
　Trey Yuen

**CONTINENTAL**
　Sazerac

**CREOLE/CAJUN**
　Antoine's
　Arnaud's
　Bouligny
　Caribbean Room
　Christian's
　Commander's Palace

**CREOLE/CAJUN**
　Copeland's
　Delmonico's
　Galatoire's
　K–Paul's Louisiana Kitchen
　La Cuisine
　LeRuth's
　Mr. B's

**DELICATESSEN**
　Martin Wine Cellar Deli

**ECLECTIC**
　Clancy's
　Gautreau's
　Indulgence
　Jonathan
　Upperline

**FAMILY RESTAURANT**
　Bozo's
　Delmonico
　Wise Cafeteria

**FAST FOOD**
Camellia Grill
Central Grocery
Mother's
Parasol's

**FRENCH**
Crozier's
Henri
Le Château
Les Continents
Versailles

**GERMAN**
Willy Coln's Chalet

**HAMBURGERS/HOT DOGS**
Bud's Broiler
Camellia Grill
Lee's Old Fashioned
   Hamburgers

**HOTEL DINING ROOM**
Caribbean Room
Grill Room
Henri
Les Continents
Rib Room
Sazerac

**ICE CREAM**
Angelo Brocato

**INDIAN**
Keswany's

**ITALIAN**
La Riviera
La Trattoria Roma
Lenfant's
Mosca's
Occhipinti's
Ristorante Pastore

**ITALIAN**
Toney's Spaghetti House
Tony Angello's

**JAPANESE**
Shogun

**KOREAN**
Genghis Khan

**MEXICAN**
Castillo's
El Patio

**NIGHTCLUB/RESTAURANT**
Blue Room

**OPEN LATE**
Café du Monde
Morning Call

**PIZZA**
Pizza Shack

**SEAFOOD**
Acme Oyster House
Bozo's
Bruning's
Casamento's

**STEAKS AND CHOPS**
Charlie's
Crescent City Steak House
Ruth's Chris Steak House

**SUBURBAN**
Del Frisco's (Gretna)
Le Château (Gretna)
Morning Call (Metairie)
Mosca's (Waggaman)
Pizza Shack (Metairie)
Ruth's Chris Steak House
   (Metairie)

**THAI**
Mai Tai

**WINE BAR/RESTAURANT**
Flagons

**UNIQUE PROPERTIES**
Café du Monde
Central Grocery
Mother's
Parasol's

**YUGOSLAVIAN**
Drago's

Down near the wide end of the Mississippi River, the citizens of New Orleans and the rest of southern Louisiana cook and enjoy what is arguably America's greatest regional cuisine. In the city it's called Creole and purveyed in almost every restaurant, even the ethnic ones. In the surrounding bayou country the word for the food is Cajun, and you'll find it mostly in home kitchens. And while one can easily start an argument by saying that Creole and Cajun are the same thing, they are certainly much more like each other than like anything else.

So what *is* Creole-Cajun food? Like all other wide-ranging cuisines, it's hard to define, but a key characteristic is *more:* more pepper, more salt, more oils, and, above all, more flavor. Creole–Cajun food has an intensity that leaves no doubt that you've had something to eat.

New Orleans food owes a lot of its distinction to its raw materials. The city is surrounded by some of the world's richest breeding grounds for seafood, particularly of the crustacean variety. Three varieties of shrimp, blue crabs in hard and soft shells, and crawfish are among the best of their kind in the world, and their conveniently staggered seasons keep seafood lovers happy. Superb oysters are available in such abundance that figuring out new things to do with them is a full-time task in restaurants. Speckled trout (a saltwater fish) and its cousin the redfish (a variety of bass) are the finny friends of choice, although there are many other varieties available fresh.

During the last five years or so, there has been a major redefinition of Creole-Cajun cooking in New Orleans. It was long overdue: A lot of kitchens and ideas were getting pretty tired. The principal upshot is that the food has been lightened up considerably and better ingredients are being used, while the distinctive flavor barrage remains. Many enthusiastic new chefs have appeared and everybody seems to be taking Creole–Cajun food more seriously.

The vogue for indigenous American cuisine has brought Creole–Cajun into a national prominence it has never before had. But take it from one who loves the stuff and tries it wherever he goes: The real thing can only be had in New Orleans.

*Thomas G. Fitzmorris is the publisher of* The New Orleans Menu, *a monthly critical review of New Orleans dining.*

---

## ACME OYSTER HOUSE
### In the French Quarter, 724 Iberville Street
#### 504–523–8928

Here is a classic old oyster bar, right to the marble top which you walk up to and ask for a dozen raw. While the man begins opening them, get a Dixie beer from the side bar and, if you want to fit in, make a sauce of catsup, horseradish, and hot sauce. However, the Acme's oysters are easily fine enough to be eaten *au naturel.* There are sandwiches at tables, but oysters are what you should be eating.

*Price: Oysters are about $4.50 per dozen*
*Open Mon.–Sat. for lunch only; closed Sun.*
*Accepts no credit cards*

---

## ANGELO BROCATO
### 214 North Carrollton Avenue   504–486–1465
### In French Quarter, 537 St. Ann   504–525–9676

This is an authentic Italian *gelateria,* in its third generation of manufacturing the definitive local versions of *spumone,* lemon ice, *terrancino, cannoli,* and a host of other Italian confections. The stuff is made at the Mid-City location, but both parlors are pleasant and old-fashioned in atmosphere and operation. The *cappuccino* is good, too.

*Price: About $10 per person*
*Open daily*
*Accepts no credit cards*

# ANTOINE'S

In the French Quarter, 713 St. Louis Street
504-581-4422

Antoine's, founded in 1840, is the oldest restaurant in New Orleans (one of the oldest in the world under one family's ownership), and still one of the most influential. A host of classic Creole dishes were first realized here, and they are still the order of the day. The kitchen works in the old, rather heavy style; almost every dish begins with a roux of butter and flour. While it's chic among locals to disdain Antoine's, everybody eats here once in a while—especially when showing off the town to visitors. They begin with oysters, either the unique spinach-less Rockefellers (and who's to say they're wrong —Antoine's invented the dish) or the terrific fried oysters Foch with their irresistible thick brown Colbert sauce (which is also good on other seafood). When crawfish are in season (roughly Halloween to Memorial Day) they also make a fine *etouffée*. Beyond those things, avoid seafood as an entrée and stick with the superb meat and fowl dishes. Tenderloin beef in a choice of shapes is accompanied by some great sauces, the best of which are the *marchand de vin* (a marrow-enriched red wine affair) and *Medicis* (a brown sauce with bell pepper). Almost absurdly rich but great anyway is chicken *Rochambeau,* sautéed and slathered with the restaurant's weird, lemony *béarnaise* and an almost Chinese-style slightly-sweet brown sauce.

The toasty loaves of French bread are the best in town. *Soufflée* potatoes —thin, fried, and puffed up like balloons—are as tasty as they are interesting. And the coffee is a fine example of one of New Orleans' greatest joys. There's only one good dessert, but it's glorious: baked Alaska, a core of ice cream covered with meringue. Be sure to order it at the beginning of the meal.

However, this just barely scratches the surface of the 138-dish menu, all in French with no explanations. This is why regulars insist on being served by "their" waiter, who in addition to putting together combinations to order gets them into the restaurant through the back door. I would instead advise you to go to Antoine's at lunch. Although the menu and prices are the same (not cheap), the food and service are better because the place isn't mobbed.

There is much ado about which room is the best; the preferred one is the dark, Germanic Large Annex, although the front room with its mirrors and bright lights is nice by day. After dining, take a walk around; the place could be turned into a museum with few changes. And get a load of the wine cellar, a very good one with more than 35,000 bottles.

*Price: About $25 per person*
*Open Mon.–Sat. for lunch and dinner; closed Sun.*
*Accepts all major credit cards*

# ARNAUD'S
## In the French Quarter, 813 Bienville Street
### 504-523-5433

This sixty-year-old restaurant, considered to be the city's best in the thirties and forties, took a long downward slide until it was grandly restored in 1978. The new proprietors had the good taste to retain the look of the place, with its tile floors, wall of beveled-glass windows, and ceiling fans. Better still, they kept the best of Arnaud's distinctive cooking and filled out the rest of the long menu with more up-to-date stuff. All of it succeeds. Kick the meal off with shrimp Arnaud, the best version of New Orleans-style shrimp *rémoulade,* with its ruddy, mustardy cold sauce. Also good are the *escargots en croûte,* the assortment of baked oysters, and the soups, particularly the shrimp bisque and oysters stewed in cream.

Arnaud's most famous entrée is its trout *meunière,* but that has fallen on hard times. Instead, get the pretty and tasty pompano in pastry, or pompano with crab meat. The poultry selections include a wonderful Cornish hen stuffed with *pâté* and a quail in a light white wine sauce. Good beef: *tournedos Charlemond* has an artichoke, a good *béarnaise,* and a mushroom.

The best dessert is a premier version of a New Orleans specialty: bread pudding. This one is cinnamony and custardy, and will show disbelievers why the dish is the city's favorite dessert. Good rich coffee.

*Price: About $25 per person*
*Open daily for lunch and dinner*
*Accepts all major credit cards*

---

# BLUE ROOM
## In the Fairmont Hotel, 123 Baronne Street
### 504-529-4744

The Blue Room is a supper club of the old school. Nightly, save Sundays, there is big-name entertainment, abetted by a big band that plays for dancing. Light dinners are served at the 8 P.M. seating, but you're probably better off having dinner at the adjacent Sazerac first and then coming here.

At the noon hour, the Blue Room mounts the city's best buffet, with superb foodstuffs in bounteous quantities.

*Price: Buffet about $20 per person; dinner (without entertainment charge) about $30 per person; entertainment charges range from $10 to $25, depending on the act*
*Open Sun.–Fri. for lunch and dinner; Sat. for dinner only*
*Accepts all major credit cards*

# BOULIGNY
## 4100 Magazine Street
### 504-891-4444

A striking, modern, airy new restaurant carved from an old firehouse, Bouligny is a popular uptown place serving up-to-date Creole food at moderate prices. Start with the thick, intense gumbo of chicken and *andouille* (a Cajun ham-and-garlic sausage) or the shrimp *rémoulade* in an avocado. There are good entrées throughout the menu: trout *meunière,* soft-shell crabs, veal with crawfish, grilled redfish, and roast duckling with julienne vegetables. The daily specials are also consistently tasty stuff. There are half a dozen or so wine specials served by the glass, and a good list by the bottle. The only weakness is the dessert selection. On Sundays, there is a superb brunch featuring, among other things, Creole-style *frittati.*

*Price: About $10 per person for lunch; $20 per person for dinner*
*Open daily for lunch and dinner*
*Accepts all major credit cards*

---

# BOZO'S
## 3117 21 Street (*one block from Causeway Boulevard*)
### 504-831-8666

Bozo's is, for my money, the best traditional seafood restaurant in town, for two distinctions: All the seafood is very fresh and extremely well-selected, and everything is fried to order and comes out crackling hot. The kitchen has windows through which you may observe the meticulous operation: no mass production, each kind of seafood fried in its own oil, and the owner, Chris "Bozo" Vodonovich, doing a lot of the cooking himself between talks with regulars. Start at the oyster bar, which is a great one. Then, at the table, have a cup of the unusual light gumbo. If they're in season, get some boiled crawfish, which are eaten by pulling them apart at the middle, squeezing the tip of the tail to extract the meat, and sucking the head to get the fat. The fried oysters, shrimp, and catfish are all as good as they get. The broiled shrimp are well peppered, light, and unforgettable. And the stuffed crab, while small, has much more crab than is the norm elsewhere. Avoid the optional French fries and potato salad. Service is efficient.

*Price: About $6 per person*
*Open Tues.–Sat. for lunch and dinner; closed Sun. and Mon.*
*Accepts all major credit cards*

# BRENNAN'S

## In the French Quarter, 417 Royal Street
### 504-525-9711

Brennan's invented from whole cloth something called the "grand Creole breakfast" about thirty years ago, and the meal has made the restaurant famous. With good reason: The original poached egg dishes, with their dozens of under- and overlayers and sauces, are terrific food, and you'd be hard-pressed to find more artfully poached eggs than those served here. The best are eggs St. Charles (atop fried trout), Sardou (creamed spinach and artichokes with hollandaise), and Hussarde (Canadian bacon and *marchand de vin* sauce). The oyster soup that starts off the meal and the bananas Foster that finish it, along with the hot French bread and thick coffee served throughout, complete a memorable meal. Now the bad news: The prices are high (bet you've never spent $25 for breakfast before), the apparent lack of a dress code in recent years has made the place feel like a hotel coffee shop, reservations are not always promptly honored, and there is a propensity to feed in herds on busy days. Lunch and dinner are okay, but haven't changed in the fifteen years since the more experienced side of the Brennan family went to Commander's Palace.

One more bright spot: The wine list is terrific, with an especially strong range in Bordeaux at prices that sometimes seem like mistakes on the low side.

*Price: About $25 per person for breakfast or lunch; $35 per person for dinner*
*Open daily for breakfast, lunch, and dinner*
*Accepts all major credit cards*

# BRUNING'S

## West End Park
### 504-282-9395

West End Park used to be the prime gathering spot for New Orleanians looking for seafood, but for the most part the restaurants there have gotten pretty bad and survive because of their views over the lake. Bruning's is an exception. It's an old place on stilts over the water, and its dining room is complete with a classic fixture of places like this: a sink at which you can wash your hands after eating a big tray of spicy boiled seafood. Depending on the season, you can get shrimp, crabs, and crawfish at prices that will shock those unused to them (for example, $9 for a *dozen* boiled crabs). The fried seafood is pretty good, although not always served immediately after its cooking.

*Price: About $10 per person*
*Open Thurs.–Tues. for lunch and dinner; closed Wed.*
*Accepts Visa and MasterCard*

---

## BUD'S BROILER
### Various locations around town; see phone book

Bud's is a local chain of hamburger-and-hot-dog places with a difference: The meats are grilled over live charcoal as the only heat source. At their best, Bud's burgers are memorable, but the consistency is less than perfect. The components are good, though: The meat is fresh, the cheese is grated Cheddar, the buns are toasted, and the hickory smoke sauce is decent. The restaurants have that Texas barbecue-joint look and are far from fastidious, but the experience is more fun than the standard national franchise.

*Price: About $2 per person*
*No credit cards accepted*

---

## CAFÉ DU MONDE
### In the French Market, 800 Decatur Street
**504-561-9235**

This is the last remaining coffee stand in the French Market, and *the* great rendezvous after any evening's entertainment in New Orleans. The coffee is classic, powerful dark-roast with chicory, so strong that it must be drunk with the hot milk that enters the cup at the same time as does the coffee. The food item is the *beignet,* a square doughnut covered with enough powdered sugar to ensure a mess when you laugh while biting into a hot one. This place is pure New Orleans and a must-visit on any itinerary.

*Price: About $1.25 per person*
*Open 24 hours a day*
*No credit cards accepted*

# CAMELLIA GRILL
## 626 South Carrollton Avenue
### 504-866-9573

A glitzy diner with a maître d' and linen napkins for counter seating, the very popular Camellia Grill cooks up a great hamburger, a variety of deli-style sandwiches, omelets fluffed up to twice the conventional size, superb pecan pie, and one of the few decent cheesecakes in New Orleans. The waiters and grill cooks are famous for their patter.

*Price: About $5 per person*
*Open daily for breakfast, lunch, and dinner*
*No credit cards accepted*

# CARIBBEAN ROOM
## In the Pontchartrain Hotel, 2031 St. Charles Avenue
### 504-524-3178

The C-Room (as it is known by its many local adherents) is one of the most romantic dining rooms in town, with big plush banquettes, large tables, and a burbling fountain. It is highly thought of by many, although the evolution of cuisine and service seems to have ended twenty years ago. The menu combines Creole with the very different Southern style of cooking and a smattering of Continental stuff. You can have a wonderful meal here if you don't go far afield of the specialties. Those are: crab meat Remick, a rich, mustardy casserole with the beautiful crab meat seen in many dishes here; trout *Véronique;* oysters *en brochette;* trout Eugene, with an artichoke-and-crab meat sauce; and the larger beef and lamb roasts. The mile-high pie, created here, is the dessert everybody gets; it serves three or four.

*Price: About $40 per person*
*Open Sun.–Fri. for lunch and dinner; Sat. for dinner only*
*Accepts all major credit cards*

# CASAMENTO'S
## 4330 Magazine Street
### 504-895-9761

Casamento's scrubbed-clean tiled interior reminds most who see it of a bath-room. The lights are bright and the echoing sounds are on the loud side as you eat a dozen oysters at the bar, and then retire to a table to eat more oysters, these fried to order to a crackly crunch, served with or without the restaurant's unique pan bread around the bivalves. The French fries are rare for being fresh-cut. There is a smattering of other seafood and a few Italian dishes, but the main item is oysters. And that is why, in obeisance to the mythical prohibition against eating oysters in months with no "R," Casamento's closes for the entire summer every year.

*Price: About $10 per person*
*Open Tues.–Sun. for lunch and dinner; closed Mon.*
*No credit cards accepted*

---

# CASTILLO'S
## 620 Conti Street
### 504-523-9226

The big dining room has brick walls and floors and a general shabbiness, and the service is slow. However, here is some of the best Mexican food in the area. Start with *caldo xochil,* the *cilantro*-scented chicken soup. The entrées include fine versions of chicken with a peppery, black *mole;* pork *médaillons* with a unique burned-black, oily pepper sauce; and *enchiladas de res,* with a stuffing of very spicy beef *picadillo. Flan* and Mexican hot chocolate round out a better meal than you thought you were going to get.

*Price: About $8 per person*
*Open Mon.–Sat. for lunch and dinner; closed Sun.*
*Accepts Visa and MasterCard*

---

# CENTRAL GROCERY
## 923 Decatur Street (*across from the French Market*)
### 504-523-1620

Here was created one of the city's unique sandwich specialties, the *muffuletta.* It's a large, seeded, round Italian loaf with layers of ham, *mortadella,* Provolone, *mozzarella,* and Genoa salami, made distinctive by the addition of a garlicky olive salad. One *muffuletta* is enough for two, and you'll have to find somewhere else to eat it, because this is strictly a takeout place. It's also a real grocery, with lots of great-smelling imported foods.

*Price: About $3 per person*
*Open Mon.–Sat. from 8 A.M.–5:30 P.M.*
*No credit cards accepted*

# CHARLIE'S
## 4510 Dryades (*one block from Napoleon*)
### 504-895-9705

Charlie's is not much to look at. Its service seems brusque (actually, the waiters are mostly first-generation Italian-Americans for whom conversation is not a comfortable art). And you would not have to look hard to find beef of better quality than they use here. But the cooking has real excitement—the steaks really do sizzle in a pool of New Orleans-style butter sauce. The small T-bone is more than anybody should be able to eat and is the best choice. The salad is a quarter-head of lettuce with thinly sliced onions and the most powerful Roquefort dressing imaginable. The onion rings are superb, light and crisp. And all the potatoes are fresh and good. No menu; finding out what's what is part of the fun.

*Price: About $15 per person*
*Open Mon.–Fri. for lunch and dinner; Sat. for dinner only; closed Sun.*
*Accepts all major credit cards*

---

# CHRISTIAN'S
## 3835 Iberville Street (*one block from Canal Street*)
### 504-482-4924

The restaurant is in a renovated church, but the name is that of the owner, Chris Ansel, who is a member of the family that owns Galatoire's and who has borrowed much of that restaurant's style. Christian's has developed a distinctive cuisine, however, and it is one of the most popular restaurants among locals. Be sure to reserve well in advance.

Start with the oysters Roland—an herbal casserole—or the smoked salmon, which the restaurant cures itself. Seafood dominates the entrée section. Shrimp *Madeleine* has a creamy sauce rich with essence of the shellfish. The light peppercorn sauce on the redfish *au poivre* is masterful. An excellent Creole-style *bouillabaisse* is chunky with all manner of local seafood. And a salmon stuffed with salmon *mousse* is vivid.

The meat entrées include an excellent filet mignon with a variety of sauces, veal with *morels,* and a *cuisine minceur* chicken with blackberry vinegar. All of this is good stuff.

The wine list is straightforward and attractively priced. The desserts are few and just okay.

*Price: About $25 per person*
*Open Mon.–Sat. for lunch and dinner; closed Sun.*
*Accepts all major credit cards*

# CLANCY'S

### 6100 Annunciation Street at Webster Street
### 504-895-1111

Clancy's took over and renovated (but not too much) an old neighborhood bar and installed a kitchen which does some of the most eclectic food in town. The standard menu is pretty good; the attached sheet of specials is better, though, and there's also a list of *recited* specials, some Creole but many not. Start off with the rabbit sausage *en croûte* with its great peppercorn sauce, the fine bubbly *escargots,* or the *gravlax.* Skip soup and salad and pay only fleeting attention to what's coming out of the mesquite pit that day. This smoked stuff is the restaurant's signature food, but it's inconsistent. (The mesquite-grilled shrimp are usually good, though.) Among the specials that appear with some regularity are Cornish hen *diablo,* a fine preparation of that meat with a spicy, slightly sweet sauce; some interesting essays with liver; freshwater trout (as opposed to the saltwater variety usually served in New Orleans), and carpet-bagger steak, stuffed with oysters. The wine list is surprisingly good, with not only a good selection of the expected French and California bottles but also a lot of offbeat wines. Tremendous coffee. The service is more peculiar than good; you're never quite sure who your waiter is.

*Price: About $25 per person*
*Open Mon.–Fri. for lunch and dinner; Sat. for dinner only; closed Sun.*
*Accepts all major credit cards*

# COMMANDER'S PALACE

### 1403 Washington Avenue
### 504-899-8221

When the Brennan family split some fifteen years ago, the elder side reestablished its headquarters in this lovely old restaurant in the center of the Garden District. There Ella and Dick Brennan embarked on a program of culinary innovation that has brought them to the preeminent position in the New Orleans dining-out scene. The menu combines imaginative versions of the Creole verities with dishes on the cutting edge of American cuisine into an exciting array of offerings. Meanwhile, you are sitting in the cheery Garden Room overlooking a fine oak-shaded courtyard or in one of the beautiful antique rooms, served by user-friendly waiters.

There are some good oyster dishes and a wonderful shrimp *rémoulade* among the appetizers, but I usually start with a soup. The turtle soup is the best Creole version anywhere, thick with turtle meat from the local swamps and rather spicy. The daily *potages* are also superb, particularly those with crab meat.

The seafood is of the first rank: trout with pecans, redfish Grieg (with crab meat in a light, spicy sauce), and in season enormous, nutty soft-shell crabs and crawfish in a plethora of forms. The veal is pretty, too, especially a pale pink veal chop grilled over hickory to a satisfying char. Steaks are prime and grilled accurately with a distinctive Creole seasoning; the filet with *demi-glace* has almost too much flavor.

Dinner is a packed house at Commander's, but the busiest meal here is brunch on weekends. A lighter menu prevails, with many of the wonderful Brennan egg dishes, while a jazz trio of some of New Orleans' best old-time musicians stroll around.

The dessert to get is a *soufflé* of bread pudding, unless you like chocolate —in which case you will find more than a few dense, rich things. Also dense and rich is the coffee. The wine list centers on an extensive catalog of California bottles, but it's well-balanced across the board.

The only problems you are likely to encounter here derive from the large volume Commander's does. However, the house corrects the few irregularities immediately without argument. Not much gets in the way of an enjoyable time, that being a Brennan—and New Orleans—specialty.

*Price: About $35 per person*
*Open daily for lunch and dinner*
*Accepts all major credit cards*

---

# COPELAND'S

1001 South Clearview Parkway, Jefferson   504-733-7843
701 Veterans Boulevard, Metairie   504-831-9449
4338 St. Charles Avenue   504-897-2325

Copeland's is the new chain launched in 1982 by Al Copeland, who created Popeyes Fried Chicken. The three restaurants (and there are more abuilding) look like the most frivolous kind of suburban "fun" joints, with ferns and fake antiques and busy bars in their centers. But the kitchen is very serious and makes very strong culinary statements in an enormous menu. Much of it is inspired by the food of K-Paul's (see page 551), ranging from a blackened redfish that's consistently better than the original to pasta dishes at the parody level. There's a hickory grill over which flanks of lamb ribs are brought to a thrilling char. And a plate of red beans for under a dollar that rank among the best. Avoid anything containing tasso, anything Mexican, or anything fried, and the chances of a great meal are high. All the foodstuffs are fresh, and even the ice creams are prepared on the premises. The prices are very low.

These places have made a major impact on the upper-middle tier of the New Orleans restaurant business.

*Price: About $12 per person*
*Open daily for lunch and dinner*
*Accepts all major credit cards*

---

## CRESCENT CITY STEAK HOUSE
### 1001 North Broad Street
**504-821-3271**

When the Yugoslavian owner of this rather odd little restaurant opened it more than fifty years ago, he set the style and the standard by which New Orleans steak houses operate even now. The style is to broil steaks to a bit of exterior char and serve them in a substantial lake of sizzling butter—a cholesterol overkill that tastes just great. The standard is to serve USDA Prime beef, never frozen, from the best sources. Other steak houses have eclipsed the Crescent City—the weirdness of the tiled place, with its mysterious private, curtained booths, limits the clientele to the few hardcore regulars—but it still serves some of the best steaks in town. Have Lyonnaise potatoes with them, but avoid all other side dishes.

*Price: About $20 per person*
*Open Tues.–Sun. for lunch and dinner; closed Mon.*
*Accepts all major credit cards*

---

## CROZIER'S
### 7033 Read Lane, New Orleans East
**504-241-8220**

It may come as a surprise that there are not many French restaurants untouched by the Creole influence in New Orleans. This little *bistro* has been, for a little over ten years, the Frenchest place in town, as well as one of the most reliable. The menu is brief and contains few surprises. But here you will find flawlessly executed versions of *coq au vin,* steak *au poivre,* sweetbreads *meunière, tournedos* topped with *foie gras,* and shrimp in a cream sauce (odd-sounding, but perhaps the best dish in the restaurant), various veal specials, and trout with capers or fennel. For starters, there's *pâté de campagne, escargots,* and daily *potages,* all of unassailable merit. A distinctive pie-shaped bread pudding for dessert is about the only concession to localism. Service is casual but good, and the wine list is minimal but well matched to the food. At lunch there is lighter fare, such as *quiches,* omelets, and salads, all made with equal care. To many, this is the best restaurant in the area.

*Price: About $35 per person*
*Open Tues.–Fri. for lunch and dinner; Sat. for dinner only; closed Sun. and Mon.*
*Accepts American Express, Visa, and MasterCard*

---

## DEL FRISCO'S
### 14 West Bank Expressway (*across the side street from Cavaretta's Furniture*), Gretna
### 504-368-2222

This is a new operation that has become extremely successful by doing everything just a little bit better and less expensively than the market leader. The place is plain vanilla, but the steaks are of the absolute top-quality beef, trimmed better than any I've ever seen, and broiled with just a little butter. Good side dishes, too: fried *calamari,* shrimp *rémoulade,* oniony potatoes *au gratin,* and a good peanut butter pie for dessert. The service is unusually accommodating.

*Price: About $25 per person*
*Open Mon.–Fri. for lunch and dinner; Sat. for dinner only; Sun. from 3 P.M.*
*only when the New Orleans Saints are playing in town*
*Accepts all major credit cards*

---

## DELMONICO'S
### 1300 St. Charles Avenue
### 504-525-4937

From the outside, this old place looks fancy and expensive, but inside it's all charm and accessibility, with a menu full of Creole basics at alarmingly low prices. The clientele is mostly uptown families who come regularly, and they mostly eat seafood. The baked oysters, shrimp *rémoulade,* and turtle soup make good starters, as does the seafood gumbo, which is one of the best in town. From there the kitchen sallies forth through the length and breadth of local seafood cookery. Particularly good are catfish *meunière,* served with stuffed shrimp; trout *amandine;* broiled red snapper; soft-shell crabs in season, and a mixed seafood brochette. There are good daily specials. The house salad of marinated vegetables is superb, and the desserts are tiny but good.

*Price: About $10 per person for lunch; $15 per person for dinner*
*Open daily for lunch and dinner*
*Accepts all major credit cards*

# DRAGO'S LAKEVIEW
## 3232 North Arnoult Road, Metairie
### 504-888-9254

Drago's started out as a standard seafood restaurant, and it's still good in that capacity. But some years ago the owner decided to share the Yugo food he likes and knows how to cook, so now we can enjoy *mučkalika* (grilled pork with green peppers), *sarma* (stuffed cabbage rolls), *musaka* (a very herbal variation on the Greek dish of similar name), and some half-dozen different preparations of squid. The flavors are sort of a hybrid of Greek and Middle Eastern cooking, but not exactly. Whatever the label, it's good and offbeat.

*Price: About $15 per person*
*Open Mon.–Sat. for lunch and dinner*
*All major credit cards accepted*

# EL PATIO
## 3244 Georgia Avenue (*one block east of Williams Boulevard at 33 Street*), Kenner
### 504-443-1188

El Patio is the most ambitious and clearly the best Mexican restaurant in a city not rich with that cuisine. The small place is operated by a large family, all of whose members seem to bounce easily back and forth between cooking, waiting tables, singing, and playing the guitar. The menu has much variety. Start off with the *seviche* of redfish in lime juice, the elegant black bean soup with chopped raw onions, or the avocado-and-*tortilla* soup. Entrées: squid stuffed with crab meat in a white sauce is lovely to look at and beguilingly good to taste; the squid also finds itself, with ink, in a gritty, filling, and delectable *arroz con calamares*. Chicken comes with many different sauces; the *mole* is a particularly good one. Local seafoods get all sorts of very Mexican treatments rarely seen in America. And if "Mexican" to you means *tortillas* with stuff in or around them, you will find versions here as good as any.

The dessert *flan* has the marvelous distinctive flavor of Mexican vanilla.

*Price: About $15 per person*
*Open Mon.–Sat. for dinner only; closed Sun.*
*Accepts American Express, Visa, and MasterCard*

# FLAGONS
## 3222 Magazine Street
### 504-895-6471

At this writing, Flagons is the only wine bar in New Orleans, but it's a good one by any standard. Using nitrogen to prevent spoilage of open bottles, they keep forty or more wines on hand for sale by the glass, and hundreds more by the bottle. The stuff is always in perfect condition, it's well-handled and served at the right temperature. The by-the-glass list always has a couple of rare things along with unusual current bottlings. The owners are serious wine buffs who select well.

There's a small menu of food designed to go with wine, and the place recently opened a dining room with a professional kitchen for real meals.

*Price: About $10–$15 per person*
*Open daily for lunch and dinner*
*Accepts all major credit cards*

# FORTUNE GARDENS
## 3804 Williams Boulevard, Kenner
### 504-443-4114

In a city not blessed with many good Chinese restaurants, Fortune Gardens stands out through the agency of a rather adventuresome menu. Spiced jellyfish, smoked fish, and pickled cabbage—all great cold first courses—are unique. As is the best entrée in the house, a rice-leaf-smoked chicken, cut into pieces with the bones still in place, irresistible with a silky smokiness. Dishes with the spicy, orange *yu-shiang* sauce and the whole braised fish are among other memorable offerings. There is nothing exceptional about the premises or service.

*Price: About $10 per person*
*Open daily for lunch and dinner*
*Accepts all major credit cards*

# GALATOIRE'S
## In the French Quarter, 209 Bourbon Street
### 504-525-2021

If you've never come to New Orleans before and you have time for only one meal, it should be here. You won't need a reservation, because you can't get one; Galatoire's is as famous for its line as for its food. (The line can be avoided by dining between about 1:30 and 6:00 P.M.; the restaurant serves all afternoon, is never empty, and has the same menu and prices all the time.) Galatoire's really *looks* New Orleans: It's one long room lined with mirrors, motionless ceiling fans, and naked light bulbs that blink every time a streetcar starts up somewhere. The waiters are more effective than elegant; wine buckets are placed on an empty chair or on the floor.

Seafood is the ticket at Galatoire's. Start with the shrimp *rémoulade,* oysters *en brochette,* crab meat *maison,* or any crawfish dish in season. Skip soup. Have a green salad with garlic. Then comes the toasty trout *meunière* or the rich, spicy trout Marguery, the two house specialties. But much else in that menu book is as good. When pompano is available, the broiled version is probably the best fish dish served in New Orleans. Crab meat Yvonne, buttery with artichokes and mushrooms, is good and light. Crab meat Sardou has an underlayer of spinach and artichokes with hollandaise. Stuffed eggplant with seafood is a great version of a local specialty. Meat is not as big a deal, but they do a memorable pair of grilled lamb chops with *béarnaise,* and the beef is nothing to sneer at.

For dessert, there are funny little *crêpes* stuffed with currant jelly and flooded (but not flamed) with Grand Marnier. And Galatoire's has *the best* coffee in New Orleans, which is saying something.

*Price: About $20 per person*
*Open Tues.–Sun. for lunch and dinner; closed Mon.*
*No credit cards accepted*

---

# GAUTREAU'S
## 1728 Soniat Street at Danneel Street
### 504-899-7397

The premises formerly housed an old pharmacy, and remnants of that heritage remain in the pressed-tin ceiling, tile floors, and handsome glass cases where wine is kept. Gautreau's is small, rather loud, and very popular, owing to its service of very consistent, creative, and moderately priced *nouvelle* Creole food. There's a whole new menu daily, including about six different offerings in three courses. Particularly good have been the soups, the various treatments of filet mignon, and the scrupulously fresh fish. There are some interesting forays into Mexican food. Some great, rich pies for dessert. At lunchtime, several large salads of top-notch quality form a good part of the menu.

*Price: About $25 per person*
*Open Mon.–Fri. for lunch and dinner; Sat. for dinner only; closed Sun.*
*Accepts Visa and MasterCard only*

# GENGHIS KHAN

## 4053 Tulane Avenue (*near South Carrollton Avenue*)
### 504-482-4044

Operated by a first violinist with the New Orleans Symphony, this very popular place serves an abbreviated menu of very accessible Korean food. Start off with *kimchee* (a hot pickled cabbage), spinach *namul* (marinated and nutty-tasting), or *kim* (a seaweed wrapper into which you can insert rice or almost anything else). *Bulgoki* is the national dish of Korea—marinated grilled beef, with a thick, slightly sweet sauce. But better still are the whole fried fish, the very spicy chicken Imperial, and the Chongol hot pot. Most nights, there is live classical music, often performed by the very talented owner.

*Price: About $15 per person*
*Open daily for dinner only*
*Accepts American Express, Visa, and MasterCard*

# GRILL ROOM

## In the Windsor Court Hotel, 300 Gravier Street
### 504-523-6000

A handsome, bright dining room decorated with much large original art and things like a Lalique crystal table, the Grill Room made a big splash when it opened in 1983 with its wine cellar, assembled by purchasing the large collections of two local Bordeaux fanatics. The food and service are at least up to the wine. The style is New American with more than a little Creole. As the name implies, there's an extensive listing of grilled foods, the fish being especially good. With the exception of oysters Peacock (a fine, spicy original baked oyster dish) and the superb, multicolored house salad of avocado, egg, bacon, and greens, stick with the list of specials. These have been completely unpredictable and, for the most part, exciting, offbeat dishes. Service is just slightly less elegant than the place promises, but it's still close to the best in town.

*Price: About $50 per person*
*Open daily for breakfast, lunch, and dinner*
*All major credit cards accepted*

# HENRI

## In the Hotel Méridien, 614 Canal Street
### 504-525-6500

The French-owned Méridien chain's practice in its flagship restaurants is to connect them spiritually with great places in France. In this case, the mother ship is L'Auberge de L'Ill in Alsace, and its chef consulted on Henri's menu and installed many of his dishes in this lovely, smallish room. Shades of green run from the mural of a topiary garden to an altar-like edifice of green marble behind the bar. The food in its first year has been sublime: Start with the *potage* of frogs legs and watercress, the gossamer salmon *soufflé,* or the crawfish salad with mango. The best entrées have been an array of chicken *paillards* in a light truffle sauce, served with a side bowl of *spätzle*-like noodles with finger-size pieces of *foie gras* in cheese and cream, glazed on top; a filet mignon of venison, ideally grilled and served with a natural sauce; and a pastry-wrapped squab with cabbage. For dessert is a *gratin* of *sabayon* with strawberries and a peach poached in vanilla syrup. The wine list and the service still need work, but this food shows polish and flavor in ways not previously seen in New Orleans.

The restaurant entrance is actually on Common Street.

*Price: About $40 per person*
*Open daily for lunch and dinner*
*Accepts all major credit cards*

# INDULGENCE

## In the Garden District, 1501 Washington Avenue
### 504-899-4411

Co-owner Frank Bailey is a food writer who's also a restaurateur, or perhaps vice versa. Indulgence began as a catering business that started serving lunches and then became a hit big enough to justify a real restaurant. The new Garden District Indulgence is a lovely little café, bright and cheery by day and intimate at night. The food is a very understated variety of New American -*cum*-Creole using superb fresh ingredients. The quail were killed less than a day before cooking, the bread is baked on the premises, and even the peas are shucked from fresh pods. The menu changes daily, although some specialties have emerged: fresh pasta with homemade sausage, Creole oyster soup, sautéed redfish with herb butter, sweetbreads *meunière,* veal chops with Madeira, and, for dessert, a stunning white chocolate *mousse* pie. Service and the wine list, like the food, are simple but flawless. A lot of restaurateurs from other places come here; perhaps it takes being one of those to appreciate this food.

*Price: About $30 per person*
*Garden District location open Mon.–Fri. for lunch and dinner; Sat. for dinner only; closed Sun.*
*Accepts American Express, Visa, and MasterCard*

---

# JONATHAN
## In the French Quarter, 714 North Rampart Street (*across from Armstrong Park*)
### 504-586-1930

In terms of architectural design, this is probably the most distinguished restaurant in town. It's three floors of artful, unaffected Art Deco, including among the many items of decor an astounding two-story glass mural. The music is from the thirties and forties and the waiters work with a kind of happy elegance that seems to have been imported from a Fred Astaire film.

The kitchen innovates with earnestness, pursuing mostly American fare but not hesitating to mess around with Creole, Mexican, Indian, Italian, or whatever. The trout *mousse* with dill mayonnaise, the *pâté maison,* and crab meat *Entremont* (with artichoke and spinach) make good starters. As do the soups; the variations on vichyssoise are particularly good. The long list of specials is a good place to start looking for an entrée—you're likely to find almost anything there—but a favorite standard item is the broiled calf's liver *à l'orange,* a tremendous dish for liver lovers. Also good is *tournedos* Thomas, with its *marchand de vin* and *béarnaise* sauces and fresh sautéed spinach. The active pastry department puts out fine pastries and cakes, with fertile fields for chocolate lovers. The lounge is lovely and makes great *cappuccino.*

*Price: About $40 per person*
*Open daily for dinner only*
*Accepts all major credit cards*

---

# KESWANY'S
## 200 Broadway, Uptown Square
### 504-833-3456

New Orleans has never been very receptive to ethnic cuisines, and so this, the area's only Indian restaurant, is relatively new and struggling. The food is not at fault, however. There are *tandoori* ovens for the preparation of chicken and lamb, roasted to a dry tenderness; *naan,* a bread baked on the wall of the clay ovens, is also good. The curry selection is broad, and includes the ultra-spicy *vindaloos.* A variety of entrées is prepared by mixing this or that with the imported *basmati* rice. An awful-looking but delectable dish called *saag* is lamb mixed with dark, sautéed spinach and oil. A particular specialty is the very filling vegetarian *thali,* a succession of some dozen small courses which change daily. The raw materials and the cooking are of a high level.

*Price: About $15 per person*
*Open daily for lunch and dinner*
*Accepts all major credit cards*

---

# K-PAUL'S LOUISIANA KITCHEN
## In the French Quarter, 416 Chartres Street
### 504-524-7394

The success of K-Paul's began when Paul Prudhomme—then chef at Commander's Palace—moved into a minimally redecorated Quarter dive with a menu of many of the same dishes he's serving now, but back then at prices in the $5–$10 range. This handwritten list of daily specials was so good that a line formed at all open hours. The line is much longer now and is completely unavoidable unless the town is empty.

Prudhomme makes much of his Cajun heritage, but the fact is that his cooking veers all over the road, incorporating ideas from many cuisines. What makes it of a piece are the levels of pepper, salt, cream, butter, and certain spices (most notably cumin), which are at the far extreme even by Creole–Cajun standards. The famous dish is blackened redfish, a fillet charred on the outside in a hot skillet with lots of seasonings. Cajun popcorn is also famous, although the creation was not the dish (you have always been able to get fried crawfish tails in New Orleans restaurants) but the appealing name. Less well-known but probably the best dish in the house is trout Czarina, with a rough-edged butter sauce with julienne vegetables and a reasonable seasoning level. The various poultry dishes, which use birds raised on the restaurant's own farm, are also lustily spicy, good stuff. Probably the spiciest dishes of all are the gumbos, the *etouffées,* and the jambalayas, which should bring sweat to your brow no matter what you're used to eating.

Prudhomme combines an extremely original style of cooking, a religious fervor for the kitchen, and a matchless gift for saying interesting things. He has inspired a large number of young chefs and has almost single-handedly generated a national interest in Louisiana cooking. When a new Creole-Cajun place opens in another city, it's usually a copy of K-Paul's. But it's hard to find other Cajun or Creole food that's anything like this. And some of the dishes which glossaries in national media proclaim as traditional Cajun fare are unique to K-Paul's.

Success has made K-Paul's somewhat less attractive. Prices have risen considerably. After the ordeal of waiting in line, you are read a list of rules which include the likelihood that you will share a table with strangers. The napkins are paper and there are no tablecloths.

*Price: About $30 per person*
*Open Mon.–Fri. for dinner only; closed Sat. and Sun.*
*Accepts American Express*

---

## LA CUISINE
### 225 West Harrison Avenue, Lakeview
### 504-456-5154

A moderately priced restaurant with an army of dedicated regulars, La Cuisine serves a comfortable, familiar brand of Creole cooking that's so consistent and such a bargain that it's worth the usual wait for a table. It's at its peak during crawfish season, when it offers a five-course dinner of the mudbugs in every imaginable form, all delectable. Variety is the style of the restaurant in its other dishes: the baked oyster platter has three different kinds, the most popular redfish is the one with oysters, crab meat, and shrimp on top of it, and trout can be had with three different sauces on the same plate. By all rights this should be a hodgepodge, but the stuff is great. The waitresses are old-school (regardless of their age) and can be expected to call you "dawlin'."

*Price: About $15 per person*
*Open Tues.–Sat. for lunch and dinner; closed Sun. and Mon.*
*Accepts all major credit cards*

# LA RIVIERA

## 4506 Shores Drive, Metairie
### 504-888-6238

The dining room is overly decorated, the waiters look like lugubrious young studs, the customers are all regulars, and the chef is famous hereabouts for one dish not on the menu: crab meat (or, in season, crawfish) *ravioli* in a sauce of cream, cheese, and seafood stock. It is in fact very good, as is the broiled Italian-style trout, with its unforgettable herb complement. The rest of the food is good enough but not world-class.

*Price: About $20 per person*
*Open Mon.–Sat. for dinner only; closed Sun.*
*Accepts all major credit cards*

# LA TRATTORIA ROMA

## In the French Quarter, 611 Decatur Street
### 504-523-9814

This new little place has become enormously popular among local Italian-cuisine aficionados for serving dishes other than the Sicilian-style stuff universal in New Orleans. The place is dark, crowded, and a little uncomfortable, but the food delivers some real excitement. The pastas cover a wide range of shapes and sauces; especially good are *linguine alla puttanesca* (tomato chunks, garlic, capers, and olives) and *rigatoni* with four cheeses. Soups also change daily and tend to be highly aromatic and irresistible. Main courses: *coniglio in salmi* is a tender marinated rabbit, sautéed with garlic; *grigliato misto* is a crusty mixed grill of Italian sausage, beef, and liver; *quaglie in tegame* is a pair of quails with a richness of *prosciutto,* peas, mushrooms, and tomatoes all around. The dessert to get is the breathtaking *zabaglione.* The wine list is far and away the best collection of Italian wines in the city.

*Price: About $20 per person*
*Open Mon.–Fri. for lunch and dinner; Sat. for dinner only; closed Sun.*
*Accepts all major credit cards*

# LE CHÂTEAU
## 1000 Behrman Highway, Gretna
### 504-392-4690

Le Château is the kind of restaurant that's very common in New York but had been unheard of around New Orleans. The menu is entirely classical French, but the execution is so skillful as to avoid any labeling of the stuff as corny. The kitchen is particularly skillful in the pastry department, and the many *en croûte* dishes are as good for their pastry wrappers as for their contents. And this is one of the two or three New Orleans restaurants where you can get a decent dessert *soufflé.*

The appetizer specials tend to be better than the standard items, although the mussels *marinière* are wonderfully aromatic. The lobster bisque is the best of the soups. The salads contain better lettuces than the iceberg ubiquitous in these parts. The best entrées include salmon *en croûte,* a steamed pheasant Souvaroff (stuffed with *pâté* and grandly carved for two at the table), a *vol-au-vent* filled with sweetbreads in a convincingly spicy and rich sauce, a masterful steak *au poivre* of the creamy variety, a textbook *tournedos Rossini,* and good specials involving flown-in French fish.

For dessert, those *soufflés* are hard to pass up, but there is a heavily laden table of excellent cakes and pastries. The wine list includes a large collection of rare Bordeaux in an inaccessible price range, and a selection of more down-to-earth bottles that's adequate but not much more. Service is overseen by the owner's wife, who handles most of the tableside ministrations with unhesitating élan. The premises are a bit too noisy and suburban-looking for this kind of restaurant, but dinner here is still a pleasure.

*Price: About $35 per person*
*Open Mon.–Fri. for lunch and dinner; Sat. for dinner only; closed Sun.*
*Accepts all major credit cards*

# LEE'S OLD FASHIONED HAMBURGERS
## Various locations around town; see phone book

Lee's traces its history through at least two sets of owners back to 1905, and calls itself the original New Orleans hamburger. The patties are thick and fresh (although not always grilled to order). What makes them good is the colossal amount of onions with which they are grilled. The finished product is a fine hamburger with good fresh dressings. Side orders are not much; the premises are clean and attractive.

*Price: About $2 per person*
*No credit cards accepted*

# LENFANT'S
## 5236 Canal Boulevard, Lakeview
### 504-486-1512

An old, recently renovated landmark, Lenfant's has never been as good as it is these days. The place is cleft in twain: The north side, with a sort of Italian-Deco look, is a formal dining room. The south holds a very active disco with neon and glass bricks; they'll serve you dinner in there, too. The kitchen's style is that of one of the owners, Nick Mosca, who works to a large degree in the style of his family's restaurant (see page 559). But the menu goes beyond Creole–Italian classics such as oysters Mosca and chicken grandee to include a spectacular baby veal sirloin with three sauces; trout interlaid with shrimp *mousse;* rack of lamb with *couscous;* and roast duckling with raspberries, all wonderful food. There's a good pastry department here that keeps the table of pastries in the dining room well laden. And aromatic hot popovers are served throughout the meal. Service is very good, and the level of *joie de vivre* is high.

*Price: About $30 per person*
*Open Tues.–Fri. for lunch; Tues.–Sat. for dinner; closed Sun. and Mon.*
*Accepts all major credit cards*

# LE RUTH'S
## 636 Franklin Avenue, Gretna
### 504-362-4914

After twenty years of stunning culinary success, LeRuth's has entered its second generation, with the sons of Warren LeRuth now in charge and the old man across the street experimenting with food as if he were in a laboratory. The chemical-equation approach to cooking has always marked the food here, but in a very rewarding way: LeRuth's continues to be among the most consistent restaurants around, particularly in its specialties.

The restaurant occupies a renovated house that's unremarkable except for the 25,000 bottles of wine in the temperature-controlled attic (see, there are no basements in sub-sea-level New Orleans) and the art on the walls (some corny, some Picasso originals). The style of the food is clearly Creole, but with a complexity of flavor rarely found elsewhere. Great examples of that are the crab meat St. Francis (a shell filled with a rich, herbal, spicy, buttery concoction) and the oyster and artichoke soup (hearty, memorable, and a real trend-setter hereabouts).

The menu is a selection of rather large *table d'hôte* dinners; the five courses bring a lot of food, so come hungry. While there are many specials, you'd be best off sticking to the regular menu unless a special *really* sounds appealing. My favorite entrée is the roasted duck, rich and smoky and stuffed with an oyster dressing: unforgettable. The rack of American spring lamb is marinated and ideally roasted, served with a large pile of fried parsley. The best seafoods are the soft-shell crabs *meunière* with crab meat and trout Oliva. And LeRuth's serves what is to my palate the best steak in town, a 16-ounce prime strip broiled to an agreeable exterior char and juicy interior, with a New Orleans-style lake of butter sauce.

For dessert, the various fruit ices are vivid and the macaroon bread pudding is original and rich. Good coffee rounds out a satisfying meal. The wine list is surprisingly short and mostly French; most of the cellar is filled with bottles waiting to be ready to drink. LeRuth's really does refrain from selling a wine before its time, a rare restraint.

*Price: About $35 per person*
*Open Mon.–Sat. for dinner only; closed Sun.*
*Accepts Visa and MasterCard*

# LES CONTINENTS
## In the Inter-Continental Hotel, 444 St. Charles Avenue
### 504-525-5566

A very long but relatively narrow room curiously decorated with odd bits of modern art and carnival-beads-looking chandeliers and entertained with live classical guitar music, this is a New York-style French restaurant working just this side of the *nouvelle* line. It is distinguished by the kitchen's importing of unusual fresh fish from exotic zones, and by its occasional importing of an entire staff from a restaurant in France. In the latter case, the French chef involved installs his own menu, no matter how unreceptive Americans are to a list with three kidney dishes on it. So to the most enthusiastic gourmets this has been a fascinating and very consistent restaurant. The menu changes four times a year, so specifics can't be named. One area of special merit is cheese, which is perfectly served from a beautiful, large selection on a cart.

*Price: About $50 per person*
*Open daily for breakfast, lunch, and dinner*
*Accepts all major credit cards*

# MAI TAI

## 714 West Bank Expressway, Gretna
### 504-367-4646

The Mai Tai was the first New Orleans restaurant to offer the singular, usually spicy cuisine of Thailand, and it is pretty good at it. Start with the Thai tray selection of appetizers, the best of which are some chicken wings stuffed with a beguiling pork mixture. Good soups, especially the chicken broth with coconut milk and lemon grass. There are several daily specials, and the one to look for is the green curry of anything—it's rich and intense. Baked stuffed giant squid and a wonderful fish cake called *todd munn* are other specialties. There's also a more down-to-earth platter of chicken and shrimp with a smooth but spicy sauce.

*Price: About $12 per person*
*Open Mon.–Sat. for lunch and dinner; closed Sun.*
*Accepts American Express, Visa, and MasterCard*

# MARTIN WINE CELLAR DELI

## 3827 Baronne Street
### 504-899-7411

Inside the city's pre-eminent wine store is the closest thing to a real deli you'll find in these parts. The sandwiches are made with superb fresh breads piled high with premium-quality meats and cheeses (nothing kosher about this place). And you can even get a po' boy sandwich. Since you can buy a bottle of wine from the tremendous retail stock and drink it on the spot, this deli has what amounts to the best wine list in the city.

*Price: About $4 per person*
*Open daily for lunch and dinner*
*Accepts Visa and MasterCard*

# MR. B'S

## In the French Quarter, 201 Royal Street
### 504-523-2078

Mr. B's first opened as the casual junior restaurant of Commander's Palace, a role it has outgrown. Now it has an appetizing style all its own and a very comfortable feel: rather masculine, with dark walls and dividers in a very large room. The food is an interesting amalgam of old Creole and New American, with the addition of some delicious stuff from an open hickory grill. In fact, Mr. B's hickory-grilled redfish was the forerunner of the now ubiquitous (and, if you ask me, much less appetizing) blackened redfish.

Good starters include oysters Maras, a rather light but intensely-flavored poaching with a reduced sauce; gumbo ya-ya, a highly-seasoned and very satisfying chicken-andouille gumbo; and beer-battered shrimp. Any fish or poultry that comes off the grill is a winner, but the kitchen has a deft hand with the sauté pan as well and makes some great light sauces for its seafood specials. There's also a good deal of pasta of note. The dessert to get is bread pudding, rich and fresh.

The wine list is all-California and very good, as is the live pianist on hand at dinner.

*Price: About $25 per person*
*Open daily for lunch and dinner*
*All major credit cards accepted*

---

# MORNING CALL
## 3325 Seventh Avenue, Metairie
### 504-885-4068

The Morning Call used to be at the other end of the French Market from the Café du Monde, but when the market was renovated a decade ago, the Morning Call moved its antique operation to the suburbs, where it does even more business than before. For locals, *café au lait* and *beignets* is an indispensable element of a night on the town. The Morning Call's products are a little better and more consistent than those of the Café du Monde, but there never was any atmosphere here.

*Price: About $1.25 per person*
*Open 24 hours a day*
*No credit cards accepted*

# MOSCA'S

*Highway 90, Waggaman (about 4 miles past the West Bank
side of the Huey P. Long Bridge, on the left)*
504-436-9942

Mosca's defines the concept of Creole-Italian, offering a style of cooking you'll
find nowhere else. The restaurant is a rather shabby-looking white house in
the middle of the swamp on the highway out of town. Still, it's always
mobbed with locals and the few visitors who can find it. Service is country
style, with portions generally big enough for at least two people. The best way
to eat at Mosca's is with about six or eight, because then you can get all the
great specialties. These are: marinated crab salad; Italian oysters, a giant casserole with herbs, bread crumbs, and olive oil; Italian shrimp, big ones roasted
with whole pods of garlic; chicken grandee, broiled with Italian sausage (made
on the premises) and mushrooms; any kind of game bird that's available,
roasted to a fine moistness with no small amount of herbs and olive oil. And
spaghetti *bordelaise,* with a light sauce of garlic and butter. You get all the
oil and garlic you always wanted at Mosca's, but somehow the food never gets
gross. The wine list is good enough; the vino is served in tumblers. Very casual
service. Reservations are essential.

*Price: About $25 per person*
*Open Tues.–Sat. for dinner only; closed Sun. and Mon.*
*No credit cards accepted*

# MOTHER'S

## 401 Poydras Street
504-523-9656

Mother's dates back to the 1930s and is still one of the best buys in town for
a lavish breakfast of meat, sausage, eggs, grits, biscuits, and coffee. Mother's
is the top practitioner of the other classic New Orleans sandwich, the po' boy.
It's a long piece of French bread stuffed with whatever, and the whatever to
get at Mother's is the baked ham with roast beef gravy. (Ask for some "debris,"
the bits and ends of the meat.) But the turkey and roast beef are also wonderful,
as are the homey and rib-sticking plate specials. Mother's always has a long
line, but it moves fast, and there are enough characters hanging around to keep
you amused.

*Price: About $3 per person*
*Open Tues.–Sat. for breakfast and lunch only; closed Sun. and Mon.*
*No credit cards accepted*

# OCCHIPINTI'S

## 2712 North Arnoult Street, Metairie (*between I-10 and Veterans Boulevard*)
### 504-888-1131

Anecdote: Frank Occhipinti, who for many years has been the master of a kind of restaurant I call Suburban Creole, had a falling-out with his partners and was kicked out of a place called the Red Onion. So he bought a piece of property a block away and erected this place, which looked exactly like the Red Onion. The crowds moved here, the Red Onion is gone, and Occhipinti continues to put out a menu of very consistent Italian and Creole food. Start with the great *vermicelli marinara,* crab meat or *escargots* in artichoke butter, or the various baked oysters. The roasts are the best shots among the entrées: marinated rack of lamb, grilled-to-order prime ribs, and prime steaks. This is probably the best place in New Orleans to get a Maine lobster (understandably not a big item hereabouts). The list of veal specialties is long and the preparations are deft. They'll also do just about anything you can imagine with fresh seafood. Lunches, very popular, are very inexpensive. The restaurant is huge and has an active lounge with a pianist.

*Price: About $30 per person.*
*Open Mon.–Fri. for lunch and dinner; Sat. for dinner only; closed Sun.*
*Accepts all major credit cards*

# PARASOL'S

## 2533 Constance Street (*one block from Magazine at Third*)
### 504-895-9675

In the center of the Irish Channel neighborhood, Parasol's whips up the definitive roast beef po' boy, sloppy and delicious with gravy and mayonnaise and dressings of lettuce, tomato, and pickle. Also superb are the oyster, shrimp, and fish po' boys, known as "loaves," and eaten with just butter and hot sauce on the bread. A lot of local color can be observed here in the half hour it takes them to make a sandwich.

*Price: About $3 per person*
*Open Mon. and Wed.–Sat. for lunch and dinner; closed Tues. and Sun.*
*No credit cards accepted*

# PEKING

6600 Morrison Road (*at Interstate 10 in the Kenilworth Mall*),
New Orleans East
504-241-3321

Looking like any of a hundred boring neighborhood Chinese restaurants, the Peking is worth a trip across town for some of the best Szechuan and Mandarin food in the area. The fried dumplings have a great meat-and-herb stuffing and a powerful garlic-and-soy sauce. The shrimp toast are delectable little tetrahedrons of shrimp forcemeat with a nose-filling ginger-plum sauce. The hot-and-sour soup is rich and perfect for sinus trouble. Peking chicken is fried lightly with layers of nuts and sesame seeds and a highly original white sauce. Stir-fried pork or beef strings, *ma-po* bean curd, sautéed string beans with shrimp, and chicken with red pepper are the best of the spicy things. Service is iffy, but the food is consistently good.

*Price: About $12 per person*
*Open daily for lunch and dinner*
*Accepts American Express, Visa, and MasterCard*

---

# PIZZA SHACK

612 Sena Drive (*just off Veterans Boulevard*), Metairie
504-833-5882

New Orleans is not a great pizza town, but this unlikely place—operated by people with an unmistakable Spanish accent—is nothing but good. The pizzas are prepared to order and have a fine, thin, perfectly baked crust, covered with a pleasant, herbal sauce, good cheese, and fresh vegetables and meats. Not much on atmosphere; the sign in front has been out for a long time, but it is still in business making fine pizza pies.

*Price: About $8.50 for large sausage pizza*
*Open Tues.–Sun. for lunch and dinner; closed Mon.*
*Accepts Visa and MasterCard*

# RIB ROOM

In the French Quarter, in the Royal Orleans Hotel,
621 St. Louis Street
504-529-7045

As dining rooms in exclusive hotels go, this is a rather casual one, but it has a good specialty: a rotisserie filling an entire wall in the dining room. On its spits various birds and roasts rotate before open flames. The results are some pretty good food, very simply prepared. Other good dishes are the shrimp brochette, prime ribs of roast beef, *fettuccine* with a thick, tan sauce of cream and *morels*, and what the fanatics agree is the best chocolate *mousse* in New Orleans, thick and intense.

*Price: About $40 per person*
*Open Mon.–Sat. for lunch and dinner; Sun. for dinner only*
*Accepts all major credit cards*

# RISTORANTE PASTORE

301 Tchoupitoulas Street
504-524-1122

Several handsome, high-ceilinged, conservative modern rooms in odd shapes make up the second attempt by the owners to get New Orleanians to go for good Northern Italian food. The menu is extensive in items many local Italian places don't even have—*risotto,* for example, and seafood. Start with the *funghi trifolati,* a trio of fried mushrooms in herb butter, or the snails, or the *gnocchi,* or the angel's hair pasta in its spicy red sauce. There are some fine soups, including small, thin made-there *ravioli* in a light beef broth. In addition to Italian manifestations of seafood, you see the occasional blackened redfish and trout *meunière.* Veal is available in many forms; best is the *vitello primavera* with artichokes, and the veal Marsala. Service attempts to be elegant but comes out a little stiff.

*Price: About $24 per person*
*Open Mon.–Sat. for dinner only; closed Sun.*
*Accepts all major credit cards*

# RUTH'S CHRIS STEAK HOUSE
## 711 North Broad Street    504-482-9278
## 3633 Veterans Boulevard, Metairie    504-888-3600

Begun decades ago by a defector from the Crescent City named Chris, and later bought by present owner Ruth Fertel, this outfit is the high-profile New Orleans steak house and the restaurant of choice of the far end of the macho politics-and-sports crowd. The beef is of superior quality and served in an ideally aromatic version of the local butter sauce. At its best, it's a memorable steak. One could only wish that it were *always* at its best. The waitresses, every one of whom seems to be waiting on you, are determined to get it right, though. Side dishes include fantastic, fresh, fried potatoes in several shapes, fine baked spuds, and popular but kitschy *au gratin* vegetables covered with Cheddar. Mediocre desserts, and an oddly priced but extensive wine list. The Broad Street location is thought of as the "real" Ruth's Chris, but the food is similar at both.

*Price: About $25 per person*
*Open daily for lunch and dinner*
*All major credit cards accepted*

# SAZERAC
## In the Fairmont Hotel, 123 Baronne Street
### 504-529-4733

The Sazerac embodies the most traditional kind of dining-room elegance, which to some may come off as corniness: red velvet walls, plush banquettes, waiters in various antique high dress, lace-like tablecloths, and a singer-virtuoso accordionist duo who've been there so long I think it's safe to say they always will be. The menu has been branching out into new styles lately, but this is still the place to come if you want to have *blinis* with caviar, truffled *foie gras terrine* from Strasbourg, double *consommé* with quail eggs, rich lobster bisque, *chateaubriand,* that kind of thing. Everything—and I mean *everything* —receives some sort of tableside ministration on the gueridon. They do the best steak tartare in town here (mainly because they do it before you and you can tell them what to put in and leave out), and the bake shop produces the best pastries and cakes around. The wine list is exceptionally good; naturally, there is a *sommelier* who goes through even the forgotten ceremonies.

*Price: About $50 per person*
*Open Mon.–Fri. for lunch and dinner; Sat. and Sun. for dinner only*
*Accepts all major credit cards*

# SHOGUN
## 1414 Veterans Boulevard, Metairie
### 504-833-7477

By general agreement among the local *sushi* junkies, this is the top place for the enjoyment of raw fish. The focus of action is the *sushi* bar horseshoe, with its squat glass cases filled with tuna, yellowtail, squid, octopus, sea urchin, quail eggs, salmon, crab, shrimp, and lots of other stuff, all very fresh and assembled with élan by the chefs. There's another bar at which you can partake of skewers of marinated grilled meats and *tempura*-battered fried seafood, and these too are good. Or you can eat any of the above at the light wooden tables, if you can find one. Very popular.

*Price: About $10 per person*
*Open Mon., Wed.–Fri. for lunch and dinner; Sat.–Mon. for dinner only; closed Tues.*
*Accepts all major credit cards*

# TONEY'S SPAGHETTI HOUSE
## In the French Quarter, 212 Bourbon Street
### 504-568-9556

In the French Quarter (and especially on Bourbon Street) there are lots of places that look like good restaurants but which are actually tourist traps. Toney's, with its gaudy neon signs inside and out, looks like a tourist trap but serves terrific food at bargain prices. Spaghetti with a thick, slightly sweet red sauce is a specialty, but the best dish is the stuffed macaroni, a pair of big pasta sheets wrapped around a mixture of veal, cheese, garlic, and breading. This is especially good with Italian sausage on the side. The veal makes an adequate scallopine. Eggplant and chicken *parmigiana* are also good. There is pizza, a substantial amount of seafood, and a list of tasty, inexpensive daily specials which are more Creole than Italian. In the morning, Toney's serves a fine breakfast with great buttermilk biscuits. It's noisy and the waitresses are perfunctory, but the place is fun, good, and cheap.

*Price: About $7 per person*
*Open Mon.–Sat. for breakfast, lunch, and dinner; closed Sun.*
*Accepts American Express, Visa, and MasterCard*

# TONY ANGELLO'S
## 6262 Fleur de Lis Drive, Lakeview
### 504-488-0888

Tony Angello's phone number was unlisted when his present place first opened, which gives you an idea of the fervor of his following. It's hard to get a table here if you're not a regular, but the trouble is worth it. The menu is hardly unusual fare—very basic Sicilian–American cooking—but the executions are superb. A typical meal at Tony Angello's will contain nothing identifiable as the entrée; it's a procession of small courses like the lobster casserole, *fettuccine*, artichoke-and-oyster soup, eggplant Tina (like a *lasagne*, but with eggplant instead of pasta), marinated vegetable salad, trout Rosa (with crab meat), buster crabs (small soft-shells), *calamari*, and veal *piccata*. All of this is good, comfortable food. The lemon ice-box pie is the house dessert. Service is a bit rushed and the dining room is loud and dark. Check out the antique radios during the inevitable wait in the bar.

*Price: About $25 per person*
*Open Tues.–Sat. for dinner only; closed Sun. and Mon.*
*Accepts American Express, Visa, and MasterCard*

# TREY YUEN
## 600 North Causeway, Mandeville
### 504-626-4476

A striking Oriental temple built with hand-carved walls and ceilings imported from China, Trey Yuen is the grandest Chinese restaurant in the New Orleans area and one of the best. Despite the size of the place, there's usually a wait for a table, during which you can "ooh" and "ahh" at the fountains and exotic fish. The menu is surprisingly everyday until you learn about the specials, which incorporate much local seafood with unusual preparations. On the standard menu, though, you can find good hot-and-sour soup, lemon chicken, *wor shu op*, tea-smoked duck, and a variety of dishes made with a wonderfully complex, spicy, ruddy *tong-cho* sauce. If you call ahead and can assemble a party of eight, they'll do a banquet for you in a grand private room with some of the most exotic stuff you've ever put a chopstick to. Service is just okay; but the wine list is far above average for a Chinese place.

*Price: About $15 per person*
*Open Wed.–Fri. and Sun. for lunch and dinner; Sat. and Mon. for dinner only;*
*closed Tues.*
*All major credit cards accepted*

# UPPERLINE
### 1413 Upperline (*one block from St. Charles Avenue*)
### 504-891-9822

Owner-chef Jason Clevenger was a pioneer in the art—brand-new around here five years ago but now a commonplace—of grilling fish. Now that he has his own restaurant he's still at it, but his imagination is active and the menu full of very fine *nouvelle* Creole dishes. Among the better starters are a seafood sausage, shrimp *rémoulade* with two sauces, and some well-made, offbeat soups *du jour*. Besides the grilled fish—of which there are several varieties daily, all excellent—you can have as an entrée a fine roast duck with the sauce of the season, some pretty essays with veal, and pizza. Pizza? Yes, the gourmet variety that's in vogue these days. The best is the goat cheese-and-tomato variety, with a great crust and no gloppy sauce. The wine and dessert lists are short but good enough, and service is better than average. Upperline is rather small, but recent additions have made it less noisy and less claustrophobic.

*Price: About $25 per person*
*Open Tues.–Sat. for lunch and dinner; Sun. for dinner only; closed Mon.*
*Accepts all major credit cards*

# VERSAILLES
### 2100 St. Charles Avenue
### 504-524-2535

The long main dining room is laid out along an accordion-fold of windows overlooking the avenue and its streetcar tracks. It, as well as the other dining rooms and the orientation of the chef-owner Gunter Preuss, comes from the European hotel dining room tradition, but there's nothing humdrum about the food. The range of the kitchen is wide—in fact, they boast that they can prepare just about anything you feel like eating, given the availability of ingredients—and there are nightly specials that show their command and creativity.

Start off with the *pâtés* and sausages made on the premises, or the crab meat *Florentine* (a rich variation on Rockefeller sauce), or the great snails with their heady brown sauce inside a *pistolette* loaf of French bread. The soups are good and light, and the undefined salads—you just tell them what you want—are very well assembled.

The entrée specialty is veal with an elegant, aromatic crab meat-and-herb stuffing, but the veal in general is excellent. The rack of lamb and the various dishes with a filet mignon in the center (*Helder, Rossini, Périgourdine, au poivre,* etc.) are as good as they get. The quail stuffed with a light *mousse* and moistened with Champagne sauce and the duck with port are also superb.

Pastry specials and *mousses* make up the dessert list. The wine list is extensive and well chosen, with the best selection of German bottles in the city. Service is okay but not distinguished. The main flaw of the Versailles is a sedate ambience which may not appeal to everyone.

*Price: About $40 per person*
*Open Mon.–Sat. for dinner only; closed Sun.*
*All major credit cards accepted*

---

## WILLY COLN'S CHALET
### 2505 Whitney Avenue, Gretna
**504-361-3860**

Only about a third of the menu is German, but the chef is from Cologne and his renditions of classic German dishes are the only good ones in town. During May and October and on Thursday nights, they really get into it, with a special German menu complete with a choice of some ten sausages, homemade sauerkraut, and an oom-pah band. Then, as always, the best dish is a roasted veal shank for two, with fresh vegetables in the natural juices.

The non-German food is good, too. There's a Bahamian seafood chowder with lots of fish and spice that gets a meal off to a good start, as well as a similar-tasting redfish Caribbean style. The duckling with green peppercorns and the filet with black peppercorns are other hits. The best dessert is the light Black Forest cake, but the chef does good pastries across the board. Service is okay but not polished; the wine list is quite good, with a lot of German bottles and a respectable selection from France and California, too.

*Price: About $30 per person*
*Open Thurs. and Fri. for lunch and dinner; Sat. and Tues. for dinner only;*
*closed Sun. and Mon.*
*Accepts all major credit cards*

---

## WISE CAFETERIA
### 909 South Jefferson Davis Parkway
**504-488-7811**

Families eat inexpensively—but usually very poorly—in cafeterias. Wise's is the great exception. It does superb versions not only of the cafeteria standards, but also of many Creole specialties. You can always get a great plate of red beans and rice, a lusty bowl of gumbo, fried and broiled seafood (if it's frozen, they tell you on a sign), and bread pudding here. The roast beef, ham, and boiled brisket are always of superior quality and freshness. And there's a good selection of vegetables and desserts.

*Price: About $5 per person*
*Open Sun.–Fri. for lunch and dinner; closed Sat.*
*No credit cards accepted*

# NEW YORK

## By John F. Mariani

**AMERICAN**
An American Place
Arizona 206
Carolina
The Coach House
Huberts
Texarkana

**BAR**
Maxwell's Plum
McSorley's Old Ale House
Oak Bar
P. J. Clarke's

**BARBECUE**
Carolina
Smokey's Pit

**BRAZILIAN**
Cabana Carioca

**BREAKFAST**
American Festival Café
Fraunces Tavern
The Silver Palace

**CARIBBEAN**
Provechos

**CHINESE**
Auntie Yuan
Chez Vong
Pig Heaven
Shun Lee Palace
The Silver Palace
Wong Kee

**CONTINENTAL**
Aurora
Cellar in the Sky
The Four Seasons
The Terrace

**CRAB HOUSE**
Sidewalkers'

**CUBAN**
Sabor
Victor's Café 52

**CZECH**
Vašata

**DELICATESSEN**
Katz's
Nathan's Famous

## ECLECTIC
Arcadia
Arizona 206
Café des Artistes
The Four Seasons
Gotham Bar and Grill
Jams
Lavin's
Maxwell's Plum
The Quilted Giraffe
Woods Gramercy

## ETHIOPIAN
Abyssinia

## FAMILY RESTAURANT
American Festival Café
Serendipity 3

## FRENCH
Brasserie
Café 58
Chanterelle
La Caravelle
La Côte Basque
La Petite Marmite
La Récolte
La Réserve
La Tulipe
Le Bernardin
Le Cirque
Le Perigord
Le Régence
Lutèce
Maxime's
Montrachet
Nicole's
The Odeon
Petrossian
Prunelle
Quatorze

## GREEK
Xenia

## HAMBURGERS/HOT DOGS
J. G. Melon
Nathan's Famous
P. J. Clarke's
Sabrett's

## HOTEL DINING ROOM
Café Pierre
La Récolte
Le Régence
Maurice
Nicole's

## HUNGARIAN
Mocca Restaurant

## ICE CREAM
Sedutto
Serendipity 3

## INDIAN
Bombay Palace
Nirvana
Nirvana Club One
Raga

## ITALIAN
Alfredo
Amerigo's
Barbetta
Campiello
Contrapunto
Dieci
Felidia
Il Monello
Il Mulino
Il Nido
Lello Ristorante
Marcello
Parioli Romanissimo
Sandro's

**JAPANESE**
Hatsuhana
Mitsukoshi
Nippon

**KOREAN**
Woo Lae Oak of Seoul

**MEXICAN**
Arizona 206
Café Marimba
Rosa Mexicano

**OPEN LATE**
Brasserie
The Odeon

**PANORAMA**
Nirvana
Nirvana Club One
The Terrace
Windows on the World

**PIZZA**
John's

**RUSSIAN**
Petrossian
The Russian Tea Room

**SEAFOOD**
The Grand Central Oyster Bar
& Restaurant
Le Bernardin
Le Régence
The Manhattan Ocean Club

**SOUL FOOD**
Sylvia's

**SPANISH**
The Ballroom
Meson Botin

**STEAKS AND CHOPS**
Amerigo's
Palm
Palm Too
Smith & Wollensky

**SUBURBAN**
Maxime's
*(Many more suburban New York
restaurants are listed in the
appendix of this book.)*

**SWISS**
Swiss Chalet/Chalet Suisse

**THAI**
Bangkok Cuisine

**UNIQUE PROPERTIES**
Fraunces Tavern
Katz's Delicatessen
Maxwell's Plum
Nathan's Famous
Petrossian

**VIETNAMESE**
Indochine

**WINE BAR/RESTAURANT**
Lavin's
Soho Kitchen and Bar

The restaurants of New York, like the restaurants of Paris, are inextricably bound to the social, political, and economic life of the city. As soon as the Dutch settled New Amsterdam there was a tavern built by Governor Kieft because he had tired of entertaining dignitaries at home and because his contract with the West India Company stipulated the tavern would sell only the company's liquors. George Washington bade farewell to his troops at Fraunces Tavern in 1783, and the reconstructed building still houses an evocative restaurant in the Wall Street area.

New York was also home to the first modern restaurants, like Delmonico's, Rector's, and Louis Sherry's, in the nineteenth century—cavernous places where tycoons and trenchermen like Diamond Jim Brady achieved feats of gluttony unmatched by any since Lucullus. It was to New York that European immigrants, brought their own culinary diversity by opening trattorias, rathskellers, and delicatessens, alongside the established beer halls, oyster palaces, and cafeterias that lined the streets from Greenwich Village to Harlem. It was in New York that the term "Café Society" was coined and the speakeasy born, and in 1939, at the New York World's Fair, Americans were introduced to international cuisines that immediately afterwards became part of the city's gastronomy—the most noteworthy being the food at Le Pavillon, which set the standards for deluxe French dining rooms in this country for decades to come.

New York has given the world vichyssoise (created at the Ritz-Carlton), English muffins (sold by an immigrant from Bath, England), pasta primavera (first made by Sirio Maccioni of Le Cirque), and the first pizzas served outside of Naples (at Gennaro Lombardi's restaurant on Spring Street). Its Chinatown, Little Italy, Jewish Lower East Side, and German Yorkville spawned hundreds of ethnic restaurants and styles of cooking that have become part of the American kitchen.

Today, with more than 16,000 restaurants in its boroughs, New York is a citadel of extraordinary gustatory range—from Greek diners to *nouvelle cuisine* dining rooms, from *dim sum* parlors to Japanese restaurants with private *tatami* rooms, from power restaurants to simple little family eateries. Name an industry and there is sure to be a restaurant where its leaders congregate. Name a trendy hot spot, and you can be sure it will be passé by next week.

Still, New York is seriously lacking in a number of ethnic restaurants:

Minneapolis has far more Vietnamese restaurants than does New York; there are no great German restaurants left, few good Spanish, fewer Puerto Rican, and only a handful of Russian restaurants. While Washington, D.C., has at least a dozen Ethiopian eateries, New York has perhaps three or four at most.

But if you want *cassoulet* at four in the morning, or barbecued ribs at midnight, you can find them in New York. The friendliest, the haughtiest, the most generous, and the chintziest restaurateurs and service staffs are to be found here, too, and for as many suave captains as there are on the East Side, there are many bumbling out-of-work actors waitering on the West. You can be sure you'll find the highest and lowest priced food in New York, but generally it will cost you more to dine here than in any other city. Largely this is the function of real estate prices for restaurants, of union wages, and of a supportive public who will pay almost anything to be where the action is—which is not necessarily the same as going where the best food is.

The following list barely scratches the surface of New York's better restaurants, and an omission is not necessarily an indication of a restaurant's being second-rate. We do have our tourist traps and we have some terribly overrated dining rooms. The selection that follows is, I hope, a good cross section of the best in their category and places that will give a visitor a sense of New York's gastronomic character.

*John F. Mariani is the author of* The Dictionary of American Food & Drink *(Ticknor & Fields, 1983) and* Eating Out: Fearless Dining in Ethnic Restaurants *(Quill, 1985). He wrote* Playboy's *"Critics' Choice: America's Best Restaurants" (1984) and compiled* Esquire *magazine's "Cheers!" selection of outstanding restaurants and bars (1984 and 1985). He has reviewed restaurants for* The New York Times, Cue, USA TODAY, *and* WNEW–TV, *and currently writes the "Country Tables" column for* Country Living's Country Cooking *magazine and "Matters of Taste" for* MD *Magazine. Mr. Mariani was honored by* Cook's *magazine in the* Who's Who in American Cooking *awards for 1985.*

# ABYSSINIA
## 35 Grand Street (*near Thompson Street*)
### 212-226-5959

One of a mere handful of Ethiopian restaurants in New York, this smacks of true authenticity—you sit on stools, eat with your fingers from a large platter of food, scoop up the stews and morsels with the *crêpe*-like *injera,* and sip on honey wine. The atmosphere is a bit dreary, but the staff is helpful in educating you in the ways of Ethiopian cuisine, with its hotly spiced lamb, chicken, fish, and vegetable dishes like *yekik wot* (split peas), *doro wat* (chicken with a hard-boiled egg), and *kitfo* (the national dish, something like steak tartare).

*Price: About $20 per person*
*Open Tues.–Sun. for dinner only; closed Mon.*
*Accepts American Express*

---

## ALFREDO
### 240 Central Park South (*off Columbus Circle*)
#### 212-246-7050

There are three completely unrelated Italian restaurants in Manhattan called "Alfredo," but this is easily the best of them. The dining room is getting a theatrical re-design (the place is a favorite of opera stars from the Met), and owner Gianni Minale looks a little like Rossano Brazzi. There are some delightful regional specialties here—veal sausage braised with *radicchio* and *arugula,* yellow peppers stuffed with black olives, and perfect *risotto alla milanese* prepared on the spot. The simpler entrées are the better ones, and most of the pastas are rich without being heavy. The wine list is solid in Italian selections.

*Price: About $25–$30 per person*
*Open Mon.–Fri. for lunch and dinner; Sat. for dinner only; closed Sun.*
*Accepts all major credit cards*

---

## AMERICAN FESTIVAL CAFÉ
### At Rockefeller Plaza, 20 West 50 Street
#### 212-246-6699

It's difficult to imagine a more beautiful spot for a restaurant than under the gaze of the gilded Prometheus and the majesty of Rockefeller Center, and that is why The American Festival Café is jammed at lunch, both on the ice-skating rink (during summer) and in the dining room itself, which is decorated with some remarkably fine folk art. This is a wonderful place for breakfast, specifically the changing theme meals like a "Plantation Breakfast" that may begin with biscuits, muffins, and fruits, and goes on to rice waffles, ham steaks, Thomas Jefferson's chicken hash, and Creole shrimp *fricassee* with scrambled eggs; or a great spot for the family while waiting for a show at Radio City Music Hall around the block. At Christmas, there's no better spot to take the family for good food and a little ice skating on the adjacent rink.

*Price: About $7.95 for breakfast; about $20–$25 per persom for dinner*
*Open daily for breakfast, lunch, and dinner*
*Accepts all major credit cards*

# AMERIGO'S
### 3587 East Tremont Avenue, Bronx
#### 212-792-3600

For forty years Amerigo's has been one of New York's finest Italian restaurants. This is not your "red sauce-white sauce" Bronx spaghetti house; owners Tony and Anna Cortese run a careful kitchen where sauces are perfectly balanced—*pesto* with fragrant basil, garlic, olive oil, *pignoli,* and *parmigiano; bolognese* with more vegetables than meat or tomato; *provinciale* with assertive capers and black olives. *Prosciutto* is cut so thin that you could read *Il Progresso* through it, and the melon it lies atop is as sweet as candy. Chicken soup is made with whole chickens. *Gnocchi* actually taste of potato, and the *fettuccine all' Alfredo* is a paragon dish of butter, cream, and cheese. But where most Italian restaurants fall down in the entrée department, Amerigo's soars—from some of the best prime sirloins in New York to an *osso buco* that would be the envy of any Milanese chef. Veal dishes range from a *paillard* in parsley butter to a scallopine with diced *prosciutto* and Marsala wine to a superb veal chop. Ask for an *arugula* salad or steamed broccoli with olive oil, and tell them you want the *espresso "ristretto"* (very rich and concentrated). The dessert cart offers a fair selection of Italian and French pastries (some from Dumas Patisserie), the ice cream is from Sedutto (see page 616), and the wine list has good bottlings from almost every region of Italy. What K-Paul's Louisiana Kitchen is to Cajun food, Amerigo's is to Italian-American cooking—lusty, abundant, rich, highly seasoned, and based on only the very finest ingredients. About a 20-minute drive from midtown; in a very safe neighborhood. Free parking.

*Price: About $20–$25 per person*
*Open Wed.–Mon. for lunch and dinner; closed Tues.*
*Accepts all major credit cards*

# AN AMERICAN PLACE
### 969 Lexington Avenue (*at 70 Street*)
#### 212-517-7660

Larry Forgione has been a leader in the renaissance of American cooking since his days at The River Café, and his An American Place has become a central meeting place for gourmets, food writers, and foreigners who want to know where American restaurants are headed. Here, in a small dining room of sedate but intimate ambience, Forgione and his crew, having receded from some of the extravagances of the past, now turn out marvels of flavor and texture. His herb *crêpes* with Calistoga goat cheese and sweet onion sauce has been copied all over the country, and he instigated the current rage for farm-raised chickens. Forgione is fascinated by sources—oysters from Cape Cod, ham from Virginia, even endive from the Bronx—and is as respectful of old recipes as he is geared for the new. Indeed, one of his best desserts is based on his grandmother's chocolate cake and his *charlotte russe* seems sprung from a nineteenth-century cookbook. An American Place is one of those New York restaurants all gourmet pilgrims hie toward as soon as they hit town.

*Price: Fixed price at $52 per person*
*Open Mon.–Sat. for dinner only; closed Sun.*
*Accepts all major credit cards*

---

# ARCADIA
## 21 East 62 Street (*near Madison Avenue*)
### 212-223-2900

Diminutive chef Anne Rosenzweig's tiny restaurant between Fifth and Madison avenues has grown large in reputation since its opening last year. The menu reflects the changes in season and the glorious marriage of meats and fish with greens, so that there is always texture abounding in every dish. The buckwheat pasta with goat cheese is a good starter when available, and chicken *"bouillabaisse"* is a charming idea. The lobster club sandwich is outrageous for its price but exquisite for its flavor. Desserts are always rich and completely satisfying. The room is too small for intimate conversation, and you'll probably wait for your reserved table, though the management seems genuinely apologetic for this chronic inconvenience. The Paul Davis murals are peacefully pastoral, even though they look as if Bugs Bunny or Daffy Duck is about to spring from behind one of the trees. This is a bellwether restaurant of fine taste.

*Price: Fixed price at $45 per person*
*Open Mon.–Fri. for lunch and dinner; Sat. for dinner only; closed Sun.*
*Accepts American Express, Visa, and MasterCard*

---

# ARIZONA 206
## 206 East 60 Street (*near Third Avenue*)
### 212-838-0440

On first appearance, Arizona 206 looks and sounds like a gimmick, as in, "let's open a New Wave Mexican restaurant right near Bloomingdales," but don't be fooled by the stark plaster walls, raw wood, loud crowd, and broil-or-freeze ventilation. Arizona 206 is one of the most exciting restaurants to hit town in a while, the brainchild of owner Joe Santo and consultant Clark Wolfe, who wanted a casual and fun restaurant but one that served really good food based on the sunny flavors of the Southwest. Young chef Brendan Walsh has delivered precisely that. His dishes are beautifully presented without ever bordering on the precious, and his forceful use of chile peppers and high seasonings is impeccably balanced by bright vegetables and legumes, resulting in luscious creations such as venison with sour cream and black beans, goat cheese cornmeal ravioli in chile butter sauce, a salad of lentils and collard greens, barbecued quail, and grilled salmon, and some sumptuous desserts, which include pine nut tart, walnut-chocolate cake with *espresso* ice cream, and a wonderful compote of warm fruit and cool vanilla ice cream. The margaritas have bits of lime zest in them and the small wine list is well chosen, as is the staff, who combine youth with exuberance in fine measure.

*Price: About $25 per person*
*Open daily for lunch and dinner*
*Accepts all major credit cards*

---

## AUNTIE YUAN
### 1191A First Avenue (*near 64 Street*)
### 212-744-4040

If you're used to Chinese food served on Formica and use sign language to make yourself understood, Auntie Yuan will be a shock. The place is very sleek, with black the dominant non-color, pin-lights shining on brilliantly flourishing flowers, and a well-prepared staff that tries to "make up a menu for you." What they don't tell you is how much that menu will cost, and it's going to be plenty. The food, however, is refined and generally delicious, based on the finest imported ingredients.

*Price: Tasting menu $38; other fixed-price dinners at $24 and $26; à la carte,*
*about $25 per person*
*Open daily for lunch and dinner*
*Accepts American Express*

---

## AURORA
### 60 East 49 Street (*near Madison Avenue*)
### 212-692-9292

Aurora was designed by owner Joe Baum, to appeal to the same powerful business crowd that flocks to The Four Seasons (which Baum also had a hand in some years back), and, in a few short months, it has succeeded in building a clientele that wants lots of room between tables, soft leather banquettes, and a menu that is substantial but not too fussy. Some of the design in the dining room—bulbous pink lights, space cadet chairs, and china with little gumballs in the pattern—lacks the majesty you might expect, and, at this early writing, the service staff is not yet able to keep up with Gerard Pangaud's kitchen. But Pangaud turns out some impeccably tasteful food—lightly sautéed sweetbreads, blushing pink kidneys with mushrooms, a wondrous lobster in ginger and Sauternes, and some of the finest desserts in the city, including a chocolate cake that may well be the best dessert I've ever had.

Prices are, sad to say, beyond belief: $9 for three Roquefort-filled ravioli and most entrées at dinner are upwards of $25–$30. The wine list is excellent, and the bar, set square as you enter through a charming portico, is a great spot to talk about rumors of a corporate takeover.

*Price: About $50 per person*
*Open Mon.–Fri. for lunch and dinner; Sat. for dinner only; closed Sun.*
*Accepts all major credit cards*

---

# THE BALLROOM
## 253 West 28 Street (*near Eighth Avenue*)
### 212-244-3005

The Ballroom—convenient to Madison Square Garden—is a great place to go for a light meal of Spanish appetizers called *tapas*. These little plates of anchovies in grape leaves, curried mussels, *chorizo* sausage, *seviche,* and dozens of others are irresistible, but don't ignore the very fine entrées too. Chef Felipe Rojas-Lombardi is a master of earthy Spanish cuisine. The Marion Pinto mural of New York School painters is fascinating, and there is a cabaret out back that draws top talent.

*Price:* Tapas *range from about $2.50–$7.00; full meals about $25–$30*
*Open Tues.–Sat. for dinner only*
*Accepts all major credit cards*

# BANGKOK CUISINE
## 885 Eighth Avenue (*near 53 Street*)
### 212-581-6370

New York has a good number of Thai eateries, and this was one of the first and is still one of the best. Don't count on elegance: This is real storefront decor, complete with fish tank. The food can be fiercely hot, so ask them to temper it if you don't want to risk having scar tissue form after the third bite. But the seasonings back up the heat admirably. The *sates* are good appetizers, the chicken, pork, and whole fish dishes are exciting, and the noodles like *pad thai* are very satisfying. There's Thai beer to put out the fires. Desserts are worth a try, if only for once in your life.

*Price: About $15 per person*
*Open Mon.–Sat. for lunch and dinner; Sun. for dinner only*
*Accepts American Express, Visa, and MasterCard*

---

# BARBETTA
## 321 West 46 Street (*near Eighth Avenue*)
### 212-246-9171

The claim by the Maioglio family that Barbetta is New York's oldest full-scale Italian restaurant (1906) has never been challenged, and time has only improved this evocative dining room in the Theater District. The elegant main room—in peach and rococo molding—is a splendid space, but in summer the garden out back has, understandably, the preferred tables. The menu here offers an amalgam of Italian standards, but you should definitely choose the Piedmont specialties Barbetta is known for—*risotto alla piemontese, bagna cauda, fonduta,* and the many game dishes offered in season. In fall and winter you can get *fettuccine* showered with white truffles (which will cost you plenty). With these order one of the many Piedmont wines like Barolo, Barbaresco, or Gavi, and end with *granita di caffè.* There's a very good pre-theater menu at $32 per person, but it's nice to relax after the theater crowd has left and order without having to rush off anywhere else that evening.

*Price: About $30–$35 per person*
*Open Mon.–Sat. for lunch and dinner*
*Accepts all major credit cards*

# BOMBAY PALACE

30 West 52 Street (*near Fifth Avenue*)

212-541-7777

Bombay Palace, now six-and-a-half years old, is the flagship in a carefully nurtured chain of restaurants run by Sant Chatwal, and, more for its consistency than for its diversity, it is probably New York's best Indian restaurant. Though not so pretty as Raga (see page 614), nor so well situated as Nirvana Club One (see page 608), Bombay Palace runs a careful, friendly dining room serving fresh Indian delicacies, from the appetizers of *samosas* and *pakoras* to the *tandoori* specialties, from the *thali* vegetarian platter to the rich desserts, from the layered *paratha* to the puffy *naan* breads. The room is pleasant, as is the bar with its complimentary finger food, and the $9.95 luncheon buffet is a very good bargain.

*Price: About $20 per person*
*Open daily for lunch and dinner*
*Accepts all major credit cards*

# BRASSERIE

100 East 53 Street (*near Park Avenue*)

212-751-4840

If you want a quick bite to eat at four in the morning (or two in the afternoon, or ten at night) and can't face another hamburger or pastrami sandwich, head for the Brasserie—open twenty-four hours, every day of the year. The brasserie fare—*quiche, cassoulet,* onion soup, and *choucroute*—can be pretty good, served with a minimum of fuss.

*Price: About $15–$20 per person*
*Open daily 24 hours a day*
*Accepts all major credit cards*

# CABANA CARIOCA

## 123 West 45 Street (*near Avenue of the Americas*)
### 212-581-8088

Be not bothered by the dingy stairs you must climb to get to this funny little Brazilian restaurant with its tacky artwork, thickly varnished wood paneling, and excess of tables and chairs. This is one of New York's friendliest restaurants, filled with Brazilians who come here for the gargantuan pots of mixed seafood, black beans, rice, and cold beer. The portion of *feijoada* (pork, sausage, black beans, kale, orange, and *manioc* flour) is enough to feed a family of four, and prices are amazingly low. There's a second Cabana Carioca just down the block.

*Price: About $15 per person*
*Open daily for lunch and dinner*
*Accepts all major credit cards*

# CAFÉ DES ARTISTES

## 1 West 67 Street (*near Central Park West*)
### 212-877-3500

Anyone who is not stirred romantically by the Café des Artistes' Howard Chandler Christy murals of Jazz Age girls cavorting nude in sun-dappled forest should consult a gerontologist on the state of his health. The rest of Café des Artistes—which last year celebrated its seventy-fifth anniversary—is every inch as romantic, while the menu, overseen by chef André Guillou, is full of the kinds of foods that make you feel wonderful—abundant *charcuterie, confit* of duck, a rich *bourride,* leg of lamb with *flageolet* beans, and some of the best desserts in New York, including owner George Lang's *Ilona torte,* based on his Hungarian mother's recipe. This has long been a special place, and its proximity to Lincoln Center makes it fit for a feast before or after the arias. Service is a match for the food and decor. The menu changes daily.

*Price: About $25–$30 per person*
*Open daily for lunch and dinner*
*Accepts all major credit cards*

# CAFÉ 58

## 232 East 58 Street (*near Second Avenue*)
### 212-758-5665

For a long time now this has been the place to come for French country fare —*saucisson chaud, lapin à la moutarde, choucroute garni, pied de porc grillé, cervelle au beurre noir, crème caramel,* and so on—at moderate prices and in an atmo-sphere of complete comfort. It's as close to a true bistro as you'll find in New York, and the city's French community forms the most faithful clientele here.

*Price: About $18–$20 per person*
*Open Mon.–Sat. for lunch and dinner; Sun. for dinner only*
*Accepts all major credit cards*

---

## CAFÉ MARIMBA
### 1115 Third Avenue (*entrance on 65 Street*)
### 212-935-1161

A subterranean, beautifully lighted, casual, and loud Mexican restaurant serv-ing an unusual menu of dishes such as *gorditas, chilaquiles, ensalada de jícama y berros, higaldo encebollado,* and good ice creams—all orchestrated by Zarela Martinez. Don't expect highly seasoned food, however. This is somewhat refined Mexican cookery.

*Price: About $25 per person*
*Open daily for dinner only*
*Accepts American Express and Diner's Club*

---

## CAFÉ PIERRE
### In the Pierre Hotel, 2 East 61 Street (*at Fifth Avenue*)
### 212-838-8000

You don't get much more swank than this—a Valerian Rybar-designed, grand deluxe, wear-your-best-duds dining room all in grays and *trompe l'oeil,* but with none of the stuffiness that usually hangs on such trappings. It's a beautiful room, and the menu is a reasonable blend of the classic and the *nouvelle.* Portions may be a bit on the lean side, and some dishes look too pretty to eat, but the food is quite serious and generally delicious. This is one of a very few hotel dining rooms in New York where you'd actually book a reservation whether or not you were staying upstairs in the opulent Pierre Hotel. In the afternoons there's tea offered in the rotunda adjacent to the restaurant.

*Price: About $40–$50 per person*
*Open daily for breakfast, lunch, and dinner*
*Accepts all major credit cards*

# CAMPIELLO
## 1466 First Avenue (*near 76 Street*)
### 212-472-3333

Parioli Romanissimo (see page 610) is a tough act to follow, but Campiello
has occupied the former's old location admirably, and the kitchen is very
strong here. The decor is somewhat somber, and the place could use some
better lighting, but there's no need to brighten the food, which is of a very
high order, despite the clichés evident on the printed card. Ask for the specials,
and you'll enjoy wonderful dishes like shrimp with *prosciutto, ricotta-*and-
spinach *malfatti* with fresh tomato sauce, *pappardelle con funghi* with cream,
perfect lobster *fra diavolo* in a bright tomato-flecked broth, and the finest *pasta
e fagioli* I've ever encountered. Entrées are a little anticlimactic after this, but
the lamb with sage is pink and nicely done. The fruit and *tartufo* dessert are
good, the *espresso* excellent, and the wine list small but solid.

*Price: About $25–$30 per person*
*Open daily for dinner only*
*Accepts all major credit cards*

# CAROLINA
## 355 West 46 Street (*near Eighth Avenue*)
### 212-245-0058

With all the so-called New American gimmickry in restaurants these days, it's
nice to find a spot that serves first-rate American classics in surroundings that
don't seem self-consciously "down home." Carolina, in the Theater District,
is a charmer—a folk quilt on the wall, a shiny zinc bar, a skylighted back
room, and very amiable service by a young crew—and you find a lot of
visiting actors who come here for the chili pepper *soufflé,* grilled shrimp,
biscuits and cornbread, ham with cherry sauce, and a chocolate mud cake that
will knock your socks off. The barbecued ribs are among the juiciest and best
charred around town. The wine list is small but well chosen.

*Price: About $20–$25 per person*
*Open Mon.–Fri. for lunch and dinner; Sat. and Sun. for dinner only*
*Accepts American Express, Visa, and MasterCard*

# CELLAR IN THE SKY
## 1 World Trade Center
### 212-938-1111

This is the best restaurant (of twenty-two!) in the World Trade Center complex, and, with only 36 seats, it's a tough reservation to make on short notice. Cellar in the Sky is designed to show off international food and wines at their best, so twice a month the menu is changed—seven courses and five wines for a fixed price of $70. There is usually a selection of canapés, then a *terrine* or *pâté,* then a fish course, then meat, poultry, or game, a fine selection of cheeses, dessert, and chocolates—all with wines selected by Kevin Zraly, one of this country's most knowledgeable cellar masters.

The dining room itself is surrounded by metal racks full of wines, which unfortunately block your view from the 107 floor of the World Trade Center. But people come here for the food and wine more than for the spectacle, and they are rarely disappointed.

*Price: Fixed price at $70 per person, complete with wines*
*Open Mon.–Sat. for one seating only at 7:30 P.M.; closed Sun.*
*Accepts all major credit cards*

# CHANTERELLE
## 89 Grand Street (*on Greene Street*)
### 212-966-6960

Chanterelle is a matter of taste; some find it a little cold, though few gourmets would argue with the high level of cooking here. Located on a corner in Soho, the place is so stark as to make you think they ran out of money to decorate it. It is also tiny—no more than a dozen tables—which makes reservations a little tough to come by. Chef David Waltuck is very serious, but never wacky in his ideas. So you will have a luscious seafood sausage, shimmering *foie gras,* good Muscovy duck breast, and superb desserts. There is also a generous cheese selection and a good wine list. Your reception may be a bit precious.

*Price: Fixed price at $50 and $65 per person*
*Open Tues.–Sat. for dinner only; closed Sun. and Mon.*
*Accepts American Express, Visa, and MasterCard*

# CHEZ VONG
## 220 East 46 Street (*near Third Avenue*)
### 212-867-1111

Chez Vong, which has a branch in Paris, resembles the kind of opulent, antique-crammed Chinese restaurants you'll find in Hong Kong and on Taiwan—places where money is no object. It is the kind of place where you book private parties, for there are nine private rooms, while the main dining room will dazzle you with its lavishness. Even the menu itself looks like a courtly manuscript. The cuisine ranges the Mainland—from Szechuan to Peking—mostly with superior results. The dumplings are delicate, the Peking duck a model of form, and the whole fish dishes aromatic and full of ginger and other seasonings. The service staff is friendly but a bit slow. The wine list is probably the best in any Chinese restaurant in New York. None of this comes cheap.

*Price: About $25–$30 per person*
*Open Mon.–Fri. for lunch and dinner; Sat. and Sun. for dinner only*
*Accepts all major credit cards*

# THE COACH HOUSE
## 110 Waverly Place (*near Washington Square*)
### 212-777-0303

A whole generation of American chefs is just now beginning to realize the achievements of Leon Lianides, Greek-born owner of The Coach House for thirty-five years, in bringing each dish on his deceptively simple menu to its highest degree of taste. From the celebrated black bean soup to the perfectly grilled shrimp, from the homey corn sticks to the crispy roasted lamb chops, from the ethereal *dacquoise* to the balanced pecan pie, the dishes at the Coach House are models of form and flavor. The peppery crab cakes have launched a new interest in that humble item; and Paul Bocuse is said to have called Lianides' black-pepper steak the best he'd ever tasted. Personally I count his striped bass poached in court bouillon as one of the finest dishes I have ever eaten, and it is with difficulty that I must always choose between that or the grilled striped bass with dill sauce. Some have criticized The Coach House for never changing its menu, but that is like criticizing Greg Louganis for never changing his diving style. When you are at the top of your form, there is little reason to change anything.

The Coach House's decor is a nice blend of Washington Square nostalgia and Early American antiques, with a magnificent central chandelier and exquisite English and American paintings. The smaller upstairs room is not nearly so pretty. Service is genial, mostly by waiters who have been with Mr. Lianides for a long while. The wine list is solid, with some especially good California bottlings.

*Price: About $35 per person; fixed-price dinners at $28.50–$36.00 per person*
*Open Tues.–Sun. for dinner only; closed Mon.*
*Accepts all major credit cards*

---

# CONTRAPUNTO
## 200 East 60 Street (*on Third Avenue*)
### 212-751-8616

This smart-looking, bright second-story dining room with wrap-around windows over Third Avenue is a well-realized concept built around a dozen or so pastas ranging from the traditional to the exotic—most with excellent results. The place is casual and not too expensive, usually filled with people who've just exited a movie or Bloomingdale's across the street. Entrées and desserts are well worth ordering too.

*Price: About $20–$25 per person*
*Open Mon.–Sat. for lunch and dinner; Sun. for dinner only*
*Accepts all major credit cards*

---

# DIECI
## 1568 First Avenue (*near 81 Street*)
### 212-628-6565

Dieci has a very faithful neighborhood clientele who know what most New Yorkers do not yet know: that the Italian menu here is far more interesting than better-known places in the same district and served with far more friendliness. Dieci gets its phalanx of limos outside, but owner Joe Franco is more devoted to good food than to star searches. He has his own *mozzarella* made and would not sully it with any tomato that was not bright red. The veal salad with beans is a delight, and I've not yet had a single disappointing pasta here. Even *penne alla vodka* (usually a dumb dish elsewhere) has real snap from the peppers marinated in the vodka. *Penne all' abbruzzese* is full of zest, and *cappellini alla primavera* a fine rendering of a much-abused dish. There's good *carpaccio*, and pray the chef has some wild mushrooms to sauté in garlic and oil. Then move on to the veal *alla giardino*—a lightly breaded scallopine topped with crisp greens and a vinaigrette that sets the whole thing up. The chocolate *tartufo* is a good finish; *espresso* is well made. The wine list has some rarities on it, but most bottlings are fairly priced.

*Price: About $30–$35 per person*
*Open daily for dinner only*
*Accepts American Express, Visa, and MasterCard*

---

# FELIDIA
## 243 East 58 Street (*near Second Avenue*)
### 212-758-1479

New York may have more Italian restaurants than Florence and Naples combined, but most serve up a tired card of Italian-American clichés. Felidia, run by Felice and Lidia Bastianich (whose first names give the restaurant its name, which just happens to be a goddess of good fortune), specializes in the cooking of the North (the family is from Istria), and the menu changes seasonally—*risotto* with cuttlefish, pasta with quail, a Triestine soup called *yota* made with white beans, pork, and sauerkraut, a dish called *krafi* made with several cheeses, veal, rum, lemon, and orange rind, and—*grazie Dio!*—good desserts. You could feast on nothing but the flat *foccacia* bread sprinkled with rosemary and onions, but put yourself in Lidia's hands, for her generous spirit aims to please, and the more open-minded the customer, the more Lidia is likely to bring out something special. The wine list is extraordinary, especially in its Piedmont and Tuscan listings.

The two dining rooms are decorated with polished dark woods and brick-work made to resemble an elegant country villa. Service can be rushed and there have been problems of overbooking, so reservations tend to pile up on one another, as do the customers by nine o'clock.

*Price: About $40 per person*
*Open Mon.–Fri. for lunch and dinner; Sat. for dinner only; closed Sun.*
*Accepts all major credit cards*

---

# THE FOUR SEASONS
## 99 East 52 Street (*near Park Avenue*)
### 212-754-9494

For its majesty and design, for its unparalleled level of service, for its magnificent wine cellar, and for its sheer professionalism, The Four Seasons ranks as one of the world's great restaurants. Set on three levels of the Seagram's Building, with rippling beaded metal draperies, a 20-foot ceiling, works by

Picasso, Miró, and Rauschenberg, a pool in the dining room, this place was designed by Philip Johnson to be a corporate cathedral, and that it is. For the daily and nightly seatings are reserved for the power elite of New York (it's especially popular in publishing circles), and some people may feel a bit intimidated. Don't be: You *can* get a table without too much advance notice, and you'll be served impeccably well. Owners Paul Kovi and Tom Margittai will see to that. The kitchen, headed by Seppi Renggli, can be brilliant, though the food is much better when it is simpler, and there are occasional lapses of good taste. But this is a unique restaurant and must be experienced as a lesson in sophistication. Brings lots and lots of money, but lunch in the Grill and a pre-theater supper are not so pricey. There is a Spa Cuisine menu for those watching their weight.

*Price: About $50–$60 per person*
*Open Mon.–Sat. for lunch and dinner; closed Sun.*
*Accepts all major credit cards*

---

## FRAUNCES TAVERN
### Broad and Pearl streets
**212-269-0144**

This historic structure (actually a reconstruction of one of New York's earliest buildings) houses a delightful museum that points up the role New York played in the period leading up to and during the Revolutionary War, and the exhibitions here are well worth a visit. This is where George Washington bade farewell to his troops on December 4, 1783, and the bar room and dining rooms are touchingly evocative. The restaurant, with its colonial motif, serves an excellent breakfast to the Wall Street crowd—Irish oatmeal, special jellies, omelets, and teas—while lunch and dinner consist of fairly conventional fare. The carpetbagger steak (with a pocket of oysters) is an unusual item, and the Yankee pot roast is an old favorite. The wine list is a big bore.

*Price: About $35 per person*
*Open Mon.–Fri. for breakfast, lunch, and dinner; closed Sat. and Sun.*
*Accepts all major credit cards*

---

## THE GOTHAM BAR AND GRILL
### 12 East 12 Street
**212-620-4020**

This was one of the first cavernous restaurants to open in the neighborhood above Greenwich Village, and for a while there the slick, boisterous crowd at this pink-green-and-black dining room subsisted on burgers and other banalities until the crowd left to go to newer caverns. So owner Jerome Kretchmer (once NYC Commissioner of Environmental Protection) retrenched, hired a bright young chef, and turned the Gotham into one of the best of the eclectic-style restaurants serving such things as duck breast *carpaccio,* grilled tuna with a *confit* of tomatoes on lemon-basil pasta, and some extraordinary desserts like a warm raspberry *gratin.* The crowds came back, this time not to preen idly but to dine well.

*Price: About $30 per person*
*Open Sun.–Fri. for lunch and dinner; Sat. for dinner only*
*Accepts all major credit cards*

---

# THE GRAND CENTRAL OYSTER BAR & RESTAURANT
## Grand Central Terminal
### 212-490-6650

There are but a handful of restaurants in the world that so perfectly express a city's character as The Oyster Bar at Grand Central. Set below street level in the majesty of Grand Central Terminal, with its constant flow of lives arriving in or leaving New York City, this grand but bare-bones restaurant pulses with the shudder of trains and the rush of feet all around it. And these are pretty impressive bare bones at that: Ochre-colored tiles arch over the dining room with its enormous windows, its takeout oyster counter, its sit-down counter, its blue-checkered tablecloths, and its blasting open kitchen. At lunch people fill the entire hall, some to wolf down the buttery clam chowder, others to gobble up a dozen oysters (from, perhaps, as many sources), others to tackle a lobster, and others to choose between a daily catch of remarkable variety—some days there's sturgeon, sometimes smelts, another time spots or triggerfish. It is inconceivable that you'll get anything but the freshest of seafood here, for the buyer at The Oyster Bar has legendary clout in the Fulton Fish Market, and he gets whatever he finds most interesting. The American white wine list is a triumph of common sense. Service may be brusque and the greeting at the front cold.

*Price: About $35 per person; more for lobster*
*Open Mon.–Fri. for lunch and dinner; closed Sat. and Sun.*
*Accepts all major credit cards*

# HATSUHANA

17 East 48 Street (*near Madison Avenue*)   212-355-3345
237 Park Avenue (*entrance on 46 Street*)   212-661-3400

Many connoisseurs of *sushi* contend that Hatsuhana is the best in town when it comes to creating the myriad delicacies of this specialized cuisine. The place is not much to look at, but is bright and cheery (the Park Avenue branch even more so with its greenhouse windows), with a quick-on-their-feet staff who pay attention to your special requests. The fish here is the epitome of freshness, and it is useless to recommend one item over another. Go for an ample selection, drink a little *sake* or Japanese beer, and take note that much of the clientele is made up of Japanese business people who know a good thing when they eat it.

*Price: About $20 per person*
*Open Mon.–Fri. for lunch and dinner; Sat. for dinner only; closed Sun.*
*Accepts all major credit cards*

# HUBERTS

102 East 22 Street (*near Park Avenue*)
212-673-3711

Len Allison and Karen Hubert are very serious about restoring the reputation of traditional, regional American cuisine by up-dating classics like Country Captain, catfish fritters, and bread pudding, while using the entire American larder to create stunning new dishes like pan-blackened salmon with a white horseradish sauce, venison with sweet potatoes *au gratin*, an Iowa blue cheese *soufflé*, and a "snow *mousse*" with *espresso* sabayon. The dining room is small, warm, and reminiscent of a fine country home in Virginia, and the staff is knowledgeable and never intrusive. There's a good selection of American wines, including some interesting New York State bottlings worth a try.

*Price: Fixed price at $42.50 per person*
*Open Mon.–Fri. for lunch and dinner; Sat. for dinner only; closed Sun.*
*Accepts American Express, Visa, and MasterCard*

# IL MONELLO
## 1460 Second Avenue (*near 76 Street*)
### 212-535-9310

Il Monello (which translates into something like "little rascal") was the first restaurant of Adi Giovanetti, who also runs the midtown Il Nido (see page 591). At both places the printed menu is nearly identical (with prices somewhat lower at Il Monello), but by relying on Signore Giovanetti for guidance (he seems to be at both places every single night) you will be treated to assorted specialties such as *ravioli* filled with pumpkin and graced with butter and sage, or a veal chop with olives and white truffles, or a perfect example of *saltimbocca*. Pray that they have the almond and chocolate *dacquoise* for dessert; it's sensational.

Il Monello is quieter and less rushed than Il Nido, and, for that—and a profusion of lighted flowers—it is ideal for a romantic dinner, when the captains and Giovanetti himself put themselves at your disposal and are always ready to suggest something new, fresh, or seasonal. The wine list has great depth.

*Price: About $35–$45 per person*
*Open Mon.–Sat. for lunch and dinner; closed Sun.*
*Accepts all major credit cards*

# IL MULINO
## 86 West 3 Street (*near Thompson Street*)
### 212-673-3783

You can safely skip all the tourist restaurants in Little Italy (if you must go, try Angelo's), and head a few blocks north to Greenwich Village, where you'll find this happy little Abruzzese restaurant packed every night with regulars who come for the beautifully seasoned cuisine at Il Mulino. Fresh basil and ripe tomatoes are used with flourish; pastas are made in the back and have exceptional lightness. The sauces are authentic. Ask for co-owner Fernando, and he'll guide you like an Italian cousin to the best in the house. The best dessert is a cold *zabaglione*.

*Price: About $25 per person*
*Open Mon.–Fri. for lunch and dinner; Sat. for dinner only; closed Sun.*
*Accepts American Express*

# IL NIDO
## 251 East 53 Street (*near Second Avenue*)
### 212-753-8450

For six years now Il Nido has been considered one of New York's most sophisticated Northern Italian restaurants, not only for its clientele and its handsome decor of dark wood beams, plaid carpet, and stucco walls, but for its exceptionally light, seasonal cuisine. Tuscan-born owner Adi Giovanetti runs Il Nido (which means a "nest" or, figuratively, a "home") with such gentility that even a harried business lunch seems more special here than at any other Italian restaurant in town, and, at night, when you take your time, Giovanetti will suggest you try a little *antipasto* of *carpaccio,* or *crostini di polenta* and chicken livers, share some *ravioli malfatti* or *risotto* with saffron and *radicchio,* and then a simple preparation of chicken with garlic and artichokes or a veal chop of extraordinary succulence. Desserts run from fair to good, the *espresso* is made the way it should be, and the wines are persuasive testimony to the owner's serious intent to show Italian gastronomy at its most impressive. The place can be noisy and it's always crowded. Most dishes are finished tableside.

*Price: About $40–$50 per person*
*Open Mon.–Sat. for lunch and dinner; closed Sun.*
*Accepts all major credit cards*

# INDOCHINE
## 430 Lafayette Street (*near Astor Place*)
### 212-505-5111

New York doesn't come close to most major American cities when it comes to Vietnamese restaurants, but Indochine is a stylish spot on the brink of the East Village serving a clientele that seems to speak a great deal of French. You might walk by it and miss it, since the sign is minuscule. The room has a greenish-yellow cast, palm leaf murals, and black-and-white tile floors. The food is moderately priced and moderately seasoned (avoid the bland spring rolls), with stuffed chicken wings, steamed fish in coconut milk, and beef salad some of the better items.

*Price: About $20 per person*
*Open daily for dinner only*
*No credit cards accepted*

# JAMS

## 154 East 79 Street (*near Lexington Avenue*)
### 212-772-6800

Jams is named after its two owners—Jonathan Waxman and Melvin Masters —whose overnight success was built on their prior reps: Waxman was chef at the heralded Michael's in Santa Monica; Masters handled marketing and publicity at Jordan Winery in Sonoma; both brought a California sensibility to the grilling of fine ingredients and a sense of seasoning based on aromatic herbs, chile peppers, and seasonal fruits. Some of the food is quite simple— roast farm chicken with shoestring potatoes, for instance—while many dishes are elaborate—swordfish with blood oranges, pasta with bay scallops and caviar—while some dishes are just plain bland, like *mozzarella* with sweet potatoes and greens. The use of baby vegetables is more affectation than good taste. But Waxman is able to coax the essence out of most ingredients, which is at the heart of California cookery.

The design of the dining room is stark white, and the noise (somewhat toned down this past year) makes it difficult for deep conversation. Good American wine list.

*Price: About $45 per person*
*Open Mon.–Fri. for lunch and dinner; Sat. for dinner only; closed Sun.*
*Accepts American Express, Visa, and MasterCard*

---

# J. G. MELON

## 1291 Third Avenue (*near 74 Street*)
### 212-744-0585

New York's prime Preppy bar, decorated with a watermelon motif (pink and green, get it?). And you'll have a good time just going for a drink or two. But Melon's (as they call it) makes one of New York's best hamburgers and cheeseburgers, which makes it worth a beeline when you're in the mood for just that item. (There's a Melon's on the West Side and one in the Hamptons, but this is the original.)

*Price: About $15 per person*
*Open daily for lunch and dinner*
*No credit cards accepted*

# JOHN'S
## 278 Bleecker Street (*off Seventh Avenue*)
### 212-243-1680

As you might expect, New York's streets are lined with good pizzerias (and many terrible ones), serving everything from a puffed-crust gooey job to a thin, crisp-crusted California stylization. John's has been on this corner of Greenwich Village for half a century, and with good reason: The pizzas—as traditional as Christmas—are the very essence of a good pie. The oven is coal-fired, the ingredients of high quality, the baking just to the point where the crust is slightly charred and a little chewy, the top blistering and well melded, the aroma breathtaking.

*Price: Under $10 per person*
*Open daily for lunch and dinner*
*No credit cards accepted*

---

# KATZ'S DELICATESSEN
## 205 East Houston Street (*at Ludlow Street*)
### 212-254-2246

One of the pleasures of New York City life is to go shopping on Sunday afternoon for marked-down designer clothes in the Orchard Street clothing shops, then to have lunch at this sprawling, loud delicatessen where you move along cafeteria-style, order a thick pastrami sandwich (or brisket, corned beef, tongue, roast beef, and so on), a hot garlicky hot dog, thick French fries, a slice of cheesecake, and that oddity of Jewish-American beverages—Dr. Brown's Cel-Ray Tonic. Sit down, nosh on a beauty of a pickle, pay your fair tab, and go home happy that such places still exist and stand out among other delis that serve meats wrapped in plastic and coleslaw made in another state. It's great for takeout, too.

*Price: Under $10 per person*
*Open daily for breakfast, lunch, and dinner*
*No credit cards accepted*

# LA CARAVELLE
## 33 West 55 Street (*near Fifth Avenue*)
### 212-586-4252

La Caravelle last year celebrated its twenty-fifth anniversary—a quarter century of classic cuisine and gentility that, alas, began to show some decline over the past few years. But its new owners, André Jammet, and former chef Roger Fessaguet, have hired a young American chef, freshened the bright red upholstery and impressionistic Jean Pages murals, and restored the luster of this grand French dining room. You may still order standard fare such as roast chicken with a cream sauce or a *paillard* of beef with sauce *béarnaise*, but you'll dine splendidly on the evening's specialties like *terrine* of *foie gras* with figs and endive or lobster with olive oil and herbs. La Caravelle's kitchen has always had a reputation for its stocks and reductions, and it shows in such simple dishes as perfectly roasted squab with wild mushrooms. Reservations are always a good idea. The wine list is very fine. La Caravelle is now better than ever and a triumph of good taste.

*Price: Fixed price at $44.25 per person*
*Open Mon.–Fri. for lunch and dinner; Sat. for dinner only; closed Sun.*
*Accepts all major credit cards*

# LA CÔTE BASQUE
## 5 East 55 Street (*near Fifth Avenue*)
### 212-688-6525

La Côte Basque, after years of going downhill, took a sharp turn uphill when taken over several years ago by Jean-Jacques Rachou, who has operated this lively, packed restaurant with its sunny murals and dark wood beams with tremendous enthusiasm and largess. You won't find more lavish dishes in any French restaurant around New York—chicken stuffed with a forcemeat of quail, a *cassoulet* of lobster and scallops in cream, a stuffed veal chop with cream and wild mushrooms, *langoustines* surrounded by artichoke hearts and mushrooms in a *beurre blanc* tinged with Pernod; a chocolate-mocha *bisquit* with chocolate sauce and raspberries, and sumptuous *soufflés*. Every dish is garnished to the hilt, and at times it all seems a bit too much. And Rachou seems to spend a bit too much time strolling the aisle rather than manning the kitchen. Still, this is a place fit for a grand splurge when you want to pamper yourself or impress the hell out of a client.

*Price: Fixed price at $45 per person*
*Open Mon.–Fri. for lunch and dinner; Sat. for dinner only; closed Sun.*
*Accepts all major credit cards*

# LA PETITE MARMITE
## 5 Mitchell Place (*49 Street and First Avenue*)
### 212-826-1084

For nearly a dozen years La Petite Marmite was a solid French restaurant serving the U.N. crowd and others who came here for strictly classical cuisine. Then, last year, the owners gutted the place and gave it a stark white and silver metal look of the 1980s and gave the menu just the amount of snap it needed —a *soufflé* of truffles, swordfish grilled with sesame and peanuts, a *jambonette de canard,* and some sumptuous desserts. They also brought prices into line with the way people want to eat today, so that La Petite Marmite (the name refers to the classic *consommé* of chicken, beef, and marrow) now provides remarkable value for this standard of cooking and is slightly cheaper than its competitors. Good wine list.

*Price: About $30 per person*
*Open Mon.–Fri. for lunch and dinner; Sat. for dinner only; closed Sun.*
*Accepts all major credit cards*

# LA RÉCOLTE
## In the Intercontinental Hotel, 110 East 49 Street (*near Lexington Avenue*)
### 212-421-4389

La Récolte has been searching for a personality for some time, going through several chefs before hiring the estimable Christian Levecque to turn this into a fine hotel dining room with a blend of hearty classics, very good game dishes, and some changing regional dinners. The restaurant itself is very roomy, perfect for a good business luncheon or a lavish dinner. Desserts are all first rate. Largely they have succeeded, though asking Levecque to do "regional dinners" detracts from his basic training and talents in turning out his own style of classic and *nouvelle.*

*Price: About $40 per person; pre-theater fixed-price at $32; "tasting menu"*
*fixed price at $42;* à la carte, *about $40 per person*
*Open Mon.–Fri. for lunch and dinner; Sat. for dinner only; closed Sun.*
*Accepts all major credit cards*

# LA RÉSERVE
## 4 West 49 Street (*near Fifth Avenue*)
### 212-247-2993

La Réserve has had three chefs in two years, which may cause some to wonder about consistency. But proprietor Jean-Louis Missud has run a level-headed operation and the kitchen has continued to produce cuisine with great beauty and finesse to match the spacious decor of patterned banquettes, etched glass, and wildlife murals by Dante Liberi. Ingredients are of the highest quality, whether they be American lamb or French turbot, and chef André Gaillard tinges dishes with whimsy—turbot scented with cloves, lamb with saffron, *sorbets* with spun sugar. The wine list is very fine and service very amicable. The pre-theater dinner is the best in town.

*Price: Fixed price at $36 per person*
*Open Mon.–Sat. for lunch and dinner; closed Sun.*
*Accepts all major credit cards*

# LA TULIPE
## 104 West 13 Street (*near Avenue of the Americas*)
### 212-691-8860

A small, very personal restaurant run by Sally and John Darr, who have dedicated themselves to cooking for exactly 80 people a night at two seatings (reservations are not easy to get on short notice) in a style that derives the best from French classicism and *nouvelle* techniques. This means very imaginative dishes with sunny, seasonal peppers, eggplant, and fennel, a touch of sesame oil on the shrimps, a squab buoyed by *couscous,* and a famous hazlenut *dacquoise* of impressive textural distinctions. The brightly lighted dining room is very loud, the staff often pompous, and there are outcries about the slowness of moving food from stove to table. But this is a significant and serious restaurant for the gourmet.

*Price: Fixed price at $48 per person*
*Open Tues.–Sat. for dinner only; closed Sun. and Mon.*
*Accepts all major credit cards*

# LAVIN'S
## 23 West 39 Street (*near Fifth Avenue*)
### 212-921-1288

Richard Lavin seems to have unquenchable enthusiasm for running his handsome restaurant in what was once the Engineers Club—with high oak walls, bentwood chairs, and a wine bar that is considered one of the best informed and stocked in the city, offering a sampling of at least fourteen wines by the glass and hundreds of others by the bottle. Unlike other wine bars in New York, however, Lavin's food is very good—eclectic, with some injudicious sweet sauces on occasion, but with some unique dishes such as salmon tartare on *radicchio* or California quail with wild rice, currants, and apricots. The pastas are better here than at all those foolish restaurants that try to outdo the Italians, and the desserts—warm chocolate cake with whipped cream, orange-flavored *crème brulée,* poached pear with *zabaglione* and candied ginger—are, in a word, scrumptious.

*Price: About $30 per person*
*Open Mon.–Fri. for lunch and dinner; closed Sat. and Sun.*
*Accepts all major credit cards*

---

# LE BERNARDIN
## 155 West 51 Street (*near Seventh Avenue*)
### 212 489-1515

Any American who complains that seafood in this country can never match the quality and freshness of that in France had better be prepared to eat his words: Le Bernardin has come to New York, serving the same kind of exquisite, simple dishes that have long made its original namesake the foremost seafood restaurant in Paris. To their great credit, owners Gilbert and Maguy Le Coze buy seafood exclusively from American waters and even they marvel at the variety obtainable. (They also print their menu in English.) Their raw tuna *carpaccio* is a lesson in freshness; the halibut in a warm vinaigrette could not be improved upon; the sea urchins in butter sauce are rich and sensual. The dining room is tastefully opulent, a mix of honey-colored wood, high ceilings, and artwork reflecting the bounty of the seas. The wine list at the moment is far from extensive. The staff, headed by *maître d'* Richard Hollocovu, includes some of New York's most experienced professionals, who balance familiarity with clear and classic grace.

*Price: Fixed price at $55 per person, with many supplements*
*Open Mon.–Sat. for lunch and dinner; closed Sun.*
*Accepts all major credit cards*

# LE CIRQUE
## 58 East 65 Street (*near Park Avenue*)
### 212-794-9292

I know of no restaurateur who does not hold Sirio Maccioni, owner of Le Cirque, in amicable esteem, for he seems able to strike the delicate balance of entrepreneur, gentleman, connoisseur, and social arbiter without the slightest flutter of snobbism. No one displays more grace under pressure than Maccioni. Le Cirque ("the circus") is, unquestionably, New York's Society restaurant—with a significant percentage of the world's most powerful business titans and heads of state (Nancy took Ronald here for lunch)—yet Maccioni, a Tuscan by birth, is able to make everybody feel welcome. Everybody, that is, except those who come with a chip on their shoulder demanding to get any table they want on a moment's notice. That goes for faithful regulars and newcomers who expect too much of a dining room that is only large enough to accommodate one-tenth of the customers who call for reservations each day.

But beyond the crush of a chic crowd is a kitchen—overseen by Alain Sailhac—that turns out French (and some Italian) cuisine that is never eccentric and always done with impeccably high taste—lobster and scallops in a light broth, barely sautéed *foie gras* with *radicchio,* a filet of beef with braised endive, the best baby lamb in the city, partridge with Swiss chard, and an assortment of beautiful dessert *soufflés.* Maccioni himself created pasta primavera (yes, pasta primavera) and Sailhac's *crème brulée* is now legendary, even in France. Whatever you do, don't just order off the menu. Ask Sirio to get the chef to make you something special. The wine list is a great one. Lunch is a bargain at $28.50.

*Price: About $40–$50 per person*
*Open Mon.–Sat. for lunch and dinner; closed Sun.*
*Accepts all major credit cards*

# LELLO RISTORANTE
## 65 East 54 Street (*near Madison Avenue*)
### 212-751-1555

Lello had been coasting along for a few years serving good, not terrific Italian cuisine, but within the last year the kitchen has revived its sense of timing and the food is now better than ever, even if the menu still seems a bit of a cliché. The *bresaola* and *carpaccio* are full of flavor, the buffalo *mozzarella* rich and creamy, and all the pastas are winning combinations of fresh noodles and light sauces. No one's seafood sauces are better, and the chef does well with his seafood entrées too—the red snapper grilled with oil and garlic is superlative, the *scampi infernali* full of gusto. The fruit tarts, chocolate cake, and cheesecake are all well worth ordering, and you'll have no trouble finding almost any good Italian wine you desire here.

*Price: About $30–$35 per person*
*Open Mon.–Fri. for lunch and dinner; Sat. for dinner only; closed Sun.*
*Accepts all major credit cards*

---

# LE PÈRIGORD
## 405 East 52 Street (*near First Avenue*)
### 212-755-6244

Owner George Briguet has kept Le Perigord at the highest levels of deluxe French dining for more than a decade now. Its sedate but romantic decor is married to a wonderfully inventive menu prepared by the energetic young chef, Antoine Bouterin. You may be assured that simple classics like rack of lamb and truffled *consommé* will be perfectly rendered, but you will also be delighted with engaging dishes like a salad of *fois gras* with white radish, sole in a garlic cream, and apple *soufflé*. The wine list is full of fine bottlings, the staff is cheerful, and George himself is the very soul of French *joie de vivre*.

*Price: Fixed price at $39 per person*
*Open Mon.–Fri. for lunch and dinner; Sat. for dinner only; closed Sun.*
*Accepts all major credit cards*

---

# LE RÉGENCE
## In the Hotel Plaza Athenée, 37 East 64 Street (*near Park Avenue*)
### 212-734-9100

Le Régence hardly resembles the restaurant at the Plaza Athenée in Paris, but both bespeak a formality I sometimes worry has gone out of style. But, no, here it is—12-foot vaulted ceilings, grand chandeliers, and an aqua-and-white color scheme that seems straight out of *House and Garden* circa 1953. But it is all quite new and a fit dining room for chef Daniel Boulud's refined cuisine. There's no wondering where Boulud's talents lie: they are in seafood cookery. The fish and shellfish preparations here—*ravioli* stuffed with lobster, red snapper in a saffron cream, or red mullet broiled over fennel—are among the finest in the city, and the desserts have gotten better and better.

*Price: Fixed price at $47.50 per person*
*Open daily for breakfast, lunch, and dinner*
*Accepts all major credit cards*

---

# LUTÈCE
## 249 East 50 Street (*near Second Avenue*)
### 212-752-2225

Lutèce has been showered with so many national and international honors— four stars from *The New York Times,* three toques from *Gault-Millau,* first place in *Playboy*'s "Critics' Choice" poll for 1980 and 1984—that you might be led to expect chef-owner André Soltner is a magician. But no, he is merely a master, who, with *sous-chef* Christian Bertrand, has devoted himself to finding the best way to approach each ingredient, each technique, each preparation, so that his puff pastry will be perfectly flaky, his turbot perfectly succulent, his lamb perfectly pink, and his seasonings perfectly in balance with the essential flavor of the dish. Soltner is not out to dazzle or surprise anyone, for he is still in awe of French classicism, which is reflected in his basic lunch and dinner menus. So his *foie gras* in *brioche* is a study in flawless technique, his roast chicken the epitome of understatement, and his *coq au vin* in Riesling the sublimation of country cooking (Soltner hails from Alsace). But go beyond the expected, ask him to make you something special (the *menu dégustation* is ideal for this), and he will take your breath away with a *brochet* (pike) cooked with little more than a *mirepoix* and butter; a *mousse* of cod in puff pastry and cream; *soupe au crabe;* or a cold lemon *soufflé* with roasted almonds. *Sorbets* are properly tart; smoked salmon has just the right fat content; fruit tarts are the pick of the season.

Lutèce is fairly small, with a minuscule bar and an open kitchen you pass as you enter a pleasant small dining room opening onto a larger orangerie room; the two upstairs dining rooms are quite formal. Service can be either exemplary and helpful or, depending on your captain, perfunctory and brusque. Soltner himself usually comes out after service to ask you how you liked your meal—and he is sincerely interested in your honest opinion. The wine list is one of the finest in the world, but don't neglect the card of twenty or so wines priced under $25, personally chosen by Soltner.

You may have to wait up to a month for a dinner reservation at Lutèce, but it will be well worth the anticipation.

*Price: About $50 per person; menu dégustation $70 per person*
*Open Tues.–Fri. for lunch and dinner; Sat. and Mon. for dinner only; closed Sun.*
*Accepts all major credit cards*

# MANHATTAN OCEAN CLUB
## 57 West 58 Street (near Avenue of the Americas)
### 212-371-7777

If the Manhattan Ocean Club served only simply grilled seafood, it would rank with the best fish houses in the city. But add to that some swank, a three-level dining area fitted out with green marble and Picasso ceramics, install an imaginative chef named Steve Mellina in the kitchen, and you have a first-class seafood restaurant serving unusual preparations like clams in a filbert nut *pesto, ravioli* stuffed with lobster, shrimp, crab, and asparagus, and some excellent chocolate desserts and frozen *soufflés*.

*Price: About $40; more for lobster and some other dishes*
*Open Mon.–Fri. for lunch and dinner; Sat. and Sun. for dinner only*
*Accepts all major credit cards*

# MARCELLO
## 1354 First Avenue (near 73 Street)
### 212-744-4400

Does this neighborhood need still another fancy Italian restaurant where dinner will cost you a cool $80 or more for two? *Perchè non?,* as this new entry proves with its superb menu of authentic Italian cooking—bright sun-dried tomatoes and yellow peppers, *funghi porcini* with *polenta,* magnificent *fettuccine* with rich *mascarpone* cheese, *ziti* with beans, lamb chops with rosemary, and a wonderful orange *sorbetto.* Marcello's wine list is very carefully culled to provide some new imports worth sampling. Service is earnest, the sound level high, and the whole place has a casual polish that makes an evening here delightful.

*Price: About $30 per person*
*Open daily for dinner only*
*Accepts all major credit cards*

# MARIO'S
## 2342 Arthur Avenue, Bronx
### 212-584-1188

Mario's has been around since 1919, and anyone who ever wanted to be elected to political office in New York has been here, along with assorted New York Yankees, and fans who grew up in this lively market section of the Bronx. Mario's is as old-fashioned as it is consistent—from good pizzas to made-on-the-spot tomato sauces that cover *al dente* pastas and good veal. Mario's, more than any place in Little Italy, has the right stuff and, with its plaster statues and photos of the Miglucci family's kids, is a little museum of Italian–American decor. Ask Momma Miglucci for her pickled carrots and peppers, but have some ice water nearby.

*Price: About $20 per person*
*Open Tues.–Sun. for lunch and dinner; closed Mon.*
*Accepts all major credit cards*

---

# MAURICE
## In the Parker-Meridien Hotel, 118 West 57 Street (*near Avenue of the Americas*)
### 212-245-7788

There's no doubt that you will eat splendidly at Maurice, but there's also a chance you may leave hungry. Portions, along the guidelines and menus set up by consulting chef Alain Senderens of Paris' Lucas Carton Senderens, are small, preciously presented, and cost about as much as things can in New York. The atmosphere is a bit overwhelming, too, just off the Parker-Meridien's hallway, and service is inconsistent, sometimes as professional as you'll find in France, sometimes as amateurish as in the Catskills. Those caveats aside, I must say you'll dine exquisitely on such dishes as *ravioli* stuffed with scallops in a thyme-butter sauce, sweetbreads in soy and vinegar, a *confit* of lamb, chocolate *sorbet,* and luscious apple tart with whipped cream.

*Price: About $50–$60 per person*
*Open Mon.–Fri. for lunch and dinner; Sat. and Sun. for dinner only*
*Accepts all major credit cards*

# MAXIME'S
## Tomahawk Road, Granite Springs
### 914-248-7200

No true gastronome should fail to drive up to the sylvan territory that is home to Maxime's—a little over an hour from Manhattan—for here is a true gem in the wilderness, as fine a French restaurant as you'll find anywhere in America and a splendid approximation of the best rural restaurants that dot the French countryside. Chef-owner Maxime Ribera, who hails from Brittany, had long experience in France, Manhattan, and Miami before settling in this lovely spot in the nearly non-existent town of Granite Springs in Westchester County. Now, after decades of cooking, he has created a cuisine according to his own likes and dislikes, a blend of strong classicism with some enlightened modern concepts. Sauces are never heavy, reductions never imbalanced, dishes never overelaborated. He gets at the essential flavors of his meats, poultry, game, and seafood, so that his *soupe des pecheurs* tastes of the sea, his roast rabbit of the forest, his pear in puff pastry of the orchard, and his braised turnips of the garden. He prefers pan juices to a thickened gravy and fresh local duck liver to half-cooked French *foie gras*.

The wine list is long and fairly priced, and the service staff, overseen by wife Hugette, could give lessons in etiquette to haughtier colleagues in New York. Maxime's is well worth a drive on its own, through the woods and lake country that make this a restful retreat at any time of the year.

*Price: Fixed price at $39 per person*
*Open Wed.–Sun. for lunch and dinner; closed Mon. and Tues.*
*Accepts all major credit cards*

# MAXWELL'S PLUM
## 1181 First Avenue (*at 64 Street*)
### 212-628-2100

Two decades have done nothing to tarnish the garish splendor of entrepreneur Warner LeRoy's restaurant and "gathering place" (that is, singles bar), and its extravagant decor—dark wood, brass accents, Tiffany lamps, Art Nouveau stained glass, and center bar—was the inspiration for hundreds of imitators around the country. But now all the imitators look hopelessly dated while Maxwell's (there's a branch in San Francisco) still has a palpable style—as if Sammy Davis, Jr., and Oscar Wilde had gone into restaurant design.

The food at Maxwell's has always been a competent balance of burgers and modernism, but the results have been consistently inconsistent over the years. Now, with the hiring of Mark Peel and Nancy Silverton, former chefs at Hollywood's Spago, the kitchen shows signs of real spark and imagination—from scrumptious pizzas (à la L.A.) and grilled lobster with deep-fried spinach to exceptionally delicious desserts like Nancy's signature chocolate raspberry *terrine* and wonderfully flavorful cookies. The wines are well chosen and the service, at least in the upper-level dining room, quite professional. The bar crowd is as handsome as ever.

*Price: About $30 per person*
*Open daily for lunch and dinner*
*Accepts all major credit cards*

---

## McSORLEY'S OLD ALE HOUSE
### 15 East 7 Street (*near Second Avenue*)
#### 212-473-8800

New Yorkers have been going to McSorley's for more than six score years now, and it's as popular a hangout now as it was when it opened in 1854. It looks just about the way it did back then too—sawdust on the floor, a pot-bellied stove, and bar offerings that begin and end with McSorley's own ale and a platter of Cheddar cheese with onions and mustard. The place barred women from entering with or without escort until the 1970s, and just this summer they finally added a ladies' room. Don't expect anything here but a bawdy slice of New York history, but a true and authentic one it has remained.

*Price: Two mugs of ale for $1.50*
*Open daily*
*No credit cards accepted*

---

## MESON BOTIN
### 145 West 58 Street (*near Avenue of the Americas*)
#### 212-265-4567

An excellent Spanish wine list, shrimp with garlic sauce, a hefty *paella,* a loin of pork in a sauce of Spanish ham and wine, and a nice eggy *flan*—what more can one ask of a Spanish restaurant in a city with so few choices? Meson Botin delivers all these in abundance in an atmosphere heavy with shields and swords and other Iberian weaponry that seem standard decor in Spanish restaurants. Don't let them sit you in the auxiliary room out back.

*Price: About $20–$25 per person*
*Open Mon.–Fri. for lunch and dinner; Sat. and Sun. for dinner only*
*Accepts all major credit cards*

## MITSUKOSHI
### 461 Park Avenue (*off 57 Street*)
#### 212-935-6444

A very refined Japanese restaurant downstairs from an equally refined Japanese department store. The blond woods and kimono–clad waitresses are perfect counterpoint for the *sushi* and *sashimi* served here with ultimate grace. The *tofu* served in an ice cold bowl with shredded vegetables is refreshing in summer, while the light soups are warming in winter. Even the desserts here are a cut above the norm for Japanese dining rooms.

*Price: About $35 per person*
*Open Mon.–Fri. for lunch and dinner; closed Sat. and Sun.*
*Accepts all major credit cards*

## MOCCA HUNGARIAN RESTAURANT
### 1588 Second Avenue (*near 82 Street*)
#### 212-734-6470

Mocca looks as if it might have opened sometime after the turn of the century, but it's really only four years old. The illusion occurs because the management has minimally spruced up the old tin, patterned ceiling, the red-white-green-and-black tile floor, and the low lighting that once characterized little Middle European restaurants in this neighborhood. Mocca has a very faithful clientele —faithful to the hearty and hefty portions of well-made, standard Hungarian fare such as chopped liver, stuffed cabbage, and chicken *paprikash*. You nibble on cucumbers sprinkled with paprika, sip on "Bull's Blood" Hungarian wine, and let yourself slide into sentimentality—from which you awake when they serve you the less than dreamy *palacsinta crêpes*. Prices seem a throwback to another era.

*Price: About $15 per person*
*Open daily for lunch and dinner*
*No credit cards accepted*

# MONTRACHET
## 239 West Broadway (*near White Street*)
### 212-219-2777

Montrachet is the perfect neighborhood French restaurant. Just as you'd find a wonderful little place in some avant-garde *arrondissement* on Paris's Left Bank, so, too, you'll find Montrachet set in TriBeCa, currently Gotham's artistic crucible. Stark but warm, casual but chic, friendly but never fawning, Montrachet has a very personal style as expressed by owner Drew Nieporent and chef David Bouley—an enchanting balance of the treasured familiar with the sensibly imaginative. The only off notes are the drab outfits on the staff who are done up like reluctant gangsters from a grade B movie of the 1930s.

The brief, understated menu hardly prepares you for the exquisite, but never fussy, cuisine that arrives at your table, and Bouley is able to draw out every flavor of every herb, every stock, every ingredient he uses—a tureen of eggplant with tomatoes and goat cheese, pigeon wrapped in savoy cabbage, main lobster in *crème fraîche,* black sea bass *"en barigoule,"* and turbot in a *bouillabaisse* sauce. Desserts are very good, perhaps only a notch below the eminence of what precedes them. Every detail shows dedication, discretion, and a desire to please customers who really love to eat here.

*Price: Fixed-price meals at $25 and $35;* à la carte, *about $30–$35 per person*
*Open Tues.–Sun. for dinner only; closed Mon.*
*Excepts all major credit cards*

---

# NATHAN'S FAMOUS
## In Coney Island, 1310 Surf Avenue (*at Stillwell Avenue*), Brooklyn 718-266-3161
## 650 86 Street (*near Seventh Avenue*), Brooklyn 718-748-4131
## King's Plaza Shopping Center, Brooklyn 718-951-7770
## 1482 Broadway (near Times Square) 212-382-0620

Nathan's Famous is as much a part of New York as the Empire State Building and the Statue of Liberty. For it was at the Coney Island original at the turn of the century that the hot dog was promoted by Nathan Handwerker into a local, then national prominence as a quintessential American food. The Nathan's hot dog (once referred to as a "Coney") is still a great frank—a long, well-seasoned, all-beef beauty grilled till glistening and slightly singed to provide just the perfect snap when bitten into. (You can buy the hot dog in packages at supermarkets.) The French fries are terrific, and the rest of the deli offerings are of high quality. Desserts and pastries are not in the same league.

*Price: Under $10 per person*
*No credit cards accepted*

---

## NICOLE'S

In the Omni Park Central Hotel, 870 Seventh Avenue (*off 56 Street*)
**212-765-5108**

If you know Flo or Lipp or La Coupole in Paris, then you will have a real sense of déjà vu at Nicole's, which is a faithful rendering (complete with many accoutrements brought from Paris) of an Alsatian brasserie—multi-colored tile floors, bentwood chairs, Art Nouveau designs, a good range of beers, and a menu specializing in *choucroute, cassoulet,* mussel bisque, *charcuterie,* oysters, and *tarte Tatin.* Its proximity to Carnegie Hall makes this a great spot after a concert.

*Price: About $20–$25 per person*
*Open daily for breakfast, lunch, and dinner*
*Accepts all major credit cards*

---

## NIPPON

155 East 52 Street (*near Lexington Avenue*)
**212-355-9020**

Nippon is New York's best all-around Japanese restaurant, complete with *sushi* bar, three private *tatami* rooms, and main dining room where you may order a succession of dishes as part of a tasting menu that may include *sushi* and *sashimi* with *daikon* and cabbage, watercress with sesame, sautéed duck breast, fried *tofu* in a broth, soft-shell crab (in season), eggplant, marinated radish, *miso* soup, beef salad, rice with black sesame and fruits, apple with kiwi and marinated mushrooms. The handsome white cypress decor has a charming informality about it, and the waitresses in their bright kimonos are as cordial as they are efficient.

*Price: About $15–$20 per person; tasting menus range*
*from $15–$40 per person*
*Open Mon.–Fri. for lunch and dinner; Sat. for dinner only; closed Sun.*
*Accepts all major credit cards*

# NIRVANA
## 30 Central Park South (*near Avenue of the Americas*)
### 212-486-5700

# NIRVANA CLUB ONE
## 1 Times Square Plaza
### 212-486-6868

Nirvana always had a magnificent view from its penthouse location of Central Park, but it used to have mediocre food. Then the kitchen was transformed by Julie Sahni, who thereafter did the same for Nirvana Club One, which has an equally magnificent view of the Great White Way. Both menus are pretty much the same, and the food is now very good (there's a worthwhile pre-theater dinner, too), with fragrant *basmati* rice and raisins, crisp light breads, entrées startling for their hotness and spiciness, and refreshing rice pudding for dessert.

*Price: About $20 per person*
*Open daily for lunch and dinner*
*Accepts all major credit cards*

# THE OAK BAR
## In the Plaza Hotel, Central Park South off Fifth Avenue
### 212-759-3000

The Oak Bar at the Plaza seems to sum up in one room the discreet sophistication of New York—even if half the people in the place are out-of-towners. The 1943 murals of New York life by Everitt Shinn, the dark, clubbish wood, the tall windows that allow a view of a Central Park sunset, and the bottles of Poland Water on the tables all bespeak a kind of John O'Hara elegance full of gray flannel, black dresses, and pearl necklaces. It's a perfect place to order a Manhattan at the start of an evening.

*Price: Depends on what you order*
*Open daily*
*Accepts all major credit cards*

# THE ODEON
## 145 West Broadway (*off Thomas Street*)
### 212-233-0507

When the TriBeCa neighborhood west and south of Greenwich Village began to attract artists to its low-rent space, rents immediately soared and eateries sprouted like mushrooms. The Odeon, a barely renovated cafeteria, was one of the first and is still the best, serving crowds late into the night a brasserie-style menu that also includes a few eclectic items like *lotte* in a warm *arugula* salad and *ravioli* stuffed with goat cheese. There are good crab cakes and the calf's liver with a sweet onion sauce is delicious. Of the steak and *frites,* the former is just fine, the latter likely to be soggy. Desserts can be just poor. Atmosphere is provided by the clientele, ranging from punk to patrician.

*Price: About $25–$30 per person*
*Open Mon.–Fri. for lunch and dinner; Sat. and Sun. for dinner only*
*Accepts American Express, Visa, and MasterCard*

# PALM
## 837 Second Avenue (*near 45 Street*)
### 212-687-2953

# PALM TOO
## 840 Second Avenue (*near 45 Street*)
### 212-697-5198

Back in 1928 Parma restaurant became Palm via the handiwork of a myopic calligrapher, and so it has remained to this day. Regulars never call it "The Palm," and regulars know you don't ask to see the menu (which is posted inside the door as you enter). You just tell the waiter (who really isn't so brusque; he just hasn't much to say) how you want your steak cooked or how large a lobster you want, and you won't be disappointed. Palm defined the New York steak house genre decades ago—sawdust on the floor, caricatures of regular customers on the walls, and the simplest of amenities. But its aged prime steaks, chops, and enormous lobsters are still the standard that every place else tries to match, as are the shrimp cocktail, the tomato salad, the cottage fries, the fried onions, and the S & S cheesecake. Palm does sell simply cooked chicken, seafood, and some pasta, but not to order the steak or lobster here would be like not looking at the ceiling in the Sistine Chapel.

The wine list is a joke (red, white, or rosé?), reservations are not taken at dinner (you've a better chance of immediate seating at Palm Too, which is nearly a twin dining room and just as good), and the bar is very cramped.

Prices for steaks are actually a bit lower than at Palm's competitors, but the 4-pound lobsters will cost you plenty.

*Price: About $35 per person; much more for lobster*
*Open Mon.–Fri. for lunch and dinner; Sat. for dinner only; closed Sun.*
*Accepts all major credit cards*

---

## PARIOLI ROMANISSIMO
### 24 East 81 Street (*near Fifth Avenue*)
### 212-288-2391

Parioli Romanissimo presents a problem for many gourmets—mainly those who consider it one of the two or three best Italian restaurants in New York but who bristle at the thought of paying $23 for a plate of pasta and $64 for a rack of lamb (for two). The only thing that may be said in defense of such prices is that the food is exquisite, the portions very generous, and the premises (set in an old town house off Fifth Avenue) beautiful. The menu is far more innovative than most of the city's Italian restaurants and includes such items as lamb *carpaccio* with a red pepper purée, freshly made *trenette* with fresh *funghi porcini* (most places use dried mushrooms), and golden roasted chicken. Desserts are also of a very high order, and the wine list—though very pricey —is solid. The staff, however, varies from the condescending to the bumbling. This is not a place any serious gastronome can afford to miss unless you can't afford it at all.

*Price: About $60 per person*
*Open Tues.–Sat. for dinner only; closed Sun. and Mon.*
*Accepts all major credit cards*

---

## PETROSSIAN
### 182 West 58 Street (*off Seventh Avenue*)
### 212-245-0303

Caviar connoisseurs know that Petrossian is the only western company allowed to choose its caviar at the Russian fisheries, and the brothers Petrossian (Christian and Armen) are very particular about how they serve such fragile fish eggs. At their restaurant (the only one of its kind in the world) they serve it in silver *présentoirs* in all its pristine nakedness—no chopped onions, no hard-boiled eggs, no sour cream to detract from the taste—and prefer you'd drink iced vodka or champagne with it. The *foie gras* tastes like fat in ecstasy, and these and other delicacies like goose *confit,* smoked eel, and fruits in syrup are sold in an elegant shop next to the sensual dining room, which is decorated with marble floors, etched glass, and gray, mink-covered banquettes. The

French cuisine is not quite so impressive. Prices are high, but you are getting the absolute best here.

*Price: Fixed price between $42 and $98 (with caviar) per person; à la carte prices vary*
*Open Mon.–Sat. for lunch and dinner; closed Sun.*
*Accepts all major credit cards*

---

# PIG HEAVEN
## 1540 Second Avenue (*near 80 Street*)
### 212-744-4333

New York has plenty of tacky-looking Chinese restaurants but few funky ones. Pig Heaven is the epitome of the latter, with a cut-out pig figure at the doorway, pink barnyard wood walls, neon lights, and limos lined up outside. The specialty here is, obviously, pork in all its varieties—minced and sautéed with corn, bell peppers, and pine nuts, steamed in dumplings, as fresh bacon with preserved winter vegetables, and—best of all—barbecued with Chinese seasonings. The seafood, like flattened shrimp with hot pepper sauce or lobster with Szechuan chili sauce, is also recommended, but desserts are not. The place gets very crowded at night and service slows down as fast as the place heats up. A great place for lunch on a Saturday afternoon, and there is takeout and delivery service offered.

*Price: About $18–$20 per person*
*Open daily for lunch and dinner*
*Accepts American Express and Diner's Club*

---

# P. J. CLARKE'S
## 915 Third Avenue (*at 55 Street*)
### 212-759-1650

"P.J.'s" or "Clarke's" (never "P.J. Clarke's" to bona fide regulars) has been around since the turn of the century, and it has the kind of red-brick-and-oak charm that newer bars have been copying for years. Even the rest rooms at Clarke's are wondrous examples of bravado plumbing, and the management has fought off all attempts to raze the building over the years. There is a great range of domestic beers and Clarke's still serves one of New York's best burgers.

*Price: About $10–$15 per person*
*Open daily for lunch and dinner*
*No credit cards accepted*

# PROVECHOS
## 21 West 17 Street (*near Fifth Avenue*)
### 212-255-2408

Provechos would make a great set for TV's *Miami Vice*—a streamlined, silver-gray diner's atmosphere with aluminum chairs, black counter, and every detail—from sugar canisters to the teeny plastic figures hung on your cocktail glass—shows great style. The food is pan-Caribbean—a little Cuban, a little Puerto Rican, a little Creole—and the appetizers, such as the baked stuffed crabs, the *pastitillo* meat pies, the *pastelon* of plantains, cheese, string beans, and meat filling, and the codfish fritters called "stamp and go," are especially well seasoned and very tasty. The daiquiris are nicely made, but the desserts are sticky and cloying. *"Buen provechos,"* by the way, is Spanish for *"bon appétit."*

*Price: About $18 per person*
*Open daily for lunch and dinner*
*Accepts American Express, Visa, and MasterCard*

# PRUNELLE
## 18 East 54 Street (*near Fifth Avenue*)
### 212-759-6410

Prunelle, named after a deep-purple plum, is as glamorous as an Hermès scarf, a Cartier watch, and Chanel perfume—a perfect place to dine with someone you adore or someone you want to let down lightly. The burled wood floors, plum-colored fabrics, mirrors, perfect lighting level, and intimate size of the room make Prunelle enchanting and never somber. The kitchen, headed by co-owner Pascal Dirringer, provides a classic menu tempered with new ideas —a salad with duck cracklings, a lobster *pot au feu,* Hawaiian river prawns in cream, and a splendid *confit de canard,* for instance—while co-owner Jacky Ruette and his staff make every effort in the dining room at establishing an ambience of discreet bonhomie. Because of its size, Prunelle never seems as crowded and intense as some of the other French restaurants off Fifth Avenue; it seems somehow more civilized.

*Price: Fixed price at $49 per person*
*Open Mon.–Fri. for lunch and dinner; Sat. and Sun. for dinner only*
*Accepts all major credit cards*

# QUATORZE
## 240 West 14 Street (*near Eighth Avenue*)
### 212-206-7006

The owners of this Chelsea restaurant have done a dedicated job of reproducing the feel and food of an Alsatian brasserie, right down to the Fernet Branca posters and yellow menu card reminiscent of Paris' Lipp. Even the loudness of the room has a *joie de vivre* about it, and the staff is friendly, even when explaining why the kitchen is way behind schedule in delivering your food. Prices are very reasonable for abundant portions of house *terrines,* chicory with bacon and hot vinaigrette, braised endive in cream, and a hearty *choucroute garnie.* Some of the specials, like a first-rate platter of lamb *médaillons* with leeks and tarragon sauce, have a higher tariff. Desserts such as apple tart and dense chocolate cake are excellent, as is the small, fairly priced list of wines.

*Price: About $25 per person*
*Open Mon.–Fri. for lunch and dinner; Sat. and Sun. for dinner only*
*Accepts American Express*

# THE QUILTED GIRAFFE
## 955 Second Avenue (*near 51 Street*)
### 212-753-5355

Despite its silly name, The Quilted Giraffe is a very serious restaurant, though also a quixotic one. For while it is capable of turning out remarkable cuisine along French *nouvelle* lines with the best American ingredients, there is also a tendency to clash one ingredient with another and one texture with another, resulting in some dishes that are very odd indeed, like *ratatouille ravioli* and steak with an *aioli*-sesame sauce or a poached pear with basil sauce. Still, when owners Barry and Susan Wine are on target, their cuisine is fascinating— ragout of lobster with a curry-Sauternes sauce, "beggar's purse" *(crêpes* filled with beluga caviar and *crème fraîche),* fresh *ricotta* with cream and a cranberry *sorbet,* and many more conventional dishes. The prices (for food and wine) are astronomical here, and for an extra ten bucks you may sample six sweets as part of the "Grand Dessert."

The atmosphere of the small dining rooms is cozy, the staff extremely well versed, and the computerized wine list quite impressive. The Quilted Giraffe, for all its quirks, is a place gastronomes pay close attention to, and for very good reasons.

*Price: Fixed price at $70 per person*
*Open Mon.–Fri. for dinner only; closed Sat. and Sun.*
*Accepts all major credit cards*

# RAGA
## 57 West 48 Street (*near Rockefeller Plaza*)
### 212-757-3450

Raga's always been one of New York's most sinuously beautiful dining rooms and the most elegant of the city's Indian restaurants—with its high ceilings, raw silk walls, and hanging musical instruments. But inconsistency has plagued its kitchen, and the later in the evening you go the less likely you are to get the cooks' best efforts. But when things click, the food is refined and very good. The butter chicken, lamb *vindaloo, mulligatawny* soup, and buttery *paratha* are excellent choices, and most of the *tandoori* dishes are very worthy. Specify the hotness you desire in your food. They will be conservative in their estimate of how hot you really like it. Desserts are not up to par.

*Price: About $25 per person*
*Open Mon.–Fri. for lunch and dinner; Sat. and Sun. for dinner only*
*Accepts all major credit cards*

# ROSA MEXICANO
## 1063 First Avenue (*at 58 Street*)
### 212-753-7407

Josefina Howard is for the moment the reigning queen of Mexican cooking in New York, having opened Rosa Mexicano two years back to crowds who had never tasted much beyond the usual *tacos, enchiladas,* and *burritos* before. Here, in a pink dining room with a handsome front bar, her staff prepares chunky *guacamole* that completely restores my faith in a dish that more often resembles green mush. Beyond that you have your choice of pork *carnitas* with a stack of wheat *tortillas,* corn-dumpling soup, red snapper with coriander, and hefty side orders of rice and black beans. The margaritas are superior to most of the slushy varieties you find around town.

*Price: About $20 per person*
*Open daily for lunch and dinner*
*Accepts all major credit cards*

# THE RUSSIAN TEA ROOM
## 150 West 57 Street
### 212-265-0947

The Russian Tea Room, but a trumpet's call from Carnegie Hall, has a dazzling glamor about it reflected in the shiny brass and bright lighting and in the glow of the celebrities who frequent the downstairs dining room. Unfortunately you may be exiled to Siberia upstairs, but this is still a good place to enjoy a shot of iced vodka and a little caviar now and again.

*Price: Fixed price at $30 per person until 9:30 P.M.; afterwards à la carte at about $30–$40 per person*
*Open daily for lunch and dinner*
*Accepts all major credit cards*

---

# SABOR
## 20 Cornelia Street (*near Bleecker Street*)
### 212-243-9579

For a long while now Sabor has been a favorite little Greenwich Village storefront restaurant for New Yorkers who want something a little different —in this case, Cuban cooking, which has a nice bit of spice to it, an abundance of sweet plantains, and some unusual coconut desserts. The poached red snapper casserole is very tasty and the *escabeche* of pickled fish has wonderful texture. Try, too, the spicy *calamarones picantes* (squid) and carbo load with the *frijoles negros* (black beans).

*Price: About $20 per person*
*Open daily for dinner only*
*Accepts American Express, Visa, and MasterCard*

---

# SABRETT'S
## Many pushcart locations all over New York

New Yorker's call them "water dogs"—these all-beef franks boiled in water and sold from carts all over the city. You'll probably find most New Yorkers outside in good weather enjoying a Sabrett's, with a soft yeast roll, a schmear of mustard or ketchup, and a mound of sauerkraut on top and a can of soda on the side. These are the preferred hot dogs at ball games too, and there's something about the dripping sausages (far blander than Nathan's [see page 606]) that can make any New Yorker's day.

*Price: Under $2 per person*
*No credit cards accepted*

# SANDRO'S
### 420 East 59 Street (*near First Avenue*)
### 212-355-5150

Here's a new Italian restaurant with a twist for midtown Manhattan: How about serving authentic country food on rustic china and charging $9 for pasta, $14 for entrées, and $2 a glass for good house wines? Wrap it all up in a bright, spacious dining room out of the way of traffic, and you've got a hit. This was owner Tony May's beautifully realized idea, and it clicks, with dishes such as *ravioli* stuffed with potato and leeks in a butter-cheese sauce, crisply fried flattened Cornish hen, a truly spicy *spaghetti alla puttanesca,* fava beans with shrimp, and roast bay lamb with rosemary. Desserts, including *granita di caffè* and *crema di polenta* with raspberry and coconut sauce, are delights, and the *espresso* and *grappas* after dinner are perfect endings. Only a Keystone Kops service staff makes an evening here less than completely satisfying.

*Price: About $25 per person*
*Open daily for dinner only*
*Accepts all major credit cards*

# SEDUTTO ICE CREAM
### Many locations throughout the city

Brooklyn-based Häagen-Dazs may have claimed a national rep for its rich premium ice cream, but Sedutto, which is made in Staten Island, is a local New York favorite, served not only from several storefronts around the city but at some of the best restaurants and ice cream parlors too. This is a gorgeous ice cream: rich, full of butterfat, of a luxuriant texture other products can't match. The vanilla and chocolate are superb, and the *biscuit tortoni* is in a class by itself.

# SERENDIPITY 3
### 225 East 60 Street (*near Third Avenue*)
### 212-838-3531

Even after twenty years Serendipity 3 seems brash, eccentric, and frolicky, like a Lolita who grew up to be one helluva woman. The place is part boutique (T-shirts, mugs, risqué greeting cards) and part ice cream parlor (though you can eat full meals here, the fare is strictly lightweight), with a clientele that ranges from Brooke Shields to nannies with their charges. The iced hot chocolate is justly famous for its ability to chill your whole head in one bite, and the sundaes are big enough to share with a group of high school cheerleaders. This is a great place after a movie or after shopping on the East Side.

*Price: Under $15 per person*
*Open daily for lunch and dinner*
*Accepts all major credit cards*

---

## SHUN LEE PALACE
### 155 East 55 Street (*near Lexington Avenue*)
### 212-371-8844

Shun Lee Palace—now in its fifteenth year—was one of the first truly elegant midtown Chinese restaurants serving a fairly refined menu and even more refined dishes off the menu as suggested by owner Michael Tong. This is the place for a banquet, at which you may try up to a dozen dishes in a marked procession of exquisite china, each one part of a modulated meal that will include steamed, fried, and roasted seafood, poultry, dumplings, meats, and sweets. The regular menu offers several fine dishes—hacked chicken, family-style eggplant, "Wang's amazing chicken," and perfect Peking duck (in three courses)—but be adventurous and rely on Mr. Tong for more special dishes like jellyfish with hot mustard and thousand-year-old eggs, river carp with ginger and scallions, and frogs' legs with broccoli. Skip desserts. The dining room in the rear is the prettiest; the front room up a few steps is more intimate.

*Price: About $20–$25 per person*
*Open daily for lunch and dinner*
*Accepts American Express, Diner's Club, and Carte Blanche*

---

## SIDEWALKERS'
### 12 West 72 Street (*near Central Park West*)
### 212-799-6070

A very casual spot serving tasty spiced crabs Maryland style, complete with printed instructions on how to eat the critters. A dozen (ranging from $22 to $30, depending on size) will easily feed two people. The gumbo is good and the sweet potatoes terrific, but most of the seafood menu is of secondary importance to those crabs.

*Price: About $25–$30 per person*
*Open daily for dinner only*
*Accepts all major credit cards*

# THE SILVER PALACE
## 50 Bowery (*near Canal Street*)
### 212-964-1204

This is New York's premier—or at least biggest—*dim sum* parlor, jammed most days of the week but absolutely overrun on Sunday mornings with Orientals and Occidentals who come here for the steaming plates of dumplings in dozens of shapes, sizes, and fillings. This is a treat.

*Price: About $12 per person*
*Open daily for breakfast, lunch, and dinner*
*Accepts all major credit cards*

# SMITH & WOLLENSKY
## 201 East 49 Street (*main entrance on Third Avenue*)
### 212-753-1530

It took a while for Smith & Wollensky to get going after opening in 1977, despite its instant steak house look of oak, planked floors, and bentwood chairs, but now the proprietors have made this into one of the city's very best steak houses, while adding to the menu the kinds of items their competitors have never cared to offer. And now the wine list is really an extraordinary collection, especially of California cabernets.

You could go just for the steak or enormous lobsters (we're talking about critters that go above 10 pounds), but you should not neglect the crab meat cocktail (sized at "under 10" to the pound), a massive veal chop, a filet mignon with pepper sauce, exceptionally good onion rings with crunch, and several toothsome desserts, including chocolate *mousse* cake and apple brown Betty. Prices are a little lower in the casual Grill to the rear. The place gets a big sports crowd.

*Price: About $35–$40 per person*
*Open Mon.–Fri. for lunch and dinner; Sat. and Sun. for dinner only*
*Accepts all major credit cards*

# SMOKEY'S PIT

230 Ninth Avenue (*near 24 Street*)   212-924-8181
685 Amsterdam Avenue (*near 94 Street*)   212-865-2900

A lot of barbecue places have opened in New York in the last year or two, but Smokey's still ranks near the top, certainly not for its atmosphere, but for its highly unusual seasonings on the ribs. You can get the ribs sauced mild, hot, or very hot, and when they ask you if you've ever had the very hot before, tell the truth: This stuff is dynamite. And the other spices are intriguing too. Best thing about the ribs is their charred exterior and meatiness to the bone.

*Price: Under $10 per person*
*Open daily for lunch and dinner*
*No credit cards accepted*

# SOHO KITCHEN AND BAR

103 Greene Street (*near Spring Street*)
212-226-9103

This enormous Soho eatery, with its abstract paintings, spotlighting, black ceiling, open kitchen, and loud rock music, gives little indication that the kitchen can turn out some exemplary fast food—pizza with sausage and cheese, French fries with their skin on, fried zucchini, and some less notable pastas. More important, even the most indefatigable oenophile will be sated by the selection of more than a hundred wines by the glass—intelligently offered in flights at a set price and including a wide range of, say, California and French Chardonnays and chenin blancs. This makes for a great deal of fun any night of the week. After midnight, champagnes are sold by the glass at discount.

*Price: About $15 per person*
*Open Mon.–Sat. for dinner only; closed Sun.*
*Accepts American Express, Visa, and MasterCard*

# SWISS CHALET/CHALET SUISSE

6 East 48 Street (*near Fifth Avenue*)
212-355-0855

What can you ask of a Swiss restaurant but that it be friendly, informal, and serve a nice selection of specialties from the cantons and some soft Swiss wines? You might be interested to know that Swiss Chalet—in addition to good food and wines—has the distinction of having invented chocolate *fondue* back in 1956 as a promotional dish. Try the smoked meats, the *rösti,* and the cheese *fondue Neuchateloise.*

*Price: About $20 per person*
*Open Mon.–Fri. for lunch and dinner; closed Sat. and Sun.*
*Accepts all major credit cards*

---

# SYLVIA'S
## 328 Lenox Avenue (*near 126 Street*)
### 212-534-9414

Sylvia's serves soul food the way it should be served—in abundance and with an integrity of spices and flavors that give you no pause to doubt its Southern farm origins. Here, in two long rooms on a not particularly savory block in Harlem, you'll be amazed at the flavor that comes through the barbecued spareribs with its sweet-sour-hot sauce, the smothered pork chops, the black-eyed peas and candied yams, and the crisp fried chicken. There are side orders of grits with butter, potato salad of real bite, collard greens, and plenty of cornbread. You'll want to take a cab to get up to Sylvia's, and you may want to have one waiting to take you back. But this is a cordial, generous spot serving the real stuff.

*Price: About $10 per person*
*Open Mon.–Sat. for breakfast, lunch, and dinner; Sun. for lunch*
*and dinner only*
*No credit cards accepted*

---

# THE TERRACE
## 400 West 119 Street (*near Amsterdam Avenue*)
### 212-666-9490

From its perch atop a Columbia University dormitory (though in no way associated with the school), The Terrace has a unique, romantic, wrap-around view of the city and of the Hudson River—quite breathtaking at twilight. The whole place seems a retreat from midtown madness, and the French-Continental menu offers some exceptional cuisine items: steamed baby shrimp with aromatic vegetables, scallops with watercress, and impeccably prepared fish. The wine list is very good, and owner Nada Bernic keeps this place running at a sophisticated level that matches its situation. The wine list is quite commendable. There's valet parking for those who drive.

*Price: About $35–$40 per person*
*Open Tues.–Fri. for lunch and dinner; Sat. for dinner only; closed Sun.*
*Accepts all major credit cards*

# TEXARKANA
## 64 West 10 Street
### 212-254-5800

Texarkana specializes in the cookery of the Gulf Coast, and that means a fair sampling of Creole and Cajun dishes. There's gumbo, and barbecued pork, and "dirty rice," and pickled shrimp, and blackened redfish—all prepared pretty well and served with dispatch by a young, eager crew. The surroundings are airy, pale-pink with arching woodwork, white tablecloths, and punctuations of western *objets d'art*. Noisy but casual, you'll enjoy yourself here and hobnob with a nice crowd.

*Price: About $25–$30 per person*
*Open daily for lunch and dinner*
*Accepts American Express*

# VAŠATA
## 339 East 75 Street (*near First Avenue*)
### 212-650-1686

Czech cuisine may at the moment be out of fashion, but when the wind-chill factor in New York drops the temperature below zero, there's no better place to be than behind a big platter of duck—all crisp and succulent—served with an equally large platter of dumplings. Or you may want to ward off the weather with boiled beef in a dill sauce, having dispatched the chicken livers and the headchesse beforehand, and finish off with *palacsintas* with apricot purée in them. All of this will cost you a very modest penny and you'll be bolstered for the night ahead.

*Price: About $15–$20 per person*
*Open Tues.–Sat. for dinner only; Sun. for lunch and dinner; closed Mon.*
*Accepts all major credit cards*

# VICTOR'S CAFÉ 52
## 236 West 52 Street (*near Broadway*)
### 212-586-7714

A sprawling Cuban restaurant that draws a festive Hispanic clientele who come for the generous portions of well-made shrimp in green sauce, garlic soup, *paella, rope vieja,* suckling roast pig, and terrific fried pork *Habanera*. The side orders of rice and black beans are pure ballast, the daiquiris freshly made, and the wine list minimal. There's also a "Roberto Duran Victory" Cuban-style steak. There's a pianist and strolling violinists on weekends.

*Price: About $20 per person*
*Open daily for lunch and dinner*
*Accepts all major credit cards*

## WINDOWS ON THE WORLD
### 1 World Trade Center
#### 212-938-1111

Everyone's heard of Windows on the World—107 stories above Manhattan, the Atlantic Ocean, and, on a very clear night, Spain. The view is spectacular, and no one visiting New York for the first time should fail to come here, at least for a drink at sundown at the City Lights Bar or some nibbles at The Hors d'Oeuvrerie, serving precisely what its name implies, and a special dining room called Cellar in the Sky (see page 583). But the restaurant most people go to—and mostly for that grand view of the western hemisphere—is called, simply, The Restaurant. The *maître d'* has all the charm of a fireplug, but the food is good. The view from the 107th floor and a good bottle of wine from one of this country's best list are well worth every effort to book a reservation here. You won't forget the view soon.

During the day Windows is a private club for local business people. Free parking if you get your ticket validated on the way out. Allow plenty of time to get to the restaurant: The concourses of the World Trade Center are confusing.

*Price: Fixed price at $29.95; á la carte about $25–$30 per person*
*Open Mon.–Fri. for dinner only; Sat. and Sun. for lunch and dinner*
*Accepts all major credit cards*

## WONG KEE
### 113 Mott Street (*near Canal Street*)
#### 212-226-9018

A small, spanking-clean little restaurant in Chinatown where you and several others may indulge in five or six dishes for under $20, and these will be very family-style Chinese dishes—duck with star anise, beef with sour cabbage, shredded pork with pan-fried noodles, and other hearty preparations. Don't expect the King's English to be spoken here. And don't order off the English menu! Point to whatever you see the Chinese families at the next table eating.

*Price: Under $10 per person*
*Open daily for lunch and dinner*
*No credit cards accepted*

# WOODS GRAMERCY
## 24 East 21 Street (*near Park Avenue*)
### 212-505-5252

There are actually three Woods locations, but this is no flashy chain. Woods pioneered *nouvelle* salads and simply cooked dishes in New York some years ago on Madison Avenue, but this most recent addition, in the Gramercy Park section, is the most romantic of the trio and attracts the publishing crowd at lunch and a fashionable clientele at night. The dining rooms are large, the tables well separated, and the staff congenial. The menu—stressing lightness —is ever changing, but count on salads with goat cheese and sun-dried tomatoes, homemade country breads, and steamed vegetables. Desserts are of a very high caliber across the board.

*Price: About $30 per person*
*Open Sun.–Fri. for lunch and dinner; Sat. for dinner only*
*Accepts all major credit cards*

# WOO LAE OAK OF SEOUL
## 77 West 46 Street (*near Avenue of the Americas*)
### 212-869-9958

Korean menus in New York may not represent the entire range of restaurants back in Seoul, but Woo Lae Oak does a nice job with grilled marinated meats and casseroles of meat and noodles—almost everything spiced up with the fiery *kim chee* condiment. Charming waitresses help you with Korean-style dining etiquette.

*Price: About $15 per person*
*Open daily for lunch and dinner*
*Accepts all major credit cards*

# XENIA
## 871 First Avenue (*near 49 Street*)
### 212-838-1191

A friendly Greek taverna with a sunny patio that is obviously preferred during good weather. The food here all tastes very fresh (despite some overcooking) —from the *tzatziki* dip of sour cream, cucumber, garlic, and dill to the baby lamb *yuvetsi* served with a light tomato sauce. The *filo* pastries could be a lot crisper than some I've had here. Service is very friendly.

*Price: About $20 per person*
*Open daily for lunch and dinner*
*Accepts all major credit cards*

# PHILADELPHIA

## By Elaine Tait

**AMERICAN**
The City Tavern
USA Café

**BAKERY**
The Pink Rose Pastry Shop

**BARBECUE**
Mama Rosa's

**BREAKFAST**
À Propos
The Commisary

**BRUNCH**
The Fountain
Restaurant La Terrasse

**CAJUN/CREOLE**
Café Nola

**CHINESE**
Hu-Nan
Joe's Peking Duck House
Lee How Fook
Tang Yean

**CONTINENTAL**
The Garden
Mirabelle
Monte Carlo Living Room
The Restaurant School

**CRAB HOUSE**
DiNardo's Famous Crabs
Walt's King of Crabs

**DINER**
Mayfair Diner

**ECLECTIC**
À Propos
City Bites
The Commissary
Frog
Marabella's
Raymond Haldeman
USA Café

**ETHIOPIAN**
Nyala

**FRENCH**
Alouette
Déjà-Vu
Deux Cheminées

**FRENCH**
  The Fountain
  La Truffe
  Le Bec Fin
  Nais

**HOT DOGS**
  Levis Hot Dogs

**HOTEL DINING ROOM**
  The Fountain

**HUNGARIAN**
  Magyar Hungarian Restaurant
    and Bakery

**INDIAN**
  Campus India
  Siva's

**IRISH**
  Downey's Drinking House &
    Dining Saloon
  Irish Pub

**ITALIAN**
  Dante & Luigi's
  Harry's Bar & Grill
  La Vigna
  Osteria Romana
  Ristorante Gaetano
  Ristorante Il Gallo Nero

**JAPANESE**
  Asakura at Tokyo Center
  Ginza

**MEXICAN**
  El Metate

**MOROCCAN**
  Marrakesh

**SEAFOOD**
  Dockside Fish Company
  Sansom Street Oyster House

**STEAKS AND CHOPS**
  Harry's Bar & Grill
  Morton's of Chicago

**SUBURBAN**
  Morgan's Bistro (Ardmore)
  Nais (Havertown)
  Spring Mill Café
    (Conshohocken)

**THAI**
  Manus Place
  Siam Cuisine

**UNIQUE PROPERTY**
  Jim's Steaks
  Reading Terminal Market

**VIETNAMESE**
  Café Da Lat
  Saigon

The mid-1970s were Philadelphia's years of great restaurant growth, a marvelously exciting time to be a restaurant critic in this city. There was a new place to review every week and—even more surprising—a majority of these early restaurants were very, very good. Yet despite favorable writeups, many of these establishments no longer exist. With so much competition, there simply wasn't enough business to allow everyone to prosper. The convention center that was to bring money from out-of-towners was slow to materialize. Atlantic City casinos siphoned off some local trade. Many pioneers became discouraged and sold out.

But that was yesterday. The bright news today is that the convention center plans seem, finally, to be moving forward. For every restaurateur who gave up, a hardy new entrepreneur has been waiting in the wings to enter this challenging arena. Many of the pioneer restaurants have changed hands, names, and menus. New locations have been found as well. We're seeing the development of new restaurant neighborhoods and all this activity is adding vitality to the dining-out scene.

A big new draw is price. Thanks to competition, restaurants have become more cost-conscious. In general, lower average checks have now made it possible for those who dined out infrequently in the past, to patronize their favorite places more than once a week.

There are even bargains in fixed-price meals at some of the top-of-the-line places like the nationally famous Le Bec Fin, which, at this writing, offers a $17 fixed-price lunch. Several restaurants, including most in Chinatown, are offering free parking to their customers, no minor attraction in a city where parking fees get higher every day.

Philadelphia restaurant food is lighter, leaner, better for you than it has ever been. It is also more flavorful and more visually attractive, thanks to an Oriental influence that springs from our large Chinese, Vietnamese, and Thai communities. And, as always, there is a feeling of friendly informality here that reflects our name as the City of Brotherly Love.

*Elaine Tait has been the restaurant critic of the* Philadelphia Inquirer *for twenty-two years. She is also the author of a popular weekly column that deals with food in an intensely personal manner. Her guidebook* Best Restaurants Philadelphia & Environs *(101 Productions), first published in 1979, is currently available in a revised edition.*

# ALOUETTE

## 528 South 5 Street (*near South Street*)
### 215-629-1126

Quietly and without much fanfare, little Alouette has become the French restaurant of choice for many discriminating Philadelphians. Kamol Phutlek's food has classic French origins, but Phutlek, who was born in Thailand, brings his own special artistry into every dish. Of special interest are the creamy yet peppery Thai curries, the silken-sauced fish dishes spiked with fresh sorrel or basil, and imaginative pastas like *capellini* sautéed in olive oil with lemon zest, *prosciutto,* and herbs. Even if you're not a dessert fanatic (I'm not), it's difficult to remain detached faced with one of Alouette's fabulous strawberry tarts or white chocolate *mousses.* But there's really very little about this restaurant that isn't first rate. The rolls, for example, are warm, crisp-crusted, and absolutely delicious. The wine list is the product of one of the city's most knowledgeable *sommeliers.*

*Price: About $35 per person*
*Open daily for dinner only*
*Accepts all major credit cards*

# À PROPOS

## 211 South Broad Street (*near Walnut Street*)
### 215-546-4424

Mesquite-grilled meats, fish, and poultry, pastas, and baby vegetables are specialties at this big, often noisy restaurant with its open, New York-style architecture and the greenhouse sidewalk café. An in-house bakery supplies excellent breads and O.K. pastries for eating here or takeout. Owners Shimon and Koby Bokovza have given Aliza Green support in making this one of the city's most exciting new restaurants.

*Price: About $25 per person*
*Open daily for breakfast, lunch, and dinner*
*Accepts all major credit cards*

## ASAKURA AT TOKYO CENTER
### 1207 Race Street (*near 12 Street*)
#### 215-988-0274

*Sushi* chefs from Tokyo man the triple *sushi* counter in Chinatown's only Japanese restaurant. Many, but not all, of the tasty rice-based tidbits they concoct are made with raw fish. My favorite exception is a vegetarian combination of avocado and cucumber wrapped in rice that has been sprinkled with toasted sesame seeds. If you like your seafood cooked, try the shrimp *tempura* made with giant shrimp. The shrimp are extraordinarily tender and the batter that coats every ingredient is so thin and delicate, you'll wonder how it stays attached. The restaurant lets you dine Western style at booths or tables or, shoeless, on cushions in the *tatami* room.

*Price: About $15 per person for a full meal*
*Open daily for lunch and dinner*
*Accepts all major credit cards*

## CAFÉ DA LAT
### 1009 South 8 Street
#### 215-627-3717

Café Da Lat, named for a Vietnamese resort city, is another neat, family-owned Vietnamese restaurant in the Italian Market. Here, against a background of tango tapes and Viet pop music, you'll find riblets of pork with a citrusy bite of lemon grass in the pepper and garlic sauce; spicy char-broiled pork on wooden skewers, lacquer-skinned roast duck with an interesting star anise scent, and at least a dozen other dishes worth ordering. Bring your own wine or beer.

*Price: About $10 per person*
*Open daily for lunch and dinner*
*No credit cards accepted*

## CAFÉ NOLA
### 328 South Street (*moving to 603 South Third Street in 1986*)
#### 215-627-2590

Nola was serving Philadelphians New Orleans Creole and Cajun food long before it became trendy. Some of us think they do it better than many of the New Orleans restaurants. Authentic ingredients are flown in regularly for crawfish pie, an *etoufée*, Cajun popcorn (deep-fried crawfish tails), blackened redfish, Acadian crab meat tart, gumbo ya-ya, and jambalaya. They'll even do a pan-blackened Cajun prime rib for beef eaters. This is one of those rare local restaurants serving Saturday lunch and the South Street crowd gives you the added bonus of entertainment with your midday meal. The restaurant also does a lively Sunday brunch.

*Price: About $30 per person*
*Open daily for lunch and dinner*
*Accepts all major credit cards*

---

## CAMPUS INDIA
### 33 South 40 Street (*near Market Street*)
### 215-243-9718

Owner Mohander Singh, a tall, handsome turbaned Indian, is one of the attractions here. His courtly manners help you overlook the restaurant's peeling paint and slightly shabby plastic upholstery. Much of the clientele is drawn from the University of Pennsylvania campus. My favorite dishes include the *lamb bhuna, keema paratha* (bread stuffed with ground meat), and *tandoori* chicken. There are also a number of appealing vegetarian dishes.

*Price: About $10 per person*
*Open daily for lunch and dinner*
*Accepts all major credit cards*

---

## CITY BITES
### 212 Walnut Street (*corner of Second and Walnut streets*)
### 215-238-1300

A grazer's and gazer's delight, City Bites was designed to entertain you with imaginative, affordable food served in a variety of zany, contemporary settings. (One is an open-sized Greek temple fitted with diner booths.) The restaurant's location makes it a good launching place for an afternoon of historic sightseeing or an equally convenient spot for collecting your thoughts after a film at the Ritz. Goodies on the menu include grilled Brie with *pesto* and garlic toast, Thai curries, gigantic pizza wedges.

*Price: About $10 per person*
*Open daily for dinner*
*Accepts all major credit cards*

# THE CITY TAVERN
## 2 Street near Walnut Street
### 215-923-6059

What looks like an original Colonial building is actually a brick-by-brick recreation of a historic tavern that was built on this site in 1773 and later demolished. Your server wears Colonial garb and can tell you as much about the history of the place as you care to hear. Food is fairly straightforward stuff —like fresh fish and roast beef. I'm one of the many Philadelphians who like to come here on a winter evening for a sherry in front of the fire or, in summer, for a lemonade in the garden. A harpsicordist adds to the atmosphere.

*Price: About $25 per person*
*Open daily for lunch and dinner*
*Accepts all major credit cards*

# THE COMMISSARY
## 1710 Sansom Street (*near 17 Street*)
### 215-569-2240

This chic downstairs cafeteria is extremely popular from morning to night with center-city professionals. The food includes predictable dishes such as classic chicken salad (with walnuts and grapes, however) and more unusual items such as breast of chicken stuffed with Roquefort. The desserts include a famous carrot cake and some of the best mixed-fruit tarts in town. Omelets are made to order. Similar, slightly lighter fare is available at the piano bar that adjoins the restaurant.

*Price: About $20 per person*
*Open Mon.–Fri. for breakfast, lunch, and dinner; Sat. and Sun. for lunch and dinner only*
*Accepts all major credit cards*

# DANTE & LUIGI'S
## 762 South 10 Street (*corner of 10 and Catherine streets*)
### 215-922-9501

One of the oldest and best of Philadelphia's Italian market restaurants, Dante & Luigi's is noisy, informal, and lovable right down to the modest prices. Homey specialties include stuffed eggplant *parmigiana* and veal with olives, artichoke hearts, and potato croquette.

*Price: About $10 per person*
*Open daily for lunch and dinner*
*No credit cards accepted*

## DÉJÀ-VU
### 1609 Pine Street (*near 16 Street*)
### 215-546-1190

Owner Salomon Montezinos' interpretation of French food is as intensely personal as the decor in this tiny, elaborately-furnished restaurant. Montezinos was one of the city's first chefs to offer diners palate-cleansing *sorbets* made with fresh herbs and blossoms. His extraordinary game dishes include young wild boar loin with cider vinegar and shallots. Now joined by chef Alain Tricot (a master pastry-maker), Déjà-Vu is even better. The wine list offers some precious vintages for big spenders as well as more affordable bottles for the rest of us. The wine cellar is available as a private dining room for those moments when you want to sup away from the crowd.

*Price: About $50 per person*
*Open Mon.–Sat. for dinner only; closed Sun.*
*Accepts all major credit cards*

## DEUX CHEMINÉES
### 251 South Camac Street (*between Locust and Spruce streets*)
### 215-985-0367

Although the cuisine offered by chef Fritz Blank is classic French and specializes in the likes of *carré d'agneau, ris de veau,* and *foie de veau Polonaise,* the sophisticated decor here is eighteenth century and reminiscent of a fine old Philadelphia home. Patrons look old-monied as well, which is understandable since the prices are commensurate with the surroundings.

*Price: About $45 per person*
*Open Mon.–Sat. for lunch and dinner; Sun. for dinner only*
*Accepts all major credit cards*

## DINARDO'S FAMOUS CRABS
### 312 Race Street (*near 3 Street*)
### 215-925-5115

The original DiNardo's (in Wilmington) is so busy you may find yourself waiting an hour or more for a table. This newer outpost serves the same meaty hard-shell crabs, cooked with the restaurant's distinctive, very peppery seasoning, but manages to get you in and out a lot faster—unless you're dining with someone like my friend Joanne, who spends hours digging every micro-morsel from a crab. Definitely a "don't dress" place; you'll feel conspicious if you arrive in anything fancier than jeans and a shirt.

*Price: Under $15 per person*
*Open Mon.–Sat. for lunch and dinner; Sun. for dinner only*
*Accepts all major credit cards*

---

## DOCKSIDE FISH COMPANY
### 815 Locust Street
### 215-925-6175

This upscale but still affordable seafood restaurant provides a pastel-walled, contemporary setting for plain and ambitious fish and shellfish combinations. In addition to grilled fresh fish and freshly opened clams and oysters, Dockside does a decent crab imperial, almond shrimp with plum sauce, and Mediterranean seafood salad. The restaurant has a special section for non-smokers. Reservations are a good idea because the place is popular with locals.

*Price: About $25 per person*
*Open Mon.–Fri. for lunch and dinner; Sat. and Sun. for dinner only; closed Mon.*
*Accepts all major credit cards*

---

## DOWNEY'S DRINKING HOUSE & DINING SALOON
### Front and South streets
### 215-629-0526

Corned beef and cabbage and Irish whiskey cake are on the menu, of course, but the attractions also include a full list of fairly simple foods and a chance to rub elbows with the sports celebs who frequent the bar here. Downey's also has some fairly obliging hours. Lunch lasts until 4 P.M.; weekday dinner starts at 4:30 and doesn't end until 10:45; on Saturday the dinner hour starts at 4 and ends at 12:30. Free valet parking is a convenience; reservations are almost a must, because Downey's is usually very busy.

*Price: About $20 per person*
*Open Mon.–Sat. for lunch and dinner; Sun. for brunch only*
*Accepts all major credit cards*

# EL METATE

### 1511 Locust Street (*near Broad Street*)
### 215-546-0181

In addition to more familiar Mexican fare like *nachos* and *burritos, tacos* and *guacamole,* El Metate offers more sophisticated dishes such as *mole poblano,* red snapper in avocado/lime butter, and *pollo con cilantro.* If you get a craving for mid-afternoon munchies, you can satisfy it between 2 and 5:30 P.M., when the restaurant serves snacks.

*Price: About $15 per person*
*Open Mon.–Fri. for lunch and dinner; Sat. and Sun. for dinner only*
*Accepts all major credit cards*

# THE FOUNTAIN

### In the Four Seasons Hotel, 1 Logan Square
### 215-963-1500

In a city of fine restaurants, The Fountain ranks up there with the best of them. Planes of gleaming marble and acres of flowering plants in the cool, elegant lobby lead to the restaurant, where you're treated to the view of the fountain for which the room is named. Food, under the direction of executive chef Jean-Marie Lacroix, is seasonally dictated and imaginatively prepared and served. If you're watching your waistline, check out the Four Seasons Alternative Menu Selections available at every meal. Excellent Sunday brunch.

The beautifully furnished extension of the hotel's lobby offers good piano music most nights and a lovely view of the Parkway at any hour.

*Price: About $35 per person*
*Open daily for lunch and dinner*
*Accepts all major credit cards*

# FROG

### 1524 Locust Street (*near Broad Street*)
### 215-735-8882

Frog packages trendy, ingredient-conscious American food in a quiet, contemporary setting. In rooms lined with interesting art and on tables graced with orchids in hand-made pottery vases, you'll eat dishes like deep-fried Brie, chèvre, and smoked *mozzarella* with grape *coulis* and grilled marinated rack of lamb with lamb essence sauce. California wine lovers should find the carefully chosen list here to their liking.

*Price: About $35 per person*
*Open Mon.–Fri. for lunch and dinner; Sat. for dinner only; Sun. for brunch only*
*Accepts all major credit cards*

---

## THE GARDEN
### 1617 Spruce Street (*near 16 Street*)
**215-546-4455**

Named for the garden that was one of the city's first *al fresco* dining locations, the Garden's indoor and outdoor dining spaces have become a year-round attraction. Food is unfussy but great. In addition to seasonal seafood specialties such as creamy oyster stews, fresh fish, and soft-shell crabs, you'll get aged prime steaks and great veal here. The *pomme frites* (fried potatoes) are winners, too. They're as thin and crisp as shreds of excelsior and absolutely delicious. The decor is understated and elegant—very much in the old money Philadelphia tradition.

*Price: About $30 per person*
*Open Mon.–Fri. for lunch and dinner; Sat. for dinner only; closed Sun.*
*Accepts all major credit cards*

---

## GINZA
### 411 South Street (*near 4 Street*)
**215-238-9921**

South Street's noise and traffic make Ginza seem like an island of serenity. Although there's a full menu, I'd stick with the well-made *sushi* here.

*Price: About $15 per person*
*Open daily for lunch and dinner*
*Accepts Visa and MasterCard*

---

## HARRY'S BAR & GRILL
### 22 South 18 Street (*near Market Street*)
**215-561-5757**

Named for the restaurant in Venice, Harry's features pastas and a variety of Italian dishes as well as 21-day aged prime steaks. In season, game and fresh fish are featured. A good deal of business is transacted over lunch and dinner in the darkly elegant, clubby room with its terra-cotta-colored walls and hunting prints.

*Price: About $35 per person*
*Open Mon.–Fri. for lunch and dinner; closed Sat. and Sun.*
*Accepts all major credit cards*

---

# HU-NAN

## 1721 Chestnut Street (*near 17 Street*)
### 215-567-5757

Hu-Nan is Philadelphia's grand, luxe Chinese restaurant, a palatial setting for some very good, very imaginative food from all of China's regions. The peppery Szechuan and Hunan dishes may be a bit tame for some fire-eaters, but try the unusual barbecued spareribs (slightly sweet) and the crisp duck. Because China lacks desserts as we know them, Hu-Nan takes liberties by adding chocolate *mousse* pie to its menu. It also offers a very good selection of wines friendly to Chinese foods. If you're on the Pritikin diet, Hu-Nan will cook some of its specialties to accommodate you.

*Price: About $15 per person*
*Open Mon.–Fri. for lunch and dinner; Sat. and Sun. for dinner only*
*Accepts all major credit cards*

---

# IRISH PUB

## 2007 Walnut Street (*near 20 Street*)
### 215-568-5603

Yes, you can get Irish stew here but more of the menu is devoted to American bar food such as chili and prime ribs. This is one of those comfy, noisy, neighborhood places where prices make it easy to dine here often.

*Price: About $10 per person*
*Open daily for lunch and dinner*
*Accepts American Express*

# JIM'S STEAKS
## 400 South Street (*corner of South and 4 streets*)
### 215-928-1911

The last time I drove by Jim's, a stretch limo was depositing a show biz celebrity at the door. That's not unusual. Anyone who has ever tasted a really well-made Philly steak sandwich like Jim's comes back for more whenever they hits town. The steaks are thinly sliced, cooked on a griddle, and then heaped high on a long crusty Italian roll. You get whatever topping turns you on. Most ask for fried onions and melted cheese with a splash of good tomato sauce, but there's also hot pepper and green pepper. You'll know from the smell of frying onions when you're within blocks of Jim's.

*Price: Under $5 for a sandwich with everything*
*Open daily for lunch and dinner*
*No credit cards accepted*

# JOE'S PEKING DUCK HOUSE
## 925 Race Street
### 215-922-3277

When's the last time you had a zany waiter in a Chinese restaurant? Joe's crew is young and wisecracking. Their chef, a graduate of the Culinary Institute of America, has a huge following, so be prepared to wait for a table on weekends. If you have a lot of time and patience, ask for the snails in black bean sauce, which takes hours to pry from their tiny shells. Otherwise stick to roast duck, or noodles with duck and broth, or mussels with black bean sauce or fresh ginger and scallions. Be prepared for yellow walls, a no-frills setting, and lots of friendly clutter. Bring your own beer or wine.

*Price: About $10 per person*
*Open daily for lunch and dinner*
*No credit cards accepted*

# LA TERRASSE
## 3432 Sansom Street (*near University of Pennsylvania*)
### 215-387-3778

This is the restaurant I think of when I'm in the mood for brunch. Live classical music, good French food, and a staff that consists, largely, of University students make the Sunday meal special here. In warm weather, windows are removed to let you stay in touch with the day. In winter, the terrace is enclosed and greenhouse-like.

*Price: Brunch about $12 per person (with a champagne mimosa)*
*Open Sun.–Fri. for lunch and dinner; Sat. for dinner only*
*Accepts all major credit cards*

---

## LA TRUFFE

### 10 South Front Street (*near Market Street*)
### 215-925-5062

Romantic-looking La Truffe also attracts a business clientele. In addition to classic French cuisine, the restaurant offers waistline-sparing *cuisine minceur* that makes up in aesthetic appeal for what it lacks in calories.

*Price: About $40 per person*
*Open Tues.–Fri. for lunch and dinner; Mon. and Sat. for dinner only; closed Sun.*
*Accepts all major credit cards*

---

## LA VIGNA

### 1100 South Front Street (*corner of Front and Federal streets*)
### 215-336-1100

Small but caring, La Vigna seats just 32, so call for a reservation first. The Northern Italian specialties include *osso buco, tortellini,* and grilled swordfish. Nice touches include free nibbles with drinks and free fruit and nuts afterwards.

*Price: About $20 per person*
*Open Mon.–Fri. for lunch and dinner; Sat. and Sun. for dinner only*
*Accepts all major credit cards*

---

## LE BEC FIN

### 1523 Walnut Street (*near 15 Street*)
### 215-567-1000

Expensive damask on the walls, enormous crystal chandeliers overhead, well-trained waiters, and a serious *sommelier* all tell you that Le Bec Fin takes seriously its status as the city's premier French restaurant.

When owner Georges Perrier is in the kitchen, as he is more often these days, the food can be pure poetry. Perrier's sauces and fish dishes are legendary for the French-born chef is no slouch when it comes to devising rich and wonderful ways with the top-quality sweetbreads, fresh *foie gras,* game and game birds, baby lamb and veal he demands from local purveyors.

Save room for dessert. The multi-tiered cart wheeled to your table holds so many temptations—from fresh raspberries with white chocolate *mousse* to buttery and beautiful tarts—that you won't be able to choose just one. Not to worry. It's something of a Le Bec Fin tradition to sample several sweets at a meal. Do let the *sommelier* help you with your wine selection. He's authoritative but not the least bit condescending. The entire Le Bec Fin staff, for that matter, is surprisingly friendly, given the imposing look and status of the place. There's a fixed-price lunch at $17.

*Price: Fixed-price dinner $60 per person*
*Open Mon.–Fri. for lunch and dinner; Sat. for dinner only; closed Sun.*
*Accepts all major credit cards*

---

## LEE HOW FOOK
### 219 North 11 Street (*between Race and Vine streets*)
### 215-925-7266

Chinese chefs eat at Lee How Fook on their day off. Does that give you a clue to the food here? Served up in a plain, often noisy setting are familiar dishes such as Peking duck and spareribs and less well-known delicacies like seaweed soup and salt cooked shrimp. The lemon chicken is unusually good, but so is just about everything I've ever eaten here. A friend, who doesn't read Chinese, points to the Chinese wall signs advertising daily specials when she orders. She's always surprised—and always delighted, she says. Bring your own beer or wine.

*Price: About $10 per person*
*Open Thurs.–Tues. for lunch and dinner; closed Wed.*
*No credit cards accepted*

---

## LEVIS HOT DOGS
### 507 South 6 Street (*near South Street*)
### 215-627-2354

How many cities have a place where they make their hot dogs and soda? Levis does both. The dogs are spicy; the soda called "champ" (short for cherry champagne) is made with Levis' homemade syrup. The place has been here for over fifty years, so they must be doing something right.

*Price: Under $2 for a soda and hot dog*
*Open daily for lunch and dinner*
*No credit cards accepted*

---

## MAGYAR HUNGARIAN RESTAURANT AND BAKERY
### 2048 Sansom Street
**215-564-2492**

Tiny Magyar is open to serve tea with delectable Hungarian pastries from noon to 4 P.M., Monday through Thursday. On Friday and Saturday evenings, there's a full dinner menu served featuring such Hungarian specialties as *gulyás* and *paprikás*. Roast pig is available by special order.

*Price: About $25 per person*
*Open Mon.–Thurs. for lunch only; Fri. and Sat. for dinner only; closed Sun.*
*Accepts all major credit cards*

---

## MAMA ROSA'S
### 3838 North Broad Street
**215-225-2177**

Mama Rosa's is located on a well-lighted, busy section of North Broad but even so, it took me months before I summoned the courage to give the place a try. One reason might be that what is now a plain but pleasant restaurant was originally a service station, and it shows. A lot of the business is takeout and a lot of the takeout is fried chicken, ribs, rice, greens, and cornbread— all pretty much state-of-the-art.

*Price: Under $10 per person*
*Open daily for lunch and dinner*
*No credit cards accepted*

# MANUS PLACE

### 4251 Walnut Street (*near University of Pennsylvania*)
### 215-386-4404

Scallops with lemon grass and stir-fried squid Thai style (with lots of pepper) are specialties at this campus Thai restaurant with the pastel-pretty decor. I've enjoyed everything I've ordered here on several visits. Portions are fairly modest, so you won't go wrong ordering more than one dish per person. Parking is always available and free in the adjacent lot. Bring your own bottle.

*Price: About $10 per person*
*Open daily for lunch and dinner*
*Accepts Visa and MasterCard*

---

# MARABELLA'S

### 1420 Locust Street (*near Broad Street*)
### 215-545-1845

Marabella's is noisy good fun but, more than that, this big, brassy café feeds you interestingly and affordably. The California-style grilled foods and wafer-crusted pizzas are great but so are Mamma Marabella's meatballs and—my favorite—her chicken soup. Arrive early if you're headed for the theater or the Academy of Music afterwards. Marabella's is busy around the clock.

*Price: About $10 per person*
*Open Mon.–Sat. for lunch and dinner; closed Sun.*
*Accepts all major credit cards*

---

# MARRAKESH

### 517 South Leithgow Street (*near South Street*)
### 215-925-5929

If you've been to Morocco, you'll know that this Marrakesh is the real McCoy right down to the unmarked doorway on a narrow city street. Knock and be received into a world of *tagines, bisteeyas,* and *couscous,* and where everyone relaxes and has a wonderful time. Reservations are recommended.

*Price: About $20 per person*
*Open daily for dinner only*
*No credit cards accepted*

# MAYFAIR DINER

7373 Frankford Avenue (*just above Cottman Avenue*)
**215-624-8886**

Classic diners are a disappearing species, and this one is so true to the original concept of crisp setting, honest food, and fast service that it's worth a trip from downtown to see and experience. Top-quality ingredients include fresh fish, fruit, and vegetables—locally produced whenever possible. Soups and desserts are homemade. At breakfast the choices include frozen or freshly-squeezed juices and real (not instant) oatmeal as well as warm *croissants*. Free parking in the lot that surrounds the diner.

*Price: Under $10 per person*
*Open daily for breakfast, lunch, and dinner*
*No credit cards accepted*

# MIRABELLE

1836 Callowhill Street (*near Logan Square*)
**215-557-9793**

Mirabelle's location may look a bit bleak but step inside and find an Art-Deco interior by one of the area's leading designers and a clientele that includes members of some of the city's best-known law firms. Lucille Canuso's food includes regional French and Italian dishes, such as *pizza rustica,* pastas, *bouillabaisse,* rack of lamb, and such daily specials as fresh pompano with hazelnut butter. A big attraction is the piano bar Wednesday through Saturday. Don't be surprised if the whole place starts singing along. You'll probably join them.

*Price: About $30 per person*
*Open daily for breakfast, lunch, and dinner*
*Accepts all major credit cards*

# MONTE CARLO LIVING ROOM

Corner of 2 and South streets
**215-925-2220**

An expensively-decorated room serves as the setting for Chef Nunzio's French and Italian specialties. Pastas are particularly enticing.

*Price: About $35 per person*
*Open daily for dinner only*
*Accepts American Express*

# MORGAN'S BISTRO
## In the Times Building (*Suburban Square*), Ardmore
### 215-642-5100

Owned by one of the leaders of Philadelphia's restaurant renaissance, this lively, caring restaurant features such contemporary American dishes as grilled duck breast and *linguine* with spicy shellfish. About half an hour's drive from downtown.

*Price: About $25 per person*
*Open daily for lunch and dinner*
*Accepts all major credit cards*

---

# MORTON'S OF CHICAGO
## 1 Logan Square
### 215-557-0724

As the name suggests, this is the local outpost of a Chicago restaurant chain that specializes in prime steaks and other no-nonsense entrées. The formula includes showing the customers the pre-cooked ingredients of the meal, so be prepared to see a slightly punchy, live lobster as well as plastic-wrapped hunks of beef, veal, or lamb. Portions are so large it's a rare diner who leaves without a doggie bag. Tables are far enough apart to make this a good business lunch or dinner destination.

*Price: About $35 per person*
*Open Mon.–Fri. for lunch and dinner; Sat. for dinner only; closed Sun.*
*Accepts all major credit cards*

---

# NAIS
## 13–17 West Benedict Avenue, Havertown
### 215-789-5983

Nais (I'm still unsure of the recommended pronunciation of the name) is a surprise in this neighborhood of fast-food franchises and pizza parlors. The chef is Thai, the food is his artistic interpretation of French cuisine. Bring your own wine. About half an hour's drive from downtown.

*Price: About $25 per person*
*Open Tues.–Sun. for dinner only; closed Mon.*
*Accepts all major credit cards*

# NYALA
123 South 18 Street (*near Sansom Street*)
**215-557-9401**

Ethiopian stews are called *wats. Injera,* the local bread, which looks like a thin sponge-rubber napkin, is used to pick up a bite of *wat.* (Spoons and forks are no-nos here.) This may sound like an Abbott-and-Costello routine, but it's actually quite appetizing and entertaining. The restaurant is located atop a long flight of dingy stairs. Don't let that discourage you.

*Price: About $15 per person*
*Open Mon.–Fri. for lunch and dinner; Sat. and Sun. for dinner only*
*Accepts all major credit cards*

# OSTERIA ROMANA
935 Ellsworth Street (*near 9 Street*)
**215-271-9191**

Pint-sized Ivana DiMarco's restaurant is located in the heart of the city's Italian market, where she finds many of the fresh ingredients for her glorious Roman cooking. Specialties include *osso buco,* angel's hair pasta with caviar, mussels in cream and brandy sauce, and, for those who order ahead, roast suckling pig. Because the restaurant is small and very popular, reservations are always a good idea.

*Price: About $30 per person*
*Open Tues.–Sat. for dinner only; closed Mon.*
*Accepts all major credit cards*

# THE PINK ROSE PASTRY SHOP
4 and Bainbridge streets
**215-592-0565**

This tiny, romantic shop moved recently from the Italian Market to the South Street area, where they now have room for eight tables. Great coffee is served in one-of-a-kind cups and saucers. The European-style cakes and pastries are almost too beautiful.

*Price: Depends on what you order*
*Open Tues.–Thurs. 8 A.M. to 11 P.M.; Fri. and Sat. 8 A.M. to midnight; Sun.*
*8 A.M. to 8 P.M.; closed Mon.*
*No credit cards accepted*

# RAYMOND HALDEMAN
## 110–112 South Front Street (*near Chestnut Street*)
### 215-925-9888

Haldeman, a popular society caterer, continues to fine-tune the menu of this big, beautiful restaurant and bar. Excellent pastas, herb-sauced fish dishes, grilled meats, and home-baked desserts are served in a choice of rooms that includes—in season—an herb garden. Free parking is available at the city-owned garage next door at lunch or dinner every day except Saturday.

*Price: About $30 per person*
*Open Mon.–Fri. for lunch and dinner; Sat. for dinner only; closed Sun.*
*Accepts all major credit cards*

# READING TERMINAL MARKET
## 12 and Arch streets
### 215-922-2317

The attractions at the Market (opened in 1893 and brought back to life in the last few years) include stands that let you sample many local specialties. Some of my favorites are Bassett's ice cream (deluxe locally made ice cream in a variety of unusual flavors); Olivieri's Prince of Steaks (famous for its "Philadelphia cheese steaks"); Fisher's soft pretzels (served warm, buttered, and with your choice of mustards by Pennsylvania Dutch vendors); and Famous 4 Street Cookie Company (the chocolate chip cookies are sensational).

*Price: Depends on what you eat*
*Open at various hours and days depending on individual stand*
*Credit cards accepted by a few stands*

# THE RESTAURANT SCHOOL
## 2119 Walnut Street (*near 21 Street*)
### 215-561-3469

It's difficult to say for certain what you'll find in the way of food and service here. This workshop of the city's well-known Restaurant School has a different staff every school term. Some are great; some are just enthusiastic. But because the price is right ($12 buys a first course and entrée) and the setting is a big, beautiful old Victorian town house, it's worth a gamble.

*Price: Under $20 per person*
*Open Tues.–Sat. for dinner only; closed Sun. and Mon.*
*Accepts all major credit cards*

## RISTORANTE GAETANO
### 705 Walnut Street (*near 7 Street*)
### 215-627-7575

Dine like guests in a historically certified Philadelphia town house. Hosts Inez and Gaetano Schinco offer a regular five-course fixed-price meal or a four-course fixed-price pre-theater menu starring the subtle dishes of Northern Italy. You get to choose entrée and dessert; the Schincos tell you what appetizer and pasta will be served that day. Included among the latter are baby *gnocchi,* silken *fettuccine* dressed with cream and Parmesan, and mini-*cannelloni* with nicely-spiced meat fillings. Veal is a favorite entrée choice here but there are interesting offerings in all meat and fish categories. Classic desserts include *zuppa inglese, crema al caramello,* and fresh fruits of the season. There's a decent selection of Italian wines at moderate prices.

*Price: Fixed-price dinner, $32 or $25*
*Open Tues.–Fri. for lunch and dinner; Tues. and Sat. for dinner only; closed*
*Sun. and Mon.*
*Accepts all major credit cards*

## RISTORANTE IL GALLO NERO
### 254 South 15 Street (*near Spruce Street*)
### 215-546-8065

Il Gallo Nero is the chic, downtown Italian restaurant, the one where they use imported *porcini,* white truffles, buffalo *mozzarella, arugula,* and *trevisse* for classic Florentine and Tuscan specialties. Pastas include artichoke and buckwheat, *cappelletti* and *cavatelli* and there are homemade *risotti* as well. For waist-watchers there's a spa menu that changes, as does the regular card, with the seasons.

*Price: About $30 per person*
*Open Mon.–Fri. for lunch and dinner; Sat. for dinner only; closed Sun.*
*Accepts all major credit cards*

# SAIGON
### 935 Washington Avenue (*near the Italian Market*)
### 215-925-9656

Saigon was one of the city's first Vietnamese restaurants and is still one of the best. Crowded into a row house, just around the corner from the Italian Market, the family-owned and -operated restaurant does especially well with Vietnamese spring rolls and grilled pork, beef, and chicken dishes.

*Price: About $10 per person*
*Open Mon.–Fri. for lunch and dinner; Sat. and Sun. for dinner only*
*No credit cards accepted*

# SANSOM STREET OYSTER HOUSE
### 1516 Sansom Street (*near 15 Street*)
### 215-567-7683

Oyster houses were a Philadelphia tradition a generation ago. This one, while not historic, is owned by a descendant of a famous oyster house family. The plain but pleasing decor includes antique oyster plates overhead. Tables are shared and there's a bit of noise sometimes, but the simply-prepared seafood here is always appealing and priced below what the more famous seafood houses charge. Try the freshly opened oysters or clams on the half shell or the broiled fish of the day. Non-smokers should know that this was one of the first center city restaurants to set up a non-smokers section. No reservations are accepted. You might find yourself waiting in line for a bit.

*Price: About $15 per person*
*Open Mon.–Sat. for lunch and dinner; closed Sun.*
*Accepts all major credit cards*

# SIAM CUISINE
### 925 Arch Street
### 215-922-7135

Siam Cuisine is the Thai restaurant with the unusual decor. Walls and printed tablecloths are colored in the desert pastels favored by contemporary designers. A series of pointed arches gives the restaurant architectural interest. Thai cooking features flavors of lemon grass, garlic, coriander, and mint. The curries are, to my taste, more appealing than Indian curries. My favorite, made with chicken and bamboo shoots, has a sauce that is at the same time peppery and soothing, thanks to a creamy, rich coconut milk base. Many of the entrées arrive, Western-style, with rice and a vegetable. Desserts include a decent coconut cake. Beer helps cool some of the curry fire. Bring your own.

*Price: About $10 per person*
*Open Tues.–Sun. for lunch and dinner; closed Mon.*
*Accepts Visa and MasterCard*

---

## SIVA'S
### 34 South Front Street (*near Chestnut Street*)
### 215-925-2700

Philadelphia's upscale Indian restaurant offers a wide range of dishes from each of that country's many regions. The sophisticated setting accounts for prices that are a cut or two above the standard Indian restaurant.

*Price: About $25 per person*
*Open Mon.–Fri. for lunch and dinner; Sat. and Sun. for dinner only*
*Accepts all major credit cards*

---

## SPRING MILL CAFÉ
### 164 Barren Hill Road, Conshohocken
### 215-828-2550

Just an easy half-hour's drive from the city, yet the café is a real country French restaurant with simple French dishes such as rabbit stew and duck with vermouth sauce. My favorite time and place to dine here? Spring, summer, or fall, when I can eat on the tiny deck just outside the kitchen door. Bring your own wine.

*Price: About $25 per person*
*Open Wed.–Sun. for lunch and dinner; closed Mon. and Tues.*
*No credit cards accepted*

---

## TANG YEAN
### 220 South 10 Street (*near Race Street*)
### 215-925-3993

Chinese health food? That's what the sign over the door of Tang Yean says. What it means is that they don't serve beef or pork here, nor do they load up the dishes with MSG or salt. You'd be surprised at how many delicious combinations can be made with chicken and seafood. My own favorites include lemon walnut chicken, chicken corn soup, and—best of all—the shrimp-stuffed eggplant slices Tang Yean coats with *tempura* batter and fries to make the coating as light as a spring snowflake. The restaurant amenities include cloth napkins and tablecloths, fresh flowers, and nice glasses for the wine you may bring. Background music is usually classical. The romantic couples I've sent here have loved it for the setting as much as for the affordable food.

*Price: About $10 per person*
*Open Wed.–Mon. for lunch and dinner; closed Tues.*
*Accepts all major credit cards*

---

## USA CAFÉ
### 1710 Sansom Street (*over the Commissary*)
### 215-569-2240

Red-and-green chile pasta with green chile *pesto* and broiled filet of beef with cumin and *jalapeño demi-glace* were on a recent menu at this restaurant, where they do imaginative things with the ingredients of the American Southwest. Tables are very close together and the place tends to be noisy, so don't come here expecting to conduct some big deal in privacy. A very good wine list specializes in American wines. Many are available by the glass.

*Price: About $30 per person*
*Open Mon.–Fri. for lunch and dinner; Sat. for dinner only; closed Sun.*
*Accepts all major credit cards*

---

## WALT'S KING OF CRABS
### 804–806 South Street (*Queen Village*)
### 215-339-9124

Walt's is about as plain a setting as you can get for hard-shell crabs. This was a slightly shabby neighborhood for a while but it's now fairly fashionable, and you may have trouble finding street parking. Dress for work. Extricating crabs from their armor plate is messy but fun.

*Price: Under $15 per person*
*Open daily for dinner only*
*No credit cards accepted*

# PHOENIX AND SCOTTSDALE

## BY ELIN JEFFORDS

**AMERICAN**
Oscar Taylor

**BAR**
Amnesia
Studebaker's

**BREAKFAST**
The Good Egg
Munchabagel

**BRUNCH**
Palm Court

**CONTINENTAL**
Chaparral Room
Orangerie

**DINER**
Ed Debevic's
Studebaker's

**FRENCH**
Bouchon
The French Corner
La Chaumière
Vincent's
The White Truffle

**GREEK**
Demetra's Kitchen

**HAMBURGERS**
Flakey Jake's

**HOTEL DINING ROOM**
Bouchon
Chaparral Room
Orangerie

**ITALIAN**
Pasta Sergio's
Tomaso's

**JAPANESE**
Shogun

**MEXICAN**
Aunt Chilada's
Fina Cocina
Restaurant Mexico
Ricardo's
Rosita's Place

**PIZZA**
Pizzafarro's

**SEAFOOD**
  Tug's

**STEAKS AND CHOPS**
  The Stockyards
  T-Bone Steak House

**THAI**
  Daa's Thai Room
  Pink Pepper

**UNIQUE PROPERTIES**
  Ed Debevic's
  The Impeccable Pig

Not so long ago, when you talked good eats hereabouts in the Valley of the Sun, you were talking cowboy steak houses or Mexican food. But the rapid growth of the area and its international reputation as a winter resort have created a respectable, though admittedly young, restaurant tradition.

Most of the major resorts boast dining rooms of genuine distinction. Travel articles routinely praise top Valley establishments. A French restaurant in Scottsdale (Vincent's) has been lauded by no less an authority than Craig Claiborne. A handful of young chefs are even becoming local celebrities.

Chain restaurants abound, but some are surprisingly good. Phoenix is the home of Big 4 Restaurants and Bobby McGee's Conglomerations, both of which have taken off nationally. *Sushi* bars are packed to the gills, and small, owner-operated places offer everything from Thai to soul food.

The most glaring shortcoming is that no restaurant has yet to develop a cuisine unique to the area based on local ingredients and culinary traditions. On the other hand, the Valley's steak houses and Mexican restaurants still rank with the best in the Southwest.

Restaurants open, close, and change hands with dizzying speed—proof that the population is becoming more receptive to the notion of dining as pure entertainment.

Because of the volatile nature of the local dining scene, I've chosen well-established restaurants that are likely to be around for a while. There are many more out there well worth taking a chance on.

*Elin Jeffords is restaurant critic for* The Arizona Republic *and was formerly food editor of* New Times Weekly, *a news and arts journal.*

# AMNESIA
## 3221 North Scottsdale Road, Scottsdale
### 602-946-7878

Lest we forget—one of the hottest spots in town featuring an adult entertainment center (pool, pente, backgammon). Light snacks and plenty of the pretty people.

*Price: Depends on what you order*
*Open daily for dinner only*
*Accepts all major credit cards*

# AUNT CHILADA'S
## 7330 North Dreamy Draw Drive (*north of Lincoln Drive and east of 16 Street*)
### 602-944-1286

Okay, so the name is kind of corny, but the restaurant's lighthearted charm totally makes up for it. Blooming flowers and overhanging trees ring the building, while at night candles in red glasses line the walkways. There are three irresistible patios for fine-weather dining and drinking. Inside the profusion of *piñatas, serapes,* and strings of chilies are colorful and appealing.

Along with the standard *tacos, tostadas,* and *tamales* are some intriguing alternatives—*calamari* steak, barbecued pork loin, chicken in raisin sauce, and sizzling *fajitas* (char-broiled flank steak seasoned with lime). Watch the *tortillas* being made by hand by Aunt C. herself. Frosty margaritas make mighty easy drinking and there's also imported beer. The youthful service folk are as bright and sassy as the rest of the place.

*Price: About $15 per person*
*Open daily for dinner only*
*Accepts all major credit cards*

# BOUCHON

At Loew's Paradise Valley Resort, 5401 North Scottsdale
Road, Scottsdale

602-947-5400

Sleek and suave, all mauves and soft-edges, Bouchon is more than just another pretty face. The menu, which changes seasonally, features a nifty listing of American regional specialties prepared with a French *nouvelle*-inspired hand.

There's cream of peanut soup, rack of lamb with cactus jelly, venison and wild mushrooms, buffalo T-bone with bourbon sauce, and crawfish in champagne butter—even desserts, such as the grapefruit cake and marzipan loaf, have a twist.

To be sure, all the proper accoutrements are present; gracious table settings, formally clad, solicitous service, a low-keyed harpist plunking in the background, and an above-average wine list.

*Price: About $35 per person*
*Open daily for dinner only; closed Sun. and Mon. during summer*
*Accepts all major credit cards*

---

# CHAPARRAL ROOM

At The Camelback Inn, 5402 East Lincoln Drive, Scottsdale

602-948-1700

The atmosphere at the Chaparral Room is rich and subdued, the service correct but not obsequious, the menu solidly in the Continental camp. Perennial favorites include *escargots* with Camembert, classic spinach salad, garlic-kissed rack of lamb for one, crisp-roasted duckling, and the scrumptious Grand Marnier *soufflé* with vanilla sauce.

Evening specials tend to be on the more adventurous side. Coffee service is extraordinary: lemon curls, shaved chocolate, whipped cream, and cinnamon are among the accompaniments. It's typical of a top-notch operation.

*Price: About $35 per person*
*Open daily for dinner only*
*Accepts all major credit cards*

# DAA'S THAI ROOM

## 7419 East Indian Plaza, Scottsdale
### 602-941-9015

From the foyer floor painted with a stylized jungle scene to the shadowbox in the back room with the exquisite Siamese dolls on display, Daa's is clearly a labor of love. Nowhere does it show up better than in the food.

The menu is lengthy and there is usually a special or two as well. Choosing can be difficult. Fortunately Daa and her staff are always happy to assist. Spicy dishes are denoted by an asterisk, and the kitchen will adjust seasonings according to taste (hot *IS* hot).

Try the fish patties with cucumber and chile sauce, the skewered beef with peanut sauce, either the beef or squid salad, hot and sour soup with chicken, pork marinated with black pepper and garlic, roast duck on spinach, curried shrimp, and either the homemade ginger or coconut ice cream. On second thought, plan another visit.

*Price: About $15 per person*
*Open daily for lunch and dinner*
*Accepts all major credit cards*

# DEMETRA'S KITCHEN

## 4110 North 49 Street (*north of Indian School Road*)
### 602-840-5646

Demetra's *is* Lilia Demetra. This is one of the most intensely personal restaurants imaginable. The lady in charge does the cooking from scratch and it's fit for the gods. All the standard Greek specialties, such as *moussaka* and lamb cooked rare, are represented. Especially estimable are the sautéed squid, lentil soup, village-style salad, marinated chicken, and feta-topped broiled fresh fish.

In between cooking chores, Demetra pops out to assure everything is running smoothly. It usually is; her staff is right on top of things. The rambling ranch-style building surrounded by greenery and decorated in cool cream and blue is a charming environment for Demetra's one-woman show.

*Price: About $20 per person*
*Open Tues.–Sun. for dinner only; closed Mon.*
*Accepts all major credit cards*

# ED DEBEVIC'S
## 2102 East Highland Avenue
### 602-956-2760

A fifties-style diner with gum-cracking waitresses, jukebox full of the appropriate musical selections, and all the burgers, fries, malts, and blue-plate specials your nostalgic little heart desires. Great place to take kids.

*Price: Under $10 per person*
*Open daily for lunch and dinner*
*Accepts American Express, Visa, and Master Card*

---

# FINA COCINA
## 19 East Adams Street
### 602-258-5315

This restaurant is in the heart of downtown, open evenings and weekends—a boon for those staying in nearby hotels. It's nothing fancy: There's no table service and the line to put in your order can move slowly. No matter, the end result is the most savory Mexican food imaginable. From the regular listing try succulent *machaca* (shredded beef laced with *chilies* and onions), juicy *pollo asado* (grilled chicken), green chili, or *carnitas* (crispy pork bits), and dessert for *chimichangas* (fried, sugar-dusted flour *tortillas* filled with chocolate or fruit). Look for the daily specials; they are exactly that.

*Price: About $5 per person*
*Open Mon.–Sat. for lunch and dinner; closed Sun.*
*No credit cards accepted*

---

# FLAKEY JAKE'S
## In The Cornerstone Shopping Center, 715 South Rural Road, Tempe
### 602-967-3192

One of the new "gourmet" hamburger establishments. The look is a little different, with the food-service area built to resemble a turn-of-the-century town and the dining area to resemble the outdoors. Cute. The burgers are outstanding—big and juicy.

*Price: Under $5 per person*
*Open daily for lunch and dinner*
*Accepts Visa and MasterCard*

## THE FRENCH CORNER
### Uptown Plaza Shopping Center, 50 East Camelback Road
#### 602-234-0245

Every town needs a centrally located, all-purpose restaurant, and it helps if it's as consistently good as The French Corner. The mood of the place is bustling and bistro-like. Hunter green, brass, and glass may not be the freshest look around, but it is pleasant.

Breakfast includes made-on-the premises *croissants* and *brioches* as well as more hearty fare like the *ratatouille* omelet. Lunch is served until late
afternoon. Dinner dishes are uniformly marvelous (try the garlicky baby lamb chops if you want your tastebuds to sing). The late-night menu is light but adequate. Desserts are also freshly made, and there's a bakery counter for takeout. The youthful service corps take their job surprisingly seriously.

*Price: About $25 per person*
*Open daily for breakfast, lunch, and dinner*
*All major credit cards accepted*

## THE GOOD EGG
### 906 East Camelback Road, Phoenix    602-274-5393
### Hilton Village, 6149 North Scottsdale Road,
### Scottsdale    602-991-5416

Even non-breakfast eaters manage to stumble out of bed for a meal at these cheery restaurants. The environs and staff are extra pleasant, the egg-oriented meals are constructed with superb quality ingredients and lots of care.

*Price: About $5 per person*
*Open daily for breakfast and lunch only*
*Accepts American Express, Visa, and MasterCard*

## THE IMPECCABLE PIG
### 7042 East Indian School Road, Scottsdale
#### 602-941-1141

Part classy country boutique and antique store, part restaurant, and totally attractive. The place is a joy, thanks mostly to a crew of flamingly idiosyncratic waiters. American-Continental selection changes daily and can be uneven.

*Price: About $25 per person*
*Open Mon.–Sat. for lunch and dinner; closed Sun.*
*Accepts American Express, Visa, and MasterCard*

---

## LA CHAUMIÈRE
### 6910 East Main Street, Scottsdale
**602-946-5115**

The name means "thatch-roofed cottage" and although there's no thatch in sight, the Valley's longest-running French restaurant lists plenty of other qualities. The main building is a cozy collection of small rooms decorated in country French. Out front there's a free-standing patio-*cum*-greenhouse for fair-weather dining.

No *nouvelle cuisine* nonsense here; the menu is classic French all the way. Delicate cream soups and vinaigrette-dressed romaine start the meal. A never-ending supply of French bread tastes exactly as it should. Fresh seafood dishes are always excellent and regulars watch for the *bouillabaisse* on special.

Other standouts include *poulet Cynthia* (with *curaçao* and champagne sauce), veal *normande,* and steak *au poivre.* Desserts are appropriately sinful, with fresh fruit tarts for the more abstemious. It's a flawlessly professional operation with one of the best service staffs around, yet there is a refreshing lack of pomp and pretense. The wine list is extensive, expensive, and excellent.

*Price: About $30 per person*
*Open daily for lunch and dinner; closed Sun. from May–December*
*Accepts all major credit cards*

---

## MUNCHABAGEL
### 511 North 7 Street
**602-264-1975**

"The Munch," as it is affectionately referred to by its legion of fans, is much more than just a bagel bakery, though the bagels are divine. The deli-style food is homey stuff—the breakfasts massive and heartwarming.

*Price: Under $5 per person*
*Open daily for breakfast, lunch, and early dinner*
*Accepts Visa and MasterCard on $10 minimum*

# ORANGERIE

## In The Arizona Biltmore, 24 Street and Missouri Avenue
### 602-954-2507

A world-class resort deserves a restaurant of the same stripe, and that's exactly what the Orangerie is. The decor is elegant and based on a sun-porch motif, with citrus colors, cascading chandeliers, and a sunny prospect over the green lawns. The hotel itself was based on an idea of Frank Lloyd Wright's, and it is a stunning example of Southwest architecture.

The menu is international in scope, and ingredients are combined in startlingly fresh ways: *tortellini* garnished with the tiniest fish broods; crayfish salad; duck with zinfandel sauce and pomegranates; sweetbreads *tempura*-style; lamb with mint, garlic, and *piñon* nuts on spinach; and shrimp with orange and pistachio sauce. There are fine, caring touches, like serving mineral water rather than tap water, a fabulous wine list, complimentary pre-dinner nibbles, long-stemmed roses for the ladies, and after-dinner confections for everyone. Service is as superbly rendered as the rest of the amenities.

*Price: About $60 per person*
*Open daily for lunch and dinner*
*Accepts all major credit cards*

# OSCAR TAYLOR

## 2420 East Camelback Road
### 602-956-5705

This is the flagship of the successful Big 4 Restaurants group, and it's as finely tuned as a restaurant can be. The decor is upscale saloon. A little deli off the foyer has takeout and the bar is *the* place for local Yuppies to see and be seen. An exhibition area outside the restaurant proper provides a "pre-cooked" view of dinner.

The menu is small and tight. Star attractions are the well-glazed ribs, mammoth veal chop, and daily fresh fish specials. A huge brick of onion rings is made from scratch and is absolutely delectable. So are the fresh-baked, assorted rolls and hedonistic desserts. The place is always packed and the staff keeps up miraculously.

*Price: About $20 per person*
*Open daily for lunch and dinner*
*All major credit cards accepted*

# PALM COURT

In the Scottsdale Conference Center, 7700 East McCormick
Parkway, Scottsdale
602-991-3400

An incredible array of high-quality viands nicely served in a contemporary
southwestern setting.

*Price: Brunch fixed price at $1.50 per person*
*Open for Sunday brunch*
*Accepts all major credit cards*

# PASTA SERGIO'S

1904 East Camelback Road
602-274-2795

This restaurant serves a remarkably effective hybrid of traditional and *nuova
cucina.* It's small and meticulously maintained. The crisp, clubby green-and-
beige decor with touches of scarlet absolutely sparkles. The service staff evinces
the same kind of attention to detail; so does the kitchen.

Classic Italian recipes are properly prepared with traditional ingredients—
*osso buco,* veal *picatta,* and *cannelloni* are precisely as they should be. Fresh and
fun are the more imaginative creations, such as wagon-wheel pasta with raisins
and pine nuts in garlic-butter sauce. Portions are huge. For the quantity and
quality provided, prices are a bargain. Beer and wine only.

*Price: Under $15 per person*
*Open daily for lunch and dinner*
*Accepts all major credit cards*

# PINK PEPPER

2003 North Scottsdale Road, Scottsdale
602-945-9300

Spare, striking, sophisticated—this is one of the best-looking restaurants
around. Done in pink, gray, and black and white, with dramatic touches, such
as jazzy neon, exotic orchid plants, and enigmatic granite and chrome spheres.

On-premises owners Annie and Tony are warmly welcoming and happy
to introduce newcomers to Thai cuisine. The food is as exciting as the decor.
Favorites include sliced chicken breast fillet on spinach leaves with a resonant

peanut sauce and toothsome squid sautéed with lemon grass, mint, ginger, and garlic. There is creamy cheesecake with a terrific macadamia nut crust for dessert.

*Price: About $15 per person*
*Open daily for lunch and dinner*
*Accepts all major credit cards*

---

# PIZZAFARRO'S
## 4225 East Camelback Road
### 602-840-7990

There are lots of locals who refuse to eat pizza anywhere but at this small, smoky spot. It's always crowded and for good reason: The produce is absolutely first class.

*Price: A large pizza with the works, $15.90*
*Open Tues.–Sun. for dinner only; closed Mon.*
*No credit cards accepted*

---

# RESTAURANT MEXICO
## 728 South Mill Avenue, Tempe
### 602-967-3280

Most Mexican restaurants in the Valley serve a style of food that originates from the northern Mexican state of Sonora, but there's a whole lot more to the cuisine of Mexico, and a sampling of it is available at this bone-plain but worthy establishment.

Service is generally prompt and helpful—the brief menu may take some explaining. Don't bypass the *huevos* (eggs) *rancheros* just because it isn't breakfast. They are satisfying any time. *Quesadillas* are made from thin corn dough patted around a choice of filling and fried. *Suaves* are soft *tacos* made with flour *tortillas* and lean pork. *Sopes* are fried *masa* (corn dough) boats piled high with chicken, beef, or Mexican sausage and soft, crumbly white cheese. Don't miss the chicken *enchiladas* with *tomatillo* sauce, but do save room for soothing homemade *flan* (custard). The beer is always cold and the college-town clientele is fun to watch.

*Price: About $5 per person*
*Open daily for lunch and dinner*
*Accepts Visa and MasterCard*

# RICARDO'S

2926 North 24 Street    602-956-5670
1402 South Priest, Tempe    602-967-7951
2017 North Scottsdale Road, Scottsdale    602-990-9516

These are the archetypal local Mexican restaurants—not too fancy, not too plain, always reliable and good. The chips are always fresh and sizzling, the hot sauce is perfectly balanced. There are those who would chose a Ricardo green *burro* over filet mignon.

*Price: About $7 per person*
*Open daily for lunch and dinner*
*Accepts Visa and MasterCard*

# ROSITA'S PLACE

1914 East Buckeye Road
602-262-9372

We are talking super-authentic here, so don't let the slightly seedy environs scare you off. The staff is warm and friendly, and English is the second language. Not to worry; merely pointing at the desired dish on the menu works fine.

Rosita's is one of the few restaurants in town that doesn't automatically provide a basket of chips. Order one and start out slowly with the hot sauce —the stuff will bring a strong man to his knees. It's practically impossible to go wrong with the entrées. The real decision is between the usual *tacos, enchiladas,* etc., or dishes like *chicharrones* (crisp-fried pork skin), *menudo* (tripe soup), chicken in *mole* sauce (made with red chilies and chocolate), and *cocido* (like a New England boiled dinner with spunk). Some dishes are available in half orders, which is a sensible option. Rosita's is half a mile from the airport, and a meal there is a great way to jet-propel yourself home.

*Price: About $6 per person*
*Open Tues.–Sun. for lunch and dinner; closed Mon.*
*Accepts no credit cards*

# SHOGUN

12615 North Tatum Boulevard, Paradise Valley
602-953-3264

There are older, larger, and more accessible Japanese restaurants in the Valley, but none is as consistently pleasing as Shogun. It's modest in size and serenely attractive.

An L-shaped *sushi* bar has two chefs turning out wonderful examples of the art. *Sushi* can also be enjoyed predinner at the table. *Tempura* and *sukiyaki* are available along with the less traditional *karage* chicken made with garlic sauce or fresh fish in *miso* sauce. Shogun serves *udon* and *soba* (noodle dishes) in various permutations including chicken, beef, egg, *tempura,* and curry. Regular dinners are complete from soup to dessert. Noodle meals include salad. Service is sweetly pampering.

*Price: About $15 per person*
*Open Mon.–Sat. for lunch and dinner; closed Sun.*
*All major credit cards accepted*

# THE STOCKYARDS
## 5001 East Washington Street
### 602-273-7378

The Stockyards restaurant started out in the forties as a modest café where the cattlemen could get a hot cuppa java before or after work.

Over the years, the fortunes (and size) of the place have waxed and waned. The territorial-style landmark building has recently been meticulously restored. Three dining rooms each have a different turn-of-the-century theme that is unhokey and effective. Visitors who don't have time to eat should at least make a stop at The 1889 Bar—it's a stunner.

It might be wise to make time to eat, however. The emphasis is on beef, hand-cut and prime. The steaks and prime rib are meticulously trimmed and done precisely to order. Go-withs include sturdy Western stuff such as cowboy beans and home fries.

Speaking of fries, a Stockyards staple is calf fries (aka "mountain oysters"), the by-product of the act that makes a bull into a steer. Tenderfeet may or may not relish them, but the flavor and texture *are* remarkably similar to oysters.

*Price: About $20 per person*
*Open Mon.–Sat. for lunch and dinner; closed Sun.*
*Accepts all major credit cards*

## STUDEBAKER'S

In The Cornerstone Shopping Center, 705 South Rural
Road, Tempe
**602-829-8495**

An All-American diner concept in the fifties mode. There is a strict dress code
and patrons must be at least 23 years old to get in. The free buffet, offered
daily from 4 P.M. to 8 P.M., is spectacular.

*Price: Less than $10 per person*
*Open nightly*
*Accepts American Express, Visa, and MasterCard*

## T-BONE STEAK HOUSE

19 Avenue South to Dobbins Road
**602-276-0945**

There are rafts of tourist-oriented cowboy steak houses in the Phoenix area.
None of them quite live up to the purebred, resolutely unfancy T-Bone Steak
House. The old adobe building hugs the lower slope of South Mountain, with
all the sprawling southwest Valley spread out below.

Grab a table by the window for a view of both the spectacular light show
and your steak being grilled over a mesquite fire in front. Making an entrée
choice won't be a problem: Only four cuts of prime beef are offered, starting
with the signature 32-ounce porterhouse at an unbelievable $13.95.

Dinner includes a small but adequate all-you-can-eat salad bar (yes, heavily
peppered, cold, canned green beans with raw onion livers *are* good atop the
lettuce). Cowboy beans served family style are the real thing—soupy and
spunkily seasoned. If that's not enough, a baked potato or serving of garlic
toast can be had *à la carte*. The no-nonsense waitresses are as efficient as a
six-shooter and when they call you "honey," they mean it.

*Price: About $10 per person*
*Open daily for dinner only*
*Accepts all major credit cards*

# TOMASO'S

3225 East Camelback Road, Phoenix   602-956-0836
7243 East Camelback Road, Scottsdale   602-947-5804
1954 South Dobson Road, Mesa   602-897-0140

It's rare for a restaurant owner to achieve excellence with one restaurant. Tomaso Maggiore has performed that miracle with three. There is a unifying theme of Mediterranean warmth and hospitality that runs through the restaurants. Decors differ slightly, but blues predominate and comfort is the key.

Maggiore insists his superlative product can be attributed to a good staff. They are that. Service is professional and accommodating, the kitchen's staff uniformly superb. The menu is the same in each restaurant; it's a lively selection of dishes from up and down the boot of Italy. Some of the simplest things are the best—*pasta e fagioli,* broccoli with garlic and oil, *mozzarella,* tomato, and basil salad, sliced tenderloin with fresh tomato, garlic, and oregano sauce, and sausage and peppers. That's not to suggest the fancier stuff isn't great, too. Desserts are made on the premises. They include wonders like cheesecake with apples and chestnuts and fresh fruit tortes. *Mangiamo!*

*Price: About $25 per person*
*Open daily for lunch and dinner*
*Accepts all major credit cards*

# TUG'S

7575 North 16 Street
602-997-0812

It's not surprising that a desert town isn't particularly noted for fresh seafood. That's changing with the help of places like this.

Tug's has a comfortable, turn-of-the-century atmosphere with high ceilings, chocolate brown walls, marble tables, and plenty of brass and leaded glass. The daily market selection is meticulously fresh and mesquite-broiled to order (no funny looks for folks who like their fish medium rare). Go-withs like the Manhattan clam chowder are much better than average. So is Tug's Special Hot Fudge Sundae (sharing is recommended). No reservations are accepted, so it's wise to dine either early or late.

*Price: Under $20 per person*
*Open daily for lunch and dinner*
*All major credit cards accepted*

# VINCENT'S
## 8711 East Pinnacle Peak Road, Scottsdale
### 602-998-0921

Some restaurants simply glow with excellence, and Vincent's is one of them. The high desert setting provides a stunning view of Scottsdale to the south, while the decor puts you in mind of nothing less than a royal European hunting lodge. It's warm, elegant, and decorated with superb antiques and tapestries. The impeccable service crew enhances the surroundings, and the wine list is commensurate with the restaurant's high standards.

Having a culinary genius in the kitchen doesn't hurt. Chef Chris Gross' magic touch has been extolled in *Travel & Leisure, Bon Appétit,* and France's *Le Figaro,* and I personally think he has surpassed the reputation of his predecessor, after whom the restaurant was named. Locals knew about it all along. Gross shops the world for raw ingredients, and everything is prepared from scratch. His *nouvelle*-inspired creations are extraordinarily imaginative —*ravioli* stuffed with snails, warm sweetbread-and-squab salad, roasted duck with a rosemary-scented reduction, and poached lobster with a clean, unsweet vanilla sauce—one glorious dish follows the last, straight through to desserts, which are masterpieces.

*Price: About $60 per person*
*Open daily for dinner only; closed Sun. and Mon. during summer*
*Accepts all major credit cards*

# THE WHITE TRUFFLE
## In The Borgata, 6166 North Scottsdale Road, Scottsdale
### 602-951-4111

A newcomer and proving to be a classy contender. Stunning black-and-white decor, well-handled country French fare, suave service, and surprisingly moderate prices for the luxe Borgata.

*Price: Under $25 per person*
*Open Mon.–Sat. for lunch and dinner; closed Sun.*
*Accepts all major credit cards*

# PITTSBURGH

## *By Robert M. Bianco*

**AFRICAN**
  Born Free

**BAR**
  Froggy's
  Mario's South Side Saloon
  The 1902 Landmark Tavern

**BARBECUE**
  Ribb House
  Wilson's Bar-B-Q

**BREAKFAST**
  DeLuca's Italian & American
    Restaurant
  Scotty's Diner

**CHINESE**
  Jimmy Tsang's Chinese
    Restaurant

**CONTINENTAL**
  Angel's Corner
  Christopher's
  Hyeholde Restaurant
  Lawrence's
  Upstairs at Brendan's

**DELICATESSEN**
  Richest Restaurant

**FAMILY**
  Great Scot

**FAST FOOD**
  Applebee's

**FRENCH**
  Café Azure
  La Normande
  Le Petit Café

**GERMAN**
  Max's Allegheny Tavern

**GREEK**
  Suzie's

**HAMBURGERS/HOT DOGS**
  Original Hot Dog Shops, Inc.
  Tessaro's Bar & Grill

**HOTEL DINING ROOM**
  The Terrace Room

## ITALIAN
Emilia Romagna Ristorante
Un Poco di Roma

## MEXICAN
Monterey Inn

## MIDDLE EASTERN
Samreny's Cedars of Lebanon
Restaurant and Lounge

## NIGHTCLUB RESTAURANT
Harper's

## OPEN LATE
Brandy's Meeting Eating &
Drinking Place
Primanti Brothers
Scotty's Diner

## PANORAMA
Christopher's
Cliffside

## PIZZA
Vincent's Pizza Park

## SEAFOOD
The Grand Concourse
Poli's Restaurant

## STEAKS AND CHOPS
The Colony

## SUBURBAN
Hyeholde Restaurant
(Coraopolis)
Un Poco di Roma (Bethel
Park)

## UNIQUE PROPERTY
Chiodo's Tavern
Isaly's
Primanti Brothers'

## VIETNAMESE
Le Vieux Saigon
Red Dragon

## WINE BAR
The Wine Restaurant

## YUGOSLAVIAN
Sarah's Restaurant and Catering

In recent years, more new restaurants per capita have opened in Pittsburgh than anyplace else in the nation. While Downtown, a compact ½-square-mile wedge of land located where the Allegheny and Monongahela rivers meet to form the Ohio, has benefited from this explosion, many of the best restaurants are located elsewhere. But too few visitors cross the rivers and climb the mountains to find them.

Pittsburgh is tiny; of the 2½ million people in the metropolitan area, only about 400,000 live in the city itself. But that 55-square-mile area is cut up into at least 75 distinct neighborhoods, in a confusion of patchwork boundaries even the residents don't understand, separated by hills, valleys, and rivers, and linked by more than 200 tunnels and bridges.

Relax, there are only a few Pittsburgh neighborhoods that the eating visitor has to master. Mt. Washington, Station Square, and the Southside are directly across the Monongahela (the "Mon") from Downtown, the Northside is across the Allegheny. Squirrel Hill, Oakland, Shadyside, and Bloomfield fan out to the east.

Most restaurants listed here are easily reached by cab, and, unless otherwise indicated, are no more than a 15-minute ride from Downtown. (But don't try to hail a cab, you have to go to a hotel or call for one.) You'll find the neighborhood location listed for all city restaurants because that is how Pittsburghers give directions.

Pittsburgh has been compared to a European provincial capital: self-reliant, rich in culture and tradition, and slightly, well, provincial. The slow, painful switch to a white-collar economy is making the city more cosmopolitan, but food trends are still slow to get here, and fleeting ones never reach us at all. Don't expect apologies for that; most Pittsburghers like their city fine the way it is.

Our restaurants are like our people, a blend of defensiveness, friendliness, bravado, and humor. No one cuisine dominates, but a relaxed style does; Pittsburghers do not like to take themselves or their restaurants too seriously. Explore a little; Pittsburgh offers good food, fair prices, and enjoyable evenings.

*Robert M. Bianco is the restaurant critic for the* Pittsburgh Press.

# ANGEL'S CORNER
## In Oakland, 405 Atwood Street
### 412-682-1879

Angel's Corner is located in a small, desanctified church, which is slightly shabby but still pretty. The temptation to be overly cute in such a location (waitresses in wings, heavenly puns) must have been great, but for the most part the owners have resisted.

The menu's accent is on seafood. It leans a bit too heavily on stuffings and cream sauces for my taste, but the quality of the ingredients is generally excellent, and the end result can be too. There is a fine wine list and adequate help to decipher it, and a good, if a little overly attentive, staff that specializes in gracious small touches. The location, on a gritty urban street lined with ethnic restaurants, is great.

*Price: About $20 per person*
*Open Mon.–Sat. for dinner only; closed Sun.*
*Accepts all major credit cards*

# APPLEBEE'S
## 411 Smithfield Street
### 412-261-2277

The best spot for a good brown-bag lunch is Applebee's. There are good *croissants* and better bagels, both of which go best with either the roast beef or the tuna salad. Applebee's two downtown locations both have good cookies and brownies, but only the Smithfield Street location has sandwiches.

*Price: About $5 per person*
*Open Mon.–Sat. for lunch and dinner; closed Sun.*
*No credit cards accepted*

# BORN FREE
## In Shadyside, 5899 Ellsworth Avenue
### 412-362-1645

In some ways, Born Free is more like a social studies project than a restaurant. The goal of the owners' of this tiny restaurant is to introduce diners to the best of African cuisine. The menu is small, but the countries represented stretch from Algeria to South Africa.

It stands to reason that no one chef can be a master of that broad a range of cooking. Born Free's reach must exceed its grasp. But, if I can't testify as to the utter authenticity of the food, I can say that it is both different and good.

Try the marinated chicken, the sweet curry shrimp, or the fish with bananas and bacon. Top off your meal with North African coffee, a light brew made with honey and spices. The food leaves you wanting to know more about African cuisine, which is just what the owners had in mind.

*Price: About $15 per person*
*Open Tues.–Sat. for dinner only; closed Sun. and Mon.*
*No credit cards accepted*

---

## BRANDY'S MEETING EATING & DRINKING PLACE
### 2323 Penn Avenue
**412-566-1000**

An exposed-brick, old wood, fern bar with a skylighted back room, a fireplace, and a jaunty atmosphere. Okay, the skylight won't mean much to you if you're there late, but the atmosphere and the crowds will get you. Sandwiches are best, or the early morning breakfast. Forgive them for having a cute name.

*Price: About $10 per person*
*Open daily for lunch and dinner*
*Accepts all major credit cards*

---

## CAFÉ AZURE
### In Oakland, 317 South Craig Street
**412-681-3533**

Café Azure is located near the Carnegie Institute on a pretty, store-lined street that is, if not quite booming, at least popping. The restaurant's outdoor patio is perfect for a balmy summer night, and its softly lit dining room is just as inviting, with warm, muted colors, soft chairs, and a shimmering wall of glass.

Café Azure is very relaxed and not very expensive. The food is mostly French (the Gallic origins of mesquite-grilled fish are suspect) and mostly fine, though consistency is a problem. Mesquite is a little too strong for most seafood; stick to the veal or shrimp dishes. Otherwise, ask the staff what to order; they are among the most expert and honest in town.

Like many Pittsburgh restaurants, Café Azure does not serve dinner on Sundays. (Always call first before going out on Sunday; policies change from week to week.) It does serve, however, one of the best Sunday brunches in town.

*Price: About $25 per person*
*Open Tues.–Sat. for lunch and dinner; closed Sun. and Mon.*
*Accepts all major credit cards*

---

# CHIODO'S TAVERN
## 107 West Eighth Avenue, Homestead
### 412-461-9307

This is the quintessential Pittsburgh mill bar. In fact, Chiodo's is so much a part of the Pittsburgh ethos that when the owner had a falling out with the local brewery, Pittsburgh Brewing Co., and stopped serving Iron City beer, it was like Lucy divorcing Desi. Thank God all is now well and you can get an "Irn" again at Chiodo's, along with just about any other beer, foreign and domestic, you can name.

When you get hungry, order the "Mystery Sandwich," which is made with whatever the cook has around that day. In these days of increasing urban homogenization, places like Chiodo's keep Pittsburgh Pittsburgh.

*Price: About $2.50 per person*
*Open daily for lunch and dinner*
*No credit cards accepted*

---

# CHRISTOPHER'S
## On Mt. Washington, 1411 Grandview Avenue
### 412-381-4500

Christopher's not only serves the best food on Mt. Washington; it is the Mount's most elegant restaurant. A glass elevator whisks you up to a large, modern room that is a tasteful and subtle celebration of Pittsburgh's steel heritage.

As three walls are glass, the largest glass walls in the country, the view can be spectacular. Or it can be pedestrian; tables on the wrong side or in the back look out on Mt. Washington itself. No Mt. Washington restaurant accepts reservations for window tables, but the consequences of not getting one, and the games played to get one, are worse here than elsewhere.

Christopher's food is excellent, particularly a stellar version of *chateaubriand.* However, most of the best dishes are only available for two and are cooked tableside, including veal *romano,* which you'd expect to find available from the kitchen for one. Couples who like tableside cooking and don't mind ordering the same thing won't find that as big a drawback as I do.

*Price: About $30 per person*
*Open Mon.–Sat. for dinner only; closed Sun.*
*Accepts all major credit cards*

---

# CLIFFSIDE
## On Mt. Washington, 1208 Grandview Avenue
### 412-431-6996

Mt. Washington, a 1200-foot cliff looming over Downtown, is a natural spot for restaurants. Here you eat suspended: the three rivers, the hills, and the entire Golden Triangle spread out before you. On a clear night, the expanse of the view and the seeming proximity of the buildings are breathtaking.

There are roads leading to Mt. Washington, most of which are more reminiscent of mountain trails than city streets. But the best way to get there is to park at the bottom and ride up on the Duquesne Incline, a hand-carved cable car that climbs the cliff on a steep, inclined plane.

Mt. Washington restaurants are more noted for their view than their food. The best combination of both is at the Cliffside, a small, dark, romantic restaurant. Same-day reservations are usually available on weekdays, but reservations must be made early in the week for the weekends.

The food is good, seafood being a best bet, though the appetizers and the desserts could be improved. Prices are fair and service is excellent.

If I had just one night in Pittsburgh, I'd go to the Cliffside. Pittsburgh does not, as yet, have a world-class restaurant, but it does have a world-class view, and it shouldn't be missed.

*Price: About $25 per person*
*Open Mon.–Sat. for dinner only; closed Sun.*
*Accepts all major credit cards*

---

# THE COLONY
## Greentree and Cochran roads, Greentree
### 412-561-2060

When I was in college, we would have called the Colony a "daddy restaurant"; a place to bring Dad (actually, to let Dad take you) when he came to visit. Ideal daddy restaurants were too expensive to swing on your own, but not so expensive that the next tuition check bounced. They were masculine and clubby, and had food that was good but never exotic. Dad already knew you were picking up strange ideas; no sense shocking him with dinner.

The Colony (about 20 minutes from downtown) fills the bill exactly. Its warm, rich interior built around an open brick grill reminds you of a small-town country club. Twenty-two dollars for a 13-ounce sirloin steak is expensive, but dinner comes with salad, potato, dessert, and a fruit tray.

And the steaks are tremendous, cooked precisely to order on the grill, and basted with a special, buttery house sauce. Not only are the steaks trimmed of every last piece of fat, they are also remarkably tender and free of gristle. If you want your steak crisp on the outside, however, you must ask; otherwise the basting keeps the steak from becoming charred.

If you crave an appetizer, both the lump crab meat and the shrimp *scampi* are very good. There are very few other items on the menu—a filet, lobster tail, a nice veal T-bone, and that's about it. And I wish the Colony would improve its salads and get rid of the aluminum foil on the baked potatoes. Other than that, it's all that a steak-loving daddy could wish.

*Price: About $30 per person*
*Open Mon.–Sat. for dinner only; closed Sun.*
*Accepts all major credit cards*

---

# DeLUCA'S ITALIAN & AMERICAN RESTAURANT
## 2015 Penn Avenue
### 412-566-2195

Freshly squeezed orange juice, Italian-French toast, and ham, sliced from the bone as you watch. Don't order anything else, this is the best breakfast in town, possibly the world (though lately they have a disconcerting habit of burning the French toast, proof, as if more were needed, that Western civilization is collapsing around us).

The waitresses are always harried and usually in a bad mood. Only smiling will help you get decent service. They are impervious to scowls and threats. DeLuca's is not for the fussy, the fainthearted, or the impatient; I've seen them throw straws at customers who annoy them. Is it worth the risk? Yes, on mornings when they don't burn the French toast. Go early on a Saturday morning and spend some time wandering the Strip, Pittsburgh's street produce market.

*Price: About $5 per person*
*Open daily for breakfast, lunch, and dinner*
*No credit cards accepted*

# EMILIA ROMAGNA RISTORANTE
## 942 Penn Avenue
### 412-765-3598

Emilia Romagna, a very good Northern Italian restaurant, is your best bet if you're looking for a restaurant right in the area of the convention center. Its success represents a triumph over its setting—a loft which formerly housed a disco.

The mirrored ceiling ball, gel lights, and speakers remain; one gets the queasy feeling that "Last Dance" may be played at any moment. The garishly orange room is cavernous, broken only by motel-like paintings suspended at random intervals by binder clips, and by huge macramé hangings. Unlike some unconventional restaurants that are purposely odd, Emilia Romagna seems bizarre by accident.

But the food will make you forget the room. Portions are huge, so, while you are encouraged to order an appetizer, pasta, and main course, share the appetizers and the pasta (don't skip them, they're very good, particularly the zucchini with hot sausage and the *fettuccine alla carbonara*).

Selections are limited, but usually the *osso buco* or the rolled stuffed veal breast are the best bets. The kitchen tends to run out of things; reservations are suggested more to help them plan than to help you get a table.

Emilia Romagna is extremely laid back, probably too much so for some tastes. Definitely don't go if you're in a hurry. Otherwise, relax, chew on the very good pizza bread between courses, and try to figure out why they've kept that mirrored ball.

*Price: About $20 per person*
*Open Mon.–Fri. for lunch and dinner; Sat. for dinner only; closed Sun.*
*Accepts all major credit cards*

# FROGGY'S
## 100 Market Street
### 412-471-3764

At one time this old brick building, located on "Firstside," the old warehouse district along the Monongahela River, was Pittsburgh's premier singles bar. But singles madness has moved on, as it is wont to do, and what's left is a large core of sports fans and young professionals. The bar is dominated by Froggy Morris, the gravel-voiced, affable owner, who seems to know everyone in Pittsburgh and is as adept at getting publicity as he is at getting customers.

Froggy's is noted more for its huge drinks than for its food, but there are good steaks and very good hamburgers available. In good weather there is a nice rooftop café looking out over other rooftops and, if you look hard, the Mon.

*Price: About $15 per person*
*Open Mon.–Sat. for lunch and dinner; closed Sun.*
*Accepts all major credit cards*

---

# THE GRAND CONCOURSE
## 1 Station Square
### 412-261-1717

Station Square is a 40-acre mixed-use development of offices, shops, and restaurants located in the Pittsburgh & Lake Erie railroad station and freight houses. The anchor and the highlight of the complex is the Grand Concourse, the restaurant that occupies the 80-year-old train terminal.

The best way to get the full, opulent effect of the Grand Concourse is to use the Smithfield Street entrance and come down the red-carpeted marble staircase (feel free to hum "Hello Dolly" as you do so). Above you stretches a beautiful, vaulted stained-glass ceiling, 60 feet long, 45 feet high. Below you is the palm tree-lined expanse of the main waiting room, with its mahogany booths and mosaic tile floor.

Of the three main dining areas in this huge restaurant, the most popular is the River Room. From this glass-enclosed room (once the waiting platform), you can watch the constant flow of river traffic on the Mon and the lights of the city across the way.

The Grand Concourse takes reservations, but you cannot reserve a table in the River Room. The wait for a table there can be long unless you get to the restaurant early.

Although the food is good, it is not as spectacular as its setting. Your best bets are the daily fish specials. Stay simple; the Grand Concourse can grill or broil a piece of fish with the best of them, but order an item like *paella* and you're asking for trouble. The restaurant also has a good Sunday buffet brunch, and full-course "early bird specials" for a very cheap $9.95.

Much of the Station Square resembles the urban playground/boutiques that are popping up everywhere, but some real history has worked its way in (including a rare Bessemer Converter). For families especially, Station Square is a must.

*Price: About $25 per person*
*Open Sun.–Fri. for lunch and dinner; Sat. for dinner only*
*Accepts all major credit cards*

# GREAT SCOT
## In Oakland, 413 South Craig Street
### 412-683-1450

Great Scot looks as if it was designed by L.L. Bean on his day off. Hunter green, light woods, green grass shades, and pictures of hunting dogs abound. And holding court over all is a smiling logo that looks a lot like Andrew Carnegie, founder of the Carnegie Institute right down the street (the Great Scot, get it?).

The menu, which changes weekly, features regional American cuisine; angels on horseback, Hangtown fry, Texas chili, and very good steaks, burgers, and desserts. Bring the family to the Institute, see the renowned dinosaur exhibit, and end up here. Not a bad day, and a pretty inexpensive one at that.

*Price: About $10 per person*
*Open Mon.–Fri. for lunch and dinner; Sat. for dinner only; Sun. for brunch*
*only*
*Accepts all major credit cards*

# HARPER'S
## 1 Oxford Center
### 412-391-1494

An intimate, warm jazz club, steel gray with crimson highlights, that's a perfect spot for a musical evening. Walt Harper is a Pittsburgh music fixture, a jazz pianist who has always had a club somewhere. When he's not performing himself, the club is host to jazz greats like Stanley Turrentine, Carmen McRae, and Mel Tormé.

The food is well-prepared and very simple; grilled items or stir-fry dominate (Harper's chef is Japanese). The food is a little pricey, but there is no cover charge, so you're paying in part for the entertainment and the ambiance.

Naturally, special tickets and advance reservations are needed when name acts are performing. On those nights, it's best to eat elsewhere; the management crowds in extra tables and chairs, and service collapses as you watch.

*Price: About $25 per person*
*Open Mon.–Sat. for lunch and dinner; closed Sun.*
*Accepts all major credit cards*

# HYEHOLDE RESTAURANT
## 190 Hyeholde Drive, Coraopolis
### 412-264-3116

Some people think that the Hyeholde, an old country manor about 5 minutes from the airport, is Pittsburgh's best restaurant. Many find this old Tudor mansion, with its secluded rooms, medieval trappings, and burning fireplaces, inestimably romantic, especially during the winter. I think the food is, at best, mediocre and overpriced, and the atmosphere is more ridiculous than sublime. There is, however, nowhere else around the airport to eat.

*Price: About $40 per person*
*Open Mon.–Fri. for lunch and dinner; Sat. for dinner only; closed Sun.*
*Accepts all major credit cards*

---

# ISALY'S
## In Oakland, 3380 Boulevard of the Allies
### 412-687-0817

Pittsburghers are addicted to chipped ham, a kind of processed ham sliced paper-thin and served while still moist on white bread. It's available everywhere, but Isaly's, home of the Klondike and the Skyscraper cone, is the supplier of choice. Transplanted residents even have Isaly's ship it to them, as our affection for chipped ham has not spread elsewhere.

*Price: About $2 a pound*
*Open Mon.–Sat. for breakfast, lunch, and dinner; closed Sun.*
*No credit cards accepted*

---

# JIMMY TSANG'S CHINESE RESTAURANT
## In Shadyside, 5700 Centre Avenue
### 412-661-4226

Pittsburgh has no Chinatown, but it does have some very good Chinese restaurants, of which Jimmy Tsang's is the best. Jimmy himself is Korean, and the menu offers some Korean dishes, but the emphasis is on Szechuan food. But remember, East Pittsburgh is not the Far East. The food here is enjoyable, but it is heavily Americanized.

Appetizers are nothing to speak of, but the soups are very good. Then try either the "E. Show" specials (slighly breaded meat served in a hot sauce) or the *kung pao* dishes. For people with a guilty addiction to sweet-and-sour dishes (you know the *cognoscenti* frown, but you eat it anyway) Jimmy's Korean version is much better than the normal, glutinous, pineapple-laden mess so often found in restaurants.

Jimmy's is too big and too crowded, and has one of the world's noisiest waiter stations (try to figure how any dishes survive that banging). Chaos may seem to reign but the service hops. In fact, it can be too fast, little niceties are lost. Your waitress is apt to be polite but slightly harried; you live in fear that someone will yell "head 'em up, move 'em out."

*Price: About $15 per person*
*Open Mon.–Sat. for lunch and dinner; Sun. from 3:30 P.M.*
*Accepts all major credit cards*

---

# LA NORMANDE
## In Shadyside, 5030 Centre Avenue
### 412-621-0744

La Normande, a small, dark, country French restaurant located, incongruously, on the ground floor of an apartment building, is the best French restaurant in Pittsburgh. In fact, for sheer food quality of any kind, only The Wine Restaurant (see page 689) comes close. Reservations are a must, particularly for weekends.

Highlights are the *foie gras,* served warm with a red wine vinaigrette, the truffle soup covered in puff pastry, the billi-bi, the Dover sole, and the imported duck breast. Seasonal game specials are also recommended. Save room for dessert, especially the *sorbets* and pastries.

Meals here, especially with wine, can be very expensive. However, there is a special $25 *table d'hôte* available on weekdays.

For those who are either intimidated by French restaurants or have had one too many encounters with snotty, superior maître d's, the service at La Normande is impeccable. It is the French ideal, seemingly effortless, with a bit of warmth added. Daily specials are always written in French, but don't hesitate to ask the staff to translate; they will do so graciously.

Unfortunately, if La Normande is a temple of fine cuisine, the temple often seems to be housing a wake. I'm not suggesting dressing the waiters in clown hats, but some lightening up of the funeral atmosphere is in order. Still, amid all the reverential hush, it is likely that you'll have an excellent meal, if a subdued one.

La Normande has a companion restaurant attached, Le Bistro, that offers simpler, cheaper dishes in a much more casual atmosphere: coats and ties are in the minority. Le Bistro is brighter and cheerier and, as a food bargain (about $15 per person), it can't be beat.

*Price: About $40 per person*
*Open Mon.–Sat. for dinner only; closed Sun.*
*Accepts all major credit cards*

---

## LAWRENCE'S RESTAURANT
### 613 Penn Avenue
### 412-391-1414

Lawrence's is in the heart of what could be called Pittsburgh's theater district, though at the moment most of the theaters are either on the drawing board or closed for renovations. Lawrence's posted closing time is 10:30 P.M., but it stays open late any time Heinz Hall (the home of the symphony, ballet, and opera) is lit.

The restaurant is comfortably formal, with fine china and crystal, waiters in tuxes and red bow ties, and a room full of attractive touches. And talk about trendy—Lawrence's offers a low-calorie, low-cholesterol menu, blessed by the American Heart Association no less, that's chock-full of food prepared without butter, salt, or cream. For those of us who are worried about our health, but are more worried that we might have to eat food prepared without butter, salt, or cream, there is a regular menu as well, with the veal dishes the best choices.

*Price: About $25 per person*
*Open Mon.–Fri. for lunch and dinner; Mon.–Sat. for dinner only; closed Sun.*
*Accepts all major credit cards*

---

## LE PETIT CAFÉ
### In Shadyside, 809 Bellefonte Street
### 412-621-9000

The most *"nouvelle"* of the Pittsburgh French restaurants. Shadyside has always been trendy; at one time it was Pittsburgh's Hippie hangout, now it's the Yuppie hangout. And Le Petit Café, located in the Bellefonte Markets, a very high-toned food emporium in the middle of the Shadyside shopping district, brings them out in droves.

The restaurant is lovely, a small bar and a pastry table the main decorations in the mauve and wine room, but it is very tiny. There is also an outdoor dining area with tables that spill onto the sidewalk from the main dining room.

Food choices vary daily and are heavily dependent on what's in season, but there are always very good filets and pastries.

When to go depends on how you feel about crowds. The restaurant is calmest late in the afternoon or on Sunday evenings. Reservations are suggested at all times.

*Price: About $25 per person*
*Open Tues.–Sun. for lunch and dinner; closed Mon.*
*Accepts all major credit cards*

---

## LE VIEUX SAIGON
### In Bloomfield, 4052 Liberty Avenue
#### 412-621-7733

Le Vieux Saigon is Pittsburgh's first upscale Vietnamese restaurant, for the others have been small storefront operations. It's very pretty, with old pictures of Saigon before the fall sharing wall space with pictures of Pittsburgh, the owner's new home. The result is sad and hopeful at the same time.

Le Vieux Saigon is the family's second restaurant. The first, Kim's Coffee House, is much smaller and overflow guests get to eat in the family's home upstairs. Kim's menu is a truncated version of Saigon's, with slightly smaller portions and lower prices. With the family's attention focused on Saigon, it's the better bet.

Saigon's menu offers a wide variety of Vietnamese dishes. The two house specials are a Vietnamese hot pot, a broth with vegetables, noodles, and quail eggs which can be eaten as is or be used to cook a variety of items (beef, squid, chicken, etc.), and a simmered beef dish.

The young waiters do their best to be helpful, but most of them are not as familiar with Vietnamese food as they should be. But there is always a family member ready to rush over to answer questions when a waiter can't; put yourself in their hands.

*Price: About $15 per person*
*Open Tues.–Sun. for lunch and dinner; closed Mon.*
*Accepts all major credit cards*

---

## MARIO'S SOUTHSIDE SALOON
### 1514 East Carson Street
#### 412-381-5610

A younger, rowdier crowd than Froggy's, but a similar atmosphere. Located in an area full of artist's lofts, antique stores, and new restaurants, Mario's is an old two-level storefront refitted as a bar. The crowd always seems to be having a great time, perhaps because of the house special, a yard-long glass of beer.

The food, mostly pasta, is filling and inexpensive. Go hungry, keep your expectations down, and you'll be all right.

*Price: About $10 per person*
*Open Mon.–Sat. for lunch and dinner; closed Sun.*
*Accepts all major credit cards*

---

# MAX'S ALLEGHENY TAVERN
## In Northside, 537 Suismon Street
### 412-231-1899

Max's Allegheny Tavern is one of the oldest neighborhood bars in one of Pittsburgh's oldest neighborhoods. The Northside used to be a separate city, Allegheny; hence the restaurant's name. Max's hasn't been duded up to look old; it is old, and the lived-in charm and infectious high spirits are delightful.

Max's would be worth a visit for the bar, the Tiffany lamps, and the player piano (complete with drums, tambourine, and accordion) alone. But the German food is actually quite good, if fairly simple. Try the *sauerbraten, Wiener Schnitzel,* or the *Würst* platter, and make sure they keep refilling your basket with the fresh homemade dark bread. There is also a very popular and filling Sunday brunch.

Max's is at its most colorful before or after a Steeler game or a Pirate game, and, because of its proximity to Three Rivers Stadium, it's often crowded. However, Max's is seldom uncrowded (early suppers are your best best), so be prepared to wait, usually about 20 minutes. Reservations are accepted for groups of five or more only. I'd rather be in the lively main room, but quieter rooms are available if you ask.

*Price: About $10 per person*
*Open daily for lunch and dinner*
*Accepts all major credit cards*

---

# MONTEREY INN
## 4068 Mt. Royal Boulevard, Shaler Township
### 412-487-7156

High-tone Mexican. Monterey Inn bills itself as "California–Mexican," meaning the food is less spicy, a bit more complex, and more expensive than at your normal Mexican restaurant. The restaurant is also much prettier, set in a stone building in the woods near North Park. It specializes in chicken and seafood dishes, including a very good chicken *molé,* but the traditional Tex–Mex dishes (*burritos, enchiladas,* etc.) and some killer margaritas are also available.

Monterey Inn is especially pretty in winter, with a fire going in the huge stone fireplace and a view of the snowy woods through the picture windows. Assuming, of course, that you are willing to make the trek out there (about 40 minutes from town over some narrow, winding roads) in the winter. If you do, make reservations; they don't deal well with walk-ins.

*Price: About $15 per person*
*Open daily for lunch and dinner*
*Accepts all major credit cards*

## THE 1902 LANDMARK TAVERN
### 24 Market Square
### 412–471–1902

1902 is packed at lunch; evenings are calmer. Highlights are a raw bar, good sandwiches, and the restaurant itself, a beautifully restored old tavern with a gorgeous, long wooden bar, tile walls, and a tin roof.

*Price: About $10 per person*
*Open Mon.–Sat. for lunch and dinner*
*Accepts all major credit cards*

## ORIGINAL HOT DOG SHOPS, INC.
### In Oakland, 3901 Forbes Avenue
### 412–621–7388

This hallmark of Pitt's campus, known as the O, the Big O, or (affectionately) the Dirty O, got national attention because of quarterback Danny Marino's attachment to its hot dogs. But Pittsburghers have been hanging out here for years, particularly late at night when nothing but a good hot dog will do.

The O's enduring popularity is due in part to nostalgia, in part to very good dogs, and in part to its huge storehouse of beer for sale by the six-pack. (Beer can be bought only from distributors or bars in Pennsylvania.) Don't confuse the Original Hot Dog with the Original Station St. Hot Dog, which has an outlet in East Liberty and a legion of fans who claim that *it* has the best hot dog in town. And don't ask how there can be more than one original; this is America, where anything is possible.

*Price: Hot dogs are about $1.25*
*Open daily for lunch and dinner*
*No credit cards accepted*

# POLI'S RESTAURANT
In Squirrel Hill, 2607 Murray Avenue
### 412-521-6400

Poli's is a Pittsburgh special, a strange blend of informal neighborhood eatery and high-priced restaurant. Built like a barn and full of people who all seem to know each other, Poli's is not the place for intimate dining. But whatever you want in seafood, including whatever is in season, Poli's has it. But stick to seafood, for nothing else on the voluminous menu is of like quality.

*Price: About $25 per person*
*Open Tues.–Sun. for lunch and dinner; closed Mon.*
*Accepts all major credit cards*

---

# PRIMANTI BROTHERS'
### 46 West 18 Street
### 412-263-2142

Primanti's, a late-night spot which opens at 11 P.M. and closes at 3 P.M., probably gets the most eclectic crowd in town. Steelworkers after a shift, truckers, college kids, Yuppies—they all end up here.

Sandwiches come with French fries and coleslaw. To save time and plates, the fries and slaw are put on the sandwich and all eaten together. At least I think it's to save time. The other explanation is that someone went goofy one night and this Pittsburgh tradition, Primanti's claim to fame, was the result.

*Price: About $2.50 per person*
*Open daily for lunch and dinner*
*No credit cards accepted*

---

# RED DRAGON
### In Hampton Plaza, Route 8, Allison Park
### 412-487-3335

There has been a heavy influx of Vietnamese into Pittsburgh, and in this country it's only a matter of time before immigrants open restaurants. It's probably part of the immigration application.

The Red Dragon is bright and cheerful, with an odd "country kitchen" look left over from a prior occupant. Like many Vietnamese restaurants, it hedges its bets and offers a Chinese menu as well. The Chinese menu is pedestrian; stick with the Vietnamese.

It is a wise idea to inquire as to a dish's spiciness. Not all Vietnamese dishes are hot, but those that are can be killers. Try the Beef Siamese (tender, rare beef served warm with fresh onions, hot peppers, and lemon) or the beef Dragon. Sometimes spicy food has heat and nothing else. This food has flavors that survive the kick.

Portions are very large and prices are low. Allison Park is a long haul from Downtown (about 35 minutes), but for people driving into town along Route 8, the Red Dragon is right off the Turnpike exit.

*Price: About $10 per person*
*Open Wed.–Mon. for lunch and dinner; closed Tues.*
*No credit cards accepted*

---

## RIBB HOUSE
### In Squirrel Hill, 2125 Murray Avenue
#### 412-521-8827

The Ribb House's ribs are the best in town; big, meaty, and tender, but not falling off the bone like those "boil 'em for an hour" places. The three flavorful sauces are excellent: the mild slightly sweet, the medium, tangy but not overpowering, the hot, hot, but not outrageous.

Problems? One, the ribs taste smoked but they don't taste grilled. Two, the restaurant is too clean and suburban looking; it doesn't feel like a rib joint. But if you're looking for ribs rather than a cultural experience, this is the place.

*Price: About $7 per person*
*Open Mon.–Sat. for dinner only; closed Sun.*
*No credit cards accepted*

---

## RICHEST RESTAURANT
### 140 6 Street
#### 412-471-7799

No schmaltz on the table, but otherwise, Richest, a fixture since the Depression, has about anything you could ask of a deli, including quarter-pound corned beef sandwiches for those who don't think that's too much of a good thing. It's about a 10-minute walk from here to the stadium, so Richest is a popular spot to stop for takeout before a game. (If all you want is a bag of bagels for the road, go to Bageland in Squirrel Hill.)

*Price: About $5 per person*
*Open Mon.–Sat. for lunch and dinner; closed Sun.*
*No credit cards accepted*

# SAMRENY'S CEDARS OF LEBANON RESTAURANT AND LOUNGE

### In Oakland, 4808 Baum Boulevard
### 412-682-1212

Pittsburgh is littered with Middle Eastern restaurants. I don't know why, Middle Eastern people do not make up a substantial part of the population. But the fact remains that most Pittsburghers are as familiar with *baba ghanooj* as they are with veal *parmigiana.*

The craze has died somewhat, but there are still more than enough of these places to go around. If you are interested in historical research, have never tried Middle Eastern food, or are just a fan, Samreny's is the classic. And the waitresses are Pittsburgh classics; they'll call you "honey" like there's no tomorrow.

*Price: About $15 per person*
*Open Tues.–Sun. for lunch and dinner; closed Mon.*
*No credit cards accepted*

---

# SARAH'S RESTAURANT AND CATERING

### In Southside, 52 South 10 Street
### 412-431-9307

Sarah's was ethnic before ethnicity was cool. "Sarah" is Sarah Evosevich, and her home-style, no-nonsense Yugoslavian cooking has made dining on the patio of her small Southside home a Pittsburgh tradition.

Dinner at Sarah's is by advance reservation only and is served family style. For $17 about fifteen items cooked at Sarah's whim will be brought to your table in bowls and on platters, and you serve yourself. While family-style dining allows you to try a great variety of items, it also means that much of the food has to be prepared ahead of time, and a lot of attention can't be paid to individual requests and preferences.

When you call for reservations, Sarah will tell you what's cooking, but she reserves the right to change her mind. You can usually count on excellent homemade sourdough bread, *podvarek* (turkey seasoned with sauerkraut stuffing), *janjetina* (roast lamb with mushrooms), and *sarma* (stuffed cabbage), plus generous helpings of vegetables and appetizers. Don't worry if any one item doesn't appeal to you. There is more good, heavy food presented than anyone could eat.

Though the room looks as if it's set up for a small outdoor graduation party (strung lights, old linens, folding chairs), men must wear ties and jackets. And

Sarah's hospitality has limits; all but the most general explanations of recipes are forbidden, and while seconds are allowed, doggy bags are not. But she provides you with good food and a unique experience. How much more do you ask of a host?

*Price: About $17 per person*
*Open daily for dinner only*
*No credit cards accepted*

---

## SCOTTY'S DINER
### 7619 Penn Avenue, Wilkinsburg
**412-241-9506**

A tiny all-night eatery whose main draw is the fun of ordering great pancakes in an old unrefurbished diner. The pancakes are big and fluffy, with just enough body to hold the butter and syrup in place. And I've never seen a straw airborne.

*Price: About $5 per person*
*Open daily for breakfast, lunch, and dinner*
*No credit cards accepted*

---

## SUZIE'S
### 130 6 Street
**412-261-6443**

There isn't much to Suzie's, a small Greek restaurant near Heinz Hall—a few tables, some wooden chairs, and the kitchen. But, to quote Tracy on Hepburn, what's there is choice.

In Greece, customers often enter the kitchen in a restaurant to choose their food. Suzie's has an interesting variation on the tradition: You enter the kitchen to get to the bathroom. It's not very elegant, but there is something reassuring about a restaurant that encourages such backstage visits, and you can use the opportunity to check out what's cooking.

The food at Suzie's is simple and prepared with a surprisingly light touch. Everything, including the bread, is freshly made. The menu offerings are traditional, some would say clichéed, Greek dishes (*kotopita, spanikopita,* stuffed grape leaves), but the preparation is far from common.

Don't miss the *tzantziki,* a cold mixture of sour cream, garlic, and cucumber, or the chicken and lemon soup. For a main course, choose any of the *filo* dishes; Suzie's touch with that buttery, paper-thin dough is masterful. Avoid only the dishes topped with *béchamel* sauce, which is dry and heavy.

For dessert, *galatoboureko,* a farina custard baked in *filo* and topped with thinned honey, is heaven. Order it when your meal comes because it takes a while to prepare.

Suzie's is inconvenient—no credit, no reservations, no liquor license. But don't let a little inconvenience keep you from one of the best buys around.

*Price: About $10 per person*
*Open Mon.–Sat. for lunch and dinner; closed Sun.*
*No credit cards accepted*

# THE TERRACE ROOM
## In the William Penn Hotel
### 412-553-5235

A grand room in a grand hotel. If you want, you can spend most of your day eating or drinking at the William Penn. Start with tea, served every weekday from 2:30 to 4:30 P.M. in the Palm Court, the ornate Edwardian lobby fronting The Terrace Room. At about 5, the pianist starts playing, and the Palm Court becomes a supremely elegant cocktail lounge.

Assuming you are still able to move, you can then head into the Terrace Room itself, a sumptuous blend of walnut and rose, one of the plushest rooms in town. Take time to study the mural, a lively old mishmash of historical figures, fiction, and fact that combines the conquering of Fort Duquesne by the British in 1758 with the relief of Fort Pitt from Indian siege in 1763.

The best choice is the prime rib, carved at your table from a standing rib. Or, for a reminder of another era, go on Friday or Saturday when a dinner-dance combination is offered with a *table d'hôte* menu. The Terrace Room also serves an elaborate Sunday brunch.

*Price: About $25 per person*
*Open daily for breakfast, lunch, and dinner*
*Accepts all major credit cards*

# TESSARO'S BAR & GRILL
## In Bloomfield, 4601 Liberty Avenue
### 412-682-6809

The Great American hamburger, freshly ground, hand-packed, thick but not overwhelming, and grilled over a wood-burning pit. This is an intense burger; it takes about a week to get the smoky taste out of your mouth.

Tessaro's is a tiny neighborhood bar that does serve a few other things, including pretty good ribs on certain nights. But the main draw is the burger.

*Price: About $3.25 for a burger*
*Open Mon.–Sat. for lunch and dinner; closed Sun.*
*Accepts all major credit cards*

# TOP OF THE TRIANGLE
## 600 Grant Street
### 412-471-4100

In a city where the hills offer so many unexpected views, it seems unsporting to ride an elevator to the top of a building for one. It is, however, more convenient.

The Top of the Triangle is located on the top floor of U.S. Steel's headquarters building, 63 stories up. The food, by Stouffers, is not particularly memorable, but the restaurant does have the good taste not to revolve.

*Price: About $25 per person*
*Open Mon.–Sat. for lunch and dinner; closed Sun.*
*Accepts all major credit cards*

# UN POCO DI ROMA
## In Bethel Park, 2930 South Park Road
### 412-833-9009

Italians are Pittsburgh's biggest single ethnic group, so it's no surprise that we're practically drowning in red sauce, most of which is pretty bad. But we also have our share of good Italian restaurants, of which Un Poco di Roma is unquestionably the best.

Un Poco di Roma is located about 30 minutes from Downtown in a tiny building that looks like an abandoned Knights of Columbus Hall, but with less charm. Don't panic, it's prettier inside than you'd guess. The menu focuses on unusual regional dishes; each month on Tuesday through Thursday, full-course dinners are offered from a different featured region.

Items to look for on the regular menu are roast duck with homemade sausage and veal stuffed with sausage. Prepare to spend the evening; service is slow, slow, slow.

While the restaurant is in the middle of nowhere, it's not really hard to find. Ask while you're making reservations, and you'll receive easy-to-follow directions.

*Price: About $25 per person*
*Open Tues.–Sun. for dinner only; closed Mon.*
*Accepts all major credit cards*

# UPSTAIRS AT BRENDAN'S
## In Shadyside, 5505 Walnut Street
### 412-683-5661

Ah, the miracle of modern technology. Upstairs at Brendan's is, as you may have guessed, located above Brendan's, a noisy, busy, tile-and-wood pub. But even though the stairway to Upstairs is right in the middle of Brendan's, the restaurant itself has been soundproofed, so that only the sound of soft conversations and the jazz pianist are heard. Amazing.

Upstairs is also surprisingly posh and subdued. Ivory and wood tones mix with lovely table settings highlighted by fresh flowers and burning tapers. Reservations are suggested, but only needed on the weekends. And don't be fooled by the casual atmosphere in the pub; upstairs, jackets are required.

Main-course choices cover a wide range from Lobster Paradise (cut up and served in its shell in a light cream sauce) to roasted duckling, with lots of beef, seafood, and veal offerings in between. At one time, the salads, vegetables, and desserts were not what one would expect from the prices and the surroundings, but they have recently been upgraded.

Upstairs at Brendan's has done its best to separate itself from Brendan's (which is a nice restaurant in its own right), but I'm sure some people will not like dressing up to cut through a crowded bar. I wouldn't bring guests Upstairs unless I knew how they'd handle downstairs.

*Price: $30 per person*
*Open Tues.–Sat. for dinner only; closed Sun.*
*Accepts all major credit cards*

# VINCENT'S PIZZA PARK
## In Forest Hills, 998 Ardmore Boulevard
### 412-271-9181

An old-time pizza parlor with huge, smoky ovens, charred pizza, and a dining room made up to look like a grape arbor. The pizza is traditional "New York-Neopolitan"-style; round, slightly thin in the middle, with thick, chewy crusts and lots of spicy tomato sauce. Despite its immense popularity, or maybe because of it, Vincent's has resisted any temptations to go high church: this is a strictly no-nonsense pizza parlor. Don't go looking for goat cheese or truffles, but almost any of the normal toppings are available. Order anything but don't overload or you'll find your pizza collapsing in the middle. Vincent's is located about 20 minutes east of Downtown.

*Price: About $8 for a large pizza*
*Open daily for dinner only*
*Accepts all major credit cards*

# WILSON'S BAR-B-Q
## In Northside, 700 North Taylor Street
### 412-231-9292

Wilson's is located on the edge of the Mexican War Streets, an area of restored brownstones on streets named after Mexican War battles and heroes. Whatever restoration is going on, it hasn't hit Wilson's. There are two tired-looking umbrella tables outside, and two more tables inside, but this is basically a takeout place.

Ribs are cooked in a huge indoor charcoal pit. The ribs can be a little fatty, but they are tasty, with a strong grilled flavor.

Wilson's two sauces are unusual, a product of their Louisiana origin. The mild sauce is watery and peppery, almost like a particularly spicy tomato sauce. But everyone comes for the hot sauce, loaded with cayenne pepper and secretly incendiary. It takes about two bites to hit, during which time you'll laugh at how provincial we Pittsburghers must be to think this is hot, and then it explodes. You've been warned.

*Price: About $7 per person*
*Open Mon.–Sat. for lunch and dinner; closed Sun.*
*No credit cards accepted*

# THE WINE RESTAURANT
## 1 Oxford Center
### 412-288-9463

The gimmick here is the nitrogen-process at the wine bar that enables you to order any one of 60 wines (from a cellar of about 400) by the taste or glass. But The Wine Restaurant, an ultra-modern restaurant in the new Oxford Center, has more than a gimmick. It also has excellent New American food, beautiful settings, and a relaxed atmosphere.

The room's position on a third-floor balcony gives it an open, airy feel. It doesn't overlook anything, but the gray wall across the way is used as a screen for a silent show of fine-art slides.

The emphasis is on fresh, high-quality ingredients. Highlights are the soups and *pâtés,* the Wisconsin veal loin *médaillons,* the Southampton duckling, and the baby lamb.

Portions are not large, to the dismay of many Pittsburghers, but that makes saving room for the wonderful desserts easier. It is possible to eat cheaply here, particularly at lunch when quick specials are offered, but most people end up spending big bucks. All things considered, however, it's worth the money.

It's best to go to The Wine Restaurant with a party of four; parties of two get lined up shoulder to shoulder along a two-crowded banquette. Reservations are recommended but are usually not essential, and dress is stylish but not necessarily formal.

While the staff is well informed, friendly, and efficient, a certain condescending bring-culture-to-the-native attitude does creep in. Spend too little time studying the wine list and the staff looks let down. Every item is described in lush detail, everything is the "freshest," the "finest," and the "best," and is served only at the ideal temperature. Restaurants should pay attention to detail, but they shouldn't force you to pay attention with them.

*Price: About $40 per person*
*Open Mon.–Sat. for lunch and dinner; closed Sun.*
*Accepts all major credit cards*

# PORTLAND

## *By Matt Kramer*

**BREAKFAST**
Bijou Café
Fuller's Restaurant
Heathman Restaurant
The Original Pancake House

**CHINESE**
Fong Chong Restaurant
Uncle Chen
Yen Ching

**CONTINENTAL**
Heathman Restaurant

**DELICATESSEN**
Dave's Delicatessen

**ECLECTIC**
Bread and Ink

**FRENCH**
L'Auberge
Le Cuisinier

**HAMBURGERS**
Bread and Ink

**HOTEL DINING ROOM**
Heathman Restaurant

**INDIAN/PAKISTANI**
Kashmir Restaurant

**ITALIAN**
Nick's Italian Café

**SEAFOOD**
Dan & Louis Oyster Bar
Jake's Famous Crawfish
Winterbourne

**STEAKS AND CHOPS**
The Ringside West

**SUBURBAN**
Nick's Italian Café
(McMinnville)

Portland is a city of 365,000 enormously contented souls. The reasons for this contentment are numerous: The city is close to some of the most spectacular scenery in the nation and the fishing is superb, as is the hunting, hiking, and outdoor sports. Perhaps because of this enchantment with the outdoors, the city has been slow in establishing standards for genuinely fine food, especially in the more demanding upper-echelon categories of restaurants.

Those looking for a sublime *haute cuisine* restaurant experience are well-advised to look elsewhere. Portland offers nothing in that category, although several restaurants purport to offer just such an experience. The essential nature of the city is restrained and down-home. The best places in town are almost invariably those that reflect this quality and capitalize on it. For example, Portland is a terrific city for breakfasts. At least half a dozen spots, such as The Bijou Café, Fuller's, and The Original Pancake House, can offer a morning wake-up of a warmth rare in most major cities.

The local wines are well worth seeking out and numerous restaurants offer at least a small selection. Many of Oregon's wineries are found within a 45-minute drive of downtown Portland. Wineries worth visiting (and wines worth tasting) include The Eyrie Vineyards, Ponzi Vineyards, Adelsheim Vineyard, Shafer Vineyard Cellars, Tualatin Vineyards, Elk Cove Vineyards, Sokol-Blosser Vineyards, and Knudsen-Erath Vineyards, among others.

*Matt Kramer is a food and wine columnist for* The Oregonian *newspaper, as well as for* Pacific Northwest *magazine.*

---

## BIJOU CAFÉ
### 132 Southwest Third Avenue
#### 503-222-3187

The Bijou is the sort of restaurant for which throngs of regulars feel great affection. A breakfast and lunch spot in the Old Town area of the city, it offers classically American eggs-and-bacon breakfasts, with homemade muffins, pancakes, waffles, fresh orange juice, roast beef hash, and so forth. These are served all day. The lunch offerings are similarly traditional, with a good chili, fine hamburgers, and milk shakes. Breakfast is served all day, reflecting owners-chefs Bonnie Allen and Kathy Hagberg's frustration at missing breakfast when they got off from work in another business prior to opening the Bijou. No reservations are accepted.

*Price: About $5 per person*
*Open daily for breakfast and lunch*
*No credit cards accepted*

---

## BREAD AND INK
### 3610 SE Hawthorne Boulevard
#### 503-239-4756

A favorite place for this reviewer and many other Portlanders, Bread and Ink represents the best of Portland. It is warm and unpretentious, and the food is excellent and equally without pretension. The best hamburger in town is here: The bun is homemade, the fixings are served in three clear-glass bowls for each diner, and the one-third pound of beef is cooked to order.

That overused word "eclectic" applies here. The lunch menu ranges from homemade sausage to Vietnamese spring rolls to cheese blintzes—all of them excellent. Daily specials are chalked up on a blackboard—you take your chances, but they're pretty good. Desserts are invariably fine. Also, there's a fine Sunday brunch in the traditional delicatessen mode.

The dinner menu is less varied than the lunch menu (although you can order from either in the early evening). Bread and Ink is fundamentally a lunch place; desserts only are served after 10 P.M. A large range of free reading material is available, from *The Economist* to *Rolling Stone*. The wine list is limited, but reasonable. In sum, if I were to take a visitor to only one restaurant in town, I'd choose Bread and Ink. It's Portland at its best.

*Price: About $10 per person*
*Open Tues.–Sun. for lunch and dinner; Sun. for brunch only; closed Mon.*
*Accepts Visa and MasterCard*

---

## DAN & LOUIS OYSTER BAR
### 208 SW Ankeny Street (*in Old Town*)
#### 503-227-5906

Can a restaurant be recommended on the basis of one dish? You bet—at least if that dish is the oyster stew with the double portion of oysters served at Dan and Louis Oyster Bar. The Wachsmuth family, who have owned Dan & Louis for decades, own their own oyster bed in Yaquina Bay, along the Oregon coast. The decor in the restaurant borders on the unbelievable: The paneled walls are covered from top to bottom with every conceivable form of naval bric-a-brac. You can't help but love it. No wine is served. Reservations are not needed.

*Price: About $8 per person*
*Open daily for lunch and dinner*
*Accepts all major credit cards*

---

## DAVE'S DELICATESSEN
### In the Justice Center building, 1110 SW Third Avenue
#### 503-222-5461

Dave's Deli is the kind of restaurant that you bought this book for: It's the place the locals know but never bother to tell outsiders about. Dave's serves Jewish food, but mostly, Dave's serves Shirley and Abe Saltman. A little genealogy is important here. Dave (now dead) was Shirley's father. Abe married Shirley and does all the cooking, while Shirley womans the cash register. Son-in-law Phil dolefully oversees the counter serving line. All of Portland's leading attorneys, bureaucrats, and department-store buyers eat here, often every day. Shirley gives them all a raft. They love it. The restaurant is newly located in the elegant Justice Center near City Hall. The old Dave's Deli was in a seedy dive farther downtown and somehow a faint air of the seediness remains, probably because most of the patrons insisted on bringing a piece of it with them—in $200 attaché cases, of course.

How's the food? Oh yes, the food. It's good. Get the *kreplach* (Jewish *ravioli*) and the cabbage rolls on Fridays. Matzoh ball soup is always available. But let's be honest, it's not really the food that makes Dave's Deli a Portland institution—it's Shirley and Abe. Say hello. No reservations are accepted.

*Price: About $4 per person*
*Open Mon.–Fri. for breakfast, lunch, and early dinner; closed Sat. and Sun.*
*No credit cards accepted*

---

## FONG CHONG RESTAURANT
### In Old Town, 301 Northwest Fourth Avenue
#### 503-220-0235

Fong Chong is a source of some of the best *dim sum* north of San Francisco. In fact, a Bay Area friend who is proficient in Chinese and has authored a substantial cookbook on Chinese food contends that Fong Chong offers *dim sum* equal to anything in San Francisco's Chinatown. It lacks only the extensiveness of some of the largest *dim sum* offerings in that area.

*Dim sum* is a Cantonese specialty and might best be described as a never-ending appetizer course. At Fong Chong, as at many such places, the waitresses push carts holding various items. You choose what looks good and pass on the rest. They total up your check by counting the number of little trays that are strewn about the table by the time you've finished your meal. As is traditional, *dim sum* is served only during lunch. The evening menu is composed of the usual array of Cantonese dishes, which also are available at lunchtime should you (foolishly) choose to forgo the *dim sum* option. Overall, the quality is superb. Reservations accepted only for parties of six or more. *Dim sum* is served every day from 11 A.M. to 3 P.M. only.

*Price: About $6 per person for* dim sum; *slightly higher for regular meals*
*Open daily for lunch and dinner*
*No credit cards accepted*

---

## FULLER'S RESTAURANT
### 136 NW Ninth Avenue
#### 503-222-5608

No one calls this Fuller's Restaurant, but that's the official name. Everyone calls it Fuller's Coffee Shop. I'm not sure Fuller's has ever seen an outsider before. The place is a local wonder. Seating is counterspace only and that for some thirty patrons at a sitting. The French toast is superb, as are the homemade cinnamon rolls. (Portland has a passion for cinnamon rolls—try those at Dave's Delicatessen as well.)

Fuller's is located in the small industry and supply house area close to the downtown core, but you'd have to know about it to even suspect that it's there. For a good, simple, cheap breakfast and lunch, this is a place worth seeking out. Fresh salmon and halibut are served for lunch in season; they even make fruitcakes every Christmas that the regulars have bought for years. No reservations are accepted.

*Price: About $4 per person*
*Open Mon.–Sat. for breakfast and lunch; closed Sun.*
*No credit cards accepted*

---

## HEATHMAN RESTAURANT
### In the Heathman Hotel, SW Broadway and Salmon Street
#### 503-241-4100; 1-800-551-0011 (toll-free outside Oregon)

The Heathman is one of Portland's newest hotels. (At this writing the Alexis —same as in Seattle—is under construction and should be open in 1986.) Located next to the renovated Performing Arts Center on Broadway, the Heathman is striving for elegance. It half makes it.

The restaurant is small, with an open kitchen. Tables are nicely appointed with very expensive glassware and the usual white tablecloth. Breakfast is predictable, but certainly worth eating. It's the most elegant setting for breakfast in town. Lunches and dinners rely heavily on fresh, local ingredients. The salmon is good, as is the lamb. Wild mushrooms are frequently on the menu. In many respects, the Heathman Restaurant is still in a shake-down period, but the efforts so far bode well. The wine list is well-thought-out and surprisingly reasonable in price.

*Price: About $15–$25 per person*
*Open daily for breakfast, lunch, and dinner*
*Accepts all major credit cards*

---

## JAKE'S FAMOUS CRAWFISH
401 SW Twelfth Avenue (*corner of Twelfth Avenue and Stark Street*)
**503-226-1419**

This is one of the most popular and overrated restaurants in Portland. Nevertheless, the salmon is very good as are some other fish dishes. If you're dying for salmon, then Jake's is certainly the place to go. Lunches and dinners are overpriced; the decor is old-fashioned and charming; the large bar is a hot pick-up spot. The wine list offers an excellent selection of Oregon wines and, like everything else in this restaurant, is overpriced. Pass on the "famous" crawfish, by the way. Reservations are advised.

*Price: About $20 per person*
*Open Mon.–Fri. for lunch and dinner; Sat. and Sun. for dinner only*
*Accepts all major credit cards*

---

## KASHMIR RESTAURANT
1022 SW Stark Street
**503-222-5247**

Either you like Indian food or you don't. I happen to be a big fan, although not an especially knowledgeable one. All I can say about the Kashmir is that it serves Northern Indian and Pakistani food in ample quantities in tackily pleasant surroundings in a storefront location. A reviewer can't pretend to be an expert in every cuisine, so the best I can pass on to you is that the food tasted pretty good to me. Portions are substantial, the chutneys are great, and no alcoholic beverages are served. I really like Kashmir, but then, I really like Indian food. Reservations are advised.

*Price: About $15 per person*
*Open Mon.–Sat. for dinner only; closed Sun.*
*Accepts most major credit cards*

# L'AUBERGE

## In the industrial area, 2601 NW Vaughn Avenue
### 503-223-3302

L'Auberge is Portland's idea of a good French restaurant and it's not a bad idea at all. The setting is a remodeled old wood structure in the industrial section of Northwest Portland. (The city is divided into NW/SW, NE/SE —the Willamette River divides the east side from the west side; and Burnside Avenue is the demarcation between north and south.)

The main dining room is exceptionally cozy, in large part owing to the substantial old-fashioned fireplace that is often used for cooking. The menu sticks fairly close to the traditional items one would expect from a country French restaurant, with some interesting twists, such as lamb marinated in pomegranate juice. Because the menu changes frequently (although not every night), it is difficult to steer you to one signature dish. Of late, the restaurant is placing increasing emphasis on fresh local ingredients. As a result, quail is often featured in one guise or another (one of the largest quail breeders in the nation is situated not far outside Portland). Fresh local mushrooms are often on the menu: *chanterelles* in the autumn, *morels* in the spring, and other delights as they appear.

Sunday night is a particularly intimate evening at L'Auberge because the bar area offers excellent hamburgers and a free movie at 9 P.M., which attracts numerous regulars winding up the weekend. The wine list is excellent, with an especially good selection of Oregon and Washington wines.

*Price: About $25 per person*
*Open daily for dinner only*
*Accepts all major credit cards*

# LE CUISINIER

## In the downtown area, 1308 West Burnside Boulevard
### 503-224-4260

This proverbial hole-in-the wall restaurant is likely the most ambitious French restaurant in town. Le Cuisinier is a one-man show. Owner-chef Karl Schaefer is attempting to upgrade the standards of French food in Portland and is definitely succeeding. Influenced (in a good way) by *nouvelle cuisine,* this 30-seat restaurant is not the place you go to impress a client or wow a date with your ability to banter with a snooty maître d': You go to eat. Portland has long had an affinity for austere restaurants, and this is the latest and, indeed, the greatest of a long line of such personal, shoestring-budget operations.

The meal usually commences with tiny, sometimes silly little hors d'oeuvres; first courses are extremely varied. Like L'Auberge, this restaurant is energetic in its pursuit of local foodstuffs. Because the chef is the only person in the impossibly small kitchen, what he finds that day at the market is what you get. This makes it hard on restaurant reviewers—there's too much variability—but fine for the diners. There's always the chance of a poor meal: The dinners extend over six courses, and the likelihood exists that at least one of the courses will not score the high points of the others. This is a small price to pay for overall excellence and seriousness. The wine list is correspondingly extensive and reasonably priced. Reservations are essential.

*Price: About $30 per person*
*Open Tues. and Thurs.–Sat. for dinner only; closed Sun., Mon., and Wed.*
*Accepts all major credit cards*

---

## NICK'S ITALIAN CAFÉ
### 521 East Third Street, McMinnville
#### 503-434-4471

This is *the* place to eat in the Oregon wine country. McMinnville, a small Willamette Valley town about 30 miles west of Portland, is on the way to the Oregon coast and near several wineries. One of Oregon's best wineries, The Eyrie Vineyards, is located in downtown McMinnville, so combining a visit to Eyrie and a visit to Nick's is a perfect idea.

Nick really runs the kitchen and a more affable, modest fellow has yet to trod this earth. The restaurant is a vaguely shabby, storefront operation that offers Nick's inimical style of feeding people, which is to say that you'll eat as if you were in an Italian home. The food is plentiful (six courses as a rule), homemade, earthy—in other words, just plain good. The wine list is almost exclusively Oregon and the prices are downright cheap. Check out Nick's. Reservations are essential.

*Price: About $20 per person*
*Open Tues.–Fri. for lunch and dinner; Mon. and Sat. for dinner only;*
*closed Sun.*
*No credit cards accepted*

---

## THE ORIGINAL PANCAKE HOUSE
### 8600 SW Barbur Boulevard
#### 503-246-9007

This is the *original* Original Pancake House. If other restaurants around the world hewed to their standards of ingredients and consistency, then you could conclude that the Millennium has arrived. The fare here is simply superb. Try the apple pancake, which is a nine-inch-diameter crusty pastry filled with layers of sliced apples and glazed with a cinnamon-infused topping. The omelets are huge, but not as fine as the various pancakes. Real cream is served in old-fashioned tiny bottles (remember those?); freshly-squeezed orange juice has been served here as if the frozen variety has yet to be invented. The Original Pancake House runs as if the 1950s had never ended. The waitresses are similarly ageless; I've haven't seen a new one yet. No reservations are accepted.

*Price: About $6 per person*
*Open Wed.–Sun. for breakfast and lunch; closed Mon. and Tues.*
*No credit cards accepted*

---

## THE RINGSIDE WEST
### 2165 West Burnside
**503-223-1513**

Located just slightly outside the downtown area, The Ringside is a blast from the past and the best steak house in town. As soon as you walk into its dimly-lit roadhouse atmosphere, with its all-male, tuxedo-clad waiters, you'll feel as if the forties have returned. The steaks are excellent and the onion rings are widely thought to be the finest in the country. Drinks are ample and inexpensive; the wine list is ho-hum. Everything is fairly priced. Reservations, made several days in advance, are essential.

*Price: About $15 per person*
*Open daily for dinner only*
*Accepts all major credit cards*

---

## UNCLE CHEN
### 529 SW Third Avenue
**503-248-1199**

This is a lovely restaurant, bright, airy, with old brick and an atrium-high ceiling. The Uncle Chen in this restaurant made his avuncular name in New York and, to paraphrase the famous H.R. Munro line—as good chefs go, he went. Uncle Chen has since gone on to open a new restaurant called Chen Dynasty (622 SW Washington).

Nevertheless, the original Uncle Chen is still plugging along and still upholding reasonable standards. All the usual Szechuan and Hunan dishes are to be found here. The portions are rather small, but the food is good and the decor exceedingly pleasant. Lunch and dinner are served. Reservations are advised.

*Price: About $10 per person*
*Open Mon.–Fri. for lunch and dinner; Sat. and Sun. for dinner only*
*Accepts all major credit cards*

---

## WINTERBOURNE
### 3520 NE Forty-second Avenue
#### 503-249-8486

Another of Portland's Trappist monk restaurants. This minuscule restaurant focuses exclusively on simply prepared fish, absolutely fresh, and served with only the most delicate of sauces, if any. The owners dislike smoking and have finally forbade it altogether. (They used to give a discount for non-smokers.) The atmosphere is non-existent, but the fish is likely the best in town. The wine list is excellent, with a good selection of Oregon wines, mostly white, of course. Located in a residential neighborhood a taxi ride from downtown, it's worth the journey. Reservations are advised.

*Price: About $20 per person*
*Open Wed.–Sat. for dinner only; closed Sun.–Tues.*
*Accepts all major credit cards*

---

## YEN CHING
### 1135 SW Washington Street
#### 503-222-1455

This Szechuan Chinese restaurant is located in the same premises as a restaurant formerly called (some years ago now) the Timber Topper. As that name suggests, the motif was Oregon timber artifacts. They are still there. No matter. The food at Yen Ching is reliably good. It's not likely to be the greatest Szechuan food that you'll ever eat, but the *moo-shoo* pork is darn good, as is the *kung-pao* chicken and the bong-bong chicken appetizer. It's an old-shoe atmosphere, with stuffed, leatherette banquettes reminiscent of old-style Cantonese restaurants in suburbia. Prices are extremely reasonable and the restaurant is deceptively large, so no reservations are ever needed.

*Price: About $10 per person*
*Open daily for lunch and dinner*
*Accepts all major credit cards*

# PROVIDENCE AND NEWPORT

## BY BILL GALE

**AMERICAN**
  The Black Pearl (Newport)
  Lloyd's (Providence)
  The Mooring (Newport)

**BARBECUE**
  Wes' House of Ribs
    (Providence)

**CHINESE**
  China Inn (Pawtucket)

**FRENCH**
  Le Bistro (Newport)
  Rue de L'Espoir (Providence)

**HEALTH FOOD**
  Amara's (Providence)

**ICE CREAM**
  Big Alice's (Providence)

**ITALIAN**
  Al Forno (Providence)
  Galleria di Gera (Providence)

**PIZZA**
  Caserta Pizzeria (Providence)

**SEAFOOD**
  Bluepoint Oyster Bar
    (Providence)

**SUBURBAN**
  Café in the Barn (Seekonk,
    Massachussets)

Once upon a time, a Rhode Islander in search of a first-rate meal had to consider making the 50-mile drive to Boston. No more. In the last decade America's smallest state has had its own mini restaurant explosion.

From the increasingly sophisticated Italian restaurants of Providence's Federal Hill section to the country inns on the way to Newport's array of French and American restaurants, Rhode Island has come a long way.

Part of the reason, of course, is the general rise in the quality of American cooking and restaurants. But a greater reason seems to be that a number of young professional chefs and restaurant managers have found Rhode Island's unique location on the New England sea coast between Boston and New York to be a place where they can live comfortably and creatively.

They have turned the state's dining-out scene from mediocrity to one worthy of note—even of a detour.

The best restaurants are in Providence and Newport. But anyone visiting either city should consider all of Rhode Island when dining out. After all, it's only an hour from one end of the state to the other, and fresh seafood and excellent Italian and French cuisine can be found in little out-of-the-way places as well as in the capital city and the summer playground.

Rhode Island's restaurant boom has been deeper than it is wide. The food of Southeast Asia is almost non-existent. There are just three Japanese and two Indian restaurants, and the cuisines of the Middle East, Middle Europe, and Spain are not yet in evidence. But for seafood, for restaurants running riffs off of classic French cuisine, and for excellent Italian food, no serious diner will go unrewarded. And the prices are generally at least a third lower than in this city/state's larger neighbors.

*Bill Gale coordinates restaurant coverage for the* Providence Journal and Bulletin.

---

# AL FORNO
## 7 Steeple Street, Providence
### 401-273-9760

A tiny place just down the hill from Brown University, Al Forno may be the toughest restaurant ticket in town.

Reservations are not taken and this handsome place with just 32 seats is often overflowing. The reason is Al Forno's inventive Italian cuisine, much of it done over wood or broiled in a charcoal oven.

Regulars know the menu changes every day but they come looking for the beautifully textured pork tenderloin with peppers and lettuce, in an orange vinaigrette, or the grilled tuna in a vinaigrette or the grilled double breast of chicken. The list goes on and is always imaginative.

But not everything at Al Forno is elaborate. The pizzas, perhaps done with Bel Paese cheese, basil, and tomatoes, are an attraction all by themselves. The clams Al Forno with pasta in a light spicy sauce over garlic or even that splendid treat grilled bread with garlic and olive oil are heaven. In the summer, almost all the vegetables are Rhode Island grown. But all year round, Al Forno is a treat.

*Price: About $20 per person*
*Open Tues.–Sat. for dinner only; closed Sun. and Mon.*
*Accepts American Express, Visa, and MasterCard*

# AMARA'S
## 63 Warren Avenue, East Providence
### 401-434-9506

After years in a colonial-era building on the street where George M. Cohan was born, Amara's has moved to new, larger quarters just across the Providence River. But thank goodness the new place has the same casual atmosphere combined with food made from freshest ingredients carefully prepared.

Although many people think of Amara's as a vegetarian restaurant, that has never really been the case. Chicken and fish (but no meat) are served. The owner, who prefers to be called just "Amara," wants to cook with no chemicals, oils, or sugars at all. Her handsome new place also meets special dietary needs.

All of this is done with flair and care. The food at Amara's is among the best in the Providence area, despite the restaurant's self-imposed restrictions. But there is no holier-than-thou feeling here. Amara's serves no alcohol, but you are free to bring your own.

*Price: About $14 per person*
*Open Tues.–Sun. for lunch and dinner; Mon. for dinner only*
*Accepts Visa and MasterCard*

# BIG ALICE'S
## 100 Hope Street, Providence
### 401-273-5812

Even in winter, there is often a line at Big Alice's. What brings the crowds is store-made ice cream made with a butterfat content of 15 to 20 percent in a wide variety of flavors.

The big seller is Oreo, made from crushed Oreo cookies. More traditional flavors are present, too, and a visit to Big Alice's is a must on the occasional summer (or winter) night. It's especially popular with Brown University students.

*Price: $1–$4*
*Open daily*
*Accepts no credit cards*

---

# THE BLACK PEARL
## Bannister's Wharf, Newport
### 401-846-5264

From front to back, the Pearl remains one of the best things about Newport. In the formal front room, elegant dinners can be had while you listen to the slap of waves on the dock.

The food here has, over the years, lightened up from the classic French style and taken on a *nouvelle* character. Seafood in season—bass, swordfish, and crab —is done splendidly unadorned. The rest of the menu runs to carefully prepared veal, duck, chops, and chicken.

The wine list is excellent. Vintages from the 1940s and 1950s are available at reasonable prices.

In the back room, the Tavern serves omelets, *crêpes,* salads, good burgers, and excellent clam chowder. At night, there is a more extensive main-course list that is cheaper but no less well prepared than in the formal front room.

In summer there's an outdoor bar that could not be more central to Newport's night life.

*Price: About $28 per person in the formal room; $18 per person in the Tavern*
*Open daily for lunch and dinner; closed in February*
*Accepts all major credit cards*

# BLUEPOINT OYSTER BAR
## 99 North Main Street, Providence
### 401-272-6145

For a city on the seacoast, Providence really ought to have more (and better) seafood restaurants. So thank goodness for the Bluepoint. From its raw bar, featuring oysters raised especially for the restaurant in a rural Rhode Island pond, to its sometimes spectacular intermingling of tastes (scrod and rhubarb, for instance) this is *the* place (in Providence) for seafood.

The atmosphere is on the casual side. The menu on a board on the back wall often has customers walking over to read it. Why they can't put up two menus is beyond understanding. Some of the tables are too close for private conversations, but the clubby friendliness makes up for a lot.

The menu changes often. But Bluepoint often has that scrod with a rhubarb sauce and wild mushrooms or perhaps the chef will do it with sun-dried tomatoes, capers, and pine nuts in a virgin olive oil base. The *scampi* over *spaghettini* is spectacular, and fresh Dover sole charcoaled with rosemary is sublime.

The wine list is especially good for American whites.

*Price: About $22 per person*
*Open daily for dinner only*
*Accepts all major credit cards*

# CAFÉ IN THE BARN
## 1590 Fall River Avenue, Seekonk, Massachusetts
### 617-336-6340

Fifteen minutes from downtown Providence, Café in the Barn provides a subdued, elegant country atmosphere and, perhaps, the most sophisticated, consistently first-rate dining in the area.

A dozen years ago, owner Guy Abelson began the Café in the Barn strictly as a luncheon restaurant. Since then, it has grown to a six-day-a-week operation. Soon a second restaurant will be opened in Providence's new Fleet Center, which is helping to make the city's downtown a showplace.

Café in the Barn's menu leans to fish, poultry, and veal. It changes often but some of the winners include *médaillons* of veal in a raspberry vinaigrette, a super leek-and-onion *confit,* and simply and beautifully done sautéed scallops. Other favorites include grilled swordfish with papaya butter and shrimp with feta, pine nuts, and spinach wrapped in *filo* dough.

Café in the Barn's success can be traced to many things, but its policy of developing chefs from within the restaurant's own staff has kept it remarkably stable over the years. It's worth a detour to Seekonk.

*Price: About $29 per person*
*Open Mon.–Sat. for lunch and dinner; Sun. for brunch only*
*Accepts American Express, Visa, and MasterCard*

---

## CASERTA PIZZERIA
### 121 Spruce Street, Providence
**401-272-3618; 401-272-3618; or 401-621-9190**

It's not easy to find Caserta's, hidden away as it is amid Italian men's social clubs and bars on a back street on Providence's Federal Hill.

But once you seek it out, Caserta's pizzas—thick-crusted with full-cream mozzarella and a tomato sauce recipe that remains a secret—will bring you back again and again. Be sure, too, to try a spicy Caserta's favorite called a Wimpy Skippy. It's a spinach pie with *pepperoni* and *mozzarella,* in which the dough is folded over the spinach and made into a sandwich.

There's nothing fancy here—they'd laugh at a pizza with basil on it—there's just a generous supply of honest Italian-American pizza.

*Price: $4.50–$9*
*Open Tues.–Sun. for lunch and dinner; closed Mon.*
*No credit cards accepted*

---

## CHINA INN
### 285 Main Street, Pawtucket
**401-723-3960**

Most of Rhode Island's good Chinese restaurants are in out-of-the-way corners of the state. The China Inn has recently moved to downtown Pawtucket, which, while not exactly in the mainstream, is still something of an improvement over other locations.

It would be difficult to eat better. China Inn puts out a wide variety of Chinese foods, preferring not to limit itself to any one region. A favorite dish is Prince's Teacher Style, a fiery concoction of peppers in hot oil, bamboo shoots, and scallions combined with your choice of chicken, beef, or shrimp. The fried dumplings and the soups—especially the sweet-and-sour—are super.

In case you can't get to Pawtucket, China Inn has a small offshoot in

Providence's historic Arcade in the midst of the financial district. It's fast food and a limited menu, but the quality is still there.

*Price: About $11 per person*
*Open daily for lunch and dinner*
*Accepts American Express, Visa, and MasterCard*

---

## GALLERIA DI GERA
### 134 Atwells Avenue, Providence
### 401-521-9459

One suspects that a lot of people would go here just for Galleria's location. It's in the heart of Federal Hill, Providence's Italian section; the second floor dining room affords a fine view of Rhode Island's ornate capitol and downtown skyline. Fortunately the food is very good, very much like what you would get in Italy and it is moderately priced. Try the seafood *Ischia* (mussels, clams, shrimp, and *calamari*) or *Milano* (shrimp and sea scallops with garlic and herbs) on pasta. Another favorite is the veal steak Napoleon, done with artichokes and Cognac.

Galleria di Gera serves some of its main courses in half portions—and those are usually enough for all but the heartiest eaters.

*Price: About $14 per person*
*Open daily for lunch and dinner*
*Accepts American Express, Visa, and MasterCard*

---

## LE BISTRO
### Bowen's Wharf, Newport
### 401-849-7778

Begun eleven years ago as a tiny restaurant serving French country food, Le Bistro has now grown to the right side of the tracks. In Newport that means a fashionable location on Bowen's Wharf in the heart of tourist country.

But owners John and Mary Philcox haven't forgotten what got them where they are: the freshest ingredients meticulously prepared in an atmosphere of casual elegance. From the local fish to a superb roast duckling in grapefruit and lime, Le Bistro is the best of Newport—and that is very good, indeed.

Lately, the restaurant has taken on Cajun and Creole foods, such as "Cajun popcorn" (shrimp dipped in a spicy batter and deep-fried), and a whopping filé gumbo.

If you're not ready (or your pocketbook is not) for a full meal, Le Bistro has a lovely little hideaway bar on the third floor. There, while enjoying a view of Newport Harbor, you can dine casually on some of the meals from the dining rooms below for about 25 percent less.

*Price: About $22 per person*
*Open daily for lunch and dinner*
*Accepts all major credit cards*

---

## LLOYD'S
### 1060 Hope Street, Providence
**401-831-9242**

If one test of a restaurant is longevity, then Lloyd's is on its way. Begun in 1950 as a deli catering to Brown University students, the restaurant, now in its third incarnation, has become one of the most popular in Providence.

While the menu still lists a superb Reuben—grilled tuna and Swiss—the place now does dinners over mesquite and ribs (from Denmark), along with chicken and fish, keeping Lloyd's hopping from noon to late night.

Owner Eliot Solomon died last year, but his wife Anita and her children and in-laws keep Lloyd's an institution. The desserts are sinful and there is a wide selection of beer from around the globe.

*Price: About $9 per person at dinner*
*Open daily for lunch and dinner (in summer, no Sun. dinner)*
*Accepts all major credit cards*

---

## THE MOORING
### Sayer's Wharf, Newport
**401-846-2260**

In the 1950s, this waterfront restaurant was a favorite of thousands of officer candidates who trained at the Newport Navy Base. Later, it became a scruffy bar. But now that Newport is a stop on the tourist route, the building has metamorphosed into a middle-of-the-road restaurant with a spectacular view of the Newport harbor.

The big thing here is lobster, broiled, boiled, or in a sandwich that is not glopped up with mayonnaise. Mussels done in a wonderfully garlicky broth are super, and there is a seafood pie filled with scallops, crab meat, and lobster. The hamburgers are plain and good.

In summer, the outdoor terrace is the place to eat. In winter, there is a huge fireplace in the dining room.

*Price: About $14 per person*
*Open daily for lunch and dinner*
*Accepts all major credit cards*

# RUE DE L'ESPOIR
## 99 Hope Street, Providence
### 401-751-8890

Known to almost everyone as "The Rue," this quiet, dark hideaway was once on the "wrong" end of Hope Street (hence the name Rue de L'Espoir).

But gentrification has caught up to The Rue, and it's now in the middle of a comeback area. One of Providence's best small theaters, Second Story, has just installed itself half a block away and the town's best ice cream parlor, Big Alice's (see page 704) is across the street.

The Rue presents a casually French menu with lots of other touches. Among their popular dishes are their own creations such as large shrimp baked in a bluefish *mousse*. Marinated grilled lamb steaks in a rosemary-*bordelaise* sauce or a simple filet mignon served with an herb butter make the Rue click, too. Dinners can also be as simple as *crêpes* and *quiches*. The desserts are made on the premises.

The atmosphere is casual. The Italian restaurant across Hope Street doesn't take reservations and its customers often wait for their call in the Rue's bar —an arrangement that makes everyone happy.

*Price: About $20 per person*
*Open Tues.–Sun. for lunch and dinner; closed Mon.*
*Accepts all major credit cards*

# WES' HOUSE OF RIBS
## 38 Dike Street, Olneyville
### 401-421-9090

What's a nice Missouri boy doing in Providence cooking ribs? Very well, thank you. West Brewton opened his ribs place in a hole-in-the-wall, and within a couple of years moved to his present location in a renovated jewelry factory. There Wes' sweet ribs and barbecued pork cooked over wood have the customers flocking in. Nothing fancy here, just good basic—cheap—down-home food.

*Price: About $7 per person*
*Open daily for lunch and dinner*
*No credit cards accepted*

# ST. LOUIS

## *By Joe Pollack*

**AMERICAN**
American Rotisserie
Balaban's
Culpeppers
1847 Restaurant
O'Connell's Pub
Richard Perry
Top of the Riverfront

**BAR**
The Village Bar

**CONTINENTAL**
Al Baker's Restaurant
Anthony's
Café Zoe
Duff's
La Veranda

**DELICATESSEN**
Kopperman's Delicatessen

**ECLECTIC**
Balaban's
Richard Perry

**FAST FOOD**
Amighetti Bakery
Culpeppers

**FRENCH**
Café de France
Chez Louis
Fio's La Fourchette
L'Auberge Bretonne
Posh's at the Park

**GREEK**
Spiro's Restaurant

**HAMBURGERS**
O'Connell's Pub
The Village Bar

**HOTEL DINING ROOM**
Posh's at the Park
Top of the Riverfront

**ICE CREAM**
Crown Candy Kitchen

**ITALIAN**
  Agostino's Colosseum Ristorante
  Agostino's Little Place
  Bar Italia
  Dominic's Restaurant
  Tony's Restaurant

**JAPANESE**
  Sansui

**PANORAMA**
  Top of the Riverfront

**PHILIPPINE**
  Manila Café

**SEAFOOD**
  Broadway Oyster Bar

**STEAKS AND CHOPS**
  Al's
  Dierdorf & Hart's Steak House

**SUBURBAN**
  1847 Restaurant (Hermann)

**THAI**
  King and I Restaurant

The heritage of St. Louis began with its founding by French fur traders in 1764, continued with a period under Spanish rule, and as the Gateway to the West, welcomed nineteenth-century Americans of practically every cultural background as they crossed the Mississippi River. Most moved on, many stayed, and yet the city spent most of the twentieth century as a meat-and-potatoes community, with an occasional desire for pasta.

Odd, perhaps, for a city where Tony Faust's rivaled Delmonico's as a gourmand's delight at the turn of the century, and where a barman at the Planter's Hotel devised the punch that still bears its name.

Odd for a city whose 1904 World's Fair gave legitimate, if disputed, claim to the creation of the ice cream cone and the hot dog roll. But perhaps exhausted by the efforts of mounting the arguably greatest fair in history, St. Louis napped until the Second World War, and its restaurateurs dozed for another decade or so.

The modern era of St. Louis cuisine began with Vince Bommarito and his brother, Anthony, who turned their father's downtown spaghetti house, Tony's, into a landmark Italian restaurant that stretched the local dining experience. More important, the employees they trained moved on to establish their own restaurants, challenging their former bosses, and the Bommaritos climbed even faster to remain a step or two ahead.

Then, in 1972, more than 300 years after Pierre Laclede and Auguste Chouteau came ashore to found the city, the real culinary revival began: the Bommaritos opened Anthony's with lighter fare and French overtones; Herb Balaban started the eclectic and trendy Central West End spot that bears his name; and Richard Perry built the Jefferson Avenue Boarding House, serving old St. Louis recipes that were a precursor to the "American cuisine" movement.

They were followed by dozens of others, who brought with them restaurants of all sizes, shapes, and cooking styles. There are still gaps in the St. Louis dining experience, but they keep shrinking. Elegant restaurants abound, and so do smaller places with a casual air in the dining room but a serious and talented chef in the kitchen.

In short, dining out in St. Louis these days is a pleasure, not a chore.

*Joe Pollack writes about restaurants and wine for the* St. Louis Post-Dispatch, *and has done so since 1972.*

# AGOSTINO'S COLOSSEUM RISTORANTE
## 12949 Olive Boulevard
### 314-434-2959

A long-time landmark on the Hill, St. Louis' Italian neighborhood, Agostino's followed the customers to the environs to serve hearty, rich, Southern Italian cuisine in a large, often-crowded room with a fairly high noise level.

The kitchen has a marvelous touch with sauces and seafood, and an acquaintance once made an entire meal of squid—appetizer, salad, entrée—with sauces and marinades that complemented each other. The red sauce of tomatoes, basil, and garlic was perfect.

Fresh *marinara* sauce, with tomatoes, garlic, and black olives, is outstanding on shrimp, and the combination of green noodles with fresh clams is superior. Rolled beef *spiedini,* with a touch of bread crumbs and more than a touch of garlic, is another favorite.

Filet *alla* John is one of the richest entrées, an aged filet whose sauce features onions, mushrooms, artichoke hearts, and peas.

Desserts are standard, including *cannoli* and a very good bananas Foster. There is a good wine list. Reservations are recommended.

*Price: About $25–$30 per person*
*Open Tues.–Sat. for dinner only; closed Sun. and Mon.*
*Accepts all major credit cards*

# AGOSTINO'S LITTLE PLACE
## 202 Manchester Road
### 314-227-7230

Once upon a time, there was a true Little Place, with seats for about twenty. Now, while the name's the same, the restaurant has moved to the far environs and expanded a lot, but the food remains impressive.

The room is dark and elegant, though the restaurant is tucked into a corner of a shopping center. Service is of highest quality.

*Prosciutto* served with either melon or lemon proves the versatility of that splendid cured ham, and a Northern Italy-style stuffed rice ball is a welcome item in a city whose Italian cuisine is primarily from the South.

Green *linguine* in a Cognac sauce highlights the pasta dishes, and the brandy works well to offer a different piquancy. Another winning sauce involves anchovies, capers, black olives, and mushrooms, and the *pesto* shows a nice balance between basil and garlic.

Among the entrées, the veal chop is tender and flavorful, and veal kidney with a mushroom and Cognac sauce is a nice change, prepared so that the kidney is tender and accepts the rather strong sauce without difficulty. Chicken breast stuffed with herbs and spices, including rosemary and thyme, produces superior flavors.

The wine list is strong in Italian imports but has some excellent California selections as well. Both *cannoli* and *zabaglione* are rich and tasty desserts.

*Price: About $25–$30 per person*
*Open Mon.–Sat. for dinner only; closed Sun.*
*Accepts American Express, Visa, and MasterCard*

---

# AL BAKER'S RESTAURANT
## 8101 Clayton Road
### 314-863-8878

The dining room is large and opulent almost to the point of being gaudy, with a large menu of Italian orientation but with plenty of seafood, steaks, and a couple of Greek items. Owners Al and Mary Baker, much into fitness, have compiled a calorie, vitamin, chemical, and cholesterol breakdown of almost every dish, available to be studied with the menu.

The wine list may be the largest in the area, with bottles representing almost every heritage and every price range.

Lots of tableside finishing, outstanding service, and a continually shifting list of about a dozen fresh seafood entrées. A red wine vinegar and scallion sauce highlights the yellowtail.

Rack of lamb is broiled with Grecian seasoning, veal is prepared in a number of Italian sauces, and steaks are cooked well. A longtime favorite is "hobo beef," sautéed tenderloin slices finished with a Dijon mustard sauce.

The pasta list is extensive, and appetizers include excellent steamed mussels, prepared simply and properly.

*Price: About $25–$30 per person*
*Open Mon.–Sat. for dinner only; closed Sun.*
*Accepts all major credit cards*

# AL'S

1200 North Main Street (*at the corner of First and Biddle streets*)
314-421-6399

North of the riverfront, in a district occupied solely by warehouses, Al's continues to serve outstanding beef and seafood, with Italian overtones. There is no menu: A waiter arrives with a large platter of beef, veal, lamb, and fish, then explains the various types of preparation and sauces, but not the prices, which are quite high.

Still, dinner at Al's is a feast, and it attracts media types and sports personalities whenever they're in town. Service is outstanding, and so is the wine list, but the latter can be confusing, too. I once asked for a brand to go with a listing that said "cabernet sauvignon," and was told, "Oh, we have three or four at that price." Two of them turned out to be from Sterling and Roudon-Smith, both 1978s, which isn't at all bad, but still confusing.

All the steaks are excellent. A filet stuffed with *prosciutto* and *mozzarella* may be gilding the lily, but is splendid. Steaks by themselves, whether filets or sirloins, are exceptional, and the giant veal chop is another winner. Lamb chops also are a good selection.

Pasta is a good side dish, and there are some Italian-style entrées, but basic steaks are the best idea. Reservations are advised.

*Price: About $30–$35 per person*
*Open Tues.–Sat. for dinner only; closed Sun. and Mon.*
*Accepts all major credit cards*

# AMERICAN ROTISSERIE

In the Omni International Hotel,
St. Louis Station, 1820 Market Street
314-241-6664

The brightest jewel in St. Louis' new downtown crown is the renovated Union Station. It took more than $150 million to turn the rotting, late-nineteenth century terminal into a spectacular array of shops and snack bars, highlighted by the Omni Hotel and its elegant, distinguished dining room. The station's Great Hall serves as lobby for the hotel and a stop for a pre-dinner drink as you admire what *New York Times* architecture critic Paul Goldberger recently called "one of the most exuberant pieces of nineteenth-century American architecture ever created."

The Rotisserie restaurant itself, with copper utensils softly gleaming along one wall of the dining room, is done in light wood paneling and a decor respectful of the space's historical integrity.

Service is outstanding, and the menu, which is much in the style of modern American cuisine, covers specialties from much of the nation. An imaginative kitchen staff is deeply committed to serving fresh meats and seafood from the region and from the coasts. Many appetizers are smoked on the premises, and all baking is done there too. Smoked goose breast, lobster *ravioli,* and smoked boar sausage lead the appetizer selection, each manifesting the flavor of origin but deftly improved by the smoking and proper spicing. Soups also are outstanding: The mussel-oyster bisque is exemplary (if not quite warm enough on occasion), and a wild rice and chicken soup is a rich, hearty beginning to a meal. Veal *médaillons* in a mushroom-cream sauce form a glorious entrée, and the poached salmon and fried catfish are both delicious. Roast beef tenderloin with a spiced bean purée and peppered cream sauce may be the best of all the entrées. The prime rib and lamb are also splendid.

There are lots of julienne seasonal vegetables, cooked lightly—some so lightly as to be practically raw. Pastries are brilliant, and the wine list is a first-rate representation of fine California vineyards, with a few good Missouri wines also available. Reservations are necessary and vital on weekends.

*Price: About $25–$30 per person*
*Open daily for lunch and dinner*
*Accepts all major credit cards*

---

# AMIGHETTI BAKERY
## 5141 Wilson Avenue
### 314-776-2855

For many years, Amighetti's Bakery was strictly that, a bakery providing classic Italian-style loaves to the Hill neighborhood and to the area's better restaurants.

The rise of the hero sandwich shifted the emphasis, and while Amighetti's remains a wonderful bakery, it has now encompassed a sandwich shop, a *gelateria,* even a bar. The Amighetti sandwich, stuffed with roast beef, *mortadella,* salami, cheese, tomatoes, and other tasty items, is truly delicious and so popular that a special takeout window has been established for those who drive out from downtown to bring back a load for the office.

Sidewalk tables offer a nice view of the heart of the Hill, an Italian neighborhood for almost a century and home of fire hydrants painted red, white, and green. *Gelato* is rich and flavorful, and the diner never knows who'll wander by during lunch or an afternoon snack.

*Price: Sandwiches under $5*
*Open Mon.–Sat. for lunch and dinner; closed Sun.*
*No credit cards accepted*

# ANTHONY'S
## 10 South Broadway
### 314-231-2434

When Vince and Tony Bommarito decided to expand, in the spring of 1972, they decided on something very different from Tony's—and they got it.

Anthony's is in a big, steel-and-glass building across the street from Busch Stadium, and the interior is smoked glass and chrome, with islands of light for each table.

The menu is wide-ranging, more French than anything else, with an Italian touch here and there. Tony Bommarito runs Anthony's, but the two are close and consult often.

Freshly made soups, light and bright, include a wonderful cucumber bisque and a spectacular vichyssoise. Mussels and *escargots* both arrive in the classic style, with lots of garlic in the sauce and excellent bread for dunking into it.

Watercress complements the spinach salad in a nice style, adding its own flavor.

Calf's liver, lightly cooked and still pink, comes in a fresh tomato sauce. Duck in orange sauce is cooked the way it should be; lamb chops are fork-tender. Beef tenderloin hunter style has a sauce of fresh vegetables and wine. Fresh fruit tarts lead the dessert array.

Service is outstanding, as in both Bommarito establishments, and the wine list is attractive, but on the expensive side.

*Price: About $35–$40 per person*
*Open Mon.–Sat. for dinner only; closed Sun.*
*Accepts Visa and MasterCard*

# BALABAN'S
## 405 North Euclid Avenue
### 314-361-8085

Herb Balaban was one of the leaders in the St. Louis restaurant revolution of 1972 when he opened a casual, eclectic spot among the antique shops and bars of the city's Central West End.

Success led to expansion, but the kitchen failed to keep up and the restaurant leveled off in the second rank. In the last eighteen months, however, both kitchen and dining room have a new feel and a new look, and the restaurant is again among the city's leaders.

Boniface Herb and his red-haired, Texas-born wife, Adelaide, now have a flashy, Art Deco dining room, replete with huge French theatrical posters from the thirties, and a kitchen that emphasizes fresh, seasonal ingredients that are simply, but beautifully, prepared.

Balaban's experiments with the new, the non–Midwestern traditional, like Hudson River shad roe in season or lamb kidneys as an appetizer. Fresh fish, or fish smoked on the premises, is featured, and exotic vegetables are regular items.

Roast duck and beef Wellington have long been menu standards, along with a classic cold cucumber soup, but they now are supplemented by tiny clams, soft-shell crabs, Pacific salmon, sweetbreads, lobsters, and a variety of other items offered on a daily basis. There's a sauce *du jour* for beef *tournedos* or chicken breasts, and preparation is both simple and innovative.

The wine list is large, though rather expensive, with some top California labels.

Balaban's long has represented "trendy" and "in" to a certain class of St. Louisan, which makes it extremely fashionable, and equally noisy, especially on weekends.

The sidewalk café serves all day, every day; the dining room has a special dinner menu, and live entertainment, on Mondays. Reservations accepted only until 7 P.M. and on Mondays.

*Price: About $30–$35 per person*
*Open daily for breakfast, lunch, and dinner*
*Accepts American Express, Visa, and MasterCard*

---

# BAR ITALIA
## 4656 Maryland Avenue
### 314-361-7010

In a city whose Italian tradition includes Joe Garagiola, Yogi Berra, and toasted *ravioli*, this small restaurant in the city's Central West End may be its final example of a *trattoria*.

Opened as a pastry-coffee-*gelato* spot, it soon added a handful of simple dishes, all from recipes of families that emigrated from Italy.

Home-made *tortellini*, light and flavorful, comes with a different sauce every day, and the veal stew, flavored with sausage and served on *polenta*, is simple, yet elegant. Sausage roll, with hard-boiled egg in the middle, is piquant, as are steamed mussels in a garlic-laden broth. *Salsa verde*, heavy on garlic and pine nuts, is good enough to spread on bread.

Pastries are extremely rich, yet not overly sweet, and always different. A fig-and-pine-nut pie was unusual and delicious, and the fruitcake has so much fruit and nuts there's barely room for the cake.

*Gelati,* coffees, wines, aperitifs, and digestives also are authentically Italian, and extremely good. No reservations.

*Price: About $12 per person*
*Open Mon.–Sat. for lunch and dinner; closed Sun.*
*Accepts American Express, Visa, and MasterCard*

---

## BROADWAY OYSTER BAR
### 736 South Broadway
**314-621-9606**

A funky little spot, with a long, narrow bar and a rear dining room with non-matching furniture—and no sign in front—but the best oysters in town and an oyster loaf that rivals anything I've ever eaten.

Oysters are always perfectly fresh, arriving daily from New Orleans, and they're served in a variety of ways. A very hot sauce accompanies the raw ones, which are juicy and tangy from the gulf; the loaf offers sautéed oysters, not fried, but sautéed with lots of butter, garlic, parsley, and Tabasco before being stuffed into a French loaf; oysters Elan involves sautéeing with artichoke hearts in a cream sauce; and the Rockefellers have a piquant topping that is different but outstanding.

Mussels are steamed to order, there's crawfish from time to time, redfish once a week or so, and seviche that's a meal. It's an undistinguished looking place, just off downtown, with loud music at night.

*Price: Oysters $5 a dozen; oyster loaf $4.25; other prices comparable*
*Open daily for lunch and dinner*
*No credit cards accepted*

---

## CAFÉ DE FRANCE
### 410 Olive Street
**314-231-2204**

Marcel Keraval and his brother-in-law, Jean-Claude Guillossou, brought elegant French dining to St. Louis when they opened L'Auberge Bretonne in 1976. Success bred expansion, and Keraval moved into the heart of downtown while Guillossou remained in the original location.

This is *the* lunch spot for the downtown crowd, and an equally sumptuous, highly romantic dinner locale, with high ceilings and cut-glass chandeliers offering a lovely aura of tranquility.

Keraval, who grew up in Normandy (his brother-in-law is from Brittany), is a matchless baker, and his pastry abilities are on display throughout the meal. A salmon *napoleon* appetizer, alternating layers of fresh and smoked salmon in flaky napoleon dough, and his hot quail *pâté en croûte,* are sensational.

An oyster-cucumber casserole is another imaginative, delicious appetizer, and Keraval makes a thick, creamy, chilled tomato bisque, flavored with dill and served with croutons topped with anchovies, and garlic on the side.

Traditional main courses include duckling, either roasted or sautéed, frogs legs in puff pastry, marvelous fresh salmon, stuffed with chicken livers and wrapped in chicory, and sweetbreads with *morels.* Sauces are light and presentation is impressive, with dishes looking as attractive as they taste.

The wine list is wide-ranging, and Keraval's talents shine at dessert time, with a rich chocolate Martinique, dark chocolate in a pastry shell, or a strawberry charlotte russe to complement a series of magnificent *soufflés.* Reservations are advised.

*Price: About $30–$35 per person*
*Open Mon.–Fri. for lunch and dinner; Sat. for dinner only*
*Accepts all major credit cards*

---

# CAFÉ ZOE
## 1923 Park Avenue
### 314-241-9122

It's hard to imagine a restaurant building a reputation on chicken salad, but that's what happened in this remodeled storefront in an area with a lot of rehab work going on.

A very popular lunch spot, with a *nouvelle* touch to items like duck salad with red grapes or Oriental chicken salad, but with superior presentation and excellent food from a small, but nicely varied menu.

Chicken breast is marinated in olive oil and lemon, in the Italian style, then broiled with fresh rosemary for a delicate flavor. *Pesto* sauce, heavy with cream and fresh tomatoes, does wonders for shrimp.

Good, if limited wine list, and excellent desserts, many made by Richard Perry.

*Price: About $12–$15 per person*
*Open Mon.–Sat. for lunch; Fri. and Sat. for dinner; closed Sun.*
*Accepts all major credit cards*

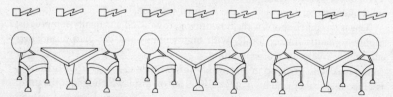

# CHEZ LOUIS
## 26 North Meramec Avenue, Clayton
### 314-863-8400

Bright and cheerful, its walls covered with gallery posters, Chez Louis brings outstanding lunches and dinners to the Clayton area, the county seat of St. Louis County.

One of the best wine lists in the city is here, and good selections are served by the glass.

The menu is fairly classic, with lighter sauces and marvelously rich desserts. Smoked duck makes a first-rate appetizer salad, with fresh endive complementing the smokiness of the fowl. Scallops in lobster sauce are creamy, tender, and smooth.

Most entrées are rather simple, without a lot of *en croûte* service or over-rich sauces, but the sea bass with clams has a memorable flavor, and fresh tuna is brightened by a hearty *béarnaise* sauce. Lamb chops Provençale are nicely garlicked.

Chocolate *gavroche* heads the dessert menu, its dark, dark richness nicely tempered by orange rind, the chocolate sinfully smooth and delightful. Home-made ice creams and a passing dessert cart are other temptations.

Owner Morton Meyer has opened Café Bernard next door, sharing the kitchen and offering less complex fare in a *bistro*-type atmosphere, and he also has plans to renovate the many-gabled building that houses both into an elegant small hotel.

*Price: About $30 per person*
*Open Mon.–Fri. for lunch and dinner; Sat. for dinner only; closed Sun.*
*Accepts all major credit cards*

# CROWN CANDY KITCHEN
## 1401 St. Louis Avenue
### 314-621-9650

Ten minutes north of downtown, one finds a time warp—a real 1930s soda fountain, complete with Coca-Cola signs above it. Counter stools and Formica-topped tables in small booths, glassware of the correct style for ice cream sodas, sundaes, and malts—and they bring the frosted metal shaker to the table.

Opened before the First World War and not redecorated since the Second (though rebuilt after a fire), the Crown attracts downtown businessmen who have a sweet tooth at lunchtime, along with neighborhood people in an eclectic mix.

Candy and ice creams are made on the premises and they are outstanding; strawberry is a June sensation. Sandwiches are available, and they're reminiscent of the old-time luncheonette, too.

*Price: Ice cream dishes under $2*
*Open daily*
*No credit cards accepted*

---

## CULPEPPERS
### 300 North Euclid Avenue
### 314-361-2828

A noisy bar, and a predominant position in the city's trendy, fashionable, and usually interesting Central West End, but the sandwiches and soups are as rewarding as the people-watching, and the kitchen stays open until midnight. The wait for tables is shorter and the noise level much lower in the downstairs dining area.

In the long-ago days of Gaslight Square, Herb Glazier and Sam Deitsch owned the Opera House; Deitsch is now at the Washington Square Bar & Grill in San Francisco; Glazier remained here and his current partner, Mary McCabe, has a touch with soups that makes them the best in town: always two, one cream-based (artichoke the favorite, but also chicken, onion, spinach, and others) and one regular (oxtail, chicken-mushroom, Italian sausage, etc.), with a tangy, splendid *gazpacho* during the summer. Another summer hit is McCabe's seviche, using only bay scallops.

Sandwiches are large and include burgers, but the barbecued pork steaks and the traditional BLT take on new glamor and are outstanding, along with a locally made Polish sausage that is very garlicky and peppery and is served on a sourdough roll. Chicken wings are deservedly popular.

*Price: Sandwiches in the $3.50–$5 range; soups $2.25*
*Open daily for lunch and dinner*
*Accepts all major credit cards*

---

## DIERDORF & HART'S STEAK HOUSE
### 323 West Port Plaza  314-878-1801
### In St. Louis Union Station, 18 and Market streets
### 314-421-1772

Just what one would expect from a pair of retired football stars, Dan Dierdorf and Jim Hart—big, thick steaks nicely served in two large, bustling restaurants, one in a shopping-entertainment center in St. Louis County, the other in the newly renovated and remodeled Union Station, downtown.

The big T-bone has superior flavor, with the grilling quite proper and the beef done as you requested it. Sirloin, even thicker, is rich and hearty, and the lobster tail is exceptionally good, arriving tender and juicy, avoiding the drying-out process that too many restaurants force the dish to endure.

Appetizers are standard, but salads are impressive, with a delicious, nicely flavored Caesar heading the list, and the standard green salad manifesting a nice mix of fresh greens and a good oil and vinegar dressing.

The wine list is proper, too, with plenty of hearty reds available at reasonable prices. Reservations are advised.

*Price: About $30 per person*
*Open daily for lunch and dinner*
*Accepts all major credit cards*

# DOMINIC'S RESTAURANT
## 5101 Wilson Avenue
### 314-771-1632

When Giovanni Galati became a waiter at Tony's, he had a problem. There already was a waiter named John, and one named Giovanni, and house rules, like those of Equity, precluded two waiters with the same name. Giovanni became Dominic.

Some years later, when he opened his own *alta cucina* Italian restaurant, there was no problem—the restaurant became Dominic's, and so it has remained, with his wife, Jackie, as the hostess, and her mother, now retired, cooking up the superb sauces.

With soft lights and elegant service, Dominic's is a lovely place to dine; there is a good deal of tableside finishing, wonderful touches with fresh items, and a lot of love and imagination coming from the kitchen.

Like most St. Louis restaurants, most dishes have Southern Italian overtones, but the shrimp Dijon offers a superior combination of light cream and fresh tomatoes, and the pastas are fresh and cooked to order. Fresh mussels are a splendid addition to green noodles, and a salmon-curry sauce improves *fettuccine.*

Dominic's has a wide choice of entrées, with seafood, veal, beef, and chicken. The chicken breast with fresh fruit and champagne sauce is deservedly one of the most popular dishes. Capers give a nice piquancy to veal, and the classic *piccata,* with lemon and wine, shows sauce-making at its finest.

The wine list is extensive. For diners seeking classic cuisine in the largely

Italian Hill neighborhood, Dominic's leads the pack. Reservations are advised.

*Price: About $30 per person*
*Open Tues.–Sat. for dinner only; closed Sun. and Mon.*
*Accepts all major credit cards*

---

# DUFF'S
## 392 North Euclid Avenue
### 314-361-0522

Perhaps the best value for the dining dollar in St. Louis is Duff's, offering a roomful of mix-and-match furniture and a casual aura occasionally reminiscent of the sixties.

In the kitchen, however, there is real talent, and the wine list is superior, at moderate prices.

The menu changes bi-monthly, with about half of the eight entrées changing each time to fit the season. Two of the almost-permanent fixtures are chicken Marsala, in a creamy, rich sauce heavy with fresh mushrooms, served on buttered noodles, and the pepper steak, a sirloin heavily encrusted with black pepper, perfectly cooked inside.

*Caponata,* chilled eggplant marinated and blended with onions, capers, and pine nuts, is a rich appetizer, and the barbecued shrimp, in a New Orleans-type hot sauce, is a winner.

There's always a fresh fish entrée, such as bluefish broiled and topped with a delicate smoked salmon butter, and chicken *saltimbocca* is covered with sharp *prosciutto* and a touch of sage.

The wine list is enhanced with some monthly bargains, and glorious pies lead the dessert choices.

*Price: About $12–$15 per person*
*Open Tues.–Sun. for lunch and dinner; closed Mon.*
*Accepts all major credit cards*

---

# 1847 RESTAURANT
## At Stone Hill Winery, Hermann
### 314-486-3479

Less than two hours southwest of St. Louis, on the grounds of the Stone Hill Winery, the 1847 Restaurant commemorates the founding of the Missouri wine industry, a rebounding factor in the state's economy. The region was settled by Germans, who found the Missouri River reminiscent of the Rhine, and the area still has a strong German flavor.

Stone Hill is one of the state's top wineries, and the property is an historic site. The restaurant, in a remodeled barn, offers traditional American fare with some wonderful touches, including a selection of homemade *pâtés* that are extremely impressive, both the smooth *terrines* or the rough country style.

Steaks and chops are excellent, and the kitchen does some superb things with local fowl and fish, often smoked on the premises.

Vegetables often come from the immediate area, and the fresh breads and pastries, baked there, give an almost French touch to American country cooking.

Local wines are featured: Stone Hill makes a dark, hearty, rich red called Norton with a taste like a cabernet or zinfandel, and the Vidal is a light, brisk white wine, similar to a light Chardonnay. Good sparkling wines, too.

Hermann is about a 90-minute drive from St. Louis, and allows visits to other wineries in the area. Between Hermann and St. Louis is Augusta, home of the state's top producer of white wines, Mount Pleasant Winery. Reservations are vital on weekends.

*Price: About $20 per person*
*Open daily for lunch and dinner*
*Accepts all major credit cards*

---

# FIO'S LA FOURCHETTE

1013 South Brentwood Blvd. (*on the west side of the Galleria, formerly Westroads Shopping Center*)

### 314-863-6866

Those who take a condescending air toward restaurants in shopping centers have a different attitude after they sample the French cuisine at Fio's, a relative newcomer that has made a major impact.

Swiss-born and trained, Fio Antognini is the chef; his wife, Lisa, is out front in the softly lighted, quiet restaurant where the cuisine is a happy blend of classic and *nouvelle*.

Fio's offers a four-course dinner with less than 750 calories, and a tasting menu of six courses, plus *à la carte* selections, and everything can be mixed or matched. The wine list is excellent, if slightly expensive.

Like so many good restaurants these days, Fio's takes advantage of seasonal availability, which sometimes means Belon oysters, other times Missouri trout or Alaskan salmon.

*Pâtés* are made on the premises, and the veal-pistachio combination is one of the best. Another fine appetizer involves brandied veal *mousse* and Brie, baked in puff pastry for an elegant, smooth flavor.

Grilled sweetbreads with leeks, their flavors merging perfectly, are a favorite entrée on the low-cal menu, with richer dishes including a perfectly roasted duck with fennel and rosemary, a tender, delicious tenderloin stuffed with Roquefort, and veal *médaillons* in a sauce of mushrooms, brandy, and cream.

Classic *soufflés* head the dessert list, and are prepared in classic style, hot and steamy with a rich interior. The day's pastries can be as simple as a pear tart, as complex as a *gâteau*. Ice cream and sherbets are also homemade. Reservations are advised.

*Price: About $30–$35 per person*
*Open Mon.–Sat. for dinner only; closed Sun.*
*Accepts all major credit cards*

---

# KING AND I RESTAURANT
## 3226 South Grand Boulevard
### 314-771-1777

The fiery cuisine of Southeast Asia is nicely prepared at this small, informal spot, but watch out for the peppers.

Thai specialties include noodles with soy sauce, pork in curry and peanut sauce, stir-fried chicken with ginger and wood ear mushrooms, curried beef, and shrimp curry soup with lemon grass. All are excellent.

Cold dishes, even more fiery, are led by a tender, burning squid and beef broiled with chili powder and lime juice in which the contrasting flavors blend nicely.

Chinese items, both mild and hot, are also available.

*Price: About $12 per person*
*Open Tues.–Fri. for lunch and dinner; Sat. and Sun. for dinner only; closed Mon.*
*Accepts all major credit cards*

---

# KOPPERMAN'S DELICATESSEN
## 386 North Euclid Avenue
### 314-361-0100

Part grocery store, part delicatessen, Kopperman's is the sort of place where the prospective diner can check the display cases before reading the menu. In a city where no one really has the hang of New York–style pastrami, this is the closest version. Sandwiches are large and generally excellent, barbecued ribs wonderfully tangy, and the chicken soup rich and hearty. The feel is casual, and there's sidewalk seating with a nice passing parade on pleasant days. No reservations are accepted.

*Price: Sandwiches in the $4–$5 range; entrées slightly higher*
*Open daily*
*Accepts all major credit cards*

---

# L'AUBERGE BRETONNE
## 10411 Clayton Road
### 314-993-8890

Jean-Claude Guillossou left the security of a plush country club to open a haute cuisine French restaurant, bringing his brother-in-law from Omaha to work with him. Marcel Keraval subsequently moved downtown and Guillossou took larger suburban quarters, across the road from the fancy shopping center that houses Saks and Neiman-Marcus.

Cuisine is more *nouvelle* than classic these days, with many fruit-based sauces, but the kitchen turns out superior meals from start to finish.

Sautéed duck liver, in a tangy pepper sauce, is a tasty and piquant appetizer, and the *pâtés* include a combination of duck and sweetbreads that blend beautifully in texture and flavor. Salmon sausage, served cold, has a hint of dill, and the cucumber soup is light and smooth.

Rack of lamb and *chateaubriand,* each served for two, are impressively carved at tableside, and the lamb is redolent with rosemary and other fresh herbs.

Raspberry vinegar sets off fresh calf's liver in impressive style, and grapes and pears are served with the sweetbreads. Salmon with sorrel sauce comes in a flaky puff pastry, with excellent results.

The wine list is large. The noise level occasionally is bothersome. Desserts include elegant *soufflés* and a collection of pastries, with outstanding fruit tarts. Reservations are advised.

*Price: About $30–$35 per person*
*Open Mon.–Fri. for lunch and dinner; Sat. for dinner only; closed Sun.*
*Accepts all major credit cards*

---

# LA VERANDA
## 607 North Lindbergh Boulevard
### 314-997-7118

La Phoenix may be a better name, considering the adventures of owner-chef David Slay, a young man of considerable talent. He first opened three years ago, remodeling a fast-food spot, and was a great success. He then moved to larger and more expensive quarters, found it more than he could handle, and returned to the smaller, less-formal location. Now he's moved and expanded once more.

Slay, whose family has been in the restaurant business here since before the First World War, serves a very thin, tomato-less, light, crisp pizza as an appetizer, then features delicately grilled fresh fish, veal, and beef, plus some pasta dishes that boast delicate, imaginative sauces.

Mussels in a tangy pepper-and-tomato sauce are excellent, and bow-tie pasta with a Gorgonzola cheese sauce is a delight.

Breads and desserts are baked on the premises, the latter highlighted by a *zabaglione* creation that is poured onto a plate, then slipped under the broiler just long enough for a light browning and a little thickening. After that, it's topped with fresh fruit.

The wine list is modest, but adequate, and service is relaxed but effective.

*Price: About $15–$20 per person*
*Open daily for breakfast, lunch, and dinner*
*Accepts all major credit cards*

---

# MANILA CAFÉ
## 2650 Cherokee Street
### 314-772-3184

The city's only outpost for Filipino cooking is a small, spotless place on the South Side that is part grocery store. The cuisine is tangy, with considerable ginger and garlic, and everything is freshly cooked.

*Lumpia* is similar to egg roll, but the *lumpia de Manila* is a monster shrimp, wrapped with meat and vegetables and then a light batter. Outstanding pork *adobo* involves vinegar, soy, and bay leaves, and pork *Afritada* is braised with fresh vegetables.

Bean thread noodles and rice stick noodles, in a variety of meat or vegetarian sauces, are a popular side dish, and the chicken curry has a lovely tang, moderated by the use of coconut milk. No liquor license.

*Price: About $10 per person*
*Open Mon.–Sat. for lunch and dinner; closed Sun.*
*Accepts all major credit cards*

# O'CONNELL'S PUB

### 4652 Shaw Avenue (*at Kingshighway*)
### 314-773-6600

No one in the area—and maybe not in the nation—matches O'Connell's for hamburgers. They're huge, fat, juicy, grilled over charcoal, and served on toasted buns by the speediest, most efficient waitresses in town. For those reasons, it attracts the most wide-ranging mix of customers for lunch. The evening crowd is younger.

Roast beef, served in huge amounts on French bread, is surprisingly good, and Italian sausage with grilled green peppers is also a winner. French fries are fresh and all that's needed, except for possibly a glass of draft beer or ale, with both Guinness and Watney's available on draft. No reservations are accepted.

*Price: Hamburgers about $3*
*Open Mon.–Sat. for lunch and dinner; closed Sun.*
*No credit cards accepted*

---

# POSH'S AT THE PARK

### In the Park Terrace Airport Hilton Hotel, 10330 Natural Bridge
### 314-426-5500

A very elegant restaurant, and an excellent one, in a newly remodeled hotel just across the road from the airport. Far and away the best hotel dining room in the area, and one of the best dining rooms, period.

The cuisine is very *nouvelle*, with lots of lightly cooked vegetables and light sauces, but the presentation and preparation are exquisite. It's the only dining room in town that makes not only its own pastries, but also its own chocolates.

The *feuilletée* of snails in garlic cream sauce is outstanding, and a lobster *pâté* is delicate enough to melt in the mouth, with the full flavor of the lobster coming through. Duck *consommé* has a light hint of ginger that makes it special, and the lobster bisque is rich and hearty.

An orange sauce emphasizes lamb in elegant style, the lamb tender and perfectly prepared, and a wild mushroom compote accompanies delicious duck in port wine sauce, prepared on the rare side. *Morels* in a cream sauce make the ideal complement for a hearty, well-prepared beef tenderloin.

The wine list is large and expensive, but includes some superior bottles.

Chocolate *mousse* and Grand Marnier *soufflé* lead the traditional desserts in classic style, the former very dark, slightly grainy in the very best sense, the latter cooked to the perfect moment, rich, sweet, and light. Raspberry *napoleon,* with fresh fruit, is another charmer. Reservations are recommended.

*Price: About $40 per person*
*Open daily for dinner only*
*Accepts all major credit cards*

---

# RICHARD PERRY
## 3265 South Jefferson Avenue
### 314-771-4100

Richard Perry brought the New American Cuisine to St. Louis and was, perhaps, a national pioneer when he opened the Jefferson Avenue Boarding House in 1972, featuring five-course, no-choice meals based on old St. Louis recipes, served in boardinghouse style.

As times changed, so did the menu and, eventually, the name of the restaurant. Today, the renovated three-story building (Perry lives on the top floor) is the site of the exceptional meals, with the baking and smoking done on the premises and a wine list that is the city's best in terms of American offerings.

The cuisine is modern American, with French *nouvelle* overtones, with an elegant air and impeccable presentation. Smoked scallops, delicate and delicious, are a splendid appetizer, and Perry's seafood sausage is exceptional. *Pâtés* vary from season to season but are always excellent, and tomato pasta with crab meat sauce is deservedly popular.

Poached salmon with sorrel sauce is one of the many fresh seafood entrées from a menu that includes many lighter offerings based on veal or chicken, complemented with fresh vegetables and two or three different home-baked breads.

Desserts are special—fruit tarts, unusual pies, and a triple chocolate cake that is not only special, but sinful.

*Price: About $30 per person*
*Open Sun.–Fri. for lunch and dinner; open Sat. for dinner only*
*Accepts all major credit cards*

---

# SANSUI
## 4949 West Pine Boulevard
### 314-367-2020

For the hungry diner in real need of a *sushi* fix, Sansui has an excellent selection and a talented chef. Variety depends, but the selection is always adequate, sometimes extremely impressive, with everything fresh and then prepared in elegant style. The other Japanese dishes in the light-wood restaurant are adequate, but they don't reach the quality of the *sushi*.

*Price: About $10 for a large appetizer; a full meal will double or triple that*
*Open Mon.–Sat. for lunch and dinner; closed Sun.*
*Accepts all major credit cards*

## SPIRO'S RESTAURANT
### 3122 Watson Road
### 314-645-8383

When Larry Karagiannis earned a master's degree in history at the University of Missouri–St. Louis, he hoped to teach, but no jobs were available. So he opened a small Greek restaurant across the street from the campus—and now has three Greek restaurants in the area.

The Watson Road location is my favorite, mainly because Larry is there, and he prepares some of the best steak tartare I've ever sampled, using only a chef's knife. The result is sensational, even though it isn't Greek, but his treatment gives the meat a texture a grinder never can.

The Greek dishes, such as *moussaka, pastichio* and *dolmades,* are excellent, and some specialities—like pan-fried smelts and a combination of pan-fried liver and sweetbreads—are exceptional.

Lamb chops and various shish kebab combinations are nicely marinated. The *saganaki* appetizer gets the meal off to a proper start.

Desserts are standard, but admirably prepared, with delicate, very rich *baklava* heading the list.

*Price: About $15–$20 per person*
*Open Mon.–Fri. for lunch and dinner; open Sat. and Sun. for dinner only*
*Accepts American Express, Visa, and MasterCard*

## TONY'S RESTAURANT
### 826 North Broadway
### 314-231-7007

Tony's is the benchmark by which St. Louis restaurants are measured, and have been for more than 25 years. From the outside it is little more than a plain brick building on the edge of downtown, across the street from a bus station. But St. Louisans beat a path to its front door, then wait patiently, because owner Vince Bommarito will not take reservations.

Service is stylish and impeccable, occasionally errs on the side of being cloying, but Bommarito's various traffic and kitchen systems work perfectly and without confusion. Newcomers are fascinated when the captain leads a party upstairs by climbing backwards.

It's a rare occasion when Bommarito is not on hand himself, and few owners take more pride in their establishments. Tours of the kitchen are offered, and the journey is a marvelous experience. He also is an expert at orchestrating a meal, starting with the type of entrée and building appetizers, pasta, and side dishes around it for the best complement of color, texture, flavor, and richness.

Bommarito changed the face of Italian fare for St. Louisans. His innovations include fresh fish and vegetables, wonderful gimmicks like fresh figs instead of melon with *prosciutto,* new dishes like a giant veal chop that have been copied all over town.

The fare is original and ever-changing; *antipasto* items vary from day to day. But simple seafood dishes and perfectly aged beef are complemented by superb pastas. For something different, try the fried potatoes cooked in olive oil with onions and black olives.

The wine list is extensive, strong in Italians but with fine French and California and the best of the Missouri wines, too, like the Seyval Blanc from Mount Pleasant Winery in nearby Augusta. No reservations are accepted.

*Price: About $35 per person*
*Open Tues.–Sat. for dinner only; closed Sun. and Mon.*
*Accepts Visa and MasterCard*

---

## TOP OF THE RIVERFRONT
### In the Clarion Hotel, 200 South 4 Street
#### 314-241-3191

This rooftop, revolving restaurant provides some of the finest views of St. Louis, including the Arch, the Mississippi River, the fast-changing downtown, Busch Stadium, and the Anheuser-Busch brewery.

But unlike many restaurants where the scenery is all and food nothing, the meals at the Top of the Riverfront range from good to very good, making it an ideal spot for a visitor who wants a good look at the city.

The menu is wide-ranging American, including beef, chicken, lamb, and a handful of seafood items. The broiled shrimp dusted with sunflower seeds is unusual and quite good, and the duck with garlic, honey, and thyme is a winner. Basic steaks are nicely prepared, the chicken *galantine* makes an impressive appetizer, and a rolling wine cart, with samples, is an easy way to check labels before ordering. Not a great selection, but adequate.

*Price: About $25 per person*
*Open daily for lunch and dinner*
*Accepts all major credit cards*

# THE VILLAGE BAR

## 12247 Manchester Boulevard
### 314-821-4532

Three television screens and a shuffleboard alley attract the sports fans, but the flat-grill hamburgers (as opposed to charcoal broiled) are worth the journey to the suburbs. Besides, it's rare to see a suburban bar with a city look—no ferns, no macramé. Burgers are fresh, perfectly cooked, and delicious. The Village batters its own onion rings and mushrooms, and changes oil often, to produce those dishes in a wonderful, old-fashioned style, where the flavor of the vegetable remains pre-eminent. Other sandwiches are served, too. There's an honor system whereby customers keep their own tabs during lunch.

*Prices: Hamburgers about $2*
*Open daily for lunch and dinner*
*No credit cards accepted*

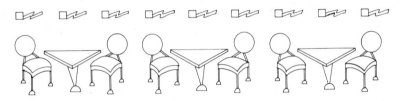

# SALT LAKE CITY

## *By Donna Lou Morgan*

**AMERICAN**
Rustlers Lodge
Tokyo Joe's

**BREAKFAST**
Bill & Nadas Café

**BRUNCH**
Grill

**CHINESE**
Fong Ling Restaurant

**CONTINENTAL**
Bird's Café
Café Mariposa at Silver
Lake/Huggery
Glitretind Gourmet Room
Lamb's Grill
Le Parisien
Liaison Restaurant
Metro Café
Millcreek Inn

**DELICATESSEN**
Marianne's Delicatessen
Siegfried's Delicatessen
The Uppercrust

**FRENCH**
La Caille at Quail Run
Le Parisien

**GERMAN**
Finn's Restaurant
Marianne's Delicatessen
Siegfried's Delicatessen

**HAMBURGERS/HOT DOGS**
Hires Drive-In

**HOTEL DINING ROOM**
Grill
Little America Restaurant
Roof Restaurant

**ITALIAN**
Confetti Ristorante
Nino's Restaurant

**JAPANESE**
Kyoto Restaurant
Mikado

**MEXICAN**
Keyhole Mexican Restaurant
Rio Grande Café

**SEAFOOD**
Market Street Broiler
Market Street Grill
Oceans Restaurant and Oyster
Café

**SOUL FOOD**
Taylor Café

**SPANISH**
La Frontera Café

**STEAKS AND CHOPS**
Rustlers Lodge
The Steak Pit

**SUBURBAN**
Café Mariposa at Silver
Lake/Huggery (Park City)
Glitretind Gourmet Room
(Park City)
Keyhole Mexican Restaurant
(Snowbird)
Millcreek Inn (Millcreek
Canyon)
Rustlers Lodge (Alta Ski resort)
Tokyo Joe's (Park City)

**VEGETARIAN**
R. J. Wheatfields Restaurant
and Bakery

**VIETNAMESE**
The Orient

S alt Lake City has come a long way from what it was in 1847 when Brigham Young and the band of Mormon followers came upon the valley. Then it was nothing more than a stark, intimidating desert wilderness, but the city has now blossomed into an industrial and tourist center. It is the cuisine capital of the area.

This city has an extraordinary past and an unusual present. It was settled by orderly and industrious Mormons. The influence of these members of the Church of Jesus Christ of Latter-Day Saints is still strongly felt, although there are a vast number of non-members living in the area.

Changes have taken place on the restaurant scene. More and more restaurateurs have staked out claims. There are now fine Italian, French, German, Spanish, Oriental, Continental/International, Vietnamese, Thai, New American, and others dotting the valley.

Although Mormon religious prohibitions against alcohol once discouraged investment in grand cafés or exclusive eating establishments, this is no longer the case. Liquor by the drink is still prohibited, but most restaurants now have liquor stores on the premises where mini-bottles and fine wine may be purchased. There has been a steady increase in restaurants, private clubs (where liquor by the drink may be served), and entertainment facilities—all aimed toward excellence.

The environs also bring excellent eating pleasures via delightful restaurants in posh ski areas offering not only fine food but fantastic scenery. These are a must for visitors to the area.

Many good family-type eating establishments can be found in Salt Lake City. Steak-and-potato cafés are on the decline. Most hotel restaurants have exceptionally fine food, which was not the case a few years ago. Most are moderately priced.

The majority of restaurants in Salt Lake City offer lunch and dinner; some breakfast. Many have Sunday brunch. Reservations are recommended. As for dress, jackets with ties are in order for men in the finer restaurants; for women, dresses or pantsuits are acceptable.

A certain undefinable, affable spirit pervades Utah country, and it reaches into friendly, courteous service most often encountered in Salt Lake City restaurants.

*Donna Lou Morgan is food editor of* The Salt Lake Tribune.

## BILL & NADAS CAFÉ
### 479 South 600 East
#### 801-364-7166

You're in a peacock blue "Olds" cruising—looking for a tiptop breakfast stop. Bill & Nadas could be just what you're after. How about bacon and eggs, pancakes, and waffles? Or how about brains and eggs or baked stuffed veal heart? Maybe just milk toast. The jukebox will play the right background music while you enjoy this fine food. The special is waffles with two eggs for just $1.30. Many say they serve the best coffee in town. Don't miss this experience.

*Price: About $3.35 to $3.55 for breakfast specialties*
*Open 24 hours a day*
*Accepts all major credit cards*

# BIRD'S CAFÉ
## 59 East 1700 South
### 801-466-1051

An intimate grill atmosphere, San Francisco-style, is featured at chef-owner Dennis Bird's upbeat restaurant, where the finest of fresh fish, pasta dishes, and Continental specialties are served at lunch and dinner. A chalkboard menu that changes daily presents such items as scallops *au gratin* and grilled lamb chops, with a blue-plate special offered daily. Dark wood emphasized by brass gives an elegant setting for this very fine restaurant. Liquor store on premises. Reservations are recommended.

*Price: About $14.50 per person*
*Open Tues.–Sat. for lunch and dinner; closed Sun. and Mon.*
*Accepts all major credit cards*

# THE CAFÉ MARIPOSA AT SILVER LAKE
## The Huggery, Deer Valley, Park City
### 801-649-1005

"Eclectic" rather than traditional seems best to sum up the fare at Mariposa (by winter) and The Huggery (by summer). A pleasant 45-minute drive from Salt Lake takes you to this wonderful spot, located in one of the most famous ski areas in the world. You'll know it's worth the trip when you see the excellent, diversified menu offered by Chef Franklin Biggs, who has remarkable kitchen skill. The establishment has freshness as its cornerstone, with choice cuts of meat, the finest fish and seafood, duck, game, and poultry. During the summer months, cocktails and hors d'oeuvres are served on the deck beginning at 5 p.m. each evening. The rustic elegance balances ageless antiques with the beauties of today, including fresh wild flowers picked on the mountainside. Don't miss the king salmon served with Oriental black bean sauce. For a sweet finale, enjoy nectarine ice cream with caramel sauce. The excellent food and awesome view make you know the trip is well worth it. Liquor store on premises. Reservations are recommended.

*Price: About $25–$30 per person*
*Open Tues.–Sat. for dinner only; closed Sun. and Mon.*
*Accepts all major credit cards*

# CONFETTI RISTORANTE
## 147 East South Temple
### 801-355-5392

Perhaps the finest food in Salt Lake City is served in this classy restaurant. A very extensive menu covers an enormous range of Italian dishes, including colorful *antipasto,* homemade pasta—*cannelloni, tortellini, capellini*—all enriched with superb sauces. Pasta standouts are the *tagliatelle* and *fettuccine all' Alfredo,* both prepared at the table with flair. Veal Marsala and *piccata* are both excellent. Don't miss the grilled fresh fish, meat, and poultry specialties. Enjoy a wide range of elegant desserts. Black tie to tennis shoes are welcome. Lots of back-patting warmth, coziness, and—occasionally—noise. The kitchen goes easy on oil and tomatoes, but not on garlic. Validated parking. Liquor store on premises. Reservations are recommended.

*Price: About $15 per person*
*Open Mon.–Sat. for lunch and dinner; closed Sun.*
*Accepts all major credit cards*

# FINN'S RESTAURANT
## 2675 Parley's Way
### 801-466-4682

This intimate suburban restaurant is a gathering place for hearty souls who enjoy *sauerbraten* with fried cabbage, *bratwurst, Wiener Schnitzel,* and a wide array of German specialties. Black and white breads are savored by guests along with pastries made daily at the restaurant. Locals who know Germany swear this is "absolutely authentic." The menu offers seven appetizers, ten European entrées, eight specialties from the broiler, and four desserts. Large portions of everything. Liquor store on premises. Reservations are recommended.

*Price: About $13.95–$20.95 per person*
*Open Tues.–Sat. for dinner only; closed Sun. and Mon.*
*Accepts all major credit cards*

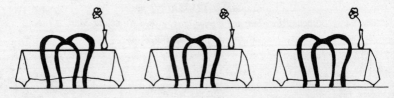

# FONG LING RESTAURANT
## 3698 East 7000 South
### 801-943-8199

Chinese chefs trained by masters of Oriental cooking present exquisite Cantonese and Mandarin dishes, with dozens of specialty items and delicacies. Seafood of all types is presented in the most artistic and tempting ways in an authentic, tranquil atmosphere. Service is unsurpassed. Specialties include sweet-and-sour yellow fish, prawns in spicy sauce, and steamed chicken with green onion sauce. A wide menu, but be sure to order "pot stickers" (fried dumplings) as an appetizer or the *pu-pu* tray of palate pleasers to whet any appetite. Waiting for a table is usually short time, but reservations are accepted.

*Price: About $10 per person*
*Open Mon.–Fri. for lunch and dinner; Sat. and Sun. from 2:30 P.M.*
*Accepts all major credit cards*

# GLITRETIND GOURMET ROOM
## In Stein Eriksen Lodge, Park City
### 801-649-3700

This elegant, traditional Norwegian mountain lodge presents a spectacular view of snow-capped mountains. Enjoy the roaring fireplace that makes for a cozy atmosphere in the candlelit dining area. By summer, enjoy the cool comfort of the clear mountain air. To complement the beauty of the ski area, the dining room offers superb food to appeal to every palate. Specialties include rack of lamb, steak, lobster, and a tempting array of fancy desserts. Enjoy these in this spectacular mountain setting, about 45 minutes from downtown. Liquor store on premises. Reservations are recommended.

*Price: About $15–$20 per person*
*Open Mon.–Fri. for lunch and dinner; Sat. and Sun. for dinner only*
*Accepts all major credit cards*

# GRILL
## In the Westin Hotel Utah, South Temple at Main Street
### 801-531-1000

Linen-topped tables gleam against chafing dishes and trays, centered with armful-sized bouquets of fresh flowers as an army of chefs stand at their posts assisting brunch diners. Seated in comfortable upholstered chairs placed on thick carpeting, customers relax as the warm wood paneling comforts the eye. A pianist plays soothing music during the brunch. For comfort, variety, and quantity, the Grill rates high. It has not sacrificed quality for quantity. All dishes are well prepared and some, such as the pastries, are outstanding. A variety of breads, *croissants,* and hard and sweet rolls tempt the diner. Reservations are recommended.

*Price: Brunch $11.95 per person; other meals $1.95–$11.95*
*Open daily for breakfast, lunch, and dinner*
*Accepts all major credit cards*

---

## HIRES DRIVE-IN
### 425 South 700 East
**801-364-4582**

Salt Lake hamburger lovers have been driving to this spot for a quarter of a century to purchase what they feel to be the finest hamburger this side of heaven. This is the home of the sensational "Big H Sandwich"—fine quality freshly ground beef with lettuce, tomatoes, and cheese on a sourdough bun. A memorable experience when eaten with a Hires root beer.

*Price: $1.35 to $1.55 per person (for hamburgers)*
*Open Mon.–Sat. for lunch and dinner; closed Sun.*
*No credit cards accepted*

---

## KEYHOLE MEXICAN RESTAURANT
### In the Cliff Club at Snowbird Ski Resort
**801-521-6040**

It's worth the 45-minute trip from town to enjoy the beautiful mountains in summer or winter while savoring some of the finest Mexican cuisine in the area. While you watch skiers schuss down the runs, munch on *nachos* and other appetizers while the chef prepares *enchilada del Mar,* trout *chorizo, chilies rellenos,* and excellent combination dishes. Don't miss the spectacular beef *tostados* with shredded beef, chopped onions, mounds of shredded lettuce, and mellow cheese atop crispy *tortillas.* Tasteful, simple Mexican decor. Because this is a private club, alcoholic drinks are served. Reservations are recommended.

*Price: About $10 per person*
*Open Mon.–Sat. for dinner only; closed Sun.*
*Accepts all major credit cards*

# KYOTO RESTAURANT
## 1080 East 1300 South
### 801-487-3525

Exquisite Japanese cuisine in a beautiful setting brings to diners centuries-old Japanese dishes served from the upbeat kitchen by Japanese chefs trained expertly in the art. Specialties include salmon *teriyaki* and tuna *sashimi*. The menu is not very expansive, but every item is carefully prepared and served with an eye to detail. This small eatery features prompt and courteous service and an atmosphere that is relatively authentic. The food, however, is totally authentic. Check the handwritten sign headlined "Today's Fish." Tuna *teriyaki*, broiled mackerel, and mild-tasting butterfish are likely candidates. There's also a beautifully flavored chicken *teriyaki*. Don't be tempted by *tempura*, as it's greasy and often too heavily battered. There's a new *sushi* bar in the restaurant. No liquor store on premises. Reservations are recommended.

*Price: Under $10 per person*
*Open Tues.–Fri. for lunch and dinner; Sat. for dinner only; closed Sun. and*
*Mon.*
*Accepts all major credit cards*

# LA CAILLE AT QUAIL RUN
## 9565 Wasatch Boulevard
### 801-942-1751

A replica of an eighteenth-century French château houses this country restaurant where fine dining is featured. Guests look out over the formal gardens of the estate while enjoying the rustic beauty of the dining room. Dinner specialties include lobster, duck *de la saison*, veal, and rack of lamb. Sunday evening they serve Basque cuisine at its finest. Eggs Benedict and salmon are Sunday brunch favorites. Service is excellent. Valet parking. Liquor store on premises. Reservations are recommended.

*Price: Sunday brunch, $13.50 per person (10 A.M.–1 P.M.); Basque dinner, $15*
*per person (6 P.M.–9 P.M.); dinner, $18–$28 per person (6 P.M.–9 P.M.)*
*Open Mon.–Sat. for dinner only; Sun. for brunch and dinner*
*Accepts all major credit cards*

# LA FRONTERA CAFÉ
## 1236 West 400 South
### 801-532-3158

Enjoy smothered *burritos* with cheese or the large combination plate along with other unique and tempting Mexican specialties in an atmosphere of Old Mexico. Don't forget to try the homemade *salsa* for a tastebud warmer. *Huevos rancheros, chorizo con huevos, enchiladas, tacos, burritos,* and other South-of-the border specialties are all recommended. Liquor store on premises. Reservations are not accepted.

*Prices: About $4–$6 per person*
*Open daily for breakfast, lunch, and dinner*
*No credit cards accepted*

---

# LAMB'S GRILL
## 169 South Main Street
### 801-364-7166

You'll feel like a pampered guest at this fine restaurant located in the heart of Salt Lake City, noted for its quality and service. Breakfast specialties range from the usual bacon and eggs to trout and snapper. Lamb shanks, braised sirloin tips, and corned beef and cabbage rate high with diners. Soups are some of the finest in town. Liquor store on premises. No reservations necessary.

*Price: About $11 per person*
*Open Mon.–Sat. for lunch and dinner*
*Accepts all major credit cards*

---

# LE PARISIEN
## 417 South 300 East
### 801-364-5223

This charming *bistro* in the heart of Salt Lake City offers a creative menu specializing in French and Italian cuisine at their best. The rustic French setting gives way to specialties such as *quiche Lorraine* and exquisitely prepared Dover sole. The *lasagne* is considered to be best in town. Liquor store on premises. No reservations required.

*Price: About $7–$15 per person*
*Open Mon.–Fri. for lunch and dinner; Sat. for dinner only; closed Sun.*
*Accepts all major credit cards*

# LIAISON RESTAURANT
## 1352 South 2100 East
### 801-583-8144

In many ways, Liaison resembles an intimate New York *bistro;* the elegantly decorated restaurant can serve only 34 guests at a time, and the excellent menu selections have a smack of goodness reminiscent of the best in the Big Apple. Chef-owner A.H. "Bub" Horne received his training in New York and has skillfully adapted the menu to appeal to a sophisticated local palate. The creative and flexible menu includes top-quality meats, with the freshest seafood and poultry topped with contemporary or classical garnishes and sauces. Don't miss the wide variety of appetizers and pastries made daily on the premises. Soups are of the finest quality. Veal stir-fry is a favorite entrée. And the Double Chestnut Chocolate Cake seems to please everybody. The Sunday brunch is of superb quality. Reservations are recommended.

*Price: About $15–$20 per person*
*Open Mon.–Fri. for lunch and dinner; Sat. for dinner only; Sun. for brunch*
*Accepts all major credit cards*

# LITTLE AMERICA RESTAURANT
## In the Little America Hotel, 500 South Main Street
### 801-363-6781

Enjoy the candlelit atmosphere in the spacious, but intimate dining room of Little America. The johnny-on-the-spot service by hospitable, efficient waiters and waitresses makes the delicious and authentic Continental cuisine even better. Specialties include filet mignon, lobster tail, prime rib, pepper steak, lamb chops, baked salmon, and other seafood specialties. Liquor store on premises. Reservations are recommended.

*Price: About $15–$18.95 per person*
*Open daily for lunch and dinner*
*Accepts all major credit cards*

# MARIANNE'S DELICATESSEN
## 149 West 200 South
### 801-364-0513

Spend an afternoon in "old Germany" at this deli where German specialties are featured along with general delicatessen items. Enjoy tempting *Rouladen, sauerbraten,* and *bratwurst* with crusty German black and white breads, plus elegant pastrics. Old friends meet daily at this colorful eating spot where authentic German fare is king.

*Price: About˙$2–$5 per person*
*Open Mon.–Sat. for lunch only; closed Sun.*
*Accepts all major credit cards*

---

## MARKET STREET GRILL
60 Post Office Place
801-322-4668

---

## MARKET STREET BROILER
258 South 1300 East
801-583-8808

Excellence characterizes the operation of these spacious and contemporary-styled restaurants where tiptop service and fine food bring customers back again and again. The Grill is in the heart of the city; the Broiler only 15 minutes away. Specialties are similar at these sister restaurants. Start with seafood cocktail, chowder, and sourdough bread. Save room for well-prepared salmon, haibut, sautéed harbor scallops, and red snapper with citrus. No reservations are accepted. Liquor store on premises.

*Price: About $12–$24 per person*
*Open Mon.–Sat. for breakfast, lunch, and dinner; closed Sun.*
*Accepts all major credit cards*

---

## METRO CAFÉ
39 Post Office Place
801-532-2226

Reflecting the twenties Café Society, this tiptop eatery has both an exterior and interior design of inviting simplicity. The crisp neon logo and white porcelain floor of the entrance are classy; the mauve and beige pastel hues of the interior are a backdrop for the central focus of Metro Café's lighted deli case and bar, resplendent with luscious desserts, salads, fresh seafood, iced beverages, and gourmet embellishments. Small bistro tables, in addition to customary dining tables and booths, invite before-and-after-theater sippers and nibblers. It is all unique yet comfortable throughout. There is a wide variety of appetizers for the "lite" crowd and entrées to please demanding gourmets and gourmands alike. Specialties include shrimp and asparagus *Alfredo,* which is a crowd pleaser. Liquor store on premises. Reservations are recommended.

*Price: About $5.75–$13.95 per person*
*Open Mon.–Fri. for lunch and dinner; Sat. for dinner only; closed Sun.*
*Accepts all major credit cards*

---

## MIKADO
### 67 West First South
**801-328-0929**

Step into old, enchanting Japan for authentic Japanese cuisine prepared by top Japanese chefs. Gracious living is preserved in a fast-moving world with leisurely dining in a private room or booth. Kimono-clad hostesses will prepare cuisine at tableside with an aura of grace, gentle charm, and unobtrusive hospitality. There's also a *sushi* bar in the restaurant. Specialties include shrimp *tempura, teriyaki* steaks, expertly prepared by owner-chef Jerry Tsuyuki. Throw yourself on the mercy of the chef and be surprised by dishes that include barbecued chicken, *sashimi* (raw tuna and octopus), and soup—all cooked to order, so avoid dining here if you're in a hurry. Liquor store on premises. Reservations are recommended.

*Price: About $10–$16 per person*
*Open Mon.–Sat. for dinner only; closed Sun.*
*Accepts all major credit cards*

---

## MILLCREEK INN
### Millcreek Canyon
**801-278-7927**

Nestled on a mountainside amid quaking aspens and pines is charming Millcreek Inn, where fine Continental cuisine is served daily. The exquisite view sets the stage for such specialties as Chicken Jerusalem, veal Marsala, grilled salmon steaks, and roast duckling. The owner-manager Dean Himmelman serves nothing but the freshest of fresh. Chocolate truffles are favorites for satisfying the sweet tooth along with an awesome array of luscious desserts. Liquor store on premises. Reservations are recommended. About a 30-minute drive.

*Price: About $11.50–$18 per person; $7.50 Saturdays all-day barbecue*
*Open Thurs.–Fri. for lunch and dinner; Sat. all-day barbecue until 5 P.M.; then dinner; Sun. for brunch only; closed Mon., Tues., Wed.*
*Accepts all major credit cards*

# NINO'S RESTAURANT
## 136 East South Temple
### 801-359-0506

A magnificent, panoramic view of the area inspires creativity for chef-owner Antonino Carilli as he orchestrates the serving of tempting Italian cuisine. Elegance prevails in decor and in menu selections, which range from sassy pasta dishes to lamb specialties, *torta pasqualina,* roast lamb with rosemary, *cozze ripieni,* and desserts that are rarely equaled. Liquor store on the premises. Reservations are recommended.

*Price: About $20 per person*
*Open Mon.–Fri. for lunch and dinner; Sat. for dinner only; closed Sun.*
*Accepts all major credit cards*

# OCEANS RESTAURANT AND OYSTER CAFÉ
## 4760 South 900 East
### 801-261-0115

This is Nantucket Island in Utah. Fresh fish is brought in daily from the East Coast, the Gulf, and the Great Lakes. Boston scrod, lemon sole, king salmon, striped bass, Lake Superior whitefish, lake and mountain stream trout, and pickerel are among the choices. You'll be served lots of it. Enjoy dining in a warm, inviting Southern California-style beach-front atmosphere. Choose from an enormous selection of fish and seafood, grilled over mesquite or as you like it. The Oyster Café offers a light menu of appetizers and fun specialties. Great service in a pleasing atmosphere. Liquor store on premises. Reservations are recommended.

*Price: About $15 per person*
*Open Mon.–Fri. for lunch and dinner; Sat. for dinner only; closed Sun.*
*Accepts all major credit cards*

# THE ORIENT
## 4768 South Redwood Road
### 801-966-3659

Don't let the size and simple decor of this restaurant fool you. The Orient is one of the finest restaurants in the area, featuring excellent Vietnamese cuisine, prepared and served with artistry while the diner enjoys the soft music and friendly atmosphere of this tiny restaurant. Owned by Chef Nguyen Dao Van, the eating establishment has a reputation for serving expertly seasoned specialties from Vietnam. Favorite entrées include stuffed Cornish hen, coconut shrimp, spring roll, egg roll, shrimp stir-fry. Reservations are recommended.

*Price: Under $10 per person*
*Open daily for lunch and dinner*
*Accepts all major credit cards*

---

## RIO GRANDE CAFÉ
### 270 South Rio Grande
**801-364-3302**

This old restored railroad station used to be the scene of hellos and good-byes. Now it welcomes guests with very hot and not-so-hot Mexican cuisine, depending on the hardiness of your palate. All the food is good, but don't miss the chili, *taco* salad, and *chalupas*. Manuel, the manager, meets everyone with a warm smile (he's the one with the toothpick) and suggestions for the day's special. The chicken *enchiladas* and the combination dinners are tops. Delightful Mexican decor. Better for lunch than dinner. Liquor store on premises. Reservations are not accepted.

*Price: Under $10 per person*
*Open daily for lunch and dinner*
*Accepts all major credit cards*

---

## R. J. WHEATFIELDS RESTAURANT AND BAKERY
### 620 Trolley Square
**801-364-8963**

Owner John Canepari sees to it that his big barn of a restaurant, with its many nineteenth-century touches, remains a popular dispenser of fine "natural foods." Located toward the north end of Trolley Square, this has become the favorite eating place of the upbeat who look for vegetarian nutrition plus attractive and delicious specialties. The very excellent wheat bread and savory soups are favored by many. The *quiche* is superb, as is a vegetable-combo dish topped with gooey melted cheese. Service is generally good. Mesquite-grilled fish is the hottest new item on the menu. Liquor store on premises. Reservations are not accepted.

*Price: About $5 per person*
*Open Mon.–Sat. for breakfast, lunch, and dinner; Sun. for brunch*
*and dinner only*
*Accepts all major credit cards*

---

# ROOF RESTAURANT
## In the Westin Hotel Utah, Main Street at South Temple
### 801-531-1000

The spectacular view matches the superb cuisine served in the Continental manner at the Roof Restaurant. French cuisine is served expertly and with flair in the contemporary chic decor with its European chairs, rust linens, and fresh flowers. The menu is largely influenced by *cuisine minceur*. Of the fish dishes, which far outnumber the meat, poached bass in mint-flavored *béarnaise* and lobster in red wine sauce might be among the specialties. Baked salmon is a favorite with diners, along with veal Oscar and rack of lamb. No liquor store. Reservations are recommended.

*Price: About $18–$23.50 per person*
*Open Mon.–Fri. for lunch and dinner; Sat. and Sun. for dinner only*
*Accepts all major credit cards*

---

# RUSTLERS LODGE
## Alta Ski Resort
### 801-532-4061

One of the West's most spectacular dining rooms is this lodge, about a 45-minute drive from downtown, where guests enjoy good French and Continental food while gazing at fantastic ski country. The menu offers fare to tempt all palates. Seafood and fish specialties outnumber meat items, although the steak lover is still honored with the best the chef can offer. Elegant desserts pamper the sweet tooth of diners. Each specialty is made to order and served with flair. Liquor store on premises. Reservations are recommended.

*Price: About $15 per person*
*Open Tues.–Sat. for dinner only; Sun. for brunch; closed Mon.*
*Accepts all major credit cards*

# SIEGFRIED'S DELICATESSEN
## 69 West 300 South
### 801-355-3891

"As you like it" German specialties are featured at this friendly deli where favorite lunch dishes might be the *Bratwurst* plate with two salads or pork steak with German salad—each prepared with careful authenticity for members of the German community and those who pretend they are. Imported deli items are available for the "faithful."

*Price: Under $10 per person*
*Open Mon.–Fri. for breakfast and lunch; Sat. until 6 P.M.; closed Sun.*
*Accepts all major credit cards*

# THE STEAK PIT
## Snowbird Ski Resort
### 801-521-6040

Considered to be one of the finest steak restaurants in the West, The Steak Pit has a rustic decor with polished wood tables and booths. Choice cuts of steak are served in this char-house-style restaurant about a 45-minute drive from downtown. Specialties include prime rib, rack of lamb, lobster, swordfish, crab, halibut, and scallop dishes nightly. All entrées are reasonably priced and include a crispy salad and freshly baked bread. Liquor store on premises. Great service. Reservations are recommended.

*Price: About $10–$24 per person*
*Open daily for dinner only*
*Accepts all major credit cards*

# TAYLOR CAFÉ
## 521 West Second South
### 801-328-1705

Ophelia Taylor sees to it that each guest is welcomed to her fine restaurant where she serves the best soul food in the region. Bite into her tempting fried or barbecued chicken served with expertly prepared greens, salads, and soups, and you'll see why. Don't bother to go unless you're ready to eat heartily. Reservations are recommended.

*Price: $12.50 and up per person*
*Open Sun., Mon., Wed.–Fri. for lunch and dinner; Sat. for dinner only; closed Tues.*
*No credit cards accepted*

# TOKYO JOE'S
In the Park Hotel, 605 Main Street, Park City
### 801-649-5637

Bogie lives! At least at this restaurant named after a Humphrey Bogart movie, and furnished with stained glass, rosewood, brass, and lots of Bogie photos for a nostalgic look. The dinner menu is extensive and artistically presented by the chef. Fish is served steamed, baked, or sautéed, never grilled or fried. Entrées include red snapper in sherry sauce, baked salmon, oysters *olé* with *tequila,* fresh tuna served in plum sauce, and preparations of clams, mussels, and Dungeness crab legs. Chicken, baby back ribs, and prime rib please most diners. An interesting concept here is the chowder bar. Three basic chowders are available including seafood, *cioppino,* and cheese with beer. Nine condiments are available to add to the savory chowders, served in round sourdough loaves of bread. Desserts are made on the premises daily. Liquor store on premises. Reservations are recommended.

*Price: About $15–$20 per person*
*Open daily for lunch and dinner*
*Accepts all major credit cards*

# THE UPPERCRUST
1362 Foothill Drive
### 801-583-5155

This very sophisticated establishment has earned a reputation for high culinary standards. It's a Yuppie gathering place where customers can purchase tempting *quiche* or perhaps chicken pasta salad to be eaten in the tastefully decorated café-type area or taken home to serve to spiffy guests. Save room for sweet delights like mocha chocolate torte or Grand Marnier cheesecake. Finest breads and pastries baked on premises daily. The pasta salads, vegetable salads, and fancy desserts rate high with customers. Upbeat decor to match service.

*Price: About $10 per person*
*Open daily for breakfast, lunch, and early dinner; Sat. until 11 P.M.*
*Accepts all major credit cards*

# SAN DIEGO AND ENVIRONS

## BY LESLIE JAMES

**AMERICAN**
Dobson's

**BAR**
Bully's (various locations)

**BELGIAN**
The Belgian Lion (Ocean Beach)

**BREAKFAST**
Baltimore Bagel Co. (La Jolla; Pacific Beach)

**CALIFORNIA**
926

**CHINESE**
Chung King Loh (Solana Beach)
Imperial Mandarin

**ECLECTIC**
Gustaf Anders (La Jolla)
Mille Fleur (Rancho Santa Fe)
Piret's (Mission Hills, La Jolla, Grossmont, Encinitas)

**FAST FOOD**
Canora's Sandwich Shop
El Indio
Esperanto (Pacific Beach)
Fuji-San (Pacific Beach)

**HAMBURGERS**
Bully's (various locations)

**HOTEL DINING ROOM**
Sheppard's

**ITALIAN**
The Pasta Place (La Jolla)
When in Rome (Encinitas)

**JAPANESE**
Fuji San (Pacific Beach)
Sushi Bar Kazumi
Tengu

**MEXICAN**
Carnitas Uruapan (Tijuana)
El Abajeno de Guadalajara (Tijuana)
El Indio
Guadalajara Grill (Tijuana)

**MEXICAN**
La Fonda Roberto's (Chula
Vista)
La Fonda Robert's (Tijuana)

**SEAFOOD**
The Fish Market (Del Mar)
George's at the Cove (La Jolla)
Old Trieste (Clairemont)
Papagayo

**STEAKS AND CHOPS**
Bully's (La Jolla, Mission
Village, del Mar)

J ust ten years ago, dining in San Diego pretty much consisted of mediocre Mexican food and self-service salad bars. Today, owing both to the national preoccupation with food and a regional pride in "California cuisine," the story is decidedly different and significantly tastier. Many young, imaginative chefs, trained in the ways of Berkeley's Chez Panisse, have opened eateries that are dedicated to the glorious produce and seafood available locally. Vietnamese restaurants abound, with several tiny, family-owned places on each block of El Cajon Boulevard, to the east of the downtown area. And Korean, Cuban, and Afghan restaurants have joined the classic French, predictable Chinese, and Americanized German and Greek dining rooms in the city. In addition, the heart of downtown San Diego is undergoing an ambitious revitalization project, with dozens of new restaurants scheduled to open this year.

Despite the growing sophistication of the dining-out public, many San Diegans still prefer ambience and gimmicks to grand food. You'll find many of these restaurants, many chains and many spots, offering spectacular views along with not-so-spectacular food.

Weekend brunch is a city institution. Happy hour—a time to enjoy the sunset, a glass of wine, and a few oysters on the half-shell—is as popular with the locals as with the tourists. And many of San Diego's most memorable meals consist of a sandwich, an icy beer, and a few chocolate chip cookies—all tucked into a humble brown bag and eaten while watching a decidedly not-so-humble sunset on the water.

Most people also love going over the border to Tijuana, Mexico, just a 20-minute drive from downtown San Diego, where you'll find a wide variety of good restaurants with festive atmospheres. Visitors need not worry about the water or the fruits and vegetables—only about the traffic and the potential wait to get back across the border. The Tijuana restaurants I've included here are popular with Mexicans and "gringos" alike.

*Leslie James is restaurant critic for* The San Diego Union.

# BALTIMORE BAGEL CO.
## 7523B Fay Avenue, La Jolla   619-456-0716
## 1772B Garnet Avenue, Pacific Beach   619-272-9321

The bagels (everything from plain to chocolate chip) are hot from the oven, the fillings fresh and imaginative. There's even a kosher version of the Egg McMuffin. The strongest drink is Dr. Brown's cream soda.

*Price: Under $10 per person*
*Open daily for breakfast, lunch, and dinner*
*No credit cards accepted*

---

# THE BELGIAN LION
## 2265 Bacon Street, Ocean Beach
### 619-295-6151

Lusty provincial fare (*cassoulet,* duckling with sauerkraut, and *confit de canard*) is served by the talented Coulon family. The decor is nondescript, but the atmosphere is charged by the warm and enthusiastic personality of the proprietors. Excellent service.

*Price: About $25–$30 per person*
*Open Tues.–Sat. for dinner only; closed Sun. and Mon.*
*Accepts all major credit cards*

---

# BULLY'S
## 5755 La Jolla Boulevard, La Jolla   619-459-2768
## 2401 Camino Del Rio South, Mission Village   619-291-2665
## 1404 Camino Del Mar, Del Mar   619-755-1660

Bully's is a singles bar extraordinaire, but people of all ages and marital status come here for the best hamburger in town, excellent prime rib, and steaks with all the trimmings—and good cheap drinks. The decor is standard for a bar: darkness and red plastic booths. No reservations, and there's almost always a wait.

*Price: About $15–$20 per person*
*Open daily for dinner; Mon.–Fri. for lunch only*
*Accepts all major credit cards*

# CANORA'S SANDWICH SHOP
## 3715 India Street, San Diego
### 619-291-5938

This tiny shop offers eighty-seven different sandwich varieties, with prices ranging from $1.69 for the peanut butter, honey, and banana to $3.49 for the tortas made with pita bread, meats, cheese, and hot sauce. The specialty of the house is "Sue's Delight"—described as "a grilled sandwich with tuna on the bottom, guacamole on top, and Cheddar cheese and tomato in the middle."

*Price: Under $10 per person*
*Open Mon.–Sat. for lunch and dinner; closed Sun.*
*No credit cards accepted*

# CARNITAS URUAPAN
## Boulevard Agua Caliente, 550, Tijuana
### 706-6-81-61-81

Located a block from the racetrack Agua Caliente, this Mexican rendition of a German beer hall is always crowded, always noisy, and always rocking to the sounds of mariachi music. The specialty of the house, served on paper plates to folks sharing long wooden picnic tables, is pork, cooked in front of the building in cauldrons of boiling oil. The meat is served with chopped tomato, onion, *cilantro, frijoles,* and plenty of hot-from-the-presses *tortillas.* The idea is to roll your own *burritos.* The food and drink are terrific, and so's the party atmosphere.

*Price: Under $10 per person*
*Open daily for lunch and dinner*
*Accepts MasterCard*

# CHUNG KING LOH
## 552 Stevens Avenue, Solana Beach
### 619-481-0184

An informal neighborhood spot with an unusual variety of well-prepared Mandarin and Szechuan specialties. Don't miss the clams in black bean sauce, the onion pancakes, the dumplings, or anything else owner Molly Lee recommends. Children are welcome. Service is fast.

*Price: About $15–$20 per person*
*Open daily for lunch and dinner*
*Accepts Visa and MasterCard*

# DOBSON'S
## 956 Second Avenue, San Diego
### 619-231-6771

This is a bustling, beautifully renovated downtown bar where the people-watching is as important as the food—which is to say, very important indeed. Young French chef Jacques Pastor and his wife, Francine, can turn out good food that is simple (roast chicken and steaks with *pommes frites*) or sophisticated (mussel bisque and fish fricassees). It's a very popular spot, with an upstairs dining room surveying the action at the downstairs antique bar (it dates back to 1912). Reservations are essential.

*Price: About $20–$25 per person*
*Open Mon.–Fri. for lunch and dinner; Sat. for dinner only; closed Sun.*
*Accepts American Express, Visa, and MasterCard*

# EL ABAJENO DE GUADALAJARA
## General Sanchez Taboada, 79, Tijuana
### 706-6-84-27-88

One of Tijuana's newest restaurants, El Abajeno offers a bright, stylish decor, non-stop mariachi music, and a lengthy menu of traditional Mexican dishes.

*Price: About $15 per person*
*Open daily for lunch and dinner*
*Accepts Visa and MasterCard*

# EL INDIO
## 3695 India Street, San Diego
### 619-299-0333

There's always a long but fast-moving lunch line at this popular Mexican takeout shop. Specialties include the *burritos, chimichangas,* and crispy *quesadillas.*

*Price: Under $10 per person*
*Open daily for lunch and dinner*
*No credit cards accepted*

# ESPERANTO
## 4462 Mission Boulevard, Pacific Beach
### 619-273-9039

Slightly Americanized *croissants* are baked all day long and stuffed with a variety of cold salads, cold cuts, cheese, and smoked fish. There are also some nice pasta dishes and cold pasta salads. Beer and wine are served. Table service can be very slow.

*Price: Under $10 per person*
*Open daily for lunch and dinner*
*No credit cards accepted*

---

# THE FISH MARKET
## 640 Via de la Valle, Del Mar
### 619-755-2277

The char-grilled fish is fresh and tasty, but sometimes overcooked. Specify your preference for "just set" or undercooked fish. The offerings at the oyster bar are noteworthy. This is a noisy, informal spot that does not take reservations, and there can be long waits during the July–August racing season.

*Price: About $15–$20 per person*
*Open daily for lunch and dinner*
*Accepts American Express, Visa, and MasterCard*

---

# FUJI-SAN
## 1130 Garnet Avenue, Pacific Beach
### 619-270-5733

This is a small, family-run operation offering simple *sushi* platters and several traditional specials each day. There are a few tables in this coffee shop-grocery store, but most folks take their food a few blocks away to the beach. No alcohol.

*Price: Under $10 per person*
*Open Mon.–Sat. for lunch and dinner; closed Sun.*
*No credit cards accepted*

# GEORGE'S AT THE COVE
## 1250 Prospect Street, La Jolla
### 619-454-4244

The menu here is an international line-up of fresh fish. Those grilled over mesquite are very good and particularly recommended. The smart decor and spectacular view of La Jolla Cove make this a wonderful spot to dine. There's a nice bar, too.

*Price: About $20–$25 per person*
*Open daily for lunch and dinner*
*Accepts American Express, Visa, and MasterCard*

# GUADALAJARA GRILL
## Diego Rivera, 19, Tijuana
### 706-6-84-20-45

Zany shenanigans by the waiters, a clever *trompe l'oeil* decor, lively mariachi music, and varied, slightly Americanized menu add up to a memorable dining experience here.

*Price: About $15 per person*
*Open daily for lunch and dinner*
*Accepts MasterCard*

# GUSTAF ANDERS
## 2182 Avenida de la Playa, La Jolla
### 619-459-4499

Startlingly sleek, with a refined setting fit for extraordinary food. The dining room hasn't a swatch of color in it: Everything is done in black and white, from the mirrors and lacquered wood to the vase and flower arrangements. The art on the walls is a changing exhibit and up for sale.

Swedish chef Ulf Strandberg does brilliant work: Sonoma baby lamb is topped with a red bell pepper sauce; fresh trout is fried, then marinated in a vinaigrette, and served cold; homemade pasta is dusted luxuriously with fresh white truffles in season; and Norwegian salmon is sauced with Chardonnay and golden caviar. In fact, there is caviar galore, all to be washed down with champagnes and vodkas in the elegant but less formal Caviar Bar, where one can sup on superb sandwiches and salads. Service is impeccable and the wine list is solid.

*Price: About $35 per person*
*Open daily for lunch and dinner*
*Accepts Visa and MasterCard*

---

## IMPERIAL MANDARIN
### 3904 Convoy Street, San Diego
**619-292-1222**

The regular food here is only fair, but the Saturday and Sunday *dim sum* brunch is terrific. The roving carts proffer all the usual dumplings and buns along with such delicacies as flaky custard, rice-flour sheet-roll with shrimp, split pea pudding, and curry beef puffs. Very casual.

*Price: Under $10 per person*
*Open daily for lunch and dinner*
*Accepts Visa and MasterCard*

---

## LA FONDA ROBERTO'S
### 300 Third Avenue, Chula Vista
**619-585-3017**

Anybody who thinks that Mexican food means *tacos, tamales,* and a big *enchilada* will rejoice in this restaurant's fine regional cuisine. There's Yucatan-style roast pig, barbecued goat, *chilies* stuffed with fruits, nuts, and cheese, and chicken in a variety of complex sauces. Casual but refined atmosphere and decent service.

*Price: Under $10 per person*
*Open daily for lunch and dinner*
*Accepts Diners Club, Visa, and MasterCard*

# LA FONDA ROBERTO'S
## Carretera Ensenada (*Ensenada Road*), 356, Tijuana
### 706-6-88-64-87

You will enjoy superb regional cuisine here, including barbecued goat, Yucatan-style pork roast, stuffed chilies, and chicken in a variety of delicious sauces. The atmosphere is pleasant and casual and the owner speaks English.

*Price: Under $10 per person*
*Open daily for lunch and dinner*
*Accepts MasterCard*

# MILLE FLEUR
## 6009 Paseo Delicias, Rancho Santa Fe
### 619-756-3085

What is probably the most romantic restaurant in town serves the grand food its setting deserves with the arrival of Martin Woesle, a 26-year-old German chef who apprenticed at L'Aubergine in Munich (three Michelin stars). Salads are imaginative and made with the finest produce from the famed Chino's ranch nearby. Fresh *foie gras* is delicious here; ditto the sweetbreads sauced with veal stock and Madeira and the veal chop with fresh *morels*. Desserts are still in the fine-tuning stage at this writing. The decor is cozy and classic within an authentic Mexican *casita,* and luncheon is served in the picturesque courtyard. A pianist regales listeners in the bar Thursdays through Saturday. About a 30-minute drive from San Diego.

*Price: About $35 per person*
*Open Sun.–Fri. for lunch and dinner; Sat. for dinner only*
*Accepts all major credit cards*

# 926
## 926 Turquoise Street, San Diego
### 619-488-7500

Tucked in the back of a tiny shopping mall, 926 has an unimposing façade and a graceful but not grand decor. But the food created here by the 23-year-old chef, Doug Organ, is spectacular. Organ and co-chef Osa Sommermeyer dazzle customers with such delights as fresh oysters rolled in crushed pine nuts, sautéed, and served in a *beurre blanc;* veal *médaillons* with ginger and blood oranges; and grilled scallops in a golden tomato-butter sauce with fresh basil.

The desserts are lovely, the chocolate truffles divine. The service is polished and unpretentious.

*Price: About $35 per person*
*Open Tues.–Sat. for dinner only; closed Sun. and Mon.*
*Accepts all major credit cards*

---

## OLD TRIESTE
### 2335 Morena Boulevard, Clairemont
**619-276-1841**

This is an Old World, rather stuffy place that serves a great piece of local fish, pan-fried with gobs of butter. The rest of the menu is traditional Italian fare.

*Price: About $25–$30 per person*
*Open Tues.–Fri. for lunch and dinner; Sat. for dinner only; closed Sun. and Mon.*
*Accepts all major credit cards*

---

## PAPAGAYO
### 861 West Harbor Drive, San Diego
**619-232-7581**

Dazzling views and bright tropical decor (including a parrot motif that gives the place its name) make this one of the most pleasant spots in Seaport Village. They do wonderful mesquite-grilled fish that is first marinated in fruit juices and Mexican seasonings.

*Price: About $20 per person*
*Open daily for lunch and dinner*
*Accepts all major credit cards*

---

## THE PASTA PLACE
### 5634 La Jolla Boulevard, La Jolla
**619-454-7004**

Bright, stylish gourmet-to-go shop, where fresh pasta, prepared salads, cheese, and cold cuts share space with a dozen neatly dressed tables. Chef Will Howard has had no formal training but manages to turn out some of the best food in town: homemade *ravioli* are stuffed with *foie gras; agnolotti* with chicken, Gruyère and fresh chervil. A simple plate of spaghetti sauced with fresh tomatoes and basil becomes a meal to remember. Desserts, including a flourless chocolate cake, a tarte Tatin, and fresh fruit tarts, are glorious. Guests may choose from the selection of Italian wines on the shelves.

*Price: About $25–$30 per person*
*Open Tues.–Sat. for lunch and dinner; closed Sun. and Mon.*
*Accepts Visa and MasterCard*

---

## PIRET'S

902 West Washington Street, Mission Hills    619-297-2993
701 B. Street, San Diego    619-696-0278
La Jolla Village Square, La Jolla    619-455-7955
Grossmont Center, Grossmont    619-464-4184
897 First Street, Encinitas    619-942-5146

This stylish, casually elegant chain of bistros serves everything from *croissants* and *espresso* to *cassoulet, fettuccine* with four cheeses, and grilled chicken breast with a *jalapeño* relish. In the downtown and Encinitas restaurants there is also a superb *nouvelle* pizza, à la Wolfgang Puck. Wines, priced at retail, may be selected from the shelves. There is also a tantalizing selection of prepared foods and gourmet groceries to go. Service is decent. Reservations are not accepted.

*Price: About $20–$25 per person*
*Hours differ at each restaurant; call ahead*
*Accepts all major credit cards*

---

## SHEPPARD'S

Sheraton Harbor Island Hotel East, San Diego
619-692-2255

The kitchen here is working hard to put to rest the common American notion that hotel dining is horrible dining. The restaurant here is notable for its spaciousness, its handsome Art Deco decor, and smooth, attentive service. The menu is notable for its duckling with pear William sauce, veal with Gorgonzola, and its elaborate desserts. There is an excellent wine list.

*Price: About $30–$35 per person*
*Open daily for dinner only*
*Accepts all major credit cards*

# SUSHI BAR KAZUMI
## 7905 Engineer Road, San Diego
### 619-292-7148

Many unusual ingredients and a brilliant performance by counterman Kazumi Yokoyama make this an attractive place for *sushi* and *sashimi*. There's a limited menu of cooked foods available. Small and informal.

*Price: About $10 per person*
*Open Mon.–Fri. for lunch and dinner; Sat. and Sun. for dinner only*
*Accepts Visa and MasterCard*

# TENGU
## 8690 Aero Drive, San Diego
### 619-292-0141

Just follow all the visiting Japanese businessmen to this bright and comfortable restaurant with its extensive *sushi* bar presided over by a young and friendly master. The traditional dishes are competently prepared and beautifully presented. Lunch reservations are essential.

*Price: About $15–$20 per person*
*Open Tues.–Fri. for lunch and dinner; Sat. and Sun. for dinner only; closed Mon.*
*Accepts American Express, Visa, and MasterCard*

# WHEN IN ROME
## 828 North Highway 101, Encinitas
### 619-944-1771

This is a spacious and nicely appointed setting for delicious, authentic Italian fare. For the three young couples from Rome who run the place, the restaurant is their *castello* and they love showing off their talents to guests. Homemade pasta is wondrously light and smartly sauced. Fresh fish, grilled with olive oil and lemon juice, is as good as anything in Portofino or Puerto Ercole. Chicken *cacciatore* is the real thing. The service is good, but it gets very busy during the racing season (July and August). There is a minimal wine list. Reservations are suggested.

*Price: About $20–$25 per person*
*Open Tues.–Sun. for dinner only; closed Mon.*
*Accepts American Express, Visa, and MasterCard*

# SAN FRANCISO

## *By Patricia Unterman and Stan Sesser*

**AMERICAN**
Campton Place
Hayes Street Grill
Perry's

**AUSTRIAN**
Lipizzaner

**BREAKFAST**
Café Beaujolais
Doidge's
JoAnn's

**CALIFORNIAN**
Greens
Mustards
New Boonville Restaurant and
   Bar
Santa Fe Bar and Grill
Zuni Café

**CAMBODIAN**
Cambodia House
Phnom Penh

**CHINESE**
China House
Ton Kiang
Tung Fong
Yuet Lee Seafood

**FRENCH**
Chez Panisse
Le Castel
Masa's
Miramonte
René Verdon's Le Trianon
Rose and LeFavour (Saint
   Helena)

**ITALIAN**
Caffè Sport
Donatello
Little Joe's
Modesto Lanzone's
Ristorante Grifone

**JAPANESE**
Kabuto
Sanppo

## MEXICAN
El Tazumal
La Cumbre

## SUBURBAN
Café Beaujolais (Mendocino)
Miramonte (Saint Helena)
Mustards (Yountville)
New Boonville Restaurant and
 Bar (Boonville)
Rose and LeFavour (Saint
 Helena)

## THAI
Khan Toke Thai House
Plearn Thai Cuisine

## VEGETARIAN
Greens

## VIETNAMESE
Golden Turtle
Mekong

For anyone who loves eating out, San Francisco offers an astonishing variety of great restaurants. You can have a marvelous meal night after night without repeating the same ethnic type twice for weeks. The diversity of San Francisco's population, the bounty of the Pacific Ocean, the abundance of California's farms, and the great wines of the nearby Napa Valley all contribute to the quality of the food scene.

In contemplating where to eat in San Francisco, it's sometimes hard to know where to start. Here are some suggestions:

—If you love Asian food, there's far more of interest than *sushi* and Chinese restaurants. For instance, San Francisco houses the nation's first two Cambodian restaurants, and the cuisine is a marvel. Try the Thai food also; Thai restaurants have been mushrooming, and some of the best are fascinating.

—For Chinese food, avoid the expensive, nationally-famous restaurants of Chinatown, since the food tends to be not nearly as good as what you can get in smaller, cheaper places. By all means sample the *dim sum,* the marvelous Chinese tea pastries served for brunch.

—The best-known restaurants don't necessarily offer the best food. This is particularly true of the some of the famed fish restaurants and some of the Italian places in North Beach. Many of the old-time famous San Francisco institutions haven't changed with the times, and there are much more exciting, newer places to eat.

—"California cuisine" may have spread across the country, but it's still worth trying here. The proximity of San Francisco to fresh produce and fish lends itself beautifully to this style of cooking, which emphasizes the freshness of ingredients.

*Patricia Unterman, an accomplished cook and part owner of two San Francisco restaurants, is the Sunday restaurant critic for the* San Francisco Chronicle. *Stan Sesser, a journalist who specializes in consumer topics, reviews restaurants each week in the Friday* San Francisco Chronicle. *Unterman and Sesser are co-authors of the book* Restaurants of San Francisco.

---

# CAFÉ BEAUJOLAIS
## 961 Ukiah Street, Mendocino
### 707-937-5614

Why go to Mendocino? For one thing, it's a relatively unspoiled coastal village, a glimpse of what Carmel might have been like decades ago. For another, it houses the best brunch place in the Bay Area. Margaret Fox, the owner-chef, has parlayed her breakfasts into a cookbook and a national reputation. The brunches are so good they'll change your concept of what this meal is like. From waffles with sour cream, wild rice, and toasted pecans in the batter to *crêpes* stuffed with fresh salmon and asparagus, the brunch specials are wonderful and innovative. The plain old omelets exceed even those in France. And Margaret's baking is astonishing. Call in winter, since they sometimes close for a couple of months.

*Price: About $10 per person*
*Open daily for breakfast and lunch and for dinner on summer weekends*
*No credit cards accepted*

---

# CAFFÈ SPORT
## 574 Green Street (*near Union Street*)
### 415-981-1251

You come for the first seating at 6:30 P.M. and you stand in the waiting area, while the waiters finish up their meals, drink wine, and smoke cigarettes in a leisurely fashion. When you finally sit down and your order gets taken, you might wait an hour for the first bite of food. At that point, everything you ordered could come at once. It's a crazy place, but if you love heaping platters of gutsy, garlicky, saucy Sicilian food, you shouldn't miss it. The *scampi* are justly famous, and you'll be tasting garlic on your breath for days. Reservations, far in advance, are essential.

*Price: About $30 per person*
*Open Tues.–Sat. for lunch and dinner; closed Sun. and Mon.*
*No credit cards accepted*

# CAMBODIA HOUSE

## 5625 Geary Boulevard (*near Twentieth Avenue*)
### 415-668-5888

Cambodia House, although the dishes are reasonably priced, manages to be one of the most elegant restaurants in the city. There are tablecloths, nice decorations, and very attentive service. So this is an Asian restaurant to go to when you want a long, relaxed meal. The owner, Pok Sonn, was an archaeology student stranded in Thailand when Cambodia became Communist. He married a Thai woman and moved to San Francisco, eventually becoming *sous-chef* at a French restaurant. The ambitious menu of 72 items shows great sophistication. Even the simple dishes, such as barbecued chicken and pork-ribs curry, are brimming with the flavors of a host of exotic spices. Try also the deep-fried whole pompano in garlic sauce.

*Price: About $15 per person*
*Open daily for dinner only*
*Accepts Visa and MasterCard*

# CAMPTON PLACE

## In the Campton Place Hotel, 340 Stockton Street (*at Union Square*)
### 415-781-5155

This quietly luxurious, small hotel dining room has become the rage in San Francisco for its very expensive, beautifully prepared American food. Chef Bradley Ogden has fused classical training with his Midwestern roots. Lots of regional ingredients appear on the menu: spiny lobster with blue corn cakes, grilled quail on deep-fried sweet potato sticks, and roasted loin of lamb on a bed of bacon and mustard greens. Meals are served on white Wedgwood, and fine California wines are poured into sparkling crystal. The breakfast is also a wonderful experience, with fresh fruit compotes, poached eggs, and Smithfield ham bathed in hollandaise. The house-made breads, rolls, and corn sticks are spectacular. Reservations, particularly for weekends, should be made two weeks in advance.

*Price: About $20 per person for breakfast; $60 per person for dinner*
*Open daily for breakfast, lunch, and dinner*
*Accepts all major credit cards*

# CHEZ PANISSE
1517 Shattuck Avenue (*between Cedar and Vine streets*),
Berkeley
### 415-548-5525; Café 415-548-5049

This was where it all started in the early 1970s—the brilliant idea of Alice Waters to open a Berkeley neighborhood restaurant that would discard the traditional notion of French food in America. There would be a fixed-price dinner, no choices, and all the cooking would take advantage of whatever was absolutely fresh and in season. The menu for the week would be decided only the weekend before, and things would change depending on what the suppliers had that morning.

Now Chez Panisse, with its simple but perfectly prepared food, is nationally famous, and Alice Waters has spawned a host of imitators. But Panisse itself keeps innovating, and keeps getting better. The problem is booking a table for the $45 fixed-price dinner; you must reserve weeks in advance unless you're lucky enough to fall upon a last-minute cancellation. These days, the five-course dinners frequently have a Northern Italian influence, due to the presence of chef Paul Bertolli, who received much of his training in Italy. But the concept and presentation are just the same.

The café upstairs does not take reservations, and you should come at an odd hour or else plan on a long wait. The café turns out crusty individual pizzas in a wood-burning oven, an ever-changing array of salads, pastas, and specials. The same rarefied standards that made the downstairs restaurant so well known apply to the café, but prices are much lower. The experience of eating both upstairs and down is enhanced by the most sensitive attention to detail, so that everything that touches your senses, from the bread to the flowers, expands them.

*Price: $45 fixed-price dinner downstairs; about $25 in the café*
*Open Tues.–Sat. for dinner only; closed Sun. and Mon.*
*Accepts all major credit cards*

# CHINA HOUSE
501 Balboa Street
### 415-386-8858

Increasingly, the area of San Francisco just north of Golden Gate Park, called the Richmond, is becoming the city's largest Chinese neighborhood. The restaurants are following, and this is one of the best. It's more elegant and more expensive than most, but the food is very special. Cecilia Chung grew up in

Shanghai and, as she explains to her guests while making the rounds of her tables, the cooking at China House represents dishes from many provinces, all prepared in the Shanghai style. The food is refined, lively, and interesting. Shredded fish with pine nuts, a minced pork dish called *kuo-cha,* and a clay pot creation called Yang Chow Lion's Head are among the best dishes here.

*Price: About $20 a person*
*Open daily for lunch and dinner*
*Accepts all major credit cards*

---

# DONATELLO
## In the Pacific Plaza Hotel, 501 Post Street
### 415-441-7182

Many visitors to San Francisco have heard about some of the famous Italian restaurants of North Beach, like Vanessi's and Washington Square Bar & Grill. If they confine their Italian meals to North Beach, however, they're missing the best Italian restaurant in the city—the elegant, expensive Donatello, located downtown near Union Square. Donatello has always offered a wide range of interesting Northern Italian dishes, but now this is being supplemented by a $54 fixed-price menu (including wines) that changes every few days.

No other Italian restaurant in San Francisco regularly offers this level and variety of dishes and wines night after night. Frequently Donatello hosts guest chefs from Italy who cook regional specialties as well. The restaurant is beautifully decorated; service is attentive, and the dazzling choice of regional specialties put to shame the stock menus that most other Italian restaurants trot out.

*Price: About $40 per person; $54 with wines on the fixed-price dinner*
*Open daily for lunch and dinner*
*Accepts all major credit cards*

---

# EL TAZUMAL
## 3522 Twentieth Street (*near Mission Street*)
### 415-647-9880

One page of the menu is Mexican, one page Salvadoran, and it adds up to one of the best restaurants in San Francisco's Mission district. El Tazumal is run by a Salvadoran couple; the loquacious, helpful husband waits on tables, and the wife does the cooking. The dining room is cheerful and well kept. On the Salvadoran side, don't miss the *lengua en salsa,* beef tongue cooked to buttery softness in a sauce of onions, red and green peppers, and fresh tomatoes, seasoned with cumin, fresh coriander, and garlic. The Mexican dishes are wholesome and huge. Fresh green chilies are used in *chilies rellenos,* stuffed to bursting with Jack cheese and treated to a cooked-that-day tomato sauce. *Enchiladas suizas,* corn tortillas filled with Jack cheese and green onions, are smothered in green chili sauce and sour cream. This restaurant dispenses the nourishment of a lovingly run family operation.

*Price: About $12 per person*
*Open daily for lunch and dinner*
*No credit cards accepted*

---

## GOLDEN TURTLE
### 308 Fifth Avenue (*near Clement Street*)
### 415-221-5285

This Vietnamese restaurant specializes in delicious marinated meats skewered and cooked over charcoal, rich stir-fried dishes, and delicate salads. Though it's located in a modest neighborhood storefront, more than usual has been done to make the dining room warm and comfortable. The family that runs Golden Turtle is as gracious and personable as if they were entertaining at home.

*Price: About $18 per person*
*Open Tues.–Fri. for dinner only; Sat. and Sunday for lunch and dinner; closed Mon.*
*Accepts Visa and MasterCard*

---

## GREENS
### Building A of Fort Mason Center (*next to the San Francisco Marina Green*)
### 415-771-6222

The chefs at Greens, a vegetarian restaurant owned and run by the San Francisco Zen Center, have been influenced by Berkeley's Chez Panisse. Greens' style of cooking couples innovation with use of remarkably fresh produce. Much of it is picked that day at the Zen Center's Green Gulch farm. Combine this food with a magnificent setting on the bay looking out at the Golden Gate Bridge through floor-to-ceiling windows and you'll understand why Greens is jammed day after day. For lunch there are Provençal pizzas, lovely soups and salads, and imaginative pastas. Dinner is *à la carte* during the week, with a fixed-price five-course meal on Fridays and Saturdays. House-made pastries and wonderful fresh breads are available at the table and at a bakery counter. For weekend dinners, reserve weeks in advance.

*Price: About $25 per person*
*Open Tues.–Sat. for lunch and dinner; Sun. for brunch; closed Mon.*
*Accepts Visa and MasterCard*

---

## HAYES STREET GRILL
### 320 Hayes Street (*near Franklin Street*)
### 415-863-5545

Many of San Francisco's older, well-known fish restaurants have been out-classed by a host of new places that grill over mesquite. You never have to ask at these restaurants whether the fish is fresh; you never have to worry about the fish coming to your table overcooked. Hayes Street Grill, near the Symphony Hall and opera house, was one of the first of these new-style fish restaurants. A couple of years ago it doubled in size, but it's still wildly popular, with virtually every table filled. The fresh fish of the day is listed on a blackboard; there's also a growing list of sauté dishes. The wine list is an extensive and well-chosen tour of boutique California wineries. Reservations accepted one week in advance. (Editor's note: Hayes Street Grill is partly owned by Patricia Unterman. Stan Sesser has written this review exclusively.)

*Price: About $30 per person*
*Open Mon.–Fri. for lunch and dinner; Sat. for dinner only; closed Sun.*
*Accepts Visa and MasterCard*

---

## JOANN'S
### 1131 El Camino Real (*across from the Kaiser Hospital*), South San Francisco
### 415-872-2810

This is the classic three-star hash house—Formica tables, fluorescent lights, a grill along one wall, and some of the best food anywhere. Pumpkin pancakes, Mexican-style scrambled eggs, and French toast from home-baked orange bread are typical of the specials that prove irresistible. But don't pass up the omelets either; they're soft, fluffy, and filled with wonderful ingredients. You have your choice of several kinds of home-baked muffins each day, including a fabulous apple-nut. There will be a wait on weekends, but it's worth it.

*Price: About $8 a person*
*Open Tues.–Sun. for breakfast and lunch only; closed Mon.*
*No credit cards accepted*

# KABUTO
## 5116 Geary Boulevard (*at Fifteenth Avenue*)
### 415-752-5652

This is the restaurant of choice for *sushi* in San Francisco. Sachio, the *sushi* chef-owner, flashes his knives like a warrior while turning out the most delicate and gorgeous creations. The tunas—red and white—are generously cut for *sashimi*. Such popular *sushi* as the grilled and basted freshwater eel, fresh local halibut, shrimp, and red clam are all carefully composed. Unlike other *sushi* bars, Kabuto has a blackboard of daily specials, such as fresh oysters gently warmed on the half-shell glazed with a seasoned soy sauce or a whole steamed Spanish mackerel swimming in a shiny brown *miso* sea.

*Price: About $20 per person*
*Open daily for dinner only*
*Accepts all major credit cards*

# KHAN TOKE THAI HOUSE
## 5937 Geary Boulevard (*at Twenty-fourth Street*)
### 415-668-6654

This was one of the first Thai restaurants in the Bay Area, and it's still one of the best. Although the prices are only a dollar or two per dish more than at bare-bones Thai restaurants, it has a pleasurable atmosphere too. You check your shoes at the door and sit at low tables in peaceful, candlelit rooms decorated with Thai ornaments. Pork balls with Oriental fine herbs are a must as a starter; you make a "sandwich" in a wonton skin of deep-fried meatballs, diced ginger, garlic, hot green peppers, and peanuts. Then go on to the curry dishes, and a great example of a Thai omelet stuffed with ground pork and vegetables.

*Price: About $15–$20 a person*
*Open daily for dinner only*
*Accepts Visa and MasterCard*

# LA CUMBRE
## 515 Valencia Street (*at Sixteenth Street*)
### 415-863-8205

La Cumbre makes the best *burrito* in town, and a good *burrito* ranks at the head of the list of desirable San Francisco Mexican food. The handsome adobe-and-tile restaurant with colorful murals is built around serving this one item. You order the *burritos* yourself at two stations on a long cooking line, one for the famous grilled steak *burritos,* another for barbecued pork, chicken, tongue, and tripe. A *burrito,* in effect, is an entire dinner wrapped in a huge *tortilla,* and no *burrito* beats these.

*Price: About $3 per person*
*Open daily for lunch and dinner*
*No credit cards accepted*

---

# LE CASTEL
## 3235 Sacramento Street (*near Presidio Avenue*)
### 415-921-7115

Le Castel inhabits a smartly converted residence with three small dining rooms swathed in soft pinks and beiges connected by Alhambraesque arches. The food is as stylish as the ambience, and plates are brought to tables as elegantly arranged as the rooms. The small menu offers some delicious and not-often-seen dishes, such as the traditional calf's brains in brown butter, beef marrow on toast, and a lovely Alsatian-style pheasant on a bed of cabbage perfumed with caraway and juniper berries. Take the recommendations of Fritz Frankel, the Alsatian-born owner, who keeps the service faultless. This is what intimate, romantic dining should be all about.

*Price: About $50 per person*
*Open Mon.–Sat. for lunch and dinner; closed Sun.*
*Accepts all major credit cards*

---

# LIPIZZANER
## 2223 Union Street (*at Fillmore Street*)
### 415-921-3424

This jewelbox of a restaurant puts out food that one might encounter at the best restaurants in Vienna or Salzburg. The young chef, trained in hotel kitchens and restaurants throughout Europe, decided to open his own little place with his wife, who runs the dining room. His *Wiener Schnitzel* redefines the dish. Whole Dover sole with *morel-*infused cream sauce, crisply sautéed sweetbreads that melt in your mouth, and a delicious filet of beef stuffed with bacon and herbs are other specialties. Save room for warm apple flan or Viennese hazelnut *crêpes.* Reservations are essential.

*Price: About $40 per person*
*Open Mon.–Sat. for dinner only; closed Sun.*
*Accepts Visa and MasterCard*

# LITTLE JOE'S
## 523 Broadway (*near Columbus Avenue*)
### 415-433-4343

Little Joe's new North Beach location is in a large, warehouse-type space across the street from Vanessi's. The famous open cooking line, where athletic sauté chefs work at breakneck speed in sight of the whole restaurant, has been lengthened a bit, but only to accommodate more patrons. The menu has stayed exactly the same. There's still the *al dente* spaghetti with *pesto* made with fresh basil and the glistening brown roast half chicken scented with rosemary. Saucy veal *saltimbocca,* boiled beef brisket, beef tongue with a piquant green sauce, and *calamari* in red wine come in huge portions that will hold you all day. It's fun and it's cheap. No reservations are accepted.

*Price: About $15–$20 per person*
*Open Mon.–Sat. for lunch and dinner; closed Sun.*
*No credit cards accepted*

---

# MASA'S
## 648 Bush Street (*between Stockton and Powell streets*)
### 415-989-7154

Masa Kobayashi started out in New York, moved to the Napa Valley, and then to San Francisco. His carefully crafted classic French cooking, combined with his artistic presentations, gave him a national reputation. His tragic death in 1984, at the hands of a murderer who's never been found, took from us one of our great chefs.

Fortunately, Bill Galloway, who had worked under Masa as *sous-chef,* has succeeded in maintaining the same high standards. Happily, this is one French restaurant where the food tastes as fantastic as it looks. You have a choice of a fixed-price meal or ordering *à la carte.* Either way, you end up with a fabulously rich meal with rainbows of perfectly executed sauces on every plate. Seasonal specials are always added to the regular menu. While there isn't a loser on the menu, the fish appetizers and game birds as entrées are always great.

The intimate dining room, which is elegant but not at all pretentious, has just 14 tables. So reservations are hard to come by; normally you have to call at 10 A.M. exactly three weeks in advance.

*Price: About $60 per person*
*Open Tues.–Sat. for dinner only; closed Sun. and Mon.*
*Accepts all major credit cards*

# MEKONG
## 730 Larkin Street
### 415-928-8989

Mekong is one of the Vietnamese businesses that have sprung up along two blocks of what used to be the Tenderloin, San Francisco's skid-row area. Because of the influx of Vietnamese families, the whole character of the neighborhood is changing. Mekong is unpretentious, cheap, and delicious. The six-page menu offers breakfast, lunch, and dinner, and lots of snacks you can stop in for at midday. The classic Vietnamese dishes—Imperial rolls, five-spice chicken, and the like—are done beautifully here. You can also eat more exotic fare, such as a marvelous coconut chicken sautéed in lemon grass.

*Price: About $13 per person*
*Open daily for breakfast, lunch, and dinner*
*No credit cards accepted*

# MIRAMONTE
## 1327 Railroad Avenue, Saint Helena
### 707-963-3970

This is perhaps the greatest wine-country restaurant. The vineyards lie all around it, the air is soft and warm, and the food marvelous. The cooking of chef Udo Nechutny represents the best of modern French cuisine with its juxtaposition of raw and cooked foods, unexpected combinations of ingredients, and a Japanese-influenced sensitivity to color and arrangement. The creative, five-course meals are rich and complex but never ponderous. The restaurant inhabits the ground floor of the old Miramonte Hotel, refurbished into light and airy dining rooms with pristine white walls framed by polished blond wood. There is a courtyard for summertime dining. The California wine list is excellent and reasonably priced. Reserve well in advance for weekends.

*Price: About $50 per person*
*Open Wed.–Sat. for dinner only; Sun. for lunch only; closed Mon. and Tues.*
*No credit cards accepted*

# MODESTO LANZONE'S
Opera Plaza (*between Van Ness Avenue and Franklin Street,*
*Golden Gate, and Turk Street*)
415-928-0400

The original Modesto's at Ghirardelli Square has been eclipsed by the new branch at Opera Plaza. At Ghirardelli, you often find yourself treated like a tourist, and the food is at that level, too. While not everything at Opera Plaza is consistently wonderful, your chance for an excellent meal is far better, particularly if you skip the printed menu and order the specials. You dine at large tables in comfortable chairs surrounded by museum-quality modern art. The waiters wear tuxedos and wheel the food out in carts. The cooking is Northern Italian, prepared with a light hand. Standouts include the house-made pastas, particularly the more unusual-sounding ones.

*Price: About $35 per person*
*Open Mon.–Fri. for lunch and dinner; Sat. for dinner only; closed Sun.*
*Accepts all major credit cards*

# MUSTARDS
7399 St. Helena Highway (*just north of Yountville*)
707-944-2424

Mustards in the Napa Valley has been such a huge success that the owners have opened two similar places, Fog City Diner in San Francisco and Rio Grill in Carmel. The restaurant offers superb California cuisine in a very pleasant, informal atmosphere, and at very reasonable prices. The old wood-framed building, which was once a cheese store, now houses a mesquite grill and a wood-burning brick oven, turning out such dishes as rabbit, duck, grilled fish, and grilled eggplant. It's quintessential California cuisine—fresh, simple, and very tasty.

*Price: About $30 per person*
*Open daily for lunch and dinner*
*Accepts Visa and MasterCard*

# NEW BOONVILLE RESTAURANT AND BAR

Highway 128, Boonville (*Take 101 north from San Francisco, west on 128; about a 45-minute drive*)
**707-895-3478**

If you want to explore a magnificent area of the California coast, go up to Mendocino, and stop at the Boonville on the way. This rambling, weather-beaten white building in the center of a no-stoplight town may be the only example of what the national food and restaurant media have been obsessed with for the last several years: an authentic, truly local California restaurant. The Boonville is an ideal, a passion, a wild dream made to come true by Vernon and Charlene Rollins, who decided to open a restaurant that only served food grown and raised on the grounds. So far, they've laid out a huge garden, with a pen of honking ducks and a family of goats nearby. The interior of the ground floor has been divided into several art-filled dining rooms; the rest of the building will someday be restored into a hotel.

Everything is simple, everything is fresh, and everything is wonderful. If you walk through the garden after you've ordered, you may find Charlene out picking the vegetables for your meal. Never have salads been fresher or more elegant, never have pizzas featured a crispier crust. The hamburger alone —with fresh sautéed spinach, goat cheese, and home-baked bun—is worth the three-hour trip. The grilled meats (particularly the rabbit) and the sautéed vegetables are astonishing. If berry ice cream is offered for dessert, you can be sure the berries were picked that morning.

*Price: About $30 per person*
*Open daily for lunch and dinner*
*No credit cards accepted*

# PERRY'S

1944 Union Street
**415-922-9022**

Perry's serves some of the best pub food in town and has been turning it out consistently for years. Any item you choose from the posted menu of generous salads and hearty meat dishes will be fresh and carefully cooked to order. Fried chicken attains new heights of crispness. Perry's huge hamburgers have the reputation of being the best in San Francisco, especially when accompanied by golden disks of fried potatoes. When you put your name on the waiting list, request a table at the back, away from the noisy, smoky bar.

*Price: About $15 per person*
*Open daily for breakfast, lunch, and dinner*
*Accepts all major credit cards*

---

# PHNOM PENH
## 631 Larkin Street (*at Eddy Street*)
### 415-775-5979

There's at least one bright side to all the travails of Cambodia. Many refugees have settled in San Francisco, and now we have the first two exclusively Cambodian restaurants in the country. It's a remarkable cuisine, using many Thai ingredients but cooking them in a different style. It's less oily, a little less hot, and more delicate than Thai food. Phnom Penh is a tiny place that somehow manages to sandwich a Thai dancer into the proceedings. Don't miss the stuffed eggplant, which could be the most ethereal eggplant dish you've ever tasted. Reservations are essential.

*Price: About $15 per person*
*Open Mon.–Sat. for lunch and dinner; closed Sun.*
*Accepts Visa and MasterCard*

---

# PLEARN THAI CUISINE
## 2050 University Avenue (*just below Shattuck Avenue*), Berkeley
### 415-841-2148

Plearn is not only the best Thai restaurant in the Bay Area; it's one of the best of any sort. Since it moved to a new and much larger location near the University of California campus, the lines have become even longer and the food even better. Plearn Kundhikanjana, the charismatic chef and owner, blends spices, herbs, and other seasonings to produce dishes of remarkable complexity. Moreover, she manages to maintain consistently high quality. Lots of her dishes are fiery hot, but the heat never drowns out the other flavors; there's always a bouquet of tastes and aromas. Try the fish cakes, the fiery *calamari* salad, and the curry dishes; then cool off with boneless stuffed chicken wings and one of the many noodle specialties. No reservations are accepted and long lines abound.

*Price: About $15 per person*
*Open Mon.–Sat. for lunch and dinner; closed Sun.*
*Accepts Visa and MasterCard*

# RENÉ VERDON'S LE TRIANON
## 242 O'Farrell Street
### 415-982-9353

This is the best of San Francisco's long-established downtown French restaurants, though it lacks the innovation that makes restaurants like Masa's and Miramonte so splendid. The menu is large, the preparations refined, the wines elegant, and the prices high. René Verdon, the chef-owner, has an exalted reputation among his peers, and he is capable of turning out exquisite dishes. His fish cookery is unsurpassed—poached Dover sole in a shiny sea of vermouth cream, *mousseline* of scallops and salmon, and warm oysters with curry, cream, and spinach. But there are some clunkers on his overly-large menu. Order the nightly specials or choose the fish. The fancy dining room decor dates from the early 1970s, and it wasn't breaking any new ground then.

*Price: About $60 per person*
*Open Mon.–Sat. for dinner only; closed Sun.*
*Accepts all major credit cards*

# RISTORANTE GRIFONE
## 1609 Powell Street (*at Vallejo Street*)
### 415-397-8458

Beware of the Italian restaurants of North Beach. Some of the most famous offer food that's often disappointing. They're fun for a drink, but consider going to Grifone for dinner. This is a friendly, modestly priced, unpretentious Italian restaurant with excellent pasta and veal dishes. Start with the *linguine* with shellfish or the *gnocchi* with *pesto* sauce and then move on to any of the veal offerings. There's also a superb, tender steak in a reduced red-wine sauce called *medallioni filetto*. Reservations are essential.

*Price: About $30 per person*
*Open Mon.–Sat. for dinner only; closed Sun.*
*Accepts all major credit cards*

# ROSE AND LeFAVOUR
## 1420 Main Street, Saint Helena
### 707-963-1681

This is about the closest a restaurant can offer to eating in someone's home. The fixed-price menu is planned for each day for exactly the number of people who have reservations. There is one seating only, and the meal takes three hours. Six-plus courses are served on elegant china. The food is as elegant as the appointments and is appropriate to the unique experience of dining at Rose and LeFavour. Oddly enough, this is one restaurant where the brilliance of each individual dish does not determine the success of the meal. Some are a bit flat, and others not as exciting as the menu descriptions suggest. Yet the concept of the meal—a series of small, very creative dishes masterminded by chef Bruce LeFavour—makes this a unique dining experience. And the dishes that work can be gems. Reservations are required.

*Price: About $50 per person*
*Open Wed.–Sat. for dinner only; Sun. for lunch only; closed Mon.–Tues.*
*No credit cards accepted*

---

## SANPPO
### 1702 Post Street
#### 415-346-3486

This informal Japantown restaurant offers a wide range of homey, country-style Japanese dishes that are always perfectly prepared and amazingly inexpensive. This means that you will probably have to wait for a place—possibly a shared place—during the busiest times. The *sushi* and *sashimi* are bright-tasting and fresh; the *tempuras* are light and crisp; the *nabemonos* (a meal in one pot) beautifully arranged and chock-full of high-quality ingredients. Try the *gyoza,* succulent meat-filled dumplings.

*Price: About $15 per person*
*Open Tues.–Sat. for lunch and dinner; Sun. for dinner only; closed Mon.*
*No credit cards accepted*

---

## SANTA FE BAR AND GRILL
### 1310 University Avenue, Berkeley
#### 415-841-4740

Jeremiah Tower, a creative cook who has gained a national reputation, designed the menu and trained the chefs in this large, lively restaurant in a converted old train depot. It's still as good as when Tower was in the kitchen every night. The menu is built around mesquite-grilled dishes augmented by a variety of trend-setting appetizers and some French-inspired creations. Always good are the warm salads of barely wilted greens tossed with sautéed bacon or *pancetta* and garnished with California goat cheese. From the grill, don't miss the squab marinated in raspberry vinegar or the grilled Petaluma duck with curly endive and red cabbage. Each day three or four types of grilled fish are offered, usually with a flavored butter melting on top. For dessert see if you can catch the warm fruit *gratin*. Because the restaurant is large and busy, inconsistencies do occur.

*Price: About $30 per person*
*Open daily for lunch and dinner*
*Accepts all major credit cards*

---

## TON KIANG

638 Broadway (*at Stockton Street*)   415-421-2015
3148 Geary Boulevard   415-752-4440
5827 Geary Boulevard   415-387-8273

The Broadway location was one of the first restaurants in the U.S. to offer Hakka cuisine, and Ton Kiang almost immediately became popular. The Hakka are Cantonese who migrated south from Northern China, retaining their own dialect, costume, and cooking style. The most intriguing dishes are listed among the Hakka specialties, a separate section of the menu. Salt-baked chicken looks hardly cooked, yet its flesh is snowy white, succulent, and aromatic of garlic and coriander. Bean curd stuffed with a spicy pork sausage is napped in a beautiful clear sauce perfumed with wisps of scallion and fresh coriander leaves. The humble surroundings at the Broadway location are no reflection on the quality of the food. The other locations are more cheerful and the menus are identical.

*Price: About $15 per person*
*Open daily for lunch and dinner*
*Accepts Visa and MasterCard*

---

## TUNG FONG

808 Pacific Avenue (*just above Stockton Street*)
415-362-7115

If you're having just one lunch in San Francisco, make it *dim sum*. This is the Chinese tea lunch—a variety of dumplings, filled pastry crescents, egg rolls, meat-filled buns, aluminum foil-wrapped packages of chicken, tiny salads, meat or seafood balls, or pickles. The place to have it is Tung Fong, a friendly little restaurant with similar food—but very different style—from the huge *dim sum* houses of Hong Kong. (If you like football-field-sized restaurants, try Asia Garden for *dim sum;* it's just down the street.) The variations of *dim sum* are endless, but hot or cold, these delectable tidbits always come on small plates in small portions, and the diner always gets to choose from a cart or tray of them. At the end of lunch, the waiter counts the empty dishes at your table to tally up the check. The chef-owner of Tung Fong comes from Shanghai, and her creations have a Northern Chinese spiciness that is an unexpected delight.

*Price: About $7 per person*
*Open Thurs.–Tues. for breakfast and lunch only; closed Wed.*
*No credit cards accepted*

---

## YUET LEE SEAFOOD
### 1300 Stockton Street (*at Broadway*)
#### 415-982-6020

This Hong Kong-style seafood and noodle house stir-fries in intensely hot woks, a technique that produces moist and fragrant fish and shellfish dishes without smothering them in sauces. Most of the fish is alive minutes before you eat it and part of the experience is choosing a wriggling crab or an eel from a tank. The chosen creature quickly becomes a gorgeous dish, generally seasoned with disks of ginger, slashes of scallion, and flecks of red pepper. You can find seafood here that appears nowhere else, such as scallops still in their shells and baby abalone and fresh shrimp, for which prices are high. But you won't be disappointed with the more modest steamed rockfish, and dabs, and rex sole. Always begin your meal with an order of dry, fried salt-and-pepper squid. Bring your own beer or wine.

*Price: About $15–$30 per person*
*Open Wed.–Mon. for lunch and dinner; closed Tues.*
*No credit cards accepted*

---

## ZUNI CAFÉ
### 1658 Market Street (*between Franklin and Gough streets*)
#### 415-552-2522

This is one of the most splendid, little unknown restaurants in San Francisco. It started with a Southwestern motif, but the menu has branched out in many directions, brought together by the idea of the freshest ingredients impeccably prepared. You can start at a cold seafood bar with oysters, littleneck clams, crayfish, or fresh scallops. Vegetables, often mesquite-grilled with beautiful sauces, are always outstanding. The simple grilled dishes, such as rabbit, *poussin,* and various fish, are done with remarkable expertise. It's a friendly, white-washed place, where you can dress informally and drink excellent California wines.

*Price: About $30 per person*
*Open daily for lunch and dinner*
*No credit cards accepted*

# SEATTLE

## BY SCHUYLER INGLE

**BREAKFAST**
Lowell's
Streamliner Diner

**CHINESE**
Green Village

**ECLECTIC**
Café Sport
Chez Shea
Green Lake Grill
The Other Place

**FRENCH**
Dominique's Place
Le Gourmand

**ITALIAN**
Bravo Pagliaccio
Il Bistro
Il Terrazzo Carmine
Pink Door
Settebello

**JAPANESE**
Nikko
Takara

**PANORAMA**
Chez Shea
Pink Door
Ray's Boathouse

**PIZZA**
Andre's
New York Pizza Place
Piecora

**SEAFOOD**
Browny's Rain City Grill
Browny's Seafood Broiler
McCormick and Schmick's
Ray's Boathouse

**SUBURBAN**
Bravo Pagliaccio

**THAI**
Bangkok Café

Ten years ago dining choices in Seattle were a simple thing for the traveler: Canlis' for an expensive steak, The Other Place for an elegant Continental meal reflective of French *nouvelle cuisine,* and Ray's Boathouse for seafood. There were also a smattering of small French restaurants of the duck *à l'orange* and *ratatouille* stripe. The chef-owners had come to Seattle with the World's Fair in 1962 and, Frenchmen that they were, they recognized the quality and abundance of Pacific Northwest bounty: seafood, shellfish, wild mushrooms, game, fruit, and seasonal vegetables—and they stayed.

Seattle's culinary revolution is all of five or six years old. But city restaurateurs have wasted little time catching up and leaving far behind the days of meat-heavy menus and meals made mostly of fried foods and processed ingredients. Fresh and seasonal products are key elements in Seattle's food scene today. While there may not be any truly great restaurants in Seattle that can go head to head with the best the world has to offer, the range, quality, and value of meals served in Seattle's best restaurants will satisfy even the most curmudgeonly diner.

With the proliferation of good, adventuresome restaurants, the sophistication of the Seattle diner has become more refined. Restaurateurs admit that meals they were proud to serve five years ago they wouldn't think of putting on their tables today. So this is a city in transition, from good, to better, to best—a city where jaded palettes and culinary cynicism are unknown foreign bodies. The meals you enjoy in Seattle may be some of the best of your life.

*Schuyler Ingle is food editor and restaurant critic for* The Weekly.

---

## ANDRÉ'S
### 5402 20 Avenue NW
#### 206-783-0479

André Goldberg is French, but he trained as a baker in Seattle, and now he has forsaken that for pizza. His restaurant is all of 360 square feet. So what you are likely to be doing here is waiting for your takeout pizza. It's worth the wait, both in terms of the thicker-style crust (you will eat it all), the sauce, and the best quality ingredients on top. Reasonable prices. If it's summer, think about a pizza and a picnic at nearby Commodore Park at the Hiram Chittenden Locks.

*Price: Under $10 per person*
*Open Mon.–Fri. for lunch and dinner; Sat. for dinner only; closed Sun.*
*No credit cards accepted*

---

## BANGKOK CAFÉ
### 219 Broadway Avenue East
### 206-328-1660

Seattle has experienced a recent flowering of Thai restaurants and everyone seems to have their favorites. Many of these establishments cater to a Western palate, rather than educating the foreign tongue to a new and wonderful taste experience. If there is an operative philosophy at Bangkok Café, it is pride in Thailand and the heritage to be shared in its food.

Standards like *thom yum goong,* the sweet-and-sour shrimp soup with small mushrooms and lemon grass, has a distinctly clear taste at Bangkok Café, the sign of good broth. The curry beef and the traditional-style barbecue chicken are outstanding. The shrimp sautéed in garlic, onion, and ginger is enough to make you want to book passage the next day to Bangkok. All that and the sweetness so typical of Thai service.

*Price: About $7.50 per person*
*Open daily for lunch and dinner*
*Accepts Visa and MasterCard*

---

## BRAVO PAGLIACCIO
### 10733 Northup Way
### 206-827-8585

Suburbs of Seattle are generically known as the "North End" or the "East Side." Strictly speaking, the East Side takes in several communities, all of them booming, including Kirkland and Bellevue. Lots of business is conducted on the East Side, particularly of the computer and software kind. So a restaurant with a particular ambience and style is in order. Bravo fits the bill, for its understated interior, for the staff trained to serve and not harass, and for the food. It can be sublime.

The pizza is some of the best, in this case baked in Seattle's first wood-fired pizza oven. Grilled meats and poultry, along with various pastas, are also specialties of the house. The tone here is friendly but reserved. The food is splendid, but at the same time does not detract from the business at hand, whether it be social or business.

*Price: About $15 per person*
*Open Sun.–Fri. for lunch and dinner; Sat. for dinner only*
*Accepts American Express, Visa, and MasterCard*

---

## BROWNY'S SEAFOOD BROILER
### 638 NW Richmond Beach Road
#### 206-542-4766

Owner-chef Mike Brown got his start at Ray's, so this follows the tradition of attention to quality, and then proceeds on into a little more adventuresomeness. *Calamari* sautéed with fiddlehead ferns and Pernod, for example. Or fresh halibut in parchment paper with Madeira butter and wild mushrooms. Or fresh Alaska spot prawns baked with artichoke hearts and Italian tomatoes in fresh herb-and-garlic marinade. Browny's is far enough out in the north end of Seattle that it is really a suburban restaurant. It is also well worth the slight extra effort it will take to get out there.

As this book goes to press, Mike Brown has just opened Browny's Rain City Grill at 2359 Tenth Avenue E (206-325-5003), with emphasis on pastas and grilled meats. It promises to be a good place to consider if you want to get a bite after 10 P.M. That's not the easiest thing to do in Seattle.

*Price: About $20 per person*
*Open Mon.–Fri. for lunch and dinner; Sat. and Sun. for dinner only*
*Accepts all major credit cards*

---

## CAFÉ SPORT
### 2020 Western Avenue
#### 206-443-6000

Café Sport is a consistently good, creative restaurant, lunch or dinner, day or night, winter or summer. You can't lose. Like any of the restaurants in and around the Pike Place Market, it's little more than a stroll from the major downtown hotels and shopping area. What you will be served, however, is worth a serious hike.

Addicts line up for the grilled chicken and spicy noodle salad. The clams or mussels steamed in fresh ginger butter work like a good marriage. Fish entrées might include grilled Idaho brook trout served with a green peppercorn and lemon-cream sauce, or baked Pacific ling cod with a tomato and fresh thyme *coulis*. Look for excellent game in the fall and winter. In summer, when local fruits and berries come in, expect to see the likes of a Washington-grown veal chop in black currant sauce. Finally, you will find the prices at Café Sport incredibly reasonable.

*Price: About $15 per person*
*Open Mon.–Sat. for lunch and dinner; closed Sun.*
*Accepts all major credit cards*

---

## CHEZ SHEA
### Pike Place Market
#### 206-467-9990

With nine tables and attentive service, Chez Shea may well be Seattle's most romantic restaurant. Windows look out over the Pike Place Market and the boat and ferry traffic on the Sound, giving the restaurant a sense of spaciousness beyond its actual confines. The food is consistently innovative and grand.

Dinner is fixed-price and four course starting with an appetizer that, depending on the time of year, might be smoked salmon tartare with black bread and watercress mayonnaise. The second course could be a *gâteau* of wild mushrooms sautéed with shallots and herbs, layered between *crêpes,* baked, and served with a lemon-cream sauce. I have yet to have anything but well-executed, exciting entrées at Chez Shea. A loin of lamb roasted with rhubarb and ginger sauce, fresh halibut poached with roasted Anaheim chili sauce, fresh rabbit braised with mustard and finished with a golden raisin sauce all taste as wonderful as they sound. The lunch menu is *à la carte,* offering a selection of several appetizers and six entrées, all according to what is seasonally available.

*Price: Fixed price at $24 per person*
*Open Tues.–Sat. for lunch and dinner; closed Sun.*
*Accepts all major credit cards*

---

## DOMINIQUE'S PLACE
### 1927 43 Avenue East
#### 206-329-6620

Chef-owner Dominique Place is a sorcerer with fire and herbs, witching up flavors with his sauces like no other chef in Seattle. In simple dishes such as a salad of fresh Oregon scallops with a fennel dressing, each green in the salad and each scallop very politely introduce themselves to the palate, then withdraw so that other flavors might have their moments of the diner's attention. His pepper steak is a benchmark experience. An almond and saffron soup is particularly memorable for its magic.

The restaurant is of the Provincial charm school, all copper pots, dried flowers, and fire flickering at the hearth. When the warm days and long, balmy evenings of Seattle summer arrive, Dominique's serves meals outside at umbrella-shaded tables.

*Price: About $30 per person*
*Open daily for lunch and dinner*
*Accepts all major credit cards*

## GREEN LAKE GRILL
### 7200 East Green Lake Drive North
#### 206-524-0365

Karl Beckley, owner-chef of the Green Lake Grill, has been a dominant force in the education of Seattle's palette, pushing the city on from fried, processed foods to lightly cooked seasonal fare of the most exquisite kind. He has managed to produce a radical cuisine that at the same time is non-threatening: relaxed chic. The restaurant is a combination of black-and-white tile floors, high ceilings, contemporary art, white linen, as well as green booth seating that harks back to lunch counter dining.

Beckley changes the menu with each season. His blue fin tuna grilled with *tamari, sake,* lemon, and ginger will make you forget you have ever craved a fat steak. He has a deft hand with rabbit, whether in a tomato sauce or prepared with fresh apricots in a Riesling sauce. His *linguine* with smoked salmon and Jack Daniels whiskey is sublime. During the season, don't fail to order the Olympia oyster appetizer, a true delicacy and treat from the Pacific Northwest. The mussels and clams steamed in a wine broth are satisfying, as is the duck *ravioli* with ginger sauce. If the weather is right, cross the street and finish the experience with a stroll around Green Lake.

*Price: About $15 per person*
*Open Mon.–Fri. for lunch and dinner; Sat. and Sun. for dinner only*
*Accepts all major credit cards*

## GREEN VILLAGE
### 605½ South King Street
#### 206-624-3634

Just about the time Chinese food in Seattle had taken on generic qualities, along came Green Village, a small upstairs restaurant in the International District. Something special was happening, something different and difficult to identify. Joby Liu, the young chef, is the answer. He has come to cooking with a sense of tradition, but not after growing up in a family-run restaurant. So he doesn't repeat as if by rote the same cooking found in nine out of ten Chinese restaurants. He gives it a fresh touch, an enthusiasm, and it shows.

The cold shredded chicken with chile sauce is unworldly. His hot-and-sour soup will help you redefine the experience of this standard. Oil-dripped chicken, hot scallops or squid, twice-cooked pork, sautéed bean cake with hot sauce—these and many other dishes are alive with flavor, not tired from a lack of imagination. Green Village can re-establish a lost faith in the merits of Chinese cuisine.

*Price: About $5 per person*
*Open Wed.–Mon. for lunch and dinner; closed Tues.*
*Accepts Visa and MasterCard*

---

# IL BISTRO
## Pike Place Market
### 206-682-3049

If Il Bistro has one hallmark, it is atmosphere: dark corners, white linen, golden light, and low ceilings. And it's a restaurant within walking distance of downtown hotels, making it a place to do business, to entertain, to hold court. The bar is a world all its own in Seattle, a definite plus.

The menu is brief and announces that this is not the place to expect aggressive culinary innovation. What is served, though, can be quite good. The *tagliarellini alla marinara,* heavy on the garlic and crushed red peppers, is popular. So too is the lamb, usually a special, and the *tortellini alla panna,* served with a white cream sauce. Il Bistro is a safe bet to host a small party and impress the guests.

*Price: About $25 per person*
*Open daily for dinner only*
*Accepts all major credit cards*

---

# IL TERRAZZO CARMINE
## 411 First Avenue South
### 206-467-7797

Riding on a crest of enthusiasm for high-end Italian cuisine, Carmine Smeraldo opened one of the more stylish restaurants in the city and set a steady example for the way things Italian should taste. The interior is open, high ceilinged, and warm. The terrace, a particular treat during Seattle's summer, looks out onto a small brick plaza with running water and a low-lying waterfall.

Smeraldo dodges the current regional chic among Italian restaurants, and, instead, presents dishes from all parts of Italy. His aim is to take what is traditional and at the heart of Italian cooking and to update it for today's taste and sense of lightness. Game is a particular strength at Il Terrazzo. A roast pheasant finished in Amarone wine and grape sauce is memorable. Smeraldo's veal loin, filled with prawns and spinach and served with a garlic and wine sauce, is as much a showpiece as it is delicious. But his real forté is the pasta of the day, taking what is at hand in the market and working around *fettuccine*. In winter and early spring, his sweetbreads and sun-dried tomatoes with *fettuccine* has been outstanding. In the warmer days of summer, the pasta special is more likely to be a purée of sun-dried tomatoes with asparagus tips in a cream sauce. The rabbit he serves on the lunch menu is not to be missed.

*Price: About $20 per person*
*Open Mon.–Fri. for lunch and dinner; Sat. for dinner only; closed Sun.*
*Accepts all major credit cards*

---

# LE GOURMAND
## 425 NW Market Street
### 206-784-3463

Le Gourmand has an atmosphere unlike any other restaurant in Seattle. This is a small restaurant not unlike the dining room of a European country inn: quiet and restrained. The people who surround you just happen to be speaking English. But this isn't to say the mood is stiff. Not with the way food is served at Le Gourmand. The orders come to the table on large platters and the diner serves himself. The menu is so small that a party of four can simply order the entire thing and everyone can have a taste. The price is fixed and reasonable.

Chef-owners Robin Sanders and Bruce Naftaly have worked their way through some of Seattle's finest restaurants, always leaving their indelible marks, before opening Le Gourmand. The restaurant is exactly as they want it: very small and open for dinner four nights a week. They have a deserved reputation for ferreting out the finest of local ingredients, then making them sing on the plate with sauces of classic complexity. Don't plan on dieting at Le Gourmand. But do plan on a peak Pacific Northwest experience. A recent evening began with a *terrine* of rabbit livers, then lamb rib chops with mustard, and steamed scallops in the shell with Riesling and fennel, followed by a spinach salad with sherry vinaigrette, and Vashon Island goat's milk cheese with walnut toast. All of it magnificent. Reservations are essential.

*Price: Fixed price at $18 per person*
*Open Wed.–Sat. for dinner only*
*Accepts all major credit cards*

# LOWELL'S
## Pike Place Market
### 206-622-2036

Breakfast at Lowell's, particularly in the middle of the week, is getting down to hard-core Seattle. The service is cafeteria style, though orders are delivered to tables, many of which have an unexcelled view of Puget Sound and the waterfront. Located smack dab in the middle of the Pike Place Market, you may find yourself sharing a table with vegetable brokers and fishmongers. Yours may be the only English spoken. Good eggs, good muffins, good coffee, an atmosphere that can't be bottled: What more could anyone want?

*Price: About $4 per person*
*Open Mon.–Sat. for breakfast and lunch only; closed Sun.*
*Accepts all major credit cards*

# McCORMICK AND SCHMICK'S
## 1103 First Avenue
### 206-623-5500

This downtown restaurant has the look of an establishment that has been serving fine seafood and grilled meat and poultry to bankers and timber barons since the turn of the century. But it's new. And it's a good downtown restaurant specializing in seafood. The menu changes daily according to what's available, but during the appropriate season pay close attention to the oysters on the half shell. Westcott Bay oysters and the native Olympias are among the best oysters in the world. Much the same can be said of the Manila clams and the Penn Cove mussels. Choosing among the simplest preparations— broiled swordfish and grilled king salmon with a pepper vinaigrette—can be a safer bet than selections that require too much of the saucier's skill for success.

*Price: About $15 per person*
*Open daily for lunch and dinner*
*Accepts all major credit cards*

# NEW YORK PIZZA PLACE
## First and Columbia avenues
### 206-467-6699

For New Yorkers, a home away from home. Order a slice, fold it in half, close your eyes, and feel the oil run down your arm: true to life. The hero sandwiches are modeled after a namesake in Brooklyn. The *antipasto* salad makes it all a splendid, and cheap, lunch.

*Price: About $3–$5 per person.*
*Open Mon.–Sat. for lunch and dinner; closed Sun.*
*No credit cards accepted*

---

# NIKKO
## 1306 South King Street
### 206-322-4641

Owner-chef Shiro Kashiba is, quite simply, one of the more innovative chefs in the city. He works within the traditions of the Japanese kitchen. The restaurant itself offers fairly standard fare. The real reason to try Nikko is the *sushi* bar. Kashiba has a way with local seafood—fish such as smelt and salmon, shellfish like oysters and clams—that is wholly different from anything being done in other city restaurants. Nothing is left unexplored. His half-a-rockfish head cooked in a special sauce is enlightening. Kashiba can take the delicate bones of sole and produce a deep-fried version like potato chips. It's best to assure him you are interested in what's fresh and creative at the *sushi* bar, then sit back and watch it unfold. That is unless you are likely to know about and order monkfish liver on your own.

*Price: About $20 per person at the* sushi *bar*
*Open Mon.–Sat. for dinner only; closed Sun.*
*Accepts all major credit cards*

---

# THE OTHER PLACE
## 319 Union Avenue
### 206-623-7340

Ten years ago The Other Place brought to Seattle the first shadings of *nouvelle cuisine* in line with the ideas of Les Frères Troisgros. Today the restaurant is something of a grande dame, surrounded by stylish restaurants with distinct New American edges. Such is the speed of the transformation of the Seattle culinary scene. The Other Place, nonetheless, can often be the best restaurant Seattle has to offer. Other times it can be much, much less. The wine list wins national awards.

In its ten years The Other Place has taken maximum advantage of local products. In the fall, don't be surprised to see antelope on the menu or wild boar as well as venison. Appetizers such as poached sable fish, warm cured lamb salad, or Oregon scallops with chives and red ginger are superb. The impromptu salad of seasonal greens, all grown and gathered for The Other Place by Pragtree Farm, is of particular interest.

*Price: Fixed price from $16–$28 per person*
*Open Mon.–Fri. for lunch and dinner; Sat. for dinner only; closed Sun.*
*Accepts all major credit cards*

---

## PIECORA'S
### 1401 East Madison Avenue
**206-322-9411**

The owners are two New York boys in Seattle doing the real thing. A tiny restaurant with no atmosphere and great thin-crust pizza in a very simple presentation.

*Price: For a large pizza with a topping, $9.00*
*Open daily for lunch and dinner*
*No credit cards accepted*

---

## PINK DOOR
### Post Alley, Pike Place Market
**206-682-3241**

Through the summer, twilight in Seattle will last well after 9 P.M. On a warm night, there is no better restaurant deck than the one at the Pink Door. The view west takes in the Pike Place Market, the waterfront, and the ferry boats coming and going. All that and good food and a full service bar.

Dining at the Pink Door at night is a simple thing. The meal comes in four courses—*antipasto,* pasta, entrée with vegetable, and salad—and the price is fixed, either $12.50 or $14.00. *Cioppino* is the house special and other entrées include a fresh seafood, chicken, and a meat, whether lamb or veal. The lunch menu offers a wider range of choices (I tend to alternate between *insalata di mare* and pasta and broccoli) and the same magnificent deck for those who enjoy the sun and the view.

*Price: Fixed price from $12.50–$14 per person*
*Open Tues.–Sat. for lunch and dinner; closed Mon. and Sun.*
*Accepts Visa and MasterCard*

# RAY'S BOATHOUSE
## 6049 Seaview Avenue NW
### 206-789-3770

You will find no better seafood quality than the fare offered at Ray's because the restaurant can boast the best seafood buyers working in Seattle restaurants. That, and a view across Shilshole Bay that makes the visitor wonder why he doesn't live in Seattle, are the two great selling points of this restaurant. The presentation is straightforward: ginger steamed black cod with soy sauce and scallions, grilled salmon fillets, baked halved prawns. You may find yourself tasting it all for the first time, however: The product of the highest quality is a hallmark here. But so, too, is the best frozen product come winter when the salmon no longer run. Try the Bruce Gore Sea frozen salmon in the middle of winter. Chances are, like Julia Child, you won't be able to tell it apart from the best of the fresh during the season. Such is Ray's attentiveness to their product.

*Price: About $18 per person*
*Open daily for lunch and dinner*
*Accepts all major credit cards*

# SETTEBELLO
## 1525 East Olive Way
### 206-323-7772

When the Northern Italian wave hit Seattle, Settebello established itself as the first, as well as the last, word on that subject. It has had some rocky times, some problems with consistency, some problems with service, but has never failed to be a place to treat the well-informed palate to a little broadening. The interior is clean lined, white tiled, spare, and chic, all notions reflected in the food. Particular strengths include a remarkable inventiveness with pasta. The touch with grilled meats is both deft and simple, emphasizing the essential flavor. There is no better *antipasti* served in Seattle. The three-course lunch at Settebello is the deal of the city—$8.75, no menu. Whatever is fresh and looks good that day is served in four courses.

*Price: About $16 per person*
*Open Mon.–Fri. for lunch and dinner; Sat. for dinner only; closed Sun.*
*Accepts all major credit cards*

## STREAMLINER DINER
### 397 Winslow Way East, Bainbridge Island
#### 206-842-8595

Café-style breakfast with great cooks slinging the hash: that's part of the attraction of the Streamliner Diner. That and the ferry boat ride it takes to get there. Pick a splendid morning, go down to the ferry terminal on the Seattle waterfront, and catch the Winslow ferry. Half an hour later, invigorated by the ride, walk up into Winslow for breakfast. These people know how to cook eggs, make omelets, toast toast, bake muffins, and flip pancakes. You will have more trouble walking back to the ferry than you did arriving. For dessert, enjoy the Seattle waterfront and skyline at the end of the return ride.

*Price: About $3.50 per person*
*Open daily for breakfast and lunch*
*Accepts Visa and MasterCard*

## TAKARA
### Pike Place Market, Hillclimb
#### 206-682-8609

While Takara has a good *sushi* bar and is proud of its *sushi* chef, the real difference here is a menu that consists mostly of appetizers. Slices of geoduck clam rolled in flour and sautéed in butter and herbs are quintessential Northwest with a Japanese edge. Small taste treats such as deep-fried cubes of *tofu* served in a radish sauce are available alongside such standard dishes as *teriyaki, sukiyaki,* and *ton-katsu.* The diner has the opportunity at Takara to create his own meal of many small dishes, and it's difficult to get much more traditional than that. Another possibility is a lunchtime takeout to enjoy on the nearby ferry to Winslow and back—an hour-long round trip.

*Price: About $10 per person*
*Open Mon.–Sat. for lunch and dinner; closed Sun.*
*Accepts all major credit cards*

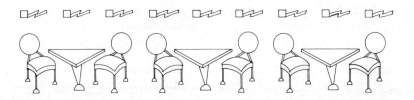

# WASHINGTON, D.C.

## By Ellen Brown

**AMERICAN**
American Café
The Florida Avenue Grill
Foggy Bottom Café
Nicholas
Old Ebbit Grill

**ASIAN**
Germaine's Asian Cuisine

**BREAKFAST**
Clyde's of Georgetown
The Florida Avenue Grill

**CAJUN/CREOLE**
New Orleans Café
New Orleans Emporium

**CHINESE**
China Coral
House of Hunan

**CUBAN**
Omega

**ECLECTIC**
The Inn at Little Washington
    (Washington, Virginia)
Restaurant Nora
Suzanne's
209½
Windows

**ETHIOPIAN**
Meskerem

**FAST FOOD**
American Café

**FRENCH**
Aux Beau Champs
Jean-Louis at Watergate
Jean-Pierre
La Brasserie
La Chaumière
L'Auberge Chez François (Great
    Falls, Virginia)
Le Pavillion
Maison Blanche

**HAMBURGERS**
Foggy Bottom Café

**HOTEL DINING ROOM**
Aux Beau Champs

**INDIAN/PAKISTANI**
Shezan

**ITALIAN**
Cantina d'Italia
Galileo
Rossini's Ristorante d'Italia
Vincenzo

**LATIN AMERICAN**
El Caribe

**MEXICAN**
Enriqueta's

**MOROCCAN**
Marrakesh Restaurant

**NIGHTCLUB/RESTAURANT**
F. Scott's

**PIZZA**
Geppetto

**PRE-THEATER**
    **RESTAURANT**
Foggy Bottom Café

**SEAFOOD**
China Coral

**STEAKS AND CHOPS**
Gary's

**SUBURBAN/REGIONAL**
China Coral (Bethesda,
    Maryland)
East Wind Restaurant
    (Alexandria, Virginia)
The Inn at Little Washington
    (Washington, Virginia)
L'Auberge Chez François (Great
    Falls, Virginia)

**VIETNAMESE**
East Wind Restaurant

**WINE BAR/RESTAURANT**
Suzanne's

Washington's restaurant scene has made the kind of progress during the past decade that would be envied by many of the government's negotiators. But while a local bank welcomes travelers to National Airport with a photo of the Jefferson Memorial and the slogan "Welcome to the Most Important City in the World," dining in the nation's capital is hardly part of that claim.

If you're lucky, food is the third priority at many of the city's restaurants, especially the downtown power lunch places. Who goes there is always first, and a Henry Kissinger or Ted Kennedy patronizing a spot with regularity can increase its business far faster than hiring a world-class chef. Next in order of importance is usually the size of the drinks, followed by either the food or ambiance.

This traditionally unfortunate state of affairs has improved greatly, but Washington still has a long way to come to match the culinary sophistication of some other major cities. Trends do not start here; and the number of truly first-class restaurants can be counted on one hand.

What the city does offer, however, is perhaps one of the greatest ranges of moderately priced ethnic spots, reflecting the location as the site of other nation's embassies as well as our own government. The hypothesis is that when we open diplomatic relations with a country, the first ambassador's brother-in-law tags along and starts a restaurant featuring the nation's cuisine, or the first embassy chef departs after a short time to make his mark on the restaurant world.

Within the city you'll find more Ethiopian restaurants than in any city except Addis Ababa. The United Nations panoply of ethnic foods includes excellent Vietnamese, Nepalese, Moroccan, Afghan, and Peruvian.

As with most urban sites, space is at a premium and rents are high, so it's the exception rather than the rule that you'll be able to hear yourself think at a meal. Tables are jammed together, which is why any lobbyist would love the one next to a senator's.

*Ellen Brown is the author of* Cooking with the New American Chefs *(Harper & Row, 1985) and* The Great Chefs of Chicago *(Avon Books, 1985). She is former food editor of the Washington-based* USA Today *and currently a frequent contributor to the Home Entertaining column of the* Washington Post Sunday

Magazine. *She was honored by* Cook's *Magazine in their Who's Who in American Cooking awards for 1985.*

## AMERICAN CAFÉ

1211 Wisconsin Avenue NW *(Georgetown)*   202-337-3600
227 Massachusetts Avenue NE *(Capitol Hill)*   202-547-8200
5252 Wisconsin Avenue NW *(Upper NW)*   202-363-5400
Other locations in Vienna, Va., Baltimore, Md., and Fair Oaks Mall in Fairfax, Va

The Georgetown location claims to have served the first *croissant* sandwich in the country, and although the interior of the flagship is more than a decade old, the design is still fresh and the food continues to be innovative. Fans of American Café feared that quality would decline as the restaurant became a local chain, but that, fortunately, has not been the case.

Although there is an extensive list of daily specials, many of them carefully mesquite-grilled, the salads and sandwiches have become staples and are consistently excellent. You can't go wrong with the salad sampler plate for a light meal or the Tennessee barbecue. Recent menu additions have been pizzas in cornmeal crusts, deep dish and a bit doughy, but filled with goodies. And the Cajun cornbread that now accompanies many dishes is savory and wonderful.

Many locations have markets attached, or offer takeout complete with all utensils. American Café is a wonderful place to pick up a picnic to take to the Mall or for a concert at Wolf Trap. The restaurants are crowded all day long, and should be considered the best places to "grab a bite" but not to dine, since the noise level and casualness preclude lingering.

*Price: About $12 per person*
*Open daily for lunch and dinner*
*Accepts all major credit cards*

## AUX BEAUX CHAMPS

In the Four Seasons Hotel, 2800 Pennsylvania Avenue NW
202-342-0444

With space between tables to ensure private conversation being as rare in Washington as a non-humid day in August, the dining room at the Four Seasons Hotel (located a floor below the lobby) pairs elegant and commodious surroundings with excellent food.

The dining room, with a floral-patterned carpet and such touches as antique Chinese urns filled with lavish flower arrangements, is open for three meals a day and an excellent Sunday brunch.

A Four Seasons Alternative Menu (500 calories for an appetizer and entrée) is available at lunch and dinner that now accounts for about half of the lunch business. You'll never know it's "diet food," as a recent dinner of a cream of scallop soup followed by a *paillard* of chicken in spinach and lemon sauce with perfectly sautéed vegetables proved.

The menu changes daily, and always includes a succulent lamb preparation, such as a tenderloin with tarragon and wild mushrooms, and many excellent fish dishes.

For business dinners for up to twelve, there is Le Petit Champ, perhaps the most elegant small private room in town. The wine list is moderately good, but highly priced.

*Price: About $40 per person*
*Open daily for breakfast, lunch, and dinner*
*Accepts all major credit cards*

---

# CANTINA D'ITALIA
## 1214-A 18 Street NW
### 202-659-1830

The red-green-and-white striped plastic sign with blinking white lights and heavily stuccoed walls decorated with plaster masks and panels of tapestry would lead you to think Cantina d'Italia would be serving pizza and Chef Boy-ar-dee. But, luckily for Washington diners, the food is far more contemporary and fresher than the heavy decor. And it has been that way now for two decades. The menu at Cantina changes weekly.

Cantina serves a variety of *antipasti,* and the vegetable salads are always made from the freshest and ripest ingredients. His selection of seafood can run up to a dozen items each night. Each of the *antipasti* is made in small batches, so you never have the sense that anything you eat is tired from the night before.

The pastas are a must, cooked to perfection and with sauces ranging from standard preparations done with well-balanced sauces to complex constructions, such as a mixture of green basil-and-red tomato noodles in olive oil with garlic and diced *mozzarella,* or *gnocchi* flavored with Parmesan cheese and served on a bed of fresh tomato sauce.

While veal dishes tend to be well prepared, try the rabbit and duck entrées, not frequently seen on Italian menus in Washington. The rabbit with fresh rosemary sauce and duck with Italian sausage and raisins are standouts.

Portions at Cantina are huge, harkening back to the era when it opened. The wine list is of considerable length and depth with Italian vintages.

*Price: About $40 per person*
*Open Mon.–Fri. for lunch and dinner; closed Sat. and Sun.*
*Accepts all major credit cards*

---

## CHINA CORAL
### 6900 Wisconsin Avenue, Bethesda, Maryland
### 301-656-1203

While Washington now hosts many Chinese restaurants with elegant interiors, this suburban spot—with floral print Formica tables and black plastic chairs —serves the best *dim sum* and Chinese treatments of seafood in town.

You realize the emphasis on fish when you walk in and are greeted by live lobster and fish tanks. Not only does China Coral offer the largest selection of seafood—including conch, frog, squid, abalone, and sea cucumber—they also know to the cook it. Never has fish come to the table overcooked.

Some of the best offerings are the sautéed stuffed scallops, stir-fried conch with chicken livers, and crispy flounder. You'll also find that frogs legs and squid are welcome alternatives prepared in *kung pao* sauce or with black beans and garlic; lobster is well treated with ginger, while scallions and abalone is quite delicate in oyster sauce.

China Coral does not roll *dim sum* carts around the room, but that is the only authentic touch lacking. The *dim sum* menu (which may also be enjoyed takeout) has about 35 items, from standards such as steamed shrimp or pork dumplings, to curried squid, stuffed duck feet, and about six sweet pastries, with the sweet lotus bean paste bun a favorite.

For the less adventurous, the renditions of baked pork buns and spring rolls should not be overlooked. Reservations are suggested for weekends.

*Price: About $20 per person for dinner; $8 per person for* dim sum *lunch*
*Open daily for lunch and dinner*
*Accepts all major credit cards*

---

## CLYDE'S OF GEORGETOWN
### 3236 M Street NW
### 202-333-9180

While the Clyde's chain has expanded in recent years to encompass suburban locations (and the owners also count the Old Ebbitt Grill [see page 819] among their holdings), the original Clyde's still features the best omelets in town, and they're almost a tradition for a relaxed Sunday morning.

While the restaurant, dating from the mid-nineteenth century, was expanded a few years ago to include another bar and a skylit atrium room with a jungle of plants in the rear, ask to sit in the Omelet Room, with old framed prints on the walls and hard antique wooden banquettes. Before you will be a pair of chefs with gas burners doing little except adding fillings to eggs and flipping their wrists with great skill to enclose such fillings as bacon, potatoes, and sautéed onions; Swiss cheese and spinach; Clyde's famous chili (sold canned at the counter if you become addicted); or just about any combination you can envision.

Begin with one of the champagne drinks or a lip-pursing Bloody Mary, served with a sticky rum bun, then choose an omelet and relive your Saturday night.

The service is efficient, in fact you can feel hurried if a line is forming. No reservations for Sunday or Saturday breakfast.

*Price: About $6 per person*
*Open daily for breakfast, lunch, and dinner*
*Accepts all major credit cards*

---

# EAST WIND RESTAURANT
## 809 King Street, Alexandria, Virginia
### 703-836-1515

Old Town Alexandria is like a suburban Georgetown, with gaslit streets and eighteenth-century buildings painted in authentic colors and filled with shops and restaurants.

While there are many Vietnamese restaurants in the District, East Wind has been attracting patrons from across the Potomac devoted to its spicy cinnamon beef and wax rhapsodically over the lemon grass chicken.

In this pocket of history, the dining room is remarkably contemporary, with plum-colored carpet and rough-hewn wood walls topped with a terra-cotta color that gives warmth to the room. There are few Oriental touches and exotic African flowers topping the wooden tables. There is also a rock sound track.

East Wind does excellent renditions of Vietnamese standards, such as crispy *cha gio* rolls, grilled skewers of both pork and beef, and *pho,* a soup of sliced beef on rice noodles in a most delicate broth.

The complex seasoning of Vietnamese cuisine is most apparent in some of the fish preparations, such as *tom kho hue,* which combines crunchy shrimp and pork slices in a hot peppery sauce, and a dish not found on other Vietnamese menus in the area: baby squids stuffed with shrimp, crab meat, and ground pork and then cooked in a red wine sauce blended with pineapple juice.

The menu is not extensive, but none of the dishes have been anything but excellent. Limited wines but a few good beers.

*Price: About $15 per person*
*Open Mon.–Fri. for lunch and dinner; Sat. and Sun. for dinner only*
*Accepts all major credit cards*

---

# EL CARIBE
## 3288 M Street NW
### 202-338-3121

Even though the country of origin may be listed on a menu, Latin American cooking is hardly distinguishable from Spanish, although one should certainly not expect the *enchiladas* or *tacos* of Mexican cuisine.

This restaurant, dimly lit with dusty wine bottles set on a wooden ledge separating the wood and stuccoed parts of the wall, offers a reasonably priced meal of well-prepared standard items.

Begin with a pitcher of margaritas, which they do very well, or a pitcher of the slightly overly fruity *sangria.*

Fried squid has been the consistently best appetizer, and then the choice is divided between such Spanish dishes as an excellent *paella* available either as all-seafood or with chicken, or a *zarzuela de mariscos* in which the seafood is simmered in a tangy sauce.

Personal favorites are the beef tongue in a spicy tomato sauce and squid stuffed with ham and seafood. Some of the South American casseroles include pork with bananas and a selection of root vegetables or a delicately spiced hen braised in sherry.

Forget dessert, except perhaps the *flan.* There are some interesting Argentinian and Spanish wines on the limited menu. Reservations are suggested, but there is a small bar in which to wait if you're without them.

*Price: About $20 per person*
*Open Mon.–Sat. for lunch and dinner; closed Sun.*
*Accepts all major credit cards*

---

# ENRIQUETA'S
## 2811 M Street NW, Georgetown
### 202-338-7772

In a national restaurant scene in which Taco Bell is becoming the standard, it's wonderful that some Mexican restaurants have retained a sense of authenticity and still present Mexican food as you'd find it South of the Border.

Certainly, there are some *tortilla* specialties—including delicious *tamales* and a wide selection of *enchiladas*. But these are not the only options, nor the best choices by and large. The *mole* sauce has been consistently good and the chili-laced *salsa* is another option for topping chicken. The fish and seafood dishes, simply prepared or sauced, have been uniformly fresh and flavorful.

One problem with the spot is that it is a small restaurant, and tables are packed in about as tightly as passengers on a Mexican bus. The atmosphere is festive, with painted Mexican rush-seated chairs and all the appropriate brightly-colored accessories, one in which you feel most comfortable when dressed casually.

Mexican beer is the best choice with the meals, since the *sangria* is terribly sweet.

*Price: About $12 per person*
*Open Mon.–Sat. for lunch and dinner; closed Sun.*
*Accepts all major credit cards*

---

# THE FLORIDA AVENUE GRILL
## 1100 Florida Avenue NW
### 202-265-1586

Just when you think the Southern traditional breakfast—perhaps that region's most important contribution to American culinary history—can only be found by trekking the mountains of the Carolinas, you hit upon a treasure like The Florida Avenue Grill.

The red plastic stools placed before the pink plastic counter give the grill the appearance of the sort of diner popular when it opened in 1944. Since that time, it was never segregated, while many Washington restaurants from that era cannot make that claim.

The Wilson family, who runs the restaurant, dishes up plates of pan-fried chicken, greens, slightly too sweet cornbread, and great potato salad for lunch and dinner, but it's the breakfast that attracts Yuppies from Georgetown and families from the environs.

You'll find mountains of great pancakes, canned corned beef hash "doctored" with freshly sautéed onions, home fried potatoes, and apples cooked in their skins. You'll hear the clanking of spatulas as they turn your eggs to order. No alcoholic beverages have ever been served. No reservations are taken.

*Price: About $4 per person*
*Open Mon.–Sat. for breakfast, lunch, and dinner; closed Sun.*
*No credit cards accepted*

# FOGGY BOTTOM CAFÉ
## In the River Inn, 924 25 Street NW
### 202-338-8707

While the Kennedy Center is within the trill of a soprano, very few good restaurants have opened that could be termed "convenient to the Kennedy Center." This small, sophisticated room off the lobby of a lesser-known hotel has been justly lauded. You can sip a Kir and belt down a burger prior to a concert (tell them you have a curtain time, and they will tell you what to order to make it) or you can linger and enjoy one of the specialties, such as the best *tempura* in town (regardless of the fact that this is not a Japanese restaurant) or ribs with a honey-barbecue sauce that rival any in the South.

The more sophisticated options (served in the pale-beige room decorated with brilliantly colored Lowell Nesbitt silkscreens of tulips) change nightly, and the pastas are always extremely good, as is the fish.

The Foggy Bottom Café does justice to simple burgers or complex sauces, such as the watercress-mustard sauce served on liver.

The room is noisy, and tables for two are close together. The service can be erratic. Reservations are suggested at all times.

*Price: About $20 per person*
*Open daily for lunch and dinner*
*Accepts all major credit cards*

# F. SCOTT'S
## 1232 36 Street NW
### 202-965-1789

Although positioned near Georgetown University, this is definitely an "adult spot," where black tie would not seem out of place but not wearing a jacket and tie would. F. Scott's is all glitz and glamor. But if you want to combine dinner and dancing, or want a late-night snack while nuzzling on the dance floor, this is the place to go.

F. Scott's has tiny tables, and if you really want to eat, the best location is in the small room on the lower level to the right of the dance floor. The best bet for dining is to graze on a number of appetizers, or go with one of the pastas or simple meat preparations. The kitchen is like a commisary for this restaurant and two others next door, and anything complex seems to allude them. So don't worry about the food. It's there and more than edible if you want to eat it, but you're really at F. Scott's to have a good time.

Reservations are suggested, especially if you want to eat and not perch at the bar, and there is free valet parking, which is a necessity in that neighborhood.

*Price: About $25 per person*
*Open daily for dinner only*
*Accepts all major credit cards*

---

# GALILEO
## 2014 P Street NW
### 202-293-7191

What Washington was lacking, and finally got when Galileo opened in late 1984, was an innovative Italian restaurant serving moderately priced food. Not only are the prices for food and wine within reason at Galileo, but the food is fabulous, with the best pastas in town and some unusual *risotto* dishes not found on any other menus.

The *antipasti* are limited but may include anything from zucchini flowers stuffed with Gorgonzola to small pizzas. For a light dinner, the suggestion is to split one of the pastas and then to select a few entrées. The pastas include examples made with basil, saffron, beet, and other flavors along with the standards, and the treatment can be with crayfish in tomato sauce, veal *ragù,* or bacon-and-cream sauce.

The staff, professional and efficient, moves gracefully around the L-shaped low-ceilinged room with its rust-colored carpet and floral tapestry banquettes. The menu changes for lunch and dinner each night and may feature anything from simply elegant grilled salmon or grouper to a loin of veal with wild mushrooms, baked squab with chives and tomato, or braised shrimp in a Barbera wine sauce.

After a few courses, all of which are ample, the desserts should be limited to a few *sorbets* or the lighter pastries. Cream-filled *cannoli* were too much one evening.

Reservations are a must for lunch and dinner at Galileo, and should be made well in advance for a weekend night.

*Price: About $20 per person*
*Open Mon.–Fri. for lunch and dinner; Sat. for dinner only; closed Sun.*
*Accepts all major credit cards*

# GARY'S
## 1800 M Street NW
### 202-463-6470

Gary's has the sort of masculine feel you expect from a steak house frequented by the city's political and legal community. You are greeted by a pair of etched-glass panels in a caricature style similar to Hirschfeld's, and proceed past a dimly lit bar with comfortable high-backed brocade chairs. The main dining room, with a dark-green accent wall, has the white-linened tables spread far enough apart so that you can really talk with a dinner companion. The smaller back dining room, with red wing-back chairs, has a cozy feel.

"Keep it simple" is the order of the day—the freshest oysters and clams for an appetizer; then dig into one of the well-aged steaks. Unlike many of the other steak houses in town, Gary's also includes some seafood on the menu; the broiled swordfish is always a good choice.

Everything is *à la carte,* so the cost of a meal can mount up quickly with just a vegetable and potato to go with the steak. The wine list is adequate if not inspired. Reservations are required for lunch and recommended for dinner

*Price: About $35 per person*
*Open Mon.–Fri. for lunch and dinner; Sat. for dinner only; closed Sun.*
*Accepts all major credit cards*

# GEPPETTO
## 2917 M Street NW
### 202-333-2602

There's a full Italian menu framed in front of this brown Georgetown store-front, but the reason why there's a line in front from before sunset to late into the evening is the pizza.

While the higher-than-average cost of toppings can remove pizza from its bargain meal category, the best pie here is the plain "pizza blanca," topped with a combination of cheeses (primarily Parmesan) and butter on a crispy light crust—perfection just as is, complemented by a tossed salad for a wonderful meal.

If you insist on tomato sauce, there are both thin- and thick-crust pizzas to enjoy in the pleasant, if always noisy and crowded, atmosphere. The noisy front room should be avoided, if possible, but that is the luck of the draw, since there's never an empty table. No reservations are taken.

*Price: About $8 per person*
*Open daily for lunch and dinner*
*Accepts all major credit cards*

# GERMAINE'S ASIAN CUISINE

2400 Wisconsin Avenue NW (*near Georgetown*)

202-965-1185

The menu at this skylit restaurant, in subtle tones of tan and decorated with stunning photo murals of Asia, not only reflects the distinct cuisines of Indonesia, Japan, India, Vietnam, and China, but also the creative spark imparted to dishes by Germaine Swanson.

You can travel an entire continent in one meal, either blending nuances of seasoning or selecting a menu to reflect the sharp contrasts between the cuisines. While not all dishes are uniformly successful, one of the marks of Germaine's is the freshness and quality of the raw ingredients. Another thing separating this restaurant from others in Washington is the extensive wine list, not found at even the most overpriced upscale Chinese restaurants downtown.

Of the starters, the most flavorful are the "bon bon chicken," scallop salad akin to a seviche, *pho ga* (the traditional Vietnamese soup served in a rich broth), and the Indonesian *sates* with a satiny peanut sauce.

"Pine cone fish," a Germaine's specialty, is a deeply scored fresh fish that stiffens to resemble a pine cone when brought to the table. It has been consistently a delight, regardless of the species of the fish. Look first to the listing of daily specials, as that's where Germaine's personality emerges. It can be an Oriental version of soft-shell crabs or a combination such as chicken stuffed with a spicy shrimp paste.

Not all dishes are stellar, and, in general, avoid fried foods as they have been greasy on some occasions. Reservations are suggested at all times.

*Price: About $25 per person*
*Open Mon.–Fri. for lunch and dinner; Sat. and Sun. for dinner only*
*Accepts all major credit cards*

# HOUSE OF HUNAN

1900 K Street NW

202-293-9111

While the downtown options for Chinese food served in attractive surroundings have proliferated over the past few years, few spots serve good food with the consistency of the House of Hunan.

Diners are greeted by a carved relief dragon and then escorted into the small dining room with rattan peacock chairs. The tables are jammed together—one of the restaurant's drawbacks—and service is highly erratic, but the food is worth suffering through the problems.

The best appetizers include crispy shrimp balls, similar to shrimp toast but with a far lighter filling, a fiery hot sweet-and-sour cabbage, and marinated smoked carp. Of the soups, the shredded pork and pickled cabbage is perhaps the best, and the minced squab and scallop soup makes for an unusual combination.

The Peking duck is excellent, but not carved at tableside, perhaps because there is little room between the tables. Dishes that have been ordered with success on many occasions are duck with gingerroot, orange beef, lamb with spring onions, and shredded beef with garlic-and-black-bean sauce, in which the beef is combined with a julienne of bean curd.

As with many Chinese restaurants, forget dessert, but this one does offer a passable wine list in addition to a number of imported beers. Reservations are suggested for dinner.

*Price: About $15 per person*
*Open daily for lunch and dinner*
*Accepts all major credit cards*

---

# THE INN AT LITTLE WASHINGTON
## Washington, Virginia
### 703-675-3800

This restaurant, nestled in the foothills of the Shenandoah Mountains about 75 miles from Washington, is one of the best in the country, well worth the two-hour drive. In fact, the spot is so popular with Washingtonians that reservations are necessary more than a month in advance for a Saturday night in the summer.

Chef Patrick O'Connell and his partner, Reinhardt Lynch, who runs the front of the house, have created the ambiance of a three-star French *auberge* with some superb examples of New American Cuisine.

The converted turn-of-the-century garage has every surface treated, with subtlety as great as that on the plate. Joyce Evans, who has decorated rooms at Buckingham Palace, created a design scheme with everything from *faux bois* walls to a gilded ceiling. The wooden tables are crowned by hanging light fixtures with salmon-colored pleated and flounced taffeta shades, and it's a treat to have dessert and coffee in the manicured garden, where frogs croak from their lily pond homes.

The menu at the Inn changes nightly, with emphasis placed on an updating of foods native to Virginia or that can successfully be grown there—such as the hams and corn or the newly harvested *shiitake* mushrooms—but O'Connell also draws from the total American larder.

Recent stellar starters have included sautéed American duck *foie gras* on a bed of black-eyed peas with Virginia ham and smoked goose breast; a cold cream of corn soup; mussels in a red pepper butter; red pepper soup flavored with fennel and *jalapeño* chili; and feathery light corn *crêpes* topped with sour cream and salmon caviar.

O'Connell does a number of *intermezzo* and dessert *sorbets,* and if either the tart grapefruit *sorbet* or one with Earl Grey tea as the base is listed, it's well worth it.

The entrée options range from simple preparations of beef and veal, which appeal to the locals, to complex constructions of ingredients and flavors. The sweetbreads may be arranged with sautéed snow peas in a three-mustard sauce, or sautéed with crab meat, capers, and lemon butter. A favorite is the rare-grilled duck breast with tart fresh currants in a sauce sweetened slightly with port, while O'Connell's presentation of Peacock Beef, from a concept derived from traditional Japanese *negimaki,* is superb, with *médaillons* of thinly sliced beef wrapped around a scallion in a rich reduction flavored with a hint of ginger.

Desserts continue at the same high standard. The grapefruit tart, bourbon pecan tart, white chocolate ice cream topped with rich dark chocolate sauce, and fruit *sorbets* should not be missed.

The wine list is not up to the rest of the menu. It does contain some Virginia wines—which at present should be viewed as curiosities rather than options —and a limited list of California and European vintages.

The service is as graceful as possible, and the staff is very knowledgeable. Reservations are a necessity.

*Price: About $40 per person*
*Open Wed.–Sun. for dinner only; closed Mon. and Tues.*
*Accepts all major credit cards*

---

# JEAN-LOUIS AT WATERGATE
In the Watergate Hotel, 2650 Virginia Avenue NW
### 202-298-4488

Although the hot contest remains between Jean-Louis Palladin and Yannick Cam (of Le Pavillon; see page 814) as to who is the city's best chef, with camps on both sides squaring off, my vote goes to the curly-haired culinary wizard from Condom, France, who was wooed to open this restaurant two levels below the elegant lobby of the Watergate Hotel five years ago.

Dinner at Jean-Louis is a must for any visitor to Washington, and if you have only one meal it should be here.

You enter by passing the glass-fronted wine cellars, floor to ceiling cases, racks of bottles, and a certificate from *The Wine Spectator* proclaiming the list as a Grand Award winner in the country.

The dining room, with panels of beige silk hung above a band of mirrors above the banquette, seats only 42 at well-spaced tables in two alcoves that divide the space into asymmetrical parts.

Your options at dinner are by the number of courses, the menu written each evening in the chef's curvilinear script with English translations typed underneath. He makes suggestions, but diners are free to select from any menu and substitute at will. A recent five-course dinner began with his complementary hors d'oeuvre—that night crispy rings of perfectly fried squid and a fried quail egg on a crouton of French bread surrounded by a halo of Beluga caviar.

Among the two dozen or so dishes offered each evening are a slice of American duck *foie gras* quickly seared and served with a peach sauce; *médaillons* of lobster on a base of corn purée in a *beurre blanc;* Palladin's version of crab cakes, which are chunks of Chesapeake crab bound by a lobster *mousseline* in a tomato butter; rare squab breast on a bed of sautéed cabbage and Smithfield ham; and capon breast with a garnish of crisply fried artichoke heart slivers.

Palladin's range of ingredients and flavors has greatly expanded since his move to the U.S., and dinners are perhaps the best food value in Washington. The cost of the fresh heart of palm he imports from Brazil for his salads and his caviar bill alone give the diner reason enough to pause. He refuses to think about food cost when devising his daily menu, because, he believes, it would limit his creativity.

Always save room for dessert, and while the *sorbets* and fruit tarts are wonderful, Jean-Louis is a chocoholic's paradise.

The service is as professional and unobtrusive as any encountered in the best restaurants of Paris. Reservations are a must.

*Price: About $50–$90 per person, depending on the number of courses*
*Open Mon.–Sat. for dinner only; closed Sun.*
*Accepts all major credit cards*

---

# JEAN-PIERRE
## 1835 K Street NW
### 202-466-2022

When the interior of Jean-Pierre received a much-needed facelift in 1984, the bastion of French restaurants on the "K Street Strip" also underwent a delightful lightening of the food as well. Jean-Pierre is once again one of the city's culinary leaders, and a wonderful spot for either a business or personal meal.

The small bar is decorated with a soft-mauve-patterned carpet and warm plaid wallpaper, and the dining room, broken into sections with mirrored columns, is one of the most romantic in the city. The ceiling is muted mirrors, and the silk walls of pale pink create an environment that is sophisticated and subtle. Tables are set fairly far apart, too.

The printed menu, which changes seasonally, is still fairly conservative, with the mussel soup and house *terrine* as outstanding starters. The trout amandine and duck with green peppercorn sauce, along with the beef preparations, are consistently good. But do not decide on a meal until you hear the specials list that chef Gerard Vettraino is concocting for the evening. The options are far more interesting.

The wine list is adequate without being stellar, and the service is always professional. Reservations are suggested at all times.

*Price: About $30 per person*
*Open Mon.–Fri. for lunch and dinner; Sat. for dinner only; closed Sun.*
*Accepts all major credit cards*

---

# LA BRASSERIE
## 239 Massachusetts Avenue NE
### 202-546-6066

When this restaurant, located within the shadow of the Capitol Building, opened, it was enjoyed for the café atmosphere and food implied in the name. But La Brasserie has matured into a serious, and rather expensive, French restaurant serving a mixture of *nouvelle* and classic dishes.

The two upstairs dining rooms look almost Colonial, with a pineapple-print wallpaper and fringed curtains in one, and soft-peach walls with gilt framed oils in the front room. Downstairs, the tile floor and contemporary prints depicting food give the space a more sophisticated tenor. During the summer the outside garden with striped umbrellas is glorious on a not-too-hot day.

In general, the printed, seasonally changing menu is more conservative than the nightly specials, which are tacked inside the menu rather than recited at tableside. The options can range from a velvety cold avocado soup to a hearty *pâté maison* or selection of salads for starters. On the menu you'll find pretty standard dishes—all of them well executed—such as breast of duck with *cassis* sauce and mussels *provençale.* But look on the card and see that duck can also be ordered with a black olive sauce, and the rockfish is served topped with cardamom and mangoes rather than the orange preparation featured nightly.

The desserts, in general, tend to be overly sweet and harken back to the *bistro* days, while the wine list as well lacks the depth one expects from a serious restaurant. Service can be erratic, especially at lunch.

*Price: About $25 per person*
*Open Mon.–Sat. for lunch and dinner; Sun. for dinner only*
*Accepts all major credit cards*

# LA CHAUMIÈRE
## 2813 M Street NW, Georgetown
### 202-338-1784

This country French restaurant specializing in seafood is a winter delight, when the fireplace in the center of the room, with its stuccoed and wood walls and French decorative touches, is blazing. It's a cozy space, and it has a reasonably priced menu with a host of nightly specials that are usually more interesting than the classic French fare on the printed menu.

There are also daily specials—those wonderful French casseroles like *cassoulet* and *choucroute* and *bouillabaisse,* done with the freshest of fish. Seafood is the strength of the menu and the kitchen, and when meat has been ordered it has been slightly disappointing. But there's nothing wrong with sticking with some of the plumpest mussels in town, steamed in a perfect balance of wine and herbs, or sometimes topped with a flavorful *au gratin* treatment, or swordfish or salmon cooked perfectly with a *beurre blanc.*

The wine list follows suit with the rest of the meal—it is well priced and adequate, if lacking in rare or great vintages.

*Price: About $20 per person*
*Open Mon.–Fri. for lunch and dinner; Sat. for dinner only; closed Sun.*
*Accepts all major credit cards*

# L'AUBERGE CHEZ FRANÇOIS
## 332 Springvale Road, Great Falls, Virginia
### 703-759-3800

While Great Falls is considered suburban Washington, once you leave the highway and reach this rustic inn, the atmosphere and attitude are one of the French countryside.

L'Auberge Chez François is a popular spot, and reservations for weekend nights are usually made more than a month in advance. It proves that people like to feel pampered, and you will be. The service is exceptional and gliding, even if the food, on occasion, has a few rough spots.

The menu changes seasonally and has remained rather classically French, with only a few nods to *nouvelle cuisine* in the sauces. The garlic sausage in puff pastry with horseradish and an appetizer of hot veal tongue were quite good, although a selection of *pâtés* (at an additional charge to the rather reasonable fixed-price menu) lacked character.

Of recent entrée selections the braised sweetbreads with truffles and Madeira sauce and a tenderloin of lamb with a light tarragon sauce were outstanding.

Desserts are the weakest part of the menu, but the ice creams and *sorbets* are excellent; the pastries are disappointing. The wine list is wonderful and one of the most reasonably priced in the region. Reservations are a necessity.

*Price: About $20 per person*
*Open Tues.–Sat. for dinner only; closed Sun. and Mon.*
*Accepts all major credit cards*

---

# LE PAVILLION
## 1050 Connecticut Avenue NW
### 202-833-3846

Subtle and delicate are the two best descriptors for this *nouvelle* French restaurant, located on the second level of a pink marble-and-glass tower. It's almost ironic that Duke Ziebert's, that bastion of the corned beef sandwich, is across the floor; no two restaurants could be further apart in food or philosophy.

Diners are greeted by a bright floral mural tucked into a curvilinear niche, and the 70-seat dining room is the epitome of quiet elegance. The room is arranged around a round Lalique crystal table, with mottled pale-pink walls, brass wall sconces, a soundtrack of classical music, and peach brocade chairs that harmonize with the environment but do not match it. The tables are placed far enough apart for private conversation, and the ever-changing panorama of downtown Washington is visible from the tranquility of the restaurant.

Chef and owner Yannick Cam, whose wife, Janet, is responsible for the front of the house, creates dishes that are intellectual and refined, and presents them in a restrained way. This is *nouvelle cuisine* at its ethereal edge; it's for people who want to eat with their eyes and heads as much as their mouths. Portions are small, and even with a five-course dinner you may not leave feeling satiated. Le Pavillion is not the place to have dinner with someone whose idea of *haute cuisine* is veal Oscar or half a cow on the plate. You would not only be wasting a lot of money; chances are they wouldn't enjoy it. This is a restaurant for the astute palate, to catch nuances of flavors.

Another caveat: Count on at least three hours for dinner and probably more like four. And saying you're in a hurry will not matter.

The menu changes frequently, so don't expect to find these exact dishes. However, these will give you an idea of Cam's style: The beet *ravioli* in chive sauce and hot Belon oysters with a subtle purée of leeks and anchovies are superb; however, the contrast in flavors between the delicacy of *médaillons* of lobster paired with snow peas in a salad is a bit too sharp. His *terrines,* such as one with *langoustines* and turbot with a hint of rosemary or his shrimp with lobster and wild mushrooms, are always excellent.

Cam's game and duck dishes have always been stellar, with a favorite being a *magret* of duck for which the garnish of pears in a Graves wine sauce were fashioned into delicate olives. If the *terrine* of *chocolate à la Negresco* is available, it's a must.

The wine list is one of the best in town, although you pay for the rare bottles handily.

*Price: Fixed price at $55 and $70 per person*
*Open Mon.–Fri. for lunch and dinner; Sat. for dinner only; closed Sun.*
*Accepts all major credit cards*

---

# MAISON BLANCHE
## 1725 F Street NW
### 202-842-0070

If you're in Washington on business and need a power spot for lunch, this is about your best bet. Instead of bland potted chicken or side of beef, you can eat reasonably well-executed, if conservative, French food in elegant surroundings that provide the luxury of space for private conversation.

Maison Blanche is a block from the White House (hence its name) and in sight of the wedding cake-like Old Executive Office Building. It's a masculine room, with brown velvet chairs, wood paneling, and silk valances swagged over the windows. The gold silk floral brocade on the walls and the crystal chandeliers give it a stately aura.

The menu is predictable—from the *petite marmite* and lobster bisque as soups and *coquilles St. Jacques* and *pâtés* as appetizers to the steak Diane and *chateaubriand*—perhaps the most popular entrées spotted on servers' trays.

But one can get more inspired food by selecting from the daily specials, which tend to be more *nouvelle,* or at least more interesting.

The service at Maison Blanche is smooth and professional, although it can verge on the rushed for the early pre-theater seating. The wine list is extensive, though one of the pricier ones in town. But most of the diners don't care, since they are all on expense accounts. Reservations are recommended at all times.

*Price: About $45 per person*
*Open Mon.–Fri. for lunch and dinner; Sat. for dinner only; closed Sun.*
*Accepts all major credit cards*

# MARRAKESH RESTAURANT
## 617 New York Avenue NW
### 202-393-9393

Marrakesh is a combination O'Farrell's Ice Cream Parlor for adults and premier North African restaurant. It's a wonderful place to go for a relaxed evening with friends or to test the humor level of a possible business partner.

The plain pink exterior (and you have to knock to be admitted) conceals a lavishly colored high-ceilinged dining room. Wear comfortable clothes, because you will be seated on either low banquettes with huge silk bolster pillows or on leather stools around low brass tables. After the waiter washes your hands over a brass bowl, you are handed your napkins for the evening —unmatched bath towels that look like they came out of detergent boxes.

You are then given a seven-course menu, starting with a selection of salads, such as eggplant in cumin and carrots in coriander, a *pastilla* stuffed with chicken and almonds in a flaky *filo* dough crust, a choice of chicken (the lemon and olives being the best), either lamb brochettes or lamb with almonds and honey (a better option), *couscous,* a basket of fruit, and ending with Moroccan pastries similar to *baklava.* And you eat it all with your hands.

The O'Farrell's analogy occurs a few times an evening when the lights are dimmed even further, a belly-dance version of "Happy Birthday" comes belting over the sound system, and a waiter delivers a pastry with sparkler to a table. It's not uncommon for people to get up and dance toward the end of the evening.

A dinner at Marrakesh is the evening's entertainment; don't plan on anything else except maybe some dancing. Open seven days a week.

*Price: About $17 per person*
*Open daily for dinner only*
*No credit cards accepted*

# MESKEREM
## 2434 18 Street NW
### 202-462-2100

There are currently eleven Ethiopian restaurants in Washington, and most of them are located next door to one another on a block of 18 Street in the Adams–Morgan section of the city. For many Americans, the first visit to any of these restaurants provides their first experience since being in a high chair when it is *de rigueur* to eat with one's hands.

Meskerem, a new addition to the block, is perhaps the most attractive

Ethiopian spot in town, featuring a finesse rarely exhibited elsewhere. Like all the restaurants in town, the mainstay of the menu is the stews—intensely colored *wats* and more delicate *alechas,* made with meat and in vegetarian versions, and such novelties as *kitfo,* the Ethiopian first cousin to steak tartare.

*Sambusas,* which are similar to Indian *samosas,* are the only appetizer of note, and the renditions of stews are excellent, with an unusual shrimp *wat* outstanding.

While most Ethiopian restaurants are dark and depressing, Meskerem is filled with sunlight and decorated with traditional woven straw tables surrounded by ample stools instead of chairs.

The service is efficient, if leisurely, and if you're craving Ethiopian food and the restaurant is full, don't despair. You have about nine others within a few blocks.

*Price: About $15 per person*
*Open daily for lunch and dinner*
*Accepts all major credit cards*

---

# NEW ORLEANS CAFÉ
## 1790 Columbia Road NW (*Adams-Morgan section*)
### 202-234-5111

Washingtonians' first exposure to the authentic flavors of New Orleans was at this casual restaurant, where you could eat fried crawfish balls for breakfast or eggs Sardou for dinner, a *muffuletta* or a bowl of gumbo all day long. Or end an evening the way they do in the French Quarter, with a basket of *beignets* and a cup of chicory coffee while dressed in evening clothes.

If you don't mind putting up with a lot of noise and confusion, the New Orleans Café, fairly sparse and tile-floored, is one of the best food buys in town. In addition to the idiosyncrasy that breakfast, lunch, and dinner are served simultaneously from early morning to late at night, there are also such wonderful specials as roast pork with oyster dressing and a pork barbecue that may not be part of Creole tradition, but has the flavors of the South.

Reservations are accepted for parties of six or more, and if you have to wait for a table (which you probably will), there's now a lovely bar around the corner above the New Orleans Emporium, the upscale relative of the café.

*Price: About $10 per person*
*Open daily for breakfast, lunch, and dinner*
*Accepts all major credit cards*

# NEW ORLEANS EMPORIUM
## 2477 18 Street NW
### 202-328-3421

When the Cajun craze reached Washington in 1984, the city may have lagged behind others in the acceptance of *etouffé* and blackened redfish, but the offerings at this bastion of Louisiana-style cooking are first-rate and on a par with food sampled in their region of origin.

The restaurant, located in the rejuvenated Adams–Morgan section of the city, gives the feel of New Orleans. You walk down the steps and the plant-filled atrium resembles the courtyards behind iron gates in the French Quarter. The pale-green walls and tile-floored bar (with an elegant green marble bar on the street level for drinking or waiting for a table) are casual but most attractive.

The menu is divided by species of seafood rather than courses, which makes it ideal for a snack or "grazing" dinner, as well as for a more traditional composition or sequence. Outstanding are the barbecued shrimp, shrimp *etouffé*, crawfish *boulettes* (similar to croquettes and served with a spicy *rémoulade* sauce), oysters Bienville, and redfish sautéed with a pecan-lemon sauce.

Do not overlook the nightly specials, which can be anything from a shark bisque to a crawfish *boudin blanc,* and save room for bread pudding for dessert. The wine list is extremely small, but there are specials in that category, too. Weekend brunch offers some wonderful egg dishes.

Service is excellent, although the room tends to be noisy when crowded.

*Price: About $20 per person*
*Open daily for lunch and dinner*
*Accepts all major credit cards*

# NICHOLAS
## In the Mayflower Hotel, 1127 Connecticut Avenue NW
### 202-347-8900

When this grande dame of Washington hotels was renovated in 1984, a small intimate corner was carved out for a restaurant specializing in New American Cuisine. Named for Chef Nicholas, who was the first chef of the hotel, Nicholas does an artful job with combinations and presentations.

The room, decorated in subtle tones of grays and beige with big comfortable cushions for those seated on banquettes, provides a tranquil space in the middle of downtown Washington. The formally dressed staff is efficient and the service gliding.

The menu changes frequently, but some starters of note have been the *terrine* of anglerfish with yellow peppers and a salad of rare squab in a hazelnut vinaigrette. Buffalo in a red wine sauce and monkfish sliced into *médaillons* and sautéed with Chesapeake crab meat were both deemed excellent on a few visits.

The restaurant does not have a distinct personality, however the basis for all dishes are use of American products handled with deft *nouvelle* French technique, and an interesting combination of flavors within the dishes.

For a business lunch or dinner, the private dining room for about twenty is one of the most attractive around. Reservations are suggested at all times.

*Price: About $30 per person*
*Open Mon.–Fri. for lunch and dinner; Sat. and Sun. for dinner only*
*Accepts all major credit cards*

---

# OLD EBBITT GRILL
## 675 15 Street NW
### 202-347-4801

The "old" Old Ebbitt Grill was a Washington landmark, and news of its demolition was greeted in 1983 with the horror one would expect if the White House were making room for a condominium project. For more than a century diners had wended their way up creaking stairs to the Omelet Room, or hoisted a beer while standing beneath a carved bear that had belonged to Alexander Hamilton.

When the "new" Old Ebbitt opened in 1984, purists still scowled, but many diners were delighted. The bar, complete with antique beer mug collection and carved bears, was transplanted around the corner in its entirety, and in lieu of the creaky steps, there was a choice of a seafood bar, an elegant dining room with etched-glass panels separating seating areas, and a back dining room with a frescoed ceiling.

The menu, formerly limited to burgers and eggs, also received an expansion and uplifting. Both the lunch and dinner menu change daily, and include some excellent pastas like a first-rate *cannelloni* with spinach and *mortadella,* and a spaghetti with four cheeses. You can dine lightly on traditional crab cake sandwiches, or elegantly on veal scallopine or baked scrod.

In addition to five imported beers on tap, there are at least eight wines by the glass, and a respectable wine list. Save room for one of the homemade ice creams or pecan pie for dessert.

Open until 1 A.M. seven nights a week.

*Price: About $15 per person*
*Open Mon.–Sat. for breakfast, lunch, and dinner; Sun. for brunch and dinner*
*Accepts all major credit cards*

# OMEGA
## 1858 Columbia Road NW
### 202-462-1732

Omega is the K-Paul's of Washington. There are bare plastic tables, no atmosphere whatsoever, and the restaurant has become an institution, owing to its huge portions of delicious Cuban food.

The fried squid has never been anything but stellar, and the bowl of black beans with rice that is automatically placed on the table has a subtle level of spicing. The bilingual menu features such Cuban standards as *ropa vieja, paella,* and a wonderful pork stew. The portions are huge, and the quality is consistently high.

Omega takes no reservations, so expect a wait at prime meal times, but there is a full bar to make the waiting easier.

*Price: About $9 per person*
*Open Tues.–Sun. for lunch and dinner; closed Mon.*
*Accepts all major credit cards*

# RESTAURANT NORA
## 2132 Florida Avenue NW
### 202-462-5143

Nora Pouillon made headlines when she first opened about five years ago for the quality of her ingredients and the innovation of her dishes, all served at a reasonable cost.

Restaurant Nora continues to innovate, but prices are now comparable to the highest in the city. Part of the reason is the cost of the ingredients; she makes "additive-free cuisine." Her meats are raised for her in Northern Virginia, and fed chemical- and antibiotic-free feed, as are the hens that lay her eggs and the cows for her cream. In addition to her own herb garden on R Street, she imports herbs during the winter months that meet her specifications. Working with farmers is nothing new to California restaurateurs, but it makes Nora almost alone in Washington.

The environment, however, is casual. Diners are ushered up a short flight of steps from the entry bar to find brick walls, pale-beige wood tables, and quilts hanging as decoration. The menu changes nightly, and it's a personal cuisine incorporating everything from traditional American dishes to Moroccan chicken *couscous* and Indonesian pork *saté.* She has a deft hand with herbs and wild mushrooms, as well as pastas.

Desserts are always excellent and include many fruit tarts, fruit *sorbets,* and a chocolate-almond cake that has remained a favorite for years.

*Price: About $35 per person*
*Open Mon.–Fri. for lunch and dinner; Sat. for dinner only; closed Sun.*
*No credit cards accepted*

---

## ROSSINI'S RISTORANTE D'ITALIA
### 5507 Connecticut Avenue NW
#### 202-244-7774

The outer boundaries of Northwest Washington have few culinary delights, and Rossini's, opened in early 1985, is certainly one of them. Do not be put off by the plastic decor with violins and other musical mementos around the walls—all nods to the composer for whom the restaurant was named. The food is top-notch and reasonably priced.

The Gildenhorn family, who not only own Rossini's but also the other restaurants on the block, hired the chef formerly with Romeo and Juliet after the demise of that downtown restaurant. His pasta and veal preparations are stellar.

Start with a *fettuccine* or *tortellini alla panna,* or perfectly cooked asparagus Parmesan, and then enjoy any of the buttery veal dishes, including such favorites as *alla zingara* (with peppers, onions, mushrooms, and white wine) or *alla Napolitana,* with crab meat and cream sauce.

Since they also own the fish market a few doors down, you can never go wrong with the soft-shell crabs (in season) or the simple sauté of shrimp with garlic and white wine.

The pastries are made by the Watergate Pastry, one of the best in the city, and the wine list of all-Italian wines is one of the best bargains in town.

*Price: About $25 per person*
*Open Mon.–Fri. for lunch and dinner; Sat. and Sun. for dinner only*
*Accepts all major credit cards*

---

## SHEZAN
### 913 19 Street NW
#### 202-659-5555

Shezan, with related restaurants in New York and London, is actually a Pakistani rather than totally Indian restaurant, but the menu is extensive enough to give samplings of food from all areas of the Indian subcontinent.

Diners are greeted on the first floor by a stunning contemporary bar with polished brass ceiling. They then walk downstairs to the dining room. The plum-carpeted walls and framed Pakistani fabrics hanging above the plum banquettes make this one of the most sensual dining rooms in the city. While the back portion of the dining room is private, the front part overlooks the ground floor of an adjacent shopping mall and should be avoided if possible.

It's a perfect place to take guests who may not care for Indian food, since the non-Indian offerings are equally well prepared, including a chicken breast stuffed with buttered mushrooms, capers, and fried parsley, and a steak with a mushroom sauce laced with Madeira.

But what you should order are some of the specialties: lamb cooked in a butter sauce with browned onions, ginger, and a hint of garlic; *tandoori* preparations from simple meats and chicken to sauced dishes; and a delightful range of vegetarian entrées, such as chick-peas with tamarind and coriander and sliced potatoes with whole cumin seed.

Service tends to be a bit slow, even if the intention for a quick meal is announced.

*Price: About $25 per person*
*Open Mon.–Fri. for lunch and dinner; Sat. for dinner only; closed Sun.*
*Accepts all major credit cards*

---

# SUZANNE'S
## 1735 Connecticut Avenue NW
### 202-483-4633

Usually, to find a wine list with the length and depth of the one at Suzanne's (the restaurant is located above Suzanne Riefers' gourmet takeout that has been feeding the Dupont Circle area for five years), you would have to pay a premium for the entrées served with your wine.

Not true here, where the menu changes nightly in the understandably crowded and quite noisy dining room. Suzanne's is popular with true food lovers rather than with those who care more about the china pattern than what is on the plate. People who appreciate excellent food and fine wine have tried to keep Suzanne's a secret, but with little success, judging from the line at dinner.

Some of the most successful recent starters were a smoked trout *mousse,* a clam-and-leek soup, and a venison *pâté.* In addition to hearty options for entrées each night—such as lamb *médaillons* with Creole mustard sauce, rare grilled tuna steak with *pesto,* or a veal chop with *cèpes*—there are always a few main dish salads, such as a wonderful mélange of wild mushrooms with Westphalian ham over greens, and some light options like asparagus-and-leek strudel or bay scallops with sun-dried tomatoes.

Always save room for dessert, since Suzanne's is known for its pastries, also served at her café housed in the Phillips Collection.

Reservations are only taken for parties of five or more, and only from Monday to Thursday evenings.

*Price: About $20 per person*
*Open for lunch and dinner Mon.–Sat.; closed Sun.*
*Accepts Visa and MasterCard*

---

# 209½
## 209½ Pennsylvania Avenue SE
### 202-544-6352

This storefront restaurant in the rejuvenated Capitol Building area was the first outpost of New American Cuisine in the city, and it continues to serve exciting food in a sophisticated setting.

It's the sort of interior one expects to find in New York—a light-green pressed tile ceiling, with walls of beige grasscloth and a rich dark-green carpet. The art is a combination of original Dali lithographs and some old prints for contrast.

The menu changes seasonally. Some recent appetizers of note were green *gazpacho* with *cilantro,* a cold *fettuccine primavera,* and artichokes in a basil sauce, while at lunch the lighter options might include a salmon tartare dressed with mustard and dill similar to a gravlax, or what has become a local favorite, the Julia Child Salad—fresh breast of chicken tossed with vegetables in an herbed mayonnaise and served with eggplant *provençale.*

At dinner, the options are limited to about six items on the menu itself, but the server will double that number verbally. Outstanding are the fillet "red, white, and bleu" *bleu* cheese, with Cognac, garlic, and fresh chives enlivening the sauce; and scallops *Niçoise,* with hazelnuts, vermouth, and garlic complementing the sweetness of the scallops.

The sour cream-chocolate cake or one of the ice creams is the best ending for a dinner. The wine list is short, but well priced. Reservations are suggested at all times.

*Price: About $30 per person*
*Open Mon.–Fri. for lunch and dinner; Sat. for dinner only; closed Sun.*
*Accepts all major credit cards*

# VINCENZO
## 1606 20 Street NW
### 202-667-0047

A few years ago this seafood restaurant preparing *pesce* in the Italian manner was considered the best Italian food—and perhaps the best seafood, too—that the city had to offer.

The consistency rating has dropped somewhat during the past few years, and recent visits have produced a range from spectacular and subtle meals to ones that could only be deemed mediocre.

It's a shame, because the two dining rooms, located a few steps down from street level near Dupont Circle, are so decidedly stark and attractive, with simple white walls and tiled floors. The front room is the place to be seated; you won't be, however, unless they know you or your picture from *The Washington Post.*

When the kitchen is "on," seafood is grilled to perfection and the pasta is *al dente,* with sauces that meld into a perfect unity. When the kitchen is "off," the *antipasti* taste like leftovers, presented on plates instead of from the cart, and there is a greasy aftertaste to the *fritto misto.*

The service vacillates in the same manner. One night it's courteous and professional; the next night you are the "forgotten table." The wine list, with a number of nice Italian whites to accompany the fish preparations, is rather high priced.

Reservations are necessary, and even with a reservation expect to stand for a few minutes.

*Price: About $30 per person*
*Open Mon.–Fri. for lunch and dinner; Sat. for dinner only; closed Sun.*
*Accepts all major credit cards*

# WINDOWS
## 1000 Wilson Boulevard, Arlington, Virginia
### 703-527-4430

Although it was 1985 before the first California cuisine arrived on the Potomac, when Windows opened last year natives got an excellent introduction to a style that had already raged like a brushfire of mesquite elsewhere.

The restaurant, decorated in pale tones of pink and detailed with etched glass, is situated on the eighth floor of the *USA Today* building, and commands a view of the Potomac and monuments unmatched by any other dining spot.

In addition to the two-level room, there is a spacious bar serving light fare at cocktail time.

Chef-owner Henry Dinardo creates a lengthy list of nightly specials to complement the set, seasonally changing, menu. Some of the better appetizer choices are an iced parsley soup, smoked salmon grilled lightly over mesquite with a champagne and papaya vinaigrette, and an intensely flavored *pâté* that is a smooth blend of liver, brandy, and Madeira.

The mesquite grilling is light, never overpowering the delicate flavors of any ingredient. Excellent choices are the swordfish served with an orange and almond butter, salmon napped in a *beurre blanc* with American caviar, and veal with wild mushrooms.

What would any California-style restaurant be without the pizzas and *calzone;* ranging from shrimp, mussels, and *mozzarella* to a topping of garlic-and-fennel sausage and sautéed vegetables?

The ice creams and fruit tarts are the best desserts; the wine list is extensive and includes some lesser known California and French vineyards. Reservations are suggested at all times.

*Price: About $35 per person*
*Open Mon.–Fri. for lunch and dinner; Sat. and Sun. for dinner only*
*Accepts all major credit cards*

# MORE
# RECOMMENDED
# RESTAURANTS

The following list of recommended restaurants represents a wide range of good eating in those cities and towns not covered in separate chapters in this book. They include some of this editor's personal favorites—from deluxe dining rooms to charming little eateries where you'll get a good meal or a special sense of the region.

—John F. Mariani

## ALABAMA ■ Birmingham

### HIGHLANDS A BAR AND GRILL
2011 Eleventh Avenue South
**205-939-1400**

One of the best new Southern restaurants with real style—a broad dining room in salmon-peach and a fine oyster bar in deep green, all set in the newly gentrified Five Points South section of town. Chef-owner Frank Stitt III does a wonderful job with a menu that changes daily and includes local quail and trout; the oysters are abundant and fresh. This is easily the classiest place in town and it well deserves its growing rep.

*Price: About $25 per person*
*Open Mon.–Fri. for lunch and dinner; Sat. for dinner only; closed Sun.*
*Accepts all major credit cards*

# JOHN'S RESTAURANT
## 112 21 Street
### 205-322-6014

A very popular, casual restaurant that more-or-less resembles a very expensive luncheonette. The waitresses are all Southern charm and the cooks serve good American staples—fried fish, gumbo, and freshly made coleslaw.

*Price: About $10 per person*
*Open Mon.–Sat. for lunch and dinner; closed Sun.*
*Accepts Visa, MasterCard, and Diners Club*

---

# SILVERSANDS CAFÉ
## 328 Sixteenth Avenue
### 205-254-9570

Known as "Jabos" to the locals, this lively soul food restaurant serves everything from delicious oxtail stew to buttery cornbread and fried chicken. The decor is barebones, enlivened only by some religious art in garish colors. Don't expect much refinement, just good black Southern cooking.

*Price: Under $10 per person*
*Open Tues.–Sun. for breakfast, lunch, and dinner; closed Mon.*
*No credit cards accepted*

# CONNECTICUT ▪ Farmington

---

# APRICOTS
## 1593 Farmington Avenue (*Route 4*)
### 203-673-5405

The pleasure of sitting at a window table overlooking the river would be reason enough to come here, but the menu is also quite interesting and the chef a good one. The menu statement that the kitchen does not serve *nouvelle cuisine* but instead serves *"cuisine eclectique"* is as pretentious as some of the exotica tastes, but the grilled meats and chocolate *marjolaine* are superbly rendered.

*Price: Fixed price $33.50 per person and* à la carte
*Open daily for lunch and dinner*
*Accepts all major credit cards*

## LA GRANGE AT THE HOMESTEAD INN
420 Field Point Road
**203-869-7500**

This is one of the most beautifully restored country homes in the country, a labor of love of Lessie Davison and Nancy Smith, and to stay here is to get a real feel for Connecticut style. To eat here is to eat well, for chef Jacques Theabeault is a classicist and does splendidly with *terrines,* veal with wild mushrooms, stuffed salmon, and *crème brulée.* The wine list is solid, though quite expensive. Have a cocktail in the Chocolate Bar before dinner. La Grange is best in autumn and winter. Then again, it's also glorious in spring and summer.

*Price: About $35 per person*
*Open Mon.–Fri. for lunch and dinner; Sat. and Sun. for dinner only*
*Accepts all major credit cards*

## RESTAURANT JEAN-LOUIS
61 Lewis Street
**203-622-8450**

Jean-Louis is one of this country's most significant restaurants, mainly because it embodies in one small, elegant dining room with deep armchairs, rosy accents, and black marble china the very best concepts of the true *nouvelle cuisine* without any of its eccentricities. [*N.B.:* A recent fire has caused a complete renovation as we go to press.] Chef-owner Jean-Louis Gérin was head chef at Paris' celebrated Guy Savoy, and his imagination is as fertile as his energy is boundless. You may feast on lobster in a citron sauce, red snapper with coriander seeds, impeccably roasted lamb, and densely flavored *sorbets* and desserts. The best idea is to go with the six-course *menu dégustation,* which will give you some inkling of Gérin's extraordinary range.

*Price: About $36 per person;* menu dégustation *$43*
*Open Mon.–Fri. for lunch and dinner; Sat. for dinner only; closed Sun.*
*Accepts all major credit cards*

# CONNECTICUT ▪ Hartford

## L'AMERICAIN
### 2 Hartford Square West
#### 203-522-6500

Hartford's best and most sylish dining room. It has a smart facade of brick and
the interior is composed of several distinct rooms, some cozy and Colonial,
the main room bright and airy, with a Pop Art portrait of Goethe on one wall.
It's a delight to sit in the foyer before a fire and have a drink. The menu is
an interesting mix of French and American items, drawing on the seasons and
the local larder for dishes like butternut squash soup and pork sausage.

*Price: About $30–$40 per person*
*Open Mon.–Fri. for lunch and dinner; Sat. for dinner only; closed Sun.*
*Accepts all major credit cards*

# CONNECTICUT ▪ New Haven

## DELMONACO'S
### 232 Wooster Street
#### 203-865-1109

A generous Italian restaurant that is very popular locally for its traditional
Italian-American fare. The place is big, noisy, but always friendly, and the
waiters are well trained to please the customers. The scallops, *spaghetti alla
carbonara,* and veal chop are hefty and satisfying and meant to be shared.

*Price: About $25 per person*
*Open Sun.–Mon., Wed.–Fri. for lunch and dinner; Sat. for dinner only; closed
Tues.*
*Accepts all major credit cards*

# FLORIDA ▪ Lake Buena Vista

## ARTHUR'S 27
### In the Buena Vista Palace Hotel
#### 800-327-2990

The panorama from the top floor is twinkling and romantic even if it is of
the surrounding Orlando area. There are seatings each evening from seven

o'clock on and and table settings are lavish. You'll sit on rounded banquettes and dine on Chef Charles Dekranis' sometimes too elaborate *nouvelle cuisine.* The menu is a fixed-price seven-course meal, and this is a serious restaurant in this area and a special night for anyone. Prepare to spend at least three hours.

*Price: Fixed price $45 per person*
*Open daily for dinner only*
*Accepts all major credit cards*

---

## CHEFS DE FRANCE
### at EPCOT Center
### 305-824-4321

Overseen by Paul Bocuse, Roger Vergé, and Gaston Lenôre, this French pavilion restaurant serves good *bistro* food. The problem here—as at all the EPCOT restaurants—is that you must make your reservations as you enter in the morning and wait around until that night to dine. The place is always jammed to the French windows with families, and the place can get noisy and rushed. But they do a good job under great pressure, and if you let yourself go, you'll have a good time. The simpler dishes are the better ones.

*Price: About $25 per person*
*Open daily for lunch and dinner*
*Accepts all major credit cards*

---

## MARRAKESH
### at EPCOT Center
### 305-824-4321

As with the other EPCOT restaurants, you have to book in the morning when you enter in hope of lasting the day till you get in that night. But you'll enjoy yourself immensely here. This place is a delight, a respite from the crowds outside, and an authentic Moroccan feast with specialties such as *couscous, bastila,* a *tagine* of chicken, and wonderful butter cookies. Try the Moroccan red wine, but definitely skip the white. There are belly dancers, but they are rated "PG."

*Price: About $20 per person*
*Open daily for lunch and dinner*
*Accepts all major credit cards*

# LOUISIANA ▪ Baton Rouge

## JUBAN'S
### 3735 Perkins Road
#### 504-346-8422

A stylish Creole restaurant with romantic small dining rooms. It's tucked away in a shopping center and doesn't look like much from the road, but once inside it has all the charm of Louisiana gentility. The wallpaper has a crawfish pattern and the menu has a Creole bent. The trout Jason is recommended.

*Price: About $25–$30 per person*
*Open Mon.–Fri. for lunch and dinner; Sat. for dinner only; closed Sun.*
*Accepts all major credit cards*

# MASSACHUSETTS ▪ Sturbridge

## PUBLICK HOUSE
### On the Common
#### 617-347-3313

This large, impeccably kept country inn has a long history of hospitality and there's never any skimping on the meal portions. Of the several dining rooms, the newly expanded main room is the liveliest and brightest, while the others are very comfortable and cozy in the eighteenth-century style. The menu is strictly American and mostly New England style; the sticky pecan buns are irresistible. The lamb chops and other simply done items are the best, and there are abundant, well-prepared side orders. But the real reason to go to the Publick House is for the gargantuan $7.95 country breakfast—pancakes, ham, sausage, chicken with dumplings, and several others pickings from the buffet. Bring a very hearty appetite.

*Price: About $20 per person*
*Open daily for breakfast, lunch, and dinner*
*Accepts all major credit cards*

# MASSACHUSETTS ▪ Yarmouthport

### THE CRANBERRY MOOSE
43 Main Street (*Route 6A*)
**617-362-8153**

The whimsy of the name does nothing for the seriousness of a kitchen that really knows how to reduce a sauce, grill meats, and cook a fish to succulence. The food is New American, with good New England common sense, and the interior and exterior are in the kempt Cape Cod style with antiques, boat models, and framed ships' logs. The small wine list is well chosen. Don't miss the homemade ice cream.

*Price: About $30 per person*
*Open Thurs.–Sun. for dinner only; closed Mon.–Wed.*
*Accepts all major credit cards*

# MICHIGAN ▪ Grand Rapids

### CYGNUS
In the Grand Amway Plaza
**616-774-0214**

A very beautiful dining room with a dance floor set on top of the hotel with a splendid view of the surrounding area. The food is quite eclectic and not everything clicks. But it's easily the best food in town and the service could not possibly be better.

*Price: About $35 per person*
*Open Mon.–Sat. for dinner only; closed Sun.*
*Accepts all major credit cards*

# NEW JERSEY ▪ Alpine

### PRINCE MAXIMILIAN
At the Tamcrest Country Club, Route 9W
and Montammy Drive
**201-767-1313**

Located on the grounds of the Tamcrest Country Club, this is a posh dining room complete with grand piano, greenhouse windows, marble floors, and a view over the golf course green that makes this a wonderful retreat, no more than 10 minutes from the George Washington Bridge. The changing menu includes first-rate preparations like smoked duck and tangerine salad, mussels with fennel, grilled shrimp with *radicchio,* ribeye steak with *shiitake* mushrooms, and a fine array of cakes and tarts. The kitchen is slow, the staff well meaning, and the wine list only fair.

*Price: About $30 per person; fixed-price dinners at $30 and $35*
*Open Tues.–Thurs. for lunch and dinner; Fri. for dinner only; Sat. for breakfast and dinner; Sun. for breakfast and brunch*
*Accepts all major credit cards*

# NEW JERSEY ■ Chatham

---

## THE TARRAGON TREE
### Main Street
### 201-635-7333

You could easily drive right by this charming little flowery restaurant, for there's nothing to announce its presence. Once inside you'll enjoy well-prepared New American cuisine and a fine selection of wines, all served in a very pretty dining room with flowered wallpaper.

*Price: About $40 per person; Fri. and Sat. fixed price $42 per person*
*Open Tues.–Fri. for lunch and dinner; Sat. and Mon. for dinner only; closed Sun.*
*Accepts all major credit cards*

# NEW YORK ■ Bronxville

---

## A TASTE OF CHINA
### 840 New Rochelle Road
### 914-668-1160

This is a modern, bright Chinese restaurant serving Szechuan and Hunan specialties. The most special of all is the beggar's chicken, an aromatic dish wrapped in pastry and cut open at your table. The staff is very friendly: Ask Thomas to guide you to the best items.

*Price: About $15 per person*
*Open daily for lunch and dinner*
*Accepts all major credit cards*

# NEW YORK ▪ Buffalo

## ANCHOR BAR & RESTAURANT
### 1047 Main Street
#### 716-886-8920

Back in 1964, Teressa Bellisimo fried up some chicken wings and served them with a blue cheese dipping sauce and red hot sauce to perk them up. They became a sensation, and now Buffalo chicken wings are served throughout the country. Success certainly has not gone to the Anchor's head—it still looks like a rough-and-tumble bar-restaurant with the most garish of color schemes and low lighting. But you come here for one thing and one thing only, and they are still the best made anywhere.

*Price: About $12 per person*
*Open daily for lunch and dinner*
*Accepts Visa and MasterCard*

## RUE FRANKLIN WEST
### 341 Franklin Street
#### 716-852-4416

This small, pretty, sophisticated dining room is the best in the region, serving a solid French country menu with some novel flourishes. You may linger here and have a very romantic evening. Prices are moderate for this kind of food, service, and wine.

*Price: About $25 per person*
*Open Tues.–Sat. for dinner only; closed Sun. and Mon.*
*Accepts all major credit cards*

# NEW YORK ▪ Croton Falls

## MONA TRATTORIA
### Route 22
#### 914-277-4580

Here, in a delightfully sprawling mansion in woodsy surroundings, you will find the only real Bolognese restaurant I know of in this country, and the specialties—such as *lasagne verde, ravioletti alla bolognese,* and *petto di tacchino* —are the best items on the menu. The wine list is of interest, too.

*Price: About $25–$30 per person*
*Open Wed.–Sun. for lunch and dinner; closed Mon. and Tues.*
*Accepts American Express*

# NEW YORK ▪ Harrison

## JILLYFLOWER'S
### 309 Halstead Avenue
### 914-835-1898

This is an up-and-coming restaurant with an energetic chef-owner named Mark Filippo and co-owner Michael Denslow up front. The pleasant suburban casualness of the dining room does not prepare you for some first-rate French cuisine—snails in cream and garlic, *soupe de poisson* based on a Roger Vergé idea, lamb ragout, sea trout with leeks, turbot with *shiitake* mushrooms and snap beans. Desserts are not yet up to par. Plan on a 40-minute drive from Manhattan.

*Price: About $26–$30 per person*
*Open Mon.–Fri. for lunch and dinner; Sat. for dinner only; closed Sun.*
*Accepts all major credit cards*

# NEW YORK ▪ Hastings-on-Hudson

## BUFFET DE LA GARE
### 155 Southside Avenue
### 914-478-1671

With its tin ceilings, mirrored bar, and casual atmosphere, this is a happy little bistro near the Hudson River. Chef-owner Gwaenel Goulet and his wife, Annie, run the place to a fare-thee-well, and the food runs from the hearty *rillettes* and *terrines* to delicious veal with *morels* and a first-rate chocolate *marjolaine* with *crème à l'anglaise.* Prices are very fair. There is a selection of well-tariffed *bourgeois crus* wines available.

*Price: About $25 per person*
*Open Tues.–Fri. for lunch and dinner; Sat. and Sun. for dinner only; closed Mon.*
*Accepts all major credit cards*

# NEW YORK ▪ Mamaroneck

## CHINA LION
### 1160 Boston Post Road
### 914-381-2320

Conveniently located on Route 1 and not far from the New England Thru-way, this is a commendable Chinese restaurant with a large capacity and thoroughly affable staff. The spicy dishes are excellent—General Tso's chicken, dumplings in hot peanut sauce, and whole sea bass—but the subtler dishes are superb—Peking duck (always available), lobster *soong,* and nightly specials. Ask owner Bob Poons for advice.

*Price: About $15 per person*
*Open daily for lunch and dinner*
*Accepts all major credit cards*

# NEW YORK ▪ North Salem

## AUBERGE MAXIME
### Ridgefield Road *(at the juncture of Routes 121 and 116)*
### 914-669-5450

If you wish to take a lovely drive through the woods and lake country above Manhattan (about an hour and ten minutes away), stop here for lunch or dinner. Auberge Maxime is the epitome of the French country inn—provincial prints, beamed ceilings, copper cookware, and a cheery bar—with an amiable staff serving a menu of such classics as sweetbreads with wild mushrooms and cream, crisp roast chicken, and several duck preparations, including the famous Tour d'Argent's pressed duck (order a day in advance), the recipe for which chef-owner Bernard LeBris picked up while working at that venerable Parisian restaurant. The wine list is exceptionally fine.

*Price: Fixed price $39 per person*
*Open Thurs. and Fri. and Sun.–Tues. for lunch and dinner; Sat. for dinner*
*only; closed Wed.*
*Accepts all major credit cards*

# NEW YORK ▪ Rye

## LA PANETIÈRE
### 530 Milton Road
### 914-967-8140

As close as you'll come to a dining room in Provence, La Panetière is a newcomer that has built an enviable reputation for creative cuisine: oysters in a sauce of leeks, a *"méli-mélo"* of seafood, roast pigeon with turnips, and other delicacies. Owner Jacques Loupiac and Chef Yves Gonachon have long experience in American dining rooms but give La Panetière a particularly Gallic feeling and flavor. About a 40-minute drive from Manhattan.

*Price: About $35 per person*
*Open Tues.–Fri. and Sun. for lunch and dinner; Sat. for dinner only; closed Mon.*
*Accepts all major credit cards*

# NEW YORK ▪ Stony Brook

## THREE VILLAGE INN
### Main Street
### 516-751-0555

Stony Brook is one of the loveliest North Shore towns, and the Three Village Inn has long been a boon to travelers through these parts. It's set right near the water, and ducks waddle about the grounds of the inn (there are rooms to rent). The dining rooms are Colonial in design and the menu traditional American— rarely rising to any real gastronomic heights, but certainly a good meal for a fair price. Desserts like Indian pudding are nostalgic and completely satisfying.

*Price: About $15–$20 per person*
*Open daily for lunch and dinner*
*Accepts all major credit cards*

# NEW YORK ▪ Stormville

## HARRALDS
### Route 52
### 914-878-6595

Impeccable attention to detail has always characterized this fine Continental restaurant about 65 miles from Manhattan. Owner Harrald Boerger always seems thrilled that you've come and he makes sure the lights in the trees twinkle, the classical music is low, the fireplace is lighted, the extraordinary wine list is in perfect condition, and the menu is explained in detail. Wife Ava handles the kitchen and turns out sumptuous cuisine, from good soups to crusted rack of lamb and a good selection of desserts.

*Price: Fixed price $45 per person*
*Open Wed.–Sat. for dinner only; closed Sun.–Tues.*
*No credit cards accepted*

# NEW YORK ▪ South Salem

## THE HORSE AND HOUND
### Spring Street
#### 914-763-3108

This is a unique restaurant—dedicated to serving a complete menu of game, from *pâtés* of pheasant or rabbit to hearty platters of bear, and just about every wild species in between—including lion and rattlesnake on occasion. The restaurant is housed in a 1749 structure, and chef-owner Claus Hattasch keeps the fires burning in fall and winter. The wine list has exceptional depth and is fairly priced too.

*Price: About $20–$25 per person; fixed-price five-course dinner Saturday only, $37*
*Open daily for dinner; Sun. for brunch*
*Accepts all major credit cards*

## RENÉ CHARDAIN
### Route 123 and West Lane
#### 914-533-6200

Fine French country fare served in an equally fine 1900 mansion designed by Stanford White. The place is surrounded by woods and lakes and makes for an enchanting night out in the country, a little over an hour from Manhattan. The Chardain family runs the restaurant and sets a sensible table of classics bolstered by imaginative, beautifully seasoned innovations. With René and his daughter Linda in the kitchen and Madame Chardain as hostess, this is a fine example of a French family restaurant.

*Price: About $30–$35 per person*
*Open Tues.–Sat. for dinner only; closed Sun. and Mon.*
*Accepts all major credit cards*

# NEW YORK ▪ Tuckahoe

## SALERNO'S OLD TOWN COACH HOUSE
### 100 Main Street
### 914-793-1557

Salerno's has a modest exterior and a simple, old-fashioned suburban interior with a good bar in the middle and a blackboard menu of specialties that stresses some of the best steaks and chops around (the Salerno family owns a meat market next door) but includes some excellent seafood preparations too, such as sole done in a buttery champagne sauce. Desserts are of little interest here, but the small wine list has some great buys. This is a casual spot, with a very loyal local clientele. They don't take reservations, so be prepared for a wait around 7 P.M.

*Price: About $25 per person*
*Open Tues.–Sun. for dinner only; closed Mon.*
*Accepts no credit cards*

# NEW YORK ▪ Yonkers

## HUNAN VILLAGE
### 1828 Central Park Avenue
### 914-779-2272

This is an excellent Chinese restaurant, with emphasis on spicy specials. The appetizers are not very interesting, but the range of the kitchen is very wide when it come to various Hunan and Shanghai dishes such as chicken velvet, bean curd with pork, cellophane sesame noodles, and shrimp with walnuts. The man to see here is owner Paul Chou, who is delighted to help out with a special menu or banquet.

*Price: About $15 per person*
*Open daily for lunch and dinner*
*Accepts all major credit cards*

# NORTH CAROLINA ▪ Raleigh

## GRIFFIN'S RESTAURANT
### 4011 Old Wake Forest Road
#### 919-876-0125

Everybody in Raleigh knows that this is the best place around for hearty Southern breakfasts. Griffin's doesn't look much different from any other shopping mall luncheonette, but the food is fresh and fast—high biscuits, country ham, grits, and pancakes, with an endless flow of coffee.

*Price: Under $10 per person*
*Open Mon.–Fri. for breakfast, lunch, and dinner; Sat. for breakfast and lunch only; closed Sun.*
*No credit cards accepted*

# RHODE ISLAND ▪ Cranston

## TWIN OAKS
### 100 Sabra Street
#### 401-781-9693

An exemplary family-style restaurant—enormous, casual, complete with hostess who calls your name over a loudspeaker when your table is ready. Things move fast here, and the waiters have the speed of a tight end. The portions are enormous, and a full-course meal will include shrimp cocktail, rolls and butter, salad, soup, entrée, and dessert. While you wait, have a drink at the bar and look out over the river in back.

*Price: About $15–$18.50 per person*
*Open Tues.–Sun. for lunch and dinner; closed Mon.*
*Accepts all major credit cards*

# TENNESSEE ▪ Nashville

## ARTHUR'S OF NASHVILLE
### The Mall at Green Hills
#### 615-383-8841

Set in a suburban shopping mall, this is Music City's premier deluxe restaurant —very swank but also very formal, and the waiters swoon over every table detailing the fixed meal (at a fixed price) you will have that evening. You sit on overstuffed banquettes, listen to the piano music, and enjoy Continental cuisine and good wines. Afterwards you'll be offered an after-dinner drink and —for the men—cigars.

*Price: Fixed price $35 per person*
*Open Mon.–Fri. for lunch and dinner; Sat. for dinner only; closed Sun.*
*Accepts all major credit cards*

## THE HERMITAGE
### In the Hermitage Hotel, 231 Sixth Avenue
#### 615-244-3121

A grand old dining room in the basement of the refurbished Hermitage Hotel. The nostalgic look and feel of the room—Dinah Shore started out singing here at the age of nineteen—with its dark oak and its potted ferns works on everyone who dines here on the commendable Continental cuisine. There's a great bar next door.

*Price: About $25 per person*
*Open daily for lunch and dinner*
*Accepts all major credit cards*

## SATSUMA
### 417 Union Street
#### 615-256-0760

A real old-fashioned ladies lunchroom—although everybody in town of both sexes goes here for the homemade sandwiches, main courses of chicken salad, and scrumptious Southern desserts. Buy one of their cookbooks at the cash register.

*Price: Under $10 per person*
*Open Mon.–Fri. for lunch only; closed Sat. and Sun.*
*No credit cards accepted*

# TEXAS ■ Fort Worth

## ANGELO'S
### 2533 White Settlement Road
#### 817-332-0357

This is how Texans like their barbecue—in a dark, bar-like atmosphere where you line up and tell the guy behind the counter what you want, and what everyone wants is the sliced barbecue on a roll. The best potable is an icy beer. The desserts come from a vending machine on your way out.

*Price: Under $10 per person*
*Open Mon.–Sat. for lunch and dinner; closed Sun.*
*No credit cards accepted*

## THE PARIS COFFEE SHOP
### 704 West Magnolia Street
#### 817-335-2041

Everybody but everybody goes to the Paris—a big breakfast-luncheon spot where politicians hobnob with truckers and cowboys with debs. The reason is some good down-home food prepared in a very old-fashioned (often overcooked) way—chicken-fried steak, chili, and *enchiladas*.

*Price: Under $10 per person*
*Open Mon.–Fri. for breakfast and lunch; Sat. for breakfast only; closed Sun.*
*No credit cards accepted*

# TEXAS ■ Lockhart

## KREUZ MARKET
### 208 South Commerce Street
#### 512-398-2361

Pronounced "Krytz" by the locals, this is a big place which nearly always has a line outside at lunch. The reason is one thing only—perfectly barbecued beef brisket, sausage, and pork chops, dark and chewy on the outside and purply-pink on the inside. It's all served—without benefit of any side orders but white bread, pickles, and *jalapeño* peppers—on butcher paper. You sit at long school-cafeteria tables and drink Lone Star beer and have one helluva good time. Dessert is limited to gumballs.

*Price: Under $10 per person*
*Open Mon.–Sat. for breakfast, lunch, and dinner (closes 6–6:30 P.M.); closed Sun.*
*No credit cards accepted*

# VERMONT ▪ Montpelier

## TUBBS RESTAURANT
### 24 Elm Street
**802-229-9202**

Tubbs Restaurant is the proving ground for second-year students at America's most serious culinary school, the New England Culinary Institute, located here in the ski country of Vermont. The cozy dining room is a wonderful spot for a special meal at a very modest price—only $20 for three courses—with a menu that changes daily and includes everything from excellent fresh rolls to delectable ice creams. In between the French food is a nice balance of classic and modern, under the direction of instructor Michel LeBorgne. Of course, you may get an "A" student or a cook who deserves an "F," but generally this is food of a very high caliber. Wines are very reasonable. Check out the bakery next door, La Brioche, for morning pastries and a first-rate *croissant*.

*Price: Fixed-price meals about $20 per person; also* à la carte
*Open Mon.–Fri. for lunch and dinner; Sat. for dinner only; closed Sun.*
*Accepts all major credit cards*

# VIRGINIA ▪ Lynchburg

## BARBARA'S COUNTRY COOKING
### 2034 Lake Side Drive
**804-237-6279**

Very down-home food at very cheap prices. The decor is straight diner-class. You can't believe the prices for the amount of food you'll get here—big portions of fried chicken, country-style steak, prime ribs, mashed potatoes, barbecue, rolls and butter, vegetables, and strawberry shortcake, all served by idealized Southern waitresses with an equal amount of affection and sass.

*Price: Under $10 per person*
*Open daily for breakfast, lunch, and dinner*
*No credit cards accepted*

# VIRGINIA ■ Richmond

## HALFWAY HOUSE
### 10301 Jefferson Davis Highway
#### 804-275-1760

The structure dates back to the eighteenth century, and the basement restaurant is about the coziest spot you'll find in the state—rough walls, blue-patterned china, wooden tables, and a stone floor. The menu never changes at the Halfway (so-called because it was a waystop halfway between Richmond and Washington), but you'll dine well on Sally Lunn and sweet rolls, good pan-fried chicken, Western ham with pineapple, pecan pie, and gingerbread with whipped cream. The waiters are cheery and very courteous. The wine list is very poor and quite expensive.

*Price: About $20–$25 per person*
*Open Mon.–Sat. for dinner only; Sun. for lunch and dinner*
*Accepts all major credit cards*

---

## SALLY BELL'S KITCHEN
### 708 West Grace Street
#### 804-644-2838

One of the great old bakeries of the South, established in 1926, and it seems not a day older than when it opened. It was originally called "Sara Lee's," but a bigger bakery got hold of that trademark and so Sally Bell's it is today. The rolls, biscuits, and muffins are paragons of Southern baking, and the small sandwiches with Virginia ham, cream cheese, and other fillings are of a kind you haven't seen in years and then they probably never tasted quite so good. Get a boxed lunch and eat it on some green lawn or over at the Museum of Fine Arts. Sally Bell's is a real gem.

*Price: Under $10 per person*
*Open Mon.–Fri. from 8 A.M.–4 P.M.; closed Sat. and Sun.*
*No credit cards accepted*

# VIRGINIA ▪ Williamsburg

## CHOWNING'S TAVERN
### Duke of Gloucester Street
**804-229-2141**

One of several rustic taverns at Historic Williamsburg serving traditional American fare. The specialties are Brunswick stew, Welsh rarebit, and shrub. The tavern dates back to 1766, though the present structure is a respectful recreation.

*Price: About $12–$15 per person*
*Open daily for lunch and dinner*
*Accepts American Express, Visa, and MasterCard*

## THE TRELLIS
### Duke of Gloucester Street
**804-229-8610**

Owner-chef Marc Desaulniers is one of this country's most creative chefs and his cooking plucks the very essences of flavors from every green, every morsel of poultry, and every fish. He loves nothing better than to combine many ingredients together in lavish profusion and so his dishes have layers of flavor. All of this New American cookery is served up on a very Olde American street in historic Williamsburg, though The Trellis—with its pretty patio and several interior dining rooms—has a fine sedate modernism about it. The best room fronts Duke of Gloucester Street. The prices here are remarkably low for this high level of cuisine.

*Price: About $20 per person*
*Open Mon.–Sat. for lunch and dinner; Sun. for brunch only*
*Accepts all major credit cards*

# INDEX

# NOTES

# NOTES